Peter OF THE Prairies
The Red River Diaries of
PETER GARRIOCH
1837 - 1847

*Fur Trader Teacher
Contrarian Smuggler Trail-Blazer*

Peter of the Prairies
The Red River Diaries of
Peter Garrioch
1837 - 1847

*Fur Trader Teacher
Contrarian Smuggler Trail-Blazer*

Edited and annotated by

Dale Gibson
Durlene Germscheid
&
Sandra Mosher Anderson

Based on the manuscript and unpublished typescript and notes of the diarist's nephew, George Henry Gunn (1865 – 1945)

PETER OF THE PRAIRIES
The Red River Diaries of Peter Garrioch

Copyright © Sandra Mosher Anderson, 2025

All rights reserved. No part of this publication may be reproduced, stored in a retrieval system, or transmitted in any form or by any means, electronic, mechanical, photocopying, recording, or otherwise, without written permission of the author and publisher.

Published by Sandra Mosher Anderson, Edmonton, Alberta, Canada

ISBN:
    Paperback   978-1-77354-594-3
    ebook   978-1-77354-595-0

Publication assistance by
PageMaster Publishing
PageMaster.ca

Contents

Prologue and Acknowledgments 1

Abbreviations 5

Introduction 7

Chapter 1 – Roots 22
1768 – 1837

Chapter 2 – From Red River To St. Peter's 41
1837

Chapter 3 – Labouring & Teaching At St. Peters 84
1837-1838

Chapter 4 – Kenyon College 118
1838-1839

Chapter 5 – Trading On The Missouri 135
1842-1844

Chapter 6 – St. Peter's, St. Paul's & the Crow Wing Trail ... 168
1844

Chapter 7 – Free Trade Struggles & Romantic Entanglements ... 224
1845

Chapter 8 – Traveling Again as Unrest Grows at Red River ... 262
1845-1846

Chapter 9 – The Pleasures of Smuggling & Family Pressures ... 308
1846 - 1847

Chapter 10 – After the Diaries 357
1847 - 1888

Appendix I – Petitions 391

Appendix II – Peter's Peregrinations: The Map 417

Appendix III – Garrioch Family Photographs 430

Bibliography 436

Prologue and Acknowledgments

It is as a diarist that Peter Garrioch (1811-1888), teacher, free trader, trail-blazer, contrarian, smuggler, missionary, farmer, community leader, politician, postmaster, and justice of the peace, has taken his place in the history of Rupert's Land and Western Canada. In 1837, when in his mid-twenties, he began to keep a sporadic personal journal, setting down in a distinctive, often humorous, sometimes angry, voice both his own activities and the momentous, picayune, comic, tragic, or everyday events of the frontier life he observed around him. Peter Garrioch's diaries merit a wider readership than they have received to date.

Although some of his diaries appear to have been lost, a reasonably intact ten-year run of entries – from 1837 to 1847 – has survived and is located in the Archives of Manitoba, where the excellent staff have offered every possible assistance to the editors.

The Archives' holdings include Peter Garrioch's original handwritten texts for much of that 1837-1847 series, although the first year's entries appear now to exist only as typewritten transcriptions. Those transcriptions were made many decades ago by the Reverend Mr. George Henry Gunn (1865-1945) ("Gunn"), the diarist's nephew and a talented amateur historian. Gunn's unique contextual and editorial contributions to his uncle's diaries will be described in more detail in the Introduction.

Decades after Gunn surrendered his labours to death, three other editors have taken up the cause, spurred by an encounter between the first of these, law professor and keen legal historian Dale Gibson, and Manitoba historian and archivist *par excellence*, Dr. Anne Lindsay. In an acknowledgment that he drafted in October, 2018, for this book, Dale Gibson described the significance of that encounter:

> It was Anne Lindsay, that resourceful and enthusiastic researcher of prairie history, who introduced me to Peter Garrioch. That was many years ago, while I was working at the Manitoba Archives on another project. I encountered Anne who, after enquiring what I was doing, said: "You'll find some useful stuff in Peter Garrioch's diaries." When I, looking blank, asked: "Whose diaries?" Anne was good enough to tell me a little about Peter and his remarkable journals, adding: 'Don't just stop with what you need. Read

them all – they're great fun!' I took her advice, was hugely informed and entertained by the diaries, and resolved to attempt, when my then-current book was complete, to try bringing them to the notice of a wider readership.

The book project to which Dale was referring in this passage is his massive and comprehensive, two-volume account of the legal system established and operated by the Hudson's Bay Company for its Rupert's Land territories at Red River. The first volume is entitled *Law, Life & Government at Red River, Vol. 1: Settlement and Governance, 1812-1872* (Montreal & Kingston: McGill-Queen's University Press, 2015). It places the Quarterly Court of Assiniboia in its societal context, operating as it did as a microcosm of life in Rupert's Land for the sixty years prior to its demise in the aftermath of Riel's rebellion and the birth of the Province of Manitoba. The second volume, *Law, Life & Government at Red River: 1844-1872, Vol. 2: Annotated Records of the General Quarterly Court of Assiniboia* (McGill-Queen's, 2015), contains in full the Court's records during the same era, together with explanatory annotations. Peter Garrioch wrote his diaries during the middle of that period, and Dale's volumes, liberally drawn upon by the fourth editor in completing the present book, appear so often in the notes to subsequent chapters as to require space-saving abbreviations (Gibson, *LLG, I*, and Gibson, *LLG, II*).

At some point near the completion of that work, which had frequently drawn him from our home in Edmonton to the Archives of Manitoba, and now already fascinated by Peter Garrioch's diaries, Dale approached his long-time friend and former colleague at the Manitoba Human Rights Commission, Durlene Germscheid, to join him in the new project as co-editor. He described the genesis and forward movement of the new book project thus:

> And when Anne learned that I and my co-editor had finally embarked on that adventure, she undertook some gratuitous research, deluging us with useful tit-bits. Our gratitude to Anne is huge. Interviews with several of Peter's descendants were also useful and much appreciated, and valuable material was found in the Manitoba Archives, the Provincial Library of Manitoba, the Portage la Prairie Public Library, and the Archives of the Minnesota Historical Society in St. Paul, Minnesota. The employees we encountered in each of those institutions were unfailingly and courteously of great assistance.

Unfortunately, after years of work, Durlene did not live to see the completion of the project. Dale described her collaboration as follows:

> I must now painfully record the passing of my co-editor, Durlene Germscheid, before our book was quite finished, and acknowledge my deep gratitude for her invaluable contributions to the project. A self-made woman of uncommon humanity, towering intelligence, great energy, and sharply-focused determination, Durlene's principal lifetime contributions were to her family and friends and, in her capacity as an investigating officer and later Executive Director of the Manitoba Human Rights Commission, to the advancement of civil liberties in her province and her country. But Durlene was also

a keen and talented genealogical researcher, with a published history of her own family to her credit, and when I proposed that we join forces to publish and supplement the Garrioch diaries she agreed enthusiastically, participating unstintingly in all aspects of the work until the time, when the book was close to completion, that her final illness prevented her full participation. Even then, she took pains to ensure that her files were in meticulous order before being passed over to me. Without Durlene Germscheid's involvement, it is highly unlikely that Peter Garrioch's diaries would ever be published.

Dale continued to labour on the Garrioch project until illness caused him, too, to slow down and finally to cease being able to do the work he cared about so much. Sadly, before he could witness the publication of the Garrioch diaries, Dale also died, and it has fallen to me to see the project to completion. Dale and Durlene, the diaries' second and third editors, were so well organized that what remained to be done was manageable, and it has in any case been a task I have undertaken with love and appreciation for them and their considerable accomplishments.

This is a welcome opportunity to pay tribute to Dale Gibson, my husband of thirty years. Raised in Winnipeg, he became a leading constitutional law scholar who *inter alia* advised the federal and Manitoba governments on the patriation of the *Canadian Charter of Rights and Freedoms*. He was a prolific and widely-published author in many areas of the law, a masterful litigator who appeared in all levels of Canadian courts, an admired law professor in both Alberta and Manitoba and honoured University of Manitoba professor *Emeritus*, and, true to his roots, an expert Prairie legal historian. A cherished friend, collaborator, and colleague to many across Canada and beyond, less widely known is that he was also a prolific poet, journal-keeper, visual artist, story-writer, and essayist. It was a profound privilege to live and work alongside this brilliant, energetic, curious, courageous, and wonderfully loving man and to share the harmonious, adventurous, and joyful marriage we had until the day Dale died, January 29, 2022.

As *de facto* fourth (and, I hope, final) editor of the Garrioch diaries, I owe boundless thanks to Jennifer S. H. Brown, Professor *Emerita* of History, University of Winnipeg, and the now-retired Director and Publications Editor of the Centre for Rupert's Land Studies at the University of Winnipeg, and to Anne Lindsay, whose Ph.D. in History, devotion to her prolific archival pursuits at the Archives of Manitoba and elsewhere, and experience working for the Centre for Rupert's Land Studies and subsequently as archivist and researcher with the Truth and Reconciliation Commission of Canada, the National Centre for Truth and Reconciliation, and the Office of the Special Interlocutor (Manitoba), have contributed to this publication enormously, both during Dale's time and mine. In particular, Jennifer and Anne have graciously offered their encouragement and deep founts of relevant historical knowledge and perspectives to me as I have worked to provide Peter Garrioch's diaries with expanded historical context. They have applied their expertise to fill the lacunae in mine with such gratifying effect as to ensure that Peter Garrioch's colourful voice can now finally come accurately to life, assisted by his now-even-more-numerous admiring editors.

Finally, it is my pleasure to offer my thanks to Dale's and my great friend, Dr. Merrill Distad, Associate University Librarian and University Archivist *Emeritus*, University of Alberta, who has applied his historical wisdom and vast experience in both fine-tuning and copy-editing to this book and has thereby saved me from many errors. Any errors which do remain are, of course, my own responsibility.

It has truly taken a village to raise this book.

Sandra Mosher Anderson
(B.A., M.A., Ph.D, LLB)

Abbreviations

ADRL = Archives of the Diocese of Rupert's Land

AFC = American Fur Company

AM = Archives of Manitoba

CE = *Canadian Encyclopedia*, 2nd ed.

CMS = Church Missionary Society

CMSA/AM = Church Missionary Society, Archives of Manitoba

DCB = *Dictionary of Canadian Biography*

DMB = *Dictionary of Manitoba Biography*

Gibson, *LLG, I & II* = Dale Gibson, *Law, Life, and Government at Red River, Vol. 1: Settlement and Governance, 1812-1872; Vol. II: Annotated Records of the General Quarterly Court of Assiniboia*

HBC or "the Company" = Hudson's Bay Company

HBCA/AM = Hudson's Bay Company Archives, Archives of Manitoba

LAC = Library and Archives Canada

MFC = Missouri Fur Company

NWC = North-West Company

Introduction

Peter Garrioch was born[1] in Rupert's Land, the vast territory of the Hudson's Bay Company (HBC aka The Company) in north-central North America, to which the Company had laid claim in 1670, a claim backed up by economic clout and monopolistic colonialism rather than by clear legal entitlement. In the year of Peter's birth, the HBC conveyed to the 5th Earl of Selkirk a property 116,000 square miles in size surrounding the junction of Rupert's Land's Red and Assiniboine Rivers for the purpose of establishing the Red River Settlement – the first significant non-Indigenous population centre in that part of what is now Canada.

Peter's father was William Garrioch, an Orkney-born HBC employee;[2] his mother was Nancy Cook, the daughter of larger-than-life fur trader William Hemmings Cook and Kahnawpawamakan, his Cree wife. After postings further west, William and Nancy were making their way back from Edmonton House to take up his new position at Swan River, on the

---

1   Peter's son, Kemper Garrioch gave his father's birthdate as July 4, 1812, when it was actually July 5, 1811, and Peter's marriage to Kemper's mother, Margaret McKenzie, as December 24, 1850: Kemper Garrioch to George Gunn, September 12, 1914. (Archives of Manitoba (AM): George H. Gunn *fonds*, MG9 A78-1, Box 2 #8). But the actual marriage date was considerably earlier. (Marriage, Peter Garrioch and Margaret McKenzie, 28 February 1849, in Hudson's Bay Company Archives/Archives of Manitoba) (HBCA/AM): Extracts from registers of baptisms, marriages and burials in Rupert's Land sent to the Governor and Committee, E.4/2, f.113, confirmed in the Archives of the Diocese of Rupert's Land, Winnipeg (ADRL): MG25 G62, no. 5252). Peter died on December 6, 1888. (Vital Statistics Manitoba, online index; Métis Museum website).

2   After the Charter was granted in May, 1670, to the "*Governor* and Company of Adventurers of England trading into Hudson's Bay," as the Hudson's Bay Company was known, its ships began using the northernmost county of Scotland, the Orkney Islands, as a supply stop before embarking on the long voyage to Hudson's Bay. There they found a ready supply of young men eager to sign on to work as labourers and boatmen in territory as hardscrabble as their own islands. By the late 1700s, fully 80 percent of the HBC's workforce of approximately 500 were Orkneymen, many of them with careers of 20 years or more and, like William Garrioch, rising to positions of authority in the various Rupert's Land trading posts and settlements, some of which were like expat Orkney communities. When the HBC merged with the Northwest Company in 1821 and men were let go from the HBC's employ, many elected to stay rather than return home to the Orkneys, and a sizable number settled at Red River. Arthur Ray, "Hudson's Bay Company," *Canadian Encyclopedia,* 2nd ed. (Edmonton: Hurtig, 1988), pp. 1022-3.

western shore of Lake Manitoba, when Peter was born somewhere short of their destination.[3] In 1822, after fifteen years' service at several remote trading posts, William retired from the HBC. He and Nancy had moved with their several children to Red River the previous year and settled near Cook's retirement home there. And, before long, Peter began to display some of the characteristics that would eventually result in his many distinctive contributions over time to the Red River community, to Portage la Prairie and environs, and to the Minnesota Territory – in his multiple roles of teacher, fur trader, blazer of trails, contrarian, smuggler, lay missionary, farmer, politician, postmaster, justice of the peace, and diary-keeper.

Enter the indefatigable Reverend George Henry Gunn ("Gunn") (1865-1945), a skilled amateur historian, a respected Manitoba cleric,[4] and Peter's nephew.[5] Gunn's Red River pedigree was as venerable as that of Peter Garrioch, stemming from his grandfather Donald Gunn, who came to Rupert's Land from Scotland in 1813 and settled ten years later at Red River, where Donald enriched the community as farmer, teacher, justice of the peace, historian,[6] and influential elder[7] until his death in 1878. Both families, the Garriochs and the Gunns, had literary interests and included a number of school teachers.[8] The Garrioch and Gunn families merged when Peter's sister Emma married George's father John Gunn about 1855, with the result that

---

3   The precise location of the birth is not easily established and has even been described as having taken place on an island along the route to Swan River.

4   Gunn attended the University of Manitoba in 1894, then various seminaries, including Union Theological Seminary, from 1895 through 1903. He was ordained as a Presbyterian minister in 1897 and served in various places in North Dakota, British Columbia, and Ontario until 1905, when he returned to Manitoba and joined the staff at the *Manitoba Free Press*.

5   George Henry Gunn's father was John Gunn (1826-1898), M.L.A. for St. Andrews-North from 1874 to 1879, son of Donald Gunn (1797-1878) and Margaret Swain (married 1819). On February 2, 1855, John married Garrioch's sister, Emma (1824-1921) and they had nine children, including George Henry. This means that G. H. Gunn was the grandson on his father's side of Donald Gunn and on his maternal side, grandson of William Garrioch. Both his father, John, and his two grandfathers were teachers. It should be noted that Gunn has sometimes been identified as Henry George Gunn rather than as he identified himself for his transcripts, George H. Gunn.

6   His posthumous *History of Manitoba from the Earliest Settlement to 1835* by the Late Hon. Donald Gunn, was supplemented by: *And from 1835 to the Admission of the Province into the Dominion*, by Charles R. Tuttle (Ottawa: Maclean, Roger, 1880). (http://www.ourroots.ca/e/roots/113c0005.jpg.) He was also a corresponding secretary to the Smithsonian Institute, as reported by his grandson. J.J. Gunn, *Echoes of the Red*, (Toronto: Macmillan, 1930), p. 1.

7   Donald Gunn was a member of the first legislative council of Manitoba. J.J. Gunn, *Echoes*, p.1.

8   The "Gunngarrioch" clan spawned several writers in the next generation after Peter's: George Henry Gunn (1865-1945) was one of eight children born to Peter's sister, Emma, and John Gunn, M.P.P.; it was he who devoted a considerable part of his life to transcribing and annotating Peter's diaries, as detailed in the Introduction. See the Bibliography for a list of some of his prolific writings in history, biography, and versifying.

In stark contrast, his older brother, John J. Gunn (1861-1907) appears to have written nothing about his uncle Peter. It is possible that the reason for this is that he was too busy with his extensive apiary business and his position as president of the Manitoba Bee-Keepers' Association, founded in 1903, or had simply not yet gotten round to it, since he died prematurely, in his forties, gored to death on his farm at East Selkirk, on September 22, 1907, by a bull that had gotten loose in the stable and killed him as soon as he entered, after which his wife of two years, "came along and, seeing what had happened, fought the bull off with a pitchfork and dragged Mr. Gunn out," an incident that was widely reported: *Winnipeg Tribune* (September 23, 1907); *Winnipeg Free Press & Prairie Farmer* (September 25, 1907); *Edmonton Daily Bulletin* (September 23, 1907); *Windsor Star (Ont.)* (September 24, 1907); & *The Province (Vancouver)* (September 24, 1907).

However, J. J. Gunn did leave behind a collection of fictional stories in the romantic "heroic Indian" vein and a few historical observations, all published with an introduction by his widow, Eleanor F. Gunn, in J.J. Gunn, *Echoes*, from which are drawn some materials about trip men in the Red River Settlement (see Chap. 4, n. 262) and about the HBC's system of bartering with Indigenous fur trappers – to their unknowing disadvantage (see Chap. 6, n. 346). Oddly, in a short chapter entitled "An Old-Time School – A Reminiscence," J. J. Gunn makes no mention of his uncle Peter's teaching career, despite the fact that he writes: "But we believe the labourer to be worth some sort of hire and as the projectors [*sic.* protectors?] of these schools derive not fortune from their labours, why, then, they should at all events have fame, so here goes for one of them [the school in the centre of Selkirk] at least." J.J. Gunn, *Echoes*, p. 119.

The third literary nephew was Alfred Campbell Garrioch (1848-1934), son of Peter's brother John, and Eliza Campbell. He was an exceptional linguist, with several vocabularies of English, Cree, and Beaver words to his credit and a translation of the Gospel of Mark into Beaver. A. C. Garrioch wrote *The Far and Furry North: A Story of Life and Love and Travel in the Days of the Hudson's Bay Company* (Winnipeg: Douglass-McIntyre, 1925), a work of fiction, and *A Hatchet Mark in Duplicate* (Toronto: Ryerson Press, 1929), both loosely based on his ministry at the Anglican mission in Dunvegan in the Peace River country, to which he was assigned in 1888. The adventures recounted in the book were reviewed in some detail in the *Winnipeg Evening Tribune* (March 14, 1930, p. 15). The *Winnipeg Tribune Magazine* (July 27, 1935, p. 8) contains a lengthy article by A. C. Garrioch's daughter, Verena L. Garrioch, on the "First Schools on Portage Plains," in which she details school-related experiences of her father and Peter Garrioch, drawn from the former's *Journal*, which she says he started to keep at about age 17, in late 1865. (See Chap. 10, text at nn. 731-738)

After A. C. Garrioch left Dunvegan in 1891 and returned to Red River, he wrote *First Furrows: A History of the Early Settlement of the Red River Country, including that of Portage la Prairie* (Winnipeg: Stovel Company, 1923), and *The Correction Line* (Winnipeg, Stovel Company, 1933), in both of which he paid tribute to his uncle Peter (see Chap. 9, ending). Not to be outdone, in an unpublished article entitled: "Correcting the Correction Line; a Review of A.C. Garrioch's book, The Correction Line," n. d. AM; MG9 A78-1, A78-3, George Gunn took his cousin to task over the second book. Along with chiding him about his prolixity in both words and topics ("its nebulous scope and lack of unity of aim," which led to Gunn "stubb[ing] his bare toes against those hidden excrescenses of bias and misinterpretation of fact hidden, here and there, beneath its lucent flow"), a condition with which Gunn himself was certainly afflicted, Gunn spotted some particular errors as well, which he asserted could not be excused merely because A. C. was close to the events, since George, too, was there for most of them. But, he wrote, it was an admirable work, except for: "1. That I have all my life been a participant in the affairs of which it treats; 2. that before the book was

George inherited an intense interest in the Garrioch clan as well as in his own. He named his Lockport home north of Winnipeg "Gunngarrioch," occasionally wrote under the name "Garrioch Gunn," and resolved to publish Peter Garrioch's diaries. When his ecclesiastical career was firmly enough established to permit him to pursue his historical avocation, Gunn acquired the surviving original handwritten texts of his uncle's diaries,[9] including the now-missing 1837-8 originals, and transcribed them, with scrupulous care[10] and a view to publication.[11] The Garrioch diaries' holdings in the Archives of Manitoba include Garrioch's originals for much of the period 1837- 1847, plus the typescript of Gunn's comprehensive transcriptions.[12] Since then, they have come to the occasional attention of both historians and at least one author of historical fiction.[13]

---

commenced, my esteemed kinsman, the Author, was good enough to discuss the project with me and to seek my advice which, I see, like a prudent man, he has carefully refrained from following; 3. that, at his solicitation, I contributed material to it that he has, by an oversight quite pardonable in a man of his years, forgotten to acknowledge...."

9   See Gunn's description of this gathering process in "Peter Garrioch: Teacher, Trader, Traveler, Diarist" (AM: Gunn MG-9 A78-3). There he wrote that the first of two of the diaries was, "in the hands of another daughter, Mrs. Alice Chaplin, Charles St., Winnipeg" (AM: Gunn, MG9 A78-3, p. 4), Peter's youngest child, born March 31, 1870, who married Henry Edward Chaplin. She was undoubtedly the Mrs. H. E. Chaplin of Winnipeg who is listed by the Archives of Manitoba as the donor of Peter Garrioch's original diaries.

10 Transcription was not always an easy task, either for Gunn or for the present editors. Peter's handwriting was far from the best, and some entries – especially those from his time at Kenyon College – were written on loose sheets of paper, making their sequence difficult to determine. Based on the observed high quality of Gunn's 1838-47 transcriptions, however, the present editors have considered those for the first year's entries to be reliable as well.

11 Gunn acknowledged encouragement from others: "Among these I would mention Prof. O. G. Libby of North Dakota University, secretary of the Historical Society of that state, who, earliest of any, recognized the historical value of these diaries and suggested their publication." AM: Gunn "Peter Garrioch: Teacher, Trader, Traveler, Diarist."

12 AM: Gunn MG2 C38: Peter Garrioch, originals and typescript, & MG-9 A78-3: The Journal of Peter Garrioch, edited with notes by George H. Gunn.

13 A later Manitoba teacher and writer, Olive Elsie Knox (1903-1982), wrote both fictional accounts of the Red River settlement, mixing together actual events and personalities, with historical materials, many of which were published by the Manitoba Historical Society, which awarded her a Centennial Medal in 1970. In *Red River Shadows* (Toronto: MacMillan, 1948), she sourced historical accounts, including the 1857 parliamentary investigation into the HBC's administration of the colony (see Appendix I – Petitions), and, as well, she stated, "the unpublished diaries of Colonel Crofton 1846 (Winnipeg Public Library) and Peter Garrioch, 1843-1847, also supplied information on the life of the settlement."

Interestingly, Peter himself becomes a character in the Knox novel, at a point where he, Sinclair, Sayer, William Cook and several fictional characters are on their way to Norman Kittson's post at Pembina, in accordance with Peter's account of their "smuggling" escapade (see Chap. 9). She

Along with his intense interest in his and his uncle's family, Gunn seems to have found Peter's diaries themselves fascinating enough to have devoted years of effort not only to transcribe them, but also to provide detailed explanatory notes. These notes contain a wealth of Manitoba geographical, social, and personal history, identifying people, locating places, and elaborating on events mentioned by Garrioch. Gunn also wove the vast information he collected for his project into additional stand-alone essays, such as: "Peter Garrioch: Teacher, Trader, Traveler, Diarist,"[14] "Peter Garrioch, His Life and Times,"[15] and "Peter Garrioch at St. Peter's, 1837,"[16] and appended an article he wrote, entitled "Garrioch's School at St. Peters, Minnesota, 1837-1838," to his typescript.[17] As well, a number of notebooks preserved among the Gunn Papers at the Archives of Manitoba[18] testify to the energy and meticulousness with which he pursued this information, in libraries and by means of personal interviews and site inspections, in Manitoba, North Dakota, and Minnesota. Explaining, verifying, and correcting every possible uncertain journal reference became a passion for him – one that occupied a considerable part of his busy

---

wrote that Peter, "whose own love-life was none too smooth," grinned at the fictional heroine and "the way she included herself as one of them, and then picking up the map, he followed the smugglers out to their mounts" (p. 237). Knox's later account of the *Sayer* trial is both accurate and effectively described (pp. 273-289). *Red River Shadows* has been described as falling into the category of "sentimental adventure stories" (a term which also applies to J. J. Gunn's stories) by Carol Fairbanks, *Prairie Women: Images in American and Canadian Fiction* (New Haven: Yale University Press, 1986), p. 129, and one that shows complex characters, "who respect Indians and their traditions and come close to recreating the white-Indian relationship which characterized the early years of the Red River settlement." *Red River Shadows* received a glowing review in the *Winnipeg Tribune* (October 16, 1948, p. 11) upon publication.

14   This is a nine-page forward clearly in Gunn's style and designed to set out the diary's provenance in some detail. From its page numbering, it is the first in the series of Gunn typescripts which form AM: Gunn MG 9 A78-3, despite the fact that the type font is different from that employed in the remainder of MG-9 A78-3.

15   This is a forty-two-page introduction to the diaries, forming part of the diaries' file AM: Gunn MG-9 A78-3 in the Archives of Manitoba, the conclusion of which sets out Gunn's mission in publishing them: "In the Journal which he has left behind…mutilated and fragmentary as it is, we have his monument; – a monument that, I believe, because of its fundamental relationship to our history, will still survive when much of the more pretentious writings of more pretentious writers will have been forgotten."

16   *Minnesota History* XX (1939), pp. 119-128. This is an overview of Peter's experiences, emphasizing journeys and events that are treated in the diaries, which are themselves liberally quoted. There is no overarching analysis and no reference to the provenance of the diaries.

17   Appendix B, Gunn, pp. 367-370. (see text below and Chap. 3, nn. 225,227)

18   AM: Gunn MG-9 A78-1.

life, and may well have been, at least in part, what prevented his ever publishing more than one small portion of the diaries, if indeed he did even that.[19]

More generally, but also consuming of his time, Gunn was also instrumental in establishing historical societies, the first of which was the Lord Selkirk Society, which he characterized as "an exclusive club or association, composed entirely of the descendants of the actual original settlers of the Red river settlement; the purpose of the club being to represent the original 'pilgrim father' of the country in the midst of this present day civilization, and to act as an agency in collecting and preserving the historic and legendary lore pertaining to the early settlement and families, in danger at present of being lost." He envisioned the building of a headquarters for the work, including a library, museum, and reading room.[20] The organization was named the Lord Selkirk Association, and Gunn became its secretary.[21] By 1915, its meetings were drawing crowds of two hundred or more, "representing six generations of descendants of sturdy colonists, who laid the industrial, political and social foundations of this western country."[22] He was also heavily involved in the Manitoba Historical Society, at a 1927 meeting of which he read a paper that, "had to do with the Journal of Peter Garrioch, covering the period of Manitoba history from 1837 to 1847. At the conclusion of Mr. Gunn's paper, Prof. Chester Martin commented upon the value of the Garrioch Journal, as covering a portion of Manitoba's annals hitherto in a large measure dark to the historian."[23]

The Gunn typescript preserved in the HBC Archives (Archives of Manitoba), MG9 A78-3, contains 391 consecutively-numbered pages, consisting of:

Peter Garrioch: Teacher, Trader, Traveler, Diarist, by George Henry Gunn – pp. 1 - 9

Peter Garrioch, His Life and Times, by George H. Gunn – pp. 10 - 42

The Garrioch Journal, Part I: Journal of a Trip from Red River Settlement to St. Peter's Minn., and on to Prairie du Chien, 1837-1838 – pp. 43 - 135

The Garrioch Journal, Part II: Experiences at Kenyon College, 1838-1839 – pp. 136 - 147

---

19   More essay-like and organized less like a diary would be, "Smuggling" was a retrospectively-written account of a trading escapade, begun by Garrioch, he records, on February 24, 1847, towards the end of his diary-writing. The occurrence of World War II at a time when Gunn's editorial work was well advanced probably delayed publication of his typescript of the diaries and accompanying documents until declining health precluded his doing more. Gunn died December 22, 1945, at Selkirk General Hospital in his 80th year. He lived at Lot 167, Gonor, Manitoba, at the time.

20   *Daily Free Press and Prairie Farmer, Winnipeg* (November 11, 1908), p. 15.

21   *Daily Free Press and Prairie Farmer, Winnipeg* (December 1, 1909), p. 17, & *ibid* (February 16, 1910), p. 6.

22   *Manitoba Free Press*, (February 13, 1915).

23   *Free Press Evening Bulletin (Winnipeg)* (February 26, 1927), p. 13.

Introduction

> The Garrioch Journal, Part III: Fur Trading on the Missouri, 1842-1844 – pp. 148 - 179
>
> The Garrioch Journal, Part IV: Account of a Trip Made by Steamboat and Red River Cart from Fort Garry to Galena, Illinois, and Back, in 1844 – pp. 180 - 234
>
> The Garrioch Journal, Part V: Home Journal – 1845-1847 – pp. 235 - 324
>
> The Garrioch Journal, Part VI: Seven Days' Experience or the Pleasures of Smuggling, Being the Account of a Fur-Smuggling Expedition of the Free Traders to Pembina, in which the Author took Part, in 1846 – pp. 325 - 364
>
> Appendix A: Extract from the Minutes of Council of Assiniboia, Passed at Fort Garry, June 10th, 1845 – pp. 365 - 366
>
> Appendix B: Garrioch's School at St. Peter's, Minnesota, 1837-1838 – pp. 367- 370
>
> Appendix C: Governmental and Judicial System of Assiniboia – pp. 371 - 380
>
> Appendix D: August 29, 1845, Petition to Governor Alexander Christie & his reply – pp. 381 - 385
>
> Appendix E: Process of Cutting Up or "Turning Out" the Buffalo in Use among the Hunters on the Buffalo Plains – pp. 386 - 387
>
> Appendix F: Text of Petition Prepared by Rev. G. A. Belcourt of the Baie St. Paul Mission and Signed by 977 Red River Settlers in May, 1846. Translated from the French – pp. 388 - 391.

Although we have preserved Gunn's consecutive pagination within our edition of the Garrioch diaries, we have chosen to organize our edition of the Gunn typescript somewhat differently, breaking the text into our own chapters (see the Table of Contents). Dale also added bolded descriptive subheadings throughout, in order to enhance the reader's appreciation of the distinct topics within Garrioch's narrative, and Sandra has preserved them as Dale wrote them because they serve both a distinctive clarifying function and distill the essence of Peter's topics.

Whether the diarist ever did write with the possibility of publication in mind is a matter of divided opinion. The 39-page document entitled "Pleasures of Smuggling,"[24] which greatly expands on

---

24 "Seven Days' Experience or the Pleasures of Smuggling, Being the Account of a Fur-Smuggling Expedition of the Free Traders to Pembina, in which the Author took Part, in 1846" (AM: Gunn, pp. 325-364). Although Dale thought that Gunn had published it in the *Nor'-Wester* or *Winnipeg Free Press*, Sandra has been able to find only one publication of it, and that a partial one, embedded in the section "Garrioch Family," pp. 373 ff. in Manitoba Village History Committee, *Many Trails of Manitou-Wapah* (Alonsa, Man., 1993). *Many Trails* contains a severely truncated version of Gunn's transcript of "Smuggling," found on a scant four pages (pp. 375-378), whereas Gunn's transcript of it in its initial state, incorporated here into Chap. 9, is fifty pages long (Gunn, pp. 325-375). Even though pp. 325-340 of Gunn's transcript is faithfully reproduced in the *Many Trails* excerpt, everything from the middle of Gunn's pp. 340 to 375 is omitted. No explanation of the source or the fact that the account is severely attenuated is provided.

Others had at least the *Pleasures of Smuggling* in mind for publication, as shown by a letter dated September 25, 1928, now residing in the George Gunn fonds in the Archives of Manitoba

an adventurous journey recorded only very tersely in the regular diary – into which it has been inserted in this edition – and was clearly penned well after the events described, certainly seems to have been intended for publication;[25] but Gunn thought the rest of the journal was intended solely for Peter Garrioch's own eyes and those of his family members:

> His sole purpose in keeping these diaries was, as he himself states, to preserve for his own gratification, in the more retired years of his life, the memory of the various incidents and events that had gone to make up the sum of his experiences in the days of his youthful and manly vigor. Later in life, as he conned them over and began to appreciate their possible interest to others than himself, this original motive was supplemented by the equally natural and unpretentious one of transmitting them to his children, as momentoes [sic] which might be treasured with a purely filial and domestic regard and handed on; thus keeping alive, for a while at least, in the minds of those nearest to him, that brief immortality of memory which seems so dear and natural to every human heart.[26]

One editor of the present publication – Durlene – adopted Gunn's view; the others do not. Sandra shares Dale's view that numerous clues throughout the diary, beginning with the

---

("Correspondence, 1891-1942," MG9 A78-1, A78-3), from C. G. Libby, secretary of the State Historical Society of North Dakota, to the Arthur H. Clark Company in Cleveland, Ohio, offering a number of manuscripts to them for publication, including: "The Garrioch fur trade war with the Hudson Bay Company, 1844, Red River Valley," which appears an obvious reference to *Pleasures of Smuggling*. That Gunn had a copy of the letter in his possession indicates that he shared with others a more than passing interest in publishing his uncle's works. Peter's diaries were also on the radar of the Minnesota Historical Society. On April 21, 1938, its curator of manuscripts, Grace Lee Nute, wrote to Gunn soliciting an article about Peter's diary for St. Paul's centennial celebration, "not too lengthy, on the connections of Garrioch with early St. Paul…and almost anything in the diary about this region will be pertinent.:" Gunn complied by writing: "Peter Garrioch at St. Peter's, 1837." *Minnesota History* 20 (1939), pp. 119-128.

25 Not only is it vividly written throughout, but it contains rhetorical flourishes fit for a stage audience, such as: "There can be but little merit to tell the world that we removed our packs and saddles from the backs of our horses, gave the poor animals full liberty to find food suitable to their respective tastes, kindled a fire, and sat down to eat and drink – drowning the toils and vexations of the past day in a kettle running over with a gallon of the delicious tea plant's juice – or that we went to bed and slept, and rose again the following morning. And yet we did all that. But my nimble pen has here taken undue advantage of my momentary absence. Suffice it to say, as a supplement to the doings of this day, that the succeeding night was as welcome to our fagged bodies and weary minds as ever night was to mortal man." (Chap. 9, towards the conclusion of the May 6, 1846, entry).

26 Gunn, "Peter Garrioch: Teacher, Trader, Traveler, Diarist," pp. 2-3. Another example of Peter's retroactive writing was his summary, written at the beginning of January, 1844, of events and adventures dating back into 1842. (Chap. 5, text between nn. 266-296). His rationale for doing so is interesting; the purpose of reducing them to writing was to prevent them from sliding into oblivion.

reference to, "you who have kind and tender mothers" in the third paragraph of the first entry of his diaries,"[27] indicate that the writer often contemplated a wider future audience as he wrote, although he never seemed to have succeeded in pursuing publication. This view is strengthened by the fact that, as Gunn went on to acknowledge (without providing specific evidence for who did the deleting), "portions containing purely private matter were deleted by Mr. Garrioch himself, while the MSS. were still in his custody." Had no publication been intended, there would have been no need to destroy or suppress anything. Being rather too polite to suggest that Peter's family and friends might have expunged portions of his diaries due to their (to them) embarrassing or scandalous content, Gunn attributed further depredation to the scattering among various relatives and friends after his death of the various "blank-books" and loose papers on which Peter had recorded his diary entries.[28]

Gunn described the disjunctive character of his uncle's diary books:

> In writing his journals, Mr. Garrioch had to avail himself of such materials as might be obtainable in the country, at that time, when proper blank-books for the making of such records were not lying around, ready to the hand of every incipient journalist, as they are with us today. As a result, these diaries were kept in a number of blank-books of various sizes and shapes, sometimes eked out with additions of ordinary foolscap, sewed into the covers with ordinary needle and thread; and in one instance, viz., the journal of his experiences at Kenyon College, on separate sheets of paper, insecurely fastened together by the same primitive method. In the latter case, through the giving way of the sewing, the bulk of the MS. became lost, leaf by leaf; the merest fragment falling into the hands of the present editor. Whether this occurred while the MS. was still in Mr. Garrioch's keeping or afterwards I have no present means of knowing. The other diaries, three in number, passed, upon his decease, into the hands of three separate individuals; and only two of these, including the account of the smuggling expedition to Pembina, which forms the concluding part of the present publication, has so far been recovered.[29]

Gunn also outlined his acquisition of various portions of the diaries. One part came from Peter's daughter, Mrs. Margaret Seymour, who obtained it from her father and "treasured it up" to Gunn in 1911. Gunn described it thus:

> The original of this portion of Mr. Garrioch's Journal is a thin, closely written, paperboard covered book of the ordinary day-journal type, foolscap size and about three quarter of an inch thick, with some added pages of ordinary "cap" sewed in by the author as already said, for the purpose of providing additional space. Inserted in this

---

27 Chap. 2, entry for June 14, 1837. See also Chap. 2, entry for July 12, 1837: "Ah, traveler...."
28 AM: Gunn, "Peter Garrioch: Teacher, Trader, Traveler, Diarist," pp. 3-4.
29 Ibid., p. 4.

journal also, as a loose leaf MS., was the account of the Pembina fur-smuggling trip…
and the fragmentary remains of the Kenyon College diary.[30]

The second portion came from Miss Olive Treilhard,[31] a granddaughter of Peter's, who obtained it from her mother, "as a momento of her late father at the time of his death." Gunn said of it:

> This MS….is in the form of a paper-covered note book with a leather back, about five by seven inches in dimensions and a little over an inch thick. Only half of this little book, however, had been utilized for journal purposes, and contains Part 1. of the present work.

The other half, Gunn said, consists of a series of biblical exercises, probably part of Garrioch's studies at Kenyon College and not included in his transcription.

But the third portion, as described to Gunn by Kemper Garrioch, Peter's son, "who had very clear and positive recollections concerning the missing record," was said to have been Peter's "most valuable and interesting of the series," but had been lost by Gunn's time. According to what Kemper conveyed to Gunn, it "covered the period from about 1847…up to 1870 or therealong, and comprised a larger bulk – some two inches in thickness – than that contained in all the recovered documents combined."[32] Gunn continued:

> …judging by the accounts of it obtained from members of the family, by far the largest portion of the diaries, it was by far the largest and most complete of the three; Mr. Garrioch having been at special pains to treat the incidents contained therein in as full and detailed a manner as possible. He himself regarded this latter journal, so I am told, as the most valuable and interesting of the series. In form, this MS. was a paper-board covered book about nine by thirteen inches square and some two inches in thickness, opening across the shorter dimension instead of in the customary way….This MS. disappeared, however, just when or how nobody appears to know; but it has not been seen

---

30   *Ibid.*, p. 5.

31   Olive Trailhard was the daughter of Peter and Margaret's fifth child, Emeline (b. April 22, 1858). Emeline married Ernest Sydney Treilhard on June 2, 1882, and Olive was one of their five children. Born in London, Treilhard came to Portage la Prairie *circa* 1880, and moved with his family to Winnipeg in 1904. Sometime before 1914, they moved to Victoria, where he died on May 4, 1934. *Winnipeg Free Press* (May 14, 1934), p. 4. Daughter Olive, born in Portage la Prairie, resided in Victoria for 50 years before her death on July 20, 1973, at age 85. *Victoria Times Colonist* (August 1, 1973), p. 40.

32   AM: Gunn, "Peter Garrioch: Teacher, Trader, Traveler, Diarist," pp. 5-6. It should be kept in mind that, judging from the fact that Kemper gave Gunn wrong dates for both his father's birth and his parents' marriage, Kemper was not the most reliable of sources.

> by any of my informants subsequent to its author's decease. It may still, of course, be in the hands of some unknown relative or friend....[33]

Gunn mourned the loss of such a significant treasure, but expressed hope that "the passage of time may yet bring it to light."[34] Unfortunately, the present editors know of no such happy event.

The editors of the current publication resolved, when we undertook to bring Peter's diaries into print, that we would exercise our own independent editorial judgment throughout and would work primarily from the original manuscripts where we could. We concurred in many of Gunn's editorial decisions, found his numerous and scrupulously detailed notes of great value, and have accordingly adopted a sizable portion of those notes and included them with minimal or no revision in our own text and notes. Although they were written long ago – in the 1930s and 1940s – we consider those we retained to be much too useful or too interesting to abandon. It would have been foolhardy to scrap so valuable a resource altogether. It should be kept in mind that, since the Gunn notes generally appear on the same page in the typescript as the entry to which they are connected, it was not felt necessary in our own notes always to cite the typescript page. Nor was it felt necessary to preface the Gunn notes with "AM" (Archives of Manitoba) when they are simply part of that typescript.

Readers must always bear in mind when reading a Gunn note, however, that it was written long after Garrioch wrote his diaries and eighty or ninety years before this book is being published. When, for example, a note describes Peter's location at some point in the diary narrative as being a certain number of miles distant from some community or landmark with which Gunn was familiar, the place in question might well have – indeed, probably has – expanded since then to embrace that very location. Conversely, the community might no longer exist, or might have another name. Even geographic features identified by our predecessor could well have changed in name or in appearance – or might have disappeared altogether. Although we have made no attempt to verify the accuracy of Gunn's topographical observations, we believe him to have been a scrupulous and honest historian and a tireless explorer of the storied and physically interesting territory Canadian prairie-dwellers share with our southerly neighbours.

It is not possible to date with any degree of precision the beginning and termination of Gunn's transcription of the Garrioch diaries, nor the, presumably, later notes he prepared. He must have started by tracking down the parts of the diary held by family members, as he described in "Peter Garrioch: Teacher, Trader, Traveler, Diarist" sometime after Peter's death in 1888. Olive Trailhard, from whom Gunn obtained a portion of the diary, was not even born until after her parents' marriage in 1882 and appears to have been an adult when she gave her portion

---

33   *Ibid.*, p. 6.

34   *Ibid.*

to Gunn.[35] To transcribe the various diary parts would have been a time-consuming job and would have necessarily preceded the preparation of Gunn's voluminous notes. The fact that he was corresponding with Peter's son, Kemper, in 1914, about Peter's family chronology shows that the process of gathering materials for his notes took place over many years, which is not surprising given his busy career and his involvement in the formation of at least two active historical societies. We know that he quoted freely from Peter's diaries when he wrote his 1939 article "Peter Garrioch at St. Peter's, 1837," and read from them during an address in 1927 to the Manitoba Historical Society. In short, Gunn's typescripts, with their notes, were the product of decades of work spanning at least the first 40 years of the 20th century.

In addition, we decided that the diaries needed to be supplemented from other sources. Like all of us, Peter Garrioch was a product of his antecedents and his times, and we felt that some knowledge of his family background and influences would enrich a reading of his accounts. Moreover, the surviving diaries cover the span of only about a decade of his life, after which he lived another 41 years, and was involved in other noteworthy activities. Our transcriptions of the original entries are therefore preceded by a chapter dealing with Peter's ancestry and activities prior to setting off for distant places on June 14, 1837, with his pregnant mare Peskee and his dog Lillipoot, and are followed by a chapter describing the years subsequent to the final surviving diary entry from June, 1847.[36]

While Peter Garrioch was a gifted story-teller with a vivid, inventive style, he had almost no experience writing for publication, and that inexperience, coupled in places with youthful self-consciousness and facetiousness, sometimes resulted – especially in earlier entries – in wordier and more florid accounts than were prudent or useful. The opening chapters are also afflicted with what today might be considered an excess of pious phraseology in service of his early intention to study theology at Kenyon College. His writing appears more authentically "Peter" once he abandoned that ambition and returned to pursuits more congenial to his character.

Nevertheless, Peter occasionally mistook one word for another, and sometimes let his expressive exuberance get seriously out of hand. And despite being an experienced schoolteacher, Peter was an atrocious speller. The editors have therefore found it appropriate to make a number of minor changes to the raw text of the diary entries. We have also added subject headings, explanatory

---

35   See above, n. 31.

36   Aided by the many invaluable contextual and archival clues supplied by Dr. Anne Lindsay, Sandra has adopted a slightly different approach, considerably expanding the footnotes with material from many sources of information about Red River and Rupert's Land society in the hope that providing a comprehensive context for Peter's lively diaries will enrich and enlighten the reader even further. It is hoped that these materials will act as bridges between Peter's diaries and his readers, without co-opting him in support of current interests or agendas, in the sense described by Jennifer S. H. Brown in her illuminating article "Documentary Editing: Whose Voices?" *Occasional Papers of the Champlain Society* (Toronto, 1992), pp. 1-14, esp. pp. 5 & 7.

paragraphs, and notes – many of the latter containing Gunn's valuable contributions – and have made minor insertions, deletions, substitutions, and re-arrangements here and there to the text of the diaries. That editorial tinkering calls for a few words of additional explanation.

One of the most important – and difficult – tasks of all editors is to assist authors in presenting their writing to their readers in the most effective manner possible without significantly compromising the authors' own voices or messages.[37] With living authors, that process commonly involves much discussion and debate between author and editor. In the case of posthumous writing, however, the editors themselves must bear the full responsibility for that final polish. Reverend Gunn recognized that many minor editorial revisions were called for,[38] and so did we.

Although it would have been wrong to eliminate Garrioch's substantive content or to seriously suppress his distinctive style, it would have been equally wrong to place his diaries before the public marred by small errors and excesses that any competent editor would have insisted upon removing had the author sought publication during his lifetime. We have therefore made small revisions – chiefly corrections and deletions rather than substitutions or additions – that we believe any editor would have persuaded the diarist to make. Except for his reference to having, "in a few instances…straightened out, or cut out, phrases or personal references that might not have proven agreeable to living relatives of those concerned, and that were not anyway, of the essence of the record," what Gunn wrote about his editorial practices aligns with our views:

> I have not sought to interfere with any picture drawn, nor to tone down what to some might appear too realistic, nor even to straighten out, to any extent, defects due to faulty composition or the overweening desire of the author, at times, to be facetious. An indispensable requirement in the reproduction of a work of this kind is fidelity to the original; and, the MS. having come to us as it is, we can do no other than to reproduce it as originally written, trusting to the good sense and fairness of the reader to make allowance for whatever he may happen upon that does not seem to accord with his critical standards.[39]

We believe we have performed our role responsibly, and we dare to think that both Peter Garrioch and George Henry Gunn would have been satisfied with the result. Specifically, we have corrected spelling and grammar, employed modern punctuation, occasionally changed

---

37 Sandra is of the view that Dale's faithfulness to Peter's text, so well transcribed by Gunn, while interpolating subheadings and explanatory paragraphs throughout, reflects Dale's profound respect for Peter's voice, a central principle of authentic documentary editing, as emphasized by Brown, "Documentary Editing," pp. 1-14,

38 Gunn acknowledged his editorial hand in the ordinary way of making "corrections in spelling, punctuation, the arrangement of the contents in orderly divisions," and so forth, commensurate with our approach. AM: Gunn, "Peter Garrioch: Teacher, Trader, Traveler, Diarist," p. 9.

39 *Ibid.*

paragraphing and sentence structure, and removed awkward, redundant, or inappropriate expressions. To assist readers to recognize our editorial tweaking, we have employed the following flags:

- **Bolded type,** mainly in paragraphs of our own inserted between paragraphs in the diary text, as a means of filling in gaps in the narrative or offering needed explanations;
- Square brackets [ ], for editors' comments within the text;
- Three dots within square brackets [...], for the few significant within-text deletions;
- Text within square brackets ['text'], for insertions into the text.
- Numbers between italicized brackets {245}, to record the page numbers in the Gunn typescript, Archives of Manitoba MG 9 A78-3.
- Footnote references to Gunn, occasionally followed by a page number (e.g., "Gunn, p. 173"), to indicate pages in the unpublished Gunn typescript.

The days of the week Peter cited for particular dates – or perhaps it was the dates themselves – were often mistaken. Date inconsistencies were corrected with calendars of the relevant years in hand, and in the absence of other evidence, we elected to consider the day of the week, rather than the date, to have been accurate where day and date were inconsistent with each other. These, and corrections of spelling, punctuation, and grammar have not been flagged.

Since Durlene's death, a document of which she (and, apparently, Gunn) was unaware has come to light: a map that appears from the handwriting to have possibly been drawn by Garrioch himself (see Appendix II – Maps). It is a fair copy of an earlier, very similar, but less legible, map pasted on two centre-facing pages of the original diary. The map portrays, in schematic form, the extensive expanse of north-central North America over which Peter's travels took him, with his routes ostensibly indicated by dotted lines. Its caption reads: "MS Map accompanying Journal of a Trip from R. R. Settlement to Galena Ill., and Back, in 1844, & Showing Routes Taken by Author in His Various Travels." It seems that at some point after recording the Galena trip (Chapter 6), which he may have sensed would be his last, the diarist decided, as he had without known success in the case of his earlier tale of fur smuggling, to find some way of making the account public. And while he (or someone else, as discussed by Sandra in Appendix II) was at it, he threw in a visual guide to all his other major peregrinations as well.

The care with which this fair copy of Garrioch's earlier map was prepared, and the fact that it was labelled as "MS. [manuscript] Map" and referred to Peter as "Author," seems to confirm that Peter had at least occasionally entertained or even expressed the hope that his diaries would eventually be published. It is gratifying that Gunn and the present editors have at long last been able to help him fulfill that wish.

Two final comments may be in order. One concerns the pronunciation of Peter's surname; the other relates to the appropriate words with which to describe his ethnicity and that of the many other Rupertslanders of whole or partial Indigenous ancestry. Nowadays many of those whose last name is Garrioch pronounce it "Garreeok." We believe, but cannot prove, that some also did so in Peter's day. Peter himself, however – and others who knew him – pronounced his surname "Garrick," consistent with Scots and Orkney pronunciations.

In the years when Peter was writing his diary, persons of predominantly Indigenous ancestry were called – by themselves as well as by others – "Indians;" and those of significantly mixed Indigenous and European blood were known as "Half-Breeds" (the latter term modified by "French" or "English" if greater precision were thought necessary). The term "Métis" was not yet in common use – if used at all. While "Indians" and "Half-Breeds" were certainly often considered by many non-Indigenous others in the community to be persons of lower social status than those who lacked – or thought they lacked – any Aboriginal connection, those *terms* were generally considered by the entire community, including the persons themselves, to be purely descriptive, not pejorative.[40] To be true to the era and locale when and where the Garrioch diaries were written, the editors have therefore preserved "Indian" and "Half-Breed" where they appear in the transcribed text and, in part, in our own commentaries.

To sum up: any editor of an historical document such as Peter Garrioch's diaries needs to listen carefully to the voice of the writer and free it to launch itself towards the reader, however many years and changed contexts lie between writer and reader. Dale asked himself: who is the reader in this case?[41] His answer, Sandra believes, is that the reader in this case is not just the academic scholar, but anyone who is willing to be transported into the pleasure aroused by the humour, sagacity, courage, and authenticity of a lively, mid-19th-century Rupertslander whose world has disappeared, but whose wonderful voice has not.

---

40   As Jennifer S. H. Brown noted in *An Ethnohistorian in Rupert's Land: Unfinished Conversations* (Edmonton: Athabasca University Press, 2017), pp. 56-58, terms such as "half-breed" and "Indian" were still in flux during the period in which Peter was writing. This was in part due to the recent amalgamation between the HBC and the Northwest Company which tended to tie the evolution of the term "half-breed" to more negative concepts (such as "half-bred"), aided by George Simpson's use of the term "half-breed" in its pejorative sense, rather than the neutral and descriptive sense in which Peter continued to use it. "Métis" was not in use at the time, except among French speakers elsewhere than Red River. Brown suggests a return to the use of more neutral terms, such as "native-born," "of mixed ancestry," or "of mixed descent."

41   See Laura Millar Coles, "Looking Backward; Reaching Forward: The Champlain Society and Publishing," in *Occasional Papers of the Champlain Society*, pp. 15-35, & esp. p. 28.

Chapter 1

Roots

1768 – 1837

Peter's emigré grandfather, the prolific William Hemmings Cook

The story of Peter Garrioch tells us much about life on the Canadian prairies in the late eighteenth and early nineteenth centuries. It begins with his maternal grandfather William Hemmings Cook, a successful fur-trader, prominent Red River settler, eccentric, and prolific begetter of offspring.

Born in London, England, on May 30, 1768,[42] Cook was still in his teens when he entered the North American fur trade. Arriving on the shores of Hudson's Bay at age 18, he spent the next four years at York Factory on Hudson's Bay as a Hudson's Bay Company clerk. Then, in September, 1790, he was placed in charge of a small, inland fur-trading operation on the Nelson River. The following year he established Chatham House on Wintering Lake to compete with a nearby North West Company post, and remained there as Master until 1794.

After a year's leave in England, Cook returned to a series of increasingly responsible and higher-paid postings until, in 1810, he was appointed Chief Factor at York Factory on Hudson's Bay, responsible for that key operation, and also for a number of York Factory's several "dependency posts." During the winter of 1811-12, Cook's primary responsibility was the provisioning and transportation of a group of Scottish and Irish immigrants who, under the sponsorship of the Scottish Earl of Selkirk and the leadership of prairie pioneer Miles Macdonell, were wintering at York on their way south to establish Selkirk's Red River Settlement at the junction of the Red and Assiniboine Rivers in what is now Manitoba – a community where he would spend the final third of his life.

---

42   Unless otherwise indicated, all Cook references are to Irene M. Spry, "Cook, William Hemmings," *Dictionary of Canadian Biography* (University of Toronto Press, 1966+) VII, pp. 206-207, & sources noted therein. Although Spry states that Cook was born in 1768, census records for 1827, 1834, 1838, and 1840, as well as his burial record, indicate that his birth was two years earlier, in 1766. Ancestry.com.

Cook seems to have had at least three "country wives" – a term commonly applied to Indigenous women with whom European and Canadian fur-traders, in the absence of any clergy, often formed marital unions of varied durations "in the customary style" with local women. The journal of York Factory cleric Charles Bourke makes reference to Cook's wives in an entry for May 1, 1812: "Governor Cook [...] maintains 3 wives locked up. He keeps the keys himself, & I am informed he is so exhausted that a man who saw him but a few years ago would not, after some absence, know him to be the same."[43]

Although it was unlikely that he actually kept his wives "locked up" often or for long, it does appear that Cook's prolific marital arrangements failed to meet with the approval of some of his peers. Later that month, for example, Miles Macdonell wrote, with obvious disdain: "The present chief of Y[ork] F[actory] has three wives, by whom he has numerous issue. One he has discarded for being old, the other two are younger, and live with him at the Factory."[44]

It was the first of Cook's country wives, a woman called Kahnapawanakan, who is of greatest significance to the present account. That union, which seems to have been formed early in young Cook's first year at York Factory, led without much delay to the birth of their first child, a girl named Nancy Cook, who would in time become the link between the Cooks and the Garriochs. By the time Cook left for England, the union had produced two more children; and upon his return they resumed the relationship, resulting in at least one more child, and possibly several more.[45] Kahnapawanakan, who died in 1813,[46] was likely the wife Macdonell described the previous year as having been "discarded for being too old."

All of these pejorative remarks suggest that, while Cook was a talented man, he did not feel inhibited by mainstream Christian religious teachings about marriage and morality, and could be deliberately provocative, setting the stage for sometimes tense interpersonal relationships

---

43 AM: Selkirk Papers, Reel 187, MG2/A1, Vol. 67, pp. 1768-9. Is the implication that frequent relations with his three wives were responsible for Cook's exhaustion? The reliability of Charles Bourke's statement about Cook's behaviour is put in some question due to his poor reputation with Miles Macdonell, first governor of the Red River Colony, who wrote to Lord Selkirk from York Factory on October 1, 1811, that he was, "not fully satisfied with the Revd. Charles Bourke, & could wish to know what character he bore in his own Country...." In the next paragraph, however, Macdonell commented, while acknowledging Cook's adherence to his duty, that Cook was one of the Company's many servants who, "have families with Indian women.... Many of these are worth money & can afford to pay well for land." He asked Selkirk for, "instructions concerning such people." It is apparent that Cook's many Aboriginal wives were a matter of some notoriety and affected his reputation.

44 AM: Selkirk Papers, Reel 171, MG2/A1, Vol. 2, pp. 376/377: Miles Macdonell, Nelson Encampment, to Selkirk (May 31, 1812).

45 The biography of William Hemmings Cook (1768-1846) in redriverancestry.ca lists seven children of Cook and Kahnapawanakan: Nancy, Jane, Joseph, James, Samuel, Jeremiah and Margaret.

46 Ancestry.com.

in which his detractors could draw on Cook's personal life to discredit him. His marital and familial arrangements hit a nerve at a sensitive time in the British Empire's attitude towards the people it was colonizing.[47] At the same time, he apparently cared genuinely for his family, in his own way.

The exact number and identity of Cook's other wives are subject to some disagreement. Irene Spry mentions Mith-coo-coo-man-e'squaw (Mary Cocking), the daughter of explorer Matthew Cocking, whom Cook married in the customary fashion about 1808, also her half-sister, Wash-e-soo-e'squaw (Mary Budd), who may have become Cook's third wife by 1811, and suggests that there might have been others.[48] Other views differ in details. What is clear is that Mary Cocking eventually became his permanent wife, to whom he was legally wed in March, 1838, prompting one cynical observer to comment that Cook did so with the "intention of bringing his 35 years' courtship to an early close."[49] This remark by Simpson – and the attention he paid to Cook's marriages – should also be seen in the context of Simpson's efforts[50] to have HBC officers marry

---

47 Anne Lindsay sums it up well: "The British Empire at this time was actively trying to find a way out of the whole chattel slavery business, so claiming that [Cook's] women were being locked up and kept essentially as sexual slaves would have played into all sorts of anxieties about that, and about miscegenation, and about the moral character of the men of the realm who were going across great distances largely unsupervised and could be falling into all sorts of bad customs that would destroy their moral character and ultimately render British manhood unfit to rule. It was a complicated time to be a British man. People really felt that there could be Divine judgement wrought on Britain for her participation in chattel slavery, and that the British Empire could be snatched away if British values were being torn asunder by people (mostly men) 'going native' as they used to say. Bourke's fairly brief description of Cook seems to have leveraged some of these great fears. [On the other hand,] Captain Cook was a role model/symbol of what British colonialism and British manhood should look like: he was at heart a family man who always went home to his wife, and only uplifted the Indigenous people he encountered…." Email from Lindsay to Anderson (June 7, 2023).

48 Irene M. Spry, "William Hemmings Cook," *DCB* VII, pp. 206-207.

49 Simpson to Ross, HBCA/AM: MG1 D20/201, Microfilm Reel 311 (quoted in text below).

50 This effort on Simpson's part has not escaped strong modern condemnation, e.g., "When Simpson came to Rupertsland he took as a country wife, Betsy, daughter of Chief Factor William Sinclair St. and soon tired of her. He then acquired Margaret Taylor, daughter of a HBC man at York Factory. He abandoned her, while pregnant with their second child. There were also two other associations, each of which produced a child…. Finally he topped all of his gross acts towards country ladies when he went to England and returned in 1830 married to his cousin Francis Simpson, to live in the Red River Settlement where he eventually began the construction of a new headquarters at the site now known as Lower Fort Garry. With Simpson was his colleague John McTavish who had also married an English girl, having put aside his country wife of seventeen years even though they had six children living. Both men gave dowries to HBC employees to take over their ex-wives. As a result of these despicable actions, officers who remained devoted to their country wives turned with scorn on McTavish but were afraid of openly criticizing the powerful Governor.

"A new and painful era had begun. Leading officers who attempted to introduce their Métis wives to Francis Simpson were directly rebuffed by Simpson in person. This reduced the possibility of

non-Indigenous wives and the growing pressure across the fur trade for couples to marry in a Christian ceremony.[51]

It is indisputable that William Hemmings Cook had many children. While the ultimate number, as in the case of his wives, is uncertain, it is known that as early as 1815 he acknowledged ten sons and daughters, and that his will left bequests for eleven children and one grandchild, as well as for his "beloved wife Mary."[52] Irene Spry's biographical sketch points out that, "[h]is descendants included not only countless Cooks but also Garriochs, Budds, Calders, Wrens, and Erasmuses," and suggests that, "[i]t was his children and their progeny who constituted his most notable contribution to western Canada." And she concludes with Peter Garrioch's later tribute to his grandfather as: "the father of us all."[53]

Retiring from the Hudson's Bay Company in 1819 after more than 30 years in the fur trade, Cook and those of his family who remained with him settled at Red River about 1820 on two large lots,[54] comprising 500 acres in total, that faced each other across the Red River in areas

---

female company to a very few, mostly the wives of missionaries, women [who] may have been very dull company compared with the better travelled and broadly educated mixed-blood wives of some senior fur trade officers. Mrs. Simpson must have had a very unhappy time here and in 1833 her husband moved the headquarters to Lachine, Quebec.

"Probably for the average Métis life went on, not too much affected by the bickering in the upper levels of the settlement. It should be remembered that at this time only a very few people were European. The Métis were gaining strength as an independent people who could trade freely in the land of their birth. The settlement at White Horse Plains began to grow and was quite permanent, strengthening the idea of legal ownership in the area the need to have their rights guaranteed.

"One of those who openly traded privately, in spite of the wishes of the HBC, was Peter Garrioch…." Man.VHC, *Many Trails*, p. 13.

51   See Sylvia Van Kirk, *Many Tender Ties: Women in Fur-Trade Society, 1670-1870* (Norman: University of Oklahoma Press, 1983), which outlines the evolving mores of supplementing weddings *à la façon du pays* with ceremonies "joining in Holy wedlock," sometimes, as in Cook's case, after decades. In contrast, Simpson himself brought a British wife back to Red River, despite having left an Indigenous partner waiting after returning to England for a time, and his behaviour shaped Rupert's Land family evolution for decades. Jennifer S. H. Brown, *Strangers in Blood: Fur Trade Company Families in Indian Country* (Vancouver: University of British Columbia Press, 1980), pp. 123-130, 132-137, 144, 151-15, & 212-218; Jennifer S. H. Brown, "Partial Truths: A Closer Look at Fur Trade Marriage," in Theodore Binnema, *et al.*, eds., *From Rupert's Land to Canada* (Edmonton: University of Alberta Press, 2001), pp. 59-77.

52   Not only did Cook himself recognize his many children by leaving bequests in his will for them, but also his sister left a bequest for his eight Hudson's Bay children in her will of 1827, if he should die before her. HBCA/AM: A. 36/10, fol. 5. See Brown, *Strangers in Blood*, p. 109.

53   Spry, "William Hemmings Cook," *DCB* VII, pp. 206-207, and Chapter 8, diary entry for February 23, 1846.

54   Lots 155 (west – Image Plain) and 578 (east). Image Plain was one of the seven original parishes of Red River. Six miles down river from St. John's and just north of Kildonan, it was the locale of the

later called West and East St. Paul respectively. The lots were a retirement emolument from the Hudson's Bay Company – awarded along with a £100 per annum, seven-year pension.

Although he served on the Red River Settlement's governing Council of Assiniboia from time to time thereafter, Cook could not be considered to have been a very influential elder. Friendly and kind-hearted at times, mercurial and disputatious at others, he was described by George Simpson, the HBC's perspicacious, if not always fair-minded, North American Governor, as:

> a most extraordinary mixture of generous eccentricity, religion, drunkenness, and misanthropy. He cannot live with . . . [his closest neighbours] because they are too sober and penurious for him, yet he must be near them to enjoy their conversation; he cannot live with . . . [another neighbour] because both in and out of his cups he engrosses the whole of the conversation, and he has changed his residence about a dozen different times for as many ridiculous reasons.

After remarking that Cook, "has changed his residence about a dozen times for as many ridiculous reasons" Simpson concluded: "He is now turning his attention to farming and rearing cattle, but has not solidity to do any good."[55] This concluding prediction was accurate, for by 1843, when Cook's name last appeared in the census returns, he had only 20 acres under cultivation. He died in 1846.

Peter's Indigenous mother, Nancy Cook

It was in the early 1800s, while Cook was still in his prime and rapidly climbing the HBC promotion ladder, that his recently-widowed daughter Nancy[56] met William Garrioch, a young

---

second English parish. It was founded by the Reverend David Jones of the Church of England in 1825. This church was St. Paul's, but on the establishment of St. Andrew's near the Grand Rapids on the Red in 1829, it became known as the Middle Church. Douglas Kemp, "The Red River Parish," *Manitoba Pageant* 8:1 (September, 1962), pp. 20-23.

55 George Simpson to Andrew Colvile (20 May, 1822). AM: Selkirk Papers, Vol. 24, p. 71, nr. 112. In this context, it should be remembered that Simpson had a poor opinion of the Red River Settlement in general and by the early 1820s had a reputation as "mean-spirited and deficient in humanity." John S. Galbraith, *The Little Emperor: Governor Simpson of the Hudson's Bay Company* (Toronto: MacMillan, 1976), pp. 71-73, & 167-169. Cook's appointment to the council occurred on May 29, 1822, and he participated in various judicial and administrative proceedings. See E.H. Oliver, *The Canadian North-West: Its Early Development and Legislative Records: Minutes of the Councils of the Red River Colony and the Northern Department of Rupert's Land* (Ottawa, Government Printing Bureau, 1914), I, pp. 220, & 239 ff.

56 The scrip affidavit for Nancy Garrioch shows that she was born in 1785 to William Hemmings Cook and Kahnawpawamakan "(Cree Indian)." Library and Archives Canada: RG15-D-II-8-a, Vol. 1321, Microfilm reel: C-14928. Her first marriage was to James Sutherland, born c.1785, with

Chapter 1 – Roots

Orkneyman employed by the Company – as Cook had once been – as a York Factory clerk. Their "country marriage" took place around 1810 at Fort Pelly in accordance with Aboriginal custom, but they formally married on May 27, 1821, in Swan River, a ceremony that also included baptism for their children Harriet, John, Margaret, Peter, and Sally.[57]

Peter's Orkney father, the 'Inactive' William Garrioch

William Garrioch was born in Stromness, Orkney Islands, about 1787.[58] Apparently his family had sufficient means to provide him with an education, as he taught school there before deciding, in 1807 at age 20, to leave home and family and embark on a New World adventure that lasted a lifetime. Because the Hudson's Bay Company maintained an agent in the Orkneys and drew heavily on Orkneymen to staff its North American operations, young William was aware of employment prospects in North America. Added encouragement likely came from his father, whom one source identifies as, "Magnus Garrioch [...] a tailor [for the HBC] at Moose Factory until 1795, when Magnus returned to Scotland."[59]

Such an adventure would have suited William's interests and qualifications well, for it involved teaching. The HBC's Governor and Committee was giving consideration in early 1807 to establishing schools at some of its major Rupert's Land posts, and must have given the company's Stromness agent, David Geddes, advance notice of the possible future need for promising teachers. Geddes apparently responded somewhat prematurely, proposing William Garrioch as the first of the teachers, and asking what salary to offer the young man. London responded:

> With respect to schoolmasters being appointed to the Factories the mode to be adopted for that purpose is not quite concluded[.] The person whom you say was a parochial schoolmaster [...] will enter as a writer at £15 p ann for 5 years[,] the usual term & wages for writers on their first engagement[.] If he officiates as schoolmaster when he arrives in the Bay he will be allowed the same pay as others in the like station but I cannot say what that may be as it is not yet determined by the Board.[60]

---

whom she had a son, James Sutherland, Jr., born c.1803, whose father appears to have died not long after his son's birth. Around 1810, James' mother Nancy became the "Country wife" of William Garrioch. Red River Ancestry: "William Hemmings Cook;" & "James Sutherland, c.1803-1844."

57   HBCA/AM: Extract from registers of baptisms, marriages and burials in Rupert's Land sent to the Governor and Committee, E.4/1b folio 196, E.4/1a folio 34. Unfortunately, surviving missionary journals tell us nothing about this day..

58   Another source, Red River Ancestry, listed his birth date as c.1779, but two documents in the HBCA/AM confirm the later date: Garrioch's employment contract (A.32/16, fol. 23), and a "List of Servants, 1818-1819" at Swan River (A.30/16, fol. 10d-11).

59   Red River Ancestry.

60   HBCA/AM: A.5/4, fol. 171.

Apparently satisfied with those rather vague prospects, William signed a three-year contract on June 11, 1807, "at the rate of fifteen pounds p. year", and the HBC's York Factory Journal reported in an entry for the following March: "Mr. Garrock [sic] acting as schoolmaster," and on October 14 of that year that "Mr. Garrock [...] continues a diligent schoolmaster." Although the identity of his pupils is not disclosed, they were probably primarily the children of Company employees.

The same source discloses that the young man was at that point also carrying out a variety of other duties, including taking care of the post's guns and traps and hunting fox, grouse, and partridge for the post's kitchen.[61] And it appears that his role as HBC schoolmaster ended after that first year – not because of any recorded deficiency on his part, but because the Company may have thought better of its educational experiment. Garrioch was thereafter posted to Edmonton House in 1808,[62] and remained in western and southern Rupert's Land, actively involved in the fur trade, for the rest of his employment with the Company.[63]

At Edmonton House William Garrioch seems to have done well. The post records for the 1809-10 "outfit" (business year), state that, "His excellent character entitles him to £30 per ann from this date," plus a £13 "bounty,"[64] and his commendable performance there (plus, perhaps, a good word in an appropriate ear from his father-in-law William Hemmings Cook?) led to his promotion to second-in-command of the smaller Swan River establishment, considerably closer to Red River, in the summer of 1811. William was later described as the first teacher in Middlechurch, Manitoba.[65]

Peter's birth and large family

Peter Garrioch, his parents' second child, was born that summer also – on July 5, 1811. The exact location is not altogether certain, but it was said to have occurred on an island in a lake while the little family was in transit to Swan River. William's promotion would likely have taken effect June 1 – the first day of the new outfit (business year) – and he and his pregnant wife and first-born daughter Mary[66] would probably have left Edmonton House in the hope of reaching

---

61 HBCA/AM; B.239/f/114.

62 HBCA/AM; B.239/d/145/fol. 11.

63 A search file on William Garrioch maintained by the Archives of Manitoba that includes an extensive collection of his employment records discloses no return to schoolmaster responsibilities under the Hudson's Bay Company. However, Binnema, *From Rupert's Land,* p. 139, n. 2, indicates he taught for the Church Missionary Society in Red River from 1822.

64 HBCA/AM: B.239/d/145, fol. 5 & fol. 2.

65 *The Lethbridge Herald* (December 7, 1934).

66 This child, who did not survive childhood, was identified by descendants.

their new home at Swan River before their soon-expected second child arrived. They did not quite succeed.

The Reverend George Gunn, whose unpublished earlier edition of the Garrioch diaries has been so valuable a resource for the editors of the present volume, asserted in a long-ago article in *Minnesota History*[67] that Peter "was born [...] on an island in Lake Winnipeg, where his parents were forced to encamp while on a journey from Norway House to Swan River [...]" with an Aboriginal woman acting as midwife. That assertion was based on a letter from Peter's eldest son Kemper.[68]

While it seems unlikely that William, Nancy, and Mary Garrioch, who were journeying eastward from Fort Edmonton to take up residence at Swan River, would have traveled via Norway House, a considerable distance to the east of their destination, it is not altogether implausible that they might have done so. Perhaps William had some business reason to visit Norway House before proceeding to his ultimate destination. And it is certainly highly plausible that if Peter was born before they arrived there, they might have chosen an island – whether in Lake Winnipeg or, more probably, in Cedar Lake or thereabouts – as a suitable location for the unavoidable blessed event. Four more children were born to the Garriochs while they were at Swan River: a son, John, and three daughters, Margaret, Sally, and Harriet. Sadly, Mary – her parents' eldest child – died in 1816, leaving five-year-old Peter as the eldest sibling.

While at Swan River, William continued to be regarded as a reliable and dedicated employee, but he was not thought to be a promising trader. From the records, he seems to have been the post's manager, rather than one of its active traders, for much of the time he was there. In May, 1813, for example, a superior officer wrote: "Mr. Garrioch, who remains here in charge all summer & who is very worthy of the trust, will get the furs packed here during my absence."[69] The following year's entry described William as: "An assiduous young man, better qualified for the business of the storehouse than that of the Indian trade."[70] He did also spend a good deal of time in the field during those years, however, and likely improved his trading skills as a result. An 1816 assessment described him as "A very steady young man capable of conducting the trade

---

[67] George Henry Gunn, "Peter Garrioch at St. Peter's, 1837." *Minnesota History* 20 (1939), pp. 119-128, at p. 119..,

[68] The September 12, 1914, letter from Peter Garrioch's son Kemper Garrioch to Gunn says his father was born July 4, 1812, somewhere on Lake Winnipeg. AM: Gunn Papers. The present editors have retained the July 5, 1811 date of birth, however, on the basis of Peter's own claim that it was so, written on the cover of his diary. In addition, Gunn himself gives the date as July 5, 1811, in "Peter Garrioch at St. Peter's, 1837," p. 119, disregarding what Kemper had told him 35 years earlier.

[69] HBCA/AM: B.176/a/1.

[70] HBCA/AM: A.30/14.

of a District;"[71] and the Swan River records for 1818/1819 stated that he was: "Sober, honest and a good accomptant [sic] & has a tolerable knowledge of the inland trade."[72] The latter description may have been written by Peter's father-in-law, with whom he traveled during that period.

The HBC's final known assessment of William Garrioch was recorded in 1822 in Governor George Simpson's cold, but probably accurate words:

> An honest good creature, but inactive and does not possess talent as a Clerk or Trader[.] [H]as saved about £500. [B]urdened with a large Family on account of which he is not disposable. [R]esigned this season [...][73]

The Garriochs remained at Swan River until 1821,[74] when William took his family to live at the Red River Settlement. That was the year when the Hudson's Bay Company and its former arch-rival North-West Company agreed to merge under the name of the former. The amalgamation resulted in a massive lay-off/retirement of redundant employees, who included William Garrioch the following year. It wasn't an employment change that William welcomed. Historian Marcel Giraud noted William's comment to Governor George Simpson. "I candidly confess that nothing but the necessity of the times could ever have induced me to become a settler at the Red River," he wrote, and pointed out that he was "unaccustomed to labour"[75] of the type involved in transforming primordial prairie into productive farm land. With no viable alternative immediately available, however, William proceeded to do just that. At Red River, he and his family took up residence in St. John's parish, on property adjoining that of Nancy's father. Of their five children, Peter was then about nine or ten and Harriet, the youngest, was a toddler aged two or three years.

Soon after arriving at Red River, where there existed a church and clergy, William and Nancy Garrioch formalized their country marriage. The wedding, conducted by the Reverend John West, took place on the 27th of May, 1821, in the Anglican Church. Nancy and their five surviving

---

71   HBCA/AM: A.30/12-15.

72   HBCA/AM: A.30/16, fol. 10d-11.

73   HBCA/AM: B.239/f/12.

74   Although HBC records date his retirement from 1822 (HBCA/AM: B.239/f/12), the family is known to have been at Red River by at least May, 1821. Perhaps a period of terminal leave was a retirement inducement.

75   Marcel Giraud, *The Métis in the Canadian West*, George Woodcock trans. (Lincoln & Edmonton: University of Nebraska & University of Alberta Presses, 1986), II, *passim*. William was sworn in as a special constable in October, 1823, along with Donald Gunn, Cuthbert Grant, Andrew McDermott, James Hargrave, et al. Rev. Dr. George Bryce and Charles N. Bell, "Original Letters and other Documents relating to the Selkirk Settlement," *Manitoba Historical Society Transactions*, Series 1, nr. 33 (January, 1889).

children were baptised that same day. Nancy's father, William Hemmings Cook, did not share her eagerness for formal confirmation of marital status, however. Almost 15 years later, on February 20, 1836, Governor George Simpson's cousin Thomas Simpson remarked in a letter from Red River to his friend Donald Ross that, amid much recent talk in the settlement about …"marrying all of us unhappy bachelors":

> [O]ld Mr. Cook has stood manfully forth and declared his intention of bringing his 35 years' courtship to an early close. The temporary delay, he says, is caused by a sudden turn for literature which his mistress has taken, to gratify which he has the walls of his den chalked with the alphabet in large characters. As soon as she has gone through this ordeal there will be no further obstacle, he says, to the fatal ceremony.…[76]

Cook managed to delay his own "fatal ceremony" for another two years before finally succumbing to respectability in 1838.

Four more children were born to William and Nancy Garrioch after their union was officially solemnized: Gavin, Emma, Ann, and William. And for young Peter and his siblings those years appear generally to have been stable ones, undoubtedly nourished in part by the proximity of their grandfather, whose relationship with his grandchildren was very warm.

The Family's stability threatened by flood

In 1825, with the family's new home presumably in sufficiently good order, William found employment more suitable to his interests and talents than sod-busting. Reverend David Jones, an Anglican missionary who had come to Red River in 1823 to take over the mission established in the St. John's area of the settlement by Reverend John West, had need of a teacher for the mission's school, the previous teacher having left, and William Garrioch, who had been instructing his own and neighbours' children at his home, was a willing and able replacement.[77] William's first letter to the sponsoring Church Missionary Society in London reflected both the

---

76   HBCA: MG1 D20/201, Microfilm Reel 311.

77   *The Missionary Register, Missionary Papers, Mission Book, North-West Canada, CC 1 M 1*, empire. amdigital.co.uk, (December, 1826), p. 624, says that he took charge of the Mission School at R.R. Presumably Peter was among his pupils, although by 1825, Peter was 14 years old. Given the fact that Peter himself later became a teacher, as did several brothers and cousins, one can assume that his father gave care to his schooling well before that. The mixed-ancestry community placed great store in education, especially as a means of broadening opportunity, and it has been said that "company servants who had a suitable background were given time to teach the children of families there. It is possible that at the time young Métis at Company posts had at least as good a chance of gaining an elementary education as many of the poor boys in Britain," and by 1821, when the HBC combined with the NWC, "the Red River Settlement had a large number of well educated and cultured men and women of mixed blood." Man.VHC, *Many Trails*, pp. 11-12.

enthusiasm he felt about returning to his first profession on a full-time basis and the excessive formalism with which he sometimes expressed himself:

> Permit one who is an entire stranger to you to intrude himself on your notice, by acknowledging his acceptance of appointment, to succeed Mr. Harbridge, as schoolmaster in the Church Missionary School in this place, under the superintendence & direction of our dearly beloved & faithful minister, the Rev'd Mr. Jones. Permit me also, sir, to desire an interest in your prayers, that I may be enabled to discharge the duties of that situation to which God in his providence is now calling me in a manner that will be calculated to promote his own glory, so that consequently my friends may not have cause to repent the choice they have made, nor the feelings of the Society be hurt by my subsequent conduct in their service.[78]

William's 1826 report to the Church Missionary Society[79] revealed that one of his six pupils was his young son and namesake William. His other students were three who came from the Rocky Mountain area, two prairie Cree, and one "Esquimeaux" (Inuit). That fifteen-year-old Peter was not among his charges suggests that someone other than his father – probably Reverend Jones – taught the older children.

The family's stability, along with that of most other Red River residents, was shaken seriously in May, 1826, when the greatest flood ever known to strike the Red River Settlement forced the abandonment of Fort Garry and destroyed almost every other building in the settlement. Much of the destruction was caused by floating ice that split trees and demolished houses. Fortunately, although eight settlers and several Natives along the Assiniboine River were reported to have drowned, Hudson's Bay Company boats among others were able to rescue many people stranded on rooftops.[80]

---

78   AM: Microfilm Reel 87 (June 20, 1825). William Garrioch "assumed the reigns [sic]" of the school on August 4, 1825, on the authority of Reverend David Jones: CMSA/AM: Section V, Missions to the Americas Mission Bk 1, *North-West America, p. 126.* By this time, Peter would have been of school age, but there is no reference known to the editors of what kind of schooling he received. It is tempting to think that he just fit into his father's classes, but neither the age level nor type of classes taught by William are known. Peter may have been part of the cohort of older boys taught by someone else, such as the Reverend Jones.

79   *Ibid.* (August 8, 1826).

80   See J. M. Bumsted: "Early Flooding in Red River, 1776-1861" in his *Thomas Scott's Body and Other Essays on Manitoba History* (Winnipeg: University of Manitoba Press, 2000), pp. 77-89. Bumsted refers to only five deaths, but he may not have taken account of casualties outside the settlement proper. More details, including ones pertaining to William Garrioch and his family, are contained in Reverend David Jones' Journal: "Sunday, May 7th, 1826. Very few could attend church this day. Mr. Cochran preached in the morning from Job V 6:7 This is a happy day in England, but a very melancholy one in Red River; Still, we could say I trust from the heart, 'to whom should we go thou hast the words of Eternal life.'"

Chapter 1 – Roots

J.M. Bumsted's account of the flood quotes from a settler's letter to an English acquaintance stating that, "the only buildings which have not been carried away or so much injured as not to deserve notice," were "the three churches, the residence of the clergy, and the house of our

> "May 13, 1826… Since last Monday Morning Mr. Cochran, Mr. Garrioch [the teacher at the school, William Garrioch], and myself have been endeavouring to secure all the property we could belonging both to ourselves & the Church Missionary Society, and tho' we were gradually during that time up to the middle in water we suffered no inconvenience in regard to our health…. About 10 o'clock last night, the water entered the church over the threshold of the door, and the appearance as was presented to us this morning was a very dreary one, still we cling to the hope that the river is nearly at its height. An immense number of Log-houses are floating down through the plains at the back of our premises this morning. Among others I noticed one of the watch towers of Fort Garry, accompanied with a whole range of Stockades from before New Fort Douglas. Indeed, it is more than probable the buildings will be swept away now, for being all build of wood they become buoyant as soon as the water reaches the roofs unless some additional [?] added. We were busy all this day preparing a stage in case the water should continue to swell; on which for safety's sake Mr. & Mrs. Cochran took up their abode in the evening; and indeed it was well they did for in the evening the water burst into our dwelling and in a few minutes stood 1 ½ feet [0.46 m] deep on the floor.
>
> "May 15, 1826, Last night we passed with little or no rest; the wind blew a storm all night, which shook our stage in an alarming manner. During the night the water rose six inches which is a great deal considering the extent of surface which it now occupies. As far as the eye can reach nothing is seen but water all the people are dispersed in quest of high eminences with their cattle and property.
>
> "After breakfast we were reluctantly compelled to abandon the premises. We had no other resource left, our house had five feet [1.5m] [of] water on the floor, and the church six feet and a half. The houses being all of wood there seemed no prospect of their remaining much longer unless the water should abate. We placed all the property not wanted with us in the loft of the church, with two views, the water was hitherto six feet under the beams, so that it would be sometime before it was in danger there of being damaged; in addition to this thought the weight would repel the buoyancy of the building.
>
> "About 1 pm a Settler came alongside of the stage with a boat and took off Mr. & Mrs. Cochran, myself & domestics; leaving behind until the morning Mr. Garrioch and family, together with the Indian School [children].
>
> "May 16th 1826 Last night I felt uneasy the moment I arrived in consequence of the necessity under which I had been placed of leaving the Indian Boys on the Stage at the Mission house, and I lost no time in applying to Mr. McKenzie the Chief Officer in charge at Fort Garry for a boat which was obligingly given me this morning, with which I left the encampment at 1/2 past 3 in the morning for the Stage and safely embarked all the individuals there with whom I reached the camp again about 12. On my arrival, Mr. McKenzie strongly advised me to send for all our property, he stated it as his opinion that all buildings of every description would be carried away; as the waters continue to increase in every direction with great rapidity; accordingly, Mr. Cochran took a Boat back again and brought away all he could and returned about 12 at night. Mr. Cochran on his return said that all our fences, Garden, Stockades, as well as those about the church yard were swept away; and that the current about the buildings was as strong as to make the probability of their destruction amount almost to certainty." CMSA/AM: Section V, Missions to the Americas Mission Bk 1, *North*-West *America*.

social prayer meeting," plus "the windmill,"[81] all of which had been constructed on high ground. Livestock losses were extensive – a depressing setback to a community that had been slowly building its herds over the past several years from expensive breeding stock imported from the United States. Some settlers, including most of the colony's Swiss and German populations – about 250 in all – soon left the area altogether and emigrated to the United States.

Although it is not known precisely how the Garrioch family was affected by the flood in terms of immediate property loss, "Mr. Garrioch and family, together with the Indian School [children]" had to wait overnight for another rescue boat after Reverend Jones and Reverend and Mrs. Cockran had been evacuated from the rising flood waters so vividly described by Reverend Jones.[82] Peter was 15 at the time, and the harrowing experience must have left a mark on him.

Nevertheless, it seems likely that the Garriochs, along with the majority of settlers who chose to remain at Red River, "sprang back to life very quickly," in Bumsted's words, when the waters receded.[83] According to a contemporary source whom Bumsted quotes, the community repaired, re-built, seeded, and cultivated their devastated properties, "with as much enthusiasm as if no misfortunes had ever befallen them." The ensuing summer brought fine growing weather, and autumn produced a bumper harvest. In the 1827 census of Red River, taken the following

---

81   John Pritchard's observation in a letter to England, quoted in Bumsted, "Early Flooding," p. 82.

82   *Ibid.*

83   Another description of the flood and the ensuing recovery is found in the account of Father George-Antoine Belcourt, who figures later in Peter's diaries: "In 1825, the snow fell the 15th of October in great quantity, and remained on the ground. Still more fell during the winter, which was one of the coldest which had passed for twenty-five years. The snow melted suddenly about the last of April. The water had already risen in the streams as high as the banks, when the ice, which had scarcely diminished in thickness, was dragged away by the violence of the current, and taking a straight course, rooted up trees and demolished edifices and whatever found itself in its way. The water rose five feet in the church of St. Boniface, nearly opposite the mouth of the river Assiniboine, which is one of the most elevated spots in that vicinity.

"The fish, the principal resource of the inhabitants at this season of the year, were dispersed in this immense extent of water, and the fishermen were not able to take them. To crown their misfortunes, the bison that were ordinarily found in abundance near the river Pembina, went away, and about fifteen persons who had calculated on this resource, perished from hunger. The waters did not retire entirely till the 20th of July; when some persons risked sowing barley, which came to maturity.

"After so many scourges of different kinds, one would think that the survivors would have been ready to abandon forever a country which offered only disasters and difficulties. Some of them did indeed leave and go to the United States; others lived like the savages, by hunting and fishing, for several years, after which they returned to the culture of the earth; at last, having had good crops during several years, the remembrance of their misfortunes was effaced." Father G. A. Belcourt, "The Department of the Hudson's Bay," *Collections of the Minnesota Historical Society* I (St. Paul: Ramaley, Chaney, 1872), pp. 220-221.

spring, William Garrioch was recorded as having a house and stable, a mare, five calves, three cows and an ox, as well as a cart, a plough, a canoe, and five acres under cultivation.

Two years later, however, William moved his family north to higher ground in the St. Andrews area, as a number of others who had lived through the crisis were doing, and there, on lots 42 and 43, he built "Orkney Cottage," the home in which his and Nancy's children would grow to adulthood.

While his main motive for moving was doubtless to reduce the risk of ever being flooded again, the decision may also have been influenced by other factors. Greater proximity to the Hudson's Bay Company's establishment at Lower Fort Garry could have been one of those additional factors; but of much more likely significance to the family was the warm, eventually life-long, friendship with Reverend William Cockran[84]. A rough-hewn, plain-speaking man of astonishing energy and unshakeable determination to minister thoroughly to the colony's Indigenous and mixed-blood populations – as well as to teach them the farming skills they would need in their increasingly Europeanized surroundings – Cockran planned to establish a church in the St. Andrews area. And although he did not do so until 1829, it is highly probable that his intentions were known to the Garriochs, as well as to others who wished to be part of his new congregation. The presence of other Orkney-born, former HBC employees, and their mixed-blood country-born offspring, who had moved or were moving to the area for similar reasons, likely constituted yet another inducement.

William's health began to fail in 1827-28. His 1828 report to the Christian Missionary Society[85] disclosed that:

> For upwards of two years I have had a complaint in my breast which has gradually been getting worse, & which obliged me last winter to apply for medical advice, & I derived very little benefit from the medicines I took. After some time, I made a second application to the Colonial Surgeon, who candidly told me that ...the best thing I could do was to give over singing; as tho' he did not consider the symptoms at present dangerous, yet if I continued to sing, there was danger of bringing myself under a consumption.

But he nevertheless assured Society officials:

> I went on, anxious to discharge my duty to the utmost, till my lungs got so weak that I could not read a chapter in the Bible without difficulty, & then reluctantly told Mr. Jones that I could take the risk no longer. This was about the middle of last June. I desire to thank God that, weak as I was, I never lost one day from school, tho' I was often very uneasy in it.

---

84   See below, Chap. 3, n. 206, on Cockran's pedagogy, and Chap. 10, *passim*.

85   CMSA/AM: Microfilm Reel 87 (August 9, 1828)..

Yet he hoped to continue carrying out his teaching duties:

> I am happy to be able now to add that since I did take Mr. Bunn's advice, or rather was compelled by my weakness to take it, my health has been so much improved that I hope still to be able to go on with the school, except it be a regulation of your Society that no schoolmaster should be eligible to hold his situation as such, the strength of whose lungs will not permit him to lead the singing in divine worship.

His reasoning was that so many others were dependent on his financial support:

> ...I have a large family of nine children by a native woman. I have poor old parents in Orkney, unable to work & now verging on their threescore & ten, to whom I had not [until] now been able to offer any assistance, had not God brought me here.

Provided that the Society had no objection to his doing so:

> Yet none of these considerations, deeply interesting as they are to the feelings of a father solicitous for the welfare of whose children, or to a son anxious for the comfort of his parents, would move me with a wish to remain as a burden on your Society a day longer than I was able in some measure to perform the duties they expected of me....

The Society did not ask William to resign at that point, and he did not do so voluntarily. His next report, in 1829,[86] announced, however, that:

> Instead of getting better I grew worse, & since last March I have not been able to read aloud a chapter of any length without giving me considerable pain.... I have therefore come to the determination to send home my resignation to your Society this year, & may the Lord provide you with one to succeed me better qualified for the work, & more successful in it than I have been....

Notwithstanding that unequivocal announcement, William stayed on for yet another year, until October 1, 1830. And even his final report in 1830, in which he announced that he had indeed resigned at long last, seemed to indicate that he had only done so because his hand had been forced by Reverend Jones: "Although I am happy to say that my health is much better," he wrote, "I have consented, at Mr. Jones' request, to stop [teaching]," adding that he had done so "in the expectation of your Society sending me one out by the ship to succeed me...." Jones also felt that the replacement must come from "home."[87]

---

86   CMSA/AM: Microfilm, Reel 8 (August 4, 1829).

87   Jones to CMS (August 7, 1830). CMSA/AM: Microfilm Reel 87.

William's replacement was William R. Smith who reported to the Church Missionary Society that, "a number of Swampy Cree Indians came here the last autumn, and are dwelling within reach of the School, [and] have increased the number of my day Scholars."[88] In a subsequent report, Smith lamented the uncertain future of the school, remarking that,

> as the time drew nigh for me to depart …I may truly say it was a Season of trial, when I reflected that there would be about 100 children cast off again and likewise a number of Poor Indians who had travelled some hundreds of miles on purpose," and who had, "established themselves in the vicinity of the Missionary Establishment so as to get instruction themselves & for their children.[89]

Peter as Teacher

It is known, however, that by 1832 William's 21-year-old son Peter Garrioch – the principal subject of this account – was teaching in the mission schoolrooms.[90] In 1835, having moved a paying boarding school to the Lower Church and securing the future of the local day school after all by leaving it open on the original site, Reverends Jones and Cockran reported that the local school was operating under Peter Garrioch, a local Métis teacher they described as "a young man of steady and correct habits…," with an enrolment of, "50 children, *viz*. 11 Scotch Highlander children, 20 [Métis], and 18 Indian boys or girls."[91] After noting that Smith had given up the school for various reasons, the chief of which were "the salary being reduced to too low a scale and himself a man of rather improvident habits," Jones stated further that:

> The School is now under the charge of Peter Garrioch, a son of our friend W. Garrioch formerly in the Society's employ. A steady and I trust (I am really afraid to speak with any degree of positiveness) a very religious young man. The school has thriven wonderfully under him since the management was committed to him.[92]

---

88 Mr. W.R. Smith to the Secretaries of CMS (August 8, 1832). CMSA/AM: Section V, Missions to the Americas Mission Bk 1, North-West America.

89 Mr. W.R. Smith to the Secretaries of CMS (*August 1, 1834*). Original Papers Letters and Papers of individual missionaries, catechists, and others, William Robert Smith, 1831-1845. CMSA/AM: Missions to the Americas, Bk 2, *North*-West *America*.

90 S.M. Johnson and T.F. Bredin, "David Thomas Jones," *DCB* VII, pp. 454-455.

91 "Report of the state of Religion, Morality, and Education at the Red River Settlement and Grand Rapids by the Revd Messr^s Jones and Cockran," [1835] in CMSA/AM: Section V, Missions to the Americas Mission Bk 2, *North*-West *America*.

92 *Ibid*. Rev. David Jones to the Clerical Secretary (August 10, 1835).

Unfortunately, as he wrote on May 16, 1837, Jones was "in difficulty again because Peter Garrioch has resigned."

Peter continued to teach there until his 1837 departure for the United States in search of the theological education with which his diary opens. Had he in fact started his pedagogical career even earlier than that? Had William's reluctance to retire until Reverend Jones pressured him to do so, and his pointed desire to be replaced by someone from England, been influenced by a desire not to be supplanted by his own son? We may never know.

It appears clear, however, that although William may have provided much less emotional support to his children than did their mother and their grandfather, his influence on at least Peter's and John's career path was powerful. William and Peter were not the only Garriochs to teach at Red River. After Peter set off on the various adventures recorded in his diary, brother John took over his pedagogical duties at the mission school.[93]

On January 14, 1832, the first of William and Nancy's children left the nest when Margaret married William Gaddy,[94] later to become a renowned buffalo hunter, and the young couple moved into the home of Gaddy's parents on Lot 42, close to her grandfather's homestead.

The Garrioch family prospered moderately over the years thereafter. The 1835 census indicates that William had twenty acres under cultivation by then and possessed two horses and two

---

93   Among the little information we have about John's teaching career is that he was farming and teaching school in Portage La Prairie by the time brother William Garrioch, Jr. pulled up stakes in St. Peter's in 1862 and moved to join the family in Portage La Prairie. Mrs. Norquay, the widow of John Norquay, Premier of Manitoba from 1878 until 1888, recalled that she attended the school at Park's Creek, where John Garrioch was the teacher. Born in 1842 at Park's Creek, she recalled that, "the children would take with them to school a bannock each to eat at the noon hour, and after they had eaten their bannocks they would play 'cross-tag,' 'wolf,' 'button' and other games. In the winter as many of them as could find room on an old buffalo robe, which they would use as a toboggan, would slide down the river bank. 'The first thing every morning at school was the reading of a chapter of the Bible,' the old lady recalled. 'After recess there would be another chapter. And school closed in the afternoon with prayer. The desks were sloping boards along the wall. The little children who were beginners had cards with the alphabet and little words on them. In the winter most of the girls used to come wearing coats made with two-point 'H.B.' blankets, with a leather cord to hold them together. And we wore woollen caps and moccasins, of course, outside of duffels made of the white or blue blanket-cloth and coming up to the knees and tied there to keep the snow out. At the school we had slates and slate-pencils. A boy or girl who had no pencil used a lump of clay instead, and if there were little pieces of stone in it they scratched the slate and you could rub the writing off, but not the scratches…." W. J. Healy, *Women of Red River* (Winnipeg Women's Canadian Club, 1923), pp. 49-50.

94   On Gaddy, Mary Cocking, Peter Garrioch, & Henry Budd see R. Beaumont & L. Barkwell, The Virtual Museum of Metis History and Culture (Saskatoon: Gabriel Dumont Institute of Native Studies and Applied Research).

dozen cattle. The household was stated to comprise nine persons, which appears to confirm that all the Garrioch offspring, other than Margaret, were still at home.

That does not necessarily rule out temporary absences from the home hearth, of course. Although Peter's teaching responsibilities must have kept him close to Orkney Cottage much of the time, it is difficult to believe that the restless young man his diaries show him to have been did not find ample opportunity to partake in the more robust activities that engaged most of his male contemporaries. Although the specific non-teaching activities in which Peter likely took part at this point in his life are unknown to the editors, the considerable skill in wilderness travel, hunting, and fur-trapping he had obviously acquired by the time the diary opens suggest considerable early outdoor experience.

He was also beginning to take an interest in his own importance. It was 1835 when Peter purchased the large, leather-bound record book in which most of his surviving diary entries would later be written. The young man clearly intended to make something of his life, and the idea of recording his exploits for posterity was in his mind as early as the year he acquired that book and wrote the following on the title page:

1835

The Life of [subsequently erased name]

Who was born in the year 1811, July 5

[the latter date – which was Peter's birthdate – unsuccessfully erased][95]

It would be some two years later before Peter actually began to chronicle his life, and the erasures in the foregoing entry suggest that he may have had second thoughts during that interval about either his career ambitions or his diarizing intentions. Other notations on that same page of the then otherwise-empty record book offer glimpses, however, of an original and critical mind – one that would soon be filling its pages with wise, woolly, and wild observations on a wide range of topics.

---

95   The inside covers of the bound volume of Peter's journal (AM: MG-2 C-38) bears a mix of later random and not-so-random notations and scribbles, some illegible. For example, Peter recorded the annual expenses of various categories of police and magistrates in the amount of £460, from which he listed the amount of £200 as sufficient for those expenses, and the remainder of £260 could be better appropriated to public improvements, as £60 ("this would ditch 2 miles") and £200 ("This would purchase a printing press and hire a printer with one Devil [apprentice] for a year.")

The inside back page of the bound volume is crowded with calculations, jottings, experimental spellings, and doodles, which often overlap each other. There is a list of persons who appear to be Councilors of Assiniboia, and a calculation concluding "£2.5.1½ – Amt. of duty for 1844." The name of Peter's yearned-for Isabella is repeated many times, concluding: "Fortunately, Isabella McKenzie is a witless wind-headed Creature" The "Fortunately" may be unconnected to the comment about Isabella, since there are several trial spellings of the word above it.

Those first jottings concerned a recent change in the Settlement's governance. In February, 1835, the Hudson's Bay Company's North American Governor-in-Chief George Simpson persuaded the Council of Assiniboia – the Company-controlled local government of the area – to institute a major re-structuring of the Red River Settlement's theretofore quite primitive policing and judicial system.[96] The new arrangements would be expensive – too much so for Peter Garrioch's liking. After calculating that the total annual cost of the 62 proposed law-enforcement and magisterial personnel would be £460, which he considered exorbitant, he noted on the blank journal's title page that after subtracting the £200 he estimated as a sufficient expenditure for those purposes, the remaining £260 could be used to excavate two miles of ditches along Settlement roads, purchase a much-needed printing press, and have enough left over to provide a year's salaries for a printer and helper to operate the press!

So the young man whose observations of life at Red River and in other parts of North-Central North America from 1837 to 1847 would later be recorded in his diaries can be seen to have already been, at the age of 24, serious, concerned about public affairs, rather imaginative, critical of authority, and keen about the dissemination of information in print – the latter characteristic interesting in light of lack of firm evidence as to whether he ever intended to publish his diary.

Let us now turn to the diary itself.

---

96 See, generally, Gibson, *LLG, I*, pp. 36 ff.

Chapter 2

From Red River To St. Peter's[97]

1837

When, in the middle of June, 1837, Peter Garrioch finally began using his journal for its intended purpose, it was to record his probable first extended travel away from home – a journey he hoped would lead to a career in the service of God. His plan was to study theology in the United States and become a Protestant missionary. The young man was no stereotypical, sober-sided student of divinity, however. It was a light-hearted, fun-loving, if devoutly Christian and occasionally pompous young man who took leave of his friends and loved ones on an early summer morning.

Farewell to Orkney Cottage

This 14th day of June, 1837 – Wednesday[98] – will be ever memorable to the author of this little, but very important, journal as being the day of his first leaving home for a protracted absence, after a nursing of five and twenty years by his mammy's fireside: the commencement of that era in which he betook himself to traveling, directing his course due southward.

I mounted my mare Peskee on the above date, on the banks of the Red River by the door of the good old Orkney Cottage.[99] Little Lillipoot [Peter's dog] was at my heels,

---

97   St. Peter's was the collective name for the encampments around the Fort Snelling military post that became the nucleus of the modern twin cities of Minneapolis and St. Paul, Minnesota.

98   This first diary entry begins on page {43} of the Gunn typescript. Gunn devoted the first 42 pages to his two Introductions, "Peter Garrioch: Teacher, Trader, Traveler, Diarist," & "Garrioch, Life and Times," which have been borrowed from, but not reproduced, in this edition. Gunn's pagination will continue to be recorded in the diary entries in order to facilitate comparison with his manuscript. The reader is reminded that the interpolated subheadings in the diary text and the comments, both in bolded type, are Dale's.

99   Gunn: "Mr. Garrioch's paternal home. The Garrioch homestead of this date was lot 40, St. Paul's Parish, and was located on the west bank of the Red River, about eight miles north of the present

anxiously waiting for the signal. All being ready, we bade a kind farewell to our nearest and dearest friends in the midst of tears, sighs, and throbbings of heart. My Lillipoot, however, excepted; for he, not having acquired the art of crying, and having no ears to squat and prick up alternatively as a mark of his regret in parting with dear friends, very uneasily shook his tail (of which he had about three inches) and, nodding his head towards the heels of my mare, made solemn expression of a most cordial adieu. At the word {44}[100] "Gee!" he was instantly something less than a mile in advance.

As for myself, having proceeded a few yards, nature would assert itself and, wheeling my head round, the first object that came in contact with my ocular perceptions was my good old mammy who, with head bowed and shoulder leaning against the door of the porch, watched the onward movement of our train. "Was that a dart!" say you who have kind and tender mothers[101] to leave behind when bidding a perhaps eternal adieu to a sweet and desirable home. Should this have suppressed a pure, ardent and laudable desire? No! Feeling should ever yield to her superior: duty. I went on my way, and my dear friends returned [home] weeping.

After crossing the river Assiniboine[102] we proceeded some distance and encamped within a few miles of the Stinking River.[103] Horrid idea! {45} A river to stink! Reminds me of Moses.

City of Winnipeg, where the Mausoleum Cemetery Company's mausoleum now stands" Gunn's note reflects his knowledge of Winnipeg and environs as it was in the 1930s or 1940s, long after the Garriochs' time. Today the area has a number of cemeteries close together.

100 This number and others like it, refer to the pagination of Gunn's original transcriptions.

101 Is the absence of any reference to Peter's father among the several references to his mother and "dear friends" significant? Might his father have been absent?

102 Since there was no bridge over the Assiniboine at that time, and it would be another eight years before even a ferry service was officially established, crossing the river would probably have involved hiring or being given passage in a barge large enough to transport horse, rider and dog – as well as Garrioch's brother and mount, who, as will be seen, accompanied him as far as his first encampment. For various possible routes and modes of transportation, see Rhoda R. Gilman, Carolyn Gilman, and Deborah L Miller, *The Red River Trails: Oxcart Routes between St. Paul and the Selkirk Settlement 1820-1870* (St Paul: Minnesota Historical Society, 1979).

103 La Salle River. A long note by Gunn explained, among other things, that it was originally called "La Sale" (the dirty), which would account for the name anglophones gave it in Garrioch's day. It was probably at the Stinking River encampment that Garrioch rendezvoused with the other members of the larger party with which he was to travel to Minnesota. Convoys of riders and horse or ox-drawn carts were a common form of transport between Red River and St. Peter's at the time. See: *Manitoba Names* (Winnipeg: Manitoba Conservation, 2001).

Farewell to Brother John

June 15, 1837 – Thursday.[104] Found myself rather cold and chilly last night, being exposed to the open air. It feels, however, much milder this morning.

How pleasant to have a friend – a dear brother who can strike the strings of sympathy with that delicacy of touch and sensitiveness of feeling which not even the strains of musical harmony could surpass! I had a brother. Here we parted. He felt, and I felt – what? You who have dear, beloved, brothers decide.[105]

The Procrastinating Guide

The guide not making his appearance this morning, we were obliged to proceed [without him] and, through the directions of a stranger, to make the best of our way towards the "crossing" – a place on the Red River so called, I presume, from its once being the only place used for crossing horses, carts, &c.[106] We arrived here in a very

---

104   This form of date reference will be used throughout. Garrioch generally dated his entries in a similar fashion, but his format sometimes varied.

105   Which of Peter's three brothers was the object of this poignant parting is not certain, but Gunn thought it was John, and that seems likely, since John was next in age to Peter. If so, the tenderness of Peter's words provides interesting background to the feuds in which the two would engage in later life. The device of referring to his readers' experience the nature and strength of the brothers' emotional response to the parting may suggest that he was, at least at this early stage of his journalizing, consciously writing with publication in view. It should be noted that he drew similarly on readers' own past reactions when describing his melancholy parting from his mother.

106   Ox carts, oxen, and the trials and tribulations associated with them are the objects of frequent and often humorous and light-hearted comments throughout the diaries. Given that they were so essential to Peter's trading activities and to trading and hunting in general, he did not describe the carts themselves in sufficient detail to acquaint future generations unfamiliar with them to their real character. An interesting description was provided by Anne M. Collier, *A History of Portage la Prairie & Surrounding District* (Altona, Man.: W. Friesen, 1970), pp. 31-32:

> "Many were the hardships our settlers endured while using this mode of travel: the mosquitoes, flies and other insects for which there was no repellent, the bumpy trails with bogs and creeks that were a part of the journey.... The cart was made of tough well-seasoned oak wood, throughout. There were two rough shafts, called 'trams' by the settlers, each about twelve feet in length (although the length could be as great as eighteen feet). Cross pieces were then firmly morticed into the trams with the two outer cross pieces being about six feet apart. The provided the foundation of the cart. Holes were then bored into the upper surface of the trams, vertical rails were inserted into the holes, and cross bars were set across the top of the rails. Across the rear of the cart was the tail board. (Carts in a brigade were often fastened rein to tailboard.) The nave, spokes and felloes of the wheel were 'dished' (curved) to give the Cart steadiness.

early part of the day; but we were obliged from the necessity of the case to spend the remaining part of the day at this place.

"Procrastination is the thief of time." A greater rascal than this creature could not live. Would that he could boast of a much less number of adher-{46}-ents. Who can tell the value of punctuality? He who could boast of being scrupulously punctual to even a half an hour – he, I say, can tell you the significance of a single moment. Nor does he know less who, in consequence of but five minutes' delay, witnessed a total failure and irrecoverable prostration of all his schemes.

June 16, 1837 – Friday. The night passed, having been spent with much anxiety on the part of the paymaster[107] by reason of the guide's non-arrival – and with much inconvenience and suffering on my part by reason of cold, and a severe pain in my sides and armpits (which last, I suppose, according to my mammy's prediction, was the effect of a previous vaccination). I was this morning requested by our company to ride back for

---

"The most important part of the Cart was the axle and a great deal of art went into the making of it as it was imperative that it be as smooth as possible to reduce friction. The axle was lashed to the Cart with dampened 'Shagganappe' (buffalo hide cut into narrow strips one half to one inch wide). This would shrink and hold the axle firmly. An ox-drawn Cart would travel twelve to fifteen miles in a day, and in three weeks, five of six axles would be needed. This is understandable when we take into consideration that the freight usually weighted eight hundred to one thousand pounds.

"Lubrication of the wheels was not advisable. The sand on the trails would soon clog up the axles and impede their progress. That is why we have so many histories recording the weird sounds make by approaching Carts.

"Charles Mair, a merchant and postmaster in Portage la Prairie in the 1870s, said: 'The creaking of the wheels of the Red River ox cart is indescribable. It is like no sound you ever heard in all your life, and makes your blood run cold.... To hear a thousand of these wheels groaning and creaking at the same time is a sound never to be forgotten.'

"If the sounds of approaching Carts were as bad as the above description, imaging how nerve-torturing it must have been for settlers who had to endure the sound for weeks on end!"

Gunn described the site of this Red River crossing as "About two miles south of Cartier on the CPR Rosenfeldt-Morden line. The main trail south from the Red River Settlement ran along the west side of the Red River. While Garrioch's account could be construed to indicate that the party crossed to the east side at this point, later references suggest that it remained on the west side, and that the reference to the crossing was merely intended to identify the location at which the group paused to wait for the guide."

107 The paymaster was presumably the person in charge of the procession, to whom travelers paid a fee to be included in the group, and who engaged and paid guides and others who serviced the group.

the distance of eight miles in order to ascertain the fate of our guide, or the cause of his delay.

I found him on one side of the [Stinking] River, smoking his long pipe with all the pomposity of a Mussulman,[108] and his quadruped[109] on the other, grazing beneath his shackles. A line stretched from his side of the river to that on which was his horse. I did not take time to ask him whether he had crossed the stream on the rope. He told me that a severe headache the preceding day had been the cause of his delay: such an ache, I presume, as is too frequently the case subsequent to the duping of punctuality. Headache! bellyache! boneache! and a multitude of others: the progeny of that most subtle and deceitful couple, procrastination and his consort indolence, who have ever exerted so much influence over so great port{47}ion of our race. May ye be cursed, like the serpent, even to your bellies! May ye be doomed to expire in one bed, doomed to eternal obliteration! Headache, says he! No marvel. He had sucked the cock of a beer barrel till he drew up and gulped down the very dregs!

The guide promising to be at my heels, I wheeled about, and in a little less than no time I was with my companions. So great was the heat today that our traveling became very wearisome. The beasts of burden, however, managed to drag their loads to the Scratching River. {48} What an idea! Whoever heard of a river scratching?[110]

Passenger Pigeons

June 17, 1837 – **Saturday.** Crossed the Scratching River, and proceeded to the Grand Point.[111]

---

108   Muslim.

109   Horse. Peter frequently referred to horses as quadrupeds.

110   Morris River. Gunn says: "Garrioch was not the first, nor the last, to be mystified by this curious and inelegant name, although the matter is very simple when its genesis is known. David Thompson in his Journal, 1798, speaks of it as Burr Brook. Alexander Henry Jr., 1800-1808, regularly refers to it as Rivière Gratias [an apparent corruption of grattage: scratching]. The [plant] here referred to is a species of prickly burr that grows very abundantly along streams in the rich river bottoms of the West. The relationship of 'Scratching' to prickly burrs is obvious." Both the river and the town (post office) were initially called 'Scratching'; it was not until 1882 that application was made to change both to 'Morris.' https://archive.org/details/geographicalname0000unse

111   Gunn: "There were various points so called on the Red River south of Fort Garry at that time. [T]he one here mentioned is probably a large point on the Red some four miles south of the present town of Morris. The party will encounter still another Grand Point, a couple of days' travel south of Pembina."

After leaving this point some distance, we fell in with a prodigious swarm of pigeons (ectopistes migratorious).[112] We indulged ourselves with some sport among these innocent creatures. Not being able to cross the river and so come immediately into their brooding place, we took our positions directly on the opposite side of {49} the stream. There we stood, charging and discharging in rapid succession, attempting to keep pace with the feathered travelers, who flew in such numbers and in such rapid and uninterrupted succession that we had little time to delay.

We could not, however, account for missing so much as we did. One attached the fault to his gun, a second to his powder, a third to the leaves on the trees being too thick, &c, &c. The spot we chose for our position must have been enchanted by some unheard-of enchantress. I discharged, for my share, at least a dozen charges, and brought but five of the feathered tribe to my feet. Despairing of doing better, and night hastening on, we quit our ground and, leaving the feathered creatures to weep for their departed, we proceeded (after naming the point Pigeon Point[113] from the circumstance), and made our next encampment on the banks of the Swan Lake.[114]

Sabbath

June 18, 1837 – Sunday. Having unanimously concluded to set apart the Sabbath as a day of rest for man and beast, each one spent the day as {50} he believed in his own heart. No minister, no church, no friend of souls to treat us with the kind and salutary invitations of the Gospel; no public praying and, I fear, very little private. How then, a friend might be led to ask, was your Sabbath spent? Why, as I said before: one began to read his journal, a second to discharge his gun preparatory [to] cleaning, a third to put soles on his shoes, and the rest either chatting or sleeping. Thus, shameful to relate, was the first Sabbath spent which the Lord graciously gave us in the wilderness. What a plight for Christians to be in! How could the pure soul of David have breathed

---

112 Passenger pigeons. Extraordinarily plentiful at the time Garrioch describes, these birds were extinct by 1914.

113 Gunn: "This encounter took place somewhere between St. Jean Baptiste and Letellier. There is a large point jutting out into the prairie to the west, about three miles north of the latter place, which is possibly the Pigeon Point of Garrioch."

114 Gunn was unable to "definitely locate" this lake, but speculated that it was "a little to the south of the present village of St. Jean Baptiste."

among us? But, having a lake at hand to quench the mortal thirst, few, if any, complained of having none to quench the immortal. "Poor deluded souls", said I. But 'tis vain to moralize!

The Sleepy Sentinel

June 19, 1837 – Monday. All being ready and in blessed health this morning, [we] commenced our second week's journey. We arrived at the Pembina River[115] in the early part of the afternoon, and there encamped. A {51} nocturnal watch was here organized.

The reason for setting night watches in and near US territory was concern about possible attacks from groups of Sioux Indians who inhabited the northern plains south of Rupert's Land territory, and were quite restive at times, unhappy with incursions from Métis buffalo hunters and American intruders, eventually culminating in the Battle of Grand Coteau in July, 1851.

But sorry am I to say that one of the sentinels, ere the morning watch began to dawn, was found at his post in a boisterous slumber, snoring in hot haste, his watch-piece [clock? binoculars? gun?] unconsciously in the hands of another. Another grand symptom of the epidemic influence of which I had occasion to speak before. "A great fellow to be entrusted with the lives of his fellows!" muttered I. Thanks to Fortune, my Lillipoot was there. He was then still in the land of the living. But now he's gone below – whither I do not know. Mayhap he's gone aloft.[116]

So great was the frost last night that we expected its consequences on our little settlement behind us to be of a serious nature.

---

115 They would have crossed into American territory shortly before sighting the Pembina River. Gunn: "Garrioch makes no reference to the historic American Métis settlement of Pembina on that river, close to which one of the principal cart trails passed, suggesting that the trail being followed on this occasion was some distance west of Pembina." See note to entry for July 6. See also Gunn's note about the various trails at p. 180. Gunn notes that p. 180 is missing, but in a note to the entry for April 19, 1844, Gunn states: "Upon leaving the sugar camps on the Boyne River near the site of Carman, Garrioch probably left the old buffalo hunting trail that he had been following up to this point, and struck across the country, on a course a little south of west, keeping to the south of the above-mentioned stream […] so as to pass on that side of the Back Fat [Swan] Lake instead of to the north of it. On this route he would be obliged to cross the Pembina twice, as indicated." See below, at n. 328.

116 This reference in the entry for June 19, 1837, to the future death of Garrioch's watch-dog Lillipoot on July 19, 1837 indicates that at least some portions of the journal were written retrospectively.

Bob the Ox

June 20, 1837 – Tuesday. A bridge[117] having been completed on the previous evening for the purpose of conveying over teams, {52} carts, baggage, &c., we unceremoniously arose and went ahead. All having crossed the river in safety, a general start was to take place. An accidental circumstance, however, rather protracted our delay. For the sake of those to whom it may possibly afford some matter of grateful titillation,[118] I shall give a precise relation of the occurrence.

When, after crossing the Pembina River, all were ready to start, we were not a little surprised to see our friend Mickle John,[119] instead of following the example of the rest, unhitching his ox Bob and, with a long muscular rope, tying him to a stump of no diminutive proportions. John took up his gun (for my friend was a sportsman) and, without a single word, directed his course to the very centre of a forest which to him was situated within striking distance of his Bob and baggage.

Not being able to unravel the purpose of so mysterious a procedure, I and the guide, having mounted our quadrupeds, rode up to my friend to ascertain the meaning of his singular movements. We had not put many questions to John with respect to his present and future intentions before he very frankly gave us to understand, and that in monosyllabic style, that he was man enough to see to his own ways. He told us that he did not intend to go further that day; and so we might go when we chose, and

---

117 The bridges upon which the party relied so heavily from this point onwards, and seem largely to have constructed themselves, were simple affairs, probably consisting of little more than two or three long tree trunks spanning the stream, covered by smaller logs placed at right angles to the main spans, in the manner of a 'corduroy' road.

118 Garrioch's full description of these potential readers was "those who may have the blessed future privilege of perusing my journal of facts," which seems at least as compatible with the view that he was writing solely for family members as that he had a public audience in mind. The self-consciousness and unnecessary wordiness of the passage, typical of a number of others that the editors have pared, diminished considerably as the journal progressed and Peter's writing style became less self-consciously mannered.

119 This name defeated Gunn, who wrote: "It is impossible to determine with certainty even what his true name was, whether Mickle John, Mickeljohn, or John Mickle, although the latter seems the most probable. I have not succeeded in finding anyone who could enlighten me, either as to the name or the further history of the one who bore it." The *Canadian Oxford Dictionary*, 2nd ed., defines mickle as a reference to bulk, or a large size, which in the current context might mean something like "Big John," or "Bulky John." Gunn's suggestion that Mickle might be the man's surname gains some support from a later entry (June 26) in which Garrioch addresses him as "Mr. Mickle," but the rarity of that usage saps the suggestion's strength. Might "Mickle" not be just a slight corruption of Michael?

Chapter 2 – From Red River To St. Peter's

he would do the same. {53} Finding him incorrigibly tenacious and refractory, and perfectly inaccessible to either remonstrance or solicitation, we left him to ruminate on the bizarre productions of his own whims.

We had not proceeded far, however, though some distance, before the rest of our company were most unexpectedly greeted with an alarming and confusing noise, composed of bawling of men, shrieking of women, crying of children, bellowing of cattle, rattling of cartwheels, kettles, dishes, &c., &c. Instantly, we wheeled our quadrupeds round to ascertain the cause, expecting every moment to hear the discharging of guns, or to see the feathered weapons of some enemy, by whom we supposed our company were being massacred. To our indescribable surprise, we saw the oxen, with their carts of women, children, kettles, &c., &c., running most furiously in every direction but the right. At the same moment, we espied Bob, my friend's ox, at the very tail of the last cart on the road, dashing along with all his might in a most majestic manner, and with all the importance of one who congratulates himself upon some noble and unheard-of achievement; or as one who had dispersed a multitude with a single nod of his head. The spectacle was truly alarming and terrifying.

The whole resulted from John having acted as he did. Bob, finding himself too closely confined, and deserted of all his companions, could not bear the distressing idea (and who could?) of being left with no other companion than the solitary stump to which he was attached. Preferring to have company of his own choosing, and thinking {54} it no harm to use desperate means in a desperate case, [he] made an effort so powerful and heroic that he succeeded not only to extricate himself, but to eradicate the stump to which his master had so shamefully attached him. Elate[d] with that laudable exultation which so noble an exploit must have produced, Bob could not help acting with his limbs what his intense feelings suggested.

Lost in the exuberance of his laurels, he assumed the speed of a steed. The stateliness of his appearance, accompanied with the [bouncing] of the stump (still at the end of Bob's rope) seemed to produce feelings of the most fearful nature in the [other] poor animals that, heavily loaded as they were, they each yielded to the temptation to get out of the way by galloping off in whatever direction seemed to them most convenient. Had Bob been satisfied to stay with the first one he came up with, all might have been well, but (mark the effects of success), exalted with joy or ostentation, he rushed on through the whole caravan. Then, wheeling suddenly around, with an air of victory, wonder and contempt, [Bob] stood amazed at the results of his glorious deeds.

Fortunately, nothing sustained any damage of consequence. Enquiry was made for Mickle, but he could neither be seen nor heard of. Presently, however, he made his appearance from among the brush, and, walking up quietly to his ox, and with eyes of anger flashing in his head, he led away poor Bob without uttering a word. Only upon being told that his ox had been likely to do much harm, he replied that {55} if his ox had not been disturbed he would not have done so.

Mickle John's Mutiny

Everything being again set in order, we resumed our journey. One of our companions, Lindsey, followed [Mickle John] back, attempting to persuade him to bear us company as usual. He, however, briefly informed Mr. L. that he wanted nothing of our company, as we were all nothing but a set of d--n rascals and scoundrels – at the same time threatening to defend himself with firearms should any of us attempt to come near to disturb him. He talked of building there, or at least of the great probability of it, and his remaining there a year or so. The dunce could not be persuaded that the ox had broken loose of his own accord, but constantly and confidently affirmed it to be the work of some person in our company, who had been hired by Governor Simpson, or the government, to do so. He drew the very same conclusion in re-{56}-gard to our guide's delay, before referred to. We left the old fool in the midst of his speculative notions and hastened on our journey.

Scarcely, however, had we proceeded two miles, when, upon looking back, we perceived a huge cloud of smoke, ascending in a most triumphant and majestic manner, just about where we had left the man. We concluded that the fire was kindled with no other intent than that of gratifying the revengeful thirst of the splenetic madman. Thus ended this exciting and memorable scene.

Night drew on and we encamped. We had not been long here before we espied old Mickle's vehicle at a distance, rolling leisurely after us. Disdaining, however, to come into our company, he very adeptly steered his course some considerable distance to the right of us, and encamped at a point of the river about two miles beyond our camp. "Poor little soul" I muttered. But why enlarge?

Mickle John Resists Arrest

June 21, 1837 – Wednesday. In passing my friend John's hut this morning, some of our company picked up a plate, knife and fork, all belonging to me, and some other

Chapter 2 – From Red River To St. Peter's

articles belonging to one of our adventurers, which [were] in Mickle's cart, and which John thought fit to disencumber himself of. {57} He was careful, however, to place them in a perpendicular position, so as more readily to come in contact with the eye. John believed in enchantments, with all his heart and something more. Suspecting, therefore, that our articles were pregnant with no small quantum of that pernicious and horrid principle of which he believed us all to have possession in an uncommon degree, he dreaded to come into contact with anything that had passed through our hands. He most scrupulously avoided us and ours, lest he should be contaminated in body and soul.

Mickle had taken the precaution, after traveling a few miles before us and getting out of our sight, to thrust himself clandestinely into the heart of a forest which lay a few hundred yards from our road. Nothing could be more amusing than to hear John, after we had traveled a little beyond him, strike up and go the full round of one of the most spirited airs of the aborigines; with strains, too, so charming and so elevating that the nerves of my soul were almost soothed into a grateful slumber. What add-{58}-ed much to the beauty of the desert songster's air was occasionally striking his lips with such regularity and rapidity (so making the war-whoop) with the palm of his hand, as would almost have made an organist envious. We proceeded, however, without paying any attention to the songster. After traveling about five miles beyond him, we discovered, upon looking back, the smoke of another fire ascending the air in a most gloomy and fearful manner.

We halted here and took breakfast. At this juncture we were suddenly visited by a herd of jumping deer, which I believe were the first quadrupeds of the desert we saw since we left Red River Settlement. Quite a number of firepieces were discharged at the harmless creatures, but happily to no purpose. After breakfast, we prosecuted our journey. But what was our feeling when we espied another of Mickle's electric achievements.[120] One would almost have supposed him to be so highly electrified as to leave after him a train of fire issuing from his heels.

We hastened on to Grand Point,[121] {59} and there encamped for the night. It was proposed that my friend John should be here apprehended, and made to give an

---

120 Fire. "Electric" was one of Garrioch's favourite adjectives. See below, n. 133.

121 Of this second Grand Point the group encountered, Gunn commented: "This is, no doubt, 'the Grand Point, south of the Bois Percé' mentioned by Alexander Henry in his Journal. The party are now a couple of days' travel, about 30 miles, south of Pembina. This would bring them in the

account of his inglorious deeds. No small part of the evening's conversation had underlying it the thought that Mickle could and would be made to expiate his crimes. But my friend was no chicken. And when and how this was to be effected was the query and the quirk, for one advised this manner, and another that. Mickle, however, was as wise as any of us, and [let] us all know that he was just as great a man on his hill as we were on ours. He moreover gave us to understand that we had to conduct ourselves with the strictest decorum so soon as we intruded within his prescribed limits.

Among the various plans suggested for the apprehension of Mickle, the following was deemed the most practicable. The plan was that he should be seized, deprived of his arms (not his arms of flesh), bound hand and foot, and carried to Lac Traverse[122] in his own cart. {60} Here he was to give a full and complete account of his conduct, or the consequence was to be – exactly and precisely as it might be. With the view of immediately putting this plan into execution, two men of our party, supposed to be the most gallant, were dispatched to invite John, who had encamped within a mile of us, over to our company. John, however, was most happily endowed with something more of that invaluable faculty – discernment – than we had most foolishly surmised.

He dared our gallant ambassadors to advance within forty or fifty yards of his premises. No, my friend was not to be scared at trifles – at matters of mere moonshine. Nor was he to be led as a lamb to the slaughter by the pretensions of a band of "scoundrels." John had all this time his gun in his hands, and threatened to discharge it upon them if they insisted upon approaching any nearer. Perceiving that Mickle was rather too dangerous a fool to sport with, our ambassadors deemed it most prudent to keep a safe distance, and, failing teetotally in their object, returned crestfallen to camp. Thus

---

neighbourhood of the present Drayton, North Dakota. Here there are two extensive loops of the Red River: one jutting out into [...] Minnesota [territory] and the other into the Dakota prairie. The latter of these loops, contiguous to the extreme western apex of which Drayton is located, constitutes a conspicuous westward projection of the timberline and, being situated at the climax of a long westward sweep of the river, would naturally be on their direct line of travel, which was generally 'from point to point.' This latter projection is undoubtedly the Grand Point both of Garrioch and Henry."

122 Gunn: "In the original manuscript, this name is given, wherever used, as "Lac Tra Viere," such being Mr. Garrioch's phonetic spelling of its French pronunciation. It may be further added that the method was used by him in all other instances, throughout this journal, where French names, either of people or places, had to be recorded. Not being a French scholar, and probably never having seen any of these names in print, he had no alternative than to do the best he could, and spell them phonetically – as they sounded to his ear."

our grand scheme ended: a sad disgrace to our party, and another feather in John's bonnet. Go ahead, friend! Bravo! So be it to all those who wish to break thy peace.

Mickle John's Progress

June 22, 1837 – Thursday. A fair and pleasant day. Took breakfast at the first Salt River.[123] A bridge having been erected over it, everything {61} was taken across with little trouble and no damage.

We had seen Mickle previous to our crossing this river, several miles behind us, steering his course due west. Whether his intention was to ascertain the extent of the great prairie, or to [travel] to the west of the Rocky Mountains, I did not take the trouble to ask him. 'Twas a pity. Much have I often lost by being ashamed to confess my ignorance.

{62} Mickle being asked, on the day of his separating from our party, what he would do in the event of the creeks being high, answered that he would get over somehow – and, if not, well and good. John well knew he was on the safe side. He kept a sharp lookout, and always took great care not to out-travel us, nor to come too near. If we came to a river and rested or camped, he did the same at a convenient distance behind us. Then, after we had traveled some distance beyond the river or creek, John would sneak after us. If he chanced at times to advance upon us too rapidly, he would invariably make a halt and sneak about the bushes a while, till the bridge was ready for him. This was the "how" that John alluded to, on being asked how he was to get over the rivers. Was I not correct that my friend had an uncommon share of discerning powers? Undoubtedly.

---

123   Gunn: "Park River. This stream rises in the southward continuation of the Pembina Mountains, in the southeast corner of Cavalier County, North Dakota. The principal town on the stream is Grafton [North Dakota]. To [the] stream the following names have been applied: Park River (Rivière aux Parcs), Salt River as above, and sometimes Forked River. The first of these names is of very early origin. Alexander Henry Jr. found it in use on his arrival there in 1800, and states that the name is derived 'from the fact that the Assiniboines once made a park or pond on this river for buffalo.' The second name, apparently in most common use in Mr. Garrioch's time, originates in the saline character of the water in its lower reaches. Some seven miles below Grafton is a salt lake about ¾ mile long by ½ mile wide. Such salt lakes are by no means uncommon in the Red River valley, both to the north as well as to the south of the boundary. Alexander Henry, in his journals, speaks of several notable ones, and has a good deal to say of the above in particular. During his stay at the mouth of this stream, it was his custom to manufacture the salt he required from the water of this lake. The earliest trail going south, which is the one our travelers are following, crossed this stream close to its junction with the Red."

The weather being excessively warm this day, thereby rendering traveling very oppressive to man and beast, we were under the necessity of halting and resting for some time. The want of water also obliged us to do so; for so brackish and unpleasant was the water of the Salt River that we could not make any use of it. We encamped at a lake called the Big Swan Lake.[124] Here our guide annihilated the life of a grey {63} deer, and wounded another.

Eclipse?

June 23, 1837 – Friday. Sorry am I to say, that the same sloth who had been found snoring at his post was last night, being his second watch, found guilty of the same breach of duty. Charity has hitherto prevented me from exposing the young scoundrel; but next time he is guilty of the same impropriety I shall be very apt to give him a rub.

The atmospherical regions, today, presented so singular an appearance that some were of the opinion that the sun was eclipsed. The sky became so darkened that our noonday presented the appearance of twilight. The day, however, was very pleasant and, the oppressiveness of heat not being felt on account of the cloudy state of the aerial regions, our beasts of burden seemed to step their way pretty cheerfully. We traveled to the Walnut Point,[125] the third point on the Red River from the Big Salt River,[126] and then encamped. {64}

---

124   A note by Gunn speculates that this large lake may have been a combination, at a time of higher water levels, of two later smaller lakes located about a mile west of the Red River in the northeast corner of Pulaski County on the line of the old trail, just nine miles south of the mouth of the Park River, and fourteen or fifteen miles south of Grand Point (Drayton), the party's last night encampment.

125   Gunn's lengthy note says, in part: "I am inclined to think they must have camped near the south edge of Walsh County, probably in the vicinity of Welshville Post Office. This would give them eight or nine miles for the day's travel, which, together with the construction of a bridge over the Big Salt River, would make a fairly good day, and leave them about the proper distance from Turtle River, to make that point for breakfast the following morning. The name 'Walnut,' however, for a locality where no walnuts grow, is a puzzle I have failed to solve."

126   According to Gunn, this is a stream that rises in the Pembina Mountains "immediately south of the sources of the Park River," and does not become salty until it passes through the previously-mentioned Salt Lake on its way to the Red River. Its upper reaches, he said, were sometimes called the Forest River.

The Very Centre of Danger: Sioux Country

June 24, 1837 – Saturday. Came to Turtle River[127] about 8 o'clock this morning, where, a bridge being speedily erected over the stream and all and everything being taken over safely, we proceeded and encamped at Tully's Creek,[128] a creek so named from the circumstance of David Tully having, at that place, most unfortunately lost his life and family.[129] Pity that man should be so often his own murderer! The fatality of imprudence, how sure and unavoidable![130]

{65} The waters of the Turtle River, like those of the Salt Rivers, were so brackish and unpleasant that we could not make any use of them, except in the way of boiling, high seasoning and high sweetening. So there was a fine composition: China tea, salt water, and maple sugar! {66}

---

127   Gunn: "Turtle River, like those already noted, heads in the high country south of the Pembina Mountains which forms the western boundary of the Red River valley. It flows into the Red near a place called Stoughton, in the extreme northeast corner of Grand Forks County."

128   Gunn: "This small stream, now known as English Coulee [flows] into the Red River about three miles below Grand Forks. It cuts the grounds of the University of North Dakota, constituting one of the principal decorative features of the handsome campus of that institution. Though forming a quite considerable channel in the prairie, especially as it approaches the Red River, Tully's Creek is now mostly a dry ravine, except in its deepest parts, or while the spring freshets are on."

129   Gunn: "The tragic affair of David Tully occurred about the year 1823. In the summer of that year, this unfortunate man, while traveling with his wife and their three children on their way from Red River Settlement to Fort Snelling, Minnesota, was set upon near this place by a band of Sioux, and slaughtered in a most horrible manner, his wife and helpless infant sharing his fate. The other two children, John and Andrew, were taken captive and carried by the Indians to the neighbourhood of the Minnesota, or St. Peter's, River, as it was then called. The elder of these two boys, John, was about five years of age, and the younger, Andrew, about three. These children were not long afterwards discovered and ransomed by the authorities at Fort Snelling, to which place they were taken. John was taken into the family of Colonel Snelling, Commandant of the Fort, but afterwards died of lockjaw [tetanus] as a result of a cut in the ankle received while using an axe. The younger was taken and cared for by Major Clark, also an officer of the Fort, who later put him in an orphanage in New York, in which city he grew to manhood, afterwards becoming a respected citizen of Brooklyn. Prior to the above events, David Tully had occupied the position of blacksmith on the Earl of Selkirk's establishment at Fort Garry, now Winnipeg, where a number of his relatives of the same name still reside. Accounts of the above affair may be seen in Mrs. Snelling's reminiscences in *Pioneer Women of the West*; also in Neill's *History of Minnesota*; Ross' *Red River Settlement*, & [Donald] Gunn's *History of Manitoba* (p. 238). The best and fullest account, however, is to be found in Mrs. Charlotte O. Van Cleve's *Lifelong Memories of Fort Snelling* (pp. 49-60). Mrs. Van Cleve was a daughter of Major Clark, who adopted Andrew Tully."

130   Although Gunn's note tells us that Tully and his family were killed by Sioux, Garrioch seems to have considered him a self-murderer because of the imprudence of traveling alone through Sioux country.

Sabbath travel

June 25, 1837 – Sunday. Being now in the heart of the wilderness, and consequently in the very centre of danger, our guide was exceedingly anxious to proceed, with the view of getting over all the danger which we apprehended from the wild sons of the forest with all possible speed. Therefore, as some could not travel, and the rest tarry, the state of the case made it necessary for all to march.

Faithless mortals. "If," said I "we all had faith but as a grain of mustard seed, we would not have acted thus." Through all our journey hitherto, we had preserved the Holy Day sacred to ourselves and quadrupeds. The Great I Am, I believe every soul believed, had been our shield and guard even to the Turtle River. Did they then suppose He tarried there, and would not travel with us any further? Great is thy faith and profound thy reasoning, O thou vain and creeping mortal! As a matter of course, from the nature of the circumstances, there must have been but little praying, reading or singing today. How it was with myself I dare not say. For with such a one as myself is, there [have] been many changes; sometimes ascending, sometimes descending, &c.

Such pious interjections remind us that Garrioch was on his way to enroll in a theological college. His equivocal concluding remarks about his own behaviour prefigure other, stronger, self-rebukes to come.

We passed the Grand Forks this day; that is, the conjunction of the Red and Sioux Rivers, which is about 3 or 4 miles above Tully's Creek. {67} From this point the course of the Red River inclines to a south-easterly direction, and that of the Sioux River to a south-westerly. This latter river takes its source, or rises, from Lac Traverse.[131]

Mickle John Returns to the Fold

June 26, 1837 – Monday. The weather being very wet and disagreeable, we traveled but a few miles, and then encamped on the north side of Goose River.[132]

---

131 Gunn: "Garrioch here follows what was no doubt a commonly accepted idea with regard to these two branches of the Red River at that time. The Red Lake River, with its source in Red Lake, Minnesota, he regards as the true Red River; while that which takes the "south-westerly" course, as he says, he calls the Sioux River, and declares its source to be in Lake Traverse. Modern geography, however has revised this conception; and what Garrioch calls the Sioux River, in conjunction with the Ottertail Lake and River system, heading in Elbow Lake, Minnesota, is now regarded as the Red River proper."

132 Gunn: "The Rivière aux Outardes of the French: a considerable stream, about 80 miles in length, which rises in Nelson County and flows in a southeasterly course through Grand Forks, Steele and

I should have mentioned that my friend Mickle had finally joined our company, after having deserted us several days. At his first leaving us, nothing less than a mile between us would please John. He however, from time to time, made his distance of separation narrower, till he drew in within a few hundred yards of us. After camping one evening, Mickle having encamped but a short distance from us, I resolved to go, with the approbation of our party, and invite the old gentleman to come over and enjoy the advantages of our society as formerly. I took the very judicious precaution, however, of going on my expedition {68} with no other arms than such as nature had provided me with – not even a toothpick in my pockets.

Mickle was busy cooking. John would never eat out of another's dish; nor would he let another eat out of the same dish with him; but my friend was of a kind turn: he would offer you something to eat, and a cup of tea or coffee, at any time. Well prepared was he with all such luxuries, and with the necessary utensils for preparing them. The moment John discovered from my actions that I was advancing towards his premises, he left his culinaries, which he was quite busily engaged in by the fire, hastened to his cart, and, removing his gun out of it from its horizontal position, perpendicularized it right by his side. Said I to myself: "I am a gone dog if I intrude."

I went on, however, pretending to be perfectly regardless of his several movements by pacing my way very slowly, with my arms hanging at their full length, my head stooping, and my whole self inclining forward and downward. Thus assuming the attitude of a profound reasoner or a naturalist, I was anxious to impress upon the mind of John that I was lost in the profundity of my cogitations, arising from the perplexing influence of some abstruse science. Presently I found myself on the opposite side of John's extended fire.

"How are you Mr. Mickle?"

"Thanks, quite well. How are you, Mr. Garrioch? Take a seat." (Throwing his tent, which he had neatly tied up, across the fire [for me to sit on]). {69}

After the common order of salutation had been formally discharged on both sides, I commenced expostulating with him, with professions of sympathetic feeling and expression, as to the obvious propriety of his once more joining our party; protesting at the same time the very grateful and pleasing sensation his doing so would produce

---

Traill Counties, North Dakota, joining the Red River about a mile east of the village of Caledonia."

throughout our company. I and my colleagues had got clean out of sugar, and, knowing that John had abundance, I resolved, having now got him in a jocular humour, to venture on his eatables. I inquired whether he would lend me a few pounds of sugar till we arrived at St. Peter's, where I could return him the kindness. He cheerfully let me have as much as I wanted, on credit. "Ah," said I, "see what it is to be a gentleman, and a man of profession, too!"

It is sufficient to say that John joined our party the following morning.

Pursuing Master Grim

June 27, 1837 – Tuesday. A convenient bridge being erected over the river, we proceeded on our journey.

We had just entered the great prairie once more, which had been intercepted from our view for some distance by shrubbery, &c., when our oculars suddenly came in contact with the apparition of a huge carnivorous quadruped, stalking over the prairie in a most stately manner. Master Grim – for it was a bear of no diminutive stature – paced his way with all the importance of a monarch, directing his course towards the river.

Doubtless Grim was king of that realm, and was on his way home after a protracted tour of surveying the boundaries of his extended dominions. Just then, when he intercepted our way, his cogit-{70}-ations were profound. They were evidently not of a perplexing or melancholy kind, but such as fall to the lot of few to enjoy. Master Grim was returning, apparently, loaded with laurels, drunk with the blood of the slain, and surfeited with the flesh of his foes.

Some of our party, however, were curious enough to ascertain the majestic monarch's condition, not to give much credence to appearances. Two or three of our most gallant party accordingly fleeted on their way to compliment Master Grim. My quadruped, being too dignified with the protuberance of an advanced pregnancy, fairly shuddered at the idea of contaminating her forthcoming progeny with blood-reeking sensations. For me, therefore, to follow the chase was quite impracticable.

The guide, being foremost, was first at the heels of old Grim. His quadruped, however, had a mind of reconnoitering him before proceeding further. Instantly, he wheeled on the tips of his hinders; and thus was formed the strange position of "tail to tail." A lash or two [having] removed in some measure the prejudice of his quadruped, the guide redoubled his perseverance. Old Grim, being rather hard put to, and perceiving

Chapter 2 – From Red River To St. Peter's

the superior velocity of his pursuers, could not bear the idea of being thus shamefully [pursued in] his central dominions. With an air of disdain, Grim quit the position of a hunted prey and, as-{71}-sum[ing] that of a champion, [stopped].

Precisely at this juncture, the guide came in contact with Master Grim's tail. So unexpected was [this] that our sportsman's quadruped bounded against the side of the poor animal, and went rolling some distance beyond him, while the guide's head came into violent contact with the rear end of Master Grim – with such force as might have resulted in inseparable cohesion, had it not been for the hair which Old Grim had, most fortunately, on the surface of his pigmy behind. It was fortunate, too, that our guide's head was protected by a similar abundance of the same material.

[Re-]mounting his quadruped, [he] gave Old Grim a second chase. What do I say? In despair [after falling again from his horse,] our guide jumped to his feet, and, horizontalizing his electric[133] instrument, presented Old Grim with a discharge of the same. Most happily for the old gentleman, [the bullet] simply skinned over his ridge, and, but slightly chafing the upper part of his skin, returned to its native soil.

Now hotly pursued by another daring intruder – Lindsey – Grim most judiciously had recourse to the liquid element for the safety of his majesty's person. He knew well this would baffle his antagonists. After landing on the opposite shore, he stood a while on the bank, {72} seemingly pleased at having defeated the vicious intentions of his violent intruders; and, having gazed on his foe with an air of dauntless intrepidity, prepared to retire. Lindsey, having lost all hope, as a parting message sent him a lead bullet to examine. The champion turned his head very coolly, and, with a look that indicated the utmost contempt, retired to his palace in peace. Our aspirants being disappointed of their prey and their fame, deprived of their laurels, and having made some addition to old Grim's [laurels], "Sic," said I, "transit gloria mundi!"[134]

It is worthy of remark that in this as in every other instance in which we fell in with any wild animals, Mickle could never be persuaded that they were in reality such animals as they appeared to be, but merely their skins employed by those whom the Governor

---

133 Garrioch's figurative use of "electric" at this very early stage of understanding of electricity was probably intended to convey the swift and shocking impact of a firearm. It may be recalled that the same term was used above, n. 120, in reference to Mickle John's fire-setting escapades.

134 "So passes worldly glory."

had hired to spy out Mickle's liberty, and who, for fear of being detected in their natural garb by the vigilance of John, counterfeited those pseudoties.

After a very pleasant travel, we concluded the toils of the day at a point called Turtle Point.[135]

A Wild State of the Aerial Regions

June 28, 1837 – Wednesday. After a march of two or three hours this morn-{73}-ing, we came to the Goose Grass River;[136] and, as soon as a bridge had been erected, we proceeded on our journey. When the "old heads" thought it was time to conclude, we encamped.[137]

Before we retired, the sky, which had presented so serene and pleasant an appearance throughout the day, we now perceived to be assuming a very different aspect – one which plainly indicated a change in the weather. About ten o'clock in the night, we fully realized the prognostications of the aerial signs. The heavens became dark, wild and gloomy. The thunders rolled along, peal after peal, with a most astounding roar. The vivid lightenings flashed with unremitting fire, which, for some minutes at a time, turned our Egyptian darkness into almost day. The winds rose, and began to exhibit {74} wild and howling fury. The scene presented a grand, majestic, and terrifying appearance. A more grandly awful scene could scarce be imagined. The most vivid imagination might stagger at the attempt.

This picturesque and wild state of the aerial regions had been but a few minutes in operation when the waters from above began to tumble down in torrents. And now we could not [see], enveloped in thick mists of darkness. Such was the fury of the wind,

---

135 In the original manuscript, this sentence precedes the previous paragraph. As to the location, and the party's slow progress, Gunn wrote: "Somewhere in the immediate neighborhood of a place now called Hague, North Dakota. The building of a bridge over the Goose River, and the bear hunt seem to have interfered considerably with the day's travel. The party, if we have rightly located Walnut Point, has made a scant six miles since crossing the Goose River."

136 Gunn: "The stream referred to here is evidently Elm River. It rises, in its main channel, in the extreme southwest corner of Traill County, North Dakota, some three miles northwest of the present town of Galesburg, by which it passes. From this point it runs northeasterly to near the town of Blanchard; thence southeasterly to its junction with the Red River in Elm River Township in the extreme southeast corner of Traill County. The exact point of junction is ¼ mile north of the village of Quincy."

137 Gunn: "The encampment must have been about opposite Georgetown, Minnesota. This would make to the credit of the day a bridge over the Goose Grass River, and about 15 miles traveled."

that (notwithstanding we were surrounded by the loaded carts, which we were in the habit of placing in a circular form to serve as a battery in time of danger and attack) all hands could scarcely keep their tents from being carried away. In a few moments after the storm commenced we found ourselves almost swimming in our beds. When morning came, Norton, who had been on the watch, wrung, I presume, some gallons of water from his leather breeches.

On the whole, this night seemed to be so awfully grand and majestic that I never witnessed such another. It had doubtless the salutary influence of driving at least some of us to reflect upon the conduct of our past lives. For such was the terrific {75} appearance of the scene, that some faithless ones among us were ready to conclude that the Day of the Lord was at hand. Some made one conclusion and some another. However, when the cause of the fear and apprehension had all gone by, the effects produced took their flight with it. And soon, very soon, each one again went on as it seemed good in his own eyes. "Poor thoughtless children," says I. "Deluded mortals!" Yet the Lord, in much mercy, spared our lives.

Mrs. McIntyre at Sporting Point

June 29, 1837 – Thursday. Our route, which had been remarkably dry and pleasant hitherto, was this morning, after the last night's rain, exceedingly disagreeable from the vast quantity of water that stood on the earth's surface.

We traveled to the River Cheyenne,[138] and then took {76} breakfast. This is the largest, and one of the most important, streams we have met with since we left [the] Assiniboine. Its course being somewhat west or northwest, it flows into the Sioux River.[139] All having gained the opposite bank of this stream through the medium of a constructed bridge, we proceeded to the second point of the Red River from the

---

138 Gunn: "A good deal of latitude seems to have been used by early travelers and writers with reference to the form and spelling of this name, which Alexander Henry Jr. informs us (Coues' *Henry*, I, p. 145) is derived "from a numerous tribe of Indians who inhabited its upper part." Henry himself uses the form Schian, or Rivière des Schians. The name has its origin in the French "chien," the Dog Indian tribe formerly occupying this territory. The Cheyenne River is the longest and most important tributary of the Red River lying wholly within the state of North Dakota. The river rises by two branches, a north and a south, about 40 miles west and south of Devil's Lake, about half way between that body of water and the Missouri Coteau. These forks soon join, however, and the united stream flows [southeast and northeast] to its junction with the Red, which takes place ten miles north of the city of Fargo."

139 Gunn's note points out that Garrioch clearly meant the Red River.

Cheyenne River, where we halted and commenced our usual occupations on such occasions.

The place we named Sporting Point[140] from the following circumstance. Mrs. McIntyre, desirous of cutting a shine and anxious to make an exhibition {77}, began to lay hold on the legs of the young men of [her] clan, who had seated themselves on the face of a bank adjoining a deep valley where we had kindled a fire, in order to drag them down the hill. One of the young braves, not being able to bear the idea of being outdone by a decrepit piece, took advantage of the old lady in an unwary moment. The youth, apparently unconcerned at the consequences, thrust the old lady from him with such force as to cause her to slide, or rather roll, precipitately down the declivity. She continued traveling in a most precipitate manner, as a cask or barrel would under the same circumstances, till she arrived at the fire we had kindled at the foot of the hill.

[W]e had determined to substantialize our fire by placing on each side of it two of the stoutest logs we could procure. The old lady came in contact with one of these logs, with such furious violence as almost to disperse every vessel we had on the fire. {78} Dazed and astounded, she stood up, looked about a little, and [although] appearing quite discouraged as the result of her novel experiment, calmly retired and attended to her business.

Where might she have stopped, had it not been for that fortunate log? Who knows where she might have halted? She might have been traveling till time should cease to tell! For, had it not been for that fortunate fire-log, she must have traveled till she arrived at the opposite log; and that would have involved herself in mysteries she, I presume, had no particular desire to pry into. The hot cinders might have reduced her to atoms; and she might have been on her progressive journey to this day – aye, to the termination of ages yet unborn! Some of her atoms might have ascended the aerial regions, and have been driven to and fro by the furious winds; some might have united themselves with the cinders which caused their disintegration, and have been subjected to all those incidental changes to which atoms are exposed; some might have aided in affording interment to other bodies. {79} Yes, she might have been traveling still, and exploring regions to us unknown.

---

140   Gunn: "The second prominent point of the Red River south of the mouth of the Cheyenne is six miles north of Fargo. Accepting this as Garrioch's 'Sporting Point' would give the party the construction of the bridge over the Cheyenne (which must have been a considerable task) and about nine miles of travel as the result of today's activities; and this point would seem a very probable locality for the evening camp."

Chapter 2 – From Red River To St. Peter's

Boundless Prairie

June 30, 1837 – Friday. We traveled till we arrived at Rice River,[141] about three o'clock in the afternoon. A bridge was erected over this river and, after a pleasant day's travel, we encamped on a point of the Sioux River lying nearly opposite to the place where Mr. Hays met with his unfortunate and melancholy fate.[142]{80}

July 1, 1837 – Saturday. Having traveled some four or five hours, we came to Graham's Point[143] so named from some old trader who had once resided {81} there. Hitherto,

---

141 Gunn: "This little river is one of the few natural features of the country that have benefited from a change of name. The early French voyageurs dubbed it Rivière aux Oiseaux Puants: River of Stinking Birds, the stinking birds referred to being turkey buzzards (cathartes aura). 'Vulture River,' the English equivalent of that, is not too bad. The name Rice River, applied to it by Garrioch, or more commonly Wild Rice River (the Rivière à la Folle Avoine of the French) has a pleasanter ring." Gunn's account goes on to point out at length that there were, however, altogether too many other Wild Rice water bodies in existence, before continuing as follows: "Wild Rice River rises in the southeast corner of Sargent County, North Dakota, on the northeastern apex of the range of hilly country known as the Coteau of the Prairies. Flowing [... in various directions, it eventually parallels] the Red, at a distance of two or three miles from it, for a space of between 35 and 40 miles, finally mingling its waters with that stream about 10 miles south of Fargo in the southeast corner of Cass County."

142 Gunn: "The incident here referred to occurred in the month of March of this same year (1837), a little over three months prior to Garrioch's making the above entry. The circumstances were as follows: On February 26, a party consisting of Martin McLeod, two young men, and the well-known guide Pierre Bottineau left the Red River Settlement on snowshoes, with Fort Snelling, Minnesota as destination. The names of the two young men were Hayes and Parys. It is stated by American authorities that they were British officers, the former being of Irish, and the latter of Polish, nationality. This little party, when at the Cheyenne River on March 17, were overtaken by a terrific blizzard which lasted several days, [and] in which both Hays and Parys perished. Mr. McLeod and the guide Bottineau, after wandering about for a considerable time – five days of which they were without food – managed at last to reach the trading house of Joseph R. Brown on Lake Traverse, and from there eventually found their way to Fort Snelling. See Neill, *History of Minnesota*, p. 452; *History of the Upper Mississippi Valley*, 1881, p. 102; *Minnesota in Three Centuries*, II, pp. 100-101; also letter of Joseph R. Brown in Minnesota History Society Archives. The point on the Red River referred to here by Garrioch as 'lying nearly opposite' to the place where this unfortunate affair occurred is probably thirteen miles south of Fargo and five miles above the mouth of the Wild Rice River. This would give a distance for the day of about 20 miles, which would just come in right to bring them to Graham's Point in, as he says, 'some four or five hours'" Gunn, p. 79, n. 2.

143 Gunn: "A point on the Red River three miles south of the site of old Fort Abercrombie, some 10 miles north of the present city of Breckenridge, Minnesota. [The present] Fort Abercrombie was built there in the fall of 1858, 21 years after Garrioch made this entry. The "old trader" after whom this point was [then] named, Captain Duncan Graham, was one of those ubiquitous, irrepressible, Scotchmen who have left their names in so many places, from east to west, over the American continent. In this particular case, the name did not stick, as it has long since ceased to be known as

our guide had scarcely been a day well enough to eat a hearty meal. This day, I am happy to say, he has been able to eat two hearty ones in the course of four or five hours. Just by making a halt, and nothing else, our traveling was knocked on the head for today. Procrastination is ever the thief of time. Give him but one minute and, five hundred and fifty-five to one, he will take ten.

July 2, 1837 – Sunday. We had decided on giving ourselves and our quadrupeds rest all this day, according to the commandment. Our guide, however, anxious to hurry out of danger, as he said (probably having left his beads and prayers at home, and having lost all confidence in anything else to guard him in this dangerous route) we were under the painful necessity of again encroaching on the [afternoon of the] sacred day.

The former part of this Sabbath, however, was, in my humble opinion, much better spent than any former one in our desert journey. Some, either through the impulse of duty or something else, spent the time in reading, singing, &c. Such as took no pleasure in these things amused themselves in either weaving some of their lengthy yarns and dealing them out "gratis for nothing," as the old nigger said, or in dreams and idle thoughts. Everyone to his taste, as Rey-{82}-nard[144] said when in the act of'

---

the name for this locality. Duncan Graham, however, is not without a memorial in the nomenclature of the state of North Dakota. The large island, or rather peninsula, in Devil's Lake still known as Graham's Island was named for him, he having had a trading establishment there in the early part of the last century.

"Particulars as to Duncan Graham's career are not very full, and authorities do not always agree. He was born in Edinburgh, Scotland, in 1772, and 20 years later emigrated to America, where he became interested in the fur trade. He was at Mackinaw when the war of 1812 broke out between England and the United States, and was made Lieutenant in a British force organized there to attack Prairie du Chien. After the capture of this place, he was raised to the rank of Captain and given command of two Mackinaw companies stationed there. At the close of the war, Captain Graham returned to his trading operations, and it was probably very shortly after this – say 1815 – that he established himself on the island at Devil's Lake. He remained there only about two years, and in 1827 was back in Prairie du Chien. Between these two dates his movements are hidden in obscurity. In the summer of 1821, Mr. Graham accompanied William Laidlaw on that historic expedition by boat from Prairie du Chien to Red River Settlement with seed grain for the Selkirk Settlers, and it is quite probable that this was the same Duncan Graham. It is probable, also, that his sojourn at Graham's Point took place in this same interval between 1817 and 1827. In 1834, he went to Wabasha, Minnesota, and he gave its name to that city. He moved to Mendota in 1847, and died there on December 5th of the same year. He was married to Hazahotewin, a sister of Chief Wayagoenagee of the Dakotah Nation, and left behind him numerous descendants through this marriage," Gunn, pp. 80-81.

144 Reynard the fabled fox, whose name became a synonym for foxes generally.

gulping down mushrooms while a wolf by his side was glutting himself with a delicious ham of mutton.

July 3, 1837 – Monday. Followed the course of the Sioux River[145] the greater part of the day, and encamped at the last point of timber on the said river at the usual time.

July 4, 1837 – Tuesday. To-day found us in the midst of an extensive prairie, where, I am sorry to say, we could not have the pleasure of commemorating the anniversary of that independence to which this blessed morning gave birth. We had, however, for the first time this season, a most inviting and reviving dessert of delicious strawberries.

We encamped on the open prairie, after traveling several miles from the river.[146] Here nothing but a boundless prospect presented itself to {83} our view. Nothing but one continuous stretch of wild and barren plains: not a tree of the most solitary or diminutive kind could be discerned throughout the vast extent of this beautiful prairie. And nothing but a little brush or scrub occasionally scattered over its surface, sometimes at a distance of many miles from each other, gave variety to the almost universal sameness of scenery. Such is the level of these prairies that even a fox could be seen on its surface at a distance of several miles, there being often neither grass nor hills to intercept the view.

---

145   Gunn: "In accordance with the accepted usage of that time among local travelers, Garrioch has consistently been calling this stream, above the Grand Forks, the Sioux River; the incorrectness of which was noted [above]. A day and a half' of travel, however, would bring them a considerable way south of the mouth of the Ottertail at Breckenridge, if this point on what is now regarded as a continuous stream can be termed a mouth. They have now, therefore, entered upon the Sioux River proper, and Garrioch's application of the name here is correct. This tributary of the Red River, which f'lows out of' Lake Traverse, is a small stream, about 35 miles in length, and of very uncertain volume, of'ten drying up entirely. Like many more of these streams, it seems to have rejoiced in a variety of names. A later name given to it was Bois des Sioux, or Sioux Wood River, which is still used, especially in the English form. This latter appellation comes from a clump of trees that formerly stood about nine miles from its mouth. This grove was said to be regarded as the most northerly undisputed limit of the Sioux territory, and hence was called Bois des Sioux, the name of the wood being transferred in time to the river."

146   Gunn: "The travelers have now crossed over the Bois des Sioux, or Sioux River, and are on its east side. They have crossed its dry bed, as indicated in the next paragraph, just north of Lake Traverse, near the present town of White Rock, Minnesota, and are camped to the south of this point, about opposite the northern end of the lake."

We passed within 20 miles of the Fort at Lac Traverse[147] to-day, and encamped under the foot of the first hills we had {84} the pleasure of seeing since we left Red River Settlement. This range of hills, or rising ground, is, I presume, what learned folks denominate [the] "height of land,"[148] for soon after this the streams change their direction.

I felt much gratified in roaming over the tops of these hills; and even my quadruped seemed to participate in the enjoyment of a circumstance so rare and pleasing. Still, however, the same scenery presented itself as before described; and nothing but the top of a hill towering above the rest, or a huge rock or stone on the side of a declivity, afforded the eye the ever desirableness of change and variety. Hitherto, the face of the country lying on our route, with the exception of such low and rising ground as was occasioned by rivers and lakes, has presented one unbroken and continuous level. From this time and place we anticipate a different condition.

In passing over the Sioux River to-day, we found its very bottom so dry and hard that the wheels of the loaded carts scarcely left an impression on its surface. This is the same river in which Mr. Ludlow rowed up his bark the year he went down to Prairie

---

147   Gunn: "Lake Traverse separates the extreme northeast corner of South Dakota from Traverse County, Minnesota. According to various early travelers, it is about 15 miles long by a mile wide; but, on reference to modern plat maps of this region, it would seem to be considerably longer than this. It was formerly called Ottertail Lake by the Indians, on account of its shape. It is the source of the Bois des Sioux or Sioux River. The lake itself lies in a deep valley, about twice its own width, the banks of which are about 100 feet in height. It is separated from Big Stone Lake, to the south, by a portage or "traverse" of between 3 or 4 miles, from which feature it [probably] derives its name. The "Fort" referred to was the post of the American Fur Company, situated down in the valley, on the east shore of the lake, not far from its southern extremity. The site is said to have been first occupied by the Hudson's Bay Company in 1812. In 1822, the Columbia Fur Company had its headquarters there; and, in 1827, when they sold out to the AFC, the latter concern continued the post. Garrioch's statement that they had "passed within 20 miles of the Fort" at this stage means that they had progressed to within that distance of it. The Fort is still some 15 miles to the southwest, and they will pass by it on the high prairie level, at least 12 miles to the east." See July 8 entry.

148   North/south continental divide. See the July 7 entry for an expression of Garrioch's pleasure at observing the effects of the divide. Gunn: "Keating also speaks of this range of hills, and states that they are 30 or 40 ft. high. The highest point of land on this great central plateau is the Coteau des Prairies, west of Lake Traverse. Its mean elevation is 1450 feet above sea level; though there are parts of it much higher than that. Lake Traverse itself is the highest water level, of any considerable body, located on the prairies between the Gulf of Mexico and the Arctic. Its elevation is 950 feet above the sea."

Chapter 2 – From Red River To St. Peter's

du Chien.[149] Both {85} we and our quadrupeds had[150] suffered some from the want of water; and, if Providence had not very seasonably sent us a shower today, we might have been in a fine predicament. In the way of firewood, we had plenty; for our teamster[151] had taken care, in leaving the last woods, to take a supply sufficient to last for three days.

Continental Divide Birthday

When the party reached the north/south continental divide – its mean elevation 1,450 feet above sea level – on Garrioch's 26th birthday, he contemplated the coincidence with mixed emotions.

July 5, 1837 – Wednesday. [This birthday morning put] me in mind of that glorious morning, the dawn of which witnessed, and but just preceded, my exit from some other unknown world into this miserable and wretched one. But sorry indeed am I to say that I could not have the pleasure of celebrating the anniversary of that important and ever-memorable event. The idea of being in the midst of a barren, groveless, and howling prairie on one's birthday is horrid. Mounted on my quadruped, however, and sweetly regaling my drooping spirits with the sweet and balmy breezes which occasionally came in contact with my olefactories while gently gliding over the tops {86} of the little hills, I could not but congratulate myself upon the fact of being exalted so high above the world: raised so many more degrees above the vanities of this earth than I was the day I tumbled into it.

The most part of this day we traveled through a watery country; which, doubtless, was occasioned by the two late showers. Thus Heaven, contrary to our apprehensions,

---

149   Gunn: "The reference here is to the expedition under William Laidlaw (not "Ludlow") undertaken in 1821 (1819-1820 according to some authorities), from Red River Settlement to Prairie du Chien, Wisconsin, and back, for the purpose of procuring seed grain for the colonists whose crops had been destroyed by grasshoppers the previous season. The party went on snowshoes and returned by boat, carrying with them a supply of the desired grain. The note goes on to cite accounts of the expedition in Neill's *History of Minnesota* (1st ed., pp. 317-318) and Donald Gunn's *History of Manitoba* (p. 214), and to comment that the expedition 'is worthy of mention as it is the only instance of heavy articles being transported the entire distance from Prairie du Chien to the Red River Settlement, with the exception of the portage between the Big Stone and Traverse Lakes, by water." Gunn tells us more about William Laidlaw in a lengthy note on p. 160 (Chap. 5, n.293).

150   The repeated use of "had" in this paragraph is further evidence of probable retrospective composition.

151   Apparently, it was not just a guide whose services were collectively engaged by the travelers.

kindly and abundantly supplied our wants. From a cursory review of our route, we concluded the distance from Red River Settlement to Lac Traverse to be 450 miles, more or less.[152]

Sioux Eloquence

July 6, 1837 – Thursday. On approaching a lake called the Lake of Big Islands,[153] we observed some Indians on the west side, sporting themselves at the expense of the harmless feathered tribes. This is the first instance of anything in the form of human beings presenting itself to our view since we left our Settlement.[154] After traveling a little farther, we halted till they came over the lake, to where we had seated ourselves under an oak tree. We found they were of the Sioux tribe. The party consisted of three men and two women. But a few words had been exchanged between them and our guide when {87} the most elderly, and apparently the most dignified, character among their party invited general attention by addressing our company, or rather treating them to a most fluent and eloquent address, [and], after a very few minutes spent in conversation, he blessed our ears a second time.

The sum and substance of his protracted harangues consisted in the recapitulation of his father's instructions when on his dying bed, viz.: that he should always avoid giving offence to a white man, whoever and whatever he was; that he should never fail to treat them with kindness; to aid them when it lay in his power; and to let them pass and repass through his country without molesting them. In so doing, his father had told him, he would be sure of procuring, not only for himself but for his children and people, the good will of the white man, and would be kindly treated by them in return. But, should he act otherwise to the whites, they would treat him and his

---

152   Gunn: "Counting by the survey, it is a little over 300 miles from their starting point to Lake Traverse. The windings of the way would probably make up another 50 miles."

153   At the conclusion of the long anecdote he began at this point, Garrioch commented: "The above lake is about 20 miles from Lac Qui Parl." Gunn offered more detail: "Big Stone Lake is here meant. This body of water, which is really an enlargement of the Minnesota River, lies immediately south of Lake Traverse, and is very similar to it. It forms the boundary between Minnesota and the south half of Roberts County, South Dakota. It is between 25 and 30 miles long by one mile in width, and lies almost at right angles to its neighbour on the north. There are several large islands in it towards the south end, the largest of which is called Chamberlain Island, on which the Sioux of that part formerly grew quantities of corn. The presence of these islands, no doubt, accounts for the name given to it here by Garrioch. About midway of its length, on the east side, was a post of the American Fur Company, established in 1822."

154   This confirms the party's failure to visit Pembina on the international border. See June 19 entry.

children and people accordingly. The very honourable (for such I considered him to be in truth) and venerable red man concluded his amicable speech by saying that all he desired of the white man in passing through his country was to give him some aid in his necessity, by furnishing him with something to eat, a little tobacco, &c.

[The Indian's presentation] having come to a conclusion, our party had the kindness to give them a little of such things as they wanted. John McIntyre,[155] the double-faced and deceitful hypocrite, was, I believe, the only one who re-{81}-fused giving them an iota of anything. After viewing each other a little while, we parted with, apparently, a most affectionate farewell.

A Laxative Lake

We discontinued our journey today, at four o'clock, on the banks of a beautiful lake,[156] in consequence of scarcity of water, our being now on high land. To our great mortification, however, we discovered when too late the water of this lake to be totally unfit for use.[157]

Necessity, however, compelled us to use it at all hazards, and in order to divest it of any injurious effect we had to boil it. For to use it otherwise would have been quite impracticable. It was so full of insects, that we had to strain every drop of it before we could sip or drink it, raw or cooked. The stench also which it emitted was so pernicious and obnoxious, that it might have put at least the reading part of us in mind of the waters of the Nile. And more than all that, such was the powerful effect of its medical virtues [that] it not only ran freely itself through the system, but sent everything lodged in the

---

155 Probably the husband of the woman who rolled down the hill on June 29. Gunn: "There was an individual of this name among the party of Selkirk colonists who came to Red River Settlement under Owen Keveny in 1812. Alexander Ross, *Red River Settlement*, (p. 45) speaks of him as 'an intelligent settler,' indicating that he was still a resident of this community after Ross came into it in 1825. In the various lists of Red River settlers found among the Selkirk Papers in the Ottawa Archives, the name John McIntyre occurs three times, but which of these is the one mentioned by Garrioch [is] impossible to say. The John McIntyre of Garrioch's caustic stricture, however, I am informed by living relatives, was at this time on his way to Iowa, where, with his family and other Red River people, he settled. The point of settlement [was] at Scotch Grove, south of Dubuque, where he lived until his death, and where his descendants still reside."

156 Gunn: "There are many small lakes along here, which makes it exceedingly difficult to identify the one mentioned with any certainty. Just which ones of these lakes they would strike would depend entirely on the course traveled, whether near to or farther from the river."

157 The word order of this sentence has been changed slightly in the interests of clarity.

intestines before it. Its {89} physical operation was equal to that of the most powerful laxative, and its effect was manifestly greater in those who had been too extravagant in its use.

South-seeking Washwater

July 7, 1837 – Friday. Came to Turnip River.[158] This river is supplied entirely by springs and, its bed being composed of stone and gravel, it presents a most beautiful crystal stream of water. The taste of its water is pleasant and agreeable, and its bottom is so firm that there is no difficulty in crossing it. This river, or rather creek, is the first stream that I have seen running south.[159] Should I gain nothing else by traveling, I have gained at least this much, viz, that I have had the pleasure of seeing water running to both poles – at least their course and direction tending towards the poles. Thus, said I, should Newton never have been born, I could at least have known that this our world was not as flat as a pancake.[160]

Having taken breakfast, I got on a huge stone in the centre of the {90} creek and, for the first time in my life, discharged the duties of a washerwoman. But either from the nature of the water in this beautiful stream, or from the manner of washing, or perhaps from some other cause unknown to me, I was well nigh washing all the skin from my fingers as well as the dirt from my shirts. What a horrid predicament! May youths take a lesson from my example, and chase bachelorhood [away].

We discontinued this day's journey within a mile or so of Fort Renville.

---

158 Gunn: "This is the little stream marked on modern maps as Pomme de Terre, or Potato River. On older maps, it is put down as Tipsinnah River or variations of that. This latter name is the Indian equivalent not of pomme de terre (potato), but of pomme blanche, the Indian turnip (psoralae esculenta) of the prairies. Garrioch's name for this river, therefore, is the correct one: Tipsinnah, Pomme Blanche, or Turnip River. It has its source in the eastern part of Grant County, Minnesota. Thence, running due south through Stevens and Swift, it joins the Minnesota a couple of miles southeast of Rush Lake, and about the same distance southwest of Appleton."

159 Gunn: "Garrioch's remark that this is the first stream he has seen flowing south is a little peculiar, in view of the fact that he must have crossed the Mustinka River shortly after passing the northern end of Lake Traverse, and that he has, for some time previous to this been proceeding along the north bank of the Minnesota. The explanation probably is that the Mustinka River, like the Bois des Sioux, was dry, as it very frequently is, and that, since striking the Minnesota, his route has lain too far back from that stream for the direction of its current to come under his observation."

160 Isaac Newton seems here to be given credit for a conclusion reached by much earlier scientists.

Chapter 2 – From Red River To St. Peter's

Visit with a Renowned Missionary

July 8, 1837 – Saturday. Removing this morning, we proceeded to Fort Renville, and halted on its adjacent banks or hills.[161] We were here, in a few moments, surrounded by numbers of spectators, the greater part of which were aborigines.

I went over to the missionary station, having received an invitation from the Doctor[162] to see him and his family. No-{91}-thing could be more agreeable, and nothing more refreshing to the mind long deprived of social and friendly intercourse, than the kindness and sociability manifested by the Doctor and his family. The consideration that I was an utter stranger, and nothing more to recommend me to them than a few black lines [of an introduction letter], in a strange land, added much to the weight of that kind feeling and attention which I met with in this family.

---

161 Gunn: "Spelled Ran Vielle in the manuscript: the trading post of Joseph Renville, the famous bois brûlé [a term commonly applied to Métis voyageurs and fur traders by reason of their dark 'burnt wood' complexions] trader, interpreter and guide. [See the note on Renville appended to the following day's entry.] This post, belonging to the American Fur Company, was on the east bank of the Minnesota River, where it leaves the lower end of Lac Qui Parl. The lake and river here are encased in a deep, wide valley with hilly, precipitate, banks. Below the banks, and between them and the river and lake, are flats of considerable extent; and down below the level of the prairie, on this bottom land, both the trading establishment and the mission were located. Mr. Garrioch's party have halted at the edge of the high bank, on the upper prairie level, overlooking the valley and the establishments down in it. This will explain Garrioch's meaning, when he says that the two establishments are "situated under the hills; so that, being overtopped by them, both places are quite invisible from the main road." The "main road" here evidently passed at some little distance back from the brink of the valley. A brief description of Fort Renville is given by Rev. Stephen R. Riggs in his *Mary and I: Forty Years with the* Sioux, p. 63."

162 Gunn: "Rev. Thomas Smith Williamson, MD, a noted pioneer Presbyterian missionary to the Sioux of Minnesota, a son of Rev. William Williamson and Mary Smith, was born in Union District, South Carolina, in 1800. He received his higher education at Jefferson College, Pennsylvania, [graduating] in 1820. Shortly after graduation, he began the study of medicine and eventually graduated from Yale in 1824. He took up the practice of medicine at Ripley, Ohio, where, in 1827, he was married to Miss Margaret Poage. In 1833, Dr. Williamson commenced the study of Theology at Lane Theological Seminary, Cincinnati, Ohio, and in 1834 was ordained. A few months later, he received an appointment as missionary to the Dakotas, and on May 15, 1835, [he and his family and staff] arrived at Fort Snelling. During his brief sojourn there, Dr. Williamson organized [at] the garrison, the first congregation ever established in Minnesota. A few weeks later, on the invitation of Joseph Renville, he moved up the Minnesota with his party and established himself at Lac Qui Parle. Gunn's account continues with a summary of Williamson's remarkable later missionary accomplishments, concluding with the observation that: Some account of his activities will be found in every work of any standing dealing with Minnesota history after 1835."

Both the Fort and Dr. Williamson's premises are situated under the hills; so that, being overtopped by them, both places {92} are quite invisible from the main road. Both the establishments are situated on the east side of the River St. Peter's.[163] The Indians among whom the Doctor carries on his missionary operations have their village and farms on the opposite side. The scenery presented to the view from these places is rather indifferent. As little more than high hills on one side and lofty timber on the other can be seen, the prospect thus obstructed on every side necessarily offers but a very limited space for the exercise of the optical organs.

This residence here being scarcely yet twelve months [old],[164] their progress in agriculture, &c, is but little. They have, however, opened a small farm, which seems to thrive well. As evidence of what the Doctor may reasonably expect in the course of his missionary labours, he has, during his short time {93} among the Indians, advanced some young men among them so far, at least in the art of writing, as to excel his own hand. They are thus enabled to correspond with him and other missionaries and with each other, and are, likewise, able to sing the praises of their God and Saviour in their own tongue, and that in the midst of the great congregation.

July 9, 1837 – Sunday. At half after ten, the Doctor, having given notice the day before to our party, commenced his service. His congregation, consisting of Yankees, French, Scotch, Irish, Half-breeds and Sioux Indians, amounted to something about forty persons. That was a mixture! I believe though, we were pretty much all of one blood after all, according to the Scriptures. This higgledy-piggledy assembly put me strongly in mind of that Scotch dish called, I think, hotch-potch. The Doctor's services were

---

163   Gunn: "Now known as the Minnesota, a name derived from the Sioux. Keating says (I, p. 328): 'The river is called in the Dakota language Watapan Menesota, which means 'The River of Turbid Water.'" E. S. Semour followed up its course in 1850, in his work *Sketches of Minnesota* (p. 105). The Minnesota rises on the Côteau de Prairies, west of Lake Traverse, the southern end of which it misses, on its way to the Mississippi, by a little over a mile. Thence it flows through Big Stone Lake and Lac Qui Parle, southeasterly and northeasterly to its junction with the Mississippi at Fort Snelling. In its upper reaches it meanders through a deep, wide valley, with steep banks; but lower down it assumes more the aspect of eastern rivers. During the earlier part of the 19th century, when communication by land first began between Fort Snelling and the Red River Settlement at Fort Garry, the course of this river was the route commonly adopted, the trail following the left bank of the stream. Later, the routes by Sauk Rapids and Crow Wing, on the Mississippi, were more generally used."

164   Gunn: "Evidently a slip here. Dr. Williamson arrived at Lac Qui Parle July 9, 1835 (Riggs, *Mary and I: Forty Years with the Sioux*, p. 386), and was consequently there nearly two years at that time."

conducted throughout, with the exception of his prayers, in the French and Indian languages, for the united benefit of the respective parties.

The morning service was concluded with prayer, offered, in the Sioux language, by Renville, the present Master of Fort {94} Renville.[165] Nothing could be more interesting than to see the savage of the wilderness assemble with the sons and daughters of the Lord in the place appointed for prayer; to hear the wild and rude sons of the forest sing the praises of their Maker and Saviour in their own uncultivated and barbarous language.

---

165   Gunn: "Joseph Renville [was] the well-known bois brûlé trader, guide and interpreter, after whom Renville Counties in Minnesota and North Dakota are named. This man, though a mixed-blood or Métis, and having slight advantages of early training and environment, was nevertheless one or the most remarkable and admirable characters to be found in the pages of our western history of that time. The son of a French trader and a pure-blooded Sioux woman, Joseph Renville first saw the light in the vicinity of the present city of St. Paul, about 1779. Keating states (I, p. 324), that he was brought up among the Indians, at Little Crow's village, and deprived of all education excepting such as his powerful mind enabled him to acquire, during his intercourse with the traders. Other authorities (Upham's *Minnesota Biographies*, p. 634) tell that he spent part of his boyhood in Canada under the instruction of a priest. On coming to manhood, he followed in his father's footsteps and became a trader; taking for a wife, also as his father had done, a pure-blooded woman of his mother's people. By reason of his great natural gifts, he soon acquired an almost unlimited influence over the latter tribe. When the war of 1812 broke out, he was selected by Colonel Dickson, who had full command of those districts, to lead the Dakotas against the American frontier forces. In this connection, he was made a captain in full standing in the British army. At the conclusion of the war, he enlisted in trade for the Hudson's Bay Company, on the head waters of the Red River; leaving that organization subsequently to permanently establish himself in the United States, thus voluntarily relinquishing his military pension from the British Government. On the amalgamation of the Hudson's Bay and NorthWest Companies in 1821, Renville, with a number of former employees of these two great concerns, banded together as a trading association and, the following year, established the Columbia Fur Company. In 1823, he accompanied the US Government expedition under Major Long to Pembina as guide and interpreter – a service which he had performed also for the Pike expedition in 1806. It was at his solicitation that Dr. Williamson, the great Sioux missionary, established himself at this point. Renville, though brought up a Roman Catholic, joined Dr. Williamson's church, together with his Sioux wife, [and] became a ruling elder, a fast friend, and [a] faithful helper of the missionary. [He assisted] in the laborious process of translating the Bible into the Sioux language, and even [in] composing the hymns used in the religious services. The slight glimpse we get of this man here in Garrioch's reference, therefore, is quite in line with what we know of him from other records; and there are few Minnesota records of that time that do not have something to say about Joseph Renville."

Renville is also discussed, along with Renville County, in Warren Upham, *Minnesota Geographic Names, Their Origin and Historic Significance, Collections of the Minnesota Historical Society* XVII (St. Paul: Minnesota Historical Society, 1920), p.455 ff.

The Doctor, having notified our party that the evening service should be conducted altogether in English, opened the meeting at 4 o'clock. The subject of the Doctor's discourse was in the following words: "Work out your own salvation with fear and trembling." The preacher's manner was engaging, his language impressive, and consequently, his whole discourse very interesting.

July 10, 1837 – Monday. A general start took place for resuming our journey. Kindly requested by the Doctor, however, to take breakfast with his family, I did so. After breakfast, I took leave, not without emotions of some regret, of my recent friends with whom I had spent two very pleasant and homely days and nights.[166] I started in pursuit of my {95} companions, who had left some hours before me by a different route. The Doctor, however, fearing that I should not be able to find the direct way, insisted upon accompanying me to the road; and, after tenderly and in a most friendly manner giving me a few words of advice – highly necessary to a stranger traveling to a strange country and people – we parted with an evident reciprocity of respect and emotions of brotherly kindness. The servant of the Lord bid me Godspeed, and I pushed ahead and went on my way rejoicing.

Farewell to Peskee, the Pregnant Quadruped

I overtook my companions at a creek called the Little Mississippi.[167] Here I was under the painful necessity of selling my quadruped, understanding by Mr. Pond (one of the missionaries)[168] and others, that there {96} was a part of the road lying between

---

166   The order of this sentence has been slightly re-arranged.

167   Gunn: "The Chippeway River must be here meant. The Dakota name for this stream, which should not be confused with the other river of that name flowing into the Mississippi below St. Paul, is Mea Wahkan Watapan: the River of the Spirit Banks, or Medicine Banks River. It rises by many branches in Pope County, Minnesota [and] flows into the Minnesota River from the north at Montevideo, in Chippewa County. This latter point, formerly known as Chippewa City, is about 10 miles down the Minnesota from Fort Renville."

168   Gunn: "Another name inseparably associated with early Minnesota missionary annals and history. There were two brothers of this name engaged in missionary work among the Dakotas at this time. The eldest of these, Samuel W. Pond, came west to Galena, Illinois as a teacher. He induced his younger brother, Gideon H., to join him as a missionary and teacher to the [Dakota] people. In 1834, they arrived at Fort Snelling; and, proceeding to the east shore of Lake Calhoun, erected there a primitive log building, and began their work. In 1836, after the arrival of Williamson [and about a year before the visit of Peter Garrioch] Gideon H. [went] as farm instructor and teacher to Lac Qui Parle (Neill, 4th ed., p. 447, and Riggs, *Mary and I: Forty Years with the Sioux*, p. 365). The Mr. Pond of Garrioch's reference, therefore, is Gideon H. Born in Washington, Conn., June

Traverse des Sioux and St. Peter's[169] so bad as to be scarcely passible for the best horses. Under present circumstances. I could by no means consider her to be among the best for traveling over bogs, from the fact that she was, most unfortunately, highly dignified with an increasing protuberance of pregnancy. And therefore, fearing the chance of risk, I concluded to let her go. Being a proverbialist by nature, I thought, as the old proverb says, that a bird in the hand is worth half a dozen in the bush. Accordingly, I sold my faithful and noble quadruped, delivering her into the hands of a stranger – and that a Frenchman, too – for the petty sum of $46.

Yes I sold my friend (for she aided me in my needs) for that trifle. It might have been worse, had I left it to chance. We were also told by certain [persons] that we should and would be at the necessity of selling our quadrupeds finally at St. Peter's for anything we could get. This last report was a most unfounded and black, perfidious falsehood: a warning to Red River emigrant folks! Yes, I {97} sold my quadruped as she stood for, as I said before, $46. Profit and loss: $17 on the wrong side.[170]

Misfortunes Begin

Here my misfortunes began, and when they will end I cannot tell. After a pleasant day's travel, we put a stop to our motion by some cause or another, and anxiously waited for the queen of . . . [Pages missing][171]

July 12, 1837 – Wednesday. After experiencing a very pleasant day's travel, we had to encamp on the open prairie, without any firewood. Fortunately the teamsters had taken a little in their carts. With this we managed to get some water warm enough to make a cup of tea. Ah, traveler, you know well the value of a pot of hot tea in your stomach after a day's hard walking don't you? I can assure you, it is not to be spoken against.

30, 1810, [Gideon Hollister Pond] was consequently at this date a young man of 27." Gunn's note concludes with a summary of Pond's subsequent illustrious career as a missionary.

169 Gunn: "Not to be confused with the town of that name now on the Minnesota River near Traverse des Sioux. The St. Peter's of those days was at the mouth of the Minnesota, adjacent to Fort Snelling."

170 He had presumably paid $63 for the horse.

171 Gunn: "Here there were several pages torn from the manuscript. Such mutilations occur from time to time throughout the various journals, and were probably deletions made by the author himself for personal reasons." It is also very possible that the pages were removed posthumously by a family member or friend.

July 13, 1837 – Thursday. In consequence of some rain, we had rather an unpleasant evening. The mosquitoes were so numerous that some of our company had little or no rest during the night.

July 14, 1837 – Friday. After taking breakfast at the side of a little lake, we passed on to a stream called the Stony Creek.[172] Finding that the stream was rather deep, the carts were unloaded previous to crossing {98} them. By so doing much time was lost. But what was done was well done.

Felling a Canoe

July 15, 1837 – Saturday. Having been informed on the preceding day by some Indians that one of them, at Mr. More's,[173] had a canoe for sale, I and my four messmates, viz.: Messrs Lindsey, Norton, Willson and Rogers,[174] made up our minds to go down to Mr. More's and purchase the canoe, so as to go down to St. Peter's by water. We accordingly took a part of our luggage with us, leaving the rest in the carts, and went down to Mr. More's. We attempted to purchase the above canoe, but without success. Not wishing to lose any of our precious time, we did not stand about trifles. Mr. More being so kind as to interpret for us, we offered a gun, three dollars, and a valuable powder horn for the {99} canoe, but all to no purpose.

---

172   Gunn: "On account of the mutilations of the manuscript, it is difficult to follow the progress of the party, or to identify the various natural features of the locality mentioned here-along. As nearly as I can judge, the travelers must be getting to near the site of New Ulm; and, if this is the case, Stony Creek is probably the small stream, marked on some maps as Little Rock River, that flows into the Minnesota from the north about ten miles above that place."

173   Gunn: "This is probably the fur trader Hazen Mooers, who figures in the early records of Minnesota. It is difficult, however, to be always certain of the gentleman's identity, for the reason that his name is seldom spelled the same way in any two of the references to it. Warren Upham, in his *Minnesota Biographies*, pp. 519-20, gives this brief account of him: "Hazen Mooers, pioneer fur trader, born near Plattsburg, N.Y., Aug. 3, 1779 died near Ft. Ridgely, Minn., in 1858. He took part in the war of 1812; entered the employ of the American Fur Company about 1820, and took charge of their trading post at Lake Traverse in 1835; afterwards established a trading post on Gray Cloud Island, and also another at Shakopee, where after 1845 he was government farmer. The later years of his life were spent on a claim near Fort Ridgely." Gunn then cites several further references to the same general effect, and concludes that: "As Mr. Mooers spent the latter years of his life "on a claim near Fort Ridgely," as stated above, the probability is rendered almost a certainty, that the "Mr. More" here mentioned is also the same; the party being now in the Fort Ridgely neighbourhood."

174   Gunn: "Of particulars of these four messmates of Garrioch I have not been able to find the slightest trace. It seems probable that they did not return to the Red River Settlement, but cast in their lot with the people of the Republic and became American citizens."

Being convinced that we had already offered too much, and determined not to be humbugged any longer, we concluded to make one ourselves. Mr. More, at the same time, advised us to do so; and very kindly offered to lend us any tools we might stand in need of. Having prepared our axes, grooving picks, &c., we commenced business in no uncertain way. We crossed the river, and soon came to a huge maple tree, which Mr. More had directed us to. We brought the tree to the ground on short notice, and mangled it to the proper dimensions by 7 o'clock in the evening. After felling the tree, I measured the diameter of the butt and found it to be 3 ¼ feet.

Night drawing nigh, we returned to our kind host; and, having previously received of him a room to lodge in, we felt ourselves happy, cheerful, and quite at home. Our supper being ready, with a spacious dish containing at least two gallons of fresh, rich and luxurious milk set before us, we supped like kings for comfort, and like Cockneys for quantity. Supper being over, and feeling somewhat fatigued from the labours of the day, we unanimously agreed to tumble into bed. In a moment, after discoursing a while on the theory of horizontalism, we found ourselves in the actual practice of the theory, as dignified as lords, as cheerful as monkeys, and as snug as so many bed-bugs.

Alone with the Lord

July 16, 1837 – Sunday. Our time being now at our own disposal, and this being the Lord's Day, we laid aside all our secular business, and each one spent the day in a way most suitable to his own feelings. Though far from a Christian country and people, and [there being] no public place to meet the people of God to worship in, I found much pleasure in contemplating the goodness of that being who has promised never to forsake those {100} who put their trust in Him. Being fully persuaded that God is ever faithful to his promises, I took particular delight in taking a retrospective of the past and gone-by days, convinced that I had realized the gracious promise. The day being very fair, I spent the greater part of it in solitary meditation.

Completing the Canoe

July 17, 1837 – Monday. The day promising to be fine, we proceeded to renew our canoe business; but, being hindered by rain, we were under the necessity of quitting for a time. The heat, moreover, became very intense and oppressive; and, the mosquitoes being very troublesome, we could not protract our labours of the day as we wished, and so we concluded in season.

July 18, 1837 – Tuesday. Having commenced our business in season this morning, we accomplished a pretty good day's work. The weather, however, being sultry and oppressive, we laboured with much difficulty. The day was so intolerably hot, that, through profuse perspiration, we lost more [weight], I believe, than we could recover for a week to come, no matter how much we might eat.

The Voyage Begins – Without Lillipoot

July 19, 1837 – Wednesday. Our canoe being now finished and in the water of the St. Peter's ready for use, we prepared for a start. We proposed buying some provisions for our journey, our stock being nearly out; but Mr. More told us he was very sorry that he was not able to meet with our wishes, as he expected to be short himself. He, however, was so kind as to let us have between 20 and 30 lbs. of flour, for which he would not accept any pay; assuring us at the same time, that, if it was in his power, he would most cheerfully let us have more.

All being ready, we bade farewell to our kind host and family, and recommenced our journey. {101} Our canoe, most unhappily, proved to be as cranky as an egg; and the consequence was, that I could not allow my poor [dog] Lillipoot a place in it. He had to do his traveling the best way he could, through thickets, bushes, grass, &c., along the banks of the river. The poor fellow followed us some distance; but, probably finding his way rather rugged and unusually irritating by being entangled so often with creeks, rivulets, &c., he concluded to proceed no further. He kept pace with us till about 12 o'clock, and then disappeared. After that we saw him no more. Poor fellow, I felt sorry for him. No doubt he fell a sacrifice to hunger and want, or to the devouring jaws of some rapacious animal of the carnivorous order. How happy would I have felt, could I but have had the privilege of carrying his mangled and mutilated carcass to the silent grave, and giving him a decent burial, who was so worthy of his kind. But alas! as a fool dies, so died he. As an ass is interred, so was he. For he fell into the hands of unmerciful foes, by neglecting to prosecute his journey with unwearied diligence. He fell a prey to the wild beasts of the desert and to the blood-thirsty fowls of the air. Or, probably, he sank under the oppressive weight of want and sad distress. Far from friends, in a wild and lonely desert, he breathed his melancholy spirit into the unknown regions of his departed kind and kindred.

The St. Peter's [River] abounds with catfish and pike. The principal part of the timber along its banks is maple, poplar, cottonwood and the willow tree. This river increases

Chapter 2 – From Red River To St. Peter's

gradually as it approaches the Mississippi. The current of its waters is considerably more rapid after it receives the Blue Earth River,[175] which is considered to be one of its most important tributaries. It appears to have derived its {102} name from the colour of the earth which abounds somewhere in the vicinity of its source. The river is remarkable for its colour and for the rapidity of its current, also for a quarry of red pipestone found near its head waters,[176] which is supposed – though I think erroneously – to be the only one in North America. The St. Peter's, I think, is also remarkable, not only for the abundance of its fish but also for the large quantities of grapes which are to be seen along its banks. Neither of these rivers [is] navigable, for vessels of any size, to any considerable distance, except in the time of high water. The Cotton River[177] is another tributary stream of the St. Peter's.

---

175   Garrioch's party did not actually encounter the Blue Earth River until July 21, but the note Gunn appended to the entry for that day seems appropriate here: "Blue Earth River, called by Nicollet the Mankato. Keating says: 'By the Dakotas it is called Makato Osa Watapa, which signifies 'the river where blue earth is gathered.' The blue earth deposits that give to the river its name are about six miles from its mouth. It is the principal tributary of the Minnesota. It rises about the centre of Kossuth County, Iowa, not far from the Des Moines, and flows due north, joining the Minnesota at Mankato, at the extreme southern apex of the great bend which the latter river takes at that point, before proceeding northeast to the Mississippi. The Blue Earth is very winding, and has many branches. The volume of water in [it] is if anything larger than that of the Minnesota above their point of junction." Upham, *Minnesota Geographic Names*, pp. 57-58, says it gives its name to the Blue Earth County. An earlier name for it was "Green River"; the name in Sioux is Makato, made up of *maka*, earth, and *to*, which in Sioux means both blue and green.

176   Gunn: "There seems to have been some misconception, in the minds of early travelers, with reference to the location of these famous red pipestone quarries. I have seen the same statement made by other writers describing these parts at a later date. I do not know of any such deposit on the headwaters of the Blue Earth River, which are over 100 miles east by south of the quarries made famous by Longfellow. A couple of the principal tributaries of the Blue Earth, the Watanwan and Chantaska Rivers, it is true, do reach over a considerable distance in that direction; but the upper part of the Des Moines River intervenes between them and these deposits. The red pipestone quarries referred to are in Pipestone County, Minnesota, between the sources of the latter stream and those of the Big Sioux, some 120 miles west by north of the location given by our journalist."

177   Gunn: "The Cottonwood River is here meant – the Rivière aux Liards of the French – so called because of the abundance of this tree on its banks. It was also called Warhoju Watapa by the Sioux (Keating, I, p. 358). It rises in the southern part of Lyon County, Minnesota, and flows east through Redwood and Brown, joining the Minnesota on the south side just below New Ulm. Its principal tributary on the north is Sleepy Eye River, which is south of the town of the same name near the centre of Brown County. Another stream paralleling it, called Little Cottonwood, joins the Minnesota about six miles farther down."

Disagreeable Companions, Hunger Pangs, and Rain

July 20, 1837 – Thursday. Encamped on a sandy beach for the purpose of avoiding disagreeable companions (mosquitoes) by whom we were so much {103} annoyed the previous night on a bank of tall and luxuriant grass. Our provisions falling short, we had to cut our allowance and retire to rest without a mouthful.

July 21, 1837 – Friday. Came to the Blue Mud River. Took breakfast at 9 o'clock this morning.

When night came, we had to jump into bed without having taken either dinner or supper. But, as evils seldom come alone, so it was in this case. After going to bed with empty stomachs (which of itself is an uncompromising evil) and in great perplexity of mind (fearing lest we should already have passed the post whence we expected to have our distressing want relieved and our most deplorable situation ameliorated), our misery was most exceedingly enhanced by the countless unwelcome visitors [mosquitos] who, out of pretended courtesy probably due to our kindness on previous occasions, affected to give us a polite and seasonable call. But it was only to make renewed attacks on our sanguinary tubes, into which they were curiously fond of dipping their suckers. Added to all this, our {104} condition was rendered, if possible, more pitiable still by the torrents of rain which descended upon us, from which we were entirely destitute of any other shelter than that which a buffalo robe and two or three threadbare blankets afforded. Under such circumstances, it is easy to conceive what the state of the feelings and mind would be.

Joyous Reunion and Scalded Hands

July 22, 1837 – Saturday. Hungry, drowsy and wet, we jumped into our canoe and cut the waters of the St Peter's in no common style. We arrived at Traverse des Sioux,[178] much to our joy, at 9 o'clock this morning. After receiving some refreshments from our former fellow travelers, who had arrived there two days before us, we purchased

---

178   Gunn: "One of the earliest-named and best-known localities on the Minnesota; both trader and missionary having located here at an early period. The site of the old Traverse des Sioux is a little below the present town of St. Peter, on the left bank of the river. The place was so called, because from this point the Sioux Indians, in whose territory it was, were in the habit of make a 'traverse,' [portage,] or short-cut, to escape the necessity of having to go round the great bend of the Minnesota, which occurs here, when traveling up and down the river." Upham, *Minnesota Geographic Names*, p. 375. This was the site of three treaties between the governor of Wisconsin [and] the Sioux in 1841 and 1851, some years after Peter's visit here in 1837.

such provisions as we considered necessary and sufficient for the remaining part of our journey. Mr. LeBlanc[179] very readily supplied our {105} wants, by letting us have such as we desired. I and one or two of my canoe-mates employed ourselves the remaining part of the day in washing. It happened with me, however, according to the proverb "More haste, less speed." I borrowed a large iron kettle to boil up my shirts, &c. in, in order to make quick work of the business. But such was the quantity of dirt, filth and lice which had accumulated upon my linens, that the operation of boiling only tended to condense the dirt with which they were so deeply impregnated. To my no small mortification, I discovered when too late that the theory of boiling dirty linen for speedy cleansing was one thing, and the practice of that theory quite another. Besides, the operation of hot linen and water on my tender and delicate hands was such as chafed and scalded them to a pitiful degree. I, with all my boasted intelligence and ingeniousness, [could not] accomplish my intention without the aid of my companions.

July 23, 1837 – Sunday. Necessity compelled me to spend the greater part of this day in writing home; for the guide was expected to return from St. Peter's in a few days, and [then] proceed homeward. Also, through the desire of my companions, we had settled upon starting the following day to proceed to Fort Snelling.

July 24, 1837 – Monday. Finding that our canoe required to be made lighter, we spent the day in doing so. Very little [else] worthy of remark this day.

July 26, 1837 – Wednesday. From the want of rest on the preceding night, traveling to-day became very irksome. Perceiving that our provisions were again likely to fall short, we were compelled to retire with barely a cup of tea in our stomachs. This

---

179   Gunn: "Louis Provencalle, a well-known French Canadian trader of that time, is here referred to. The name Le Blanc, or Le Bland, as we sometimes find it, was only a nickname. He came to the West some time before 1800, and traded for many years on the Minnesota. Reverend Stephen R. and Mrs. Riggs, who passed this point on their way up to Lac Qui Parle Sept. 5, 1837, just six weeks after Garrioch's party, also met him here, where he was located as trader, no doubt for the American Fur Company. Of this encounter, Mrs. Riggs writes ([*Mary and I:*] *Forty Years with the Sioux*, p. 49): 'Here we made the acquaintance of a somewhat remarkable French trader, by name Louis Provencalle, but commonly called Le Bland. The Indians called him Skadan: Little White. He was an old voyageur who could neither read nor write. But, by a certain force of character, he had risen to the honourable position of trader. He kept his accounts with his Indian debtors by a system of hieroglyphics.' Provencalle was still trader at Traverse des Sioux in 1843 when Riggs established his mission there; and he continued at that place for some years thereafter (Riggs, pp. 101, 114). That Le Blanc, not Le Bland, is correct for the nickname would seem to be indicated by the Indian 'Skadan,' Little White."

very naturally produced a keen desire for rest; and, fearing that we could not obtain that desirable repose which we so much stood in need of by reason of bloodthirsty creatures, we thought it advisable to continue our traveling till such time as night became so cool as to overthrow and impede their blood-thirsty intentions. With this object in view, we traveled till 10 o'clock; for, by this time, our foes, taking the hint, had retired in disappointment. We halted for an encampment, [at] a spot covered with tall and dense grass, where we spent a night of the most agreeable and comfortable kind.

St. Peter's at Last

July 27, 1837 – Thursday[180] After a night of sweet and refreshing sleep, we proceeded on our journey, and halted after a few hours traveling to take a cup of tea and some gruel. We had neither fat nor flesh to put in our gruel, but sweetened it with what sugar remained after sweetening our tea, and made it go the best way we could. We could not say, after breakfast, that we had so much as one mouthful of anything. To be sure, we had a little tea; but, without sugar, it was inferior to pure water.

Happily for us, we were within a few miles of Fort Snelling.[181] We arrived at this Fort at 2 o'clock, pm.

The Fort Snelling military post was surrounded by a small group of settlements and establishments, then known collectively as "St. Peter's," that grew eventually into the modern twin cities of Minneapolis and St. Paul. Peter Garrioch had reached the destination of this stage of his journey. The succinctness and matter-of-factness with which he recorded the fact may perhaps be attributed to exhaustion.

Other recent arrivals to the area were Protestant missionary Stephen Riggs and his young wife Mary. Mrs. Riggs' enthusiasm in a letter written to her brother from Fort Snelling on June 2, the day after their arrival, had been considerably more effusive:

> **As we passed up the Mississippi & gazed upon the sublime handiwork of 'nature's God,' we wished you were with us to gaze, to admire & to adore.... The scenery of**

---

180   Only the first part of this day's journal entry is included here. For the concluding portion, see the first journal entry in Chapter 3.

181   Gunn: "This fort, built by Colonel Snelling in 1820-21, and named by him Fort St. Anthony, occupied the high point of land formed by the junction of the Mississippi and Minnesota Rivers on the north side of the latter, just is it does today, and is too well-known to require further notice here." More detail appears in Upham, *Minnesota Geographic Names*, pp. 227-228.

the Upper Mississippi surpasses all that I have witnessed to say the least. I could give you no idea of its grandeur if I were to fill this sheet with descriptions.[182]

The subsequent correspondence of Mary Riggs, with whom Garrioch soon crossed paths, would not always be so complimentary.

---

182   MHS: "Stephen Riggs & Family Papers: Mary Anne Longley Riggs Correspondence," Minnesota Historical Society, 1837-51: 144.G.7.2F.

Chapter 3

Labouring & Teaching At St. Peters

1837-1838

Clustered at or near the confluence of the Mississippi and Minnesota (or St. Peter's) Rivers – the seminal site of the twin cities of Minneapolis and St. Paul – were the Fort Snelling military outpost, a major trading post of the American Fur Company, two missionary stations (Congregationalist/Presbyterian and Methodist[183]), and several small settler communities. One of the latter was called St. Peter's, and that name was also applied to the entire area by Peter Garrioch and others.[184] The fort, standing on high ground west of the Mississippi and north of the Minnesota, was the governmental heart of the cluster, the trading post on the other side of the Minnesota being its commercial hub. The Methodist mission, which was on the east side of the Mississippi, a site now in the modern city of St. Paul, served a Sioux village there, and the Congregationalist/Presbyterian establishment – where our subject was soon to find himself – was at Lake Harriet in what is now Minneapolis. The entire white population of the area was estimated to be 157 (many of them the Swiss settlers who had fled the Red River Settlement after the 1826 flood) at the time Garrioch was present.[185]

---

183   There was no Roman Catholic mission in the area at the time; the first resident priest was Father Lucien Galtier, who did not arrive until 1840. *Catholic Encyclopedia*.

184   Gunn: "Just what territory and settlements were included under the above name at this time is an interesting and seemingly open question. Most American authorities unhesitatingly identify St. Peters with the present Mendota, across the Minnesota River from Fort Snelling; and I have heard the same from Red River people who had made the trip there in early days. From Garrioch's use of the name, however, I think we cannot escape the conclusion that, in his conception at any rate, the name embraced the entire group of hamlets in the Fort Snelling neighbourhood. It is certain that he did not live in Mendota. He lived at the Baker Settlement. Yet he speaks of having spent the winter in St. Peter's, and it is St. Peter's that he bids farewell to when he leaves in the spring. I am inclined to think that, in general usage, the name referred to the entire group of settlements at the mouth of the Minnesota at this time."

185   See AM: Gunn, "Garrioch at St. Peter's," pp. 119-128, and Chap. 1, text associated with n. 82.

Chapter 3 – Labouring & Teaching At St. Peters 85

St. Peter's was not the final destination of Garrioch's first lengthy journey from home. From there he planned to continue on to some larger centre where he could pursue his educational goals. It being mid-summer, however, there was no immediate need to move on. Besides, his journal tells us, there was no "opportunity of going down the river at this time." Just why that should have been so at the height of the river traffic season is not certain, but it seems likely that the young man needed to earn some money before proceeding.

First, however, a little relaxation was in order. His canoe-mates having found almost immediate employment, he was on his own; but there was an historic event unfolding close to him that afternoon, offering both diversion and food for his enquiring mind.

Treaty Talks

July 27, 1837 – Thursday [continued]. The American Govern-{107}-ment were in the act of forming a treaty with the Chippewas of the Mississippi.[186] The delegate appointed to conduct the operation was Governor Dodge of the Wisconsin Territory.[187] I spent the greater part of this day in listening to the remarks of the Governor, and to the eloquent speeches of the Chippewa chieftains.

July 28, 1837 – Friday. Spent the greater part of this day also at the place of treating, which was a shade[d area] previously erected for this purpose. Several lengthy and most eloquent harangues[188] were delivered by two or three of the principal chiefs

---

186 Gunn: "This was the first treaty made by the Chippewas of Minnesota by the United States Government for the cession of their lands. Under it was included all the lands in southeastern Minnesota and southwestern Wisconsin. According to Major Taliaferro's Journal, there were 1,200 Chippewas at this treaty. It was signed July 29, 1837. (See *Minnesota in Three Centuries*, II, p. 278)."

187 Gunn: "General Henry Dodge, first Governor of Wisconsin territory – which also included Minnesota, Iowa, and the eastern halves of North and South Dakota. The new Territory was decreed April 20, 1836, and the new Governor was sworn in on July 4 of the same year. He was removed from office, for political reasons, by President Tyler in 1841. One of the first duties of Governor Dodge upon assuming office, was to make treaties with the Indians, and to extinguish their rights to such tracts of land, within his jurisdiction, as had not already been relinquished. By the treaty above described was extinguished the Ojibwa title to their Minnesota hunting grounds. Identification of the Eastern Sioux was called to Washington the following September, when a treaty was also made with them, whereby all the Sioux lands east of the Mississippi were ceded to the United States Government. This treaty was signed on September 29." Upham, *Minnesota Geographic Names*, p. 171, provides more detail about Governor Dodge, after whom Dodge County, Minnesota was named, and the treaty he made with the Ojibways on July 29, 1837, at Fort Snelling, to cede a large tract of land east of the Mississippi to the United States to open it for white settlement.

188 The fact that the term "harangue" is – surprisingly, to modern eyes - modified by "most eloquent" points to the fact that, in Peter's day, "harangue" did not carry the inevitably pejorative meaning it does today but instead was commonly used when describing Indigenous speeches. These speeches

during the treaty. The rest of the chiefs, about 20 in number, did not appear to take any active part in the way of speaking, but spent their time in consulting with each other, and dictating to those who addressed the Governor and the assembly.

The land to be purchased from the Chippewas, amounting to about a million and a half acres,[189] was valued at $800,000, out of which $100,000 was to be received by the Chippewa halfbreeds, and $70,000 by the American Fur Company for old debts due by the [Chippewa] nation to that company. The remainder, after the above deductions, was according to the treaty to be paid to the Chippewas concerned in 20 installments, covering 20 years. {108}

A More Skeptical View

While Garrioch's brief description of the treaty proceedings was accurate enough, there is nothing in it to suggest that anything he heard or observed awakened his usually alert critical sense. Mary Riggs, who was also present to observe the negotiations, came away with a much less favourable impression of them. Her long August 4, 1837, letter to her father describing her observations and opinions reads, in part, as follows:

> **About the 15th of July Governor Dodge & General Smith, the commissioners on the part of the . . . government to treat with the Indians for certain lands, arrived at Fort Snelling. Near the same time three steamboats came up bringing persons 'good, bad and indifferent' to stay and see the end. Some left when the business was only partly transacted, but thirty or forty remained until it was finished, some of whom are now on their way to the newly-purchased land with high hopes of making a fortune by locating in some place where in days to come there will be a great city.**

> **The Indians commenced coming about the first of July, but did not all arrive until the twenty-fifth. . . . They numbered between four and five hundred men besides women and children, in all probably twelve or fifteen hundred. Some of the bands came with all their hosts, while others sent only their chiefs and braves.**

---

were often delivered by a representative of a leader who was talented and trained in this area and tended to follow a particular format and structure. They were delivered in such a way as to be persuasive to those assembled where reaching consensus agreement was to be favoured (courtesy of Anne Lindsay).

189 Gunn: "In *Minnesota in Three Centuries*, II, p. 279, the following particulars are given: in consideration of the cession of this vast expanse of country, amounting to fully 60 million acres, the Indians were to receive less than two cents an acre, or $810,000 in goods and money, payable in 20 annual installments as follows: in money, $9,500; in goods, $19,000; for establishing their blacksmith shops and supplying them, $3,000; for farmers' implements, grain, etc. $1,000; in provisions, $2,000; tobacco $500. To the Chippewa halfbreeds $100,000, and to the Indian leaders for debts [owed to the American Fur Company] $100,000."

The land purchased of the Indians by the present treaty is probably as great, if not greater than, the whole state of Ohio in extent, reaching from Black River which joins the Mississippi River two hundred miles below this . . . to one hundred above. . . . It extends as near to Lake Superior as the head of the St. Croix river, being probably about three hundred miles in length and one hundred and fifty in width. The country purchased is chiefly valuable on account of its timber, but it is said by those acquainted with it is that there is also very much very good arable land.

But you will like to have a glimpse of the . . . [atmosphere] of the treaty. You are probably aware that a certain set of men called 'traders' have the principal influence in managing the Indians in the formation of treaties. These men are generally without principle, and of course they urge the Red men to sell that they may share in 'the spoils.'

The first day, after all the Indians had arrived, the Governor in council told them, by showing them a map, what country he wished to purchase. Then, after many of the chiefs and braves had spoken about various things, he told them he wished them to appoint two of their number who should speak for them on the following day. When they should go to their lodges he wished them to assemble, and smoke, and choose their speakers, and discuss the question in regard to selling this land - and give him an answer on the morrow.

That evening this was all done in due form, smoking of course not neglected.

The next morning, when they assembled together in council, after smoking again and shaking hands with the Governor, all the chiefs and braves went to their two speakers, the former took their medals received from the President of the United States, and took their feathers and put them up on those they had chosen. There seemed to be much of primitive significance in this act.

The two representatives then announced to the Governor that the Chippewas were willing to sell[190] part of their land to their great father the President, and,

---

190   Like most Europeans and non-Indigenous people, Mary Riggs understood and used the term "sell" in relation to land acquisition and disposition quite differently than did the Indigenous people with whom they were dealing, including the immediate negotiators in this instance, leading to many tragic misapprehensions. An "agreement to share the land," as John Long put it, is probably a more accurate description of what Indigenous peoples thought was occurring. The word "sell" is a one-sided, inadequate, and culturally-bound interpretation of a process that has been used since time immemorial by Indigenous people and peoples to bring outsiders into reciprocal relationships. Agreeing to share the land can be a part of this reciprocity, but the relationships created in these gatherings were mutual and ongoing, not a limited dickering over barter and exchange. Even when specific misleading as to the impact of specific terms set out in the written treaty documents is set aside, there was at least a strong element of misunderstanding on both sides of a negotiation such as described here. "Indigenous participants' signatures do not necessarily imply any understanding of, or consent to, what was written on the parchment. Their marks simply acknowledge that they were present, like witnesses at a marriage, when solemn promises were made." John S. Long, *Treaty No. 9: Making the Agreement to Share the Land in Far Northern Ontario in 1905* (Montreal & Kingston, McGill-Queen's University Press, 2010), p. 345. See also: Canada, Minister of Supply and Services Canada. *Report of the Royal Commission on Aboriginal Peoples* (Ottawa, 1996), I, pp. 119-132, & 155-199; John McLaren, et al., eds., *Despotic Dominion: Property Rights in British Settler*

taking a piece of paper, they cut it out so as to cover on the map that which they were willing to sell. At the same time they wished the commissioners to take into consideration that whatever they received for the land, it was their desire to have it in yearly payments for sixty years, supposing that the present generation would be dead by that time, and thinking it would be right that the next should provide for themselves.

When the terms of the treaty were under consideration the traders brought in a bill of account [claiming] credits against the Indians amounting to one hundred and forty thousand dollars, which they wished to secure to themselves by the terms of the treaty. This has always been the case in treaties heretofore made with the Indians, traders have received from what has been pretended to be paid to the poor and degraded Red men a part or the whole of their credits. This seems to me very unjust.

Indians are just like other people in regard to paying their debts, only more so. They always get their goods from the traders before they go out on their hunt. After they come back, if they have made a good hunt, those who are pretty honest go pay up all of their debts, while those who are not honest take their furs to some other trader and receive other goods for them. If they have had a bad hunt, all fail in paying what they owe, and if it is not paid that year it is never paid. It is said by those engaged in the trade that they do not lose more than one third of their credits.

Traders go into the country knowing these facts, and hence they make ample allowance for these bad debts. They sell blankets, ammunition, beads and such things to the Indians at two, three, five and sometimes six hundred percent. And then, to finish this hyperbole of wickedness, when the poor Indians sell their land and get flour and pork and blankets and money, these traders come and ask the government for a Benjamin's mess of it. And government gives it to them.

You may rest assured that the Indians opposed this with all their force. But they might as well oppose the furious northern blasts that sweep over our wide prairies. The traders, in this case, obtained only seventy thousand dollars, half their first claim.

In debating this point some of the old chiefs were quite eloquent. One asked 'Where are our young men? Years ago we had a great many young men, now we have only few. Where have they gone? We sent them out in bands of twenty and thirty to hunt for these traders – the Sioux [enemies of the Chippewas] found them and killed them. Thus the flower and pride of our nation have vanished, like the mist upon the hills before the rays of the morning. We have given our sons and they want more.'

The price paid these Indians by government is eight hundred thousand dollars in cash (from which the seventy thousand before mentioned is to be subtracted)

Societies (Vancouver: University of British Columbia Press, 2005); & Robert J. Talbot, *Negotiating the Numbered Treaties: An Intellectual & Political Biography of Alexander Morris* (Saskatoon: Purich Publishing, 2009).

besides some considerable amount in blankets, ammunition, provisions, tobacco, &c to be paid in annuities for 20 years.

The commissioners proposed giving them some part in farming utensils, cattle, mills, the establishment of schools among them &c, but they preferred having it given in food and clothing. How much influence the traders had on them in this decision I can not say - but I presume it was not much less than that exerted by Herodias upon her daughter when she asked for the head of St. John the Baptist…

Last <u>Sabbath</u> the treaty was concluded. The better the day the better the deed. All the chiefs signed it on that day but one, the chief of the band called the "Pillagers." He refused to sign it and would not be forced into the measure by all the bayonets in the garrison. This was a noble example of sublimity in action. I wish this Sabbath-breaking in the foundation of this treaty were trumpeted throughout the religious world. Surely such a wicked nation as the United States, God hates."[191]

Military Country Wives

Another of Mary Riggs' criticisms was directed at a practice she had observed during the few days she and Stephen had spent at Fort Benning before moving to Lake Harriet. Three days after Garrioch's arrival at the Fort she vented her outrage in a July 31, 1837, letter home to her mother at what she considered an abuse of the "country wife" custom:

Until my location here I was not aware that it was so exceedingly common for officers in the army to have two wives or more. But [only] one of course legally so. For instance at the Fort before the removal of the last troops there were but two officers who were not known to have an Indian woman, if not half-Indian children. You remember I used to cherish some partiality for the military, but I must confess the last vestige of it has departed. I am not now thinking of it in connection with the peace question, but with that of moral reform. Once in my childish simplicity I regarded the army & its discipline as a school for gentlemanly manners, but now it seems a sink of iniquity[,] a school of vice.

And oh how lamentable is the influence of such men when in authority upon the poor oppressed Indians. How diametrically opposed to that influence which we wish to exert. And yet we are all from the same Christian country. I believe however that the Indians are so discriminating that they will perceive & feel the different motives which activate us in our labors, if we daily live as disciples of Jesus, reflect his image & walk in his steps.[192]

She then turned, somewhat uncertainly, to missionaries' personal opportunities for social intercourse and the extent of St. Peters' isolation from the outside world:

It would be pleasant indeed had we good Christian society so near us [as] to encourage & warm our hearts, but I do not know certainly that any of the present

---

191 MHS: Stephen Riggs & Family Papers, 144.G.7.2F. For more on the unfair trading terms with Indigenous peoples, this time at the hands of the Hudson's Bay Company, see Chap. 6, n. 346.

192 *Ibid.*

officers & families are pious.... [But] perhaps I should not have used an expression that would imply [that we are secluded], as you will perceive by what I have written that we might have more intercourse with the gay & fashionable than in most of the mountain towns in Massachusetts. Besides this, we see friends from the States occasionally, as we have had very frequent arrivals this season. You will not deem us shut out from the world entirely while six or seven steamboats are in this port in about the same number of weeks.[193]

And she concluded that letter with a snippet of news that would have important consequences for Peter Garrioch: "Mr. Stevens thinks of leaving this station for a few weeks or months to arrange matters of a private nature – such as landed estate in Indiana, be ordained I suppose, &c &c." Stevens returned at the beginning of November, however, as Peter's entry for November 9th shows.

Visit to a Mission Extended

July 29, 1837 – Saturday. My former companions having hired themselves in the service of speculators, and [I] being left entirely alone without companions, and nothing to do, I concluded to take a walk out to Mr. Stevens' [mission] and see the reverend gentleman. Agreeable to their kind invitation, I concluded to spend the night and the following day with the family.

It was natural that the lonesome young man, inspired by his short sojourn with Dr. Williamson at Lac Qui Parle[194] three weeks previously, should choose to visit the nearest Protestant mission, and that he should accept an invitation to stay there overnight and share in the family's and the mission's Sunday activities. It offered an opportunity for educated discourse, devout exercises, and further insights into the missionary calling to which he hoped to dedicate his life. And, although Peter did not expressly record the fact in his diary, he impressed those he encountered at the mission sufficiently to be offered an extended invitation to remain longer than a "night and the following day."

The St. Peter's mission, beautifully located on the shore of Lake Harriet some seven miles distant from Fort Snelling,[195] was in the charge of the Reverend Jedediah D. Stevens, an experienced missionary of the Congregational faith. Born in 1798 in Madison County,

---

193 Ibid.

194 Upham, *Minnesota Geographic Names*, p. 288, explained that the unusual name originated with the Dakota or Sioux name, *mde*, lake, *iye*, speaks, *dan*, a diminutive suffix, *Mde Lyedan*, probably from the echoes thrown back from the bluffs that border it, or from a belief that voices were heard, but no speakers found. A missionary at Lac Qui Parle, Rev. Moses N. Adams, reported that there was a remarkable creaking, groaning, and whistling of the ice on the lake in winter and spring, caused by fluctuations of the water level in the lake. To these "voices" he attributed the Dakota and French name.

195 Garrioch estimated the distance from the Fort to the mission at six and a half or seven miles. See August 5 entry. For colourful descriptions of the trails around Lac Qui Parle, see Jon Willand,

Chapter 3 – Labouring & Teaching At St. Peters

New York, and educated there, he had begun ministering to Aboriginal people in 1827, first on Mackinaw Island and then at Green Bay, on behalf of a joint Congregationalist and Presbyterian missionary board. Two years later, the same board commissioned him to survey mission possibilities throughout what was then the Wisconsin Territory. That project, which took him as far as Fort Snelling, resulted in the creation of a mission on Lake Superior. When instructed in 1834 to establish a permanent mission among the Sioux of the Minnesota River area, he returned to Fort Snelling with his wife and a niece, only to find that Dr. Williamson had arrived there a few weeks previously with the same intention. When Stevens pressed his prior claim Williamson had relented, moving on to Lac Qui Parle.

Peter found that he was not the only guest of Reverend and Mrs. Stevens. The recently-arrived Reverend Stephen Riggs and his aforementioned wife Mary, were also staying at the Harriet Lake mission temporarily, pending their continuing on westward to replace Dr. Williamson at Lac Qui Parle.[196] While the Garrioch diary does not mention the Riggs explicitly, Mary's letters clearly establish that her and her husband's presence there overlapped with Peter's by about six weeks. It would be unimaginable that these three young people, all far from home and afire with missionary zeal, would not have spent considerable time together.

In a letter to her grandfather, dated June 22, 1837, Mary Riggs left a description of the Harriet Lake mission as it appeared at the time:

> The situation of the mission houses is very beautiful: on a little eminence, just above the shore of a lovely lake skirted with trees. Beyond, towards the fort, commences a finely undulating prairie which reaches to the rivers. About a mile north of us is Lake Calhoun, on the margin of which is an Indian village of about 20 lodges. Most of these are bark houses, some of which are 20 feet square, & others are tents of cloth or skins.
>
> The Indians come here at all hours of the day without ceremony, sometimes dressed & painted very fantastically, & again with scarcely any clothing. One came in yesterday dressed in coat, …shirt & cloth leggings – the only one I have seen with a coat excepting two boys who were in the family when we came. The most singular ornament I have seen was a large striped snake fastened among the painted hair, feathers & ribands of an Indian headdress, in such a manner that it would coil round in front & dart out its snaky head or creep down the back at pleasure. During this the Indian sat perfectly at ease, apparently much pleased at the astonishment & fear manifested by some of the family….

Lac Qui Parle and the Dakota Mission (Madison, Minn.: Lac Qui Parle County Historical Society, 1964), p. 267 ff.

196 Stephen Riggs and his wife Mary arrived at Fort Snelling on June 2, 1837, and spent about three months studying dialects of the Sioux language (e.g., Dakota, Lakota, Nakota) at the Lake Harriet Station before arriving at Lac qui Parle on September 15, according to a chronology in Willand, *Lac Qui Parle*, p. 282. Willand mentions Peter Garrioch's visit to Lac qui Parle on pp. 264-265 without providing any details.

> The Indians spend much time in feasting when they have materials. They sing together & shake their rattles while the food is cooking over a fire in the midst of their lodge. Their feasts are religious ceremonies & of many kinds to the Great Spirit, to the sun, earth, water, wood, beasts of many kinds, war armour &c. Now the corn is ready to roast for which they have been long waiting with impatient hunger, and their joy is almost full. Feasts [are held] night and day. No suffering from cold of course, [and] no concern for clothes. They are strangely benumbed with regard to the future. The little boys are amusing themselves with play, shooting birds [and] squirrels and roasting them. Many of them are entirely naked; others wear a blanket with a cloth about their middle. Women and girls from day-break to dark are driving blackbirds from their cornfields, and are far more noisy than the birds themselves.
>
> [Reverend Stevens has] made things look quite civilized. He [...has] built two houses of tamarack logs, the larger of which [for] his own family..., the lower part of the other ... [being] used for the school and religious meetings. Half a dozen boarding scholars, chiefly Half-breed girls, [...form] the nucleus of the school, ... taught by his niece, Miss Lucy C. Stevens.[197]

Not everything about the accommodations met with Mrs. Riggs' approval, of course:

> We are not troubled with all the insects which used to annoy me in Indiana, but the mosquitoes are far more abundant. At dark swarms fill our room, deafen our ears, & irritate our skin. For the last two evenings we have filled our room with smoke almost to suffocation to disperse these over officious insects.[198]

When Peter Garrioch, for whom mosquitoes would have been a minor nuisance by now, first encountered this generally impressive mission compound, he must have been strongly attracted to the place. That opinion would change before long.

July 30, 1837 – Sunday. Spent this day very agreeably, and enjoyed the valuable blessings and comforts of a Sabbath kept holy to the Great Au-{109}-thor. The congregation attending the holy services on the sacred day was but small. It was composed, however, almost entirely of such as professed to know the Lord.

---

197 The first three paragraphs are from: MHS: Stephen Riggs and Family Papers, 144.G.7.2F. The final paragraph is based on a description Gunn took from Stephen R. Riggs, *Mary and I: Forty Years with the Sioux*, pp. 41, 43. Gunn's note concluded with a summary of the Reverend Jedediah Stevens' subsequent, moderately successful, career.

198 Mary Riggs letter to her mother (July 8, 1837). MHS: Stephen Riggs and Family Papers.

Chapter 3 – Labouring & Teaching At St. Peters

A Poor Sweat-Labouring Mortal

July 31, 1837 – Monday. Not having any opportunity of going down the river at this time, there being no way of getting into business, and, disliking to remain in a stranger's house at no expense, I offered to labour with the master of the house [Reverend Stevens] for a few days, he being very much in want of assistance in his little farm. I took a jaunt to the Fort this day but, being unaccustomed to travel on stones and gravel, I suffered much inconvenience, and returned to my new home (Lake Harriet) with great difficulty.

August 1, 1837 – Tuesday. This morning I commenced to follow once more the business of a poor sweat-labouring mortal. Having been unaccustomed to labour, however, for some years back, and the day being excessively oppressive, I felt quite fatigued and much exhausted at its close.

The last of the provisions allowed by Government to the Chippewas during the Treaty was given out today. The whole allowance, I understood, was to be 100 barrels of Indian corn, 60 barrels of pork, and 60 barrels of flour – for pork weighing, each barrel, 256 pounds, and the flour and Indian corn, each barrel 196 pounds.

Discontent

August 2, 1837 – Wednesday. Nothing could make me, or I presume any other who entertained the smallest respect for his own character, feel more indignant than the humiliating treatment which my new friend was pleased to exercise upon me this morning. To be treated like a menial servant after having [attained] a rank in society at least a little superior (if a poor but honest schoolmaster can be so considered) is bad enough; but to be treated so by a stran-{110}-ger in a strange land, and by one who had made many professions of friendship, is what aggravates the matter.

My recent friend told me that, in consequence of the smallness of his table, and from his frequently receiving visits from "ladies and gentlemen" from the garrison, he would of necessity have to set two tables, and required me to sit down to meat with the menial servants – that is after the "ladies and gentlemen"! What could be more galling? Had I been treated thus in a civilized land, where it is necessary for every man to sustain his rank to a critical nicety, and had it been by a man of the world who moved in the ranks of wealth, fashion and etiquette, I should have calmly yielded to what I considered unbecoming in a missionary living in desert wilds and amid barbarous tribes. Here is a man, a Christian and a minister of the gospel of the humble, meek and lowly Jesus, sent forth to proclaim the glorious tidings of salvation to the inhabitants of savage and heathen wilds, so taken up about a few fashionable and unbelieving "ladies and gentlemen" that one who bears the character of a respectable member of society and a professor of Christian piety is deemed so unimportant as to be numbered only among those who had scarce ever taken a step from the state and condition in which nature left them. That, however, I leave for others to say. His fellow labourers, at least as worthy and competent as himself, thought as I did on the subject.[199] Having previously resolved to take the world as it came, I quietly submitted to the unkind treatment.

August 4, 1837 – Friday. After a day's hard work at haymaking, having a little leisure, I sit down to write a few lines in my diary. It is now going to eight o'clock, and I have not yet had my supper. I think I {111} shall have to go somewhere else to get some, for I feel very hungry indeed – or I must go to bed supperless. O! Here comes the messenger: "Supper! Supper!!" What welcome news!

Farewell to the Dugout Canoe

August 5, 1837 – Saturday. Took a jaunt down to the Fort, and sold my canoe, which I had bought of my companions in travel for $10. I sold it for the same. I bought a pair of booties for the purpose of walking out to the meadow in; but in attempting to walk home in them my feet became so pinched and chafed that it cost me much pain and great difficulty to reach home. The distance from the Fort to Lake Harriet is from six and a half to seven miles.

Spiritual Exercise

August 6, 1837 – Sunday. A fine and pleasant day, and much spiritual exercise throughout. All the succeeding Sabbaths were spent much in the same way as this during my residence at the place.[200]

August 7, 1837 – Monday. Agreeable to the usage of the Congregational Church of the United States, this day, being the first Monday in the month, was set aside from 5 o'clock pm for...

---

199 Gunn: "Reverend Stevens' 'fellow labourers' at the Lake Harriet Mission at this time were Reverend Stephen R. and Mrs. Riggs, Samuel W. Pond, and Lucy C. Stevens. See Neill, *History of Minnesota*, p. 447."

200 Here is more evidence of retrospective diary-writing.

Chapter 3 – Labouring & Teaching At St. Peters 95

Twenty pages of Garrioch's typescript are missing here – an excision, covering a ten day period, that Gunn estimated to involve some 3,500 words. As in the case of the first such gap, Gunn thought the deletion was probably made "by the author for private reasons." As on the previous occasion, however, it is also possible that the pages were removed posthumously by a family member or friend.

... with this celebrated and far-famed hero, he, with a final and most desperate effort, plunges his sabre into his heart! By reason of his mysterious prowess, he breaks his weapon in twain. This accounts for our being but a part of the instrument specified. {112} From first to last, the whole has been to me a source of great excitement to merriment. It is indeed very obvious, from all the brackets, parentheses, and zigzag penlines, that the whole party was under the influence, physically and morally, of some powerful stimulant which possessed the virtue of defusing a general nervous excitement.[201]

Paid Employment

Reverend Stevens was due to leave the area in early September and travel to New York City to report to the missionary society that employed him about the progress of his work. He persuaded Garrioch to remain at Lake Harriet during his absence, tending the farm and acting as a general hired man for the mission and family.

August 17, 1837 – Thursday. Made an agreement with Mr. Stevens Tuesday to stay with his family, as a common labourer at the rate of $20 per month, till he should return from his tour to New York. It was told to me that I should be treated as a member of the family. But alas!

Pay for Looking On

August 18, 1837 – Friday. Took another trip to the Fort. In returning home, I had to increase the burden of my wagon with two barrels of pork, which I left on the road on a former occasion in consequence of my wagon having broken down from the weight. I could not get an Indian to lend me any help, though they were passing continually, till I paid 25 cents. But the best of the fun was that the wife of the man who helped me demanded the same pay for looking on. She did not even touch a barrel, but it was *her* husband that helped, and she claimed pay, just as I would for lending a horse. Go it, red girls, while you're young!

---

201 The purport of this intriguing passage is a mystery to the editors. Was he describing some "penny dreadful" novel he was reading? Or some episode recorded in the foregoing missing twenty pages?

In setting the barrels right on the wagon, the edge of one of them intruded upon my toes with such violence that it made a rent in one of my new boots. Fortunately, however, my toes escaped with little injury. In the meantime, the night was fast approaching, so that it was well dark and late before I got home.

To St. Peter's Fort I went today,

And did to several persons monies pay.

Now 'tis dark, the oxen walk so slow. {113}

O dear, I'm sorry for my shoe and toe!

A Change of the Missionary Guard

Dr. Thomas Williamson, the Lac Qui Parle missionary who had so impressed Peter Garrioch, was about to move to another posting, and be replaced by Reverend Stephen Riggs and his wife Mary, who had been staying at the Harriet Lake mission for the past three months, trying to learn to converse with the natives. Williamson, apparently intending to accompany Stevens on his trip to the East, now arrived on the scene, just as the Riggs prepared to take his place at Lac Qui Parl.

August 26, 1837 – Saturday. About 9:00 o'clock pm Dr. Williamson arrived from Lac Qui Parle on a visit to Mr. Stevens. He is a worthy man, and, I believe, a heart-Christian from one end of his soul to the other.

August 31, 1837 – Thursday. Took Mr. Rigg's baggage to the Fort.[202]

September 3, 1837 – Sunday. Rode down to the Fort with Mr. Williamson, being Sunday. The congregation was very small, but the sermon was very good, indeed.

---

202 Gunn's note about Riggs was as follows: "Reverend Stephen Riggs was on his way to his first missionary appointment among the Sioux at Lac Qui Parle. This gentleman later became one of the most noted Indian missionaries of the West. He was born in Steubensville, Ohio, March 23, 1812, took his higher education at Jefferson College and Western Theological Seminary, and was licensed to preach by the Presbytery of Chillecothe, Ohio, about 1835. In 1837 he was appointed a missionary to the Sioux of the Minnesota District. In February of that year he married Miss Mary Ann Langly of Hawley, Massachusetts, and in March they started for Mr. Riggs' field of work on the Minnesota, arriving at Fort Snelling on June 1. They remained with Reverend J. D. Stevens from this time to September, when they started by Mackinaw boat up the Minnesota to [Lac Qui Parl]." The note goes on to summarize Riggs' later career, concluding: "Dr. Riggs left behind him a number of published works, viz.: a Dakota lexicon and grammar, a translation of the Bible into that language, a narrative of his experiences entitled *Mary and I: Forty Years with the Sioux*, besides other smaller works."

Chapter 3 – Labouring & Teaching At St. Peters 97

Saturday Night

September 9, 1837 – Saturday. This being Saturday night, I must be very short. Besides, I have two very great evils to contend with: the {114} Scotch fiddle I carried with me from Red River, and a houseful of bedbugs.[203]

Boarding School Behaviour

Gunn provides no guidance in his notes about what Peter's involvement may have been with the Lac Qui Parle school Peter describes below as "the boarding school," although, from his subsequent journal entries, it seems not to have been large or lasted long. The Lac Qui Parle school is mentioned in Gunn's Appendix B: "Garrioch's School at St. Peters, Minnesota, 1837-1838" as having been commenced in 1835 by Miss Sarah Poage and that it was where the Reverend Williamson commenced teaching in the Dakota language that December.

By July, 1837, Mary Riggs had disapproving words for this school:

> The school connected with this mission is almost the only thing which can be seen of the efforts now [sic] making for these Indians, & this most of us feel little confidence in, as it regards the mass of Indians. Being a boarding school, its influence must be very limited for many reasons. One obvious one is, none except they [who] have white fathers can meet even the small sum requited yearly, and few of these take much pains to educate their half Indian children when perhaps they have white wives & children, whom they care more for.[204]

Mary was more concerned about the inequities in access to schooling for the area's Indigenous children, which she attributed to the officers' habit – a matter in need of "moral reform" - of taking "two wives or more" and to the "lamentable influence of such men when in authority upon the poor oppressed Indians" which was so "diametrically opposed to that influence which we wish to exert,"[205] while Peter, perhaps still smarting from his previous teaching experience, focused on the children's comportment.

September 13, 1837 – Wednesday. The principle upon which the boarding school at this place appears to be conducted is somewhat singular. The principle seems to be this: let every child and scholar have as much liberty and as many indulgences as he would have, short only of tearing down houses and burning up the whole premises. I

---

203 Why was the fiddle an "evil"? Perhaps it was in need of repair. While this is the first suggestion that Peter Garrioch played the fiddle, doing so on a Saturday night is certainly consistent with his convivial personality.

204 Mary Riggs letter to her mother, Lake Harriet (July 31, 1837). MHS: Stephen Riggs and Family Papers.

205 *Ibid.*

am, and have been ever since I came here, so much disturbed by these boarding girls that I could scarcely do anything in the way of reading and writing after they retired to bed. For they seldom spent less than an hour or two in chatting, laughing, squealing, &c. I never knew a horde of children gratified with so many indulgences as these are.

Peter is expressing an ongoing complaint missionaries had about the lack of "discipline" Indigenous parents enforced in their families and on their children. In fact, parents guided their children's behaviours, just not in the way that missionaries were able to see or understand. Peter must have understood these cultural differences already, but appears here to be adopting the frustrated views of those teaching at CMS and other prairie schools.

Indeed, his own teaching experience was in the Indigenous cultural context where he too must have had to yield to the unruly conduct of his pupils, a course of action reflected in the observations Cockran made after a visit in 1834 to the boarding school established when the boarding component of the school was moved further north, leaving behind the day pupils for the day school where Peter was soon to teach. Since Cockran is almost certain to have been a source of advice to Peter about teaching, what Cockran wrote in the following passage about having to let the children adapt slowly to western discipline or one would have no students must have had an impact on Peter's own views and practices and are reflected in the preceding diary entry. Cockran wrote:

> **Visited the new school as usual found nine of the boys present that had been promised. They are exceedingly rude, but the Master is obliged to submit to the inconvenience. The Indian children are all allowed to do as they please with their parents. 'The children are all young and foolish,' the parents will say, 'nothing can be expected from them; time will correct their errors.' A boy may knock down his mother, and then say, 'Lay there you old dog,' and still be viewed as a promising son. Subjection from such wits into [wild as them?], cannot be expected. Were the master to enforce proper school discipline, the boys would immediately fly from him. A comfortable room to sit and sleep in, a warm fire, and regular fare – these have no allure to them when thwarted in their feelings. They can enjoy them when they can be processed without any sacrifice, but they are sensible of no inconvenience from the want of them; no more than a dog or a wolf wants experience from being driven from your establishment. If you let your stick fly at him, he will grin and run off, and make you understand, that if you will not allow him to pick your marrow bone, he will go and seek one elsewhere. In like manner would these boys act the instant you exact from them what one civilized man claimed from another. What can we do then, but carry on our pointless [frontlets?], the injunction of the Apostle, 'Let patience have her perfect work,' that we may wait, kill time and custom which have strengthened these barbarian vices, may also overturn them.[206]**

---

206 Rev. Wm. Cockran *Journal* (December 17, 1834). CMSA/AM: Missions to the Americas Mission Bk 2, North-West America, pp. 93-94. Another perspective on Rev. Cockran's teaching methods, a much darker one, using the school experience of A. C. Garrioch and his views about Cockran as the main example is found in George van der Goes Ladd, "Father Cockran and His Children: Poisonous Pedagogy on the Banks of the Red," pp, 61-71 in Barry Ferguson, ed., *The Anglican Church and the*

In the time of worship it is not uncommon to see them scattered over the room in every direction and position. Some sit while the rest are bowing before the footstool of mercy. Some stretch themselves on the forms or seats, and others in one position and another. I have frequently seen them collect together in groups under a table and sit there, either chatting, eating, or doing some unbecoming thing. I have frequently been so annoyed and pained at their conduct, and the manner in which it was connived at, that I often had a mind not to join family worship at all. What a great pity that Christians should not revere the worship of God more, and bring up children placed under their care in a more consistent manner.

World of Western Canada, 1820-1970 (Canadian Plains Research Center, University of Regina, 1991). In later years, A. C. Garrioch characterized Cockran as both powerfully protective and powerfully punitive; in other words, he operated in accordance with mid-19th century pedagogical practices, exemplified in Macallum's conduct (Chap. 5, nn. 289-290), and whose methods A. C. Garrioch also later defended in his own writings.

See Ladd, *ibid.*, p. 65, where the prevailing pedagogical goal was explained as being to make children "unconditionally obedient" by whatever means. Another excerpt there (pp. 67-68) from Cockran's report to the CMS secretaries (August 3, 1838) (CMSA/AM), expressed Cockran's racist views in extreme apocalyptic form: "…The savage says, not in his heart but aloud with his life, I will not submit to the degradation of earning my bread with the sweat of my brow; I will go forth with the beasts of the forest; join myself to them: exercise my authority over them, kill every one that comes in my way, and live upon them, when they fail I will kill my own progeny and eat them, and then lay down [*sic*] and die. (There are individuals all belonging to distinct families, in my neighbourhood, who have killed their relatives and eaten them.)" The children of whom Cockran was speaking were part of his mostly mixed-descent flock, tacitly including the Garriochs in this macabre analysis. Cockran has attracted considerable attention in modern times for his strong, but ambivalent influence in the Red River settlement area. A lengthy article which reviews the literature and balances the worst that Frits Pannekoek and George van der Goes Ladd have to say about him with the fact that he was revered by his congregants and community members generally and by the Garriochs in particular is Raymond M. Beaumont, "The Rev. William Cockran: the Man and the Image," *Manitoba History* 33 (Spring 1997), https://www.mhs.mb.ca/docs/mb_history/33/cockran_w.shtml.

It is worth noting that these sentiments about Indigenous pupils, shared by both Cockran and Garrioch, reflect the strong notions of class endemic in Red River society, with white settlers and residents on top, then those of mixed descent next, divided into subclasses according to their abilities to achieve success in occupations such as teaching, and, finally, the Indigenous population who were largely indifferent to "European" values and attitudes. These class and race divides were complicated by the evolution of marriages *à la façon du pays* and their interface with church marriages, as Garrioch had experienced in relation to the most important women in his life (his mother Nancy and his wife Margaret and her sister Isabella, Peter's yearned-for intended). See Van Kirk, *Many Tender Ties*, pp.154-168 & *passim*.

Makeshift Bedding

September 15, 1837 – Friday. My bedding having been taken away this morning by some mistake, I am obliged to make the best shift without it. To lie as comfortable as possible, I fell instinctively upon the following plan. I stretched myself on three boxes, having one under {115} each end, and the other under the middle. This was the form and substance of my bedstead. For my bedding, I slipped my pillow right under my backbone, took my greatcoat for a covering, a pair and a half of pantaloons for my pillow, and thrust my two feet into a bag. This was the best and only method I could adopt, for the whole family had retired to bed when I discovered my predicament. I suffered from the scantiness and hardness of my pillow. For, having placed it on the edge of a box without a cover, I sometimes felt as though my neck would yield and break.

September 16, 1837 – Saturday. My bedding, I understood this morning, had been put out yesterday for airing. They are now in a fine state. [It] having rained considerably last night and this morning, every bit of the bedding is as wet as dung in a gutter. Therefore, I must make a virtue of necessity by endeavouring to pass this night as I did the last.

September 17, 1837 – Sunday. I am sorry to say that I did not rest so well the last night as I did the one before. The chances, to be sure, were against the very idea of rest or comfort.

Lost in the Forest at Night

September 18, 1837 – Monday. My day's work being over, I went out, according to my usual custom, to hunt up the cattle at the setting of the sun (not that I expected them where the sun set – that would be a preposterous idea). Being overtaken by night while in the midst of a forest, and the darkness having become extremely thick and dense, till I could not see an inch through it. I very inopportunely got entangled among some bushes in such a manner – bless me! – I was like never to extricate myself.

After finding the cattle, I gave them the privilege of {116} leading the way. But, like all other inconstant souls, they abused their important trust. They precipitated me into a maze of such gloom and darkness that my oculars were as little use to me as a pair of magnifying glasses would be to a blind man. My situation might have put me in mind, forcibly, of old times, when all was chaos! Perhaps it did, but my memory has dwindled down to the limits of the utmost stretch of a bee's sight. Upon entering this dungeon-like gloom, the first salutation I received was a poke right in the side of one of my eyes by an ungrateful twig. What a mercy that it preferred entering by the side instead of the centre said I.

Having by this time lost sight, sound and smell of the cattle while detained in contending with darkness, bushes, grass, vines, &c, I resolved to compromise the matter by retrograding a few steps and making an entrance at another part. Unfortunately, I fell into a worse predicament. I came into contact with shrubbery, or something else which I could not move a step forward in without extending my two arms as far before me as their elasticity would permit, in order to clear my way and prevent anything from intruding upon my face. For the same purpose, I had sometimes to hold up my hat (for it was impossible to keep it on my head) before me with one hand, and make my way as best I could with the other.

Finding that all would not do, I turned from this place of darkness and confusion, and once more gone into an eligible route. I had not proceeded far, however, when, in the act of stooping forward as I traveled along, with my hat still in one hand, I most unexpectedly bounced my {117} head against a tree of no diminutive size. Such was the force of the thump, and such the concussion that the natural inhabitants of this forest received, that the shock reached the very inhabitants of the regions above. For the very topmost leaves shook like the leaves of an aspen. I went furiously bouncing against the side of an old stump, which made me stagger like a toper. I cannot but believe the old Devil was sneaking about there in those trees; for it seems quite unreasonable to suppose that honest nature could possibly be so indecent or malignant as to manifest such stubbornness and refractoriness as I had to contend with that night.

I had several times almost come to the conclusion to throw myself down in despair and commit myself to the auspices of chance for the night. No sooner had I done so, however, than a crowd of horrid ideas took possession of my mind, already too much excited. Three things, I may say, prevented my final determination to lie out all night. In the first place, the night was raw and cold, and I had nothing on but light clothes, such as genteel folks wear in warm weather. In the next place, I knew that before morning I should have companions enough, of such character as would suggest ideas most horrible: a toad on my brow and a lizard poking his nose into mine, then a host of infuriated mosquitoes wreaking their vengeance upon my vitality and pouring their obnoxious melodies into my ears. The third reason for my being unwilling to lie out was a fear of causing anxiety at home. {118} Not being able to improve matters by mere thinking, I re-exerted myself and, going through thick and thin, soon found myself at home.

My delay, as I had expected, had created some apprehensions. A volley had been discharged, and the second just going when I made my appearance at the door. I reached the house between the hours of nine and ten. After supper I retired and, being almost exhausted, dozed away the night in a most uncommonly pleasant manner.

Volcanic Landlady

October 2, 1837 – Monday. Finished mudding[207] business, very much to my satisfaction. It kept me employed three full, long weeks.

Many a narrow and broad hint, and many an insinuation, did my landlady treat me with during that long, long period. May it never fall to my lot to wait upon a second matron. I have tried one, and I cannot say – no, not I – that I have any particular curiosity to make a second experiment. Generally speaking, one specimen of the fair sex, not in point of fairness or beauty, however, but... is a sufficient representative of the whole train of Eve's fair and false progeny.

Was the young man asserting that his mistress had made sexual overtures during her husband's presumed prolonged absence? Another interpretation – that she was simply a demanding and hot-tempered employer – finds additional support in the following paragraphs.

In serving or assisting a lady, you must always, and particularly on washing days, have water enough about the chimneys and stoves to quench the flames of Etna or Vesuvius.

Is that not a preposterous idea: to quench the flames of an Etna or Vesuvius? The idea, I suppose, was suggested by the fact that a woman's tongue is very much like a burning mountain. I'll tell you how. I suppose then, that the acute genius who first suggested the idea compared a woman to a mountain; for they like to appear big and {119} huge anyhow. Her mind [is to] be compared to the bowels of a volcano, her mouth to the crater, the nature and feelings of her mind to the lava, and her tongue to the principle which compels the lava through the crater. I take this to be a beautiful and superb

---

207 He was presumably plastering or mortaring a log structure with clay-rich mud.

example of the manner in which things ought to be compared. But I return to the proper subject before me.

If you do not have wood, chips, sprigs, and twigs enough about her to kindle a fire large enough to boil the waters of a river or lake, if you do not have such wood as will kindle by the heat of her breath, and finally if you do not keep her swimming and roasting, and all her irons and kettles as hot and wet as herself, you may look out for snakes and furious flying cinders.

If the lady's "hints and insinuations" had indeed involved invitations to physical intimacy, readers might well wonder how Garrioch responded. However, with their references to demands for enough water and wood for a fire and for heating an iron, chores which he was likely expected to perform, these odd paragraphs are more likely simply to reflect his hot-tempered reaction to being "bossed around" by a female employer, especially in view of his sensitivity about having to take on labouring work during his prolonged stay in the area, as his entries on August 2 and August 17 have already demonstrated. Moreover, this difficult landlady appears to have fallen into a habit – perhaps from awkwardness at having to boss a man directly – of communicating ineffectively with the young man about her expectations and his performance in meeting them. In fact, all of Peter's entries from the time at the end of July 1837, when he agreed to stay on in the role of labourer, have an unusually testy character. Soon, however, his good nature began to reassert itself.

October 5, 1837 – Thursday. Commenced digging potatoes.

Mickle John Re-appears

October 7, 1837 – Saturday. I had the pleasure of seeing my old friend Mickle John today, concerning whom I heard the following anecdote: Mr. Andrew Robertson,[208] whom we had met at Traverse des Sioux, informed me that Mr. John, upon landing

---

208 "Gunn: "A pioneer trader among the Sioux. Particulars of his career are scant. Of the early and later parts, I have not been able to find anything. He was evidently of pure Scotch extraction, but was married to a mixed blood woman, Jane Anderson, a daughter of Captain Thomas A. and Margaret Aird. Margaret Aird afterwards married the trader Hazen Mooers, and after that a good deal of Robertson's activities were connected with him. In 1838 Mooers, Robertson, and J. R. Brown moved to Gray Cloud Island in the Mississippi, where they engaged in trading operations until 1847." The note continues with an outline of Robertson's activities in later years, and cites the following authorities: John H. Case, "Historical Notes of Grey Cloud Island and the Vicinity," in *Collections of the Minnesota Historical Society* XV (St. Paul, 1915), pp. 371-376, esp. p. 372; Return Ira Holcombe, "Narration of a Friendly Sioux," in *Collections of the Minnesota Historical Society* IX (St. Paul, 1901), p. 427; & *Minnesota in Three Centuries*, II, p. 329.

at St. Peter's, had a fire-billet[209] swung about his neck, tied at each end with a string. The people of the place were curious and bold enough to ask his reasons for so doing. He told them that on his way down to St. Peter's an Indian had thrown that billet at him, but [had] fortunately missed him. [Believing], however, that the Indian had been employed by some agent of the British Government, he had [hung] the piece of wood around his neck to prevent assassination. He told Mr. Robertson at the same time that if he knew the man who had employed the Indian he would blow his brains out with his gun. [He was] holding his gun in one hand, and the same gentleman he was then addressing was the very man he {120} had reference to in speaking of a British agent. Mickle had told me himself, at our first interview with Robertson at Traverse des Sioux, that he strongly suspected him of being an agent sent by the British Government to apprehend him.

The following will manifest the shrewdness and economy of my friend. Upon landing at St. Peter's, he took a cursory view of all things; but particularly examined all the canoes about the beach to see if there were any equal to or superior to his among them. Convinced that they were all inferior according to his notion, he concluded that his would be the most likely to attract attention, and be consequently in the greatest danger of being stolen, or made a ferry-boat of. To prevent the occurrence of such an evil, this unparalleled gentleman hit upon the following most ingenious and admirable plan. He drew his canoe out of the water and, having placed it on an eminence, he drove three posts on each side of it, and pinned the upper ends together, so as to bind the canoe. He then took out his chisel and hammer, and very carefully cut out a piece of from two to three feet long from the bottom of it. By keeping this piece in his trunk, as I presume he did, his canoe was in less danger of being made into a ferry-boat.

I had, during our travel on the prairie previous to our arriving at Lac Qui Parle, several conversations with Mickle, in which he always displayed a degree of eloquence, and the finest oratory I ever witnessed. In these conversations I had the best opportunities of becoming acquainted with some of his most singular and curious notions. He at one time told me that the world was in a miserable condition, and all from the ignorance and stubbornness of the ruling powers. Nor could he think that it was possible for the world {121} to improve upon its present state till the governments, and particularly those of Great Britain and the United States of America, would condescend to be

---

209 A piece of firewood, perhaps partially burned.

instructed by one superior to themselves – alluding to himself. Perceiving his drift, and being very anxious to draw something [more] out of him, I expressed my surprise in the strongest language I could manufacture, at the stupidity of mankind in turning a deaf ear to those counsels. But I soon found that Mickle was not that son of vanity I took him to be.

It was by no means the easiest of things to look through his heart; at least, it required more penetration than the milk of my Mammy's paps had infused into my bituminous brains. I uniformly failed of attaining a full disclosure of his deep and secret plans. Indeed, nothing short of the genius of a Newton could be adequate to the full unveiling of the mystic conclusions that lay hid in the recesses of John's expansive and impenetrable mind. He told me that he had brothers and sisters; but [that] they were the same as the rest of the world, and would not receive him, or give any heed to his instructions. However, as he considered himself entirely superior to them, and indeed of being superior to the human race, he was satisfied to exercise that privilege, and those superior talents and intellectual qualities which the Almighty had conferred upon him solely to His glory, and to the advancement of His eternal kingdom. Such were some of the fine specimens of the exalted and sublime {122} ideas of that universal genius.

St. Anthony Falls

October 11, 1837 – Wednesday. I had the pleasure of seeing, for the first time, the celebrated falls of St. Anthony today. I must say, however, that I was very much disappointed. They indeed present a pleasant view to the eye of the stranger, or to him who has never heard anything more of them than the name; but to one who has been accustomed to hear them spoken out in a manner calculated to awaken curiosity, and consequently comes hither with high expectations, it is inevitable that they should prove a disappointment. The fall of water may be from 10 to 15 feet, and the precipice over which they fall extends over the entire breadth of the river. These falls are altogether too little to be considered grand, and too large to be considered beautiful. The greatest satisfaction I enjoyed in visiting the falls, and what I considered most worthy of admiration, was the various and brilliant hues the waters assumed while tumbling and, as it were, sporting themselves, over the edge of the precipice.[210]

---

210 Gunn: "Every traveler that has passed this point, from the earliest French explorers down, has stood and gazed upon these falls and has had something to say about them. And what they have said is interesting, not alone as preserving to us an idea of their appearance before the greed of commercial development destroyed their original grandeur, but as a study in comparisons and,

A Water Sawmill

{123} Here also, today, I first saw a water sawmill.²¹¹ My curiosity being highly excited, I took pleasure in examining the ingenious invention. When I had arrived at the close of my investigations, I had the conceit to think I could construct one. Vain man thinks himself {124} large enough to fill a world, and seldom can he be convinced to the contrary till he is led to the grave and finds that it requires a space of but seven feet by three to contain every inch of him.

I should have stated that there is a little cascade of about 15 or 20 feet in width, with a fall of water of about 30 or 35 feet, 2 miles northwest of Fort Snelling, which is highly beautiful and engaging.²¹²

---

incidentally, in human nature. Hennepin, the first white man to visit this cataract, and who also gave it its name, declared it to be 50 or 60 feet high, and described it as: 'terrible' and 'something very astonishing.' Jonathan Carver, the Englishman, himself no inconsiderable liar, was scandalized at this exaggeration, and pronounced it but 30 feet high. Lieutenant Pike needed 16½ feet in 1806, while Major Long's party, in 1823, by actual measurement, found it to be just 15 feet. In view of these various pronouncements, Garrioch's estimate here of a maximum height of 15 feet is significant testimony as to his accuracy as an observer. Counting the rapids below as part of the falls, of course, the drop of the river would be considerably greater." Garrioch's disappointment at the spectacle presented by the falls may have been attributable to the fact that he was viewing them in October, when the volume of water involved was probably at its lowest level for the year.

Well-acquainted with the area as a native of Minneapolis, Merrill Distad comments: "Since the capping of the falls by the Army Corps of Engineers to prevent further upstream erosion, and the building of adjacent hydro-power station and locks to enable barge traffic to pass further upstream, today's passerby can scarcely imagine the *existence* of the falls, for there is no drama, let alone beauty, left to behold!" Distad to Anderson (November 26, 2023).

211 Gunn: "This old 'water sawmill' at the Falls of St. Anthony was built in 1821 by the United States Government in connection with the establishment of Fort Snelling. It was built by the soldiers under the direction of Lieutenant McCabe, one of the officers of the garrison of which Colonel Snelling was the Commandant. It stood on the west side of the Falls, and was the nucleus from which subsequently sprang the great milling industry of modern Minneapolis." Reverend Stephen R. Riggs visited the falls just before his departure for Lac Qui Parle in 1837, within a month or two of Garrioch's visit, and says (*Mary and I: Forty Years with the Sioux*, p. 24.): "The Government sawmill, with a small dwelling for the soldier occupant was then the only sign of civilization on the present site of Minneapolis." Gunn's very lengthy note continues with considerably more information about the sawmill.

212 Gunn: "The Falls of Minnehaha. This fall, which has become world-famous for its picturesque beauty, and through its association with Longfellow's heroine of the Hiawatha legends, is situated on a small stream forming the outlet of Lake Harriet and Calhoun It is 50 or 60 feet in height, but its volume is scant, dropping like a thin veil over a perpendicular rock into the chasm below. At the time when Fort Snelling was built (1819-20), it was known as Little Falls. Later it was called

Chapter 3 – Labouring & Teaching At St. Peters

October 13, 1837 – Friday. A very hard frost last night.

A Small Mishap

October 14, 1837 – Saturday. Went down to the Fort for some articles on a wagon. Unfortunately, my wagon fell into pieces and, after some trouble, I managed to tie my load on a part of it, and left the other part. It upset, at one time, right over me, but produced no serious injury. It being fine moonlight, I got home quite slick.

A Missed Opportunity

October 21, 1837 – Saturday. Being very anxious to get into the Chippewa country with the view of acquiring a thorough knowledge of the language of that people, I proposed my intention to Mr. Seymour,[213] a miss-{125}-ionary who had been some time among them, and was again on his return to his station from a visit to his friends. The gentleman and his wife, an amiable and intelligent woman, were both anxious to have me go; but he, not being superintendent of the mission, could neither invite nor insist upon my going. Unwilling to put them to any inconvenience, I gave up the idea, and submitted to my fate without a groan.

Giving Up Snuff

November 4, 1837 – Saturday. Feeling quite indisposed, I took a short walk. I had laboured under a sort of stupid and drowsy feeling for several days and, believing it to proceed altogether from an excessive use of snuff, I resolved to suspend the use of the nauseous and brain-poisoning article. To accomplish my object, I placed my snuffbox,

---

Brown's Falls after Major General Brown of the U.S. Army; which name it retained until the coming into popularity of the Hiawatha legends."

Merrill Distad notes that Gunn erred regarding the source of Minnehaha Falls. "The 'small stream,' Minnehaha Creek, has no direct connection to Lakes Harriet or Calhoun (the latter name since changed in 2018 to Bde Maka Ska). Its source is Lake Minnetonka, west of the modern city of Minneapolis."

213   Gunn: "John L. Seymour who, along with his wife, was at this time associated in Indian missionary work with the Reverends Frederick Ayer and E. F. Ely in the Leech and Sandy Lake regions. Information about him is somewhat meagre. He was born at Plymouth, Connecticut, in 1811, came to Mackinaw in 1833, to Yellow Lake [in] September 1834, and to Pokegama, or Snake River, in May 1836 (*Minnesota in Three Centuries*, II, p. 235). D. A. J. Baker, in his article "Early Schools of Minnesota," (*Minnesota Historical Society Collections*, I, p. 81), mentions a Mrs. Seymour, probably the wife of the above, as teaching at the last-mentioned in 1836; and it is, no doubt, to this place that the couple are now returning."

and a bottle of snuff which I had purchased a few days previously, constantly before me for several days in order to give my passion for that practice full scope to work, and thus give more firmness to my determination. The temptation suggested by thus placing constantly before me what had hitherto been deemed a "precious and sweet morsel" was by no means so trifling as some folk of more faith and firmness might suppose. I sometimes felt as though I could snuff up ashes, embers, or anything else. The itching and preposterous desire, however, did not survive long. It had to yield to the potent will of determination, and gave up the ghost before it.

Interrupted Studies

November 6, 1837 – Monday. While at my studies this evening, a little girl[214] living with the family as waiter, nurse, &c, came in and, making rather more noise than I wanted just at that time, I either told or requested her to make less noise. What answer do you suppose the white-headed lousy little Yankee gave me? "No, I shan't." Mysterious!![215] {126}

An Indian Threat

November 7, 1837 – Tuesday. After sitting out till three o'clock in the morning in consequence of some Indians having threatened to do something to the place or family, I took a walk around the premises with a gun in my hand but, neither proceeding nor hearing anything, I retired to rest.

Fire!!!

November 8, 1837 – Wednesday. Went down to the stacks of hay to burn about them. No sooner had I got the fire under way than the wind began to blow, and drove up the flames so furiously that the stack I was then attending was exposed to imminent danger. There being no alternative, and having no help that I could depend upon, I rushed

---

214 Gunn: "This little girl's name was Jane de Bow. She was of French parentage, and was born in New York State about 1828. She was adopted by Reverend J. D. and Mrs. Stevens, and came with them to the mission at Lake Harriet in 1835, being then seven years of age. She remained with the Stevens, and lived with them at their various places of abode until 1848, when she was married to Herman R. Gibbs. They settled on a claim at St. Anthony Park, where they afterwards resided, being the first white settlers there." Gunn's full note contains source references about her.

215 This is a much more lighthearted entry about children's deportment than that of September 13, 1837, or November 30, 1837, below..

Chapter 3 – Labouring & Teaching At St. Peters

through the flames, by which I got my beautiful eyebrows and the most prominent [parts] of my dignified moustaches and bushy whiskers singed to a ridiculous degree.

Here an incident occurred, the remembrance of which always makes me feel jocose and fine. The mistress of the house had been kind enough to send me some assistance, viz.: a squaw, an Indian idiot who served but as a third wheel to a cart, and the Yankee gal of whom I spoke before. Finding that the whole arduous duty of extinguishing the flames devolved upon me, and seeing the flames were rapidly approaching the stack, I exerted every ounce of nerve, marrow, and bone about {127} me. But, finding that all would not do, and the flames now within an inch or two of the stack, I threw my broom out of my hand in despair. Anxiety [arising] from consciousness of the responsibility resting upon me and [the sight of] all my companions scared to a state of inaction extorted an ejaculation from the very depths of my soul for assistance.

Precisely at that juncture, while running from the scorching flames and suffocating smoke, the first object that intercepted my view was a large, new, woolen blanket lying on the ground close by the side of the stack, which I had not noticed before. Without taking a second thought or asking any questions about it, I eagerly grasped the blanket and applied it with such fury and good effect, just at the very crisis of the flames laying hold of the stack, that, in the twinkling of an eye, I sent the flames to oblivion.

The blanket I necessarily abused so, I learned upon enquiry, belonged to the innocent, harmless, idiot, poor fellow. On seeing the abuse I made of his blanket, he stood as mute as a stump and looked as sour and cross as a bear. So soon as I let the blanket out of my hands, he examined it very carefully, turning it over and over, without saying a single word, but pouting all the time.[216]

Reverend Stevens Returns

November 9, 1837 – Thursday. On this evening Mr. Stevens returned. He told me, upon my enquiring, that the boat he came up in was to leave again in two or three hours. O what a disappointment! Here is cross upon cross; but, if it be the Lord's will, I am quite reconciled.

---

216   That the loss suffered by the "Indian idiot" should have made Garrioch remember himself to have felt "jocose and fine" tells us much about 19th century attitudes toward both native persons and mental disability – as well as, perhaps, a little about Peter Garrioch himself.

Frustration

The reason that the steamboat's swift turn-around was a "cross upon cross" for the diarist was that he had been aching to move on from St. Peter's before winter set in, and it seemed likely that this would be the last sailing before the Mississippi froze over. As Gunn explained: "So there Garrioch was, seven and a half miles from the boat landing, night coming on, and without a conveyance to take him and his luggage to the Fort."[217]

I did not know what to do. I sometimes thought of taking my trunk on my back and setting off. Being obliged to submit to Fate, I retired to bed with a leaden heart; and after musing a while on my sad disappointment, I embarked for the Land of Nod. {128}

November 14, 1837 – Tuesday. Learnt that there was a letter for me in [the] sutler's[218] store, but could not find out where it went.

Changing Homes & Occupations

Peter Garrioch had never been happy at Jedediah Stevens' Lake Harriet mission, and the prospect of remaining there over the winter must have been too much to bear. Shortly after Stevens' return, therefore, he set out to seek alternative quarters, and found them – along with more satisfactory employment – at the "Baker Settlement" on the other side of the Mississippi River, where he was taken under the benevolent wings of Methodist missionary David King, fur trader Benjamin Baker, and Martin McLeod, the apparent manager of Baker's trading post.

November 14, 1837 – Tuesday. Not being able to reconcile my mind to Mr. Stevens' Yankee notions, I concluded to seek for another home. With this view, I went down the

---

217   Gunn, "Peter Garrioch at St. Peter's," p. 126. Just why the newly-returned missionary could not have provided transportation was never explained, though it may well have influenced a decision Garrioch would make a few days later.

218   Gunn: "The sutler [at Fort Snelling] was Colonel Samuel C. Stanbaugh. He had Norman W. Kittson as assistant." Kittson was later to provide, from a base in Pembina, Dakota Territory, formidable fur-trade competition to the Hudson's Bay Company's Red River operations. A sutler was a civilian storekeeper or provisioner for a military establishment. A fixed sutler's store was a typical feature of military forts and posts, either located in, or nearby. At frontier forts, in hostile Indian country, the sutler's store would be in rented/leased space within the fort stockade, even if friendly Indians came there to trade. The military officer responsible for the stocking of supplies, feeding, clothing, and equipping of soldiers, was the "Quartermaster," representing the Army Quartermasters Corps. An Army Quartermaster would be a low-ranking officer, and certainly *not* a colonel, as Gunn suggested here. An officer of the rank of Colonel would almost certainly have been in command of the entire fort and its garrison of troops.

Chapter 3 – Labouring & Teaching At St. Peters

following day to the Methodist Mission at the Little Crow village.[219] Here I enquired of Reverend King, the Principal of the missionary station, who received and entertained me in a manner emphatically scriptural.

He expected a boat from the Prairie[220] laden with provisions and other necessaries for his mission.[221] But, the prospect appearing very doubtful from the advanced period of the season, I readily made up my mind to [accept] the kindness which Mr. McLeod had proposed on the preceding day: that is, of keeping a school at Mr. Baker's premises.[222]

---

219   Gunn: "This mission was established [on the east side of the Mississippi] by the Methodist Episcopal Church in May, 1837 – the same year that Garrioch visited it. Its location was at the village of Kaposia, a little below the present city of St. Paul. The chief of this particular band of Dakotas was the Little Crow known as Big Thunder, father of the notorious Little Crow who later led the uprising in 1862-63. Hence Garrioch's designation: 'the Little Crow Village.' The mission was not a success. It continued the year following, but was later moved to Red Rock, where it continued until 1842. Of the Reverend King here mentioned, not a great deal is known. Warren Upham in his *Minnesota Biographies*, p. 402, gives the following: 'David L. King, clergyman, born in Mahoning, Pennsylvania, October 31, 1816; died in Plainview, Minnesota, August 3, 1898. He was licensed to preach in 1845, settled in Rochester, Minnesota, in 1854, [and] on to a farm in Kalmar, Olmstead County.'"

220   Prairie du Chien.

221   This would have allowed Garrioch to travel south on the return trip, or would perhaps, alternatively, have made it possible for the mission to take in Garrioch as a boarder or employee.

222   Gunn: "Benjamin F. Baker, one of the early fur traders of Minnesota. Of his family history and trading activities there is very little data extant. He was known among the Indians as "Blue Beard," or Pu-tus-hinto, in the Sioux tongue. Where he hailed from, or when he arrived in Minnesota, I have not been able to ascertain. His name first appears in a list of licensed traders among the Dakotas in 1826. (Neill, p. 382). He was then stationed at Crow Island, a point on the Mississippi about 15 miles below the mouth of the Crow Wing River; and in 1832, when the Schoolcraft Expedition to Lake Itasca passed that place, he was still there (Neill, 4th ed., p. 409). In the next list of license traders given by Neill (4th ed., p. 415), 1833-34, Baker is given as at Fort Snelling, and here he remained for the next four or five years. When Nicollet started to explore the upper Mississippi, in 1835, Benjamin F. Baker was one of his chief assistants in the preparation of his outfit at Fort Snelling. (*Autobiography of Major Taliafarro, Minnesota Historical Society Collections* VI, p. 243). In 1837, Neill informs us (p. 453), 'after the treaties with the Indians were concluded, Messrs. Baker, Taylor and Franklin Steele made a claim, and commenced the improvement of the valuable water power at the Falls of the St. Croix.' He was subsequently sutler at Fort Snelling.

"Baker's chief activity, however, while at the latter place, was the operation of a trading post. This establishment was located on the north side of the Minnesota River, between the Fort and the falls of Minnehaha. Its exact site was about a mile northwest of the former place, at Coldwater Spring, the site of Col. Leavenworth's 'Camp Coldwater, of the summer of 1820. Here, and at a place known as Massie's Landing, in 1837, there seems to have been quite a number of white settlers. R. I. Holcomb (*Minn. In Three Centuries*, II, p. 81) is authority for the statement, that there were 82 such, at these two points, at that time. At the former of these localities, at any rate, Baker had his

Accordingly, after securing the unanimous consent {129} of MacLeod, King, and others, I concluded to teach the school, for the magnificent consideration of $50 and my board, for the long period of six months.

A Majestic Cave

November 15, 1837 – Wednesday. On returning this morning with Mr. King from a visit to his mission, I had the exquisite pleasure of witnessing one of the grandest and most majestic spectacles I ever laid my eyes upon. This was the celebrated and far-famed {130} Carver's Cave.[223] To such as myself, there is always something peculiarly enticing and enchanting in such specimens of Mother Nature's handiwork.

I could not be satisfied without penetrating as far into the bowels of this subterranean vault as circumstances would allow. I proceeded from the entrance with one

---

establishment; and, from that circumstance, it came to be called 'The Baker Settlement.' Here, in 1837, the year of Garrioch's arrival, he built a storehouse of massive and palatial proportions, which continued to stand as his monument for many years after he himself had disappeared from the scene. This building was afterwards used as a hotel, and later destroyed by fire. It was in some building connected with this establishment that Garrioch taught his school during the winter of 1837-38." Gunn, pp. 128-129. It is interesting that Dale wrote a note to this: "I have checked the references cited here. All are accurate. DG, June, 2016."

223   Gunn: "I am inclined to think that the cave visited by Garrioch, and here described, was not the real Carver's Cave. Not that such a visit would have been impracticable in the course of an excursion to the Methodist mission at Kaposia. On the contrary, the real Carver's Cave lay right on his road from Fort Snelling to that point, as it was situated at the foot of Dayton's Bluff, in the lower outskirts of what is now St. Paul. My reason for so thinking is that the cave Carver saw and described was practically blotted out of existence by the action of the elements years before Garrioch visited its site. In 1817, when Major Long was there, he had to creep into it on all fours, so covered up with debris was the entrance. In 1837, the same year as Garrioch's visit above described, Nicollet the scientist, who was at Fort Snelling, had to work many hours with assistants to penetrate into the little cavity that was left. (Neill, footnote, 4th ed., p. 207). There was, however, another cave, perhaps even finer than Carver's, some two or three miles farther up the river, called Fountain Cave, which has been mistaken by travelers from time to time, and described as Carver's. This one would also be right on Garrioch's road to Kaposia and, I think, there can be no doubt of its being the one described by him here. E. S. Seymour, who visited the site of both the caves in 1850, in his Sketches of Minnesota, has left us a splendid account of both as they were at the time; and his description of Fountain Cave answers perfectly to that of Garrioch above."

Upham, *Minnesota Geographic Names*, pp. 80, 443-444, describes explorer Captain Jonathan Carver, after whom Carver County was named, and both Carver's Cave and Fountain Cave, about four miles further up the Mississippi, which was sometimes, as Gunn wrote, erroneously called Carver's Cave. Fountain Cave was given its name "because a brook runs through the cavern and issues, like a fountain, at its mouth."

companion, taking the lead myself, till our torches, either from the rarefied state of the atmosphere or from some other cause, refused to sustain and protract their ignited effulgence. We were, of course, left in blackness and, being now at least 250 yards from the mouth of the cavern, it was not without some difficulty, and a little anxiety once more to behold the sun, that we effected our escape from the gloomy and direful abodes of spectres, hobgoblins, and other sweet and tender creatures of fancy.

The width of this beautiful cave, at the entrance, was about 30 feet, {131} and its height 18 feet. Upon entering it, we were introduced into a spacious concave apartment and, upon proceeding, we discovered several others – intercepted only by narrow passages – formed by the force of the stream of water running through the cave and washing away the sand from between the contiguous and more consolidated rocks. The apartments diminish in size, however, as they approach the head or termination of the cavern. The water running through the cave, and which doubtless has brought it to its present form, is a beautiful, crystal, stream – and as pleasant to the taste as any water I ever tasted. The sand, with which the walls are in great measure lined, is the best specimen that has ever come under my notice. Both to the sight and to the touch, there is no small affinity between it and wheat flour run through a moderately coarse sieve.

Report says that a soldier and two Indians formerly penetrated so far into this cave that they were never heard of any more. This report is only for children and old women who wish to have something to talk about. It is more than probable that they fell into some gulf, and were immediately metamorphosed into sturgeon, or some other sort of fish, as it was with Weesakatchak[224] in days of old, when he was thrown into the midst of the waters and cried out: "Let me be a sturgeon!"

Schoolmaster Once More

Gunn believed that Peter Garrioch's school at the Baker Settlement was the first public school in Minnesota.[225] Even if the young teacher had not appreciated the historical sig-

---

224   Gunn: "The legendary culture hero of the Crees – the Nanabozho of the Ojibwa legends. Reference is here made to one of the many metamorphoses attributed to that eccentric hero-divinity of the Indian lodges."

225   Reverend Gunn's manuscript includes, as Appendix B, a summary of early educational activities in Minnesota, concluding that Garrioch's was "the first publicly supported school for English speaking children ever attempted in Minnesota." Although he identified several earlier schools, beginning in 1832, that had operated in the territory, Gunn concluded that those were all mission

nificance of what he was doing, just having been raised once again from the menial status of "sweat labourer" to the more "superior" situation of "poor but honest schoolmaster" he had enjoyed at Red River must have been gratifying to the young man.[226] He does not seem, however, to have had a very high opinion of his "brats."

November 30, 1837 – Thursday. Opened my school[227] on the heterogeneous sys-{132}-tem. The whole number of brats that attended for the purpose of being benefitted by my notions amounted to thirty. This number was composed of English, French, Swiss, Swedes, Cree, Chippewa, Sioux, and Negro extraction. Such a composition, and such a group of geniuses, I never saw before. May it never be my privilege to meet with such another. It staggered my gifts, talents, and all the powers of "me soul," to keep up with the brights[228]. I question whether an antiquarian of the most celebrated longevity ever could produce a specimen of such dolts and dunderheads as were clustered together in my school. "Birds of a feather flock together!"

December 4, 1837 – Monday. The River St. Peter's was frozen over, and became passable on the following day.

Mr. Cratt's Christmas Ball

December 23, 1837 – Saturday. Mr. Cratt made a great dinner, or rather supper as the party collected late in the evening, and crowned it with a generous ball. I had half determined not to go but, being requested by Messrs. Baker and MacLeod, I concluded

---

schools teaching children whose first language was not English. In his view, the fact that Peter's school had been organized and funded by the local community, and that its pupils were English-speaking from the start, justified his claim.

226 Credit for opening on December 1, 1837, at the Baker Settlement near Fort Snelling, "what the writer believes to have been the 'first public school in Minnesota supported entirely by local contributions" was attributed to Peter Garrioch. The writer was Theodore C. Blegen, editor of *Minnesota History*, writing in volume XIX (1938), pp. 204-205, who derived the information from Peter's diaries, "now in the possession of Mr. George H. Gunn of Saskatoon, Saskatchewan." "Garrioch opened the Minnesota school after missing the last boat of the season bound down the Mississippi – an accident that forced him to spend the winter in the vicinity of Fort Snelling."

227 Gunn: "As my observations on Garrioch's school are a little too extended to fit in very well as a footnote, I have given them a place elsewhere. My remarks on this subject will be found as an Appendix at the close of this work." The present editors have incorporated the information in Gunn's Appendix B on schools into the commentaries in this book.

228 This word is likely "brats", instead of "brights" as recorded in Gunn's transcript, but since this portion of Peter's journal is not extant, it is not possible to check it against the original. See the Introduction.

Chapter 3 – Labouring & Teaching At St. Peters

to go and look on a little. After partaking very moderately of the good things of the table, I visited the ballroom in company with the above gentlemen. So soon as I discovered, however, that the handkerchief was beginning to flutter,[229] I concluded that my presence could be very well dispensed with, and so I cleared out for home.

Mr. Cratt, I must say in justice to his honour, acted on the basis of Scripture principles, for he invited the rich and the poor, the maimed and the blind, without reference to age or sex, to partake of the sumptuous banquet which Heaven had so gener-{133}-ously spread upon the table. Mr. Cratt is a blacksmith: a native of Canada .[230]

New Year's Thaw

January 1, 1838 – Monday. The wind having turned to the south last evening, there has been a considerable thaw and rain today.

January 2 & 3, 1838 – Tuesday and Wednesday. It rained considerably these two days also.

A Duel Honourably Settled

January 25, 1838 – Thursday. Mr. A. had sent a challenge the last evening to Mr. B., to settle some question of honour, it is foolishly and improperly termed; but, happily for both parties, the point was truly more honourably settled. Mr. B., convinced either of his own improper conduct, or of the impropriety of so base of crime as fighting a duel, came over this morning, and, without manifesting the slightest symptoms of fear, very honourably proposed to compromise the matter with Mr. A., who seemed to be as willing as the other to believe that bullets were rather dangerous things to trifle with. Thus ended the intended disgraceful tragedy. The dreadful prospects of a tomorrow's events had robbed me of a night's rest, but the final issue has more than compensated for the suffering of an anxious mind.[231]

---

229 Gunn: "The reference here is to the 'kissing dance,' much in vogue at that time."

230 "Gunn: "Oliver Cratte, according to Warren Upham, *Minnesota Biographies,* p. 148, was born in Liverpool, England, October 4, 1800. He probably migrated first to Canada, which would explain Garrioch's statement here as to his origin. He came to Minnesota in 1825, and resided in the Baker Settlement at Coldwater Spring. In 1839 he settled on the site of Wabasna, being the Government blacksmith for the Wabasna band of Sioux. He was married to a daughter of the noted Scotch trader Duncan Graham."

231 Although the identities of "A" and "B" are unknown, the tone of the entry indicates that the challenger was a friend of Garrioch's – and the ambiguous expression "came over" suggests that he

Spring

April 20, 1838 – Friday The rivers having now once more assumed their liquid state *in toto*, and the wintry winds having retired to their mother poles, the grand surface of old Mother Earth begins to deck itself with {135} all the vast and pleasing variety of green herbage, flowers, &c., with which she never fails to procure the admiration of her ungrateful sons and daughters.

Journey Resumed

May 2, 1838 – Wednesday After spending an easy but somewhat blurry and unpleasant winter at St. Peter's, during which period I spent a great part of my time among the Methodist missionaries, whose attentions and kindness were unlimited during my stay, I made arrangements with the captain of a steamboat which arrived the evening before for a passage to the Prairie. The charge for cabin passage was $12. I bade farewell to my recent friends at St. Peter's, and in 24 hours I found myself on the banks and shore at Prairie du Chien, the distance from St. Peter's to the {135} Prairie, by water, being 300 miles. We traveled on an average of 12½ miles per hour.

Prairie du Chien

Gunn described Prairie du Chien at this time and speculated about Peter Garrioch's business there: "Prairie du Chien is 132 miles south and 95 miles east of St. Paul, by the survey. It is consequently about 150 miles distant in a straight line. The distance by river is given by E. S. Seymour as 244 miles.[232]

A few words as to its condition at the time of Garrioch's visit to it may not be out of place. The place takes its name from a beautiful level prairie in which it is situated, at the confluence of the Mississippi and Wisconsin Rivers. This prairie derived its name from a Mesquakie village leader, Le Chien, whose community was nearby.[233] It was first settled by white people about 1785. In 1813 there were about 50 families there, engaged mostly in agriculture. Their common field was 4 miles long and a half mile in width. Beside this field they had three separate farms and 12 horse mills to manufacture their produce.

---

was perhaps a member of the same household, or at least someone who lived close by.

232 E. Stanford Seymour, *Sketches of Minnesota, the New England of the West, with Incidents of Travel in that Territory during the Summer of 1849* (NY: Harper, 1850), p. 276. If Seymour was correct, Garrioch's calculation of average speed must be reduced to about 10 miles per hour – still rather impressive when compared to travel by or in the company of Red River carts.

233 Lucy Eldersveld Murphy, *A Gathering of Rivers: Indians, Metis, and Mining in the Western Great Lakes, 1737-1832* (Lincoln, University of Nebraska Press, 2000), p. 45.

Chapter 3 – Labouring & Teaching At St. Peters

In 1835, 3 years before Garrioch's arrival, it was visited by a Methodist circuit rider, Reverend Alfred Brunson, who gives us the following concise account of its condition at that time: "The prairie is 9 miles long, and varying from 1 to 2 miles in width. It lies on the east of the Mississippi River, and north of the mouth of the Wisconsin. The high bluffs which rise and bound it on the east are 300 or 400 feet high, covered mostly with prairie grass, and having a little timber, and on their peaks or points presenting craggy precipices of rock. The Settlement extends the whole length of the prairie. About midway, north and south, is the village, which contains perhaps 100 houses of all descriptions. The whole French and mixed population are about 600, the Americans 200, and the garrison (Fort Crawford) contains 250 men, but their wives and children and other attendants amount to about 150 more – making the population of the place, including all descriptions, about 1,200. The garrison is built of stone, and situated at the south end of the village, commanding the river on one side and the prairie on the other."[234]

It is not known what business, if any, Garrioch had in Prairie du Chien. Probably it was simply the first stop in his journey to Gambier, Ohio, where he arrived June 5 to begin theological studies at Kenyon College – a part of his life recorded next in his journals.

A later note by Gunn elaborates importantly on the concluding two sentences quoted. Commenting on letters Garrioch wrote to Dr Williamson and to Bishop Jackson Kemper on November 18, 1838, Gunn revealed that, regardless of the young man's intentions in stopping at Prairie du Chien, doing so was instrumental in his choice of Kenyon College. Whether intentionally or accidentally, Gunn said, Garrioch had "fallen in" with Bishop Kemper at "The Prairie," and had been advised by him to pursue his intended studies at Kenyon.[235]

---

234   *Missouri Gazette* (July 31, 1813). Alfred Brunson, "A Methodist Circuit Rider's Horseback Tour from Pennsylvania to Wisconsin, 1835," *Collections of the State Historical Society of Wisconsin* XV (1900): pp. 264-291, at pp. 284-285.

235   In discussing Peter's "falling in" with Bishop Kemper, Gunn provided a fulsome description of Bishop Kemper, "a saintly and talented man," by whom "Garrioch was induced to go to Kenyon College…during his brief stay there [Prairie du Chien] in the spring of 1838." Gunn, p. 141.

Chapter 4

Kenyon College

1838-1839

The small town of Gambier, Ohio is home to a venerable and nationally-renowned institution of higher learning called Kenyon College. That is where, in June, 1838, Peter Garrioch's journal next finds him – enrolling for a challenging course of theological and other studies. Reverend Gunn's unpublished manuscript described Kenyon College and its surrounding area at that time as:

"[A]n institution of the Protestant Episcopal Church of America, and still a flourishing centre of learning under the management of that religious denomination. The village of Gambier is situated on the Vernon River, which encompasses it on three sides. It lies in the centre of a 4,000 acre tract of land, the property of Kenyon College, and is named after Lord Gambier, an English nobleman to whose generosity its founding was largely due. The village was laid out in 1826 under the direction of Bishop Chase of the Ohio Diocese, and the same year saw the College founded. In 1838, at the time of Garrioch's arrival there, the village contained some 30 or 40 dwelling houses, three stores, a printing office, a temperance hotel, and boasted a population [of 250], exclusive of the College students. A daily stage connected it with Mount Vernon, five miles to the west.

The College itself, being financed originally chiefly through the benefactions of titled Englishmen, was named after Lord Kenyon, one of its principal benefactors. It was first chartered as a theological seminary, but to this an arts college and other departments have since been added. Its equipment at the time of Garrioch's attendance was: Buildings: the main college, built of cut stone, 190 feet long and four stories high; a chapel of the same material, 100 feet long by 66 feet wide, with a basement; the grammar school, a wooden building of about 80 feet long and two stories high used as a school room and dormitories, and Milnor Hall, a brick building four stories high and about 70 feet long, with two wings attached, calculated to accommodate the Principal and 80 [student] boarders. Administration: Right Reverend C. P. McIlvaine, D. D., President;[236]

---

236 Kenyon's first President had been Bishop Chase, who resigned in 1831, and was followed by McIlvaine, about whom Gunn wrote: "Right Reverend Charles Pettit McIlvaine, D.D., Bishop of Ohio, was a son of Joseph McIlvaine, US senator from New Jersey, and it was born in Burlington,

Reverend M. T. C. Wing, Secretary and Treasurer, [and 11 others, of whom five were clergymen]. Faculty: [15 teaching staff, of whom 8, including McIlvaine and Wing, were clergymen, and one librarian]. Students: [206, including 64 theological students].

In addition to its ordinary funds, the institution owned 8,000 acres of land, which was valued in 1837 at $100,000. The annual [fees] of board and tuition for two college sessions of 20 weeks each, including room rent, light and supply of fuel, for a theological student, were $50, [and for other students] about $100 per annum."[237]

In 2018, 180 years later, Kenyon College and the Village of Gambier seem not to have changed radically in character, but rather to have intensified in the respects Gunn recorded. Gambier's non-student population in 2013 was still only 1,871, distributed among just 278 households.[238] And although the College now describes itself as a "liberal arts college," whose English department receives top billing in its literature, it still offers majors in Religious Studies, declares its religious affiliation as Episcopal, and proudly displays a coat of arms and motto in which the Christian cross is prominent. Its total enrollment in 2017-18 was 1,708. In *Forbes Magazine*'s 2011 list of "America's Best Colleges," Kenyon ranked 43 out of 650, and *U.S. News and World Report* for 2017 rated it number 26. Although the college campus is now smaller than in Garrioch's day, the September 2010, *Forbes Magazine* credited Kenyon with having "The World's Most Beautiful College Campus," England's Oxford University being considered the second most beautiful.[239]

Garrioch's journal entries for this period of his life were written on random scraps of paper, and frequently reflected more sombre and subdued moods, and much less self-confidence, than those recorded either before or after his months in Gambier.

New Jersey, January 18, 1799. He graduated from Princeton College in 1816, and was ordained priest in the Episcopal Church March 20, 1821. He was five years Rector of Christ Church, Georgetown, D.C. In 1825 he was appointed chaplain and professor of ethics at West Point. He [moved to] St. Anne's Church, Brooklyn, in 1827 and, for years later, was chosen as Professor in the University of the City of New York. Dr. McIlvaine was made Bishop of Ohio, and consecrated to that office in New York, October 31, 1832. The same year, he became President of Kenyon College, which office he retained until 1840. Bishop McIlvaine died in Florence, Italy, March 13, 1873. He was the author of many religious works which were highly regarded by contemporary scholars. See: Henry Howe: Historical Collections of Ohio, 2, 1904, Vol I, pp. 989-90.

237   Gunn, pp. 136-137.

238   Source: 2000 Census, reported by Wikipedia December 2011.

239   Source: Kenyon College website, December, 2011.

Settling In

June 5, 1838 – Tuesday. Arrival at Kenyon College. {137}

Expenses[240] at Kenyon College: .... Paid

June 6, 1838 – Wednesday.

    To 9 yds. bed stuff @ 16 2/3 ....$ 1.50

    " 1½ yds. linen   " 37 ½ .... .50

June 7, 1838 – Thursday.

    "   1 Latin grammar................... 1.00

    "   1 cot 2.50

        Received on credit, and sent: 3 blankets, 1 bed tick, 1 pillow.

[A part of the manuscript is missing here. Since the excision is followed by what appear to be two student resolutions, numbered 8 and 9, it seems likely that the missing page or pages contained the first seven.[241]]

(8) That my country and countrymen shall be ever in view, for whose sake I have come here.[242] {138}

---

240   Probably the $50 tuition/room and board fee for the year.

241   The two resolutions do not correspond to any of the rules laid out in the impressive catalogue for 1838-39 of Kenyon College's Theological Seminary of the Diocese of Ohio, so one can assume these are not official rules, but perhaps student-generated ones.

242   In the 1838-1839 catalogue, Peter is listed among the senior preparatory department students (not the theology students), of whom there were 48. All but Peter ("Red River, Hudson's Bay") appear to be from the U.S. No room number is listed opposite his name, meaning, it seems, that he took private rooms. He was among the 12 members of that class whose name was marked with an asterisk, which indicates, the catalogue explains, "the names of those Students who have left the Institution, but not in disgrace, during the year." The catalogue goes on to explain that the college is divided into four sections: the theological seminary, the college, and the senior and junior preparatory schools, the latter of which exists "to prepare young men to engage in the active duties of life, without taking a full College course." The catalogue billed the college as being located in the centre of Ohio and "in a neighborhood peculiarly free from the temptations and dangers to which young men are often exposed." Tuition for the senior preparatory department, including board, room rent, bedding, washing, fuel, lights, and physician's attendance was $120.00, plus $5.00 for books, stationary, mending, etc., or the equivalent of about $4,077 today.

Chapter 4 – Kenyon College

(9) That the Lord would give me strength to put the above humble resolutions into practice is my earnest prayer.

Studies Begin

June 8, 1838 – Friday. This day I have, in the strength of the Lord, commenced studying Latin.[243] May all that I shall ever acquire be here, at least, devoted to His glory.

June 10, 1838 – Sunday. Went out this morning in company with some pious students to attend a Sabbath School. I have met with interesting children, but very ignorant. They know not who made them. May the Lord bless our labours among them. The field is truly large, but the labourers are few.

June 12, 1838 – Tuesday. The students received their grades and their delinquencies: my initials being M. B., grade 35.[244] Delinquencies: none.

A Lost Day

June 17, 1838 – Sunday. This has been a lost day to me. O how can I redeem it? It is gone, and I have not been in the house of God. The Lord forgive me. Detained by unforeseen events was the cause of my absence from the house of prayer. May the Lord teach me the value of my time and all other blessings, that I may be anxious to improve them all to His glory and to the salvation of my soul.

Virgil & Singing & Literature

June 19, 1838 – Tuesday. I have commenced Virgil this day. It is truly a difficult study for me, considering my scanty knowledge of Latin. However, I trust to the Lord. I look to Him for understanding, memory, and every other thing I stand in need of.

June 25, 1838 – Monday. The singing, which is very interesting as well as a needful thing, I have commenced this day.

---

243 According to the 1838-39 catalogue's list of courses for senior preparatory department students, Peter would have been studying, besides Latin, English grammar, arithmetic, ancient and modern geography, Greek, book-keeping, algebra, geometry, trigonometry, surveying, natural philosophy, chemistry, rhetoric, composition, and declamation.

244 The significance of these grades is not known with certainty, but if 35 was a percentage it was not an encouraging sign. Nor is it evident why Peter should have been known as "M.B."

June 26, 1838 – Tuesday. I have this day joined the Literary Society. May the Lord bless my undertakings, that I may prosper. {139}

Early Doubts

July 2, 1838 – Monday. Commenced the study of Natural Philosophy, by Comstock. How many more studies shall I pursue, alas? These are but the beginning of those requirements that I need to fit me for usefulness. Shall these and every other branch I intend to take up redound to the glory of my God? If so, all is well; if not, may the Lord prevent my progress. Lord, teach me continually how to act.

I have this night attended a missionary meeting. How much of the missionary spirit do I possess? O Lord, increase my love for my blessed Redeemer, who loved me so much that He gave his life for me; so that my desire for the coming of His kingdom and the salvation of the world may continually increase till Thou shalt, if it be Thy will, place me in that great vineyard, which stands so much in need of labourers.

Here, less than a month after Garrioch's arrival at Kenyon College, is a strong expression of doubt that he has made the right vocational choice in life. Another clue to his uncertainty might be found in the sharp contrast between the unrestrained exuberance of his earlier (and later) journal entries and the awkward, unnatural, piousness of those made in these weeks.

July 4, 1838 – Wednesday. Attended the celebration of the American Independence for the first time. The whole seemed to be very good and well conducted. But, alas! the heat of enthusiasm seems to have too great a sway. To hear songs on musical instruments only fit for the ballroom played in the house of God is, I think, bestowing too much on man.

Potatoes Trump Classes

July 18, 1838 – Wednesday. This is almost a lost day, for I have not been in school. I took the day for working at my potatoes.[245] This is now the second day spent in like

---

245 Does this mean that students were given garden space to grow food for themselves? Or was there an obligation to pitch in to help keep the communal kitchen in provisions? Since in the 1838-1839 catalogue there is no room number after Peter's name, he may well have been boarding somewhere else and doing this work for a person who took him in as a boarder. Or did he have a patch of potatoes to help him to save on his food bill, perhaps? Still more puzzling is why he should have gone on to describe this mid-July day as perhaps the "last day" of this gardening activity.

manner. I have, however, studied my lessons as usual. I hope this will be the last day that necessity will compel me to spend so.

July 29, 1838 – Sunday. The Sunday School anniversary took place, at which were present between two and three hundred Sabbath School children.

August 5, 1838 – Sunday. The Lord's Supper was administered, and a stu-{140}-dent (Bonnar)[246] ordained Deacon.

Illness

November 3, 1838 – Saturday. Fell ill and was necessarily from school four days. But how kind indeed has the Lord been to me. He has increased my strength and permitted me again to pursue my studies. O may I live more to the Lord than I ever yet have done. O Lord, grant me grace so to do.

A Terrifying Dream

November 10, 1838 – Saturday. Was roused to my duty by a dream which I dreamt last night. I thought I was just going on my knees, after being idle for some time, when God himself, in the form of a man, spoke to me from behind me, sitting on a chair. He told me that, as I had not improved the time and many privileges which He had graciously bestowed upon me, He would remove the whole from me. After He had said this, two others appeared in the room, to whom He made known my carelessness and negligence, and they unanimously agreed in taking from me all my privileges.

Gunn noted at this point in his transcription that the conclusion of the dream is missing from the manuscript. He appears, however, to have overlooked the following three paragraphs which, although slightly out of place in the sometimes helter-skelter original journal, and lacking a syntactical linkage to the foregoing passage, substantially complete Garrioch's account of this powerful experience.

In consequence of the frowns in the countenance of the Judge, we were quite speechless. Our confusion was aggravated by the [revels] of the multitude by whom we were surrounded. Then did the Judge call upon my two companions of iniquity to give in their accounts, and when each of them had done so they were both acquitted.

---

246 Gunn: "Reverend James Bonnar, graduate in Theology of Kenyon College [...] in 1837. He was at this time Instructor in the [...] institution."

The Judge then commanded me to advance, and answer for my past conduct, [as related] by a certain one standing between us and the Judge, whom I thought was my own father. As soon as He had read to me all the particulars of my sin, I thought He doomed me to everlasting punishment, and commanded the one who stood before him to beat me with a rod of iron, which he did immediately. After he had commenced beating, which he did without enmity or intemperance, I thought he was Moses. I then cried for mercy, but in vain, for he told me that it was too late to cry for mercy, and that he knew not how to show mercy.

While I was thus crying aloud for mercy under the rod, I awoke; and beheld it was a dream – to my unspeakable joy and comfort. However, the impression which the dream made in my mind was great, and [convinced] me of the error of my ways. So great was the fear which the dream wrought on my mind that I began to despair of [illegible word], and a gloom of horror prevailed in my soul all the day long. I sometimes attempted to look for mercy through a [illegible word] saviour, but my conscience would again obstruct me, and tell me I had forfeited all hope of mercy because of my sins against God. So great was the fear and horror of my mind when I awoke that I trembled and, notwithstanding the comfort I felt in finding myself still in my bed, I could scarcely convince myself that my dream was not real.

Letters to Mentors

November 14, 1838 – Wednesday. Wrote two letters: one to Bishop Kemper, {141} the other to Dr. Williamson.

Bishop Jackson Kemper,[247] it will be remembered, was the person who, at Prairie du Chien, had advised Garrioch to come to Kenyon College to pursue his studies. Dr. Thomas

---

247   Gunn: "Right Reverend Jackson Kemper, D. D., was born in Pleasant Valley, Duchess County, New York, December 24, 1789. His paternal grandfather came to America from Kaub, on the Rhine, in 1741, settling soon afterwards in the locality above-mentioned. His grandfather was an officer in the Palatine army, while his father, Daniel Kemper, served as a colonel in the American Revolutionary War. The future bishop, Jackson Kemper, or David Jackson Kemper as he was baptized, was educated at Columbia College, New York, from which he graduated as valedictorian of his class in 1809. In 1811, he was ordained as deacon in Philadelphia, becoming an assistant to Bishop White – a position which he held for 20 years. In 1814 he was ordained priest. In 1834 he undertook for the Domestic and Foreign Missionary Society of the Protestant Episcopal Church a trip to Wisconsin to report on the establishment founded by Reverend Richard F. Cadle – of which trip he left a journal in manuscript, since published by the Wisconsin Historical Society, with valuable notes by Dr. Thwaites. The following year, at the General Conference of the American Episcopal Church, Dr. Kemper was elected as its first missionary bishop, his field being "the Northwest." In the winter

Williamson was the missionary who had so inspired him when he passed through Lac Qui Parl, and later at Harriet Lake. Did he share with these two wise counsellors his growing uncertainty about his suitability to continue following the path he was on? And did he feel compelled to write to them because one or both of them had contributed financially to make it possible for him to attend Kenyon College?

More Illness

December 4, 1838 – Tuesday. Fell ill again, and laboured under a greater degree of pain.

December 30, 1838 – Sunday. This being Sabbath, I ventured out to church after being confined to my bed for 20 days, and six more in my room. Beyond my own most sanguine expectations, I am recovering my former strength rapidly; but my eyesight remains very weak. How wonderful is the goodness of God. I pray that this affliction may be greatly blessed to my soul, and may it teach me to live nearer to my God.

Back to Classes

January 8, 1839 – Tuesday. Had the pleasure of attending Mr. Bronson's[248] interesting lectures for the first time.

January 10, 1839 – Thursday. Again attended his lectures (or declamations) and 25 cents ...

The remainder of this day's entry has been removed from the manuscript.

January 11, 1839 – Friday. Commenced attending his regular class lectures, the charge being one dollar per week, and the class consisting of 60 in {142} number.

---

of 1835 he moved to St. Louis, Missouri, where he established the headquarters of his diocese. Bishop Kemper was a saintly and talented man, held in high esteem – especially in the West, where his missionary labours had been of a most arduous and consecrated character. It was through his influence that Garrioch was induced to go to Kenyon College, having fallen in with the Bishop at Prairie du Chien during his brief stay there in the spring of 1838. See *Wisconsin Historical Society Collections*, XIV, pp. 394-95."

248   Gunn: "Reverend Sherlock Anson Bronson, D.D., L.L.D., subsequently President of Kenyon College. He graduated from the above institution in 1833 as valedictorian of his class; remained with the College as tutor and student in Theology through the session of 1834-35, graduating from the Theological Department in the latter year. He took his A.M. degree in 1836, and was subsequently made D.D. in 1848, and L.L.D. in 1885." On this occasion the Bronson lectures – on some unknown topic – seem to have been over and above the regular curriculum.

January 14, 1839 – Monday. Re-pursued my studies in full.

Discouraged

January 16, 1839 – Wednesday. Got so discouraged in Greek, after losing so much time, that I almost determined to commence again.[249]

January 17, 1839 – Thursday. Fell down one of the under pathways in the night, but received little hurt – because the Lord was there.

Student Unrest

For the next fortnight, the diaries carried echoes of dissatisfaction by other students. Garrioch's response was not what those who knew him in later life might have expected.

January 21, 1839 – Monday. General Harrison[250] sent out of school for refusing to obey authority.

January 23, 1839 – Wednesday. Appointed as... C. in the L.L.M.[251]

January 24, 1839 – Thursday. Could not get my lessons from weakness of eyes.

January 25, 1839 – Friday. Bradshaw left the hill.[252]

January 26, 1839 – Saturday. Louis commenced calling the roll.[253]

---

249 Does he mean *not* to commence again, or does he mean to start the course over from the beginning?

250 John M. Harrison of Danville, Kentucky, was a classmate of Garrioch's. Perhaps he was indeed a retired military officer; but his high-ranking title could also have been a mere nickname.

251 The meaning of these initials is lost on the editors. Perhaps they indicate an office in one of the College's student organizations, suggesting that Garrioch continued to be involved in extracurricular activities at this point. The apparent deletion or blank is in the original.

252 John W. Bradshaw was another classmate, and "the hill" was the college, which was set on a hill. Bradshaw's apparent abandonment of his studies may well have been an action Garrioch was beginning to contemplate for himself at this juncture. Like Harrison and Garrioch, Bradshaw has an asterisk next to his name, indicating he left the school before the year was out.

253 There appears to have been some restiveness among the students if the Harrison and Bradshaw incidents, and Garrioch's own increasing uncertainty, are indicative. Poor class attendance may have been a consequence. If this were the case, it would explain a decision to call attendance rolls in classes. Who "Louis" was is not known, and a "Louis" is not among the 38 students listed in the senior preparatory department in the 1838-39 catalogue. Inasmuch as no one on the faculty or administrator lists provided by Gunn had that name or initial he would seem to have been a student.

Chapter 4 – Kenyon College

January 31, 1839 – Thursday. Wrote a letter to Mr. Stevenson,[254] giving him my reasons for not signing the petition concerning the calling of the roll. General Harrison dissolved his connection with the Literary Society.

February 3, 1839 – Sunday. Mr. Arnott, lately a Methodist preacher, was ordained to the office of Deacon in the Episcopal Church by C. P. McIl-{143}-vaine. This day also, a child of Mr. Dyer's[255] [was] burned.

February 6, 1839 – Wednesday. I was this day requested to sign a petition, to be presented to the Faculty, for the readmittance of Harrison into the school. From various considerations, however, I objected [declined] it.

The Will of the Lord I Know Not

February 11, 1839 – Monday. Whatever may be the will of the Lord concerning me, I know not. My constitution is broken, and my eyesight is fast going. Two weeks from today I have done nothing towards my studies. I have lost of this session 8 weeks. While my fellow students are prosecuting their designs, and are daily improving, I am idle, and daily losing what I have already acquired with much labour.

For the last two days, the impression has been weighty on my mind that I should go to Africa or the East Indies as a missionary next summer. But how shall I know that this is the will of the Lord, or whether I {144} should return home? Today I feel quite cast down, and perfectly discouraged. The day before yesterday, I received a letter from Mr. Menard.[256] This day I fast, trusting through the grace of God to weaken the flesh, and to be strengthened in the spirit.

Dreams of Africa

February 13, 1839 – Wednesday. Spoke something to Mr. Hensel about the climate of Africa. Where he had been as a missionary, he said, was very damp. The weather

---

254   Gunn states in a note that a Robert Stevenson was a member of Garrioch's class. The 1838-39 catalogue confirms that a Robert B. Stevenson of Bellefontaine was indeed in that class.

255   A faculty member.

256   Menard's identity is not known. He is not listed among the 1838-39 catalogue's "officers of instruction and government."

continues quite rainy and foggy, sometimes for three or five months. This did not give me much encouragement to think of going to Africa as a missionary.

February 19, 1839 – Tuesday. Mr ———,[257] Governor of Liberia, delivered a lecture on colonization, which the majority of the students, and also the professors, attended. From his statement of the climate in that country, I am of the opinion that it would be very favourable to my constitution and general health.

February 20, 1839 – Wednesday. Mr. Corcle[258] and some others dismissed for improper conduct.

Aching Eyes, Opium, Snow & Uncertainty

February 23, 1839 – Saturday. Felt quite drowsy all day.

February 24, 1839 – Sunday. Could hardly keep my eyes open in church, still being quite drowsy. I believe it was occasioned by taking too much opium.[259] My eyes felt so weak this day that I had often to keep them closed a while. And could not attend the Bible lesson as usual.

February 27, 1839 – Wednesday. Not knowing what to do for my eyes, I have this morning thrown my spectacles aside to see if that will not help them.

February 28, 1839 – Thursday. Fell about nine inches of snow.

March 2, 1839 – Saturday. It snowed the greater part of the day. In the evening I went over to Dr. Cotton, to speak on the subject of con-{145}-firmation.

---

257 The blank space is in the original. The gentleman in question was Thomas Buchanan, a cousin of James Buchanan, the 15th President of the United States. The west African state of Liberia resulted from an early 19th century project by the American Colonization Society to repatriate emancipated American slaves to the African continent. Thomas Buchanan was the Society's third appointee as Liberia's Governor, serving from 1836 to 1841, and contributing much to the country's transition from tribal to national governance, and eventual indigenous leadership and independence.

258 Presumably another student.

259 For thousands of years, opium was the main analgesic known, used to treat all manner of illnesses, but it was in the early 19th century that its euphoric effects began to be paid more attention, such as in Thomas De Quincey's *Confessions of an English Opium-Eater* (1803), and leading people such as Immanuel Kant to warn of its dangers and to advocate that its use be restricted to medicinal purposes only (*Metaphysics of Morals*, 1797). This appears to be how Garrioch was employing it: for treating the pain in his eyes.

Retiring to rest this night, I felt the pain in my right eye so terribly that, if shame had not prevented it, I believe I should have cried. The thought of having lost nearly a whole session, and now feeling more pain in my eyes than I ever did before, at the very time I flattered myself that they were getting quite strong, was almost more than I could bear.

I cannot but wonder that I have so little faith. Strongly and most earnestly do I desire that I may be more submissive to the will of that Kind Being who has clothed my past life with so great and unspeakable mercies. My prayers are: "Lord, do what seemeth Thee good."

March 4, 1839 – Monday. The thermometer stood at 14° below zero.

March 7, 1839 – Thursday. Felt much gratified this evening in the lecture of Bishop McIlvaine on the departure of the children of Israel out of Egypt, till they came to Rephidim. One remark particularly pleased me very much, viz.: that being surrounded on every hand with obstacles is no argument that we are not in the path of duty. God is sometimes pleased to beset our way with many difficulties, that our faith may be tried, and that we may learn to trust in Him alone, and at all times. When the children of Israel took their departure of Egypt, they were hemmed in on every hand before they crossed the Red Sea. This was no argument that they were out of the path of their duty, for they went as the Pillar led them, and in so doing He on whom they trusted delivered them from their enemies.

March 9, 1839 – Saturday. I find my eyes to be increasing in strength very rapidly. This day I looked over three newspapers, and read several speeches, which is more than I've done for some time back. {146}

March 10, 1839 – Sunday. Found my eyes quite weak again, and continued so for some days.

March 11, 1839 – Monday. The Bible Missionary Society met at the Chapel, and, after arranging matters and raising a subscription to the amount of $56, dismissed.

A Temperance Society Throwup

March 14, 1839 – Thursday. The Temperance Society: Subscriptions to the amount of six or seven dollars were raised for the distribution of tracts on the subject. I subscribed 50 cents. An address was delivered by Milton Lightner,[260] and remarks by some others, after which we adjourned to meet in two weeks.

Soon after the wine question was proposed, including beer as I supposed, the contents of a stomach [were] forcibly thrown up onto the floor before the assembly, caused by the virtues of beer. A most unfortunate circumstance for the wine question.

Confirmation & Spring Thunder

March 17, 1839 – Sunday. I received the rite of Confirmation, together with three other males and six or seven females. A short yet appropriate and excellent address was made by the Bishop (McIlvaine) to the candidates and congregation previous to his laying on of hands. After the Confirmation, the Bishop preached from the first verse of the 15th chapter of St. John's Gospel.

After retiring to rest, and having dozed for some time, I was quite gratified to hear thunder, it being the first I heard this spring. Thunder, for the first time after the lapse of several months, on the eve of the day of my Confirmation, seemed to add weight to the solemnity of my renewed covenant with my God and Saviour; for it seemed to say, just at the time when some evil thought came across my mind, "Remember your covenant engagement, which you have this day ratified anew."

This was the last of Peter Garrioch's Kenyon College journal entries, and he seems to have withdrawn from his studies shortly thereafter. The sudden re-emergence of Peter's familiar unrestrained, jocular, voice in the final sentence of his next-to-last entry was doubtless a harbinger of that decision. And this concluding entry was also prophetic: while remaining a fully 'engaged' Christian for life, the future adventures to which the distant thunder was calling him never included theological ordination. There is no record, either, of his ever again having problems with his eyes.

It is hard not to conclude that Peter's attempt at theological studies, so quickly abandoned, was due less to a pious calling than to the desire to better himself socially. After all, nothing in his subsequent diary entries suggests he gave more than an occasional nod to conventional piety. Rather, in pursuing the opportunity to study at Kenyon College, he may well have been looking for his place in Red River society and wanting that place to be more that of a gentleman than of a voyageur.

But there were not a lot of options for gentlemanly pursuits at Red River, especially for upwardly-mobile persons of mixed descent like Peter. The fur trade was laying people off,[261]

---

260   A fellow student.

261   E.E. Rich, *Hudson's Bay Company* (New York: Macmillan, 1960), III, pp.407-409, 429-430, & 481-48; Brown, *Strangers in Blood*, pp. 205-211; & *Report of the Royal Commission on Aboriginal Peoples*, I, pp. 151-153. In *Manitoba: A History* (University of Toronto Press, 1957), p. 73. W. L.

Chapter 4 – Kenyon College

and Governor George Simpson had made it abundantly clear that the interracial offspring of traders were not going to have the same options their predecessors once had, despite the fact that many fur traders' sons had grown up expecting to follow in their fathers' footsteps. Then Simpson blocked them from employment, thereby reducing redundancy and expense at a critical time when overhunting was depleting the most valuable furs. Eventually Simpson had to walk this back a little and allow them to work in low level administrative positions, but the chance to be a gentleman was virtually non-existent for Peter and his cohort.[262] **Fur trading could provide some degree of wealth, but not the**

Morton attributes the colony's failure to grow and the slow seepage of population out of the colony to the growing settlement on the upper Mississippi to this thwarting of economic opportunity.

262 On the impact on Peter's generation of the growing distinction between "gentlemen" and "servants," held back socially and otherwise, see Brown, *Strangers in Blood*, pp. 205-209. The distinctions were less racially-motivated than they were reflective of class distinctions, although class and race cannot be completely untangled from each other: Irene M. Spry, "The Métis and Mixed-Bloods of Rupert's Land before 1870," in Jacqueline Peterson and Jennifer S. H. Brown, eds., *The New Peoples, Being and Becoming Métis in North America* (University of Manitoba Press, 1985), pp. 95-118.

Spry points out that these divisions in Red River society were "between the well-educated gentry, the officers and retired officers of the Hudson's Bay Company and those of their progeny who had achieved respectability, the clergy, and the prosperous merchants, in contrast to the mass of unlettered, unpropertied natives of the country.... James Sinclair, for example, was recognized as a "gentleman"; …this set him apart from the ordinary tripmen, whom he employed on his freighting ventures. The gap was one occasioned by ambition, affluence, education and social status as against poverty and the inferior status of employees or, at best, of hunters, petty traders or small farmers." *Ibid.*, p. 111.

As for the large number of persons employed as tripmen, freighting of all sorts was big business in Red River and well beyond. E. S. Russenholt, *The Heart of the Continent, Being the History of Assiniboia – the Truly Typical Canadian Community* (Winnipeg: MacFarland, 1968), p. 86, pointed out that *circa* 1849, the HBC paid freighters $4 to $4.50 per hundred pounds for the 500 miles between St. Paul and Fort Garry "in goods at Fort Garry prices." More than 1,500 carts were employed freighting between Assiniboia and St. Paul, and 500 more between Assiniboia and the Saskatchewan country. "Thus, 'the Company' employed 600 or 700 cart-men, in addition to 500 in the boat brigades. By extending credit to both voyageurs and cart-men, 'the Company' kept them bound by debt."

George Henry Gunn's brother, John (Introduction, nn. 6 & 8), who did not have the same keenness for history-writing as his brother George did, nevertheless wrote an extensive chapter, entitled "The Tripman of Assiniboia," pp. 24-58, in his book, *Echoes*, about the Red River tripmen, presumably on firm historical foundations. It begins: "In those days when what is now Manitoba and a goodly chunk of Uncle Sam's territory, there was a numerous important class of population, the members of which were known as Tripmen. Some few of these still remain to tell of the glories of a calling that dwindled away before steamboats and railways, and is now as completely unknown as though it had never been. The importance of this class may be judged from the fact that, when at its height, there were fully one thousand employed by the Hudson's Bay Company, and other traders, in transportation either by land or water. The Tripman proper belonged to the water, and was, in Assiniboia the successor of the voyageur of earlier days."

social status enjoyed by officers, clergy, CMS officials, medical men, HBC officials (at least those enjoying the Governor's favour), and others of the upper settler class.

As we shall begin to see in the next chapter, the adventures and challenges of the fur trade better suited Peter's contrarian personality. So long as he could avoid the humiliation he had experienced not long before at St. Peter's (Chapter 3) when forced by circumstances to support himself as a labourer and general dog's body, he was able as a young man to find sufficient satisfaction as a fur trader. An enterprising fur trader could do well financially while maintaining the freedom lacking in more staid occupations like farming.[263] **Along**

John Gunn also described the routes of the usually-French Métis composition of the tripmen, their habits, cooking, earnings, and their diminishing performance for their masters at the HBC as the Company's reach grew shorter. At the end of the chapter, he ascribed importance to their role in the eventual uprisings against the HBC: "Ordinarily happy-go-lucky, yet easily excited, fearless, athletic and fierce, we can see how serious an affray they were capable of creating over a matter that would have caused no excitement whatever in another class of men. This gave them with some the reputation of being lawless, savage and altogether bad; but without granting this in all its sweeping significance, we would recall that it was chiefly the uprising of this class and its kindred, the hunter-traders, that shook to crumbling the government machinery of the old regime and so made necessary and possible the establishment of the present order of things."

263   Spry, "The Métis and Mixed-Bloods," p. 111, where one of the class divides at the time was "between the professional farmer and the hunter and plains trader, between the sedentary population and those to whom the freedom of a wandering life out on the plains was more important than economic security and material comfort." Another scholar put it this way: "The fur trade held many attractions. Traders were men of wealth who enjoyed economic and political influence yet were not tied down to farms and the back-breaking labour required to maintain them. Moreover, the close ties of the Métis to the Indian communities gave them access to and certain advantages in dealing with the providers of furs. As cultural brokers, the Métis spoke the tribal languages and were welcome in the Indian camps. At the same time, because many of them had the rudiments of a European education, they were able to function in the world of frontier commerce. Indeed, many Métis were so adept at the trade that British and American firms attempted to hire them as agents. Most, however, continued to remain self-employed." R. David Edmunds, "'Unacquainted with the laws of the civilized world': American Attitudes toward the Métis Communities in the Old Northwest," pp. 185-194, in Peterson and Brown, *The New Peoples*, p. 188; & Raffan, *Métis and the Medicine Line: Creating a Border and Dividing a People* (Chapel Hill: University of North Carolina Press, 2015), p. 39 & *passim*, Both describe how the growing competition between Indians and people of mixed ancestry in the 1840s and 1850s led to sometimes violent disputes, but also to a growing cohesiveness among the latter themselves.

A concurring contemporary analysis of Red River society and the situation of the "half-breeds" within it was offered by Catholic missionary Father Belcourt, writing from Pembina in 1853, in the midst of his own troubles with the HBC:

"The population of the country divides itself into three classes, viz: The colonists who came from Canada or Europe, the half-breeds and their children, and the savages. The Canadians and the Europeans have brought with them that spirit of nationality which leads them to esteem themselves above the other inhabitants, half-breeds, &c. For the first, nothing is so good as at Montreal; for the others, nothing is like London. The half-breeds being more numerous, and endowed with uncommon health and strength, esteem themselves the lords of the land. Though they hold the

with that freedom, Peter seems to have relished the challenges presented by the obstacles thrown in his way by the HBC's officials (Chapters 8 & 9).[264] **In pursuing his career as a fur trader, and a free trader**[265] **at that, Peter must have realized that it would be preferable**

---

middle place between civilized and savage life, one can say, that in respect to morality, they are as good as many civilized people. Their character is gentle and benevolent. Their greatest vice is prodigality; they have also an extreme tendency to the use of strong drinks; nevertheless, the vivacity of their faith has wrought wonders among them in this respect.... Though the half-breeds lose much of their time in idleness, I do not think this owes its origin to the vice of indolence, but rather to the absence of all commercial interests; that is to say, to the want of enterprises passably lucrative, or of rewards sufficiently inviting to make them sustain the fatigues of labor. For they are capable of enduring to an astonishing degree the most horrible fatigues; and they undertake them with the greatest cheerfulness when circumstances call for it....They have a taste for music; and above all for the violin; and a great many of them know how to play.... The third class of the population of the country are the savages, who have a still stronger spirit of nationality than the other two, though they admit that they are not so skillful in other respects," Belcourt, "The Department of the Hudson's Bay," p. 224.

264 When the clever and opportunistic George Simpson was quickly promoted to Governor of the newly-combined HBC and North West Company in 1821, he began to implement a tight administrative system in Rupert's Land which involved laying-off the many employees he considered redundant, reducing wages and waste, increasing accountability, improving record-keeping, reducing the flexibility of the Factors and others on the ground to make independent decisions and to hoard supplies for their own outposts, and consolidating trade routes. At the same time, he respected Aboriginal people as business operatives and did what he needed to do to keep them on his side, even while writing that "an enlightened Indian is good for nothing." All of this had a deleterious effect on the independence of the fur traders, along with Simpson's 1822 edict that "a ledger [was to be kept] for Free Hunters throughout the Country shewing their Book Debts, hunts and Balances up to 1st June – a Balance Sheet from which ought to go home also." James Raffan, *Emperor of the North: Sir George Simpson & the Remarkable Story of the Hudson's Bay Company* (Toronto: Harper-Collins, 2007), pp. 125-149, 421-422. The deterioration in Simpson's mental state, especially between 1830 and 1832, is summarized in the introduction to Simpson's *Character Book*, which is reproduced in: Glyndwr Williams, ed., *Hudson's Bay Miscellany, 1670-1870* (Winnipeg: Hudson's Bay Record Society, 1975), pp. 151-236, where his negativity was there and elsewhere directed in full against "half-breeds," whom he labeled: "thoughtless, dissipated, and depraved." (*Ibid.*, p. 154)

265 See Gilman, *Red River Trails*, pp. 8-10, where free trade and "smuggling" activities in the area are summarized, and Peter is described as being by the time of his lengthy 1844 trading enterprise "well on his way to becoming one of the colony's most aggressive free traders." For a surprisingly empathetic early analysis of free trade issues and the unwise position the HBC was taking against its own interests, see the 1856 account by Assiniboia sheriff and councillor, Alexander Ross, *The Red River Settlement: Its Rise, Progress, and Present State* (Edmonton: Hurtig, 1972), pp. 369-372. In *Manitoba: A History*, pp. 73-74, W. L. Morton explores the notion that the HBC's efforts to suppress free trade was in fact against its own interests because, by maintaining effective monopoly of the commerce of the Northwest, Red River's economy was not able to sustain itself with farming, stock-raising, or buffalo-hunting alone. "The chief hope of economic gain, therefore, lay in trading, and the private trader at once encountered the commercial monopoly of the Hudson's Bay Company. The introduction of the free settlers into Rupert's Land had, of course, raised serious problems for the united Company with its effective monopoly of the commerce of the Northwest." In effect, the

to be a leader in the commercial side of Red River society than to strive in vain to achieve status in the "genteel" society of Rupert's Land and Red River, such as his now-abandoned aspirations to a theological career might have given him.

---

free traders' industriousness in developing their markets aided the HBC's American rivals. Petty trading among themselves was tolerated, but such trading "reached intolerable proportions only in 1844, when Norman W. Kittson opened a post for the American Fur Company at Pembina, and when a native-born generation was beginning to find the monopoly of the Company oppressive and life in Red River dull and unrewarding."

We meet Kittson often in Peter's diaries, and we recognize in both men the free traders' themes of lust for freedom, thwarting of ambition, restlessness, and resentment of the HBC's restraint measures against Peter's trading exploits. Indeed, W. L. Morton specifically names Peter Garrioch as the epitome of the "adventurous young men ... [who] began to trade with American traders on the Souris, or brought furs ...with goods imported by the Bay. The free traders themselves now carried the catch to Pembina or to St. Paul.... The almost open trade for furs with goods imported into the colony by the Company's ships, and the scarcely clandestine traffic with Pembina and St. Paul, were more than the Company could tolerate." *Manitoba, A History*, p. 75. As a result, it took steps against Peter and his fellow free traders, starting in 1844. See especially Alfred J. Gluek, *Minnesota and the Manifest Destiny of the Canadian Northwest: A Study in Canadian-American Relations* (Toronto: University of Toronto Press, 1965), pp. 47-50, 56, 76-81, where Kittson is described in detail as an established ally of James Sinclair and Andrew McDermot and a "mainspring in the whole free-trading movement", the HBC's "greatest competitor."

Chapter 5

Trading On The Missouri

1842-1844

Nearly five years had elapsed since Peter Garrioch's last known journal entry in March, 1839, and the one that opens this chapter. Although this first long passage summarizes events since the fall of 1842, three and one-half years of the diarist's life are entirely unaccounted for. The fact that he chose to ignore them in his retrospective account may suggest that he wrote them up at some point, but that they have been lost. About all we know as we pick up the broken thread is that the Red River Settlement is still his home base, and that his mother, father and family members continue to reside there. As he takes up his pen once more, Peter is 33 years of age, and still unmarried. He has hopes, however, of altering the latter circumstance.

Retrospective

{148} January 2, 1844 – Tuesday. Under the above date I intend to congregate all the events and circumstances relative to my own affairs and observations since the first of May last to the present day. To allow eight months to slide off into eternity without preserving a single memento for probable old age to advert to when such things would be memorials and handmaids to the memory, is to leave one in absolute doubt, whether he spent that period of his life in the active discharge of those duties connected with any calling in this life, or whether the whole routine of his functionaries were then reduced to a state of such dormant stupor, which the great blank in his life-book would intimate. That he was perfectly unconscious of existence during that period – That would be ridiculous! To avoid the odium of such a charge, is what induces me, but for my own satisfaction however, to fill up that vacuum of my active life, which the lapse of eight months unnoticed, has caused.[266]

---

266   At this point Garrioch seems to have had no plans to publish his journal.

In the fall of 1842 I undertook to trade for the Missouri Fur Com{149}pany,[267] having a post assigned to my charge at the Mouse River.[268]

---

267   Gunn: "The American Fur Company is meant, or more correctly still Pierre Chouteau, Jr. & Co. The American Fur Company [theoretically] ceased to exist on the Missouri after the retirement of John Jacob Astor from it in 1834, though the succeeding company, in common usage, still went by that name. There was a 'Missouri Fur Company,' with headquarters at St. Louis, in the early part of the 19th century, [but] Garrioch's 'Missouri Fur Company' [should] not be confused with [it]." For a modern overview of Peter's economic success in the trading of furs, see Gerhard J. Ens, *Homeland to Hinterland; The Changing World of the Red River Metis in the Nineteenth Century* (University of Toronto Press, 1996), pp. 84-86, where it is concluded that Peter was among the dozens of fur traders who, by the 1860s, were making $1,000 per year or more from the fur trade. Ens' conclusion seems, however, inconsistent with the Métis' complaints (Appendix I – Petitions) that the HBC was pushing the fur traders into penury with draconian duties, prohibitions on free trading in furs, and confiscation of transgressors' furs, as well as what we know of Peter's rather straightened circumstances in his later years (see Chap. 10).

268   Gunn: "The Rivière la Souris of the French, now known as the Souris River. The Souris is a considerable stream. It has the distinction of being one of the longest, as well as one of the crookedest, of the smaller rivers in the Northwest. It flows through two provinces of Canada and one state of the American Union. The territory through which it flows was formerly rich in fur-bearing and other animals of the chase; and most of the great fur companies, at one time or other, had trading posts on it. It is not clear from Garrioch's narrative just where his trading operations were carried on. The probable point, however, was at the southern extremity of its great loop southward in North Dakota, where it is joined by the small stream known as Wintering Creek." Dale and Durlene disagreed with Reverend Gunn on the latter point. They interpreted the following paragraph of the diary as indicating that Peter's post on the river was in British territory.

On the other hand, Sandra has found some authority (other than Gunn) for the location of the Souris River Post to have been on American Territory. G. A. McMorron, "Souris River Posts & David Thompson's Diary of His Historical Trip Across the Souris Plains to the Mandan Villages in the Winter of 1797-98," *Annual Report of the Manitoba Historical and Scientific Society* (1950), p. 17, wrote: "Just one brief note with regard to Peter Garrioch's post on the Mouse [Souris] River. Garrioch, whose diary covers the years 1843 to 1845, was one of the most bitter opponents of the Hudson's Bay Company monopoly. He tells us of his Mouse River post and his numerous trips between it and Red River. The site of his post is still unknown, and Garrioch has left us very little to work on. It was likely in the Melita District south of the American boundary. In one of his diary entries he tells us of experiencing 'a March thunderstorm off the tail of the Turtle Mountains' (below, entry for March 25, 1844]. His trail to and from Red River must have therefore, been along the Turtle Mountain, probably to the south, and then by way of the Back Fat Lakes, the Rock Lake chain of today. In other places [below, text at notes 293-303; Appendix II, text and nn. 848-850), he tells us he was deprived of his Mouse River post due to the authority given its agents by the United States Congress to seize all posts that 'sold ardent spirits.' His post must have been in America territory." On p. 18, McMorron gives the [erroneous] dates of 1843-1845 as the period during which Peter "operated a small post on the Mouse River south of Melita on the American side." *Ibid.,* & *passim.*

Chapter 5 – Trading On The Missouri

The French word for mouse is "souris," and the river on which Garrioch was stationed in 1842-3, a tributary of the Assiniboine, is still known in Canada as the Souris. Its southern extension in the United States, where Garrioch's post seems to have been located, was and is called the Mouse River. The company he was working for, formally called the American Fur Company, was still popularly known by the name John Jacob Aster originally gave it, the Missouri Fur Company. Peter's account of his (presumably) first trading-post responsibility opens with preparations to transport the fruits of the past winter's trading operations over the continental divide to Fort Clark, a company command post on the Missouri River.

An Inconvenient Change of Heart

After spending the winter at this post with a few Rupertian[269] families, I returned to Missouri in the beginning of April [1843[270]] with such returns as my trade afforded.[271] I had various difficulties to contend {150} with, however, before I could finally transport my trade, etc., to Fort Clark. I had hired two of the Rupertians to assist me in carrying my effects over to Missouri. But, apprehending upon secondary consideration (which, by the way, was after some time) that their horses would not be able to return to Red River in consequence of their poverty,[272] they retracted their engagement and turned back to their families.

The map of Peter's travels associated with his diaries at the Archives of Manitoba gives no guidance on the location of the Souris/Mouse River post, since, oddly, that post is not even indicated on it (Appendix II – Maps).

269   Inhabitants of Rupert's Land – a term perhaps coined by Garrioch, perhaps to differentiate them from the denizens of the United States with whom he was now in frequent contact. Some families with HBC connections still describe themselves with the variant "Rupertslanders," as Jennifer S. H. Brown learned from an interview in 1972 with Ruby and Barbara Johnstone in Selkirk and reported in *Strangers in Blood*, p. 216.

270   1843 is inserted here by hand, probably by Gunn, on p. 149 in his typescript which continues without dates indicated for Garrioch's entries, until dated entries resume on p. 166 of the Gunn typescript, at the beginning of 1844.

271   The Company's nearest post was at Fort Clark on the Missouri River, from which Garrioch had apparently traveled to Mouse River in the fall of 1842, and to which he was now returning with the furs he had traded during the winter.

272   If "poverty" was not a mistaken transcription on Gunn's part, Garrioch's meaning is difficult to fathom. The editors' best guess is that the Rupertian defectors feared that their horses' physical resources would be so depleted by the arduous journey that they would not be able to travel back to Red River thereafter.

Fortunately, I had another man to depend on, who arrived from the Turtle Mountains[273] just as the other two had made up their minds to decline going with me. With this man, I started for the Missouri, taking each of us a horse [but] being obliged to leave all my effects at my post till I could get assistance from Mr. Chardon, who {151} was then Post Master at Fort Clark.[274] Our horses, being rather of an indifferent race, became so dispirited and fagged that we were under the painful necessity of footing a great part of our way.

On the fourth day from our starting point, we crossed the Missouri at Fort Clark.[275] Mr. Chardon was glad to see us, and treated us with much kindness, as evidently manifested his sincerity.

---

273   Gunn: "A high range of hilly country lying partly in Rolette and Bottineau Counties, North Dakota, and partly in the Souris District of Manitoba. The range of hills is so called because of some real or fancied resemblance to a great turtle basking on the prairie. Its head faces a little to the west, and its tail south of east. The highest peaks are Bear Butte, to the west, and Butte St. Paul, to the southeast of the range. These buttes can be seen from a long distance across the prairie, and furnish an excellent lookout for [anyone] who might wish to have a panoramic view of the surrounding regions."

274   Gunn: "Francis A. Chardon, one of the best-known (and one of the least favourably-known) traders on the Missouri at that time. He had charge of various posts on the upper Missouri from time to time [and was at Fort Clark] in 1843. With reference to Chardon's character, Chittenden (*Early Steamboat Navigation on the Missouri*, F. P. Harper, 1903, I, p. 231) has this to say: 'Chardon was the same manner of man as was Alex Harvey.' And when we know that Alex Harvey was one of the most notorious desperados on the Missouri further comment on Chardon along this line is unnecessary. His conspiracy with Harvey in the affair at Fort McKenzie above referred to (Larpenteur, *Forty Years a Fur Trader on the Upper Missouri*, ed. Coues, Elliott, (New York, Francis P. Harper, 1898), I, pp. 218-9; Chittenden, I, pp. 694-5) fully bears out this [description]. In 1846 he was ordered out of the Indian country by the Indian Department of the US government for selling liquor to the Indians – a mandate which he does not seem to have obeyed, as he was still there in 1848, when Palliser passed through. (Palliser, p. 263)." The work of Palliser's to which Gunn was referring is *Solitary Rambles and Adventures of a Hunter in the Prairies* (London, John Murray, 1853), where on p. 263, Palliser describes being at the Fort when Chardon died after requesting Palliser to help him write his will.

275   Gunn: "This establishment, otherwise known as the Post of the Mandans, was on the south bank of the Missouri River. It was built by the American Fur Company in 1831 as the headquarters of their trade with the Mandans, Grosventres, and allied tribes in that vicinity. It stood about three quarters of a mile below the old Fort Mandan of Lewis and Clark, at a point about 56 miles above the present Bismarck, North Dakota. It was one of the most important posts of the American Fur Company on the Missouri. (See Coues' note in Larpenteur, I, pp. 142-3.)"

Reinforcements from Fort Clark

After spending two days with Mr. Chardon, I started back with three men he had ordered and my former hireling; [and] with as many horses and mules as were necessary to carry over my [buffalo] robes and other effects – which I had left at my post in the care of my house and a whole generation of mice. After traveling four days midst storms, rain, and sunshine alternately, we succeeded in opening the door of my winter residence, which I had closed mechanically when leaving it. We found everything safe, and much in the same condition as when I left, [except that] the mice had been actively employed to a small degree.

Non-Guns

It is worthy of remark that the three men who were sent to assist me had, [not one] of them, a [workable] gun or anything else in the way of weapons that might afford the means of defence in a case of necessity. One of them, to be sure, had the form and shape of a gun; but that was {152} all, for it wanted all the qualities of such a weapon. I took it out and snapped it about 10 or 15 times before I could see the least spark, notwithstanding [that] the flint was passable. My second man had also something in the shape of a gun, but it lacked in length. It measured about 2 feet; and neither the point nor the butt [was] original. I told the man that carried it not to depend on it as a gun, should we be attacked by the enemy, but as a Pugamagon.[276] My third man had also a gun, by name, but it was ridiculous to the last degree. It was about a foot and a half in length and had neither make nor shape. Like the former, it had little to do with originality, except the lock. To such a shameful degree had it been mutilated, by cutting from both ends, that it had been reduced to little else than [the flint]lock. [If] it had not been for the difference in colour of the wood and iron, one could scarcely have distinguished the stock from the barrel. It might have killed a mouse at {153} the distance of a foot; but beyond that I would not undertake to say what it could kill. It was exceedingly providential that we met with nothing which required that desperate resistance that is realized on a field of battle.

---

276   Gunn: "An Indian war club."

A Successful Haul

After a delay of five days at my post for the purpose of reviving[277] our horses and mules, we started back, leaving 2,000 pounds of [buffalo][278] grease behind under the care of a wolverine and half a dozen wolves. [We] arrived at Fort Clark on the sixth day, having encountered comparatively little inconvenience.

Miles of Buffalo Corpses

Here I remained 10 days, and then went down with Mr. Chardon to Fort Pierre in a canoe manned by three men besides ourselves. Nothing of any note occurred during our voyage. Nor was there anything to be seen that claimed particular attention, [other than] that the beaches of the {154} Missouri and other rivers were strewed with the carcasses of buffalos that had perished, either in falling through the ice in the fall, or crossing in the spring. The mangled carcasses of [buffalo] calves, also, which had perished [by reason of both] a storm that had taken place a few days before we left Fort

---

277 *Sic*? Gunn's word was "recruiting."

278 This amount seems enormous until one contemplates the massive numbers of buffalo trapped in many of the hunts in those days; for a vivid description, see pp. 406-407 in: "The Diary of Martin McLeod," ed. Grace Lee Nute, in *Manitoba History Bulletin* 4:7-8 (Aug.-Nov. 1922), pp. 351-439 & 521, published by Minnesota Historical Society Press, wherein in 1836 McLeod described how families set out with 500 or 600 carts drawn principally by oxen and smoked the meat on poles as fast as it was killed by the hunters. "It requires the flesh of twelve of the largest animals thus prepared to load a cart drawn by one ox – and allowing 600 carts in the spring season would make 7,200 of these animals killed in about a month....the Pemmican is made by drying the meat as I before mentioned. It is then beaten into small pieces and placed into a sack made of the Buffalo skin – into which is pour'd a quantity of the melted fat of the animal. When it cools, it is pressed into the sack which is sewed up. In this manner it will keep for 3 or 4 years. The sacks are various sizes but the common sizes are from 100 to 150 lbs. The usual number of horsemen attending these hunts are about 500. However not more than from two to 300 act as hunters and are those who possess the swiftest horses…. A gentleman who has lived may years in the Buffalo Country says that upon the least Calculation four to five hundred thousand of these animals are killed years on this side the Missouri." Peter's reference, a few lines below in this entry, to "[t]he mangled carcasses of [buffalo] calves, …extend[ing] for hundreds of miles on the banks of the Missouri" vividly illustrates the point. For a similarly vivid account of a buffalo hunt at the beginning of the 19th century, see "To Red River and Beyond," *The Nor'-Wester* (August 28, 1860). J. M. Bumsted offers a countervailing view of the alleged wastefulness of the buffalo hunts on the eventual decimation of the buffalo on the American continent, by pointing out the convenience of the conclusion for those invested in "taming" Indigenous peoples to a more settled way of life: *Trials & Tribulations: The Red River Settlement and the Emergence of Manitoba 1811-1870* (Great Plains Publications, 2003), pp. 95-97. In his excerpt from McLeod's journal, Gunn says it is dated at St. Peters, May, 1837: Gunn, "Buffalo Hunting in the West," MG9 A78-1, A78-3.

Clark and starving and ravenous wolves, extended for hundreds of miles on the banks of the Missouri.[279]

Fort Pierre

Fort Pierre is but an indifferent log house, but [it is] almost infinitely superior to Fort Clark. It is about three times as large as the latter, and though it has within its pickets some very mean buildings, there are others that look well for an Indian country and trade. This post has, at all seasons of the year, a great deal of employment. But particularly is this the case in the spring, when the various outposts scattered throughout the country bring in the returns of their trade. After waiting ten or fifteen days, the steamboat made its appearance. We took passage in her, and returned to Fort Clark, where we landed on our fifth day from Fort Pierre.

An Abominable Scene

Never shall I forget the abominable scene I witness{155}ed on the boat on the evening we landed. From the time we landed, which was about nine o'clock in the morning, till dusk, the boat was crowded with men, women and children of the Ree, Grosventres and Mandan tribes. The great end which these poor, ignorant, and licentious wretches had in view in flocking so eagerly to the boat appeared to me to be not so much to cohabit with the whites for the pleasure of the thing, as for the remuneration they expected after the 'rutting' business was over.[280] I cannot dignify the scene by any milder term. If I should, I could not but charge myself with detracting from common decency. Fathers and mothers led their daughters, and husbands their wives, to the obscene and abominable shrine of Venus, as parents lead their children to the sacred font of baptism, or their daughters to the Divine Altar of Matrimony.

Never, perhaps, since the days of Adam, or since public markets were first instituted, did any species of animal or goods prove more marketable, or meet with more general demand and ready sale than the hindquarters of these ignoble and prostitute females. I am perfectly justified in making use of epithets regarding these abandoned women

---

279   A note by Gunn refers to further accounts of massive exterminations of buffalo by natural forces at other times and places.

280   Examples of transactions involving women between French and British Canadians in their trade dealings with Indigenous peoples – though none so extreme and raw as this episode Peter was describing from the American fur trade river-boat frontier – are described by Jennifer S. H. Brown in *Strangers in Blood,* pp. 83-90.

which, I am aware, ought in justice to be applied to the brute creation alone, as they are totally divested of everything approaching decency, the very shadow of it even. Not the slightest regard was paid to virtuous appearance or personal qualities. If the object that was led to the shrine of ...Venus bore the semblance of a woman, it was enough. The reality was taken on, to be desirous in the secret chamber.[281] I will give a single specimen to confirm the above assertions.

A certain man in the boat, a cook by employment if I remember right, requested a free-man of the place to make arrangements with a woman for[{156} him, and bring her to his cabin. The freeman was somewhat of an eccentric turk. He went out and led in a 'harmless' one to the door of the said cook. Just at that moment the cook, who was eagerly on the lookout, met his agent with, as he supposed, a fair, or at least a young damsel in his hand. The freeman, however, gave him no time to put any questions, should he be disposed, but forthwith advised him to drag her in with all haste and close the door; for, said he, she is one of the fairest among all the tribes; and, if the other young men should see her, they will take her from you. The night had advanced and the lights were extinguished; and, her face being mantled, counterfeiting bashfulness, as instructed by the freeman, the fiery libertine had not the privilege of examining her personal qualities even by the dim light which the stars afforded. Perfectly satisfied, however, that her general appearance indicated her to be a woman, he pulled her up into his bed, and doubtless felt as independent and tranquil as if he had won a wreath of permanent glory. Poor enchanted mortal! No doubt he discovered by the glorious morning sun, who is the test and touchstone of all beauty, that his night-shade laurels were such as no one would give him a squint look for. When the bright and penetrating rays of the early sun darted into his chamber, the enchanted but miserably duped darted from his fair companion in horror, whom he had enjoyed and kissed so pleasantly all the night long.

---

281   It is notable that Gunn included this striking passage in his typescript, albeit without any note, explanatory or otherwise. Sandra has reinserted the passage, choosing Peter's language over Gunn's where they differ, since it illustrates in a single example not only a certain crudity and insensitivity on Garrioch's part to female exploitation, but also the sordid underbelly of trader/Indigenous relations at the time. Anne Lindsey points out that there are not many contemporaneous glimpses into what attitudes were toward women whom some may have construed as living in the lower echelons of society and that this passage gives additional insight into Peter Garrioch's character and class attitudes; in any event, he appears to have been genuinely shocked by what he was observing. Email from Lindsay to Anderson (June 19, 2023).

Chapter 5 – Trading On The Missouri 143

How would he ever have discovered the deception, had not the sun been gracious unto him. She scarce had an eye in her head. Her features were variously distorted through age and a long course of licentiousness and her locks had arrived at a stage between white and grey. {157}] Her strong ones [legs?] had many years bowed themselves under the weight of licentious corruption. In a word, her whole frame was tottering to its kindred dust and leaning on the verge of the grave. The duped wretch, unconscious of guilt, shame, decency or honour, paid her off her hire and sent her away with a glee. Fifty percent premium for the hind quarters of old women of the Missouri!! Better than any bank in the United States! Go it, Yankees![282]

Return to Red River

After the conclusion of the above sublime doings, the boat proceeded to Fort Union,[283] and in nine days returned to Fort Clark, whence she puffed away down to St. Louis.

After loitering about Fort Clark a few days longer, I started for Red River [overland] in company with Potchya[284] and family, and two other men. A Ree {158} strumpet completed the party.

---

282 In *The Fur Trade on the Upper Missouri, 1840-1865* (Norman: University of Oklahoma Press, 1965), p. 67, n. 30, John E. Sunder describes the maelstrom of activity at the landing of the boat passing between Fort Pierre and Fort Clark, then elaborates by referring to this passage in "Garrioche's" diary of 1844-47. In doing so, he borrowed from Garrioch's description in some detail, but treated it with scepticism: "at least Garrioche said so." Sunder provided no explanation whatsoever for his scepticism, and the fourth editor suspects it can be attributed less to any particular scepticism about its accuracy than to the distasteful content of the passage. Indeed, it is curious that, while the second and third editors chose not to include it, the Reverend Gunn did include it, and as a result, it has been restored to its place here after all.

283 Gunn: "This fort was, for quite a number of years, the most important – from both a historic and commercial point of view – of any of the great trading posts of the Missouri. It stood on the north bank of the Missouri River about three miles above the mouth of the Yellowstone River, just within the eastern boundary of Montana. It was begun in 1828 under Kenneth McKenzie […] and a large part of its historical interest comes from the fact that this gentleman made it his headquarters for almost the entire period of his fur trade career. [McKenzie fathered the woman who later became Garrioch's wife, as well as her sister, of whom more will be learned in this chapter.] Completed in 1833, Fort Union was at first christened Fort Floyd, the name Union being given to commemorate [the union of the Colombia Fur Company and the American Fur Company]. Besides being the scene of many thrilling episodes connected with the fur trade and frontier life of those early days, Fort Union had the distinction of being the temporary resting place of such distinguished travelers as George Catlin, the artist [and] Audubon the great naturalist – here being produced much of those scientific notes, beautiful drawings of plants, animals and scenery, and other material that has come down to the world as a precious legacy. (See Chittenden, *American Fur Trade*, I, p. 327.)"

284 Gunn: "Pochien: a well-known French Métis family of the Red River Settlement at that time. There were two brothers of this name. They were half brothers of William Gaddy, the great buffalo hunter

Hunting Buffalo

On our ninth day from Fort Clark, we fell in with the hunting party of Red River.[285] The hunters then divided into three different parties, and I followed that party which promenaded the prairies towards the Turtle Mountain. After wandering about the prairies with these buffalo hunters for five or six weeks, I returned to Red River in company with another man. During my stay with the hunters I had three runs, and killed two cows and two bulls. [Having] a great eye to generation, I went by couples so as to preserve a proper and regular ratio in the species!

A Gloomy and Fearful Night

The night before I reached home was to me the most gloomy and fearful one. My man had become totally fagged, and I had been under the painful necessity of contenting myself under a bower rudely afforded by a number of sapling poplars and shrubbery, which I came to precisely at the moment when the thick gathering clouds, and peals of thunder rolling from one end of the Earth to the other in rapid succession, were threatening to disgorge an overwhelming shower and tempest upon me. I had kindled a fire, the evening being cool and airish, but, having nothing to cook, I went to bed hungry. There being no water, I was perished also with excessive thirst. Having arranged my pillow and my saddle bags and other trifles, I covered myself with the only blanket I had, awaiting the consequences of the impending storm. On my back, at full length, I opened my mouth and thankfully received each blessed drop as it dreaded, till Nature unconsciously sank under the {159} power of the night. The thunders roared, the lightnings flashed, and the waters from above fell down in mighty torrents; but Peter had soon been lulled to sleep by them.

---

and Indian fighter, and were themselves noted along those same lines. Souza Pochien, the one probably referred to here, lived at this time on the east side of the Red River, just above the present Parkdale, Manitoba. In 1851 or 1852 they moved to Portage la Prairie, being among the founders of that place, but later lived at High Bluff. During the Riel uprising of 1869-70, they accompanied the Portage volunteers to Kildonan Church, and there captured Parisien after the shooting of Sutherland. They were originally Catholic, but turned Protestant, and belonged to the following of Archdeacon Cochrane. See Reverend A. C. Garrioch, *First Furrows*, pp. 228-29." Although not mentioned by name here, William Gaddy married Mary Marguerite Garrioch, daughter of William Garrioch and Nancy Cook in 1835, so he was Peter's brother-in-law. Later, after he was allowed to escape from Riel's soldiers, Geddy and his wife were eventually photographed in 1891 by George Henry Gunn: information from Métis Museum website.

285 This would be part of the annual largely-Métis spring buffalo hunt.

Peter in Love

Based on Garrioch's various previous estimates of travel times, he seems to have arrived back at Red River in early August, 1843, – his journal entries are undated for some time – and probably remained there for about a month before returning to his trade activities. Two pages were removed from the journal at this point, so whatever he wrote about the Red River visit is missing. The entry immediately following the gap suggests, however, that the deleted pages related, at least in part, to a love interest having entered Peter Garrioch's life.

He was in love with, and had apparently become at least informally engaged to, Isabella McKenzie,[286] one of two daughters of a prominent fur-trader named Kenneth McKenzie.[287] A former wintering partner with the Northwest Company who had, like Peter's father, been made redundant by that company's 1821 merger with the Hudson's Bay Company, McKenzie had joined John Jacob Astor's American Fur Company, and conducted that firm's Missouri River operations with great success for several years. There is no evidence known to the editors that Garrioch ever met him, even when engaged by the AFC, unless their paths crossed later when Garrioch visited St. Louis briefly.[288]

When McKenzie moved to the Missouri he left both his native "country wife" and their two young daughters, Isabella and Margaret, at Red River. The girls were eventually enrolled at the Red River Academy, the Anglican residential school which was at that time run by one John McCallum.[289] The Academy catered to parents who, like McKenzie, could afford sub-

---

286 The spelling of Isabella's surname varied; as many sources spelled it MacKenzie as McKenzie. She would have been in her late teens at this point.

287 Not to be confused with the even better-known Northwest Company trader, Kenneth MacKenzie, who drowned near Sault Ste. Marie in 1816. See Jean Morrison, "Kenneth MacKenzie," *DCB* V, pp. 543-544. Gluek, *Minnesota and the Manifest Destiny*, pp. 33-37, describes McKenzie and his partners William Laidlaw, Joseph Renville, et al, as "Hudson's Bay men who had deserted the Company. Without exception, they were men of little principle, energetic and unscrupulous traders making their way in a lawless environment and giving to all fur traders an infamous reputation that is too often undeserved," but in his case, McKenzie was a "thoroughly unsatisfactory servant who ignored orders, squandered Company property, and preferred the company of the Red River half-breeds to the isolation of the Souris," including urging some of them to relocate across the border, as Simpson noted sourly in 1823. See Chap. 7, entry for May 4, 1845, and n. 503.

288 See Chap. 9, entry for September 20, 1846, and nn. 679-681.

289 Gunn: "John Macallum originally hailed from Scotland and received the major portion of his higher education at King's College, Aberdeen. Having gone to London, he fell in with Reverend D. T. Jones of Red River Settlement, who induced him to accompany him upon his return there in 1833. Macallum's special mission to Red River was the establishment of a select boarding school, for the education of the sons and daughters of such in the Settlement and throughout the fur country as desired and could afford something more advanced than the ordinary parochial schools of the day. This school, which was the nucleus out of which grew the present St. John's College, [Macallum] organized, and conducted, first as a church school, later as a private enterprise assisted by the Hudson's Bay Company. Mr. Macallum was admitted to holy orders in the summer of 1844. From this date to 1847, his duties included the incumbency of St. John's parish church, in addition to his school responsibilities. He also held the office of assistant chaplain, later, chaplain

stantial tuition fees. But their mother seems to have been altogether abandoned by their father. Letitia Hargrave, the wife of the HBC's York Factory's James Hargrave (where he became Chief Factor in 1844), and history's primary source of Red River gossip (gleaned from itinerant fur traders) for this period, left a poignant vignette of the McKenzie girls and their mother. At McCallum's school, she said:

> If the mothers are not legally married they are not allowed to see their children. This [...] is fearfully cruel, for the poor unfortunate mothers did not know there was any distinction, and it is only within the last few years that anyone was so married. [...] The two [McKenzie] girls were [...] of course prohibited from having any intercourse with their mother, who is in a miserable state of destitution. The poor creature sits in some concealment at McCallums' with deer's head or some such delicacy ready cooked for her daughters, and they slip out and see her. And as she is almost naked they steal some of their own clothes and give them to her. This is a fearful fault, and the young ladies suffer for it [...].

As for how the girls were punished for meeting and aiding their mother, the same letter explained that: "Children [...] suffer from [...] severe floggings, confinement after any fault, and the total want of the following meal."[290]

The sister with whom Peter Garrioch was enamoured was Isabella. Like John Macallum, Peter had been a Red River schoolmaster, though at schools for younger children. Whether he had met Isabella and her sister as pupils when he taught at the Red River day school or

---

to the HBC, as well as that of member of the Council of Assiniboia. He died in 1849." Macallum was boys' teacher at the Red River Academy beginning in 1834 and became principal from 1836 until his death in 1849: A. C. Garrioch, *Correction Line*, p. 102. See also J. M. Bumsted, "John Macallum," *DMB*, p. 147. A dark view of his pedagogy is found in Ladd, "Father Cockran and His Children," p. 64; "unconditional obedience" was the ultimate outcome of good schooling, p. 65.

290 *The Letters of Letitia Hargrave,* edited with an introduction by Margaret Arnett Macleod. Champlain Society Publications XXVIII (Toronto, 1947), pp. 177-8: letter to Mrs. Dugald Mactavish (September 14-17, 1843). The passage begins with a stern indictment of the entire school: "They say that Mr. MacCallum's school is going to wreck. Children who have had duck geese & venison 3 times a day are supposed to suffer from breakfasts of milk & water with dry bread, severe floggings, confinement after any fault & the total want of the following meal. The boys & girls are constantly fainting but MacCallum won't change his system. Many girls have got ill, and as he makes them strip off their Indian stockings & adopt English fashions it is not surprising. They must take a certain walk every day, plunging thro' the freezing snow. They wear Indian shoes, but without the cloth stockings or leggings over them the snow gets in & I need not say that the feelings one undergoes are not comfortable." For more on this unfortunate situation, see Van Kirk, *Many Tender Ties*, p. 165. Despite the fact that his own mother and sisters were subjected to Macallum's punitive style, A. C. Garrioch "drank the cool-aid" and later defended Macallum: " so, whatever may be said about Mr. John Macallum, this, at least can never be said – that he 'spared the rod and spoiled the child.'...so that his conscientious pupils will know that he does not flog then because he can't nor because they don't deserve it, but because he respects their feelings and hated to do it." A. C. Garrioch, *Correction Line*, pp. 100-101, quoted in Ladd, "Father Cockran and His Children," p. 64.

Chapter 5 – Trading On The Missouri

Sunday school is unknown, but that seems a plausible conjecture. In any event, he now knew Isabella as a young woman, had fallen in love with her, and his love was reciprocated by the young lady.[291] **But Peter had a livelihood to earn a long way from home, and all he could do for the time being was to yearn.**

Back to the Missouri

Soon after the reception of the last letter from my fair intended, which wanted not in glowing and flowing "dears," "adieus," and "goodbyes," I took leave of my sweet, sweet damsel,[292] of all my friends, and returned again to Missouri, having made previous arrangements with the American Fur Company to trade for them at Mouse River the following winter (1843-44). On my twentieth day from Red River I arrived at the Missouri.

Mouse River Visitors

On my way thither, I called at my last winter's residence to see how the grease fared which I had left in [the] care of a wolverine and 500 wolves. I could not possibly have left the articles under more careful hands. Such was their faithfulness to their charge that not one particle was to be seen of about thirty cakes [of buffalo grease], weighing thirty pounds, which I had elevated three feet from the ground. Of six bags [of the same], which I had placed on poles extending from one beam to another, only two and a half bags remained. On examination, I found that Mr. Wolverine had walked in, not by the door, nor yet as a thief who climbs, but by digging his way under the logs of the house. There being no floor, he met no obstacles. And in went after him the whole fraternity of wolves, foxes, minks, raccoons, &c, &c, and feast{160}ed on my grease like a set of lordly rebels. Having left this grease agreeably to Mr. Chardon's orders, no fault could be found with me, nor anything required for damages.

Bad News

When I arrived at [the] Missouri, I found Mr. Ledlow[293] there, who had ar{161}rived the day before from St. Louis. The first intelligence I received from him was by no

---

291   See below, nn. 335-336, and Chap. 7, entry for March 23, 1845, and nn. 481, 482.

292   Does Peter's reference to Isabella as his "fair intended" indicate that the couple was engaged, at least informally, by this point? The present editors believe that it does.

293   Gunn: "Laidlaw is intended. This is the same William Laidlaw who figures in the note on p. 84. He came out from Scotland to Red River Settlement about 1818 in the employ of Lord Selkirk as

means pleasant, and contrary to anything I had expected. He regretted to inform me, he said, that, agreeably to orders just issued from Washington, [the Company's] limits for fur trading for the future were so much retrenched [that] they could not send [a trader] to Mouse River without incurring the displeasure of the [Indian] Agent, thus exposing their property to confiscation.

The using of ardent spirits[294] as an article of trade to the natives was what brought about the foregoing restrictions. The American Government, he said, had for several years back been attempting to put a complete stop to the dealing out of ardent spirits to the Indians, and at different times and by various methods, and could never succeed. Finding that the evil was rather on the increase than otherwise, they were now under the necessity of making use of the most rigorous measures in order to discourage the traders and compel them to relinquish every attempt to bring spiritous liquors to the country for the Indians. In the event of their being discovered selling ardent spirits to any Indian, everything in the post or place where such ardent spirits are sold was to be seized by the Agent or his Deputy, by authority of Congress.

Complex Motivation

Gunn was of the opinion that this development had a more complicated explanation than the journal records:

> **The Act of Congress prohibiting the taking of intoxicating liquors into the Indian country was passed on July 9, 1832, and was consequently no new feature of the Indian trade at this time. The [full] explanation of the situation that confronted Garrioch is to be found rather in a new departure instituted by the Indian Department in the early part of 1843: the revival of the office of Indian Agent for the tribes of the upper Missouri, and the appointment thereto of a determined and fearless incumbent in the person of Andrew Drips.**

---

superintendent of [the] experimental farm at Hayfield. (Gunn, *History of Manitoba*, p. 236.) In 1821, the experimental farm not having proven a success, he left the Red River colony and made his way south to Prairie du Chien, whence, becoming interested in the fur trade, he engaged in that pursuit [with several companies.] Of him, Chittenden says (*Fur Trade*, I, p. 387): 'Next to Kenneth Mackenzie, he was the ablest of the traders who came to the Missouri with the Columbia Fur Company.' Like Mackenzie, also, he was a great autocrat – a lordly nabob among his subordinates. He wore a military uniform and, according to Larpenteur (I, p.160), was considerable of a tyrant. [*sic*] A somewhat piquant summary of Laidlaw's character is given by the same author (I, p. 162) as follows: 'Mr. Laidlaw the Father, Mr. Denig the Son, and Mr. Jacques Bruguière the Holy Ghost, formed the Trinity at Union last winter – and a trio of greater drunkards could not have been got together.'"

294   Distilled liquor.

> The revival of this office was brought about through the instrumentality of the American Fur Company itself, for the following reason. They were at that time beset by a swarm of little opposition companies [which], small and inconspicuous, and having less at stake, could take the risks, dodge up and down the rivers, and peddle whiskey to their heart's content, thus putting at a disadvantage their giant rival, and making serious inroads into its trade.
>
> It wasn't that the AFC had any conscientious scruples about selling the Indians whiskey. They were notorious for this very thing. But they were too big and conspicuous to play the game against these small fry without taking chances they couldn't well afford to take. With whiskey eliminated altogether, they had no fear of any opposition and so, as a good piece of strategy, they used their influence to have this office revived – and to have appointed to it Drips, one of their own traders. Drips, who was a [conscientious] and energetic fellow, did not take his job as a sinecure, but instituted and carried on a vigorous campaign to break up this traffic among the opposition traders.
>
> This campaign was in full progress when Garrioch reached the Missouri in the spring of 1843. The AFC, having encouraged the campaign, was naturally on its good behaviour. They weren't using any liquor just then; and to send a man up to the Mouse River to contend against [competitors who used it] was not, in their estimation, a good business proposition.[295]

The AFC representative's explanation for closing the Mouse River post leaves little doubt that Garrioch's trading the previous season had been lubricated by ardent spirits.

In consequence of these new regulations, I was deprived of my {162} post at Mouse River; and the only alternative[s] I had [were] to go down to Fort Pierre to await Mr. Picotte's arrival from St. Louis, or to return to Red River immediately. Mr. Picotte[296] had told me in the summer to consider myself as engaged for a twelvemonth at the rate of $400.

A Quick Trip Home

Garrioch chose the second alternative – immediate return to Red River. If he shared his reasons for that decision with his diary, we will never know what they were, because there is another two-page deletion at this point. Speculation is possible, however. The likelihood that a long paddle or an expensive steamboat trip to Fort Pierre would produce employment was slender. And the now-abandoned Mouse River post, in or near British territory, offered the young man a tempting commercial opportunity. Whisky trading was just as illegal in Rupert's Land as in the United States, but enforcement was lax north of the border. So why not re-open the post under his own auspices? He would have to acquire

---

295 Gunn, pp. 161-162.

296 Gunn's note identifies this man as Honoré Picotte, a veteran fur trader who was in charge of the AFC's Fort Pierre operations at the time but was temporarily absent.

trade goods somehow, of course, but there was just enough time left for a quick trip home to obtain supplies before the trading season began. Financing such a large purchase would be difficult, but the would-be entrepreneur thought he knew how it might be arranged.

{163} I and a boy started for Red River in company with several men of the [buffalo] hunters, who were taking green leather[297] for the market. My object in going was to cancel some of my old standing debts, and to procure goods on credit for my trade at Mouse River. I started with the amount of twelve pounds sterling in [buffalo] tongues, fur, and some tobacco. Thirty shillings of this I lost – I could not find out how. Another thirty shillings I gave and squandered away unnecessarily – a new method of gaining a fortune speedily!

Messrs. Sinclair & McDermot

The first order of business at Red River was to acquire trading stock, and Garrioch lost no time entering into negotiations to do so. Approaching the Hudson's Bay Company was out of the question, because it had been granted a fur trading monopoly under its 1670 Royal Charter[298] and, although critics pointed out that such monopolies had been outlawed by Parliament, the Company was still vigorously exercising its alleged Charter rights against free traders, employing Red River's law enforcement machinery, which it controlled. He accordingly took his proposal to independent merchants James Sinclair and Andrew McDermot.

McDermot, of Irish origin, was the senior of the two. He had come to Rupert's Land as an HBC employee, but had been in business for himself long enough by this time to have become Red River's wealthiest resident. James Sinclair, born five years before Peter Garrioch, also to an HBC employee from the Orkneys and his native wife, had been educated in Scotland, and had achieved considerable success at Red River as a freelance businessman. He was also Peter's uncle, undoubtedly a factor that the younger man hoped would strengthen his suit.[299]

Both McDermot and Sinclair were opposed to the HBC's attempts to stifle free trade in furs, and were occasionally suspected of violating the Charter themselves, though they maintained an uneasy working relationship with the Company much of the time. They

---

297 Uncured buffalo robes.

298 For a recent, well-illustrated, bird's-eye view of the history of fur-trading in North America and its consequences for the peoples and animals involved, see Jonathan Faiers, *Fur: A Sensitive History* (Yale University Press, 2020), pp. 42-56.

299 Both McDermot and Sinclair are to be found in the *DCB*, and the latter is more fully treated in D. Geneva Lent, *West of the Mountains: James Sinclair and the Hudson's Bay Company* (Seattle: University of Washington Press, 1963), as well as in Gibson, *LLG*, I. The former receives extensive treatment in: Brian Richardson, "Manitoba History: The Quality of Friendship: Andrew McDermot and George Simpson," *Manitoba History* 46 (Autumn/Winter, 2003-2004): pp. 27-36. Both men are described in Gluek, *Minnesota and the Manifest Destiny*, pp. 48-69.

Chapter 5 – Trading On The Missouri

partnered with each other for particular projects, and it was as a team that would-be free trader Garrioch approached them. They would drive a hard bargain.

On my arrival at Red River, I immediately acquainted Messrs. Sinclair and McDermot of my intentions, which they were at once disposed {164} to look favourably upon. I told them that I could not give security of any kind, as I had neither money nor property; and, therefore, if they did not choose to let me have goods entirely on their own responsibility I should prefer applying to some other person. They philosophized a little on the subject, and then consented to let me have [goods] to the amount of 120 or 130 pounds sterling. The list was drawn up forthwith, with the articles and quantity specified. I was to have the said goods at credit price, which was about 25% over and above their cash selling price.

Everything having been arranged to the satisfaction of all parties, I returned homewards to spend a few days with my friends. In the meantime, the goods were to be packed up and put in readiness against my return, so as to avoid any unnecessary delay and thus enable me to proceed to Mouse River with all speed.

Mortification

"Man is born to trouble," says the divinely-inspired writer, "as the sparks fly upward." I had just escaped the crushing jaws of a vexing disappointment at the Missouri, and here I fell headlong into a worse. On my way back to Mouse River, I called in at Sinclair's for the goods alluded to above. One might conceive more readily than {165} express my confusion and infinitely greater mortification at [learning of] the retraction [of the supply] arrangements![300] They told me bluntly that, upon second

---

300   Because of covert trading by Sinclair, McDermot, and Garrioch, they were suspected of illegal activities, and their freighting contracts were cancelled for failure to pay the HBC-imposed customs duties on goods imported from St. Paul. As a result, they were upset enough to try to sue the HBC over the broken contracts and the loss of freighting fees they claimed the HBC owed them. Gibson, *LLG, I*, p. 91. The oblique references and missing passages in the diaries may be the result of an attempt by Peter or others to expunge the details. Many non-HBC merchants, including Andrew McDermot after he left the HBC's service in 1824, not just Sinclair and Garrioch, felt that the HBC had little or no right to apply tariffs to imports. Recorder Thom was probably behind the excuse proffered by Governors Simpson and Christie to reject the traders' lawsuit by asserting, outrageously, that the Quarterly Court of Assiniboia – the HBC's own court – had no direct jurisdiction over lawsuits against the HBC's monopoly. Having failed to engage the legal process, Sinclair and McDermot fell back on a resort to persuasion, presenting Christie with a list of questions about trading rights, all of which were based on the premise that as "Halfbreeds," they had an aboriginal right to trade in furs. Sinclair's August 29, 1985, petition, & Christie's September 5, 1845, response,

thought, they found they could not possibly let me have the goods without some kind of security.

Like Two Begotten of the Father of Lies

When I put the question: "Why did you not tell me so before, as you knew then as well as you do now that I had not the means of giving security?" They quibbled, sophisticated, manufactured, and lied like two begotten of the Father of Lies. The whole of their reason and reasoning, I afterwards discovered, was nothing more than that, having been informed of the favourable prospect of trade at Mouse River, they perceived that it would be much better for them to send out such articles to their own trader, Antoine Degerlai[301] and thus have all the profits to themselves; whereas if they gave me the goods they would simply have the amount back at their common credit prices, while all the profit over and above that would be mine. {166} Another object they had in view in retracting their promise was to frustrate and discourage me – to deprive me of means for carrying on in my trade.

Back at Mouse River

This setback did not prevent Garrioch returning to the Mouse River post and resuming trading in furs. Somehow – we know not how because eight pages were removed from the journal at this point – he had found a merchant or merchants willing to supply him with trade goods on credit and had headed south once more. Later journal passages will reveal that Garrioch was again on friendly terms with Sinclair, and perhaps with McDermot as

---

are reproduced in Lent, *West of the Mountains*, pp. 176-179 and are described here in Chap. 7, n. 515, and text associated with it, and in Gluek, *Minnesota and the Manifest Destiny*, pp. 56-59. See also Appendix I – Petitions.

301   Gunn: "Usually spelled Dejarlais [or Desjarlais]. In the US census of 1850, Pembina District, two Antoine Degerlais or Dejerlais are enumerated, probably father and son, hailing from Red River. The elder of these, age 54, is probably the same as Garrioch's reference. The late Mrs. Dr. Cowan of Winnipeg, daughter of Sinclair, told me that she remembered this Antoine Dejarlais very well. He was, she said, a French-Canadian trader who had spent considerable time in the US, where, in addition to following his proper vocation, he had picked up some Yankee accomplishments. Among these was that of sleight of hand. She related an amusing story of the first public entertainment she remembered to have attended as a child in what is now Winnipeg: [a show] given by Antoine Dejarlais. The show was very good, she said, but what she particularly remembered about it was the novel admission fee. Small change in currency being a scarce article then in the Red River Settlement, each patron had to present the doorkeeper with a dried buffalo sinew." For more on Antoine Desjarlais and related families, as well as Honoré Picotte, see Heather Devine, *The People who Own Themselves: Aboriginal Ethnogenesis in a Canadian Family, 1660-1900* (University of Calgary Press, 2004), *passim*.

Chapter 5 – Trading On The Missouri

well, before very long. Might the partners have been persuaded to change their minds a second time?

I arrived at Mouse River on the ninth day from my last starting point, and recommenced my trading operations with renewed vigor. And I continued thus even to the date which opened the foregoing preamble [January 2, 1844]. This leaves me now to make remarks on such of the succeeding days as may embrace anything worthy of notice.

Trading, Drinking, Singing, and Chattering

January 3, 1844 – Wednesday. Yesterday, today, and the following embrace[d] much the same subjects: trading, drinking, singing, and a great deal of chattering – as is common on such occasions.

January 10, 1844 – Wednesday. I send off Alexander Fisher to Red River, with some furs, for salt and other articles. {167} Not to be at the trouble of adverting again to the subject, I will leap twenty days before my diary, and state that he returned at the expiration of that period, having gone no further than the Back Fat Lake.[302] Their horses could not get on, on account of the great depth of the snow.[303]

January 29, 1844 – Monday. A child belonging to Baptiste Berzie[304] fell {168} into a dish of boiling fat and died of it ten days later.

---

302 Gunn: "One of the regular trails from Fort Garry to Mouse River and the Missouri in those days passed through [what is now] southwestern Manitoba, by Carman, Thorn Hill, Clearwater, and the Swan Lake country, and this was the one evidently attempted by Fisher and his party. The lake here referred to is probably Swan Lake, the most northerly of the chain – Swan, Rock, and Pelican – which forms the upper waters of the Pembina River west of the Pembina Mountains. These lakes were known to the early explorers and traders by a variety of names – all, however, having the same significance though sometimes corrupted in translation. Alexander Henry Jr., in his journal, refers to them as the 'Rib Bone Lakes, or Lacs du Placottes' (Coues: *Henry*, I, p. 82.) The term 'placotte' among the French was applied to a certain part of the buffalo in the cutting up or "turning out" process. Coues says 'Rib Bone translates the French placotte correctly. We hear of placottes where it is a matter of taking out certain rib pieces in cutting up buffalo.' Tanner says (p. 133): 'We went to Pekaukaune Sahkiegun (Buffalo Hump Lake), two days' journey from the head of the Pembinah River.' 'Buffalo Hump' and 'Back Fat' are practically synonymous terms; and Back Fat Lake seems to have been the name in most common use [by English speakers] in Garrioch's time."

303 Part of a page was deleted from the journal here.

304 Gunn: "In the Red River Settlement census records of 1840, 1843 and 1846 a Baptiste Bercier is listed, but no Berzie appears. Bercier is therefore probably meant. The family were French Métis,

January 30, 1844 – Tuesday. I traded eighty-four [musk]rats, eight swans, and two dressed skins today. For the last articles I gave one of the only two blankets I was worth. Thank heaven I still have a blanket to put under me and a robe over me.

February 3, 1844 – Saturday. Another child of Pierre Lavalee's[305] died of the scarlet fever.

February 5, 1844 – Monday. The wife of Lagress[306] died of the scarlet fever after an illness of only four days.

February 10, 1844 – Saturday. Sold one of my coats for four robes. I still have three remaining, thank fortune.

To Fort Clark

It was time to dispose of the winter's crop of traded furs, and since the HBC would seize them if he transported them back to Red River, Garrioch took them to the AFC post on the Missouri River. That company seems to have had no compunction about accepting pelts from traders not formally connected to it, regardless of their trading methods.

February 14, 1844 – Wednesday. I started, in company with three Rupertians, for the Missouri, and arrived at Fort Clark on our fourth day. The weather is exceedingly warm and favourable. Plenty of bulls, but no cows.[307]

---

and lived up the Assiniboine at what is designated in the census as Grant Town – White Horse Plain, in St. Francois Xavier."

305   Gunn: "It is very difficult to say with certainty, in some of these cases, just who is meant. These names are often spelled differently in the records, and Garrioch makes no pretense of spelling them correctly. The 1843 census shows two Pierre Lavalees. One of these lives with Bercier, and as the Pierre Lavalee of Garrioch is evidently associated with Bercier in the buffalo hunt, I think we may safely conclude that he is the one referred to. This is probably the Pierre Laviellier who was a delegate from St. Francois Xavier to the first convention of Riel in 1869, and who, as a loyalist, went to meet Commissioner [Donald A.] Smith on his way from Pembina [late that year]."

306   Gunn: "The nearest approach to this in the Red River Settlement census records is Legros, and this only appears in 1838. Antoine Legros is put down as age 43, Canadian, Catholic, [with] six children. On p. 57 of the *Records of the General Quarterly Court*, Red River Settlement, in a case against James McDermot, Andrew McDermot testifies that his son, in returning from the plains towards the Missouri quarter had met, among others, Lagraisse. All these likely referred to the same [person]. [In a supplementary note, Gunn adds: Probably Lagrace. There was a French Métis family of that name in the Northwest, one of whom was killed in the so-called Cyprus Hills massacre, north of the Montana boundary, in 1873." See also Gibson, *LLG, II: The Public Interest vs. James McDermot* (Case 18, A56), and Commentary, pp. 47-49.

307   This probably refers to the gender of buffalo sighted along the way.

{169} **February 18, 1844 – Sunday.** Received at Fort Clark intelligence of the deaths of Francis Gardepie, and Meshell Bellemaire's wife. They were both killed by the same party of Sioux – the devils![308]

After purchasing such articles as we required, we bade adieu to our kind old, Mr. Charles Primo,[309] and started back for home. {170} The snow, at this early period of the season, seems to recede before the increasing strength of the sun very rapidly. It begins to turn into pools of standing water, and will doubtless begin its running fashion in a day or two.

February 19, 1844 – Tuesday. Just in time for the good Catholic to commence his fasting, we arrived this afternoon at Mouse River. Tomorrow is the first day of Lent, or Ash Wednesday.

Four Corpses

February 21, 1844 – Wednesday. Four young men start for Red River with four corpses. They expect to be back in twenty days.[310]

Peter a Father?

While writing the above, I was privately informed that the last child begotten by John F——'s wife favoured me to a die [*sic*], and that, therefore, the report must be correct which says the child is mine. All I have to say on the subject is this: if wrestling, laughing, and mimicking with women, and kissing them when convenient, will produce generation and enable them to bring forth sweet, smiling infants, without

---

308 Gunn: "It is probable that both the parties mentioned belonged to the Red River Settlement, as Garrioch's reference would indicate that they were well known to him. In looking through the Red River census records of 1838, 1843, and 1846, I find four Gardipuis families, all living in the White Horse Plains district at Grant Town. One François Gardipuis, aged 50 in 1838, disappears from the record in 1846. In the case of the second of the parties mentioned, [the wife of] Michel Bellhumeur is no doubt meant. There are two of this name listed in the census records above referred to. They lived up the Assiniboine in the same neighbourhood as the Gardipuis, which would account for F. G. and Mrs. B. being together when killed."

309 Gunn: "Charles Primeau, a well-known fur trader on the Missouri during the 30s, 40s, and 50s."

310 Garrioch had recorded five recent deaths, three of them having occurred locally, and there may well have been others earlier in the winter that he did not mention. If local Rupertians wished to bury their deceased loved ones back at Red River, this was the time to transport them: when the impassibly deep snow had subsided somewhat, but the weather was still cold enough to preserve the remains.

any other natural or unnatural effort by either party, then I say, as the world says: the child is mine. And if the begetting of children be so easy, harmless and simple, I'll be hanged by the toes till I have not one remaining, if I don't have a family in less time than one thinks, large enough to keep the Yankees in pumpkin pies, and faith, the Paddies in roasted tatties.

While writing the last paragraph, I received information of the arrival of certain individuals from Red River and Beaver Creek.[311] {171} If information [continues to come] in such rapid succession, I shall soon be crammed up with intelligence, and become a perfect Job; but, as I have a delicious buffalo tongue roasting under the hot embers, I must pull it out and feast upon it before I can find time to hear any more information.

William Garrioch's Death

Singular and strange as it may appear, about half an hour after the above circumstance, I received the melancholy intelligence of my father's death.[312]

Mystery Solved by a Razor

From some notion or other, [I] made a clean sweep of my proud mustachios and whiskers on [receiving] the intelligence of my father's demise. This solved the problem

---

311   Gunn: "The Beaver Creek, or Fort Ellice, post of the Hudson's Bay Company. It belonged to what was known as the Swan River District, and it was located in what is now Birtle municipality in western Manitoba. The creek mentioned is a small stream, about twenty miles in length, rising in the adjacent province of Saskatchewan about midway between Welwyn and Rocanville, whence it flows in a northeasterly direction into the Assiniboine River some 4 miles below the mouth of the Qu'Appelle. All these streams flow through deep, picturesque valleys, the whole region being, in times past, a rich fur preserve and the scene of much fur trading activity. Through this circumstance, there developed in the early part of the [19th] century quite an intercourse between it and the Missouri country. American traders [cut] into the Hudson's Bay Company's trade with the Assiniboines and Crees of the district to such an extent as to force them to build a post here to counteract the opposition. This post was accordingly built in 1831 on the north bank of Beaver Creek, where it flows into the Assiniboine, and was named Fort Ellice in honour of Edward Ellice, the great North West Company partner who had been principally instrumental in bringing about the union of the two companies in 1821, and who [then became] the ruling influence in the united concern."

312   Gunn: "William Garrioch, the author's father, died January 30, 1844." HBCA/AM: Extracts from Registers of Baptisms, Marriages and Burials in Rupert's Land, E.4/2, f. 133, registers William's burial as having occurred at the Upper Church, Red River Settlement, on February 1, 1844.

of a dream which [a friend had had and]³¹³ considered very ominous and mysterious. A few nights ago he had dreamt that he saw the child [reported] to be mine. The upper part of the child's face favoured me to a die, but the lower part, from the nose downward, he could not see, as it was either covered or presented an appearance he could not understand. He had related this dream in my presence and [that of] others. The moment he heard of the news I had received from home, he came over to see me, as is customary, as a comforter or some such thing. The first thing that struck him was the novel aspect of my countenance, which the loss of my late bushy whiskers con{172}tributed. This instantly unravelled the mystery of the child's face in his dream.

Starting for Home

February 26, 1844 – Monday. Having delayed as few days as possible, I started for home on the 26th, in company with Thomas McDermot and two men.

Here, perhaps, was the solution to a second mystery. Thomas McDermot was a son of Andrew McDermot, who, along with his partner James Sinclair, had reneged on their agreement to supply Garrioch's enterprise on credit the previous autumn. Did Thomas's presence at Mouse River now indicate that the partners had relented, and agreed to back the venture after all, so long as it was overseen by the younger McDermot? Garrioch's subsequent friendly relations with at least Sinclair lends support to that hypothesis.

The Abode of a Saint

March 6, 1844 – Tuesday. Reached Red River last evening, and early this morning I entered the late abode of a saint who is now reaping the fruits of his labour in an invisible world.

Given the brevity and matter-of-fact tone of other references to his father's death (and also, perhaps, his lack of precision as to *which* "invisible world" he referred to here) might this terse comment be considered sarcastic? Or is it simply Peter's "manly" way of dealing with his grief?

March 7, 1844 – Wednesday. I have been subsequently informed that the first geese were seen on this day at the Black Hills of the Mouse River.

---

313 Garrioch simply called the person who had the dream "he," which seems, as Gunn suggests in a note, to refer to some party whose name the author has inadvertently omitted.

Brief Return to Mouse River

March 13[314], 1844 – Wednesday. Having settled such affairs as devolved upon me, I started back for Mouse River, and arrived there on my sixth day.

March 22, 1844 – Friday. We made a general start for Red River. A few Indian families were left behind, and my old Morone (an old mare).

Winter's Retreat from the Prairies

The snow[315] fled before the south wind, like grease before a furnace.

March 25, 1844 – Monday. Thundered and lightninged for the first time this season, at the tail of the Turtle Mountain.

March 27, 1844 – Wednesday. Buffaloes seen within three miles of our encampment.

The pause from Wednesday to Saturday was likely for the purpose of pursuing buffaloes – probably unsuccessfully, since no hunting spoils are subsequently reported.

March 30, 1844 – Saturday. Started again for Red River, in company with two men, at about 10 in the night, and continued traveling until about 10 the following morning, when we took breakfast. {173}

March 31, 1844 – Sunday. Resumed our journey in the evening, after resting ourselves and dogs. A great thaw. Missed our way by a mile or so. Wood very scarce, and hard to kindle a fire.

Traveling at night on Saturday and Sunday had three advantages: there was likely to be less melt water at night; resting in the daytime was warmer; and proper observance of the Sabbath was made possible. The disadvantage, as the last entry showed, was an increased likelihood of getting lost.

---

314   In the original typescript, Archives of Manitoba, MG-2 C-38, this date is recorded as March 11, but in Gunn's (MG9 A-78-3), it is March 14.

315   As recorded by Gunn, but the word in Peter's original typescript (Archives of Manitoba, MG-2 C38) is "sorrow."

April 3, 1844 – Wednesday. This and the last two days have been very warm. We have traveled the whole distance from the Pembina River to here (White Horse Plain)[316] on foot in snow and in water.

Old Orkney Cottage Again

April 4, 1844 – Thursday. Reached old Orkney Cottage, and found all my friends, according to my wishes, well.

Sugar & Isabella

The writer had been home less than a week when he set off in search of sugar. Although the famous sugar maple trees of central Canada do not flourish on the prairies, box elder trees – now sometimes called "Manitoba maples" – which also produce harvestable sweet sap in spring, are plentiful. As historian W. L. Morton once observed, although the sugar produced from the "quick, thin sap" of the local trees "was not equal to that of the sugar maple of Canada, it was sweet and helped eke out the costly refined sugar imported by York [Factory]."[317] Two favourite sites for sugar-making at Red River were "Sugar Point," near the Saulteaux village below the main Settlement on the Red, near where St. Peter's Dynevor Church stands, and les Islets de Bois, an area along what is now the Boyne River, south-west of the Settlement, near present-day Carman, Manitoba. It was to the latter

---

316 Gunn: "A place on the Assiniboine River, about eighteen miles above its junction with the Red, in the French parish of St. Francois Xavier. This name for the locality is of quite early origin. Alexander Henry Jr. uses it in his journal of the year 1806 (Coues, *Henry*, I, p. 288), and it is no doubt of much older date than that. Different theories are advanced as the origin of the name. I was recently informed by one of the oldest residents of that part that it originated in the circumstance of a white horse being used when the original river lots were laid out there by Lord Selkirk's agents or the Hudson's Bay Company, the lengths of the lots being determined by the distance at which a white horse could be seen back on the prairie. Such an explanation …is put completely out of court by Henry's use of the name in 1806, as neither Lord Selkirk nor the Hudson's Bay Company was in this vicinity until several years after that date. Another tradition is given by C. N. Bell of Winnipeg in the *Manitoba Historical Society Transactions*. This legend, said to be current among the French Métis, tells of a wonderful white horse that once frequented this vicinity, eluding all attempts at capture. This latter legend has some air of probability, but I have a feeling that the true explanation is yet to be found." Earlier notes by Gunn refer to another name for the area – Grant Town or Grantown – that was in use during the time when the community's founder and longtime leader, Cuthbert Grant, was prominent. In that regard, see Margaret MacLeod and W. L. Morton, *Cuthbert Grant of Grantown* (Toronto: McClelland and Stewart, 1974), pp. 90-94.

317 Introduction by W.L. Morton to *London Correspondence Inward from Eden Colvile, 1849-1852*, ed. E.E. Rich, Hudson's Bay Record Society Publications XIX (1956), p. xxxii. As references concerning sugar-making in Rupert's Land, Morton cited Henry, *New Light on the Greater Northwest*, I, p. 172, Margaret Arnett MacLeod: "Manitoba Sugar Maple," *The Beaver* (Spring, 1955), pp. 10-13, & "Peter Garrioch's Journal III, pp. 175-177."

location that Garrioch now headed in the hope of trading with the sugar-makers encamped there.

April 9, 1844 – Tuesday. I started back [to the White Horse Plain] with an ox and cart to meet the sugar makers, with some goods to trade [for] sugar. Spent the evening with Mr. Pascal Berlan. {174}

Garrioch's host – and long-time friend – Pascal Berlan (more commonly Berland or Bréland) was a prominent Métis leader whose middle-of-the-road political views made him popular throughout most of the Red River Settlement. He was about the same age as his sugar-seeking friend.[318]

April 10, 1844 – Wednesday. With the kind assistance of my good host, I got my ox and cart over the river, which was getting very bad. And, after getting into my cart, I went on my way thinking about sugar and Isabella![319]

---

318 Gunn: "More correctly 'Bréland.' Pascal Bréland [was] a well-known and highly respected French Métis, a native of the Red River Settlement, who lived on the north bank of the Assiniboine, in the Parish of St. Francois Xavier, just below the Roman Catholic Church. Born in 1812, his father was Pierre Bréland, and his wife a daughter of Cuthbert Grant. As hunter, trader, and patriot, Mr. Bréland was recognized as a [conservatively inclined] leader among his confreres; while his kindly disposition, good judgment, and moderation made him a valued and much sought-after counsellor with all classes. He was a member of the committee formed in 1849 by Louis Riel Sr. to secure free trade in furs. In 1850 he was appointed magistrate for the White Horse Plains district, and Petty Court judge for the same area in 1851. In 1856, he was census enumerator, a member of the [Red River] Board of Works, [and] Councillor of Assiniboia. Upon the erection of Manitoba into a province, he was elected member of the Legislature from his district, and became a member of the Legislative Council. He was also appointed a member of the Executive Council for the Northwest Territories."

319 These two entries are reproduced by McLeod and Morton, *Cuthbert Grant*, pp. 106-107, with the following commentary: "From the first years of the [Grantown] settlement, the annual sugar-making began each year before the snow had left the ground, and this meant that the women would have to slosh about, half-way up to their knees in deep snow and slush gathering the sap from the trees which the men had tapped. The sugar season was a time of much merry-making also, and it was a wonderful time for the children. Though the events recounted happened years after the people of Grantown first began to go to their sugar-lots, the free-trader, Peter Garrioch, in his unpublished diary, gives an interesting account of a trip to the sugar bush. Leaving his home at St. Andrews on the Red River, he travelled the usual route to White Horse Plain. He writes: [entries for April 10 & 11]. It was not easy to get around the country to the sugar camps, even if one was not in love, as Garrioch was with his Isabella. There were spring freshets and much water on the ground. Garrioch had difficulty in getting his cart-load of trading-goods over some streams, and some he could not attempt so had to change his course. At times, through it was raw cold weather, he had to strip and swim across streams to reconnoitre the road ahead. By the evening of April 14, he had arrived within a mile or so of the Islets de Bois camps but he was unable to get across the swampy ground in the dark, and so had to make his solitary and uncomfortable camp within sight of the

A Hot Appetizer

April 11, 1844 – Thursday. At a very early hour, I encamped three miles beyond the Stinking River.[320] I kindled a fire by the side of the stream to make a cup of tea. The wind blew very strongly and, though I apprehended some danger of it acting too freely on my fire, I walked up to my cart to take down my eatables. Before I had time to return, I heard the noise of fire, perceived a column of smoke ascending majestically, [and] hastened to the spot. The flames were sporting themselves among my clothes and various sporting and cooking implements, which I had left thrown on the ground carelessly. My poor coat never got over what it suffered, [so] I flung it into the stream with my [powder] horn. My gun simply got singed, but my shot pouch was perfectly incorporated with the flames. I succeeded, however, in extinguishing them with the help of Providence.

This experience gave me an appetite. {175} I supped, and then retired.

Baptism for Man & Ox

Garrioch's destination was an area on the upper reaches of the Scratching (now Boyne) River where copses of box elder ("Manitoba maple") trees were plentiful, and sugar makers' camps were clustered. He knew he didn't have far to go, but he wasn't sure of the exact direction.

April 12, 1844 – Friday. Proceeded to the Rivière aux Isles de Bois, the place of sugar-making.[321] Not knowing the way of sugar camps, I followed, at a venture, the trails of carts which had passed in the direction I expected to find the sugar makers. After

---

flickering fires of the merry-makers. The next day he reached the camps and, his woes forgotten, wrote of April 15 and 16 [entries for those two dates]. On continuing his sugar-trading journey farther south he reported finding other sugar-makers with 'little else to live upon but sugar.'"

320   Gunn: "This trail crossed the Rivière Sale or Stinking River [present La Salle River] in its upper part, 26 miles southwest of Winnipeg, in the vicinity of what is now Starbuck. Garrioch's camp would therefore be three miles to the southwest of this point."

321   Gunn: "Garrioch's phonetic spelling of this name is 'Riviere Eyil de Buwa.' [It] is the upper waters, of the Rivière aux Gratias (Scratching River), which flows into the Red River at Morris, Manitoba…. This portion of the system was known as Rivière aux Isles de Bois, or River of Clumps of Trees, the name having reference to the many small clumps of timber occurring along its course. These clumps of timber, in some parts, were largely composed of Manitoba Maple, or Box Elder, the tree from which all the maple sugar produced in the northwest was made. Alexander Henry Jr., in his journals of 1800-08 (Coues, *Henry*, I, pp. 66 & 480), refers to it by this name, and gives a remarkably accurate description of its course and general character. It is now known as the Boyne River. The principal places on it are Carman and Treherne."

going about a mile in water of from one to two feet, I came to a creek which took my ox nearly up to the back. I continued another quarter of a mile, through water as before, when I came to another creek which, from its depth and narrowness as well as from the rapidity of its current, I did not like to encounter with my ox and cart. I therefore stripped to the skin and, Baptist-like, bounded into the stream. Having gained the opposite shore, [I] hastened to cover my shivering and half-benumbed form with my clothes – which I had thrown over previous to my taking [to] the water. I now hastened to get to dry land, and proceeded several hundred yards with that view, through water up to my knees. {176}

The annual sugar-making ritual was a regular part of the settlements' tasks, beginning before the snow had left the ground and requiring hard sloshing about in deep snow and slush to gather the sap from the tapped trees. There was usually much merry-making during the process as well. Peter had a hard time getting his cart-load of trading goods over some streams and swampy places to get to the camps of the merry-makers where he could trade for sugar.[322]

At this moment I came in contact with another creek, which appeared to me more formidable than any I had crossed. Convinced that I could not cross such waters with my ox and cart without endangering their safety and mine, being quite alone and now scarcely able to stand from the effects of the cold water on my limbs, I hasted back to my ox and cart as fast as my almost powerless limbs would carry me, undressed at the bank as before, threw my clothes over towards the cart, and again committed my shivering carcass to the icy and merciless stream. I took up my clothes, sprang into the cart, put on what dry clothes I had, wheeled my ox round, and drove like fury to dry land. My poor ox had scarcely reached the first spot above water when he lay down under his load. The cause was doubtless the coldness of the water on his limbs.[323]

Seeing I could not proceed much farther, I collected all the dry bushes I could find, and drove off again. We did not, however, go more than another hundred yards when

---

322 These diary descriptions of Peter's efforts to get to the sugar camps to trade for sugar are quoted in MacLeod & Morton, *Cuthbert Grant*, pp. 106-107.

323 Gunn: "Garrioch [had] probably skirt[ed] the western edge of the big Boyne marsh, and got himself tangled up in the network of creeks forming the drainage into it from the northwest. Elm Creek is probably one of those mentioned as encountered. The old trail that he [was] supposed to be following crossed this stream about five miles northeast of the present Carman, about 2½ miles southeast of Barnsley. By keeping a little too much to the west he would have [had] a number of branches of the Elm Creek to contend with."

Chapter 5 – Trading On The Missouri

he [the ox] again sank to his belly. I took him out [of his harness] and made up my mind to spend the night on the open prairie.

A Peevish Prairie Fire

With about fifty willows, each the size of my little finger, I managed to boil my pot and light my pipe. In crossing the creek I had lost all my fire tackle but fortunately I had a flint gun, which {177} answered every purpose.[324]

Before I retired to bed, I kindled a fire – that is, I set fire to the prairie – which produced a grand spectacle for one in solitude and exile.[325] [I did this] partly from peevishness at my crosses, and partly from a design to let the sugar makers know that a poor soul was doomed to spend a disagreeable night in the open prairie not a mile from their camps while they were feasting on the delicious juice of the maples, and basking in their huts and cabins, sheltered from the inclemency of the weather by the expanding boughs of that propitious tree.

Wind, Rain, & a Flatulent Ox

April 13, 1844 – Saturday. Got up this morning in perfect health – far [better] than I expected after such experiences as yesterday and last night.

My ox blows like a bellows. This trouble came upon him during the night, and it continued so loud that either it or the thunder awoke me.[326] I got up in the midst of wind and rain, without any fire, and started for the river by a circuitous route. My poor ox, after lying, and attempting to lie, down several times, managed by hard driving to reach the river at the crossing place[327] by midday. Here, after kindling a fire and having something to eat, I went down to the sugar camps, driving my ox before me and leaving my cart and merchandise in the care of miserable chance.

---

324 Whether the "flint gun" was an actual pistol or a device intentionally designed for starting fires is not known. In either case sparks generated by the gun's flint mechanism was used to ignite dry leaves and twigs with which to start Garrioch's campfire and the larger conflagration he mentions next.

325 The order of the words in this sentence has been changed, and a footnote by Garrioch has been added to it.

326 The animal's problem seems to have been flatulence, brought on by some gastro-intestinal disturbance.

327 Gunn: "The old [main] trail that Garrioch [now followed] crossed the Rivière aux Isles de Bois in the vicinity of the present Carman, where there are large maple groves."

Among the Sugar Makers

April 14-15, 1844 – Sunday & Monday. Spent these two days among the sugar makers, feasting on the blood of the saccharine maple.

April 16, 1844 – Tuesday. Resumed my journey towards the Back Fat Lake, {178} taking with me Francis Astwack, whom I hired at the rate of sixteen shillings, to accompany me to that place.

Crossing the Pembina in Flood

April 18, 1844 – Thursday. Crossed the Pembina River,[328] which, however, we accomplished only with a great deal of trouble and risk – both for ourselves as well as for our animals and merchandise. We cut up a hide into lines of sufficient length to extend twice over the river. We then constructed a raft, on which we placed our trunks, bedding, etc.; and, having attached a line to each end of the raft, my man, on his horse, took one of the lines to the other side while I made the other fast on my side of the river. Having gained the opposite shore, he pulled the raft towards him and unloaded it. Then I pulled the raft to my side. We repeated the process three times before we could get everything over.

Back Fat Lake

April 19, 1844 – Friday. Killed three pheasants, and after that arrived at the south end of the Back Fat Lake, where we had the Pembina to cross again. Assisted, however, by Potchya[329] and {179} his canoe, we got over it expeditiously. Here we found four Rupertian families and several Indian ones.

---

[328] Gunn: "Upon leaving the sugar camps on the Boyne River near the site of Carman, Garrioch probably left the old buffalo hunting trail that he had been following up to this point, and struck across the country, on a course a little south of west, keeping to the south of the above-mentioned stream so as to pass on that side of the Back Fat (Swan) Lake instead of to the north of it. On this route he would be obliged to cross the Pembina twice, as indicated." See above, Chap. 2, n. 115.

[329] See above, note 284. Potchya seems to have been with the group of other "Rupertian" buffalo hunters next mentioned, who were sugar-making and hoping to encounter buffalo before long.

Chapter 5 – Trading On The Missouri 165

April 21, 1844 – Saturday. I moved a few miles downward to another set of uncircumcised bastards,[330] and spend this and the following day with them, trading sugar and whatever else I could get that was of any value.

April 22, 1844 – Monday. Proceeded to the north end of the Back Fat Lake,[331] and there I found my friend Charles Racette,[332] and "my son" and old sweetheart, <u>as it is said</u>..[333]

All the sugar makers hereabout had little else to live upon than sugar. No buffaloes could be heard of, and fowl were very scarce. During our stay we made a fishing …

End of Sugar Trading

Four pages are missing from the journal at this point, preventing our knowing whether Garrioch returned to Red River with his sweet cargo, or continued on to sell it in Missouri River country, where it might have fetched a higher price than at home.

Farewell to Isabella

Nor does the surviving journal tell us more, until some cool passing references almost a year later[334] about the writer's "sweet, sweet damsel" and "fair intended" Isabella McKenzie. Something happened to extinguish that love affair, and if the circumstances were ever recorded by Garrioch it would likely have been in the foregoing destroyed pages.

---

330   The significance of this crude term is not altogether clear. Since circumcision could not have been common anywhere in the area at the time, it must not have been used literally. If it referred to Indigenous, as is probable, and was intended to be pejorative, as the tone suggests, it may well have signified Sioux, whom Garrioch thought responsible for the recent murder of his friends.

331   Gunn: "In the neighbourhood of the present Indian Springs."

332   Gunn: "The Racettes were French Métis. They lived on the Red River south of the present Winnipeg. In the 1840 census a Charles R. is given: no age, native, Catholic, three children – this probably being the Charles Racette of the above reference."

333   This new reference to the accusation recorded on February 21 (Gunn, p. 170) that Garrioch had recently sired a child by another man's wife is interesting for two reasons, suggesting as it does that the woman in question may have been part of Charles Racette's extended family, and that she may well have been Peter Garrioch's "old sweetheart," since he did not place that expression in quotation marks, as he had with the term "my son." The underscoring is his.

334   Chap. 7, March 9, 1845 (Gunn, p. 244).

The only known explanation was provided almost a decade after the event by Red River's first historian and long-time Sheriff, Alexander Ross:

> One of the Company's officers, residing at a distance, had placed two of his daughters at the boarding school in the settlement. An English half-breed, a comely, well-behaved young man of respectable connections, was paying his addresses to one of these young ladies, and had asked her in marriage. The young lady had another suitor in the person of a Scotch lad; but her affections were in favour of the former, while her guardian, the Chief officer in Red River, preferred the latter. In his zeal to succeed in the choice he had made for the young lady, this gentleman sent for the half-breed, and reprimanded him for aspiring to the hand of a lady accustomed, as he expressed it, to the first society.[335]

Although the McKenzie girls' father was only a *former* Company officer, there can be little doubt that this account refers to Isabella McKenzie and Peter Garrioch.[336] And while Alexander Ross's retrospective recollections cannot be expected to be accurate in every detail, their substance has generally stood the test of time.

Interestingly, Ross attributed much more than just personal significance to this event. He went on to say that after the young man walked wordlessly from the interview, he shared his outrage with other members of both the anglophone and francophone mixed-blood communities, and that:

> being a leading man among his countrymen, the whole fraternity took fire at the insult. 'This is the way,' they said, 'that we half-breeds are despised and treated.' From that moment they clubbed together, in high dudgeon, and joined the French malcontents against their rulers; so that for years afterwards this spirit of combination and hatred gave rise to plots, plans, and unlawful meetings among them, which threatened, and threatens, in more or less degree, to this moment [1856] the peace and tranquility of the settlement.[337]

The prospect of Peter Garrioch's marrying Isabella McKenzie ended at that point: Ross tells us that "the Scotchman carried off the prize." Although he was undoubtedly upset by this turn of events, there seems also to have been an element of acceptance – perhaps even

---

335 Ross, *Red River Settlement*, pp. 238-9. See also Brown, *Strangers in Blood*, pp. 148-152, who places this incident in a larger context, as an example of European misogyny and HBC social and class standards affecting both Métis and Company women in the 19th century fur trade economy.

336 Margaret Arnett MacLeod, editor of *The Letters of Letitia Hargrave*, p. 177-8, reached the same conclusion as the present editors: that the "young lady" in question was Isabella McKenzie, and the "comely, well-behaved young man" was Peter Garrioch. She also revealed that the man Isabella married was one Cornelius Pruden. HBCA/AM: Extracts from Registers of Baptisms, Marriages and Burials in Rupert's Land, E.4/2 folio 89d, shows that the marriage took place on January 11, 1844.

337 Ross, *Red River Settlement*, p. 239.

some "sour grape" consolation – in his response. Among several scribbles, calculations and doodles on the cover of his surviving original journal is the name "Isabella," repeated many times over, followed by: "Fortunately Isabella McKenzie is a witless windheaded creature." Garrioch nevertheless remained in contact with the McKenzie family, with consequences to be examined later.

In the meantime, he moved swiftly onward; his next known journal entry, dated a little more than six weeks later, finding him in American territory, much further to the east, after having probably been back to Red River, in the early stages of an adventure very different in kind and significance.

Chapter 6

St. Peter's, St. Paul's & the Crow Wing Trail

1844

An Historic Journey

Just weeks after his sugar-trading expedition, Peter Garrioch set out on a precedent-setting, major trading journey to the United States, to which Gunn gave the title "Account of a Trip Made by Steamboat and Red River Cart from Fort Garry to Galena, Illinois, and Back, in 1844." Peter traveled in the company of a group of prominent free traders that included James Sinclair, Peter Hayden, James Green, and Henry Cook. They brought cattle, horses, and trade goods for sale in the United States. Whether they also carried a clandestine cargo of furs in contravention of the Hudson's Bay Company's controversial fur trade monopoly is not known, but that is unlikely given the apparent openness of the enterprise. As one of Red River's earliest large-scale trading excursions to the south, the mission had considerable commercial significance, and Peter Garrioch's return trip, leading a small party by an arduous new, alternative route, would make transportation history.

The deletion of two pages at the beginning of this portion of the journal may have deprived us of an explanation of the expedition's origins and the diarist's preparations for it. As we join them, the travelers have recently crossed the U.S. border, and are now somewhere southwest of Pembina.

Their route is a little different than the one taken by Garrioch on his 1837 trip to St. Peter's. As a note of Reverend Gunn's explains:

> The rivers crossed, and a good many of the places mentioned, on this trip do not coincide with those mentioned by Garrioch as being encountered on the trip recorded on Garrioch's first trip [Chapter 2]. In order to understand this, it must be borne in mind that these cart brigades had several different routes. One of these lay through the flat plains of the Red River Valley, keeping close to the Red all the way to near Lake Traverse, and consequently crossing the various western tributaries met with in their main streams. This was the route followed in Garrioch's first trip.

Chapter 6 – St. Peter's, St. Paul's & the Crow Wing Trail

Another way was to strike southwest along the south side of the Tongue River after leaving Pembina, following the Pembina-Devil's Lake trail to where it crossed the Cart Creek. Thence branching off and taking a course a little eastward of south, they followed the high country forming the southern continuation of the Pembina Mountains, joining the river trail again at what was then known as Graham's Point, and later as Fort Abercrombie. There was still another trail on the west side of the Red (as all the trails of this time were), known as the Wet Road, about midway between the two just described; but the two above were the ones most generally used. It is the latter of these two first-mentioned routes that our party is now following. They are traveling on the high country forming the western edge of the Red River Valley, and consequently are crossing the various streams near their sources, where they are much branched and often differently named. Tongue River, for instance, is not mentioned on the first trip, because the Pembina was crossed below where that stream falls into it.[338]

River Crossings & Suspended Tongues

{180} June 12, 1844 – Wednesday. Weather still dry and pleasant. Crossed the Tongue River today.[339] Four of our party united and purchased a calf {181} of Joe Rolette[340] for five shillings. {182}

---

338 Gunn, pp. 180-181.

339 Gunn: "The Tongue River rises on the Pembina Mountains, to the west of Olga. With its headwaters thus in Cavalier County, it flows northeasterly through Pembina, joining the Pembina River some three or four miles from the junction of that stream with the Red, near the international boundary. The name is of ancient aboriginal origin, and derives its significance from the position of the river bisecting the angle formed by the Red and Pembina. To the observant Indian, the relative positions of these three streams suggested a wide open mouth, the Red and Pembina answering to the gaping jaws, the [subject river] being the protruding tongue. This origin of the name was given me by Peter Cameron, an old resident of Tyner, who had it from Felix Letrail, a very old French Métis, now deceased, who formerly lived at Leroy, on the Pembina River. The derivation seems credible both on account of its source and reasonableness. The principal towns on the Tongue are Bathgate and Cavalier. How [the Tongue] comes to be crossed on this trip is a little puzzling; as the second route described above, which we suppose them to be [mostly] following, crosses the Pembina at the same spot as the first, and keeps to the south of the Tongue all the way. The probable explanation of this lies in still another route that was sometimes followed. This trail, instead of continuing close to the Red River all the way to Pembina, branched off to the southwest in the neighbourhood of the present town of Morris, Manitoba, proceeding, as the crow flies, to St. Joseph (Walhalla), passing by what is now Rosenfeld. Crossing the Pembina at Walhalla, it proceeded south by east, joining the trail already described as paralleling the south side of the Tongue River about midway between Mountain and Hensel. This route passed near to what is now Leyden, crossing the Tongue six or seven miles south of that point. Garrioch and his party are evidently, therefore, following this trail and hence crossing the Tongue River."

340 Gunn: "Joseph Rolette [of Pembina], after whom Rolette County, North Dakota is named, [was] a well-known character in both the Red and Mississippi valleys through this and the two subsequent

June 13, 1844 – Thursday. Crossed the Cold Water River,[341] and breakfasted {183} at Lacutpick.[342] A very sultry day. One-third of our oxen suspended their tongues.

June 14, 1844 – Friday. Crossed the Cart and Little Salt Rivers.[343] An{184}other warm day. A wheel of one of Peter Hayden's[344] carts split in two, and one of another tumbled down.

---

decades of the 19th century. His father, Jean Joseph Rolette, was a French Canadian from Quebec, said to have been educated for the priesthood. The wild life of the courier de bois, however, being more to his liking, he went to the United States, to Wisconsin Territory, and became a trader for the North-West Company. From about 1800 on, he was prominent in the Mississippi regions. He [eventually] settled at Prairie du Chien, and there, in 1820, the Joe Rolette above mentioned was born. Young Rolette was sent to New York, where he was educated under the supervision of Ramsey Crooks, then President of the American Fur Co., in whose employ [his father] now was. Later, about 1840, he was sent to open a post at Pembina.

"In 1843, Norman W. Kittsen was placed in charge of all the trading operations of the AFC in these regions, superceding young Rolette, who nevertheless remained with him as his assistant; in which capacity we find him acting in the above reference. In 1844, Kittsen had a trading post at St. Joseph, the present Walhalla of which Rolette was probably in charge. This would fit in with our conclusion, reached in the preceding note, as to the route followed by Garrioch and his party; the calf transaction with Rolette, in all likelihood, taking place there. [Rolette] later acquired considerable prominence and influence, representing the district in the Minnesota Territorial Legislature of 1853-55, and on its Territorial Council of 1855-57. He was known far and wide as "jolly Joe Rolette." He died [in 1871] at Pembina, where his memory is perpetuated in the name of one of the streets of that historic and picturesque little burgh." Gunn, p. 181.

341   Gunn: "The Cold Water River here referred to is undoubtedly one of the upper branches of the Park River. This latter stream, as previously noted, rises in three main branches on the height of land new being traversed by Garrioch's party; each of these branches being in turn bifurcated in its upper part. The traveler going south, therefore, if keeping far enough to the west, would have no less than six of these little streams to cross." Garrioch's Cold Water River was probably one of the middle two of these.

342   La Côte à Pic (Steep Hill). Gunn's complex note concludes that it was probably located "in the neighbourhood of the present Gardar, North Dakota."

343   Gunn: "The crossing of the Little Salt River, keeping to the route we have been following, would occur somewhere a few miles to the west of the present town of Park River; but I find nothing answering to this Cart River on any modern map where it could possibly be crossed on this trail unless Garrioch's party is much farther west than where we have located them."

344   Gunn: "A prominent free trader of Red River at this time. He lived, at this time, [at Red River] on Point Douglas, but subsequently moved to Pembina, North Dakota, where he permanently resided." Born in Ireland, there is some discrepancy about when Hayden was born, either about 1800 (HBCA/AM: c.1797; "Passengers England to York, 1822,") or about 1806 (Genealogical Research Library, Ontario: Canadian Genealogy Index, 1600s-1900s); & D.N. Sprague and R. P. Frye, *The Genealogy of the First Metis Nation, The Development and Dispersal of the Red River Settlement 1820-1900* (Pemmican Publications, 1988). Peter Hayden arrived in the Red River Settlement in 1822 with his uncle, Michael Hayden, a blacksmith and gunsmith, and his wife, Maria Hayden.

Chippewas, a Comet & Mental Aberration

June 15, 1844 – Saturday. Crossed the Big Salt River[345] and fell in with a small party of Chippewas, consisting of four men, two lads, and one woman. They gave us meat,

---

The 1827 census for Red River indicates that Michael Hayden and his family and his nephew Peter Hayden were living on lot 818, and that Peter Hayden was unmarried, had no dwelling house or other buildings, and no livestock, farm implements, or means of transportation: Census returns for Red River Settlement and Grantown, 1827, HBCA/AM: E.5/1 (H2-136-1-2). By 1829, Peter Hayden was married to Marie-Rose Antoinette Lagimodière, living on another lot (778), and had 3 mares, 2 cows, 3 oxen, 1 cattle, 1 cart, 1 plough, and 1 harrow. HBCA/AM: Census returns for Red River Settlement, E.5/2 (H2-136-1-2), 1828 and 1829. Hayden made his living by carting, fur trading, and selling liquor on both sides of the still-fluid border with the U.S., activities that made him a part of the Métis free trading community and, as we see throughout Peter Garrioch's diaries from 1844 on, an enthusiastic member of it. His mercurial temperament brought him into conflict with the HBC. See Chapter 8, entry for February 19, 1846, as one example.

Spirit of the Times: A Chronicle of the Turf, Agriculture, Field Sports, Literature and the Stage, 19:8 (April 14, 1849), contains a description of trading and hunting parties with reference to Hayden: "These parties usually commence their journey towards the Mississippi in May, and return in September. Peter Hayden, an Irish-man, is the pioneer of this route, and has made probably twenty journeys across this vast country, with a train of carts. He is on good terms with the Indians, half-breeds and whites, and has managed to accumulate some property in his migratory operations." The trade with St. Paul involved dressed skins, buffalo tongues, and large quantities of Indian curiosities, and the free-trader Peter Hayden and others took back dry goods, boots and shoes, and whisky. John Francis McDermott (ed.), "A Journalist at Old Fort Snelling: Some Letters of "Solitaire" Robb," *Minnesota History* 31:4, (December, 1950), pp. 209-221. At p. 217, Hayden was described thus: "One of the greatest characters belonging to this settlement [St. Paul] is an old Irish trader, named *Peter Haydon* – he has been for the past thirty years engaged in trade in the northwest, and I am informed that he has grown wealthy in the business."

Along with Peter Garrioch, Andrew McDermot, James Sinclair, Joe Green, and Alexis Goulet, Hayden was involved in the free trade disputes with the HBC in the mid-1840s. Gibson, *LLG, I*, pp. 88-91. While preparing to defend himself against seizure of his goods, Hayden set off a pistol and accidently killed a boy passing nearby, an incident vividly described by Peter in his diary entry for January 27, 1846 (Chapter 8). Hayden was acquitted of manslaughter, however, in the midst of hot disputes between the free traders and the HBC. Gibson, *LLG, II*, pp. 37-40. The *St. Paul Weekly Minnesotan* (July 23, 1853), carried on page 2 a description of the arrival at Traverse des Sioux of traders from Pembina County and the Red River Settlements numbering 133 carts with rich "spoils of the chase;" the traders included both Norman Kittson and Peter Hayden, "an old Red river trader, well remembered by the early settlers of St. Paul." Later, in the spring of 1858, Hayden was said to be living near Pembina on the border – he had moved there about 1844 – and Daniel Hunt described him as a "poor but hospitable man," quoted from the *Diary of Daniel Hunt*, which was described by McDermott in "A Journalist at Old Fort Snelling," (*ibid.*), as being in the hands of the Minnesota Historical Society in manuscript form. Hayden died in late 1874 or early 1875, and his obituary appeared in the *Nor'Wester* on January 2, 1875.

345 Gunn: "New Forest River."

and we gave them flour, powder, and ball in exchange.[346]

346　This is one of many references in Peter's diaries to bartering with Indians he encountered in his journeys and in the main these exchanges seemed unplanned and driven by circumstances and convenience. An additional example is found below in the entry for November 26, 1844. It could be said that this is "moral" exchange of goods, in contrast to the system employed by the HBC which took advantage of Indigenous people to collect wealth in addition to the imposition of duties against which Peter and his free trader colleagues fought so strongly. J. J. Gunn describes this system in an illuminating passage in a chapter entitled, appropriately, "Lo, the Poor Indian and the Hudson's Bay Company," in *Echoes of the Red*, pp. 82-85. After sarcastically describing the HBC;s reputation for probity, he continued, "In a pamphlet published in 1846 [by Alexander Isbister], entitled *A Few Words about the Hudson's Bay*, we find a 'Tariff of prices employed by the Hudson's Bay Company in licensed territory east of the Rocky Mountains.' At the time this tariff was in use 'the entire value of all the furs and other articles traded by the Company from the Indians in all its territories and possessions averaged less than £200,000 per annum. In one year it amounted to £211,000 and the net profits that year were declared at £119,000!'"

"A glance at the tariff will explain the possibility of such an extraordinary result, as well as show some rather curious angles in the reputed square dealing of the Company.

"The first item given is a gun, the first cost of which is placed at twenty-two shillings. To this should be added thirty-three and one third percent, which the Company calculated covered the cost of placing their goods in the Indian countries. This would make the net cost of the gun $7.22; and the price charged for it was twenty 'beavers'. Now the beaver was the standard of valuation when dealing with Indians; three martens were worth one beaver, one silver fox equaled four beavers, one lynx one beaver, one otter one beaver, etc. This gun was sold to the Indian for twenty beavers, which if paid in beaver skins represented a value of $162.50, as the market-value of a beaver skin is given at $8.12½. Now one would think this is a good enough price for a gun costing $7.25; but if the Indian were under the necessity of paying those twenty beavers in marten skins, his gun would cost him the fine sum of $232.50, and in silver fox skins it would cost him a round $250.00 on account of the relative values of these furs in the markets of Europe. If, however, he paid it in otter skins he got his gun for $117.50, and in lynx skins for $100.00.. But the poor Indian did not study the markets. There were many circumstances to prevent him from reading the daily papers, so as long as the Company allowed him four beavers for a silver fox, he was happy.

"Thus the profits of the Company varied on each article according to the kind of pelt they received in payment. But they do not seem to have carried any article into the country with the idea of losing on the venture. Assuming that each article was paid for in silver fox skins, they charged for one gill of powder $12.50, for 18 bullets the same, for ten gun-flints the same. The first cost of each of the last two items is given at one penny. An axe which cost the Company thirty-seven and one-half cents, cost the Indian thirty-seven and one-half dollars! While the Company bore testimony to the value of a six-gallon copper kettle in the economy of a wigwam by demanding a profit thereon of $196.00. It cost them $4.00 and they sold it for $200.00. For a plain blanket they charged $125.00 and for a striped one $150.00. The price of a coat was $150.00, that of a pair of trousers $112.50, while a cotton shirt could be had any day for $37.50, a cotton handkerchief for $12.50, six yards of gartering for the same, a four-penny mirror for the same, and a dozen brass finger-rings for $25.50, thus making it possible for an aspiring buck to play the dude in his neighbourhood for the trifling cost of $375.00. How many a vain sigh for such a possibility do the streets of Winnipeg echo.

Saw a most beautiful comet or meteor this evening. Its tail, or track, was visible for about five minutes after it disappeared. Two carts belonging to James Sinclair upset today.

June 16, 1844 – Sunday. Before we were out of bed, a man came up from Red River, having instructions to take Alex Kennedy back. Alex, {185} through the persuasion of the party, consented to go.

Alex Kennedy was a member of a prominent Red River family who suffered from what Gunn called, "fits of mental aberration." He seems to have slipped away from the Settlement without his family's knowledge.[347]

"A prominent writer on historical subjects, in making out a case for the Hudson's Bay Company as against the North-West Company, some years ago, made the statement that the former company was careful to 'foster civilizing influences.' The writer was careful not to particularize, and we are left in the dark as to what these influences were and how they were fostered. And only now we begin to think we do partly understand his meaning. But all that writer's special pleading is tame compared with this item in our tariff: one pint rum (watered), price one beaver, - which in fox skins would be $12.50. Such a price for a pint of run speaks volumes for the fatherly regard with which they looked on the untutored savage; while that word 'watered' almost waters our eyes as we read it...."

There is a lively dissection of the tariff list on page 20 of *A Few Words on the Hudson's Bay Company; with a Statement of the Grievances of the Native and Half-Caste Indians, addressed to the British Government through their Delegates Now in London*, attributed to Alexander Kennedy Isbister, published by C. Gilpin in London, 1846, https://www.canadiana.ca/view/oocihm_16731, and which incorporated the Belcourt petition of 1846 for which Garrioch helped collect signatures (Chap. 9, entry for May 28, 1846). Garrioch was involved in drafting and circulating several petitions supporting free trade and outlining the repressive practices of the HBC (see Appendix I – Petitions) and he was undoubtedly aware of the tariff system the HBC used to outplay and outmanoeuvre the Indigenous traders. These unfair trading practices with Indians were vividly described by Mary Riggs in her August 4, 1837, letter to her father, quoted in Chap. 3, text associated with n. 191-192.

347   Gunn: "A brother of Captain William Kennedy, the Arctic explorer. A younger man of fine education and accomplishments, but subject to fits of mental aberration. The 'man from Red River' was probably sent by the family or friends. The Kennedys lived on the west bank of the Red River at the head of the St. Andrews rapids, about a quarter of a mile north of old St. Andrews church". Dr. E. C. Shaw, "The Kennedys – An Unusual Western Family," *MHS Transactions*, Ser. 3, nr. 29 (1972-73) offers more information (but not on possible mental issues). On Alexander, William, and their father: "John Frederick Kennedy was born at Cumberland House in 1805. He was educated in the Orkneys and Edinburgh, Scotland, as a doctor. In 1829, he was engaged as surgeon on land or afloat in the Columbia district. Subsequently, he served as a doctor in various posts where he was also qualified to act as trader, store-keeper, and accountant. He was appointed as Chief Trader in 1847. He married an Indian woman of the Fort Simpson district and had several children. He retired in 1856 to Victoria, Vancouver Island. He died there on April 3, 1859. Alexander, Jr., was born in 1806 at Moose Lake. He was also schooled in the Orkneys and was a schoolteacher at St.

Had some rain this afternoon – the first since we left the Settlement. Our party killed two [buffalo] bulls this evening.

June 17, 1844 – Monday. Crossed the Turtle River.[348] Saw some more bulls and some deer. Encamped at a branch of the Goose River.

June 18, 1844 – Tuesday. Had an early visit from five more Chippewas. Gave them a little ammunition and tobacco. Having had something to eat, they returned to their families and we resumed our journey. Crossed another branch of the Goose River.[349]

June 19, 1844 – Wednesday. Some difficulty in crossing a little stream to-day. Wind blows strongly and pills operate well.[350]

Keeping Watch & Delicious Bathing

June 20, 1844 – Thursday. Rained about an hour to-day. Came to Goosegrass River[351] and there encamped. The first watch was kept to-night.

Andrews, Manitoba. He was a clerk of the vestry at old St. Andrew's Church and some of his precise handwriting still survives in the church records. He was said to have been very much a gentleman and an accomplished violinist." On Alexander's brother William: "The fifth child, was William, born at Cumberland House in 1814. During the absence of his father in 1819, young William was treated to the unusual event of the arrival of Sir John Franklin and his party in October. The young explorer amused himself by teaching the children at the post their first reading, writing and arithmetic during the months that he stayed there. See also "Captain William Kennedy," (Manitoba Culture, Heritage and Recreation, 1985).

348 Gunn: "Also crossed in its main stream, probably near the town of Arvilla; or between that place and Larimore, the next town west."

349 Gunn: "These upper branches of the Goose River are very difficult to identify with certainty. The two here mentioned are probably the two main branches. The party are now passing south at a distance of about thirty miles west of the Red River, probably some five or six miles to the west of the present Mayville. See note on Goose River." Gunn, p. 185 (June 18, 1944).

350 Gunn: "This 'little stream' might possibly be the upper end of the Elm River, or some small tributary of Goose, flowing in from the south. The nature and purpose of the 'pills' are unknown." See Chap. 1, text associated with n. 85, where William Garrioch indicated that he was taking pills for his weak lungs. But in the 19th century, a "pill" meant both a bark pealer/skinner and an unpleasant or boring person. The former meaning better fits the context here. It is also possible that Garrioch meant to say "piles" and to refer to piles of supplies or brush which might anchor a cart or other objects against the winds.

351 Gunn: "Probably the little stream marked on maps as Rush River, and lying wholly within Traill County. Our travelers, at this encampment, would be about in the neighborhood of Amenia. See previous note on Elm River." Goosegrass River seems to have been a spot where people in Peter's day recognized that they were crossing into in territory claimed, and likely to be defended by,

Chapter 6 – St. Peter's, St. Paul's & the Crow Wing Trail   175

The reason for this precaution was that the party was approaching an area where a risk of Sioux raids was feared. It will be recalled that similar safeguards were taken on Garrioch's 1837 trip.

{186} June 21, 1844 – Friday. Came to Maple River.[352] Had a delicious bathe and broke Henry's[353] steel. Kept my first watch to-night with Green and Moutry.[354]

Companions

Two of the three men mentioned in the foregoing entry were close associates of the diarist. Henry Cook was both Garrioch's cousin and his brother-in-law, being the child of another of William Henning Cook's daughters, as well as the husband of Garrioch's sister Harriet. He and Peter shared many adventures over the years. James Green[355]**, an American whom**

Dakota groups. Although Dakota raids were definitely something to be concerned with, there was also the possibility of safe passage under the guidance of the right people, and/or a treaty if groups were looking to, say, hunt. Getting to one's destination was more a matter of good judgement and respect for appropriate protocols than "fighting it out" in most cases. Still, keeping watch at night and taking precautions during the day was more than a prudent precaution in that area.

352   Gunn: "This, together with the one just preceding are two streams not mentioned by Garrioch as having been crossed in the former trip, comprising Part I of his journal. The reason is that, on the former occasion, the party crossed below their junction with the streams into which they flow. The one here mentioned is a tributary of the Sheyenne, flowing into it from the west about ten miles from its mouth, and about seven miles northwest of Fargo."

353   Gunn: "Henry Cook, [like Peter Garrioch, was] a grandson of Chief Factor William Hemming Cook [Chap. 1, text associated with nn. 42-55; Chap. 9, entry for March 2, 1847], former HBC Governor of York Factory. Henry Cook [also] married Garrioch's sister Harriet. He was prominently identified with the free trade movement and the fight against Hudson's Bay Company monopoly. He later lived in St. James, on the Assiniboine River west of Winnipeg, where he kept a trading establishment until he died…." Henry and Peter shared many adventures. The "steel" was an instrument made of steel that was used for either sharpening knives or striking sparks from flint.

354   Gunn: "Probably Montraille, or Montrel. In the Red River census records for the years 1838, '40, '43, and '46, a Joseph Montrel is listed as a native, Catholic, with a large family of children. In 1844 he was 41 years of age. The [family] were French Métis, and lived on the Red River south of Winnipeg. In pronunciation, either of these names would sound to Garrioch like Moutry, or Moutrie (See p. 193)."

355   Gunn p. 185(a): "James Green, an independent trader of Red River Settlement at this time. He was an American, having been born of 'Pennsylvania Dutch' stock. The date of his coming to Red River is uncertain, but Martin Macleod, who arrived at Fort Garry in the fall of 1836, mentions a Mr. Green as being one of their party…and as this tallies with the approximate date of his arrival furnished me by a son, and other old residents of the Settlement who knew him, I feel justified in concluding that this was no other than the Green of the above reference.. On his arrival at Red River Green joined the ranks of the free traders, associating himself with such men as Garrioch, James Sinclair, Henry Cook, William Hallet, &c., with whose names and activities he will be found closely associated in the succeeding pages of this journal.   James Green married Mrs. Isabella

Gunn thought had come to Red River by at least 1836, was an independent trader who would soon be battling the HBC's asserted fur-trading monopoly alongside Garrioch and other like-minded free traders.[356] **William Cook, whom we will meet in the next entry, and who will be the subject of a melancholy report at a later point, was the youngest son of**

> Gunn, a daughter of Alexander Ross, the [sheriff /] historian, and widow of William Gunn, eldest son of Donald Gunn, another pioneer historian of Manitoba. Of the issue of this marriage, a daughter still lives at Edmonton, and a son, Thomas, from whom I received many facts relative to his father's life resides in Winnipeg. In 1848 Green returned to the U.S., establishing himself in a small store and trading establishment at St. Paul. Sometime during this same year he took up a squatter's claim on the east bank of the Mississippi at Little Falls, thereby becoming the first permanent settler in what is now Morrison County, Minnesota. Here he developed a water power sawmill. Shortly after the completion of this mill in 1849, Mr. Green died suddenly and mysteriously at St. Paul [possibly of poison, since his body was "all black", according to his son's account later told to Gunn in the longer version of this note: "Note re James Green," n. d. MG9 A78-1, A78-3]. Mrs. Green and the family later returned to Red River, and lived for a time with her father. (See *History of the Upper Mississippi Valley*, Winchell, Neill, et al, Minnesota Historical Society, 1881), pp. 588-90.)" While Gunn seems to have been correct about Green's immediate family connections – James Green married Isabella Ross Gunn on November 13, 1845 (HBCA/AM: E.4/2. fol. 98) – he seems to have entertained some doubt that this was the same Green. The doubt seems to have been justified, because the Green who was initially in McLeod's party was named William and "had to be left behind at Lapointe" because he was ill. Nute, *Diary of Martin McLeod*, p. 373.

356 The HBC was well informed about what Peter and his associates were up to in this period, see Gibson, *LLG, I*, pp. 89-90, nn. 30, 38, 40 & pp. 409-410; Lent, *West of the Mountains*, pp. 169-171; & Bumsted, *Trials & Tribulations*, pp. 76, 97-98. In a series of letters written by Recorder Adam Thom in December, 1844, to Governor Christie, Thom outlined a scheme for suppressing the free traders. It would involve creating a new restrictive currency which could only be used in transactions with the HBC. While the details of the proposal are not really clear in the correspondence, it seemed to have involved requiring the principal free traders – identified as "Garrick" (undoubtedly Peter Garrioch), Green, McDermot, and Sinclair, the very companions involved in Peter's 1844 trading trips – to take out licenses from the company under which they undertook not to engage in trade with the U.S. or otherwise interfere with the HBC's prerogatives. The currency would be hedged about with similar restrictions.

In a letter to Christie dated December 7, 1844, Thom wrote that he had been thinking about the best way to protect the HBC's interests: "Of course, relying as little as possible on any extreme view of our legal rights....With respect to Garrick's Ammunition, which the imperial law for regulating foreign trade of the colonies absolutely prohibits, the absence of the ordinary machinery prevents us from effecting a strictly legal seizure and confiscation; but considering that the prohibition rests neither on fiscal nor on commercial grounds, but entirely on political considerations of the very highest importance, we are not only entitled but even bound to enforce, if possible, the prohibition, as such, by practical means. I should, therefore, strenuously recommend, even merely as a lawyer, the securing of Garrick's ammunition till he gives good sureties, maritime importers in preference, for immediately carrying it back beyond the possibility of being again smuggled into Rupert's Land. As he could hardly find such sureties, he might be offered, as a boon, the mere prime cost of his ammunition and thus be enabled to save himself the expense of removing it. But he ought not to receive one farthing for any expense incurred after fairly starting from St. Peter's with his illicit enterprise on his mind. To make sure of taking peaceable possession of the ammunition,

Chapter 6 – St. Peter's, St. Paul's & the Crow Wing Trail

William Hemming Cook, and thus Peter and Henry's uncle, although near their age. He

---

the greatest caution and secrecy must be observed, and no person whatever ought to be trusted till his [illegible words].

"With respect to Green, neither he nor his goods have, in strictness, any business here at all; and if this first attempt of the kind be tolerated there will be nothing to deter half a score of Kittsons from transferring themselves from Pembina to the.... From Kittson's own locality, ...we may conclusively gather that in the opinion of the Americans themselves Green's proceedings are wrong & unsafe – an opinion which will render his escaping with impunity doubly mischievous. But what to do, that is the question. As the intercourse with the Americans has grown up so gradually, as least with the Company's connivance [?], Green ought perhaps to be treated with as much indulgence as may be consistent with the [illegible] of his scheme; and be placed on somewhat the same footing as Garrick. He could have no reasonable ground for complaining of severity. The advantage of dealing with a foreigner is considerable. He can have, as an individual, no voice at Court, and his government, even if he were to be more rigorously treated could not espouse his cause, having passed a law, which is still in force, to prevent any British subject from doing to Americans what Green is doing to us, and having itself recognized in the international treaty of 1794 the Company's exclusive rights in the most unqualified manner. To illustrate this last point, I quote the words of the treaty: 'Art. III. It is agreed that it shall at all times be [illegible] to His Majesty's Subjects and to the citizens of the United States, and also to the Indians dwelling on either side of the said boundary line, freely to pass and repass, by land or inland navigation, into the respective Territories and Countries of the two Parties on the Continent of America (the Country within the Limits of the Hudson's Bay Company only excepted) and to navigate &c.'

"With respect to both Green and Garrick, they are both liable to lose their goods unless they report them and pay the duty of 4 p. Cent; but with Green you cannot assume this ground without admitting his right to bring goods on paying the duty – a right which, with the existing facilities of communication, would be far more pernicious to the Company than any opposition from any other quarter ever has been or ever can be." HBCA/AM: A11/95, f.4650; see also Thom's March 10, 1845 report to Simpson on these measures: HBCA/AM: D5/13, f.253 ff.

Although these behind-the-scenes machinations on the part of HBC officialdom were occurring at the same time as the trading ventures Peter was recording in his 1844 diary entries, including trading in ammunition and pushing through the Crow Wing Trail (June 18; September 17; October 3, 4, 9, & 23; November 6, 9, 14, 17, 21, 24, & 27; & December 3, 4, & 7), Peter's diary is focused on the charm of the scenery, the misadventures of his companions, encounters with Indians, including trading with them, the condition of the animals, the difficulties of the route, etc., rather than on the plans of HBC officials to thwart his activities. Conversely, it appears that the Governor and the Recorder were well aware of the details and timing of Peter's and Green's operations, as well as Kittson's.

This letter bore fruit in Governor's Christie's proclamations, referred to by Peter with heat and distain in his diary entry for February 21, 1845 (Chap. 7). See also Appendix I – Petitions.

appears to have come along on the trip as an assistant to Peter and/or Henry, rather than as a principal.

June 22, 1844 – Saturday. Started at a very early hour. Here W. Cook[357] returns back several miles for our horses. After crossing the Cheyenne {187} River, I was exceedingly annoyed with a fit of the physic.[358] Its attack was more severe than I have experienced in the last three years.

Sabbath Travel – & Divine Response?

June 23, 1844 – Sunday. A very sultry day. Rested according to the Commandment till about one o'clock, and then the good Papists thought it proper to travel.

Awful thunder and lightning. The winds blew as if they intended to spend their fury upon man and beast. The rain poured down in unmeasured torrents. Our horses and cattle took to running before the fierceness of the storm, and, in the midst of it, some of our party had to run and drive them into the circle of our encampment.

June 24, 1844 – Monday. One of our party killed a fine buck and six young geese. We encamped at the mouth of the Ottertail River[359] and I washed two shirts.

June 25, 1844 – Tuesday. Encamped at the Sioux River and my man Charles[360] {188} hurt one of his hands by pulling an ox.

---

357 Gunn: "William Cook, youngest son of Chief Factor W. H. Cook noted above [and thus the uncle of Peter Garrioch and Henry Cook]. His subsequent mental derangement and death by drowning are recorded by Garrioch later in his journal." The entry Gunn means is that for August 21, 1844 (Gunn, p. 199).

358 Probably diarrhea.

359 Gunn: "Generally now regarded as the headwaters of the Red River. It rises in the northern part of Becker County, Minnesota, not far from the source of the Mississippi, whence [it flows] to Breckenridge on the Red. On its way thither, it passes through a network of lakes, including Ottertail, Rush, Pine and a number of others. It will be noted that the travelers have now joined the trail followed on the first trip, recorded [earlier] in this journal. They are now on the Red River, and are encamped right across from Breckenridge, on the site of what is now Wahpeton, North Dakota. From this point, their route will be identical with that of the former journey [almost] until they strike the Mississippi."

360 Gunn: "Charles Laurance. No further information available."

Chapter 6 – St. Peter's, St. Paul's & the Crow Wing Trail

Inadvertent Bath & Surfeit of Eggs

June 26, 1844 – Wednesday. Crossed the Sioux [Wood] River. The carts, in crossing this river, were almost entirely submerged.[361] One of Peter Hayden's carts was turned clean over by the force of the stream, with a woman and children in it. They received no further injury, however, than a good general washing; and doubtless they needed it.

June 27, 1844 – Thursday. Crossed the Rabbit River[362] and encamped by a lake, where we collected between three and four hundred eggs.[363]

Encounters with Civilization

As the travelers approached the vicinity of St. Peters, Garrioch sought out educated members of the local population.

June 28, 1844 – Friday. Took a ride to Big Stone Lake and saw Mr. Martin McLeod,[364] who accompanied us to our encampment and spent the evening with {189} us.

---

361 Gunn: "On the first trip, the party crossed [this river], like the Israelites the Red Sea, on dry ground; here they are treated to the fate of the pursuing Egyptians. The presence or absence of water in the Sioux Wood River depended entirely upon the time and nature of the season."

362 Gunn: "A small stream flowing from the northeast into the east side of Lake Travers, near its north end. It was called by the Indians Mustincha Wu-ju, or Mustincha Watapan: Hare or Rabbit River. Like the Sioux Wood River, above noted, it is also uncertain as to its water supply. Garrioch does not mention this stream at all on the first trip; it being no doubt dry at that time. The old trail crossed it about five miles northeast of Lake Traverse."

363 Waterfowl eggs?

364 Gunn: "Known in later Minnesota history as Honorable Martin McLeod. Like many more of Minnesota's pioneers, Mr. McLeod was [a British subject]. He was born at Montreal, August 30, 1813, and came to the West about 1836, or shortly prior to that date. In the summer of that year, he accompanied 'General Dixon,' the 'Deliverer of the Indian Nations,' to Fort Garry, Red River Settlement (Neill, p. 452). The latter part of the following winter, he left Red River on showshoes, with a couple of companions, for the United States; their objective probably being Fort Snelling. When near the Cheyenne River, the party was overtaken by a terrible blizzard, in which Mr. McLeod's two traveling companions perished. McLeod [and the party's guide] survived, however. The following spring he found his way to Fort Snelling, and was there during Garrioch's sojourn at that point in 1837-8. He was engaged in the fur trade, at various posts, until 1849, when he settled at Bloomington, Minnesota, and served on the Territorial Council from that year until 1853, occupying the position of President of the Council during his last year in office. McLeod County, Minnesota is named after him. See Upham's: *Minnesota Biographies*, p. 476; *History of Hennepin County and Minneapolis* by W. H. Mitchell & J. H. Stevens, (Russell and Belfoy, 1868)." See also

June 29, 1844 – Saturday. Mr. McLeod, after he had read the whole *History of England* by Hume, returned this morning to his post and we went on our way rejoicing.

Did McLeod, a Montreal-born near-legendary Minnesota fur-trader and politician, borrow the book from Garrioch and read it overnight, or did he treat Garrioch and his companions to a reading from or verbal summary of Hume's classic?[365] Whatever happened, he seems to have left a good impression. As, no doubt, did the old friend whom the diarist next sought out.

June 30, 1844 – Sunday. Arrived at Lac qui Parle and went to hear Dr. Williamson preach.

July 1, 1844 – Monday. Left Lac qui Parle and crossed the Chippewa River. The water in this river was 8 or 10 feet above low water mark. Our crossing cost us a great deal of trouble but no damage.

July 2, 1844 – Tuesday. Encamped on the open prairie without any wood for fuel. Green's man leaves him this evening.

Drinking with the Sioux

July 3, 1844 – Wednesday. Met a large party of Sioux from the Traverse.[366] We smoked and took a glass with them. We gave them a young bull; and, after trading with them a little, we left them as merry as sailors. In consequence of the beverage with which the Sioux had treated us, some of our party, who had been complimental [of] the pernicious liquid, were like to tear each other to pieces. {190}

July 4, 1844 – Thursday. Met another party of Indians of Sioux tribe, as drunk as pipers. These offered to shoot some of our cattle. We got off, however, without sustaining any harm from them.

Nute, *Diary of Martin McLeod*, p. 373, and above, Chap. 5, n. 275, and a longer accolade-filled essay on McLeod by Gunn among his papers in the Archives of Manitoba, MG9 A78-1, A78-3..

365   Towards the conclusion of his diary, McLeod devotes considerable space to listing the remarkable number of books he read in periods of enforced rest while staying at various locations during his travels. Nute, *Diary of Martin McLeod*, p. 373.

366   Traverse des Sioux, towards which the party was headed.

Thirty-three Years Old

July 5, 1844 – Friday. This day strongly puts me in mind of the moment fate ushered me into this miserable existence. I am this day thirty-three years old; running rapidly up to the number of days allotted to man. Thirty-three years! The question rises – what portion of that time has been employed as it should have been? I confess I could not, for my life, account for half of it!

Traverse des Sioux

July 6, 1844 – Saturday. Arrived at Traverse des Sioux[367] about two o'clock. This part of the country is almost altogether covered over with water. I went down to see Mr. Riggs,[368] and took supper with him.

July 7, 1844 – Sunday. Attended public services. Mr. Riggs preached.

Rowing to St. Peter's

July 8, 1844 – Monday. We hired a boat of Mr. Riggs' to carry our luggage down in to St. Peter's. We left all our cattle and horses in care of our hired man.

July 9, 1844 – Tuesday. Left the Traverse for St. Peter's. Our cattle and horses to be taken down by land.

July 10, 1844 – Wednesday. Carried on as fast as the current and four oars could carry us.

---

367 A shallow rocky ford across the Minnesota River in the vicinity of the present city of St. Peter on that river. It was a traditional gathering place of the Dakota Sioux, and would be, seven years later, the site of that nation's treaty with the US Government. As Gunn pointed out in a note to Garrioch's first visit here (p. 96), that location must not be confused with the party's next destination: the settlement of St. Peter's (now Mendota) at the junction of the Minnesota and Mississippi Rivers. See diary entries for July 3, 6, & 7, 1844.

368 Gunn: Rev. Stephen R. Riggs. See Chap. 3, text associated with nn. 196-204, on Riggs, as well as diary entries for July 6-8, August 20, & August 31, 1844.

July 11, 1844 – Thursday. Arrived at St. Peter's.[369]

St. Paul's

Garrioch immediately crossed the Mississippi to the east bank settlement – known by then as St. Paul's in honour of the recent establishment there of a Roman Catholic mission and church of that name – where he and his companions found accommodation with prominent resident / merchant Henry Jackson.

Went down to St. Paul's[370] and took up lodging with one Jackson.[371] Our fare here was at {191} the rate of $3.00 per week. {192}

July 12, 1844 – Friday. The steamer Lynx arrived from Galena [Illinois]. In this boat I hired a [later] passage for $10.00 to Galena and back again.

---

369 The earliest permanent white settlement in Minnesota, located on the Minnesota River near where it joins the Mississippi from the west. It is now known as Mendota.

370 Then a new young community on the east bank of the Mississippi a little downstream of both the head of navigation at St. Anthony on that river and of St. Peter's on the Minnesota River. Gunn: "We have here the first mention of this name in Garrioch's journal, the reason being that, upon his visit, it had not yet begun to be applied to that locality. The name St. Paul first appeared in 1841. In that year the Catholics of Dubuque, Iowa sent out a missionary, the Reverend Lucien Galtier, to Fort Snelling. He, finding a little group of his coreligionists settled on the spot where St. Paul now is, decided to establish a mission there. He built a rude log building on a bluff overlooking the Mississippi River on what is now known as Bench Street. This simple structure was dedicated November 1, 1841, and named the Chapel of St. Paul; a name which soon attached itself to the locality and persists in the St. Paul of the present day. See *Pen Pictures of St. Paul, Minnesota*, by T. M. Newson, pp. 23-24. On pages 60-61 of that work is a picture of the infant metropolis as it was in 1847, three years after Garrioch's first visit to it – substantially the hamlet which he saw. At that time, the author says: 'St. Paul could boast of five stores, about twenty families and thirty-six children, making in all not more than fifty inhabitants, while the entire white population in the Territory could not have been more than three hundred.'"

371 Gunn: "Henry Jackson [was] one of the pioneer citizens of St. Paul. He was born in Abingdon, Virginia, February 1, 1811. In 1842, he came to Minnesota and settled on the site of the present day of St. Paul, where he opened a small store for the accommodation of both the white and Indian population. This establishment, which was the first store to be operated on the site of the present metropolis, stood on the bluff just above the lower landing, near the corner of the present Bench and Jackson Streets, the latter of which derives its name from this fact. In more senses than one, Jackson may be said to have been a 'first citizen' of St. Paul: he was first storekeeper, first justice of the peace, first postmaster, first hotel keeper, member of the first town council and of the first territorial legislature." Gunn: p. 191.

Chapter 6 – St. Peter's, St. Paul's & the Crow Wing Trail

Pig's Eye

Before leaving for Galena, Garrioch and his friends paid a visit to a disreputable part of the river bottom lands some distance south of St. Paul's known as "Pig's Eye" in honour of a one-eyed French-Canadian who dispensed whisky to Indians and others at a sordid drinking establishment located there.[372] **It was not to carouse, however, that the Rupertians went to Pig's Eye.**

July 14, 1844 – Sunday. Went down to the Pig's Eye in expectation of {193} meeting our cattle there, which had to be crossed [over the river] immediately on their arrival.

July 15, 1844 – Monday. Our men came down by the St. Peter's [trail] with the cattle and horses; all well and safe but very thin.

---

372 Gunn: "The place bearing this unusual name at that time was several miles below St. Paul. It was situated in the bottom lands of the Mississippi at the foot of Dayton's Bluff, opposite what was then Kaposia, or Little Crow's Village. This locality, then known as Grand Marais, was settled in 1839 by a number of French Canadians from the Red River country, said to have been connected with the American Fur Company. The name 'Pig's Eye' became attached to this community about 1842, at which time a notorious whiskey seller of French Canadian origin, Pierre Parrant by name, adopted it as his place of residence and centre of operations. This famous, or rather infamous [and] evil-looking fellow [was] bereft of an eye [and his] remaining optic [resembled] that of a pig. On account of this peculiarity, Parrant was nicknamed 'Pig's Eye;' the name being subsequently transferred to his place of business and then to the entire community. The name, I understand, has clung to this locality, if not up to the present at any rate to within quite recent years. Pierre Parrant and Pig's Eye [had] won a sure niche in history prior to Garrioch's visit. [In 1838 he erected] a hovel along the Mississippi, at the mouth of the small creek flowing out of Fountain Cave, in what is new upper St. Paul, about four miles below Fort Snelling, where he sold whiskey to soldiers and Indians. The following year, he built a log shanty, and plied the same trade, at the foot of what is now Robert Street. It was to this latter establishment that the grotesque sobriquet above mentioned was first attached. A young Canadian who was staying at the groggery, [wrote] a letter to [someone, and] for want of a better designation dated his missive from "Pig's Eye," receiving, in due course a reply to that address. From that time the name was applied to Parrant's shebeen, and to the little community that soon grew up around it. [When he removed] to Grand Marais about 1842 [the name] went with him and became attached to the new location. Pierre Parrant and his "Pig's Eye" may not rank with Romulus and some others as the traditional founder of a great city; but that the good people of St. Paul have no disposition to disown their "Parrant-age" is evidenced in the following piece of doggerel published in the *St. Paul Pioneer Press* on January 1, 1850:

Pig's Eye? Yes; Pig's Eye!
That's the spot! A very funny name, is it not?
Pig's Eye's the spot, to plant my city on,
To be remembered by, when I am gone.
Pig's Eye, converted thou shalt be, like Saul:
Thy name, henceforth, shall be St Paul."

The end of the trail from Traverse des Sioux being on the west side of the Mississippi and St. Paul on the east, the livestock had to be got across the river for sale. No further reference to the animals being made, it seems likely that they were successfully sold.

A Disgrace

July 21, 1844 – Sunday. Most disgraceful to the community of St. Paul's, Moutrie and Lasart[373] had a fist fight this evening.

To Galena by Steamboat

July 22, 1844 – Monday. This is the day I went on the Lynx for Galena. {194}

Galena, Illinois, a bustling lead-mining centre with a population of close to 14,000, was the largest community on the Mississippi north of St. Louis at that time – an excellent place for Peter Garrioch and the Cooks to complete their commercial mission.[374] The steamboat

---

373 Gunn: "The first-mentioned of these rioters is undoubtedly the "Moutry" of the June 21, 1844, entry, above, text at n. 354,355. The last-mentioned is not so easy to identify. There were several individuals of this name among the French Métis of Red River prior to and at that time. The difficulty of identification is increased by the fact that the name is seldom ever spelled the same in different records. We find the forms Lasart, Lesart, Lasert, La Serte, Laserte and La Cert. In the Red River census lists of 1838 there is a Louis La Certe set down as native, Catholic, no age, five children; and in the 1843 lists is a Louis Lacerte, native, Catholic, no age, no children. Either one may be the party of the reference. During the Métis uprising of 1869-70, Riel, the rebel leader called two conventions, at the first of which a Louis Lacerte was one of the two delegates from St. Norbert. At the second, a Louis Lascerte was the delegate from Pointe Coupée. As these places were in the same direction and not far apart, it is likely that the two delegates are one and the same person, and identical with one or the other of the names on the census above mentioned. [Any one of several other men with similar names] also might be Garrioch's Lasart. [Members of this family] seem to have been of a wandering disposition and not easy to keep track of."

374 Galena had been producing lead since 1814, and by 1845 its output was 27,000 tons annually. Although the decline in the use of lead in recent times has reduced its population sharply (just over 3,400 in 2010) Galena had almost 14,000 inhabitants when Peter Garriock visited. Gunn: "The following brief description of Galena, Illinois is taken from the diary of Reverend Alfred Brunson (*Wisconsin Historical Society Collections* XV, p. 280), a Methodist missionary who was there in 1835, nine years previous to Garrioch's visit. Allowing for intervening growth, this is substantially the town in which he spent the week described. Brunson says: "This is a place of great business, about 1,200 inhabitants. It is situated on a hillside on Fever River, about seven miles from the mouth. There are two streets in the town, too narrow to admit of teams passing with convenience, and one so much higher than the other that the people on the upper street can look into the chimneys of those on the lower. The hillside is but a mass of rock, and admits of no gardens worth anything. The people are most intelligent, enterprising and healthy, but too much absorbed in the cares of the world to think of religion. The trade of this mineral district occupies six or eight steamboats, which ply constantly between St. Louis and Galena, Dubuque and Prairie du Chien." Another descrip-

Chapter 6 – St. Peter's, St. Paul's & the Crow Wing Trail

Lynx **appears to have traveled the distance, which Gunn estimated as 327 miles, between St. Paul and Galena in about two days – perhaps longer going upstream.**

A Most Painful Circumstance

July 24, 1844 – Wednesday. Here it becomes my duty to note down one of the most painful circumstances that has ever come under my observation and experience.

Yesterday I had made an arrangement with W. Cook, or rather I had proposed the thing to him, to take out all the shoes and other articles I had on hand to the country [around Galena], either to peddle or barter them. I proposed allowing him a certain percentage for his trouble and expenses. William cheerfully accepted the offer. Early then this morning he hired a man, with his horse and wagon, and started for the country immediately after breakfast. In the course of the evening he returned, apparently much affected by his not succeeding as he had anticipated. He retired immediately into his bed chamber, and in a few minutes after sent for me. On my entering he fell to crying.

Upon my enquiring into the cause, he told me he could not, and finally said he would not, tell me. Upon [my] pressing the question, he told me I should become acquainted with the whole mystery in six days. He seemed to labour under dreadful foreboding of the future, and apparently evinced strong apprehension for the welfare of his particular friends and relations. I could not but feel most keenly for his miserable condition. I trembled for his safety. Though I did all in my power to conceal my agitated feelings, as operated upon by his dread and wild despair, he detected the anxiety I manifested for his most unfortunate case.

Aside from his apprehension for the future, his mind appeared to be occupied entirely with love and fortune. This led us to conclude that his mind had been operated upon by degrees by a strong attachment he had formed for a certain young lady, without

---

tion (1834) says: "The country around Galena, for a distance of forty or fifty miles east and north, was dotted with crude log furnaces for smelting the mineral, the products of all of which had to be hauled by team to this post for shipment down to St. Louis, from which place it found its way all over the country. There were several stores in the town, with well assorted stocks of goods suitable to supply the necessities of the settlers and miners, and the volume of business was surprising. (Theodore Rodolf, *Wisconsin Historical Society Collections* XV, pp. 342-343)." Gunn's note goes on to list the places Garrioch would have passed en route from St. Paul to Galena, and gives the distance traveled as 327 miles each way.

having the means or resources to support her rank and character; or, in other words, to justify their union. {195}

What had happened? Although we are never given a better explanation than this passage provides, it may be reasonable to speculate that this apparently unsuccessful youngest son of a once-powerful fur trader, whose dynamic and successful nephews were now giving him menial tasks like rounding-up their straying livestock,[375] and who had eagerly seized upon Garrioch's proposal as a way of proving himself to them and to his sweetheart back home, had been demolished emotionally by the final straw of failing as an itinerant salesman. Another hypothesis would be that the woman in question was in St. Paul, that she had promised an answer to his proposal when he returned there in six days, and that he was apprehensive about her decision.

A Perfect Maniac

July 25, 1844 – Thursday. However dreadful, what is to be must be. Poor William, as I apprehended yesterday, is this morning a perfect maniac. His reasoning powers have left him, and he is now classed with the insane.

July 26, 1844 – Friday. William grows worse, and attempts to strip himself naked. The *Lynx* leaves today for St. [Paul's] and Henry [Cook] goes in her to see after poor William.

One Sabbath – Five Church Services

July 28, 1844 – Sunday. Attended the service of the Episcopal church twice today, and once at the Presbyterian church; also a few minutes each at the Methodist and Baptist congregations.

Was the erstwhile student of theology seeking to compare and contrast denominations? Or was he just starved for Christian fellowship after so long in the wilderness?

---

375   See the entry for June 22, 1844.

The Circus

July 29, 1844 – Monday. Attended the circus in the afternoon. About 2,000 spectators. The performances were splendid and done with much taste and ability.

July 30, 1844 – Tuesday. Attended another part of the circus performance. Saw James Matheson[376] of Red River to-day. He is still the same keen old coon.

Back to St. Paul's

I spent a week at Galena; and, after seeing all that {196} could have been seen, and having made all the purchases that my limited means would allow me, I returned to [St. Paul's] on board the same steamer the *Lynx*.

William in Irons

On my arrival at St. Paul's, I found poor William much better than I had anticipated. This, however, did not continue long. In a few days a change for the worse was manifest from his conduct and appearance. Poor fellow, we could do nothing for him.

It was my purpose to make application to the commanding officer [at Fort Snelling] to take him under his charge till a favourable opportunity offered to have him conveyed to St. Louis and safely lodged in a lunatic asylum. Mr. Steele,[377] however, told me there was no use in making the application, as it [had been] with the greatest reluctance, and through unavoidable circumstances and considerations, that on a previous occasion the commanding officer had been induced to afford that lenity to [someone] labouring under a similar debility. With this failure, we had no alternative but to borrow a house for poor William and keep him closely confined [temporarily there] in iron cuffs.

Delayed Departure

With fall approaching and a very long trek ahead in order to convey themselves, a large quantity of purchased trade goods, and their unbalanced uncle back to Red River before winter, Peter Garrioch and Henry Cook were anxious to depart at the first opportuni-

---

376   Gunn: "I have no data on this individual. He was probably one of the Kildonan Mathesons, but I have not been fortunate enough to be able to place him."

377   Gunn: "Franklin Steele, a well-known resident of Fort Snelling at that time, and afterwards of Minneapolis. Steele was born in Chester County, Pennsylvania, and came to Fort Snelling in 1837, [and] the following year was appointed sutler to the garrison."

ty. But they were plagued by delays – many of them probably associated with William's condition.

Another source of delay may have been indecision as to the route they should take. Most members of the main party they had traveled with to St. Peter's were apparently intending to return to Red River the same way they had come. As we have seen, however, that trail passed through an area heavily populated by Sioux and was thought to be dangerous for Red River migrants. Garrioch and Cook eventually made their decision, completed their arrangements, and set off from St. Paul's for St. Peter's and the Minnesota River.

After spending some days at St. Paul's, trying to get off every day, we at length came to the conclusion to return by the old route. With this view, we loaded our boat at Jackson's and rowed up to Sibley's,[378] [at St. Peter's] where we intended to take in some plank for Mr. Riggs [further up the Minnesota at the Traverse], {198} which we had promised to take up [in payment] for the use of his boat.

Change of Plans

The journey had barely begun, however, when, at St. Peter's, a further frustrating delay occurred; and an encounter with a Red River-bound couple brought about a change of plans.

August 20, 1844 – Tuesday. We discovered this morning, when too late, that our boat was not sufficient to take in all our luggage and the lumber we had promised by contract to take up [to Riggs]. We were therefore driven to the awkward and unpleasant necessity of leaving all the luggage behind, belonging to Mclaughlin, Cook and myself, and started with only what belonged to Larivière and D. Ducharme,[379] and

---

378 Gunn: "Henry Hastings Sibley, one of the early Minnesota pioneers, who afterwards rose to positions of honour and trust. Born at Detroit, Michigan [in] 1811, he came west to Sault Ste. Marie [in 1829], and became a clerk for the American Fur Company at Mackinac. In 1834, when Astor sold out his interests in the AFC, Sibley became a partner in the new firm, and was sent by them to the Mississippi as their general manager of the trade with the Sioux. His headquarters were at Mendota [then St Peter's], at the mouth of the [Minnesota] River]." Gunn's note goes on to describe Sibley's subsequent illustrious career: election to the legislatures of the Wisconsin and Minnesota territories and as Governor of Minnesota after its statehood; appointment as Commander of U.S. forces to quell the Sioux uprising of 1862 and to subsequently drive hostile Sioux westward; service as Regent and President of the state university, president of the state Historical Society; and author of many historical papers. See *Lives of the Governors of Minnesota*, by James H. Baker, *Collections of the Minnesota Historical Society* XIII (1908), pp. 77-105; also Upham, *Minnesota Biographies*, p. 702."

379 Gunn: "No Christian name being given, there are no means of positively identifying the first of these parties. The note then listed several possible candidates. [The other] was Dominque Ducharme, a French Canadian who lived at St. Boniface. [He was] an active free trader, associated

300 ft. of plank {199} instead of 600 ft. Cook and I, to oblige McLaughlin, retracted our former intention of returning by the old route, and concluded to bring our carts down and return by the Sauk Rapids.[380]

This was the first mention of John McLaughlin, whom Garrioch and Cook had apparently just met. McLaughlin was an Irishman – a nephew of Red River entrepreneur Andrew McDermot, and a stranger to the North American wilds – who was traveling to the Settlement with his new bride.[381] The cousins undertook to accompany the couple through the wilderness, and, in apparent deference to their charges' safety concerns, agreed to proceed by a route that would follow the Mississippi further north before turning northwest at Sauk Rapids in order to re-connect with the normal route north of the area of greatest perceived danger. It is not known how much Peter and Henry charged the McLaughlins to shepherd them to HBC territory, but whatever it might have been must soon have seemed inadequate.

---

with Garrioch, James Sinclair, Alexis Goulet, Henry Cook, *et al.*, and [would be] a signer [as was Garrioch] of the petition addressed to the Council of Assiniboia on May 9, 1845 praying for exemption from payment of duty on goods imported from the US. (See Minutes of Council of Assiniboia, June 16, 1845. Oliver, *Canadian North-West*, I)." The Red River census for 1838 lists him as Canadian, Catholic, age 30, married, with 2 children.

380 Garrioch called these the "Sac Rapids." Gunn's note explains the origin of the name and its modern equivalent: "The Sauk Rapids of the present day, on the Mississippi above the mouth of the Osakis or Sauk River, and about 80 miles, by the old Mississippi wagon route, northwest of St. Paul. St. Cloud is on the west bank, a few miles farther down, at the junction of the two streams above mentioned. There was a trail running from Sauk Rapids northwesterly to a point near the present Breckenridge, on what was known in those days as the Sioux, Sioux Wood, or Bois des Sioux River. It is now known below Breckenridge as the Red River. The Sauk River and rapids take their name from a tribe of Indians known as the Osakis, Sauks, or Sacs, who formerly frequented that locality; hence Garrioch's 'Sac Rapids' instead of the present name."

Gunn also described the detour Garrioch *et al.* intended to take from Sauk Rapids back to the "old route: [It] ran in a northwesterly direction from Sauk Rapids, or later from St. Cloud, on the Mississippi. It went by way of Sauk Center, Alexandria, Pomme de Terre River, and what is now Breckenridge, crossing the Sioux Wood River there and proceeding north on the west side of the Red."

381 Gunn: "John McLaughlin, whose name will frequently recur in succeeding pages, was an Irish nephew of Andrew McDermot, the great Red River merchant, [who was] on his way into the Red River Settlement, upon his first arrival in the country [accompanied by a new bride.]. It was, I believe, a case of elopement, this being the honeymoon trip. A keen-witted but somewhat erratic character, he was not given to hiding his light under bushels. During his five year [subsequent stay] at Red River, he entered with zest into the various activities of the country; entering with especial zeal into the free trade field and the agitation against the Hudson's Bay Company's asserted trade monopoly. In his free trade operations he was principally associated with his uncle, McDermot." Gunn's note goes on to describe some of McLaughlin's anti-HBC activities, and states that he eventually settled in Savanna, Georgia. See Bumsted, *DMB*, p. 163.

The other two individuals mentioned – Larivière and Ducharme – may have been hired men, who presumably intended to travel home with the main party and therefore needed to have their gear taken with them to the Traverse.

While the McLaughlins waited at St. Peter's or St Paul's, the cousins therefore started for the Traverse along the Minnesota with their cargo of lumber for Reverend Riggs, their hired men, and their manacled uncle.

Tragedy

August 21, 1844 – Wednesday. This day is one not soon to be forgotten. It dates the memorable and most melancholy fate of the late, poor, and unfortunate William Cook. While sitting amusing himself, with his feet in the water over the gunwale of the boat, he sprang into the river with the intention of getting to land. His feet and hands being fettered with iron cuffs, he sank like a stone, never more to rise. The stream being deep and rapid, and there being no light craft at hand, assistance on our part was impossible. We left him in the hands and care of the Disposer of all Events, conscious that any effort on our part to save his life would be impracticable and unavailing.

The Brushing the Hunters Gave the Sioux

As Garrioch and his party continued upstream on the Minnesota River toward Traverse des Sioux – probably being hauled against the current by one or more of their horses on an adjoining towpath – they learned from someone encountered along the way of an important recent occurrence on the prairies.

August 24, 1844 – Saturday. Today we heard of the brushing the hunters gave the Sioux, out at their hunting excursions.

The "hunters" were members of the Métis buffalo brigade from Red River who had been attacked by a group of Lac Traverse Sioux. The "brushing" was the major defeat the Métis had inflicted on their attackers in response.

Realizing that this humiliation would significantly increase the risk of Sioux retaliation against any passers-by from Red River, Garrioch decided to warn his friends in the main party returning to the Settlement, who were just preparing to leave St. Peter's, and to travel by the "old route" via Lac Traverse. In addition to his concern for their safety, he knew that his own party would be more secure if he could persuade the larger group to take the Sauk Rapids trail as well.

I rode back to Sibley's to ascertain what effect the intelligence may have on the rest of our party. They determined, however, agreeable to their first intentions, to proceed on the old route.

We therefore proceeded on the following day to the Traverse.

Tragical Event of the Missouri Drovers

August 30, 1844 – Friday. Arrived at the Traverse, and found several Indians of the Sioux tribe tenting there. None of these Indians, fortunately, were of Lac Traverse.

Received intelligence of the tragical event of the Missouri drovers. {200}

A group of drovers driving cattle eastward from Missouri country had recently been set upon near Lac Traverse by a band of Sioux – possibly members of the same group defeated by the Métis.[382] The sole drover to survive the attack and subsequent wilderness ordeals had just been rescued by Reverend Steven Riggs when Garrioch arrived at Riggs' mission to deliver his partial consignment of lumber and arrange for further use of the missionary's boat.

August 31, 1844 – Saturday. Having entered upon fresh arrangements with Mr. Riggs for the use of his boat back to St. Peter's, we started for that port this morning and landed there on the 2nd September.

---

382   Gunn: "The affair here referred to took place immediately prior to the date [of the diary entry]. In the earlier part of the season, a party of American drovers had set out from Missouri, across the plains, with a drove of cattle, destined, according to some accounts, for the Indians at Fort Snelling, and for Red River according to others. There were four of these Americans. This party, when somewhere in the neighborhood of Lake Traverse, were met by a band of Sisseton Dakotas returning from an unsuccessful foray against their ancient enemies, the Ojibways. Believing the drovers to be Red River people, they conceived this to be a good opportunity to avenge themselves on the Red River buffalo hunters, with whom they were at that time on bad terms; having quite recently been roughly handled and defeated by these hardy plainsmen of the North. They accordingly [attacked], robbing the drovers of their outfit, shooting some of the cattle, and stampeding the rest. One of the men, offering resistance, was killed on the spot, and the others were taken prisoners. One of these latter, being sent with a number of Indians to round up the cattle, escaped, and was never afterwards heard of. The next morning, the other two, Turner and Bennett, were permitted to leave, but were destitute of proper clothing or means of subsistence. After wandering for four days, Turner, who could not swim, was drowned in trying to cross a deep stream. Bennett, the solitary survivor, struggled on for five days longer, subsisting on hazelnuts, and at last reached the camp of Sleepy Eyes, a friendly Sioux chief at Swan Lake, near Travers des Sioux. Here he was found by Reverend Stephen R. Riggs, at that time in charge of a mission to the Sioux at the latter point, who took charge of him, furnishing him with food and clothing, and providing for his return to his people in Missouri. A reliable first-hand account of this affair may be found in Riggs' *Mary and I: Forty Years with the Sioux*, pp. 115-117." Gunn: pp. 199-200.

On to Sauk Rapids

Although the drover's story offered additional evidence that the "old route" to Red River was a risky one, it did not cause the main party to change its plans. It might possibly have been a factor, however, in the decision of veteran free trader James Green, who was mentioned in the June 21, 1944 diary entry, to join Garrioch's little group as it prepared to move on up the Mississippi, which they now considered to be a safer way.

September 4, 1844 – **Wednesday.** Made arrangements with Moutrie[383] to conduct us to Red River, by the Sauk Rapids, for the sum of six pounds.

September 5, 1844 – **Thursday.** Moutrie told us this morning he could not go with us, as he could not find any person to take his ox and cart over to Red River from the Traverse. {201}

September 9, 1844 – **Monday.** Prepared our carts, horses, etc., for a start on the following day. We sold, today, the late William Cook's horse to Pierre Bottineau[384] for $80.00, and hired him as our guide to Bois des Sioux at the rate of $2.00 per day.

September 10, 1844 – **Tuesday.** Prevented from starting in consequence of sleet and rain.

September 11, 1844 – **Wednesday.** Bade fare-ye-well to our friends at St. Paul's, and made a regular start for Red River – home.

September 12, 1844 – **Thursday.** Our guide overtook us near Rum River.[385] {202}

---

383 This is undoubtedly the "Moutry" of earlier entries.

384 Gunn: "Another of the outstanding native pioneers of those days. Pierre Bottineau was known to every traveler, trader or resident in Minnesota, the Dakotas, and what is now Manitoba, for more than half a century, preceding and subsequent to this time. He was born in the Red River Settlement, January 1, 1817. His father was Canadian French and his mother Ojibwa. He came to Fort Snelling, Minnesota about 1837, and his subsequent occupation was principally that of guide, interpreter and hunter. There were few treaties, military or exploratory expeditions made, during this period that did not owe something to Pierre Bottineau, in one or other of these capacities. He spoke all the Indian languages, and had traveled over almost the entire Northwest. After settlers were ejected from the military reservation at Fort Snelling, he lived at St. Paul for six years. From there he moved to St. Anthony, and established a settlement at what is now known as Bottineau's Prairie. His name is also perpetuated in Bottineau County, North Dakota. See Upham, *Minnesota Biographies*, p. 66."

385 Hired at the last minute, Bottineau must have had business to complete before leaving, and agreed to catch up with the party the day after their departure. Gunn described the place where they met: "A tributary of the Mississippi, flowing into that stream from the north, about twenty-eight miles above St. Paul, known also as the Issati River, and by the Ojibways as Anoka Sippi. I have never

Another Change of Plans

September 16, 1844 – Monday. Came to the Sauk Rapids at an early part of this day.

Before the day was over, however, the travelers learned that their intended route was not as safe as they had hoped. While it would avoid the Traverse des Sioux and Lac Traverse areas, it would nevertheless take them back into a part of Sioux territory where, it now appeared, there was still a prospect of trouble.

While here taking dinner, Mr. Morrison,[386] a trader to Mr. W. {203} Akins,[387] came up to our camp on his way down to the garrison [at Fort Snelling], who stated that two different parties of the Sioux tribe had been observed loitering about that place some few days previous to our arrival.

He, as well as ourselves, entertained no doubt as to the intention of these rambling scoundrels. Their end, no doubt, was to intercept us on our way home, and wreak

---

happened across any satisfactory explanation of the origin of the name given above, by which it is now generally known. E.S. Seymour in his *Sketches of Minnesota*, p. 151, attributes it to the dark colour of the water, occasioned by the tamarack swamps through which it flows; but whether this is the true origin is doubtful. The Rum River is about 100 miles in length and is a stream of considerable size. It has its source in Mille Lacs, formerly known as Spirit Lake, whence it flows almost due south, [eventually] joining the Mississippi at the town of [Anoka]. It is about thirty yards wide at its mouth. It flows out of a heavily timbered country, and was formerly an important factor in the logging and lumbering industry of those parts."

386 Gunn: "There were two brothers of this name, William and Allen Morrison, identified with the early history of Minnesota. They were Scotch Canadians; and, like many more of that hardy stock, have left their names indelibly engraved on the map of the country. They were both engaged in the fur trade; though the name of William, the elder of the two, is remembered today chiefly on account of his achievements as an explorer. The younger brother, Allen is no doubt the gentleman referred to here. He was a well-known trader in this region at that time. Like his brother, he was born at Montreal. He came to Minnesota in 1820 at the age of 17, and traded with the Indians in the vicinity of Leech and Red Lakes. In 1833-34 he was at Mille Lacs, and later was on the upper Mississippi. He was the first settler at Crow Wing. On the formation of the Territory of Minnesota he was elected one of its first representatives. Morrison County, on the Mississippi, just above where our party now are, is named in his honour. See Neill, *History of Minnesota*, pp. 375, 416; Upham, *Minnesota Biographies, Minnesota Historical Collections* XIV, pp. 526, 527; I, pp. 417-18."

387 Gunn: "Aitkin is probably meant. There were three different traders of this name in Minnesota in the early days – William A., Alfred and John – but W. A. is no doubt the one here referred to. He was of Scotch nationality, born about 1787. He came to the Minnesota region when but a boy of 15, and entered the Indian trade. He had charge of the Fond du Lac department of the American Fur Company, with headquarters at Sandy Lake, from about 1830 on. Aitkin County and Town are named for him. (See Neill, *History of Minnesota*, pp. 405, 416; Upham, *Minnesota Biographies*, p. 6)."

their vengeance upon our property; so as to satiate vengeful feelings on us, which it was not in their power to exercise on those hunters of the Red River who had annihilated so many of their friends. Thus taking the above view of the subject, we deemed it necessary and advisable to alter our intention of going home by that route, and to prefer a safer, however difficult and arduous.

We therefore discharged our guide for the Sauk Rapids route, and unanimously a{204}greed to hire another for our intended new route.

The Crow Wing Trail

This was a momentous decision. The new route would certainly be safer from Indian depredations, because it would avoid Sioux territory altogether, continuing further north on the Mississippi before turning west through country populated chiefly by Ojibwa friendly to Métis and other Red River residents. But while Garrioch and his friends knew it would be "difficult and arduous," it is unlikely that they realized just how difficult it would prove to be. Whether they knew it or not, they had opted to carve a new trail from the Mississippi to the prairies. It would become known as the Crow Wing Trail.[388]

---

388 Gunn: "[The route] afterwards known to the inhabitants of Red River as the Crow Wing Trail is here rightly referred to by Garrioch as a "new route," as it was cut out de novo by this party; and theirs were the first vehicles to traverse it. We have here, so far as I am aware, the only extant account of the opening up of this historic old trail. The late Sir John Schultz, former Governor of Manitoba, in a contribution to the Manitoba Historical Society (Transaction 45), entitled "The Old Crow Wing Trail," has left a very interesting account of a journey made over it in 1860. He appears to be mistaken, however, in stating (p. 4) that it was opened 'under direction of William Hallett.' I am quite sure that, had Hallett been with Garrioch's party, some mention of him would be found in this Journal.

"This route left the Mississippi at the Crow Wing River, and following up that stream to near its junction with the Leaf River, a tributary flowing into it from the west. It followed the latter stream to Leaf Lake, thence crossing over to Ottertail Lake and Ottertail River. Then it followed the chain of small lakes and streams constituting the upper waters of the Ottertail or Red River northward, towards their source. Finally passing by Detroit Lake, the present popular summer resort, it kept on the higher country back from the Red River until it reached Pembina. In later years, this northern portion of the route varied, the east side of the Red being kept, sometimes, right to Fort Garry. On the present trip, the Red will be crossed to the west side at Park River. In general, however, the above fairly describes the route."

Sir John Schultz's account of his 1860 journey on the Crow Wing was made in 1894, over 30 years later, but was still vividly descriptive of the already much-used route. He was 19 years old at the time and did not explain his source for attributing the opening of the trail to William Hallett; in fact, he said: "The old Crow Wing Trail, opened in 1844 by a few adventurous spirits under direction of William Hallett, who, having been attacked by the Sioux on their way to St. Paul by Lac Travers and St. Peter, sought safety in returning by this route, many miles of which had to be cut through the woods.": "The Old Crow Wing Trail," *MHS Transactions*, Ser. 1, nr. 45 (Manitoba

Chapter 6 – St. Peter's, St. Paul's & the Crow Wing Trail

Before they could begin that historic trek, however, they had several days' further travel northward along the east side of the Mississippi's upper reaches to a trading post on Crow Island, where they hoped to engage another guide, and then to the mouth of the Crow Wing River[389] **where the trail would begin.**

September 17, 1844 – Tuesday. Crossed the Elk River near McDonald's place, {205} another trader among the Chippewas on the Mississippi.[390] Green's cart upset and its entire contents were totally submerged.

Historical Society, 1894). Significantly, he referred to "a few adventurous spirits" as being responsible for opening the trail, which could mean that Peter Garrioch was among them even though not receiving the credit for it from Schultz. Schultz's address, with an introduction to Schultz himself, is reprinted in Jim Blanchard, ed., *A Thousand Miles of Prairie: the Manitoba Historical Society and the History of Western Canada* (Winnipeg: University of Manitoba Press, 2002), pp. 107-127.

In short, there may have been multiple attributions for being "the first" to have opened up the route, but it was surely already known to Aboriginal inhabitants and perhaps the occasional Métis hunter who were early users of a route which later gained increasing popularity as time went on to the point at which Peter made use of it to avoid possible hostilities. It has been described as "an historical Métis trade route used during the Pemmican Wars of the 1700-1800s." *Alberta Native News* (June, 2002). The innovation attributable to Peter might have come from connecting different trails together, perhaps for new purposes, as much as in blazing entirely new routes.

For a detailed modern description of Garrioch's journey along the Crow Wing route, see Gilman, *Red River Trails*, pp. 9-10, & 55-57. The authors refer to its alternate name, the "Woods Trail" and provide a map of it. See also Morton's Introduction to *London Correspondence Inward from Eden Colvile*, pp. lviii-lix; as well as Morton, *Manitoba: A History*, p. 75. W. L. Morton gave Peter credit for "first opening" the Crow Wing Trail, which allowed the free traders to bring American goods to Red River and was "a trail to the east of the Red which was less exposed to stoppage by the Sioux than the older trails down the open plains of the west bank."

389   Gunn: "This stream, the Aile de Corbeau of the French, rises in a series of small lakes to the south and west of Leech Lake, in the southern portions of what are now Hubbard and Cass Counties. From Hubbard it flows south [and east] to its junction with the Mississippi. This it accomplishes just below the present village of Crow Wing, on the opposite side of the Mississippi. Brainard is about eight miles above. The distance from Crow Wing to St. Paul, by the old wagon trail, used to be reckoned about 130 miles. The country through which [the Crow Wing and its tributaries] flow is, generally speaking, heavily wooded; the principal timber being pine, tamarack, spruce, with elm, birch, etc., in the river bottoms. It was known to the early voyageurs as the Bois Forts or Strong Woods." Gunn, p. 213.

390   Gunn: "Elk River is a small stream flowing into the Mississippi from the north about twelve miles above Rum River, or thirty miles above St. Paul. It has two principal branches; the most westerly rising in a number of small streams to the north of Sauk Rapids, in Benton County, and paralleling the Mississippi practically all the way from the latter point to its junction with that river. From opposite McLeod to its mouth, its main stream lies in Sherburne County. It joins the Mississippi a few miles above the present town of Elk River, which is named from it. It is joined by another branch from the north opposite Monticello. The old wagon road from St. Paul, on the east side of the Mississippi crossed it near its mouth. At this point it is rapid and deep and about twenty

This is the first indication that the party consisted of anyone other than Garrioch, his employee Charles Laurance, Henry Cook, the McLaughlins, and a guide. A later entry[391] discloses that Cook's brother Joe was also with them, but he was not an adult. With James Green, the group comprised seven souls (eight if Green had an assistant) in all at this point.

September 22, 1844 – Sunday. Spent this day at the Apple Lake, about two miles from the Crow Island.

Crow Island & A Little Dance

September 23, 1844 – Monday. Came to the Crow Island.[392]

September 24, 1844 – Tuesday. Had an invitation to dine with Suza Bruno, Mr. Aitkin's trader. Had a little dance by way of exercise.

Waiting for a Guide

September 26, 1844 – Thursday. Still at Crow Island waiting for Mr. Morrision. We had requested the above Suza Bruno to conduct us some six or eight days till we reached some point whence we could proceed without a conductor, aided simply by his directions. For this purpose we have now waited several days, as S. B. is a hired man under yearly salary, and cannot be absent without acquainting his employer. Neither Mr. Aitken nor Mr. Morrison, his right hand man, makes his appearance, so we have concluded to make a start tomorrow at all hazards. Hitherto our traveling ha[s][393] been easy and pleasant; what has to come has yet to be learned.

---

yards wide. The party here referred to, at whose place the crossing was made, is probably Donald McDonald, a well-known trader and pioneer of those parts in the early days of Minnesota. Mr. McDonald was born in Canada, in 1803. He was, in his early life, connected with the Hudson's Bay Company, afterwards being in the employ of the American Fur Company, and stationed at various ones of their posts in Minnesota. He is said to have built one of the first houses on the east side of the Mississippi near Fort Snelling, and at one time owned a large tract of land now included in the city of St. Paul. He afterwards lived at Crow Wing. See Upham, *Minnesota Biographies*, p. 464." Gunn, p. 204.

391   October 27, 1844. Gunn, p. 217.

392   Gunn: "An island in the Mississippi about 15 miles below the mouth of the Crow Wing River. There were trading posts on this island from time to time. In 1826 the American Fur Company had a post here called Fort Biddle (*Minnesota in Three Centuries*, II, p. 54). In 1832 the Schoolcraft expedition to the source of the Mississippi, on its return journey, spent Sunday there with the trader Baker (Neill, *History of Minnesota*, p. 409). At the time of Garrioch's visit, it was in charge of W. A. Aitkin, with Allen Morrison as local trader in charge."

393   Garrioch's word was "had," suggesting that the entry was written some time after the event.

Crossing the Mississippi

September 27, 1844 – Friday. Crossed the Mississippi a little above the Crow Island. Assisted by Suza Bruno with his two large canoes, we got ov{206}er in good time and everything in good order. Our animals crossed over with their carts empty. The river at our crossing place was nowhere more than four or four and half feet deep.[394]

Runaway Wagon & Stolen Horses

September 28, 1844 – Saturday. Bought several bushels of potatoes of Suza Bruno, among us.

McLaughlin's wagon ran with great fury down the hill, while his wife was in it, and came well nigh killing the poor thing.

While I am writing, four men of our party are out in search of four of our horses who were here but an hour ago, and our men have been gone nearly that time. I am afraid that some rascally young men of the Chippewas have ridden them off. [Later] it turned out just as we suggested about our horses; for Henry overtook two or three of these young scamps riding them off {207} towards the Red Lake.

---

394   Gunn: "The route taken by Garrioch and his party does not coincide at this point with the Crow Wing Trail of later days. Travelers over this route, in the fifties and sixties, kept to the east of the Mississippi all the way to Crow Wing, opposite the mouth of the Crow Wing River, where a crossing was made a little above the mouth of that stream, the trail then following up its northern bank to near the mouth of the Leaf River, where it was crossed over to its southern, or western side. In the present instance, Garrioch and his party cross the Mississippi to the west side, some twelve or fourteen miles below the mouth of the Crow Wing, at a point which I would identify as Topeka, about three miles above the present Belle Prairie. Some old maps of Minnesota show a trail running northwesterly from this point, passing three miles west of Fort Ripley, and striking the Crow Wing River about ten miles from its mouth, somewhere in the vicinity of the present Wheelock. This is undoubtedly the trail blazed out by our party; and, although no mention of a crossing here is made, it is safe to conclude, that the party crossed over to the north side of the Crow Wing at this point; their further trail being identical with that already described in the former part of this paragraph. I have been repeatedly told by old people who traveled over this trial that it crossed the Crow Wing River three times. [I believe] this statement was based upon a misconception, these early travelers confusing the Leaf River with the upper portion of the Crow Wing. The former of these streams the trail crosses near its junction with Leaf Lake; the second crossing is that of the Crow Wing proper, just below its junction with the Leaf River, the third being that near the site of Wheelock, above indicated. [It is possible that] instead of taking [the above-described] short cut to Topeka, or Belle Prairie, [Garrioch's party followed] the south bank of the river all the way to its mouth at Crow Wing, where the Mississippi was crossed and a junction made with the regular wagon road on the east side. The distance from Belle Prairie to the crossing of the Crow Wing at Wheelock, by this short cut, would be about eighteen miles as the crow flies." Gunn, pp. 205-206.

A Small Unguided Start

September 29, 1844 – Sunday. There being quite a number of Indians about the Crow Island trading house, which is not more than a mile from where we now are, we think advisable to make a small start to-day. We traveled about six miles and then encamped.[395]

Here, in spite of our wishes to get rid of drunken Chippewas, we were visited by a large party of them. They were, however, very kind and manifested no intention of bad design. After receiving each a piece of tobacco and a little to eat, they went off quietly without molesting us or ours.

Success, Disappointment & Brush Clearing

September 30, 1844 – Monday. Rode in to the Crow Island trading house with Charles Laurance, to see after our horses and our guide. Met five or six young men of the Chippewas leading off the two horses which {208} were not to be found yesterday – fortunately before they had crossed our yesterday's trail.

Suza Bruno told us that Mr. Aitkin, instead of coming up, had sent for him from St. Peter's. This, of course, put an end to his being our guide. He promised, however, to do his best and get some old Indian to follow us the day after.[396] We could not get provisions of any kind, and we therefore hastened back to our companions.

We then harnessed up in short order and traveled about six miles before sundown.[397] We have had some little cutting and clearing brush to-day. To-morrow must be left to speak for itself.

McLaughlin Inadvertently Summons Aid

Although the diaries did not record the event at the time, an Indian guide named Nine Fingers arrived the next day, as Suza Bruno had promised, and the back-breaking work of trail-cutting began. John McLaughlin and his wife, who seem to have been paying

---

395 Gunn: "If [my] former judgment as to the point of crossing of the Mississippi and the route followed is correct, this camp would be about three miles of the site of Fort Ripley."

396 This promise was kept. See entry below for October 19, 1844. Not until the November 6, 1844. entry do we learn the guide's name: Nine Fingers.

397 Gunn: "This camp would probably be a few miles to the northwest of Lake Alexander, in the vicinity of a place now known as Rail Prairie, in the northwest corner of Morrison County."

customers, were apparently not expected to participate in the work and found other diversions.

October 1, 1844 – Tuesday. A deal of cutting and clearing through brush and lying timber. Traveled five or six more miles to-day and then unhitched.[398] Four of us went out to clear some two or three miles more before we could proceed any further.

Alarmed, however, by a number of shots in the direction of our camp, we were obliged to leave our work and run home in haste, apprehending that the shots were from Sioux on the rest of our party, or from some ill-disposed Chippewas on our cattle.

On approaching our camp, however, we discovered all safe, and found out that the reports which so alarmed us were nothing more than McLaughlin's shooting a few pine squirrels for his dinner. He fired seven or eight shots and killed but two little squirrels and {209} one wood hen.

Disheartening Conditions

Gunn's calculations indicate that the party's progress was not as good as Garrioch thought; and the going was getting more difficult by the day.

October 2, 1844 – Wednesday. The cutting and clearing to-day is almost intolerable. It is now past noon and we have scarcely yet traveled three miles. Henry and Green are away to seek out a better route if possible.

They have returned, but every account they give of the face of the country before us would be enough to dishearten any person not accustomed to crosses and difficulties.

---

398 Gunn: "By consulting any fairly accurate plat map of this district, we are forced to conclude, that the travelers were not making nearly as many miles at each stage as they thought they were. The stop here indicated was made probably a couple of miles southeast of the first crossing of the Crow Wing River, in the neighborhood of the present villages of Wheelock or Pillager." Gunn, p. 208.

Green Gets Lost

October 3, 1844 – Thursday. Cut through and traveled the distance of about three miles more.[399] About 2 o'clock Green started on foot to explore the country ahead. He left here without a coat.

October 4, 1844 – Friday. Whatever is the cause, Green has not yet returned. He [should have been] back last evening at dusk or thereabouts. We waited until about an hour after that time and then discharged four shots, supposing him to have missed his way homeward. Now that I am writing, it is noon and Green has not yet made his appearance. He must either have wandered considerably from his course to our camp, or some serious accident has befallen him. Henry Cook and McLaughlin have now been gone two hours in quest of our friend. They started on horseback with the intention of going five or six miles up the river, the course Green intended to take. It is to be hoped that all our apprehensions of his safety will be converted into a month's en{210}tertainment of merry jokes and innocent laughter. This would only be putting his own theory of the subject into practice; for he said, the very day he started, that any person who lost himself in any country whatever ought to be whipped and transported.

Green Found; Mac Lost

Good! Green returned this evening, precisely at dusk. But strange[ly], as if this particular spot were destined to be the centre of accumulated crosses and calamities, while cutting and toiling through dense and almost impassible forests, Mac [McLaughlin], who was one of the party that went out in search of Green, has got lost in his turn. At least he has not yet returned, and it is now 7 or 8 o'clock of the night.

Green tells us that he found Mac in the centre of a tamarack swamp, with his horse up to the eyes in mud and mire. Green assisted him out of this awful predicament and then had left him – each party confident to strike a course for the camp as best suited his own notion and circumstances.

That McLaughlin, the Irish greenhorn, should have chosen his own route over that of seasoned wilderness traveler Green says much about the former's foolhardy character.

---

399   Gunn: "On the theory that the last stop noted was south of the Crow Wing River due south of Pillager, the two stages of three miles each since recorded would bring their present camp to somewhere in the vicinity of Wheelock. Although no mention has been made of the fact, they must have crossed the Crow Wing, and are now traveling westward, parallel to its west bank."

Henry returned at about 2 o'clock.

Mac Among Squirrels & Fish

October 5, 1844 – Saturday. Several shots were discharged late last evening by our party for our lost man; but he either heard them not, or preferred to learn by experience, in person, the comforts and delicacies of an October night in a forest, without food or bedding or other companion than the northern traveler's chief delight: the pipe. I expect poor Mac is 'sausage fried.'

He returned this evening with all the appearance of hard times. He spent his night, he tells us, no less than five or six miles from our hut. From the time Green left him, he traveled by land and in water, through brush and through rat holes, among squirrels and among {211} fish, until cruel Fate led him to the spot where old Mother Destiny had prepared him a fine log for his pillow.

We removed to-day to the distance of a mile, when we were again obliged to encamp till we could clear another day's journey.

Mac's Fire & the Sportive Wind

While busily engaged slashing our axes through the forest before us, we observed a fire suddenly break out in the direction of our hut. I instantly hastened back on horseback to ascertain the meaning of the phenomenon. Mac's fire, it appears, had not been well secured before he left it this morning; and, taking advantage of the gentle breeze, it had scrambled up among the combustible pieces of dried and decayed pine which lay thick in every direction. Everything being thus well prepared for action, the sportive wind fluttered about Mac's fire, and fanned it with such diligence that the brush and decayed timber was soon like the vengeance of fury.

Sabbath Was Made for Man

October 6, 1844 – Sunday. Went out to cut as usual. Whether there be merit or demerit in using the Lord's Day thus, I leave to the more wise to judge. 'Necessity knows no law.' 'The Sabbath was made for man and not man for the Sabbath.' {212}

A Few Miles More, Hard Fighting, Ditto, & Repeat

October 7, 1844 – Monday. Traveled a few miles more and encamped by a creek,[400] where Henry stole some of my apples.

October 8, 1844 – Tuesday. Went about six miles to-day. First rate traveling.

October 9, 1844 – Wednesday. Only four miles to-day. Green goes out again to explore the country ahead.

October 10, 1844 – Thursday. Ditto, as Reverend Mr. Roberts[401] said.

October 11, 1844 – Friday. Cut through more brush to-day. Hard fighting.

October 12, 1844 – Saturday. Repeat it, as the physician says.

The Crossing Place

October 13, 1844 – Sunday. Went out to cut to the crossing place.[402] Hired a man of the Chippewas to conduct us to the Otter Tail for $12.00. {213}

October 14, 1844 – Monday. Crossed the Crow [Wing] River after sixteen days of hard traveling. From the Crow Island to this point where we crossed today cannot be, at the utmost, over sixty miles.[403] This would aver{214}age our traveling at a little over three and a half miles per diem.

---

400 Gunn: "The creek here referred to is probably that which flows into the Crow Wing from the north, where the town of Motley now is. Motley is only three miles west of Wheelock, which would be about right for the distance, considering their average rate of traveling through this difficult part."

401 Gunn: "The Roberts most likely [referred to] was a catechist of the Church of England, Reverend J. Roberts, who came out to Red River with Reverend Abraham Cowley in 1841. He was an appointee of the Church Missionary Society of England, and remained but two years in the country." *Ditto*, which had been in use in England since long before Roberts' lifetime, must have been one of his characteristic expressions.

402 Gunn: "The place on the Crow Wing, selected by them beforehand, where they were to cross that stream from its north to its south side. This does not indicate that there was already a recognized 'crossing place' here. The point of crossing selected at this time was probably identical with that subsequently used by all other travelers over this route, and known as the second crossing of the Crow Wing. It was a short distance below the mouth of the Leaf River, one of the principal tributaries of the Crow Wing from the west, but generally regarded by travelers of that time as the upper portion of the Crow Wing itself. It is directly northwest of the stop last noted, about nine miles W of Motley." Gunn, p. 212.

403 Gunn: "Miles negotiated under the circumstances that these were [are] apt to stretch considerably, and multiply in computation. Each one [must have] appeared like two. By the most generous mea-

Chapter 6 – St. Peter's, St. Paul's & the Crow Wing Trail   203

First Snow, Good & Awful Traveling

October 15, 1844 – Tuesday. Traveled about nine miles,[404] course due west. Good traveling at last. A few flakes of snow yesterday and today.

October 16, 1844 – Wednesday. Some more snow today. Crossed three creeks, none of them very bad.

October 17, 1844 – Thursday. Fell about two inches of snow to-day.

October 18, 1844 – Friday. Crossed more creeks today. Awful traveling. Quite a rough, rugged country

Providential Provender

October 19, 1844 – Saturday. Fine weather, but provisions almost entirely out. For dinner we had some gruel without a particle of grease or salt in it.

Just as we were gulping down the dregs of this unsavoury meal, five stock [mallard] ducks descended from the upper regions and lit in a creek by which we were taking dinner, not more than a hundred yards from our hut. Our guide[405] and Henry ran down with their guns and brought the whole five to our fire.

---

surement, and taking the longest road – viz., by the mouth of the Crow Wing River – the most that can be made between these two points, computing by the survey, is about 40 miles By the measurements of the Northern Pacific Railway, the route of which is almost identical with these old trails, the distances are: Topeka to Crow Wing at the mouth of the Crow Wing River, 16 miles, and Crow Wing to Motley, 18 miles – to which add 9 miles as the distance in a straight line from Motley to the mouth of the Leaf River, and we have 43 miles. If, on the other hand, we compute the distance by the shortcut which we believe Garrioch's party to have taken, the distance is still shorter: 33 miles by that route. It must be remembered, however, that men opening a road under the circumstances indicated above would naturally follow the line of least resistance, winding around in all directions to avoid obstacles, and consequently covering many more miles than necessary. It is possible, therefore, that Garrioch's estimate of 60 miles to this point, even by the shorter route, may not be so very much wide of the mark." Gunn, pp. 213-214.

404   Gunn: "Since crossing the Crow Wing our travelers have been paralleling the Leaf River on its south side. They are now encamped a little south of, and about midway between, the points now know respectively as Central and Lukens. Another nine miles will bring them to the site of the present town of Wadena, in the southwest corner of Wadena County."

405   This is the first indication that the Indian guide Suza Bruno promised on September 30 at Crow Island (above, commentary introducing the entry for October 1, 1844) to send to the party did indeed join it. Not until the November 6, 1844, entry will he be given a name, and that probably just the group's nick-name for him: Nine Fingers.

This was certainly providential: a God-send. Even our guide, an untutored savage, acknowledged it. Our guide also killed a fine fat bear this evening. Certainly most providential!

Cutting Ironwood

October 20, 1844 – Sunday. Came to the Dry Leaf Lake,[406] where we again {215} crossed the Crow [Wing] River.[407] Some more cutting to-day. This Dry Leaf Lake is about four miles long and one mile wide.

October 21, 1844 – Monday. Cutting very hard today: ironwood.[408] Encamped within a few miles of the Otter Tail Lake.

Pillagers & Provisions

October 22, 1844 – Tuesday. Came to the Otter Tail Lake at an early hour. Here we found about a dozen tents of the Pillagers,[409] and a black man trading for some company at La Point.

These Pillagers evinced no such disposition as we expected they would be inclined to do, from every representation that we had ever heard of their character as a tribe. They, on the contrary, evinced the greatest satisfaction in our passing through their country, and assured us that we and our property would be treated with the greatest civility, and preserved from the hands of any who should be disposed to molest.

---

406 Gunn: "The source of the Leaf River, still known by this name, or as Leaf Lake. It is situated near the centre of Ottertail County, its western extremity being only a few miles from the north end of Ottertail Lake."

407 Gunn: "The Leaf River is meant. As already noted, this stream was commonly confused, by Red River tripmen and other travelers from that quarter, with the upper portion of the Crow Wing River – this being counted as one of the three crossings of the latter stream said by them to be encountered on the Crow Wing Trail. The Leaf River flows out of the lake of the same name, and the crossing place is quite close to the latter body of water. From Wadena to this point is about fourteen miles; and in coming that distance, our travelers have passed Wadena Junction and Deer Creek."

408 Since the term "ironwood" is applied to a wide variety of trees and shrubs composed of unusually hard wood, one can only guess at which particular type slowed the party's progress here. Possibly prairie oak? See entry for November 17, 1844.

409 A term used to describe Ojibwas of the area, and the origin of the name of the present small city of Pillager, Minnesota, located on the north bank of the Crow Wing River.

The only inconvenience we sustained from these wild sons of the forest was their unaccountable eagerness for riding. It was in vain that we expostulated with them on the impracticability of our allowing them to ride our horses, as they were very poor and had still a long distance to travel. They acknowledged our reasons to be good, but would slip off unobserved and, after riding about for an hour or so, would take the horses where they found them and then sneak back to our hut with the appearance of innocence.

October 23, 1844 – Wednesday. Being entirely out of provisions, we laid in today fish, oil and rice that we deemed necessary for the remaining part of our journey home. I purchased for myself and [my] man two bushels of rice,[410] about two hundred dried fish, forty fresh [fish] and a bag of pounded fish. For the 40 fresh fish and a cod line[411] I gave a fur cap and ten pounds of coffee.

October 24, 1844 – Thursday. Having prepared and refitted ourselves for prosecuting our homeward journey, we made a start today, and encamped by a beautiful lake.[412]

More Cutting, Pheasants & Ducks, Difficult Crossing

October 25, 1844 – Friday. Spent the day in cutting. {217}

October 26, 1844 – Saturday. Had quite a sport at game. Killed several fine pheasants Purchased some ducks from Indian lads.

October 27, 1844 – Sunday. Little Joe[413] concealed himself after a slight correction from his brother and did not come up with the party till we had traveled several miles.

---

410   Gunn: "Zizania aquatica, the wild rice, so abundant in Minnesota lakes."

411   Gunn: "A small rope, about three-eighths of an inch in diameter, made usually of cotton, for use in the cod fisheries. It was brought in for the Indian trade, and was much used in the early days of the country for tethering horses, guide lines in driving, and for such other purposes where a light, pliable, yet strong rope was needed."

412   Gunn: "Rush Lake, three miles north of Ottertail. This lake is five miles long, and about three wide in its broadest part. The Ottertail River flows out of it, to the south at its southwest corner. The old trail from Ottertail City to the crossing of that stream runs almost due north and is practically identical with the Soo Line route of today. The river was crossed to the west side just south of its junction with Rush Lake. This, is no doubt, the route taken by Garrioch's party, who are now encamped somewhere on the south shore of the last-mentioned body of water."

413   Gunn inserted the handwritten comment: "Joe Cook, [young] brother of Henry Cook." Gunn, p. 217.

October 28, 1844 – Monday. Had a most awful difficulty in crossing a little stream, owing to its steep and rugged banks and soft and boggy shores. It took us from three to four hours before we got everything over. The vast quantity of variegated matter oozing from under the banks of this river would indicate, we thought, the presence of some valuable mineral. This is the third time we crossed this river.[414]

Blacky Breaks Ice

The ice on it, being from two to three inches thick, gave us no small labour in breaking our way through; and, had it not been for my ever-determined and invincible Blacky, our labours must have been infinitely more. He would get on the ice, which was considerably above his knees, with his fore legs, and stand on it till it gave way {218} under his weight. He at one time even attempted to get on the ice with his all fours, in order to make his progress more rapid; but, the ice not being sufficiently strong to bear up his whole weight, it gave way while he was in the act of drawing up his hind quarters. This, of course, made the old fellow go souse headlong into the stream. This flattened his courage for a while, but, quickly getting over his momentary repulse, he redoubled his exertions; and, in a few moments more, made himself master of the opposite bank.

In fact, were I to speak of my old Blacky in terms consonant to his merits, I should be under the necessity of allowing him a greater space in my journal than to any other dumb or reasoning animal in our party. I will therefore leave his merits and memory to be enrolled in the annals of impartial Fate and proceed to note my conceptions and experience as usual.

Beautiful Little Prairies

October 29, 1844 – Tuesday. The greatest part of our journeying, for these last three days, has been through beautiful little prairies, occasionally obstructed by thin intervening hammocks, or little forests.

North of the Divide

I should have stated that the little stream we crossed yesterday is the same which forms the Otter Tail Lake River, and falls into Red River. This little stream in its course

---

414   Gunn: "The Ottertail is here referred to. The party, it should be remembered, since leaving Ottertail, have been proceeding up the river, towards its source; whence the characterization 'little stream.' The travelers are now encamped in the neighborhood of Frazee, Minnesota."

Chapter 6 – St. Peter's, St. Paul's & the Crow Wing Trail 207

travels every point of the compass, and communicates its waters to Red River through an innumerable succession of lakes and marshes.

Abundance of Cutting

October 30, 1844 – Wednesday. Abundance of cutting, and but little traveling.

October 31, 1844 & November 1, 1844 – Thursday and Friday. Same as above.

November 2, 1844 – Saturday. Cut to a lake, which we sincerely expect {219} puts an end to our axe exercise; at least with the exception, our guide tells us, of the little we have to cut along the lake.

More Predicaments for Mac

Poor Mac got into the same predicament to-day that he did at a former period. He had started in the morning without his gun, fire tackle or anything else, intending to go only a few hundred yards to see after his horses, when lo! he did not return till dark; having traveled, as he told us, about fifty miles. Had he not fortunately come across our road which we cut out that day, he must have sacrificed his little carcass to his vanity and stubbornness, and have become a precious morsel for the raccoons and ravens.

November 3, 1844 – Sunday. Traveled to the above lake and encamped there.

We left Mac behind looking for one of his horses. Intending to stay all night, he prepared himself for the worst. 'Experience teaches fools.'

Our Last Cutting

Did our last cutting today.

Breakfast at Detroit Lake

The group had reached an unnamed lake that would later become a vacation resort called Detroit Lake[415] popular with both Minnesotans and Manitobans. It was a most welcome

---

415 Gunn: "Detroit Lake. This beautiful body of water is now so well known as a summer resort as scarcely to require comment. It lies in Becker County, towards the south side, and considerably west of its centre. Its distance from Frazee is six or seven miles, and its direction from that point northwest. The present town of Detroit lies to the north and a little to the west of it. The road

sight for the weary travelers. They were now at the edge of the prairies with which most of them were at least somewhat familiar, and over which they thought they could find their own way home. It was not to be an easy journey, however.

November 4, 1844 – Monday. Took breakfast at the last end of the lake, and then traveled till our way was intercepted by an impassible bog.

The Vast & Beautiful Prairies

November 5, 1844 – Tuesday. Traveled backwards about two miles to get round the bog, and then proceeded fairly. Unspeakably cheering to our almost wasted courage and patience, the vast and beautiful prairies we had longed for burst suddenly upon our view this evening. We could not but hail the prospect with accents of the greatest satisfac{220}tion and liveliest gratitude.

Farewell to Nine Fingers

November 6, 1844 – Wednesday. While Green and I went off with our guide, Nine Fingers,[416] to seek out some Indians who we had been told had plenty of provisions, our party went on with the carts. We traveled several miles in quest of the Indians, but, it growing late and despairing of finding any, we discharged our guide, according to arrangements made with him at Otter Tail Lake, and started back after our companions.

Lost Near a Prairie Fire with One Dried Fish

About 12 o'clock a strong wind blew up from the north and soon after a furious fire. A river,[417] however, intercepting its progress towards us, prevented it from disturbing us. Green and I traveled all day in a circuitous manner, endeavouring to find our party by

---

chopped by Garrioch's party was probably along its northeast shore. This was the regular route of the Crow Wing Trail, as subsequently established, and this lake was known to travelers over this trail for many years subsequently as 'Lake 44' in commemoration of the opening of it by Garrioch's party in 1844. The late John Henderson of Kildonan, Manitoba, told me he had once seen all the names of this party carved on a giant tree along this lake, probably at the site of the above camp."

416   Here we finally learn at least the nickname of the Indian guide who led the party on this arduous and hazardous expedition. See previous notes about him for the entries of September 30 (Gunn, p. 208) and October 19 (Gunn, p. 214).

417   Gunn: "Probably the Buffalo River, the upper portion of whose main stream passes about fourteen miles to the northwest of Detroit Lake. This river, which is of considerable size, has its source in the Buffalo and other lakes in Becker County, Minnesota, in the southern part of the White Earth Indian reservation. It follows a generally southeasterly course, [and later northwesterly] to

coming across their tracks. But, signally failing, we halted, and both of us supped on one dried sucker [fish].

November 7, 1844 – Thursday. After spending the night in a comfortable sleep, we made an early start and came to our hut of yesterday morning. Here we picked up the crumbs of dried fish for our breakfast, which we had wastefully thrown away yesterday and the day before.

Buffalo Feast

By about 10 o'clock we got up with our party. Henry here killed a [buffalo] bull.

{221} We encamped in a beautiful forest, and some of our party went back for a part of the bull. They returned about twelve in the night. We [ate] away at the old bull in extraordinary style, for his meat was somewhat better than dried fish.

Snow, Bogs, Cart Breakdown, Demise of an Ox, Loss of an Otter

November 8, 1844 – Friday. Some snow this morning. The old North begins to smell.[418] Traveled to the Boggy River.[419] In the course of our journey to-day one of my carts broke down, one of my oxen gave up,[420] and I lost a beautiful otter I had by the tail.

November 9, 1844 – Saturday. Crossed the Boggy River, a beautiful crystal stream, and proceeded to the Rice River.[421] Came in contact with an everlasting bog. Had to

---

its junction with the Red at Georgetown. Besides this main stream, Buffalo River has a southern branch of about equal volume, which rises in Ottertail County."

418   The smell of the "everlasting bog" of the next day's entry?

419   Gunn: "The stream here named is probably the south branch of the Wild Rice River. It rises in Becker County, in the northwest corner of the White Earth Indian Reservation, and but a few miles north of the upper channel of the Buffalo River."

420   Garrioch appears to have had three oxen with him on this trip, and this entry seems to record the death of his first.

421   Gunn: "Wild Rice River, the Rivière à la Folle Avoine of the French, Menomine Sippi of the Ojibways. This river, which is of a size capable of navigation by Indian canoes (or was, in early days), rises in Becker and Mahnomen Counties, not far from the sources of the Red and Mississippi Rivers. Its upper waters are within the limits of the White Earth Indian Reservation, principally

travel backwards a piece and take another {222} course – we [had] kept too near to the Red [Lake] River. Came to a creek on the prairie and there we camped.

Green in Tears

In crossing the Boggy River this morning, one of Green's carts again upset in the very centre of the stream. Should Green at any time hear of the decease of his mother, I question if it will put him to his second thoughts; but the upsetting of his cart, which was now a second time in the water, drove him to his third thoughts. That is, it drew the watery elements of his brain through the tenderest parts of his eyes.

Dozing in a Blizzard

November 10, 1844 – Sunday. Crossed the Rice River and encamped among a cluster of willows and other brush, which afforded some fuel for us and shelter for our animals. It blew, snowed and drifted for a few moments like fury; but, being weary from hard thinking as well as from bodily exercise of various kinds, we dozed away the night very agreeably – at least I did.

Mac's Horses Give Up the Ghost

November 11, 1844 – Monday. Two of Mac's horses gave up the ghost today: Tom and Peter. No wonder: they were little more than skin and bone – not so much blood in them both as Mac could boast of in one of his little fingers.

Scarce Fuel, Shrunken Bodies & Minds, Continuing Storms

November 12, 1844 – Tuesday. Another brush encampment. Scarcely fuel enough to keep up common circulation – which actually caused our animal frames to contract to an alarming degree. Even our mental parts – as many of us as possess any mentality – envinced symptoms of conceptual contraction. Indeed, had things continued as they

---

in Mahnomen County, which derives its name from it. Its general course is a little south of west, to its junction with the Red River between Hendrum and Halsted, Minnesota. [It] has also another connection with the Red through what is known as the Marsh River. This second channel leaves the main stream just east of Ada, Norman County, and joins the Red a mile below the mouth of the Goose River, nearly opposite Caledonia, North Dakota. Since leaving Detroit Lake, Garrioch's party has been heading towards the present city of Crookston. While it is difficult to determine their exact route with any certainty, it is safe to say that the probable crossing place on this stream was in the neighborhood of Faith, on the border of Norman and Mahnomen Counties."

were, we should in all probability have [shrunk to the size] of common cur dog[s], ere the Majestic Traveler had dispersed his benign beams among our shivering limbs and distended muscles.

November 13, 1844 – Wednesday. Came to River of Sandy Hills.[422] More {223} snow and storms.

November 14, 1844 – Thursday. Made a bridge over the above river. Green dries his goods today which got wet in the Boggy River.

To enable Green to dry his property during this pause, the weather must have warmed a little, at least during the day; but the cold was still a serious problem.

Cart Sideboards as Fuel

November 15, 1844 – Friday. Left the river and traveled towards the Red Lake River but, night overtaking us on account of bad traveling, we halted in the open prairie and clustered about a small fire we had constructed from the sideboards of our carts, like so many bees about a honeysuckle. Mortality here vied with our situation; but, observing that we had still some side-boards in reserve, we retired quietly, after sneaking and reconnoitering about our premises for a few moments.[423]

This river is nothing more than a large creek with almost unvaried perpendicular banks and muddy bottom.

---

422 Gunn: "The Rivière aux Buttes de Sable of the old French traders and voyageurs. Alexander Henry, Jr., who built a post on this river in the fall of 1806, informs us (Coues' *Henry*, I, p. 141), that it "derives its name from some barren, sandy hills, fifteen leagues to the east." It rises in the southeast corner of Polk County about six miles south of the source of the Clearwater River. Its main course is due west. In its upper part it is a well-defined stream with high banks, but as it approaches the lower levels it gradually dwindles away until it loses itself in a great marsh. It gathers again west of this marsh and, as a mere creek, flows into the last-mentioned stream near a place called Climax. Garrioch's party crossed the Wild Rice probably a little east of Beltrami, between that place and Fertile."

423 What did the "sneaking and reconnoitering" signify? Suspected theft?

A Ball to Flakey's Head

November 16, 1844 – Saturday. Came to the Red Lake River[424] at an early {224} hour and encamped. The river is full of running ice. Traveled five or six miles downwards to find a convenient place for crossing.

Put a ball in poor Flakey's head today to save his life.

Flakey was one of Garrioch's two remaining oxen, shot due to disease or starvation. The expression "to save his life" must have meant to save the animal further suffering or to save their own (human) lives.

Seeking a Crossing

November 17, 1844 – Sunday. Green and I set out to look for the Grand Forks and for a crossing place, but found neither.

An Oak of Antiquity

In the course of my travels today I came in contact with the stump of an oak of antiquity. I extended my arms round its butt till I discovered its circumference to measure 22 feet.[425] The trunk and limbs of this enormous stump lay extended by its side like a castle in ruins. The trunk in {225} its fall, which must have [sounded] like

---

424 Gunn: "The most important tributary of the Red River from the east. It flows out of Red Lake, a large body of water in the centre of Beltrami County, which gives it its name. Although its source is in Beltrami, its actual beginning as a river is in the northwest corner of Clearwater County, the western edge of Red Lake constituting the boundary between these two countries. From Red Lake its course [takes it past Thief River Falls, Red Lake Falls, and Crookston] to its junction with the Red at Grand Forks. At the latter place it is fully as large as the Red River. The Red Lake is a very crooked river, making excursions to many points of the compass on its way to the Red. Its main course, however, is westerly; its final junction with the Red River being, almost to a mile, due west of its exit out of Red Lake. As there were no established trails on the east side of the Red River at that time, it is impossible to determine with certainty just where Garrioch's party struck the Red Lake River. From the course they appear to have been following, however, I would conclude that it was [several miles below] Crookston. This hypothesis would work about right with the daily rate of progress recorded by Garrioch from this crossing to the mouth of Big Salt River, the next point mentioned of which we have certain knowledge."

425 Gunn: "Both the Red and Red Lake Rivers about this latitude are still notable for the size to which the timber on their banks attains; and, in those days, such immense trees as that here described were by no means uncommon. Alexander Henry, Jr. (Coues' *Henry*, I, p. 157) tells of one [stump] on the Red, near Park River, of which he says: "The size of this tree was enormous, having a hollow six feet in diameter, the rim or shell being two feet thick, including the bark." This note, although struck out in Gunn's manuscript, seems worth preserving. Garrioch's description of this

the distant roar of cannon, had broken into three pieces. The small end of the largest piece presented an open space, which doubtless was occupied as a den or resting place for bears and other large carnivorous animals during the summer season. The small end of the middle piece presented a similar cavity, and appeared to be the resting place of the smaller sort of flesh eaters, such as fox and coon; while the smallest piece, in connection with all the limbs, branches and twigs, lay in a careless mass, apparently constructed for a common shelter and rendezvous for the whole tribe of the weaker carnivorous and graminivorous strollers.

Creating a Crossing

November 18, 1844 – Monday. Prepared a place for crossing on the ice by making a trail on it with earth and throwing water on it, to cement it to the ice and to strengthen it.

November 19, 1844 – Tuesday. Got our animals and luggage over by 2 o'clock, after a deal of difficulty. Thank fortune, we have no more danger to apprehend from water, as the weather begins to get so cold that we begin to tear up whatever comes in our way for socks. This last is an infallible proof of growing ice at any time.

Blacky Does Double Duty

November 20, 1844 – Wednesday. On the 16th I had been under the pitiful necessity of extinguishing the vital spark of one of my faithful oxen to save his vitals from consumptive heavings. Today my other – for I am left with but one – appealed to my sense of honour and compassion by lying down under his burden while traveling. I was, of course, obliged to give him his liberty; and poor Blacky, after having conveyed his own burden to the halting point of today, had to retrace his steps to bring up the vehicle of his companion of burdens.

A Mirage?

November 21, 1844 – Thursday. Green saw someone today, whether a hu{226}man or a devil he did not know. Be it as it may, it was a sort of variety to see something in the shape of himself in these wild, stormy deserts, and he congratulated himself upon the circumstance.

---

oak strengthens the editors' speculation in an earlier note (October 21, 1844) that his previous reference to "ironwood" may have meant oak.

An Ox on Strike

November 22, 1844 – Friday. My ox begins to know me and takes advantage of my good nature. I was again obliged to give him his own way. Before we had proceeded more than two miles he lay down very composedly. As [if] to say: "vexation, botheration and termination," he coolly turned his head to his tail, where he placed it, much to his satisfaction but to my almost unbounded vexation. I took him out of the cart and left him. We encamped at a very late hour of night.

An Ox Thinks It Over

November 23, 1844 – Saturday. An excessive cold day. Went back on my poor old Blacky for my ox and cart. Came to the cart but my ox had eloped. I proceeded to the river,[426] and found him under the bank, quite in a princely and cogitative mood, chewing his cud. I did not think it worthwhile to ask him the nature and tendency of his cogitations, but I guess they were something like the following:

"I am now here, free and independent – free as the wind that whistles along my horns, and as independent as nature that nourishes me and provides for all my wants. Shall I remain here and rove at random and at pleasure, or shall I follow my companions of travel? Let me see. Should I remain, I shall expose my emaciated frame to the bleak and frigid palms of this rigid monster, who has already begun to insert himself into my vital parts. Nature, too, has retired to her usual dormant independen{227}ce, and she forgets her wonted propitiousness to her graminivorous offspring. My present wants scarcely penetrate the ears of her gracious majesty. Without strong food I must perish, and that in solitude, without a friend near, and, unspeakably worse, surrounded by a host of carnivorous devils who would measure the length of my languid intestines ere the vital spark had quit this emaciated frame (looking towards his tail). And again, should I return to my fellow travelers, I know what lies before me: just what my present deplorable state tells me is behind. True, my water would be sure, and in time, my food, bed and home. But to think of trudging through deep snow with a cumbrous vehicle at tail from day to day is terrible; and, worse, to be inflicted with piercing ideas every moment from the hands of an unthinking, rash youth is humiliating in the

---

426 Gunn: "The Red Lake River. The party is now proceeding on the north side of this stream, and practically parallel with it. Their course is northwesterly, with the intention of striking the Red River north of Grand Forks."

extreme and insulting to the most common mind. Die I have to, die I must, and die I will, rather than submit to such ignominious treatment."

Just at this moment I came upon him and told him my errand. He evinced considerable retractiveness, and proceeded in accordance with my wishes only through the application of those piercing ideas he had so much dreaded, and which had shocked his sensitive feelings so far as having induced him to sacrifice himself to fatal despair. Suffice it to say that we reached home before sundown.

Saw a bull.

Jettisoning Cargo

November 24, 1844 – Sunday. [We] found it necessary to leave a large portion of our loads in consequence of the increasing weakness of our animals, and [of] finding the depth of snow every day increasing. We concealed what we left at different places, in various directions {228} from our hut, [so] that, in the event of their being discovered by Indians, we might stand a chance of saving something. At this place[427] I was obliged to leave a stove, all my coffee and shot, and nearly all my tobacco, without any further precaution than thrusting into badger holes what they would admit and leaving the rest exposed or placed in the bosom of reeds and rushes.

Notwithstanding the weather was cold to the extreme, we made a start and encamped after traveling three miles.

Ox Unbound

November 25, 1844 – Monday. Here I was again obliged to leave another stove, and Henry left one. Before we had gone five miles, my ox refused to accompany us any further with his load, so we took him out of his cart and left it with a hide in it. The poor ox followed with difficulty.

Saw seven deer to-day.

---

427   Gunn: "Somewhere a few miles east of the present East Grand Forks." The abandoned items were trade goods that Garrioch, Henry, and Green had purchased in Minnesota and Illinois.

The Red River at Last

Came at last to the Red River.[428]

November 26, 1844 – Tuesday. Not being able to cross the Red River at this place, we continued our course on the east side of it as before.

Saw a fine large buck, but could not get him, tho' within only a hundred yards or so of us, owing to the rashness of one of our companions. Weather quite stormy and a considerable fall of snow. Encamped by a lake near the river.

Saulteaux Hospitality

Providentially, we encamped near the village of some of the Red Lake Indians, who had plenty of fish and dried meat. Henry and I went over to see them after dark. Found them quite hospitable and kind. After satiating our appetites with the best that two of their tents could afford, we bid them all good night and retired. One man presented us with ten or fifteen pounds of dried and fresh meat for our breakfast. Purchased a few {229} [musk]rats from a young man.

November 27, 1844 – Wednesday. Spent the greatest part of the day in eating, chatting and trading with the Indians at their lodges, smoking not excepted.

A Refreshed & Unanimous Start

November 28, 1844 – Thursday. Having provided ourselves with provisions for the rest of our journey, and having received some necessary instructions as to our proper course, and our animals being now considerably refreshed, we made a unanimous start.

After pacing three or four miles through deep snow, we halted for the day.

Today's "unanimous start" suggests that the group was not always traveling cohesively by this point – which later entries would confirm.

---

428   Gunn: "Probably about eight miles north of Grand Forks."

Lost Trail, Lost Blacky

November 29, 1844 – Friday. Encountered some difficulty in crossing a creek; and not being able to find the Red River by any possible way for our carts we made an early encampment in order to explore the country before we proceeded any further.

November 30, 1844 – Saturday. Charles could not find my old Blacky. I found, however, a trail leading towards the Red River, and, after following it about half a mile, it brought me exactly to the place we had been advised by some Indians to cross. I returned to the camp, and my companions received the intelligence with raptures.

December 1, 1844 – Sunday. We were obliged to spend yet another day at this place, on account of my horse. I and Charles started early for him; and after riding a great part of the day among the brush and thickets, Charles found him 'solitary and alone.'

Cutting, Clearing, Crossing

December 2, 1844 – Monday. Made a start once more and, after a little more cutting and clearing, gained the opposite side of the Red River by crossing it at the Big Salt River. Our horses could scarcely be persuaded to leave the water of the last mentioned stream.

{230} Came to the Little Salt River.

Blowing, Snowing, Drifting

December 3, 1844 – Tuesday. Quite a stormy morning. It blew, snowed and drifted in a fearful manner. Yesterday our traveling was pleasant and comparatively easy, both to ourselves and animals; but this day is hard both to man and beast. The snow is not deep but very hard, which causes the wheels of the carts to go through it, with much labour to the poor animals.

Came to some French Half Breeds. There were Francis Demarais[429] and his son-in-law. They had plenty of meat but no tobacco, tea or sugar.

---

429 Gunn: "The Desmarais were a numerous [family], and figured frequently in the history of those early days. Donald Gunn (*History of Manitoba*, p. 110) speaks of a Jean Baptiste Desmarais being at the Turtle River for the North West Company in 1813-14. A John Desmarais was sentenced to death at Fort Garry in 1866, for killing an Indian in a drunken row. The same summer, according to Hill (pp. 181-85); or in 1868, according to Hargrave (pp. 444-46), a Francis Desmarais was killed at Portage la Prairie by a settler upon whom he had made a vicious attack. The Francis Desmarais

Going on Alone

I had come to the conclusion to go ahead to Red River Colony on foot, when Green and his party came up just as I was starting.

Although Blacky had been found, he must have been in such poor shape that Garrioch felt he would better off pushing ahead on foot while the horse stayed with Charles, the ox, and the carts.

Green, wishing his horse in the Settlement as soon as possible, told me to take him if I chose. I did so; and a few minutes after sundown I arrived at Mr. Kittson's[430] on the

---

    of Garrioch's reference would be too old a man to be mixed up in an affair of this kind in 1868, but might have been the father of this man. Some of these Desmarais, who were all French Métis, were Catholics, and some Protestants. Several of the latter wing moved to Portage la Prairie about 1853, and were among the first settlers there; a Baptiste Desmarais and a Charles Desmarais belonging to Archdeacon Cochrane's congregation. (A. C. Garrioch, *First Furrows*, p. 80). Just who the particular Desmarais and son-in-law that Garrioch encountered here were I have not been able to ascertain."

430 Gunn: "At the site of the present Pembina, [North Dakota] at the junction of the Red and Pembina Rivers. The gentleman referred to, Norman Wolfred Kittson, was one of the best known and most influential pioneers of the Red and Mississippi valleys. A grandson of the explorer Alexander Henry, he was born at Sorel, Quebec. In 1830, when 16 years of age, he engaged with the American Fur Company and came to the West. His first post, where he remained for two years, was between the Fox and Wisconsin Rivers. He was then sent to the headwaters of the Minnesota, and later to Red Cedar River, Iowa. In 1834 he went to Fort Snelling, where he was engaged in the sutler's [provisioner's] department of that establishment until 1838. In 1839 he entered business on his own account as a fur trader near what was then known as Cold Spring, or the Baker Settlement, just above Fort. Snelling. Here he remained until 1843, when he again joined the AFC as special partner, being placed in charge of all their business on the headwaters of the Minnesota and along the British line. His headquarters were at Pembina, [on the international boundary], to which point he removed the same year. He established various trading stations throughout the district under his charge, and soon built up an extensive trade, the proceeds of which he shipped by Red River cart trains to Mendota [St. Peter's] at the mouth of the Minnesota River. In 1854 Mr. Kittson formed a partnership which Major H. W. Forbes, and entered the general Indian trade supply business in St. Paul. Their establishment, the "Saint Paul Outfit," was well known throughout the Northwest. Mr. Kittson's permanent residence in St. Paul dates from the latter year. In 1858 the firm of Forbes and Kittson was dissolved, but Kittson continued in the Red River trade until 1860; about which time he accepted the office of agent of the Hudson's Bay Company, and established a line of barges and steamers on the Red River. From his connection with this enterprise came the sobriequet, "Commodore," by which he was familiarly known in after years. Mr. Kittson was later (1873) one of the celebrated Canadian quartette, which included James J. Hill and Donald A. Smith (later Lord Strathcona), that bought out the St. Paul and Pacific Railway, thus laying the foundations not merely of immense wealth for those concerned, but of the two great railway systems of the northwestern US: the Great Northern and Northern Pacific. During his lifetime he held a number of important public offices, [including] being a member of the Council of the Minnesota Legislature,

Pembina. Poor Fox [Green's horse] {231} would not have gone much further. Both his strength and his spirits were very much fagged.

Fox Gives Up

December 4, 1844 – Wednesday. After spending a pleasant evening with Mr. Kittson, I made an early start this morning, with the intention of reaching home in the course of the evening. I was, however, sadly disappointed; for I had not gone more than two miles when Fox refused to go any further. It was, of course, worse than useless to remonstrate with the poor animal with such 'piercing ideas' as were shocking even to an ox.

I therefore wheeled about to ride back to Kittson's, {232} to leave Fox in his care till Green came up, and take it on foot myself to Red River Settlement. Fox, instead of carrying me back, could scarcely support his own weight to Kittson's. I was therefore under the painful and laborious necessity of alternately loading and pushing him onwards. I felt so weak and unwell, from the profuse perspiration occasioned by this arduous exercise, that I was obliged to defer my journey homeward till the following day.

---

for the Pembina District, from 1851 to 1855. He was also elected Mayor of St. Paul in 1858. See J. Fletcher Williams, *History of St. Paul*, pp. 147-149; Upham's *Minnesota Biographies*, p. 406; & *Minnesota in Three Centuries*."

Establishing his trading post in Pembina by 1843, Kittson opened up the cross-border trade considerably. Russenholt, *Heart of the Continent*, p. 87: "Norman Kittson, a Canadian born at Chambly, Quebec, opened a trading post at Pembina. …from this headquarters, he wove a growing business into the life of Assiniboia and of the Plains, southward to St. Paul. More and more Assiniboia Settlers venture into the one highly profitable enterprise: the fur trade. 'Company' men battle, tooth and claw, to halt such invasion of their Monopoly. …Kittson may have been the first to take Red River carts from Assiniboia to St. Paul. His 6 carts carried, southward, $1,400 worth of pelts; and freight, northward, $12,000 in merchandise. If Kittson led the way, other and bigger cart trains follow on his heels. Freight rates, paid in goods at high markup, average 20 cents per ton-mile. Freighting outfits multiply."

Kittson's pivotal role in cross-border trading during Peter's trading career and beyond is detailed in: "Norman W. Kittson and Free Trade in the Red River Settlement, 1843-1849," in Gluek, *Minnesota and the Manifest Destiny*, chap. 3. The fact that Kittson set himself up at Pembina, just over the American border, propelled Pembina into its important role as the site of much frustration for the HBC ("an ineradicable, cancerous growth, [a] threat to the Company") in its decades-long battle against free trading within its sphere of authority, as Gluek describes it, pp. 32-33, 40, 47-48, 77.

Continuing on Foot

December 5, 1844 – Thursday. After breakfast I started for home and slept at the Grand Point

Here, after I had a fire kindled, three young men of the Sottos [Saulteaux] came up, who were also on their way to the Settlement. The night was very cold; and, having nothing but leafless willows to shelter us from the piercing north wind, we were not a little annoyed at its shivering tendency [frigidity], as well as its action on the smoke of our fire.

A Humane Barbarian

I had taken nothing but a small blanket, which, aside from its utility to screen from the cold, was quite inadequate for a covering. One of my companions, however, though a barbarian, perceiving my awkward predicament, very humanely offered me one of their buffalo robes. This, with my little blanket, enabled me, in various unnatural positions, to pass the night tolerably.

A Hungry Trek

We took breakfast on one or two pounds of meat we had reserved for the purpose; but, it being too early for me, I could not take more than three mouthfuls. Even this I had to ram down by the force of the laws of necessity.

December 6, 1844 – Friday. Made an early start; and, after going ten or fifteen miles, I sincerely regretted that I had not exercised the {233} above laws to a greater extent than I had done, before we started. I felt weak and perfectly fagged, which I attributed entirely to the empty state of my stomach. This I have experienced time without number; and yet, strange to say, I am still unpardonably negligent in the care of this indispensible organ.

The Settlement

With much labour and perseverance, I reached the Halfbreeds [south of the Forks][431] by sundown. After taking a hearty meal, I hired a man with a horse and cariole to take me to A. Goulet's.[432] After another hearty meal here, I went down to [James] Sinclair's and spent the evening with him.

As One Risen from the Dead

December 7, 1844 – Saturday. Mr. Sinclair had the politeness to take me home. I was to our family as one risen from the dead. Reports, for the last month or more, had been industriously circulated through {234} the Settlement that we were all annihilated by the Sioux. My sudden appearance, therefore, was regarded more as a phantom than as a reality. However, I assured them that it was I – and so it was.

Having gone the round of family and friendly salutations, and the excitement of rumour having subsided, I made the arrangements and preparations requisite for bringing up my little property, left at the Grand Forks. And, my wearied limbs being considerably [recovered] after a few days' rest, I started, in company with brother Gavin[433] and John Kirkness.[434]

---

431   Gunn: "The French Métis settlement extending south along the Red River from what is now Winnipeg. J. Wesley Bond, who traveled this trial in 1851, says (*Minnesota and its Resources*, (Redford, 1853), p. 286) that, 'the settlement extends along both sides of the crooked river, in the shape of a long serpentine village.'"

432   Gunn: "Alexis Goulet, a well-known French Métis resident of Red River Settlement at that time. The name, in the MS., is spelled variously as Gaulay, Goulay, Gauley, Gouley, Gulley, Guley, &c. I have used the form 'Goulet' throughout, which is the correct spelling. The A. Goulet above lived up the Red River, probably in what is now St. Vital. He was a prominent free trader, closely identified with the agitation against the monopolistic rule of the Hudson's Bay Company in Rupert's Land. His father was Jacques Goulet, a French Canadian of Lower Canada, and his mother Josephine Seiveright, a daughter of John Seiveright, Chief Factor of the HBC. Alexis was frozen to death on the prairie in December, 1856."

433   Gunn: "Gavin Garrioch, third son of William Garrioch, was born at St. John's, Red River Settlement, in April, 1822. He was named after Reverend Gavin Hamilton, a friend of poet Robbie Burns, whom William had known before leaving Scotland. He married Hannah Bourke, a daughter of John Palmer Bourke of St. James, and in the fifties moved, with others of his family, to Portage la Prairie, where he resided until his death."

434   Gunn: "A Native of Orkney extraction, born in Rupert's Land in 1820. He was married to Betsy Cook, a daughter of Joseph Cook. He is put down in the 1846 and 1849 Red River census records as living at St. Peter's, [the Indian village] on the Red River north of the present Selkirk."

Pembina & an Ox's Fate

We arrived at Kittson's early on the fourth day.

Here I learned that my ox had been left behind, as he could not follow any further. The next I heard of him was that some Indians found him in the act of dying; and, in order to deliver him from the excruciating pains of the last groan, put a bullet in his head. In anatomizing his emaciated frame, they discovered his heart, the seat of life, as they told me, to be quite rotten. A wonderful discovery! I told them I had no doubt at all that the heart was well enough till they had eaten it – and it was only after that that they had found it to be rotten.

Cargo Recovered

On our fourth day from Kittson's we arrived at the Shot Lake. This is where we [had] left our goods; and I have given it this name because I lost, or missed, a bag of shot out of eight I had left. Everything else was safe and in the same good order as when we left it.

A Special Christmas Eve

[December 24, 1844 – Tuesday.] After thirteen days of very hard traveling, both day and a deal by night, we reached home once more by nine o'clock at night, being Christmas Eve.

There was much for the pilgrims to celebrate that holiday season. Although the journal tells us only that Garrioch and Sinclair returned safely to Red River – the latter no doubt much sooner than the former – we know from other sources that every person in both the main party and the diarist's smaller group, including disaster-prone John McLaughlin,[435] eventually did so, along with most of their imported goods. And since Garrioch's ill-fated third ox was the only animal whose demise was reported, it is reasonable to assume that Fox and Blacky survived the gruelling expedition as well.

---

435   During his testimony in London in June, 1857, before the Parliamentary committee struck to examine whether the HBC's licence should be renewed, McLaughlin was speaking about his view that it would be possible to sustain the colony's trade through Canada better than through the HBC's ships in Hudson's Bay, then bragged about his role in opening the Crow Wing route: "I might mention, to show you how the Americans are working their way up in that direction, that I was the first person with seven others who cut that entire route through the woods from the Mississippi and from Crow Wing River, right through, that is the route that is now used...." Great Britain. Parliament. House of Commons, *Report from the Select Committee on the Hudson's Bay Company; together with the Proceedings of the Committee, Minutes of Evidence, Appendix and Index* (London, 1857), Q. 5008, p. 279.

It was not just a matter of personal success for the particular independent traders involved in the event. As historian W. L. Morton has pointed out: "When they appeared in Red River with their American goods, it was apparent [... to everyone in the Settlement that] Red River [was] no longer dependent on York Factory [i.e., the Hudson's Bay Company] for the import of its supplies."[436] And Peter Garrioch's little party had created an alternative route for future travelers who sought to circumvent real or perceived hazards along the traditional one.

The next chapter will demonstrate, however, that although it was now indisputable that there were no insuperable physical obstacles to importation from the US, would-be importers would soon experience barriers of another kind.

---

436 Morton, Introduction to *London Correspondence Inward from Eden Colvile*, p. lix.

Chapter 7

Free Trade Struggles & Romantic Entanglements

1845

This portion of Peter's diary, here provided as Chapters 7 & 8, he subtitled: "Being a Record of Events in the Red River Settlement, Connected Principally with the Free Trade Movement, the Semi-Annual Buffalo Hunts and other Matters of Local and General Interest."

The next several years of Red River's history were marked by vigorous efforts on the part of independent entrepreneurs, of whom Peter Garrioch was one, to compete with the Hudson's Bay Company in both the fur trade and general commerce. The Company was equally determined to suppress those efforts and employed various measures for doing so.

The HBC's 1670 Royal Charter purported to grant it the "whole, entire and only" right to carry on any type of trade in, to, or from the vast territories – known as "Rupert's Land" – that had been bestowed upon it by that Charter. While many asserted that the Charter monopoly had expired, the company continued to assert it and to insist that its courts enforce it. While it was the trade in furs that the Company was most anxious to protect from competition, it was willing to tolerate independent commerce in other areas. HBC officers were, however, made nervous by the sight of free traders stocking up on goods they could use surreptitiously to trade for furs with native trappers. That nervousness was intensified by the breakthrough success, despite the hazards involved, of the recent large-scale trade expedition to the United States on the part of Garrioch and other independent Red River merchants. That successful expedition demonstrated that the American goods were available at better prices than those charged for English merchandise obtained through the HBC-controlled ocean port at York Factory.

Several measures taken by the Company in response to its concerns[437] were legal in nature, many of them devised by Adam Thom,[438] the Settlement's only trained lawyer and also the Recorder (judge) of its principal court. That may explain why Garrioch chose, after almost

---

437 For details, see Chap. 6, n. 356, and Appendix I – Petitions.

438 On Adam Thom see Roy St. George Stubbs, *Four Recorders of Rupert's Land* (Winnipeg: Peguis, 1967), pp. 1-47, & Gibson, *LLG, I, passim.*

Chapter 7 – Free Trade Struggles & Romantic Entanglements

two months' silence, to resume his diary entries by reporting on a visit to a session of that court.

February 21, 1845 - Thursday. Since my return [from trading in America] to the present date nothing has occurred, to my knowledge, worthy of notice.

This day I attended a General Court at Fort Garry,[439] the first I {236} have attended in Red River, and but the second in my life.[440]

---

439   Gunn: "There were two establishments of this name belonging to the Hudson's Bay Company in Red River at this time. The one here referred to was the original establishment, and was located on the north side of the Assiniboine River, on the point of land formed by the junction of that stream with the Red. The other fort, built by Sir George Simpson in the 1830s on the west bank of the Red River some 19 miles farther north, because of its stone construction was called the Stone Fort, but in later years Lower Fort Garry. This [latter] fort is still standing, in a good state of preservation. The name [of both] was derived from Nicolas Garry, Deputy Governor of the Hudson's Bay Company who, at the time of the union of the latter with the North-West Company, visited Red River as the HBC's representative. Being located on the site of the present city of Winnipeg, when the real estate boom struck in the beginning of the 1880s, the land on which it stood [became] very valuable, and it was sold by the Company to a private speculator, who, in 1882, had it demolished; leaving standing only the principal gateway, which is still preserved as a historic relic in the little square on Main Street near the Assiniboine known as Fort Garry Park." The General Quarterly Court sat in a small building, shared by the Settlement's jail, a short distance west of the original fort's southwest corner.

In another note (p. 235), Gunn pointed to his "full account of the judicial system of the Red River Settlement" of the time in his Appendix C, Gunn, pp. 371-380. For a much fuller account of the Quarterly Court of Assiniboia in its societal context and with the complete annotated court records, see Gibson, *LLG, I* & *LLG, II*.

440   Dale thought it possible that Garrioch may have made an earlier visit to a court, perhaps in the United States, but it is more likely that he attended court in his home area at an earlier point, perhaps on the important occasion in 1835 when the Red River court system was established. This seminal 1835 event was precipitated by the fact that, unbeknownst to many of the colonists, Lord Selkirk's estate sold the settlement to the Hudson's Bay Company that year. On February 12, 1835, a historic meeting of the Governor and Council of Assiniboia was convened at Red River by the HBC's North American Governor-in-Chief, George Simpson. After describing the Settlement's rapid growth and increasing complexity, Simpson called for consequential expansion of its government. In response to his suggestions, the Council adopted a number of important new laws, the most significant of which created the court system and police force. It would have made sense that Peter, like many others in the community, would have attended that organizing meeting, especially since one of the laws, said to be necessary to support the new police force "for the protection of the Settlement from a foreign enemy – likewise for maintaining good order at home," was designed to meet this expense by imposing a 5 percent duty on imports from England; London's approval, which was soon forthcoming, was contingent on offsetting the customs duty (borne by the HBC as Rupert's Land's chief importer) by raising prices of the goods imported by 5 percent, thus passing the cost on to consumers. However, at the Council of Assiniboia meeting called to consider resolutions, the customs duty became 7.5 percent "on all imports and exports

General Quarterly Court in Session

The Hudson's Bay Company's Charter gave it more than just the ownership of and exclusive right to trade within Rupert's Land. It also gave it the right to govern that territory, make laws for it – so long as those laws were not inconsistent with English law – and to administer justice in accordance with English and local laws. The powers of governance, legislation, and administration of justice were delegated by the HBC to local officials, subject to the over-riding authority of the Company's head office in London. The most significant of those local government institutions – and the only ones relevant to matters dealt with in the Garrioch diary – were the Governor, Council, and Quarterly Courts of Assiniboia. "Assiniboia" was the name given to the very large district of Rupert's Land within which the Red River Settlement was contained. That district, originally ceded by the Company to Lord Selkirk in 1811, embraced 116,000 square miles, and extended roughly from the height of land south of the present American border northward to the lower reaches of Lakes Winnipeg and Manitoba, and almost from Lake Superior in the east to somewhere between Brandon and the present Saskatchewan border.

The General Quarterly Court of Assiniboia was the senior judicial tribunal for the Settlement and the rest of Assiniboia. Created in 1835 by the Governor and Council of Assiniboia, the General Court sat every three months to deal with both civil and criminal

---

other than personal effects, not just 5 percent on English imports as first proposed," in order to raise additional funds, for example for the construction of the courthouse/jail and other public works. Gibson, *LLG, I*, pp. 36-38.

In his Appendix C to his transcription of Peter's diaries, Gunn quoted from the minutes of the February 12, 1835, Council of Assiniboia meeting, giving the wording of the 7th "enactment:" "That a public building intended to answer the double purpose of a court-house and gaol, be erected as early as possible at the Forks of the Red and Assiniboine Rivers. That in order to raise funds for defraying such expenses as it may be found necessary to incur, towards the maintenance of order, and the erecting of public works, an import duty shall be levied on all goods and merchandise of foreign manufacture imported into Red River, either for sale or private use, at 7½ per cent, on the amount of the invoice; and further, that an export duty of 7½ percent be levied on all goods and stores, or supplies, the growth, produce, or manufacture of Red River." Gunn went on to provide what presumably was his justification for the enactments: "In these enactments, the Settlement was now provided with all the necessary machinery for the handling of not merely civil but criminal cases. It may be remarked, too, in passing, that, theoretically at least, these laws were binding upon the Hudson's Bay Company and its officers equally with the colonist and plainsmen; even if the duty levies applying to their merchandise, without discrimination." (Gunn, pp. 375-376).

That meeting and the frustrations it generated among the Settlement's trading community provide the context for Peter's jottings on the inside cover of his new diary in which he noted down the calculations for the costs of the new court and policing arrangements as contrasted with the costs of public works, described in Chap. 1, text at note 95, and helps confirm that he may have actually attended that momentous Council of Assiniboia meeting in 1835 and then acquired and doodled in the book which was to become his diary.

Perhaps because of his contrarian, free-trading views, Peter Garrioch later came to take on prominent roles in the judicial system of the Red River settlement: see Chap. 10, text at nn. 710-714, 766-776.

Chapter 7 – Free Trade Struggles & Romantic Entanglements

litigation of a serious nature, and to hear appeals from Petty Courts that also met quarterly in each of the Settlement's three judicial districts. The Petty Courts were operated by panels of three magistrates (community elders) in each district. The General Court consisted of the Governor of Assiniboia, who presided, a judge known as the Recorder of Rupert's Land, the colony's two sheriffs (one of them known as "Warden of the Plains"), and, usually, a magistrate from each of the Petty Courts.

The General Court's first Recorder, the controversial, Scottish-born, Montreal-trained, lawyer Adam Thom, was sitting on the occasion of this courtroom visit by Peter Garrioch. Although the Court was formally chaired by the Governor, the Recorder was responsible for directing proceedings, charging juries, and deciding questions of law. His rulings could be overturned by a majority of others on the Court, but the strength of Thom's personality was such that this rarely happened.[441]

Garrioch's description of this particular judicial session was not complimentary.

The bench judicial was composed of various materials [*sic*], viz.: by Judge Thom, Governor [Alexander] Christie,[442] Dr. [John] Bunn,[443] Captain [George] Cary,[444] [James] Bird,[445] and [Alexander] Ross,[446] Esquires. Mr. [John] Black acted as Court

---

441 The Records of the General Court for the period from October 1844 to mid-1872 have survived and are held by the Archives of Manitoba. They are reproduced and annotated in Gibson, *LLG*, *II*. See also Dale and Lee Gibson, *Substantial Justice: Law and Lawyers in Manitoba: 1670-1870* (Winnipeg: Peguis, 1972), Chap. 1.

442 Veteran HBC officer Alexander Christie served as Governor of Assiniboia twice: from 1833 to 1839, and again from 1844 to 1848. See Bumsted, *DMB*, p. 50. As a local governor, Christie was subject to the superior authority of Sir George Simpson, the HBC's North American Governor, as well as of the Company's overall Governor-in-Chief in London. For details about all of the *dramatis personae* in the following notes, see Gibson, *LLG*, *I*. Gunn could not resist commenting broadly about Peter's list of names: "The names here casually set down constitute a somewhat notable group, each one of which contributed something to the history of those early Red River days. The record of their activities is to be found scattered through the many volumes that have already been written, and will grace the pages of many more still to be inscribed, dealing with this ever perennial story of the settlement and development of the Canadian West." (Gunn, p. 236).

443 Dr. John Bunn, a Rupert's Land-born, Scottish-educated, physician, served Red River loyally and well in many positions, including magistrate at this time, and – in spite of his lack of formal legal training – as Acting Recorder in later years. See Bumsted, *DMB*, p. 39, & Stubbs, *Four Recorders*, pp.91-134.

444 George Cary came to Red River to establish an (ultimately unsuccessful) experimental farm for the HBC. Like Bunn and Bird, he was a Petty Court magistrate. See Bumsted, *DMB*, p. 47.

445 James Bird, the third magistrate present at that sitting of the General Court, was a retired HBC officer who owned a large land holding on the east side of the Red River in the area now known as Bird's Hill in his honour. See Bumsted, *DMB*, p. 24. Garrioch was soon to have a run-in with Bird in the latter's additional capacity as Collector of Customs.

446 A former fur trader with a scholarly bent but a thoroughly practical approach to his responsibilities, Sheriff Alexander Ross was in charge of Red River's police force, of maintaining order in the

Clerk,[447] and Mr. [Cuthbert] Grant a mute and neutral Under Chairman.[448] The cases brought before the court were murder, theft and slander.

The murder [case involved] an Indian, who was supposed to have killed his wife in a drunken spree.[449] The thief was likewise an Indian,[450] who had taken a coat and trousers. The slander was by one McDonald, a Scotchman, who had accused James Taylor of "long fingers." James Taylor is an Orkneyman.[451] The [accused] murderer was acquitted [on that charge], there being nothing stronger than presumptive evidence against him. He was, however sentenced to six months' imprisonment for having beaten and thrown his wife, previous to her death, into the fire.[452] The thief

---

courtroom, and of enforcing judgments and orders of both the General and Petty Courts. He would later write and publish the first history of the Red River Settlement, in which he expressed the view that the General Court functioned much better before lawyer Adam Thom's appointment to its number introduced what Ross considered to be unnecessary and confusing formalism. See Bumsted, *DMB*, p. 214.

447 John Black, who trained as a court clerk in his native Scotland, accompanied Adam Thom in that capacity to Red River in 1839. He also worked for the HBC in a commercial capacity, which duties would eventually completely displace his role as Court Clerk. He left Red River and Company service altogether in 1854, but returned as *de facto* Recorder in 1862, and, like Bunn, served with great distinction in that capacity despite not being a fully-qualified lawyer, until 1869. See Bumsted, *DMB*, p. 25; Stubbs, *Four Recorders*, pp. 135-187; & Chap. 8, text at n. 567.

448 Cuthbert Grant, a colourful and once highly influential Métis leader, who had led the North-West Company force at the Battle of Seven Oaks and was largely responsible for establishing the large Métis settlement at White Horse Plains, had been given the title of "Warden of the Plains" by the HBC in 1828. In that capacity, which was formally akin to the position Sheriff Alexander Ross held with respect to Red River, but extended to all of Rupert's Land and was less routine, Grant was chiefly expected to discourage his people from engaging in crime, free trading, and other behavior upon which the Company frowned. See Bumsted, *DMB*, p. 96, & Gibson, *Substantial Justice*, pp. 11, 23, 25, & 40. Garrioch's description of Grant as an "under-chairman" is not accurate. The Court's under-chairman at this point was Recorder Thom, and Grant, like Ross, was present in his capacity as a sheriff.

449 Gibson, *LLG, II*, pp. 9-14: *Public Interest v. Keetchiwaipasse* (Case 4, A11). The name is also spelled "Keetchepewaipas" in the body of the case report.

450 Gibson, *LLG, II*, pp. 8-9: *Public Interest v. Aysassoouun*. (Case 3, A9).

451 Gunn: "James Taylor is listed in all of the Settlement census records that I have had access to. He is put down as a Protestant, hailing from Orkney. He was born in 1794, and in 1846, a year after the above incident, had eight children, 88 head of stock and 18 acres of [cultivated] land, a bonanza farmer for those days. He lived on the west side of the Red River in St. Paul's parish."

452 The death followed a New Year's Eve drinking party at which the accused had been seen to beat his wife, pushing her into a fire at one point, and then to leave the premises in her company, heading toward the Red River. Her beaten body was found the next morning beside a water hole on the river ice, the head and upper torso appearing to have been drenched. The husband was charged

was sentenced to two months imprisonment, and two weeks for having attempted to escape.[453] James Taylor, the slandered, had the satisfaction of not only losing his case but of paying the sum of one pound sterling for {237} the cost of his suit.[454]

Stuff! Stuff! Stuff!

Mr. Thom, judge for the sole benefit of the Hudson's Bay Company, gave us a long and very learned rig-ma-role about the boundary lines, the Charter Unquestionable, and the pure and disinterested goodness of that Company; informing us, that, in all his travels he had not seen a people so happy and blessed as we, and a people that had less to complain of than the people of the Settlement, &c., &c. Stuff! stuff!! stuff!!! Such is the impression on the public of this colony.

Peter Garrioch's impression of the Recorder of Rupert's Land, which he correctly also attributed to general public opinion in the Settlement, was deserved. The choice of Adam Thom as Red River's first legally-trained judge could hardly have been less appropriate.

Although he was brilliant, erudite, and energetic, and did much to shape the Court's procedures and the Settlement's laws along acceptable lines, Thom's temperament was utterly unsuited to a judicial role. Arrogant and snobbish, short-tempered with all but superiors from whom he sought favours, bigoted in matters of race, religion, and language, greedy in matters of money, self-centred, pompous and pontifical in manner, and completely uncompromising in the views he held on every topic under the sun, the man's unsuitability should have been obvious to the HBC's North American Governor George Simpson, who had recruited Thom for the post of Recorder.

While training for law in Montreal, where Simpson lived when not in the field, Thom had supported himself by journalism, and had been publicly reviled for his virulent editorials damning the French language and all other aspects of francophone culture – the language and culture of most "Rupertians." Just before leaving Montreal for Rupert's Land, Thom had assisted Lord Durham in the writing of his infamous *Report* calling for the amalgama-

---

with having killed her by battery and drowning. Autopsy evidence revealed water in the deceased's lungs, and indicated that her death was consistent with drowning. After the jury acquitted the accused of murder he was immediately charged, and convicted of, criminal assault. Gibson, *LLG*, II, pp. 9-14: *Public Interest v. Keetchiwaipasse* (Case 4, A11).

453   The sentence was actually only one month for theft and one week for escape.

454   Gunn: "The slander case arose out of a call Taylor had made at McDonald's place to pay a small sum of money to George Sutherland, a neighbour, who happened to be there. When paying over the money, Taylor remarked that "money was soon spent but hard to earn," whereupon McDonald observed: "It's not hard for you, Jamie, that have long fingers." Jamie took this as a reflection upon his honesty and brought the suit. There were only two witnesses, George Sutherland and Angus Matheson, who [both] supported McDonald in claiming that he had not meant it in that way; that, being a Gaelic man, he had not succeeded in saying in English just what he had intended; but that all he meant was that Jamie, being smart with his hands, could get along. The Court also took this view." See Gibson, *LLG*, II, pp. 7-8: *James Taylor v. Wm. McDonald* (Case 2, A7).

tion of the two Canadas in order to suppress French-Canadian culture. Simpson must have known, but not cared, that this was not someone who could win respect in a predominantly French-speaking community.

What he also knew, of course, was that Thom would be loyal to the employer that paid his extremely generous salary (£700 per annum), and it was that characteristic which prompted Garrioch to describe the Recorder as "judge for the sole benefit" of the Company.[455] Although the description was somewhat exaggerated, the company rarely being directly involved in litigation before the court, Thom did devise, in his additional role as local legal adviser to the HBC, numerous ways to legally hamper or harass free-traders like Garrioch who sought to challenge the fur-trade monopoly the company claimed under its 1670 "Charter Unquestionable." Two such devices are described next in Peter's diary.

Unprecedented Condescension!!

{238} A few days previous to the last date, the two following declarations were presented to all merchants of this colony trading in English goods – the first to be signed, and the second to be retained by each merchant as an earnest of their exalted privileges and a memorial of the HBC's invaluable favour. Pure and disinterested motives surely! Unprecedented condescension!!

The two documents referred to were: (1) a declaration by any person wishing to import goods from England on HBC ships (virtually the only ones that sailed to Rupert's Land) stating that he or she had not trafficked in furs or supplied or financed anyone who did so, and agreeing that if they later "appeared" to have done so, delivery of their imports would be delayed for a year, or the goods would be confiscated by the Company at cost;[456] and (2)

---

455   Gunn's note on Thom, p. 237, is uncompromisingly damning: "…he made himself very unpopular with the French element in Canada, by the strong attitude he took against their compatriots in the Papineau rebellion of 1837.… As incumbent of this office [Red River Recorder] he was not popular with the people of Red River. Though of unquestioned ability and possessing many fine traits, his genius was not of that tactful, diplomatic order, so absolutely necessary to handle the delicate and complicated situations constantly arising at that time within his jurisdiction. His past record, too, as a "Francophobe," destroyed his usefulness with the large French-Canadian element in the community; while his salaried relationship to the Hudson's Bay Co. gave strong grounds for the feeling among all classes that, as Garrioch here expresses it, he was 'judge for the sole benefit' of that – in many quarters – heartily detested corporation. Under the situation in which he [Thom] was here placed, he proved an unqualified failure; and so great was his unpopularity, and the distrust with which he was regarded, that he had finally to be retired." This note of Gunn's is an excerpt from a two-page essay on Adam Thom found among Gunn's papers in the Archives of Manitoba, MG9 A78-1, A78-3.

456   Gunn: "The following is [a public notice containing] the first of these two declarations here referred to: 'Whereas certain persons are known to be trafficking in furs, I hereby give notice that, in order to preclude, if possible, the necessity for adopting stronger measures for this illicit trade,

Chapter 7 – Free Trade Struggles & Romantic Entanglements

a similarly-conditioned license from the Company to sell imported English goods solely within the Settlement (see below). Since Garrioch, along with most other independent merchants, did import goods from England, he had no alternative but to submit to the restrictions set out in both documents.

The first of the above declarations, I should have stated, was returned after it was signed. Here goes the second:

{239} "On behalf of the Hudson's Bay Company, I hereby license Nancy Garrioch to trade, and also ratify her having traded, in English goods, within the limits of the Red River Settlement. This ratification and this license to be null and void from the beginning in the event of her hereafter trafficking in furs, or generally usurping any one whatever of all the privileges of the Hudson's Bay Company.

Given at Fort Garry this 7th December, 1844.

Alex. Christie, Governor of Assiniboia"[457]

---

the Hudson's Bay Company's ship will henceforward not receive at any port goods addressed to any person whatever, unless he shall, at least a week before the day appointed for the departure of the winter express, lodge at the office of Upper Fort Garry a declaration to the following effect: 'I hereby declare that since the 8th day of December instant I have neither directly nor indirectly trafficked in furs on my own account, nor given goods on credit, or advanced money to such as may be generally suspected of trafficking in furs; moreover, if before the middle of August next I shall appear to have acted contrary to any part of this declaration, I hereby agree that the Hudson's Bay Company shall be entitled either to detain my imports of next season at York Factory for a whole year, or to purchase them at the original cost of the goods alone.' I feel confident that the community at large will appreciate my motives for extending this regulation for the present to all importers without distinction; and in order to lessen as much as possible the trifling inconvenience of make the necessary declarations, the accountant has prepared a sufficient number of copies for the signature of parties.

(Signed) Alexander Christie, Governor.Upper Fort Garry,7th December, 1844'"

For the machinations of Adam Thom associated with this strategy, see Chap. 6, n. 356.

457   Gunn: "The document here transcribed by Garrioch, and referred to as the second of these declarations, was accompanied by the following proclamation: 'Whereas, under the fundamental laws of Rupert's Land, it is notoriously illegal to traffic with other countries, or in imported commodities, unless under the protection of the written license of the Hudson's Bay Company; and whereas, under the general law of England, an illegal action cannot be aided by a court of justice, whether to make the debtor pay what he owes, or the agent for what he has received, I hereby give notice, that in order to guard the fair and honest dealer against otherwise unavoidable embarrassment and less, I shall forward to every maritime importer who had lodged a declaration against trafficking in furs a license to the following effect: to which was subjoined, in blank, the license above transcribed.'"

Interestingly, it was not to Peter Garrioch that this license, with its restriction on fur-trading, was granted; but to his mother, Nancy Garrioch. That was probably because when the license was applied for, Peter was still crossing the frozen prairies on foot, and no-one in the colony knew whether he was alive or dead. Nancy no doubt conducted trading transactions at the family home when Peter was absent, and he had not arrived back at Orkney Cottage until the very day Governor Christie signed the license at distant Upper Fort Garry. Since it was Nancy, not Peter, who held the license, it was convenient that Peter escaped having to swear an oath he might otherwise have ended up contravening.

In the course of the present month I gave out goods (American) to the amount of £33, s11, d8 to young F. Gardippe,[458] and £5, s15 to Sam. Baptiste Demes,[459] to trade for fur at the Turtle Mountain quarter. In this month also, I sold a stove to Bouvet[460] for two oxen, one sled and {240} harness, and five pounds in cash.

If the goods provided to Gardippe and Demes had been English, the foregoing undertakings would have been technically violated, which was undoubtedly why Garrioch sold them only American merchandise.

February 22, 1845 – Saturday. Sold James Green two bags of shot.

Sally's Banns

February 23, 1845 – Sunday. Sister Sally published [banns of marriage] with Charles Cummings.[461]

---

458   Gunn: "This is the second François Gardipuis of the note on p. 170. The family lived up the Assiniboine at White Horse Plains, in the parish of St. Francois Xavier. This branch was French Métis."

459   Gunn: "Not in any available census record, and I have been unable to find any trace elsewhere."

460   Gunn: "François Bouvet [was] a French Canadian, born in Lower Canada in 1796. He lived near the [Red] River on Point Douglas, Winnipeg, on the lot next north of Thomas Logan's. A blacksmith by trade, he plied his calling there for many years. He left several sons, François, Louis, and Emile. Louis settled in East Lynn. Emile [lived] in St. Boniface."

461   Gunn: "Sarah ['Sally'] Garrioch, the first-mentioned of these parties was [Peter Garrioch's] third sister. She was born at Norway House June 30, 1820, and married Charles Cummings March 13, 1845, as recorded on a subsequent page. Her husband was a son of Chief Trader Cuthbert Cummings. They moved to Portage la Prairie about 1853, being among the original settlers of that place, and remained there until the time of their deaths. The reference is to the custom of 'publishing the banns,' in lieu of a marriage license, in vogue at that time." However, the date of the marriage is recorded in LAC: FA-1366 (MG25 G62) as having been March 13, 1843. See Peter's diary entries for March 8 & 13, 1845; January 3 & 5, February 17, & March 2, 1846.

Chapter 7 – Free Trade Struggles & Romantic Entanglements

February 27, 1845 – Thursday. Went up to Goulet's and sold two more bags of shot to Mr. Green.

The Norway House packet arrived.

News from Afar

Gunn explained the packet system well:

> The 'packets' of the Hudson's Bay Company were the only means of communication with distant parts of the country and the outside world known to the people of Red River [before trading caravans to the United States were instituted]. In winter they traveled by dogsled, and in summer by canoe, making on average of about 40 miles a day. Being very limited in their capacity, their burden was confined almost entirely to letters and a few newspapers. There were several of these [services], named according to their starting points: the Norway House, the Northern, the Packet from Canada, and so forth; the various outfits linking up with one another and covering the entire HBC territories. The Norway House Packet here referred to left Fort Garry usually about the tenth of December, or as soon as the lakes were sufficiently frozen for safe traveling, and would be known to the Norway House people as the Red River Packet. At this place the matter carried was all re-sorted; that intended for Saskatchewan and that for Hudson's Bay being carried to those destinations.[462]

February 28, 1845 – Friday. Received some geographical information on the Slave Lake vicinity from Mr. James McKay, one of the Northern expeditioners.[463]

---

462 Gunn, p. 240.

463 Gunn: "The reference here is to the arctic expedition under Peter Warren Dease and Thomas Simpson. The party left the Red River Settlement December 1, 1836, and returned in the spring of 1840. See *Life and Travels of Thomas Simpson* by Alexander Simpson, and *Narrative of the Discoveries of the North Coast of America,* [*effected by the Officers of the Hudson's Bay Company, during the years 1836-1839* (London: Bentley, 1843)] by Thomas Simpson. The Honourable James Simpson was born at Edmonton House, where his father was serving the Hudson's Bay Company at that time. He was educated at Red River Settlement, [and as a young man he became] famous as a steersman with the HBC boat brigades, in which capacity he was attached to the above-mentioned expedition. Thomas Simpson, in his narrative, speaks of 'McKay and Sinclair, the picked men of the party.' A possible reason for Garrioch's mentioning this encounter in this manner, so long after the return of the explorers, is that [McKay] may not have returned all the way to Red River [earlier]. [McKay] was married at Red River in June 1859 to Margaret Rowand, third daughter of HBC Chief Factor John Rowand. [In later years he] was a well-known and influential citizen of Red River [and Manitoba], occupying many positions of trust. He was a local magistrate and President of the Court of Petty Sessions for the White Horse Plains district. He [later] held the position of Superintendent of the Dominion Board of Works of the Lake of the Woods, or Dawson Road, when that enterprise was under process. Upon the erection of Manitoba into a province, he

{241} March 2, 1845 – Sunday. Sally published [her banns] the second time.

The Customs Collector Summons

Saw a notice at the Upper Church for merchants to come forward and pay the commission to Mr. James Bird. If the old fool waits till people go to him, he'd better drink more strong tea, to keep him awake.

This is the same James Bird mentioned in the February 21 entry as a magistrate member of the General Quarterly Court. He was also Assiniboia's Collector of Customs Duties, and Peter Garrioch, among others, was resisting the payment of duties demanded for goods recently imported from the United States[464]. He would not pay without a fight, and Collector Bird will be encountered again.

To-day the mail from Partridge Crop reached us.

The reason Peter was interested in mail from Partridge Crop – a small community, renamed in 1851 and now known as Fairford, on the northeast shore of Lake Manitoba – is that his brother John had recently settled there with his wife and baby as the teacher at a Methodist mission established in 1842.

Heard also through {242} Norway House packet, that great mortality had taken place in British Columbia. The cause was dysentery; the effect that 30#[465] of Doctor McLaughlin's[466] men died, and a great number of Indians of the surrounding country.

---

was appointed a member of its Executive Council, and President of that body; and, on the creation of the [province's] Legislative Council he was also called to a seat thereon, with the additional function of Speaker. He lived on the bank of the Assiniboine River in the parish of St. James, now a western suburb of Winnipeg, on an estate known as Deer Lodge."

464 Spry, "The Métis and Mixed-Bloods," cites Peter's diary at p. 103 to illustrate how Garrioch and other free traders were banding together to resist the 1845 imposition by the Council of Assiniboia of import duties on goods brought in from American territory. A detailed description of the free traders struggles against such duties, including the *Sayer* trial, is provided by Morton's Introduction to *Correspondence Inward from Eden Colvile*, pp. lix-lx & lxxvii-xciii; as well as in Morton, *Manitoba, A History*, pp. 73-93.

465 Gunn's note (p. 242) to this number is that Garrioch's original entry stated that 30 of McLaughlin's men had died, but he later appended a note stating: 'The number, it appears, was exaggerated from 3 to 30.' Gunn adds: "Peculiar Addition."

466 McLaughlin, a larger-than-life physician and fur trader, was in charge of HBC operations on the Pacific coast. Gunn's note calls him "the hero and father of Oregon," and continues: "Dr. McLaughlin was a Canadian. He was born at Rivière du Loup, Quebec, in 1784. At an early age, he entered the service of the North-West Company. On the union of the [NWC and HBC] in 1821, McLaughlin was sent across the mountains to take charge of the trade for the joint concern,

Tough Times

March 3, 1845 – Monday. Weather cold. No money. Beef getting out and all other things.

March 4, 1845 – Tuesday. Called on the old gentleman, Monkman.[467] Found {243} him as cheerful, contented, and just as speculative as ever.

March 5, 1845 – Wednesday. Old Black Legs bought a half penny's worth of tobacco.[468]

Garrioch's business must have been slow indeed for such a picayune transaction to be recorded.

March 6, 1845 – Thursday. Went up to see Green. No raisins at Fort Garry; no prunes, no currants, no figs; nothing sweeter or less sweet than sugar – a common article in this colony.

March 7, 1845 – Friday. A heavy fall of snow and very stormy.

The Impracticability of a Celebration for Sally

March 8, 1845 – Saturday. Went down to Thomas Sinclair's to see after stone hauling for the new church,[469] and to announce to Charles Cummings {244} the impracticabil-

---

arriving there in 1824. He built Fort Vancouver, on the north bank of the Columbia River near the Willamette, and here he remained until his retirement from the Company, which took place upon the final settlement of the Oregon boundary question in 1846. The remainder of his life he spent among the settlers of the Willamette Valley; dying at Oregon City, on the Willamette River, in 1857. For the latter part of McLaughlin's life see *McLaughlin and Old Oregon* [by] Eva Emery Dye."

467   Gunn's intended note on Monkman was left blank. The "old gentleman" may have been the father of Joseph Monkman, a prominent Métis who opposed and resisted the 1869-70 uprising and provisional government led by Louis Riel.

468   Gunn notes that Old Black Legs was: "an old Indian, well-known in the community at that time."

469   Gunn: "[Thomas Sinclair was a] younger brother of the James Sinclair already noted…. He lived on the west bank of the Red River, 14 miles north of the present Winnipeg, and about half a mile south of the stone church at St. Andrews Rapids. The stone church, [is] still standing, in use and good repair. It is now the oldest church building in Manitoba, if not in the entire Canadian West. The congregation at this point was established by Reverend Archdeacon Cochran in 1827, and three successive buildings followed each other on the site. In 1831, the original wooden building was replaced by a larger structure; and, in 1845, the present stone edifice, here referred to by Garrioch as "the new church," was commenced. It was completed in 1849, and dedicated by Bishop Anderson, the first Bishop of Rupert's Land, upon his arrival in the country that year. It was known to people of the locality, in those days, as the Rapids Church; or sometimes, as the Lower Church, in contradistinction to St. Paul's and St. John's, which, on account of their relative

ity of making a wedding at his forthcoming marriage with my sister Sally. Two reasons for omitting this customary ceremony [are:] the entire scarcity of luxuries, and the inexorable and almost unpardonable disposition of the majority of the family to the intentions and inclination of Sally.

As the senior surviving son of William Garrioch, Peter considered himself the head of the family; and as such he opposed a wedding celebration party for Sally and her spouse-to-be – and perhaps even the marriage itself – for a reason additional to the hard economic times. While it seems clear that he had no complaint about Charles as a person, Peter had some other objection to the marriage, other than what he described as the family's opposition to it.

What, exactly, was the family's "disposition"? Inasmuch as all of them, other than Peter, would ultimately attend the marriage service – as well as a subsequent wedding celebration party – their feelings as described by Peter in this entry would seem to have either been inaccurately stated or to have subsequently changed. Or might there be a third explanation? Could it be that what was "almost unpardonable" about the family's disposition was simply that it differed from that of head-of-the-household Peter?

And what might his non-economic objection have been? Given that the wedding banns were announced in the family's church, where the ceremony would undoubtedly also take place, the reason was not likely ecclesiastical in nature. Since we know by now that Peter was a stickler for principle, the editors speculate that this objection was a principled one too. Perhaps Sally Garrioch and Charles Cummings were cousins[470]. If that were so, however, a cousinship would not change, leaving unexplained the apparent subsequent thaw implied by the family's attendance at the later celebrations of the marriage.

March 9, 1845 – Sunday. Sally published the banns a third and last time.

---

positions, were designated Middle and Upper Church, respectively." Garrioch was presumably seeking employment hauling stone for the new building. Sinclair was probably in charge of construction operations.

470 Charles' father, Chief Factor Cuthbert Cummings (1787-1870), had "seven reputed children" with his Indigenous wife, Susette McKee, some of whom were settled in Red River and Company locations, but Cummings also had another five children by Jane, the wife he married in 1842. This means that Charles was the product of a *"marriage à la façon du pays"* and may have been, as a "half-breed," not what Peter wanted for his sister, even though Cuthbert ultimately left a portion of his estate to his first seven children. See Krista Barclay, "From Rupert's Land to Canada West: Hudson's Bay Company Families and Representations of Indigeneity in Small-Town Ontario, 1840–1980," *Journal of the Canadian Historical Association* 26:1 (2015), pp. 67–97. As well, the sheer number of Cuthbert Cummings' children increases the possibility that there could have a prior kinship connection between the Cummings and the Garriochs that made marriage between Charles and Sally unpalatable to Peter.

Chapter 7 – Free Trade Struggles & Romantic Entanglements 237

Farewell to Isabella

Saw poor . . . [this is the way Garrioch wrote it] today at Pambrun's, but not recognizing me, I paid no attention to her. I am sorry for it. She no doubt thinks that I despise her, and that I entertain hard feelings against her from what is past and gone by. You are mistaken, poor . . . I still love you, though I cannot well account for the reason. I pity your case from the bottom of my heart. Perhaps you are happy without my pity. I certainly hope you are.

The woman Garrioch avoids naming here is undoubtedly Isabella McKenzie, the sweetheart/fiancée of earlier journal entries. What had come between them since those earlier references is not known with certainty, but this entry suggests that, her relationship with Peter having been forbidden by her guardian John McCallum, Isabella did something to sever their previous relationship, having decided that Peter's rival had better prospects than his. Among a number of random, undated, jottings on the cover of his diary is the observation that "Isabella McKenzie is a witless windheaded creature," which, if it relates to her preference for the other suitor, seems, like the entry about Sally's wedding, to reflect more pity (and arrogance?) than anger.

Gunn observed:

> Isabella, daughter of Kenneth McKenzie. This young lady and her sister Margaret had been sent by their father from the Missouri, to be educated at the boarding school [then known as McCallum's School] and were consequently under the guardianship of Mr. McCallum, who evidently interpreted his powers, in this connection, as having jurisdiction over the affairs of the heart as well as those of the head. Mr. Garrioch, who later married the other sister, Margaret, had, previous to this time, fallen a willing captive to the charms of Isabella; but, there being another suiter in the field more favoured by the Principal of the school, the whole influence and authority of that gentleman was brought to bear, to the discomfiture of our Author's suit. It is to this little bit of private human history that the phrase 'Isabella's case' refers.[471]

March 11, 1845 – Tuesday. Another good fall of snow. Received a bag of pemmican as a present from Pascal Bréland.

March 12, 1845 – Wednesday. Took a ride up[stream along the Red River]. Peter Hayden[472] very ill.

---

471 Gunn, pp. 246-247. See Chap. 5, text at nn. 286-291.

472 Peter Hayden figures prominently here in Chap. 7 and at various points in Peter's diaries; for introductory background to him, see Chap. 6, n. 344.

Sister Sally Married

March 13, 1845 – Thursday. Sister Sally married to Charles Cummings. Every soul is down to the wedding, and I am left alone, like a cottage in a garden of cowcumbers.[473]

{245} **March 14, 1845 – Friday.** Went down to see the newly married couple. They look sweet and pleasant – and they look like immortality.

These entries confirm that the objection to Sally's marriage was Peter's alone. Yet he was moved to visit the couple after their union and seems to have had a "pleasant" reception from them. What did it mean that they looked like "immortality"? Perhaps that, for all her big brother's misgivings, Sally's union with Charles appeared destined to survive a long while – as indeed it did.[474]

March 15, 1845 – Saturday. A fine day with some snow. Felt for the first time this season a pain in my chest. This is occasioned, I presume, from constant sitting.

March 16, 1845 – Sunday. Strong north wind, and it thaws at a noble rate; sleet in the evening, snow in abundance before bed time.

Helping a Mission

March 18, 1845 – Tuesday. Mr. William R. Smith went about for wheat for the Partridge Crop mission.

Partridge Crop, now known as Fairford, was located on Lake Manitoba, and was the site of a recently-established Anglican mission to the native population of that area. William Smith was a widely-respected former HBC employee and Anglican catechist who was currently operating a school in the vicinity of the Garrioch home, and would soon begin a long and distinguished career as Clerk of the Council and Quarterly Courts of Assiniboia.[475] His canvass on behalf of the Partridge Crop mission on this occasion was typical of his dedication to community service.[476] John Garrioch's presence as teacher at

---

473   There may have been an excision from the journal here – perhaps of comments about Sally's wedding – although Gunn makes no reference to it. "Cowcumbers" were, no doubt, cucumbers.

474   They were married until their respective deaths, in 1893 and 1894. See above, n. 461.

475   Gibson, *LLG, I, passim*.

476   Gunn: "Partridge Crop was where the present Fairford now is – see note on p. 241. A mission of the Anglican Church was established [there] in 1842. [The mission's canvasser,] William Robert Smith, [was] one of the best known and most interesting figures [at Red River in] those days. He was born in England in 1796, and studied at Christ's Hospital, London. In 1813, he came to Rupert's Land as an apprentice clerk in the service of the Hudson's Bay Company, being stationed successively at Oxford House, Isle à la Crosse, Little Slave Lake, Lac la Biche and Norway House. In 1824

Chapter 7 – Free Trade Struggles & Romantic Entanglements   239

the mission no doubt strengthened Smith's own persuasiveness among residents of the area where John grew up.

A Domestic Tallow Trade?

I suggested this day for the first time an attempt to establish a tallow trade by domesticating buffalo calves.

The idea of using buffalo fat to produce tallow for the manufacture of candles was not new. The "grease" mentioned in Garrioch's earlier journal entries had long been a valuable byproduct of the buffalo hunt. What seems to have stimulated his proposal to raise the animals domestically for this purpose was probably the fact that the wild herds were moving further away from the Settlement, having been driven especially far by devastating prairies fires in 1844, coupled perhaps with the fact that the Hudson's Bay Company was currently going out of its way to hamper the shipment abroad of tallow from wild buffalo by free traders like Andrew McDermot and James Sinclair.[477] Garrioch may have thought that a close-at-hand domestic source of tallow would overcome both the supply and the trade monopoly problems. There is no evidence that he ever attempted to put such a scheme into operation, although he did engage in a little candle-making with the tallow on hand.

Logging, Candlemaking, Commerce

March 19, 1845 – Wednesday. The boys, not being able to find Frederick's[478] sawing logs, brought home round logs for various purposes. Frederick's bull [was] left behind.

---

he removed to the Red River Settlement and, severing his connection with the Company, settled on a farm at what was subsequently known as Little Britain, where he was one of the first settlers. In 1828 he received an appointment as [Anglican] catechist at St. John's, remaining there until 1832. [He then] moved to Middle Church, where he [operated] a private school in his own home, subsequently being placed in charge of the parochial school there. In 1848 he was appointed Clerk of the Court and Council of Assiniboia, offices which he continued to hold until 1868, when he retired on account of failing health. During Smith's long life in the Settlement he also filled, from time to time, many other offices of trust, and was, in fact, the general legal and literary factotum of the community. He died in 1869, the father of 22 children, and many others of his descendants are scattered through the Province. See also J. J. Hargraves' *Red River* (Friesen, 1871), pp. 208-212."

477   Lent, *West of the Mountains*, pp. 96-7, 167, & 170. On Sinclair see Gilman, *Red River Trails*, pp. 8 (picture)-13.

478   Gunn: "Frederick Adolphus Bird, [who will appear again] on subsequent pages of this journal, was the eldest son of George Bird and grandson of Chief Factor James Curtis Bird, noted on p. 236. He was born at Carlton House, Saskatchewan, March 18, 1823, educated at Red River Settlement, where he also learned the blacksmith's trade, a calling which he subsequently followed. In 1843, he was married to Ann Garrioch, the youngest sister of [Peter], taking up his residence in St. Paul's parish. In the spring of 1851, upon the founding of Portage la Prairie, he moved with his family to

"The boys" were Peter's brothers Gavin and William, who, along with Frederick Cook, were fetching logs felled and limbed earlier at some woodland location. "Sawing logs" might have been those of sufficient diameter to be sawn into boards or squared for beams; "round logs" being too thin for those purposes. On the other hand, sawing logs *could* have been those intended to be sawn for firewood and round logs larger ones suitable to serve as building beams. The latter interpretation finds possible support in the March 22 and 24 entries.

The two last days have been very cold, and this day very little better.

March 20, 1845 – Thursday. Made 64 candles, and sold goods to the amount of no less than two shillings and threepence!! ... [Pages missing][479]

Dreams of Columbia

Although both Great Britain and the United States claimed jurisdiction over the Columbia River and Oregon country between the mountains and the Pacific Ocean, the Hudson's Bay Company was active there, and Garrioch's relative and respected colleague James Sinclair had, in 1841, famously led a migration of former Red River residents wishing to settle in the area.[480] Its moderate climate and agricultural promise must have made it a land of dreams for prairie dwellers in the bleak days of late March. Peter Garrioch was no exception.

March 21, 1845 – Friday. Never thought so much about Columbia as I have done today. But then a question presents itself in this form: "And should you go, what can you do? Without money, without a wife, without interest and without property, and with a very limited education, what could you do?" I see I must think again.

My Intended House

March 22, 1845 – Saturday. It snows, sleets and rains, a "ferry dribblan sheer." The boys returned early this morning with ten beams for my {246} intended house, and twenty sawing logs for Frederick. They take up Frederick's logs this moment.

---

that point, where he [resided the rest of his life, occupying] the position of Postmaster for a number of years. He was also made a Councillor of the abortive "Republic of Manitobah," organized there in 1867, holding the position of Sheriff to that body. He was a member of the first Legislature of Manitoba; being elected to represent Portage la Prairie upon the creation of the province. He died [at Portage] in November 1884".

479 The dots appear to indicate another excision.
480 Lent, *West of the Mountains*, pp. 107-58.

An Easter Grudge

March 23, 1845 – Sunday. This is Easter Sunday. I did not join in the communion, from the sole reason that I could not go forward with that feeling of brotherly love which Mr. Macallum[481] had dwelt so largely upon in his preparatory discourse. The only grudge in my heart against any man was against Macallum himself, from his former conduct towards me in Isabella's case.[482]

---

481   See Chap. 5, nn. 289-290, and above, entry for March 9, 1845. Macallum ran a harsh school, according to the Reverend Benjamin McKenzie who was sent to the school in the company of his aunt Jane who was to take charge of the girls' school, while it was under the superintendency of Rev. John Macallum: "His ambition was to make good writers of all the boys …he was a very severe pedagogue. He over-estimated the value of the use of the rod…. I well remember the day of my arrival at the Academy. Getting out of the York boat, and going up the bank, I began to explore and found an open door…. With mocassined feet I could very easily enter the long, low porch to listen at the school door. It was my misfortune to hear someone being punished for unsatisfactory writing, stroke after stroke. It happened to be my own brother and that, surely, was a warning and a prophecy as to what I was to expect. Well, the prophecy came true and no mistake. It would require no prophet to foretell that I was not going to love school. And I may just as well here say that my school days under Mr. McCallum [sic] were bitter as Egyptian slavery and profited me very little." Reminiscences of Reverend Benjamin McKenzie, Ecclesiastical Diocese of Rupert's Land *Fonds*, PRL-84-59 7953.

482   *Ibid*. As Gunn noted (above), Macallum undoubtedly saw himself *in loco parentis* in this matter and may have seen it as his responsibility to make sure Isabella made a "good" marriage. Not that the Macallum was a very "nice" man but, again, marriage was not seen as purely a matter of individual choice. The "wrong" marriage could bring down a family's reputation, or a good one could vastly improve the family's security through creating new relationships. It is clear that Peter Garrioch, being somewhat deficient in both social status and reliability, was not seen as an "eligible" bachelor in the community, and this may account in part for why he remained unmarried for so long.

However, by the time of his marriage in February, 1849, four years later, Peter seems to have been acceptable enough to marry – Isabella's sister! We do not know the precise circumstances of their betrothal and wedding, since by that time, Peter had apparently ceased writing his diaries, but either his reputation had improved or Macallum was no longer in control of the McKenzie sisters as he had been in 1845, when Peter failed to secure permission to marry Isabella. In fact, in the summer of 1849, Macallum suffered an attack of jaundice from which he never rallied, and he died on October 3, 1849: Allan Levine, "John Macallum," *DCB VII*, p. 526. Peter's and Margaret's marriage occurred on February 25, 1849, several months before Macallum's catastrophic illness, (Chap. 10, text at n. 707), but it is possible that Macallum's health was already in decline by that point, and he just didn't have the energy to oppose the marriage. Another possibility is that Peter and Margaret were already living together, making marriage look better than not marrying. Or it could have been some combination of these things. It is also possible that his future wife for some reason did not have the so-called "better options" that her sister had had, or that Peter had managed to gain Kenneth McKenzie's approval directly. After all, the powerful "King of the Upper Missouri," who among other things built the Fort Union trading post, now a U.S. National Historic Site, lived until April 26, 1861. H.M. Chittenden, *The American Fur Trade of the Far West* (New

A Thought Experiment

{247} After retiring to rest last evening, my faculties refused to slumber. My eyes in vain courted and expostulated with the Goddess of Night, [but] she refused to impart her genial caresses. In losing this sweet slumber, however, I gained a very important point – one which I had never [before] been fully able to comprehend.

That [point] is: How [does] any soul of spirit differ from that of the Spirit of Spirits, or the Author of all things, with regard to omniscience and omnipresence? I discovered, when applying my mind to the task, that it was not capable of concentrating its energies on two different and separate objects at one and the same instant. I took, for instance, London and New York, and endeavoured to compass the two places [in my mind] at the same instant of time; but I found, after repeated trials, that only the almost imperceptible rapidity of the mind from one object to another induced me for a moment to think that it was capable of preserving two objects, perfect and clear, at one and the same indivisible moment. For the moment my mind compassed the two separate objects everything became imperfect; and the mind either unavoidably hung in suspense between the two objects, or the vision of the mind became imperfect and the objects enshrouded in a midst of confusion. This very forcibly convinced me of the difference between a finite and infinite mind.

This also leads me to believe that Satan, though he is Prince of {248} the Powers of the Air, is not capable of being present at more than a limited space at the same moment; nor is he capable of [making suggestions], at the same indivisible moment, to any two separate individuals. But such is the rapidity of the almost inconceivable transition of spirit from one object to another, that it is capable of exerting its energies to such a degree as almost to exclude any doubt of its being able to compass any two, or indeed any object in conceivable space in a moment of indivisible parts. This, however, could be applied only to spirits of originally a superior order, such as angels and devils, whose existence is purely spirit, and who are not, consequently, locally confined, as we are, whose spirits are limited in their operation by reason of the bodies with which they are environed.

The logical fallacy of concluding that, if a human mind cannot concentrate on more than one topic at a time, a supernatural mind like Satan's cannot do so either does not detract from the originality of this interesting little thought experiment. A practical modern

---

York, Francis Harper, 1901), I, pp. 331-362, 378, & 384-387. Chittenden writes that both sisters, Isabella and Margaret, were still living in 1900.

Chapter 7 – Free Trade Struggles & Romantic Entanglements   243

reader might find the experiment relevant to the more mundane controversy over the merits and demerits of "multi-tasking."

March 24, 1845 – Monday. Boys went off for Frederick's forge logs at the Hill.

"The Hill" was probably the area still known as Bird's Hill, northeast of Winnipeg. Frederick Bird, being a blacksmith, required a large supply of wood to fire his forge.

Spring Approaches

The first ducks of this season seen today.

March 25, 1845 – Tuesday. A fine, warm day. The snow runs down rapidly before the united force of sun and south wind.

Beede's son buried today.[483]

March 26, 1845 – Wednesday. Took a trip up to Bouvet's to see after my gun. The weather is warm and the roads on the ice begin to be very bad.

A child of James Hallett's was burned to-day.[484] Yesterday [my] brother John {249} arrived from the Partridge Crop.[485]

Collector Bird Begins to Press

March 28, 1845 – Friday. Received a note from Mr. Bird, of which the following is a true copy:

> Mr. Peter Garrioch:
>
> Will you be good enough to call some day (not Monday next) and pay the Duty, 4 percent, on the goods you brought from the States, on their price thereof . . . and also the Duty on the goods your Mother received the last

---

483 Gunn: "John Beede. He lived in St. Andrews parish, on the west bank of the Red River, below the stone church [then under construction]."

484 Gunn: "James Hallett was a brother of Willian Hallett, the well-known free trader of those days. He lived in the parish of St. James, on the north side of the Assiniboine, not far from the old St. James parish church."

485 John was serving as teacher at Partridge Crop at this point.

fall, bringing her papers with you. She has, I believe, two invoices, one from Mr. Roberts.[486]

Yours, James Bird 28 March, '45

The old coon will find that I am not quite so great an ass as he takes me to be. He tells me to call some day. It may be ten, twen{250}ty or fifty years hence; the time is not specified definitely. He seems, however, [to be] quite apprehensive, and emphatically wishes me not to call on the following Monday. Old man, you have been young and now you are old, but I assure you that you will again become young, and old enough again after that, before your most humble servant will be so stupid and impertinent as to trouble you with a call. Your humble servant knows his own place better than that. He does not like to insinuate himself into the affairs of big folk at all.

Although Garrioch was dragging his feet with respect to both the American and English duties, his chief objection, in common with other Red River traders, was to the duty which was newly imposed on imports from the United States. Although it would not take "ten, twenty, or fifty years" to resolve the matter, it would take more than a month. See the entries for April 6, 7, 9, 21, 24, and May 3 to 13 inclusive.

March 30, 1845 – Sunday. This is quite a stormy day. It snows and blows furiously.

March 31, 1845 – Monday. Some more snow and plenty of wind. [Brother] John starts off this morning for the Partridge Crop, with wind and tide in his favour.

April 1, 1845 – Tuesday. The wind still keeps to its favourite winter quarter, the north.

Tumble from a Colt

April 2, 1845 – Wednesday. Got a neat tumble from Buscuyee, Frederick's colt. The wrist of my right hand suffered a good deal by the fall. I went out with Gavin and William to the Pines [in the Bird's Hill area] for firewood, but, by the time we got there, I found the swelling and pain in my wrist had {251} so much increased that I could do little more than look on.

---

486 Gunn: "I think [Roberts] was an English merchant from whom Red River settlers were in the habit of ordering goods, by way of Hudson Bay."

Chapter 7 – Free Trade Struggles & Romantic Entanglements 245

More Logging

April 3, 1845 – Thursday. It blows and drifts like a February day. Gavin, William and Frederick out for juniper cedar [tamarack] pickets, and returned with 96 on three oxen.

April 4, 1845 - Friday. Gavin is out again to the Pines for birch wood. William and Frederick took up some wood belonging to the latter to his own place. The wind still continues to blow from the north, and cold withal.

Death in an Awful Manner

Heard today that some American traders came by their deaths in the following awful manner. Being attacked by some Indians, they defended themselves from within as long as their munitions of war lasted. When, all their powder [... was] expended, they set fire to their house – thus choosing rather to suffer death by the flames than to fall into the hands of their bloodthirsty and merciless enemies.[487]

April 5, 1845 – Saturday. Quite a cold and windy day. The wind has turned to the west.

Collector Bird Recruits the Clergy

April 6, 1845 – Sunday. Cold north wind all day. This evening Mr. Cockran[488] called up and advised me to pay the duty on my American goods, {252} at the same time

---

487 Gunn, in a handwritten interpolation on p. 252: "I have not been able to verify this incident."

488 Gunn: "Reverend William Cockran, Archdeacon of Assiniboia, third in the succession of Protestant Episcopal missionaries to arrive in the Red River Settlement. Mr. Cockran came out from England in the summer of 1825, as assistant to Reverend D. T. Jones, then in sole charge of the Christian Missionary Society's activities in Rupert's Land. [Cockran] proved himself to be the greatest missionary of any of the men sent out by that society for this work and is regarded as the virtual founder of the Anglican Church in Manitoba. An indefatigable worker, he organized congregations and built churches up and down the Red and Assiniboine Rivers; and two at any rate of the original buildings: the stone church at St. Andrews Rapids, and St. Peters Church at the Indian Settlement. The former of these congregations, established in 1827, was the first fruit of Mr. Cockran's missionary efforts in the country; the latter, his second achievement along this line, was organized in 1836. He retained the office of missionary to St. Andrews practically from its inception to 1850, having charge also of St. Peter's, and devoting his time entirely to the latter congregation from 1850 to 1856 or thereabouts. In 1856 he removed to Portage la Prairie, and there established the congregation of St. Marys; later organizing the missions of St. Margarets and St. Anns, a little further [along] the Assiniboine at what are now High Bluff and Poplar Point. In connection with the church at Portage la Prairie, Mr. Cockran also opened a school, which was

showing me a letter he had received in the morning from Mr. Bird on the same subject. The following is a true copy of this highly politic[al] and artful letter:

> My Dear Sir: White Cottage, 6th April, 1845.
>
> Knowing how solicitous you are that we should not resort to coercive measures for the collection of the import duty, I would take the liberty to again induce them to pay the little they have become liable for. I believe they have been led to think that James Sinclair is determined not to pay, and that, under his influence, they may be able to escape with impunity. But he has already assented to respect the law by promising to pay me when called upon, and an assurance of this may have some weight with them. Mr. Macallum has kindly promised to try his influence with Goulet tomorrow on the same subject.
>
> I am, Dear Sir,
>
> Respectfully yours,   James Bird."

April 7, 1845 – Monday. The wind at length got round to the south {253} side of the globe.

Someone was Lying

Suspecting the correctness of the statements in the above letter, I and Henry Cook went up to see more particularly into the matter of import duty by advising with those who were equally concerned with us in the business. [. . .] Henry alone called on James Sinclair, [and . . .] discovered that Sinclair's promising to respect the laws, &c. was nothing but a huddled-up and barefaced lie – or Sinclair himself tells a lie – for he told Henry that he never did promise to pay unless the rest [of the free traders] paid first.

---

placed under the charge of [Peter Garrioch]. Feeling his health beginning to fail in 1864, he left the country with the intention of permanently remaining in England, but returned the following year, dying shortly afterwards at Portage la Prairie (Oct. 7, 1865), on the exact day and date of his arrival in the country 40 years previously." See also Bumsted, *DMB*, p. 52. This article with expanded details is found in the George Gunn fonds at the Archives of Manitoba: "Note re Rev. William Cochrane," n.d. MG9 A78-1, A78-3.

Taxation Without Representation

So that [Sinclair's] promising to pay was only conditional, and not out of any respect he entertained for the laws of 'taxation without representation.'

When we got up to Alexis Goulet's, we did not find [him] at home, but left word with [James] Green to tell him to come down with [Peter] Hayden on the following Thursday. While in Goulet's, [Reverend] Macallum's man came in with a message that Macallum wished to see him that day. The messenger was sent home with the impression that Goulet was out on a fur trading expedition, and that he was not expected to return before the following Monday. The fact was that Alexis was out for hay, and was expected back every moment.

The misrepresentation was no mere prank. Goulet, along with the others Garrioch and Cook were arranging to meet with, was one of the free traders resisting the payment of customs duties; and Customs Collector James Bird's letter to Cockran, playing the free traders off against each other, had indicated that Reverend Macallum would be asked to undertake a similar mission to Goulet. This was a questionable tactic. Employing clergymen to influence their parishioners to do the HBC's bidding, as Collector Bird was doing, seems morally dubious today.

April 8, 1845 – **Tuesday.** South wind all day. Frederick and Gavin winnowed about 80 bushels barley.

April 9, 1845 – **Wednesday.** Southwest wind all day. Blew hard and the snow ran down into liquid like a giant in his race. The water on the sides of the river formed a rapid current before 12 o'clock.

Reverend Cockran's Advice

His Reverence, Mr. Cockran called this morning and paid me 9/2 for Mr. Cowley.[489] I handed him Mr. Bird's note, and he gave his opinion, {254} by way of advice, that we who were importers of American goods should either pay the tax demanded now and

---

[489] Gunn: "Reverend Abraham Cowley, an Anglican Church clergyman, who came out from England to Red River in 1841 as assistant to Archdeacon Cockran. He became well known and highly respected during a long life of missionary activity in the country. His first independent work was the establishment of the Indian mission at Partridge Crop, now Fairford, in 1842. Being but a catechist at the time of his arrival, he was ordained priest in 1844. In 1857, he was placed in charge of the Indian mission at St. Peters, a position which he held until 1866, at which time he was made Archdeacon. The same year he became incumbent of Mapleton, or St. Clements Parish. Garrioch must have sold something to or done some work for, Cowley."

petition Governor [-in-Chief] George Simpson for a repeal of the tax law on American goods; or present a written petition to Mr. Christie, the [Assiniboia] Governor, to be laid before the Council [of Assiniboia] on the arrival of Governor Simpson.

Pledged Not to Yield

Peter Hayden and Alexis Goulet, according to promise, came down today. Mr. Macallum's advice to Alexis Goulet was to defer his payment of the duty to the very last. This being the screening song of every one of us against the unjust measure of the Fort Garry Council, it is hard to say which of us is to pay the tax first. Five of our party, however, viz.: Peter Hayden, Alexis Goulet, St. Germain,[490] Henry Cook[491] and myself, have mutually pledged ourselves, on our word of honour, not to yield to the above requisition of the Council, unless compelled by superior coercive measures. {255}

Policemen Mustering, River Rising, Serious Eruption Looming

The day after we had been at Goulet's, it was reported that the Council were mustering policemen to apprehend certain American traders, who had taken up their lodgings at Goulet's.

---

490   Gunn: "This name was spelled in the manuscript in accordance with its local French pronunciation: "Chagerma." The name is one that recurs frequently throughout the literature of the fur trade. There were two families of St. Germain in Red River Settlement: one at Baie St. Paul on the Assiniboine, the other up the main river. The reference is probably to the latter."

491   A few days after this entry, on April 12, 1845, Reverend William Cockran wrote from Grand Rapids to John Smithurst, who had been appointed by the HBC in 1840 as company chaplain in Red River and appears to have been seen in some quarters as perhaps too diligent in ministering to his Aboriginal charges, and described to Smithurst a useful approach to handling the free trade controversy: "There has been a good deal of excitement above, by the Importers from the States, refusing to pay the Import. And I take the first opportunity of informing you of the laudable conduct of Mr. McAllum with Henry Cook. Mr. McAllum bought some bonnets from Henry and hearing that he refused to pay the Import. Mr. McAllum asked him if he had charged the import on the bonnets? to which he replied no. Mr. McAllum: "I suppose you would have charged the bonnets a little higher, if you had intended to pay the Import." "Henry: "Certainly." Mr. McAllum: "Here is the additional price, carry it to Mr. Bird, if you don't intend to pay the Import, take your bonnets home with you; for I do not intend to purchase counterband articles." As you have had dealings with Henry you may be in the same position with the said Gentleman. I give you this information, so that should you choose to act you may have an opportunity of developing your soundness of Judgment & principle. Only keep the hint private that you may not appear to act from precedent. Yours Truly Wm Cockran." https://discoverarchives.library.ualberta.ca/index.php.

April 10, 1845 – Thursday. The river begins to burst about the sides, and traveling on ice ends to-day.

April 11, 1845 – Friday. Measured 37 bushels barley [on hand], and the cattle got out to the prairie for the first time this season.

April 12, 1845 – Saturday. Saw a rainbow this evening; the first this season.

April 13, 1845 – Sunday. A report circulated on the probability of a serious eruption among the English, French and Americans.

First Thunder, False Report, Muddy Roads

April 14, 1845 – Monday. Went down to see John Spence about my barn. He was off to the Shoal Lake.[492] Some rain this evening, and the ice took a start at the Image Plains.[493] The first thunder this season was heard this evening.

April 17, 1845 – Thursday. Cold and cloudy. Heard today of some skirmish among the Sioux and some Americans, in which an American killed ten of the Sioux.

April 18, 1845 - Friday. Gavin went up to the Fort to purchase some ammunitions, &c. He says the above report is false.

{256} **April 19, 1845 - Saturday.** William Badger[494] commenced with Gavin sawing boards.

April 20, 1845 – Sunday. Very warm, but the roads very wet and muddy. One of Mr. Clouston's children dangerously ill.[495]

---

492 Gunn: "A considerable body of water, lying to the northwest of Winnipeg, and east of the southern extremity of Lake Manitoba. Being a shallow, marshy lake, as its name implies, it was a favourite rendezvous for hunters in the early days."

493 Gunn: "A large meadow or plain lying to the west of the Red River at what is now known as Middlechurch, about eight miles north of Winnipeg."

494 Gunn: "William McCorrister, a native of the Settlement, is the party here referred to, ["Badger"] being merely a nickname; [many] in the community being rechristened, after the same fashion, with some characteristic sobriquet. Mr. McCorrister lived on the east bank of the Red River, just south of the Little Britain ferry, in the parish of St. Andrews."

495 Gunn: "Robert Clouston, a native of Orkney; born in 1792. He came to the Red River Settlement at an early date and settled on the west bank of the river, in St. Paul's parish about half a mile below the present Middlechurch. He was, by trade, a watch and clock maker and repairer, and followed

Paid Mr. Bird on English Goods

April 21, 1845 – Monday. Paid Mr. Bird £1 s13 d7 for duty on English goods, but, as formerly, refused paying duty for American goods. The old gentleman expatiated largely on the respectability of my family, connections, &c. But the old fox could not come it.

April 22, 1845 – Tuesday. Sent twenty bushels wheat to W[illiam] Bird's mill.[496]

April 23, 1845 – Wednesday. William commenced ploughing with two yoke of oxen.[497]

April 24, 1845 – Thursday. Went up to the White Horse Plains to get some pemmican for John Spence. Kittson[498] arrived today and brought {257} intelligence of Owen McKenzie's death.[499]

---

this occupation, in conjunction with his other activities, the principal of which was the operation of a small general store. He also built one of the first mills in the community. He died in 1850."

496   Gunn: "William Bird, a son of [Customs Collector] James Curtis Bird. He also lived on the west side of the Red River north of Middlechurch, a lot or two south of the premises of the Mr. Clouston just noted. He was proprietor of one of the several grist windmills in the community at this time."

497   The meaning of the expression "two yoke of oxen," which Garrioch repeats with variations in later entries (see May 6 and May 19, for example), is open to speculation. A yoke was a wooden device used to harness two oxen or other animals together for purposes of ploughing or hauling, and this reference could simply mean that William employed two teams of oxen to do his work. Since it is highly unlikely that one man could drive two teams of oxen simultaneously in a straight line, however, it seems more likely that the term is used here in some other – special – sense, such as to designate the amount of ploughing or other work a team of oxen could accomplish before having to be released from the yoke for rest. By that interpretation, "two yokes" would mean two ploughing sessions – perhaps with the same animals. It might also refer to four oxen being yoked to one plough, but that would seem like overkill unless, perhaps, if unbroken land were involved.

498   Norman Kittson, an American fur trader based at Pembina who was encouraging Red River free traders to bring their furs to him rather than to the Hudson's Bay Company, whom Peter Garrioch knew, and with whom he would have many dealings. See diary entries for January 26, February 19, & May 2, 1846. Also see Bumsted, *DMB*, p. 132; Gibson, *LLG, I*, pp. 79, & 89-92; Gilman, *Red River Trails*, pp. 10-14, 23-26, & 55; & Russenholt, *Heart of the Continent*, p. 87.

499   Gunn: "The Owen McKenzie here referred to was a son, by his first wife, of Kenneth McKenzie, the great Missouri fur trader, and a brother of the previously-mentioned Margaret and Isabella McKenzie. He was himself a well-known trader on the Missouri, and was not unknown in Red River Settlement, having visited his sisters there on a number of occasions. There is something wrong about this entry, as we know that McKenzie lived for nearly 20 years after this date. The entry is probably accounted for by the prevalence [of rumour] in isolated [communities] like Red River. Owen McKenzie continued on the Missouri, trading at the various posts of the American Fur Company until [the early 1860s, when] he was shot and instantly killed by a notorious desperado of that region named Malcolm Clark. The [killing] took place on board the 'Nellie Rogers,' one of the

Sinclair's Position

James Sinclair told me today again that he did not promise to pay the bothered tax except the rest paid it.

Snow, Sunshine & Early Death

April 25, 1845 – Friday. Left the White Horse Plains by 8 o'clock through, or rather against, wind and snow. It fell about two inches of snow last night and continued to snow all this day.

April 26, 1845 – Saturday. Bought half a sturgeon to-day for one shilling. The snow is nearly all off again, for the sun begins to show his beautiful and powerful face.

April 27, 1845 – Sunday. Commenced raining at about three in the evening. Mr. Clouston's child died this evening.

April 28, 1845 – Monday. Kittson started for home.[500] Still continues {258} cloudy and rainy.

May 3, 1845 – Saturday. Some more snow this morning. Cleaned ten bushels of wheat.

Drafting a Petition

Finished the first impression of a petition to the Council.[501]

AFC's steamers on the Missouri, [and] arose out of a quarrel over some long-standing financial disagreement between the two men. McKenzie [was] drunk at the time. Also see Chittenden, *Early Steamboat Navigation on the Missouri*, II, p. 234, & Charles Larpenteur, *Forty Years a Fur Trader on the Upper Missouri*, II, p. 353."

500   It seems unlikely that Garrioch had any business, or even social, dealings with Kittson while the latter was at Red River, given the failure to mention any such and Garrioch's normal candour about his disdain for the HBC's asserted trade monopoly. Gunn inserted a handwritten note in the text (p. 257): "May have something to do with the American traders....here under April 9," meaning that there was a reference to them – and another handwritten note by Gunn – in the April 9 diary entry.

501   Gunn, p. 258 provides references to this joint free-trader petition against the duty on imports from the U.S. Although the absence of a personal pronoun in Garrioch's diary entry prevents certainty at this point, the May 6 to 9 entries, p. 260, confirm that he authored at least the first draft of that joint petition. Gunn says in his note that he was unable to locate a copy. See Appendix I – Petitions.

Curiosity

May 4, 1845 – Sunday. A delightful day. Went to the Upper Church[502] as usual, and took my seat up in the gallery out of simple curiosity.

The last reference to Garrioch's church attendance was March 23, when he declined to take communion because of his antipathy, or at least disgruntlement, toward Reverend John Macallum over the latter's refusal to countenance the young man's betrothal to Isabella McKenzie. Why had he taken himself up to the gallery (balcony) on this occasion, and what or who was the subject of his "simple curiosity"? Could it be that he chose that relatively sheltered vantage point in order to better observe Isabella and her new suitor?

Heard by Mr. McKay that Mr. [Kenneth] McKenzie, [Isabella's father][503] at Missouri had bought up all the {259} opposition concerns at that river.

---

502 Gunn: "St. John's parish church, in north Winnipeg. [It is] now called St. John's Cathedral, being the ecclesiastical seat of the Archbishop of Rupert's Land. It was called the Upper Church in contradistinction to St. Paul's and St. Andrew's, which, on account of their relative positions, were known respectively as the Middle and Lower Churches. St. John's was founded in 1820 by Reverend John West, the first missionary of the Church of England in [what is now] Western Canada. The first building on the site was erected by him in 1821. Reverend D. T. Jones succeeded Mr. West in 1823, and, under his direction, this original wooden structure gave place to one of stone, which was opened in 1834. The first Bishop to make St. John's his headquarters was the Reverend David Anderson, who came to the country in 1849; and under [whose] incumbency a still larger stone building, opened in 1862, was erected. The present building was completed, under the leadership of Archbishop Samuel Matheson, in 1926."

503 Gunn: "Kenneth McKenzie, the great fur trader of the Missouri, [would become] Garrioch's father-in-law. This notable personage was born in Inverness, Rosshire, Scotland, in 1801. He was, we are informed by Chittenden, of distinguished parentage, and a relative of Sir Alexander McKenzie, the great explorer and proprietor of the North-West Company. Of his early life little is known, except that he came to America as a young man, and was attached to one of the two great British fur trading concerns of the time.

"Just where the field of his early operations lay cannot be stated with certainty; but the probability is that it was south of the international boundary in what is now Minnesota. His career first emerges into the clear light in 1822. Being one of those thrown out of employment by the union of the NWC and the HBC the preceding year, he joined a number of associates of the fur trade similarly affected by that event. Principal among [those] were Joseph Renville and William Laidlaw, both [of whom were,] like himself, experienced traders of British origin. These young adventurers put their savings together and organized the concern known as the Columbia Fur Company, with headquarters at Lake Traverse.

"By far the ablest of these associates was Kenneth McKenzie, who soon rose to the presidency; and, under his energetic and skillful management, the new company grew, in a few years, to such proportions as to force itself upon the notice of the wealthy and powerful American Fur Company, of which John Jacob Aster was the moving spirit. This great concern, seeing their dividends disappearing, made such favourable overtures to McKenzie and his associates as to induce them to

Chapter 7 – Free Trade Struggles & Romantic Entanglements   253

sell out in 1827. The deal practically amounted to an amalgamation, McKenzie and [colleagues] entering the AFC with [almost] the same standing they had in their own concern. While all their posts in what is now Minnesota, Wisconsin, Dakota were merged into the general business of the older company, the business of the Upper Missouri district was given over to [the newcomers'] control entirely, and a [sort of] subsidiary company known as the "Upper Missouri Outfit." Of this [subsidiary] McKenzie was placed in charge; and, for the next twenty years, the fur trade on the Missouri was largely the [monopoly] of him and his associates, although he was not in active control all that time.

"McKenzie's headquarters under the new regime were at Fort Union, built by him and so named, it is said, in commemoration of [the CFC/AFC] amalgamation. Here he reigned as the "King of the Missouri," attired in a splendid military uniform, or in broadcloth and black cravat, as the occasion demanded; entertaining [from time to time], with sumptuous hospitality, travelers of royal rank like Prince Maximilian of Wied, and scientists like the great Audubon. Although maintaining the [style] of a great pasha, however, McKenzie was popular with his men, and had the faculty of attaching them to him, and getting their best work [from] them, while addressing himself to the peculiar task for which he was there, viz., the production of dividends for the fur trade. In less than four years from the time he was placed in charge of the U. M. O. [Upper Missouri Outfit], he had carried the trade into every quarter, and built forts at all the strategic points on the river.

"An interesting glimpse of the attitude of respect and almost awe, in which McKenzie was held by the understrappers [sic] of the fur trade at this time, is given us by Larpenteur, in his Forty Years a Fur Trader (I, p. 65). Referring to his first meeting with McKenzie, he says: 'Imagine my surprise, on entering Mr. Campbell's room, to find myself in the presence of Mr. McKenzie, who was at that time considered the King of the Missouri; and, from the style in which he was dressed, I thought really he was a king.'

"Like most of the men of his time and occupation, of course, McKenzie's morals were hardly of the kind ordinarily set up as Sunday School models. He was possessed, however, of a certain rugged and picturesque genius, and of some equally rugged virtues, that will always make him an outstanding figure on the pages of early Missouri history.

"Upon retirement from the fur trade McKenzie went to live in St. Louis, where he engaged in the wholesale liquor trade, a venture which did not prove a success. There he married a second time, and raised another family. He died there on April 26, 1861. See the works of Chittenden and Larpenteur on the early days on the Missouri." These paragraphs contain only part of Gunn's lengthy note on pp. 258-260.

Just how much of a "King" of the Upper Missouri fur trade McKenzie was is demonstrated by the fact that, by 1823, he was running the Columbia Fur Company which controlled the trade in that area until it was bought out by the American Fur Company in 1829. "In the course of the following six years, as head of the Upper Missouri Outfit of the American Fur Company, McKenzie secured the company's virtual monopoly over the fur trade on the Northern Great Plains. By 1834 almost 2,000 packs of bison robes a year were being collected at Fort Union as well as large quantities of

James Witford's daughter died.

First Sowing

{260} **May 5, 1845 – Monday.** A sweeter, pleasanter day than yesterday. Gavin threw into the ground this morning four bushels of wheat. This is the first this season.

There is no believing half of what people say: some say that a cat has seven lives, and others say that the moon is made of green cheese, but I say I'm a fool for writing such nonsense.

May 6, 1845 – Tuesday. Cold north wind all day. Another bushel wheat thrown into the ground.

Petition Finished

Finished my petition to the Governor and Council,[504] and ploughed a yoke in the afternoon.

May 7, 1845 – Wednesday. Strong south wind all day. Went up and left my petition with James Sinclair, to have it copied and corrected. James Sinclair paid the tax on American goods last Monday.

Gavin sow{261}ed three bushels wheat today. David Harcus[505] died.

May 8, 1845 – Thursday. Messrs James Sinclair and [John] McLaughlin call today for the first copy of my petition.

---

beaver, fox, and muskrat skins:" http://plainshumanities.uni.edu/encyclopedia/ . See Chap. 5, n. 287.

504   See above, May 3 entry and related note, as well as the next three entries, & Appendix I – Petitions, Oliver, *Canadian North-West*, I, pp. 315-27 & II, pp. 1303-5, which deals with a petition expressing their complaints, and their resolution at meetings of the Council of Assiniboia in June & July, 1845. Garrioch's entry for April 21 (Gunn, p. 256) states that he paid his English duties that day, but "as formerly" refused to pay duty on American goods."

505   At the age of 47, "poor" David Arcus had been mostly bed-ridden for the previous two years before his death on May 7, 1845. AM: Rev. William Cockran in Original Papers, Letters and Papers of Individual Missionaries, Catechists and Others 1825-1865, North-West Canada 1821-1880 CC1O16 (148-163) [empire.amdigital.co.uk], & HBCA/AM: Extracts from Registers of Baptisms, Marriages, and Burials in Rupert's Land, E.4/2 folio 138.

Chapter 7 – Free Trade Struggles & Romantic Entanglements

McLaughlin, who with his wife journeyed with Garrioch to Red River in 1844, would have been representing his uncle Andrew McDermot, the Settlement's most prominent and prosperous, free trader. As we have seen on earlier occasions, McDermot and Sinclair often collaborated.

Gavin sowed three and three quarter bushels wheat today.

May 9, 1845 – Friday. I went up to get the petition signed. It was signed by seven of us who had imported goods from St. Peter's, viz.: Peter Hayden, Henry Cook, Alexis Goulet, Dominque Ducharme, Alexander Ducharme, Charles Laurence and myself. The above petition was addressed to the Governor and Council of Red River Settlement. It was handed in [to the Governor] this evening by Peter Hayden.[506]

Note that McDermot and Sinclair, the Settlement's two largest independent importers, chose not to sign it after examining Garrioch's petition.[507]

Life Ends & Goes On

This evening old Magnus Spence and Liddy Cook[508] departed this life.

This day also my house wood came down.

This refers to a raft of logs and/or lumber for Peter Garrioch's new house that must have been assembled somewhere upstream (perhaps at James Sinclair's lot; see entry for May 16) awaiting the departure of ice from the river.

---

506   Peter Hayden, the petitioners' envoy to the Governor, was later involved in a melancholy repercussion of the ongoing tension between the free traders and the HBC. See Gibson, *LLG, I*, pp.89-91, & *LLG, II*, pp. 37-40: *Public Interest v. Peter Hayden* (Case 10, A46, 1846).

507   The refusal was not necessarily due or even partly due to the language of Garrioch's petition. While inclined to support free trading in theory, both Sinclair and McDermot had long since been co-opted, if not (in McDermot's case) actually bribed by Simpson and Christie to remain in the Company's sphere of influence and to resist getting overly enmeshed in the illegal aspects of free-trading, thereby putting their business ventures at great risk: Richardson, "The Quality of Friendship."

508   Gunn: "Magnus Spence, a native of Orkney and retired servant of the Hudson's Bay Company, had come to [the] Settlement from Moose Factory. He lived on west side of the Red River, north of Middlechurch. He was 90 years old when he died. HBAC/AM: Extracts from Registers of Baptisms, Marriages, and Burials in Rupert's, E.4/2 folio 138, or, as Rev. Cockran expressed it, he "had come to his grave in a full age, like as a shock of corn cometh in his season." Cockran, *Original Papers*, pp. 148-163. The lady mentioned was a daughter of Chief Factor W. H. Cook, already noted." For Cook see Chap. 1, *passim*.

The first whip-poor-wills heard this season at this place today.[509]

May 10, 1845 – Saturday. Took some of my wood out of the raft.

May 11, 1845 – Sunday. Attended the funeral of Liddy. A notice was stuck, as usual, on the church door by Governor Christie, requiring all the police to be up at Fort Garry on the 15th instant by 10 o'clock.

Church doors were commonly used as community bulletin boards. The occasion for this announced assemblage of the Settlement's constabulary was a looming sitting of the General Quarterly Court of Assiniboia at the little Upper Fort Garry courthouse.[510] Such general musters were common on court days, but Garrioch's recording of this particular police summons in his journal may indicate he feared that some coercive action might be taken against him and his co-petitioners over their refusal to pay customs duties on imports from the United States.

Collector Bird Tries Again

May 12, 1845 – Monday. Weather wet and stormy. Received the following note from Mr. James Bird:

> Mr. Peter Garrioch,   May 12, '45.
>
> Sir:
>
> I send Philip [his son] once more with a hope that you may {262} by this time have seen the impropriety of opposing yourself to the authorities of the place, and feel disposed to settle the account of duty due on the few goods you brought into this place from the States, more especially as your principal objection to paying – viz.: not to be the first to pay – is quite done away with, Mr. James Sinclair, Rolette and St. Germain having already paid, and there being no doubt of Goulet's following their good example. Let me prevail upon you to save yourself and me further trouble, by coming here to pay me or sending the amount due by Philip, with a statement of the goods you brought and their price in the States.
>
> Yours, James Bird

---

509   Whip-poor-wills are now a threatened species in Manitoba, and in Canada generally.

510   Gibson, *LLG, I*, pp.88-92.

Chapter 7 – Free Trade Struggles & Romantic Entanglements

The following is the answer I returned by the bearer, his gracious son Philip:

> Jas. Bird, Esq.,
>
> Sir:
>
> Perhaps you are not aware that we presented your Honourable Council with a respectful petition, stating our reasons for refusing to comply with the requisition of import duty; and requesting that requisition to be repealed on certain weighty considerations. The petition was forwarded to Governor Christie on Friday last. We have not yet heard what the opinion of the Council is on that petition, and therefore I am under the necessity of informing you that I am not at liberty to comply {263} with your official request.
>
> Your most obedient and humble servant,
>
> Peter Garrioch

A Victory of Sorts

May 13, 1845 – Tuesday. Peter Hayden came down with instructions from Governor Christie, advising us to pay the tax on American goods, and that our petition would be duly attended to. Relying on the promise of the Governor, we yielded, and addressed the following note to his Excellency, signed by our party:

> Alexander Christie Esq., Governor of Assiniboia   May 13, '45.
>
> Sir:
>
> We the undersigned, your late petitioners, take this opportunity of returning you our sincere thanks for the friendly advice you have transmitted to us by Mr. Peter Haydon, and likewise for the impartial and favourable consideration which you assure us shall be bestowed on our said petition by your Honourable Council. And therefore, fully relying on the favourable prospect before us, we do hereby assure your Excellency that it is our intention, forthwith, to settle our accounts on our imported American commodities.

Payment Without a Murmur or a Groan

Two or three hours after we had signed the above note, Mr. Bird popped in, and I settled with him without a murmur or a groan.

May 14, 1845 – Wednesday. Gavin sowed three bushels wheat. Heard this day that John Spence had returned without my barn wood.

May 15, 1845 – Thursday. The Grand or General Court day. Philip Bird {264} received his discharge[511] today. Jack Spence, the Keeper,[512] offered to give up his commission, which, however, was not granted. William McMillan, Antoine Moora,[513] Wese Batoche[514] and another I do not remember, forfeited their constables' pay for having been present at Goulet and Green's affair.[515]

May 16, 1845 – Friday. Went up to Sinclair's and bought 18 pieces of wood, from 25 to 30 feet each, for thirty shillings, to be paid sometime between this and next fall. Three more bushels of wheat sown.

---

511 Gunn: "Probably as constable" (p. 264).

512 Gunn: "Likely as Keeper of the Jail. He was a son of Magnus Spence of note on p. 261 and lived on the east bank of the Red River at the present Parkdale."

513 Probably Morin. See nn. 555 & 599.

514 Gunn: "The Christian name "Wese" was a common nickname among the French Métis, being the recognized contraction of Louison."

515 The "affair" referred to was probably a large gathering of disgruntled Métis and others at the home of free trader Alexis Goulet in late December, 1844. When Sheriff Alexander Ross investigated the assembly he noted the presence of some whose duties seemed incompatible with its tone and apparent protest purpose. These were probably the men dismissed from the police force. See Ross memorandum to Council of Assiniboia: AM: Ross Papers, MG2, C14, letter 1. Ross himself, at least upon later reflection in the mid-1850s, casts a sympathetic eye on the plight of the Métis' when trading with their Aboriginal partners because of the HBC's rules. After describing a number of examples of the invidious positions in which the HBC's rules placed the Métis traders, he wrote: "The half-breed, as already stated, cannot well abandon his own business to attend upon the Indian for nothing; and if he takes any furs; he is prosecuted for an infringement of the Company's regulations! We might multiply instances without number, all tending to establish the fact, that the existing law not only places the half-breeds in an awkward position, but operates strongly against humanity, in so far as the Indian is concerned. Any benefit the Company can derive from this law is purely imaginary, and yet, to support it, we had well nigh completed the circle of folly by upsetting Red River Colony, as shall presently appear...." Ross, *Red River Settlement*, p. 371.

May 17, 1845 – Saturday. Old Sowanas[516] departed this life last evening. "Man that is born of a woman hath but a few days to live."

Gavin sowed three bushels of wheat.

May 18, 1845 – Sunday. Went to the Lower Church with D. Pambrum.[517]

May 19, 1845 – Monday. Gavin sows two bushels more wheat today, and I ploughed two yokes.

May 20, 1845 – Tuesday. Sowed four or five bushels of potatoes and two gallons Indian corn.

HBC Increases the Pressure

Heard today that Mr. Grant with twelve men {265} started early last Sunday morning, to seize Mr. Green's fur, which was conveyed to the Pembina by six or seven men.

The HBC's "Warden of the Plains" Cuthbert Grant,[518] who was both a law enforcement officer and a prominent Métis leader, found himself in a position of uncomfortably divided

---

516   Gunn: "An old Indian, well known in the Settlement." This may have been "Sowanas", recorded in HBC's biographical records as having entered service between 1813 and 1815 at York Fort, working in the capacity of Boatman, with wages of 15£ per annum. HBCA/AM: A.30/12, fol. 25d & A.30/13, fol. 26d.

517   Was his attendance at this church a consequence of the discomfort with his accustomed church he had previously displayed? See entries for March 23 & May 4.

518   Gunn: "Cuthbert Grant, a noted leader among the French Métis of the Red River Settlement. He was of Scotch and French extraction; his father being the famous North-West Company trader of the same name, there being some family relationship between these Scotch Grants – of which Peter Grant was another – and the family of the late Lord Strathcona. Cuthbert Grant, Sr. died in 1799. The son, here mentioned by Garrioch, was born in 1796, and was left an orphan when seven years of age. Taken [under the care of the NWC, and educated] in Montreal; and [possessing those] advantages, as superior natural endowments, he became a recognized leader among his people. He took an active part, on the side of the Nor'westers, in the conflict that raged between the [NWC and the HBC] in the decade prior to 1821, and was captain of the [NWC] party at the Seven Oaks fight in 1816. Later, when peace had been restored, he settled at White Horse Plains on the Assiniboine, where he lived the life of a law-abiding and highly respected citizen, occupying various positions of public trust. At [the time of this entry] he was on the constabulary force of the Hudson's Bay Company, in which connection he is here mentioned. He was also one of the fifteen members of the Council of Assiniboia, representing thereon the French element, and having assigned to him, as his special duty, the enforcement of law and order on the buffalo plains. From this latter appointment he derived the title 'Warden of the Plains.'" Assiniboia's constabulary force had been requested by the Company to enforce the fur trade monopoly granted by its Charter and it was in that capacity

loyalties when ordered to prosecute free traders – many of whom were Métis – for violating the Company's alleged fur trade monopoly.

May 21, 1845 – Wednesday. Mr. Grant was seen at Fort Garry today, but I did not yet learn the issue of his trip.

Sowed one and a quarter bushels barley today.

May 23, 1845 – Friday. Understand that Mr. Grant had met with singular failure in his expedition, and almost got drowned at the Scratching River into the bargain for his trouble.

Sowed two bushels more barley.

May 24, 1845 – Saturday. Heard that Green had not sent off his fur as was supposed, so that Grant's parade was a mere wild goose chase.

Farm Routines

May 25, 1845 – Sunday. A very sultry day. We have put our seed in the ground, but we must now wait patiently for the showers of heaven to give it the increase. Men therefore, as usual, are beginning to be clamorous about the present drought.

May 26, 1845 – Monday. Went up to A. Goulet's with two fishers and four martins. A man arrived from Missouri. {266}

May 27, 1845 – Tuesday. Frederick and Gaddy[519] threshed fifteen bushels of wheat.

May 28, 1845 – Wednesday. Frederick and Gavin threshed ten bushels wheat.

---

that Grant and his men sought to seize free trader James Green's furs on this occasion: MacLeod & Morton, *Cuthbert Grant*, & Gibson, *LLG, I, passim.*

519   Gunn: "William Gaddy, a well-known Scotch Métis of the Settlement, said to have been one of the most daring and successful buffalo hunters and Indian fighters of his time. He was brought up in St. Paul's parish, north of the present Middlechurch, where his father settled at an early date. He married Margaret, eldest daughter of William Garrioch, and sister to the author of this journal. Later, upon the founding by Archdeacon Cockran of Portage la Prairie in 1851, he moved to that place and became one of its earliest residents, Gaddy St., in that city, being commemorative of him. He subsequently moved to Prince Albert, on the Saskatchewan, and settled on a farm at Red Deer Hill, where he died. He had no family."

Chapter 7 – Free Trade Struggles & Romantic Entanglements 261

May 29, 1845 – Thursday. Frederick and I put the frame of a cart box together. Pierre Lavalée brought down a new cart for me, for which I pay him three cwt.[520] flour.

May 30, 1845 – Friday. Washed and winnowed between twenty and thirty bushels of wheat with William. Went down to Bill's to buy a cart box of him. The Company's boats passed yesterday.[521]

May 31, 1845 – Saturday. Worked at my cart box. In the evening it commenced raining and continued till the following morning.

June 2, 1845 – Monday. Yesterday evening Mr. Rhone[522] and his party arrive{267}ed. Today I went up to the White Horse Plains.

June 3, 1845 – Tuesday. Came down and fell in with Reverend La Flesh[523] of the Catholic Church. He speaks broken English but appears to be highly intelligent, and speaks the French with remarkable fluency.

June 4, 1845 – Wednesday. Purchased a horse of Alexis La Boom Barb[524] for eight pounds; that is, £2 in flour and £2 in goods at present, the balance to be paid as I am able to in the same way.

June 5, 1845 – Thursday. Cleaned some wheat and wrote the best part of three letters, viz.: one to brother John, one to Coleburn, and another to Jackson. The two latter are merchants at St. Louis and St. Peter's.

---

520 Three hundred pounds. Cwt. was short for "hundredweight."

521 Gunn: "The spring brigade of Hudson's Bay Company boats, on their way down the Red River from Fort Garry to Norway House and York Factory." With flags flying and pipes playing whenever within sight or sound of settled areas, these brigades were popular spectacles.

522 Gunn's note speculates that Garrioch refers here to J. R. Rowand (a son of the celebrated HBC officer John Rowand), who lived near James McKay's renowned Deer Lodge in St. James Parish.

523 Reverend L-F. R. LaFlèche, who ministered to the Métis of Rupert's Land from 1844 to 1856. Bumsted, *DMB*, p. 135.

524 Gunn: "La Bombard is evidently meant, as there were people of that name among the Red River Métis of those times. The La Bombard of this entry lived probably at Baie St. Paul, or the White Horse Plains, on the Assiniboine River."

Chapter 8

Traveling Again as Unrest Grows at Red River

1845-1846

As Appendix I – Petitions illustrates, Peter's growing involvement in the struggles against the Hudson's Bay Company in favour of free trading led to numerous disappointments, the effect of which he tried to mitigate by resuming his nomadic trading adventures, among which was the following buffalo hunt. Even there, there was meddling by government officials.

Buffalo Hunt

June 10, 1845 – Tuesday. Having made all the necessary preparations, I started this day for the buffalo hunt with six carts, four oxen and three horses. I left here with but one boy to drive all these animals, intending to get the rest of my servants on the way.

June 15, 1845 – Sunday. Hired Bastaney's daughters at the Tobacco Creek. [525] {268}

June 16, 1845 – Monday. Our whole number amounts to about 100 tents this morning, being now at the Pembina.[526]

---

[525] Gunn: "This creek is really a tributary of the Scratching River. Rising by two branches, not far from Altamont and Deerwood on the northeastern slope of the Pembina Mountains, it parallels the upper waters of the above, formerly known as the Rivière aux Islettes de Bois, at a distance of about six miles to the south, losing itself also, like the above, in the marshy country to the southeast of Carman. The two branches join a couple of miles southeast of a place called Lintrathen. Its general course is east and west. The old Fort Garry trail to the buffalo plains, now being followed by Garrioch, crossed it. I have never heard the genesis of the name."

[526] Gunn: "On this trail Garrioch's party would strike the Pembina [River] near a place called McKenzie, about six miles south and a little west of Manitou, where the old crossing was."

Chapter 8 – Traveling Again as Unrest Grows at Red River

June 17, 1845 – Tuesday. Towards the morning, while sleeping on my bed, I dreamed that I saw a man precisely in that situation, between the spokes of a wheel of one of my carts, which happened to be between myself and the man. Another strong proof of the immortality of the soul.[527]

During the trip of this summer to the plains no less than 12 or 13 deaths took place. Two of the number were killed by their own friends, one wilfully and the other accidentally. The rest all died natural deaths. Our hunt almost entirely failed, notwithstanding buffaloes were numerous. It could not therefore be attributed to anything but bad management. This summer we received a visit from some American troops, whose object was to put a stop to the buffalo hunting by the Half Breeds. The Commander of the troops, 132 in number, bore the name of {269} [Captain E. V.] Summer. I brought home in six carts but 2,300 lbs. provisions, four parchments and 150 sinews.

The 2,300 pounds of "provisions" were chiefly goods, probably obtained on credit, that Garrioch had hauled to the plains in the vain expectation of trading them for buffalo meat and products. Although Red River's buffalo hunting expeditions would continue until well into the 1860s, Garrioch's cursory retrospective summary of this summer's largely wasted efforts was a portent of forthcoming changes, one of them being the increasing regulation of the United States Midwest of which the appearance Captain Summer's troops was an early manifestation. Gunn's comment about that encounter was:

> **The military expedition under Captain Summer left Fort Atkinson, Iowa, June 3, 1845, and met the Red River hunters, 180 in number, near Devil's Lake on July 19. Summer, the purpose of whose expedition was to stop the slaughter of buffalo on American soil by British hunters, was most favourably impressed by the Red River party.**

Home Again

August 12, 1845 – Tuesday. I returned from the plains and found Gavin and Ann[528] quite unwell. Nothing is yet done towards getting in the crop, and but half the hay got.

---

527 The meaning of this passage completely escapes the editors' understanding, and Reverend Gunn provided no explanatory note.

528 Gavin, 23 years old at the time of this entry, was a brother of Peter Garrioch. Ann was Peter's youngest sister, afterwards married to Frederick Bird, frequently mentioned in these pages. Ann Garrioch Bird was born at Middlechurch, St. Paul's Parish, Red River Settlement, April 6, 1826.

August 15, 1845 – Friday. A petition was prepared for the Half Breeds in general, to be presented to the American Government.

This petition, prepared by John McLaughlin – Andrew McDermot's nephew, and Peter Garrioch's greenhorn traveling companion of the previous fall and winter – was not, as the context might suggest, a complaint about interference by American troops with the Métis buffalo hunt. It was, rather, a plea for intervention by the United States to prevent the Hudson's Bay Company's allegedly illegal suppression of democracy and free trade in furs. Delivered to Washington by McLaughlin in October 1845, it was handed off by one government department to another until it eventually disappeared from sight altogether, and never received an official response.[529]

A Peace Delegation

August 20, 1845 – Wednesday. The Burnt Ground (a Sioux chief of Lac Traverse) with ...men paid us a visit. He came down to the Fort. {270} His object in coming, it appears, is to renew a peace with the Half Breeds and Saulteaux.

A considerable proportion of the local Aboriginal population were Saulteaux people, who were traditional foes of the Sioux and allies of the "half-breeds." Hostile confrontations between Sioux and "half-breed"/Saulteaux buffalo hunting parties were common, and military success was divided over time. Peace treaties of varying durations were not uncommon. The most recent such warfare had resulted in a major victory for the "half-breeds"/Saulteaux, followed by a peace overture from the Sioux. The "half-breeds", under the leadership of Cuthbert Grant, who was wearing his law-enforcement hat as the HBC's "Warden of the Plains," entered into a treaty with the Sioux – apparently without consulting

---

529 Gibson, *LLG*, I, p. 91. The petition is described also by Gluek, *Minnesota and the Manifest Destiny*, pp. 55-59, who states: "Garrioch and Sinclair were both educated men, able to articulate the sentiments of the other smugglers, and, in concert, they composed a petition to the Governor and Council of Assiniboia praying for relief from all impositions on American imports…..The free traders were not yet bent upon a lawless course. They still preferred to fight with their pens...." In Gunn's correspondence files at the Archives of Manitoba ("Correspondence, 1891-1942, MG9 A78-1, A78-3), there is a letter dated December 28, 1929, to Grace Lee Nute of the Minnesota Historical Society, copied to Gunn, from Newton D. Mereness, which contains more details of the petition's likely fate: "The petition of 'the half-breeds of the Red River settlement" which John McLaughlin sent to the Secretary of State in October, 1845, was transmitted according to the records, to the Commissioner of Indian Affairs, who, on November 4, 1845, sent it to the Secretary of War, and in the register of letters received by the Secretary of War is a note stating that it was returned to the Indian Office. A search for it in the files of the State Department, War Department and Indian Office has been unsuccessful." Mereness (1868-1961) wrote articles for the 1911 *Encyclopedia Britannica* on territorial, homestead, and states' rights. See Appendix I – Petitions, nn. 777, 796, 802, 819.

Chapter 8 – Traveling Again as Unrest Grows at Red River 265

their Saulteaux allies.[530] **Sioux Chief Burnt Ground, who had considerable experience in such negotiations,[531] now arrived at Red River in company with several followers hoping to further cement friendly relations.**

Assassination

September 1, 1845 – Monday. This morning's report says that one of the Burnt Ground's principal men was killed in the Fort by a Saulteau of the Upper Catholic Mission.[532] A Chippewa, it is said, was killed with the same ball and same charge that annihilated the poor Sioux. The murderer, it is said further, was immediately seized and cast into prison.

The assassination was committed by one Capenessesweet, a Saulteau whose people were unhappy that the peace treaty Grant had negotiated with Burnt Ground's band did not include the Saulteaux. The crime was committed in broad daylight in front of many witnesses just outside the walls of Upper Fort Garry.

September 2, 1845 – Tuesday. The Burnt Ground and his men returned to their home and country.

September 3, 1845 – Wednesday. Built the fourth stack of wheat and hauled in as much as would build another. This latter is a product of a piece of land that was neither ploughed nor sown last spring.

---

530 A remarkable correspondence between the Sioux and Métis documenting the negotiations is quoted in Ross, *Red River Settlement*, pp. 324-330. The felicitous phrases used in the quoted documents indicate good intentions on the part of the Indigenous negotiators, but Ross cynically noted that he "had never yet known an instance in which a treaty between savages held good a day, or an hour, after an advantage was to be gained by breaking it" (pp. 324-325). Ross's cynical viewpoint was and is at least as applicable to the colonial authorities in that period of whom Ross was a representative.

531 Gunn: "Other names by which we find this famous Sioux chief referred to are Wa-nen-de-ne-ko-ton-mony, Terre qui Brûle, Burnt Earth, etc. He belonged to the Sisseton branch of the Dakotan nation, in the Lake Traverse and Minnesota River regions. He made several friendly visits, accompanied by [band members], to the Red River Settlement. The first of these of which we have a record [was] in 1834. Thomas Simpson, in his work, describes [that] visit. He was accompanied on [that] occasion by 36 of his people, and narrowly escaped a serious clash with the Saulteaux of Red River, his hereditary enemies, which might have resulted seriously for the whites." See n. 561 and text associated with it, below.

532 Gunn: "On the Assiniboine River 30 miles above Fort Garry, afterwards known as Baie St. Paul. An Indian mission under the Roman Catholic church was established here by Reverend Georges Antoine Belcourt, in 1832. Belcourt called his chapel St. Paul's, which gave the locality the name it subsequently bore. It was also frequently referred to as the Upper Catholic Mission."

Trial

September 4, 1845 – Thursday. A special court was convened today to determine the case of the young man that murdered the Sioux. The jury tell us that he is to be hung on Saturday next. The public are called upon to attend on that day at Fort Garry, and are requested to take with them their firearms.

Capenessesweet was tried, found guilty, and sentenced to death by a special session of the General Quarterly Court of Assiniboia, assisted by a jury of 12, on September 4, 1845.[533]

September 4, 1845 – Friday. Spent the day in horse hunting. I could {271} not find my Dick.

Hanging

September 5, 1845 – Saturday. Went up to Fort Garry and saw the poor murderer launched into awful Eternity with a rope about his neck. He had struggled about five minutes when the vital spark ceased to give any symptoms of survival, and the spirit took its eternal flight.[534]

This was the first, and only, infliction of capital punishment at Red River, and HBC / Assiniboia authorities have often been criticized for causing it to occur. Gunn commented: "The proceeding was, probably, wholly *ultra vires*; but it had a salutary and deterrent effect, at a time when something of the kind was much needed."[535] **He was not the only commentator to suggest that the hanging was unlawful.**

One of the present editors has taken issue in print with the view that the hanging was unauthorized, pointing out that the Hudson's Bay Company's 1670 Charter, under the authority of which the General Quarterly Court functioned, sanctioned its application of both the full civil and criminal law of England in Rupert's Land in the same circumstances that would justify its application in England, and that no applicable legislation had ever countermanded that authority.[536] **Whether technically authorized under the 1670 Charter or not, the hanging impacted relationships between the Rupert's Land authorities and the**

---

533 The Court record of The Public Interest vs. Capenesseweet (erroneously dated August 4) is preserved in the Archives of Manitoba and is reproduced, with commentary, in Gibson, *LLG, II*, pp. 17-27 (Case 6, A23).

534 Alexander Ross also left a description of the event: one that stressed its solemnity and discipline: *Red River Settlement*, pp. 332-333. Gunn stated in a note to the May 6, 1846 diary entry that the executioner was reputed to be a settler called Ada Klyne.

535 Gunn, p. 271.

536 Gibson, *LLG, I*, p. 360, Gibson, *LLG, II*, pp. 17-27 at p. 26 (Case 6, A23), & Dale Gibson, "The First Hanged Was Indian: Capital Punishment in the Quarterly Court of Assiniboia," in *Papers of the Rupert's Land Colloquium*, (University of Winnipeg, Centre for Rupert's Land Studies, 2008). CD.

inhabitants of the Settlement and may have overstepped boundaries set in Indigenous law and practice.

Although Capenessesweet was not the only person to be condemned to death by an Assiniboia Court, he was the only person actually to be executed as a result of such a sentence. While Assiniboia authorities might well be criticized for not granting him the same executive clemency that had saved the lives of others sentenced to death, there was a compelling reason for not doing so: a very real threat that Red River would otherwise be subjected by a large-scale attack by Sioux warriors.[537]

Free Trade Questions for the Company

I should have stated above that, on Monday last, a document was presented to the Governor [Christie] containing a number of questions from a number of the Half Breeds. The questions had particular reference to fur trading and the peculiar rights and privileges of the Hudson's Bay Company, and of the Half Breeds[538]. The answer to the above document, of which I have preserved a true copy, was returned in a few days.[539] {272}

Sinclair, the author of the questions, had been sought out by mixed ancestry members of the settlement for advice as to their rights, if any, as descendants of those who had originally owned the land. In order to obtain the answers accurately, Sinclair decided to frame the questions in the form of a signed inquiry which could be presented to Governor Alexander Christie for response. After consulting with leading Red River persons of mixed ancestry, Sinclair presented the document to the Governor on August 29, 1845. It shows how focused he and the others were on free trade in furs as central to their rights (Appendix I – Petitions).

---

537   See Gibson, *LLG, I*, p. 360 & Gibson, *LLG, II*, pp. 17-27 at p. 26 (Case 6, A23); & Gibson, "The First Hanged."

538   This echoes the debates between the HBC and the Northwest Company around and especially after the events of Seven Oaks. The HBC took the position that, since the people of mixed ancestry were the illegitimate offspring of non-Indigenous fathers, they had no claim to Aboriginal title. The Northwest Company and Métis themselves argued that they were "sons of the soil," able to claim Aboriginal rights, including Aboriginal title to the unceded land, and that the HBC were interlopers.

539   A copy of the document Garrioch was discussing at this point appears as Appendix D towards the end of the Gunn typescript, pp. 381-385, and is reproduced, along with Christie's reply, there, as well as here in Appendix I – Petitions, and in Lent, *West of the Mountains*, pp. 176-179. The document contains a series of questions about the petitioners' trading rights and privileges believed held by the "half-breeds," including Peter Garrioch (although he was not a signatory). The questions were dismissed out of hand by Governor Alexander Christie as being based on the false "supposition that the half-breeds possess certain privileges over their fellow citizens, who have not been born in the country." The exchange bears an eerie resemblance to the divergent views held even today by Indigenous peoples and majoritarian settler/immigrants in Canada.

There were eighteen signatories, including Sinclair and Garrioch. Christie's answer was dated September 5, 1845, and showed little empathy for the plight of the petitioners, instead turning their position on its head by saying, with not unexpected sophistry:

> Your first nine queries, as well as the body of your letter, are grounded on the supposition that the half breeds possess certain privileges over their fellow citizens who have not been born in this country. Now, as British subjects, the half breeds have clearly the same rights in Scotland or in England as any person born in Great Britain, and your own sense of justice will at once see how unreasonable it would be to place Englishmen and Scotsmen on a less favourable footing in Rupert's Land than yourself......

Needless to say, the hauteur which undergirds the tone and content of Christie's reply resulted in further tensions in the Settlement and a deterioration in the relations between Governor Simpson and those with whom he could formerly get along with, such as McDermot and Sinclair.[540] Peter dealt with the situation by absenting himself from the Settlement on a lengthy trading mission.

September 7, 1845 – Sunday. Mr. Mason[541] preached among the Scotch people, and Mr. Jacobs[542] to all who would [be] at Vincent's.[543]

Having no permanent church buildings at Red River at that time, Methodists gathered for worship at private homes. The implication of this entry seems to be that the Métis and English-speaking, mixed descent, Methodist congregations met separately – chiefly,

---

540 See Lent, *West of the Mountains*, pp. 179-187, & Richardson, "The Quality of Friendship."

541 Gunn: "Reverend William Mason, a Wesleyan Methodist Missionary, who came to Rupert's Land about 1840. He engaged in mission work among the Indians, part of the time on the Winnipeg and Rainy Rivers; afterwards at Rossville, an Indian village at the southeastern extremity of Playgreen Lake, about two miles east of Norway House, north of Lake Winnipeg, [where he assisted Reverend James Evans, famous for having developed a system of written Cree syllabics and put it to effective use among the native population]. By "the Scotch people" to whom Mason [preached] is meant Lord Selkirk's Scottish colonists, who resided in Kildonan, just north of Winnipeg."

542 Gunn: "Reverend Peter Jacobs was another missionary of the Wesleyan Methodist church. He was [an] Ojibwa Indian from near Lake Simcoe where, as a boy, he was converted to Christianity. He first came to [Rupert's Land] about 1840, and was associated with the Reverends Evans and Mason of the above note. In 1842, he went to England, where he was ordained. On his return the following year he went first as missionary to Rossville, and then to the Winnipeg River. In 1847 he conducted a canoe brigade from Upper Canada to Red River, with a consignment of flour for the soldiers stationed at Fort Garry. In the summer of 1852 he made a voyage from Rice Lake to Hudson Bay and back, by way of Fort William, the Winnipeg River and Red River. He left a journal of that journey, which was published in New York in 1857. His Indian name was Pah-tah-se-ga."

543 Gunn: "John Vincent, an English mixed ancestry person; was born at Moose Factory, and lived on the west side of the Red River, in St. Paul's parish south of the present Middlechurch, where he engaged in farming."

Chapter 8 – Traveling Again as Unrest Grows at Red River

perhaps, because both geographic distance and linguistic differences dictated the development of the two groups.

September 8, 1845 – Monday. Spent another day in vain looking for my horse.

Fall Trip to the Plains

Jack Spence and his party start today for the plains and, Lord willing, I follow his example tomorrow. May the Lord direct, protect and bless me throughout my journey, as He has ever graciously done. {273}

September 9, 1845 – Tuesday. Having arranged everything at home as well as I could, I started for the buffalo hunt. I provided myself with five carts, three oxen and three horses. I left home with but a single servant, whom I allowed £1 s15 for the trip.

Less than a month had elapsed since Garrioch's return from the unsuccessful summer hunt on August 10; and although his equipage was slightly smaller than on the prior trip it was still optimistically substantial.

Encamped at the Stinking River.

Mac Gets Lost Again

September 10, 1845 – Wednesday. Encamped at the Grand Point.

Mr. McLoughlin, who is on his way to Europe [via the United States] on special business, as is his usual custom when traveling, lost himself last evening. I dined with him today. He has improved considerably in the method of traveling in this country. He begins to see the necessity of taking everything as it comes, rough or smooth, particularly with regard to diet.

John McLoughlin's many misadventures on his arduous maiden expedition with Garrioch the previous year will be recalled. On this trip he was carrying the petition from the Settlement's mixed descent population that he had prepared and would take steps to deliver[544] without discernible result to United States authorities in Washington (see August 15 entry) before proceeding to London and becoming embroiled in a bitter personal legal dispute with the Hudson's Bay Company.

---

544   See Appendix I – Petitions, pp. 5-6, & Bumsted, *Trials & Tribulations*, pp. 99-100.

Plums, Red Deer & Cannons

September 11, 1845 – Thursday. Encamped at the little lake beyond the Pembina.⁵⁴⁵ Some of us collected large quantities of prunes [wild plums].

September 12, 1845 – Friday. Several red deer were {274} brought to our camp to-day.

September 13, 1845 – Saturday. Encamped at the Cart River.⁵⁴⁶ It is said that sounds resembling the reports of cannon have at different times been heard about this river by various persons.

Good Hunt

September 16, 1845 – Tuesday. Encamped within three miles of the Lake De Checoo.⁵⁴⁷ The hunters had a run today. This day is generally the starting day from the Settlement for the fall trip. {275}

September 17, 1845 – Wednesday. Remained at the same place and had another run.

---

545 Gunn: "Garrioch's party have followed the west bank of the Red River from Fort Garry to Pembina, and are now proceeding along the trail to the south of the Tongue River, as part of the most westerly St. Paul route, as well as of the regular Devil's Lake trail. The 'little lake beyond the Pembina' here referred to is undoubtedly the slough known today as Iceland Coulee. This is a long narrow slough, to the south of the Tongue River, about four miles southwest of Pembina."

546 Gunn: "If the stream now known as Cart River – that is, the north branch of the north fork of the Park River – is here meant, Garrioch's camp would be in the vicinity of the present village of Mountain. If, however this name was applied at that time to one of the more southerly branches of the Park, …their location would be correspondingly farther south."

547 Gunn: "Chicot Lake, or Lac des Chicots is no doubt meant; this being the French name for the body of water now known as Stump Lake. The English name [is] almost a literal translation of the former. The French chicot, however, has reference more to an old decayed stub than to what in English we call a stump, and in this sense it more exactly fits the peculiar circumstance that caused it to be applied to this lake, which is the presence on its southern shore of innumerable old withered stubs, the remnants of a forest that flourished here probably several centuries ago. The land on which these trees were growing appears to have sunk, at some distant date, thus becoming submerged by the water of the lake, which not only killed the timber thus effected, but, by impregnating with the lime solution contained in it such portions of the trees as were beneath the water, has preserved to the present day the old gnarled stubs in an almost petrified state. On a visit made to this lake a few years ago, hundreds of these old whitened stubs were still in evidence along the beaches, and even below the surface of the water. This lake, called also Wandushka Lake by the Indians, is a body of very irregular shape lying to the east and somewhat south of Devil's Lake, North Dakota. It is about 10 miles in length, measured along its main axis, but is in no part much over a couple of miles, and in a large portion of its length less than a quarter of that wide. It is separated from the east end of Devil's Lake by about seven miles."

Chapter 8 – Traveling Again as Unrest Grows at Red River

September 18, 1845 – Thursday. Ditto, ditto, ditto....

September 19, 1845 – Friday. The same as yesterday, and I put 160 tongues and 50 little bosses[548] in pickle.

The "Process of Cutting Up or 'Turning Out' of the Buffalo in Use among the Hunters on the Buffalo Plains," a 1½ page description Gunn appended to his transcript of Peter's diaries, brings to vivid life the enormity of the on-the-spot effort required to process the animals killed on a buffalo hunt:

> **The hunt ended, the hunter places the animal on its knees; then he stretches out his hind legs; this position rests it on the belly. They begin by cutting off the little hump [the petite bosse], which is a mass of flesh, in weight about three pounds, on the top of the neck and attached is the large hump. Next they open the skin on the back and loosen it up, after which the animal is 'turned out'. Here are the details and the various parts of the operation.**
>
> **The two parts of the hide are raised on the sides from the shoulders back to the haunches; they are separated from the flesh below by a cartilaginous casein, or rather a thin skin;**
>
> **The fillets, sinews enveloped by flash which bind the chuck-ribs to the haunches;**
>
> **The breastcellars, two bands of fat which descend from below the shoulders to underneath the neck;**
>
> **The small fillets of the neck, little sinews enveloped by meat, which start opposite the extremities of the large fillets;**
>
> **The round, which is taken from the top of the flanks;**
>
> **The shoulder pieces;**
>
> **The undershoulders, masses of meat between the brisket and the shoulder;**
>
> **The udder, a fat portion which contains the udder; it extends under the belly and into the flanks;**
>
> **The belly, a fleshy portion which joins the sides and sustains the intestines; The first stomach, which the halfbreed regard as a titbit;**

---

548   Gunn: "In cutting up, or 'turning out' the buffalo, as the process was called, every part had its name and its proper classification as to food value, etc. The "large hump," or "boss," was the great mass of flesh and bone on the back just above the shoulder blades, corresponding to the withers of a horse. The "little boss," or "small hump," was a smaller mass of flesh of from three or four pounds weight on the back and base of the neck, immediately in front of the big boss. Both of these were considered great delicacies by the hunters, and were accordingly preserved along with the other choice parts of the animal. Reverend G. A. Belcourt, a Roman Catholic priest well known during his time in the Red River Settlement as well as in Dakota, who accompanied his parishioners to the fall hunt of 1844, has left a detailed inventory of this." See also: J. M. Bumstead, "Another Look at the Buffalo Hunt" pp.115-126 in Thomas Scott's Body and Other Essays on Early Manitoba History, Winnipeg, Manitoba, Press, 2000.

The large hump, which is highest opposite the shoulder blades; it is formed by thin large points, inclines backwards, bring in the skeleton what the row of fins is on the back of fishes. This part has a delicious taste.

The fat or suet from within the body;

The flatsides or cutlets;

The rump;

The brisket, or meat which covers the stomach;

The tongue.

The rest remains on the field; it is the heritage of the wolves.[549]

September 21, 1845 – Sunday. Still at the same place.

September 22, 1845 – Monday. Encamped within a few miles of the Devil's Lake.

---

[549] Gunn reproduces this as Appendix E on pp. 386-387 of his typescript of Peter's diaries, citing it as: "From letter of Rev. G. A. Belcourt, dated November 25, 1845, in Executive Docs., United States, 31st Cong., 1st Sess., 1849-50, VIII, Nr. 51, p. 44." A vivid description of the fall hunt in the Turtle Mountain and Souris River country after Father Belcourt arrived in September, 1845, is provided in Russenholt, *Heart of the Continent,* pp. 88-90: "Under rigid discipline, the 75 hunters approach quietly within two gunshots.... Buffalo mass together, when attacked. To overtake the cows, hunters thrust through a solid phalange of bulls. This is dangerous. 'Last year, an Indian, after his horse was knocked over, was tossed and re-tossed by an infuriated bull 20 feet into the air – caught each time on its horns.' Dangerous, too, are stray bullets flying in every direction, through the clouds of dust. The hunters fire with astonishing rapidity. Often, 3 buffalo are knocked over by a hunter within 100 yards. Some fire 5 times during a single chase. The hunter carries 3 or 4 bullets in his mouth. At full gallop, he pours powder into the muzzle of his gun; spits a bullet on top, strikes his gun-butt on the saddle, to force the round to the breech; primes his piece; and fires, point-blank, at the animal which his trained steed follows, by pressure of the rider's knees. In the first chase, 160 cows are killed. The women and boys pitch camp close by. Next day, 177 are killed. On the third day, some riders rest. Those who go out, shoot 114 cows. Next day, the harvest is 168 cows – a total of 628 cows killed in 4 days!" Then follows a description of dressing the carcass, almost identical to the one Gunn derived from Father Belcourt. Next, the processing of the meat: "The meat is cut up by the women, into long strips, hung on pole frames to dry. The choice strips are rolled into bundles. The rest in pounded into powder on a hide, shovelled together with melted fat; packed into sacks made of the raw hides. This is the pemmican that feeds Settlers and fur-men; and is traded to both 'Company' and free-traders. A cow makes about 90 pounds of pemmican and jerked meat. Ten cows are killed to make up a cart-load. Hides are stretched, scraped, and dried by the women, to make parchment and teepees. Men crack and boil bones, to get the marrow for frying. The marrow from 2 cows, stored in a bladder, weighs about 12 pounds." Another detailed description of the buffalo hunt appeared in the *Nor'-Wester* (August 28, 1900). In Appendix I – Petitions, there are more details of Father Belcourt's other activities.

Chapter 8 – Traveling Again as Unrest Grows at Red River

September 23, 1845 – Tuesday. Pitched to the east end of the above lake and had another run.

We remained here till the 3rd of October, preparing our provisions, according to the common method, for a more compact and portable condition.[550]

September 24, 1845 – Wednesday. I have this day ten cows cut up, two hundred and forty tongue in pickle, and another hundred not yet in salt. I have also about fifty small bosses.

September 25, 1845 – Thursday. Some French Half Breeds fled today from old Jack Ward[551] and his son, supposing them to be Sioux.

A Great Row, Bringing Down a Sioux, &c.

September 27, 1845 – Saturday. A great row took place this evening a{276}mong the Perrizas,[552] brought on by beer which James Johnston had brewed and sold them.

September 28, 1845 – Sunday. My poor friend Jack Spence chose this day to make a feast for his grandchild.[553]

---

550 This future date is clear evidence that Garrioch's diary entries were sometimes retroactive. The editors' unbroken need at this point in the transcription process to correct entry dates by one day also suggests that his calendar was for some other year than 1845.

551 Gunn: "An English-speaking Métis. He lived, during the latter portion of his life, with his son-in-law, Archibald Flett, on the east side of the Red River, in St. Andrews parish, just south of the Gonor road. He dropped dead, while hunting with a number of others, at the big St. Andrews marsh, known locally as 'The Bog.'" The Bog was probably the wetland area later known as the Oak Hammock Marsh.

552 Gunn: "Properly, Parisien. The Parisiens were a French Métis family, a numerous clan, of whose general disposition the above reference furnishes a sample. The family lived up the main river in the neighbourhood of St. Norbert. It was by one of this [clan] that J. H. Sutherland, son of the late Senator Sutherland of Kildonan, was shot and killed, during the first Riel rebellion. Another of the family, Narcisse Parisien lived on the west bank of the Red River in St. Andrews Parish, about ½ mile above what is now Lockport. Representatives of the family are to be found scattered throughout the Northwest, on both sides of the international boundary."

553 Spence was, or had been, the jailor at Fort Garry. See Gunn, p. 264. The nature of the "feast" is unclear – perhaps a memorial or prayer ceremony.

October 2, 1845 – Thursday. Francis Lauze [Lauzon?] saw twelve or fifteen of the Sioux. Some of them belonged to Lac Traverse and the rest to the Missouri Indians. He brought one of them to the ground, he says, with the butt of his gun.[554]

October 3, 1845 – Friday. Wese Moorah's[555] child died. The weather has been quite wet and stormy for the last four days.

Peter Garrioch's Hill

October 6, 1845 – Monday. Still at the Cheyenne River. Several of us rode out today in quest of buffalo. During this excursion, a pillar of nearly six feet high, all of stone, was erected on the peak of a prominent and beautiful hill on the north side of the River Cheyenne. I paid one gallon of good beer for the pillar, and the hill bore the ti{277}tle of "Peter Garrioch's Hill." This hill is about twenty-five miles southwest from the Devil's Lake.

Gunn tried to find Peter's hill, and reported that:

> **It is difficult to locate with certainty any of the topographical features mentioned here on account of the party's wandering around after the buffalo herds, without confining themselves to any definite trail. There are several very prominent hills, or buttes, south of Devil's Lake, such as Garrioch describes. There is the Devil's Heart and Sully's Hill, both south of the lake and north of the Cheyenne River; but neither of these could be described as southwest of the lake, to say nothing about the 25 mile distance required. There *is* such a prominent butte, however, southwest of the lake, and north of the Cheyenne, distant about 35 miles, and marked on maps of the sixties and seventies as Butte Moral. [It] is in the vicinity of Wellsburg, [and] is probably that christened by this party as 'Peter Garrioch's Hill.'**[556]

---

554 Emphasis in Gunn's typescript, p. 276.

555 Gunn: "Another of Garrioch's phonetic misspellings of [a] familiar French name. The form here given might stand for Moret, Moran, or Morin. I am inclined to think the latter is intended. The name Morin was not an uncommon one among the French Métis of the Red River, at this time, nor is it to-day. The "Antoine Moora" of p. 264 was no doubt one of the same family, possibly a brother. "Wese," as already noted, is a contraction of Louison."

556 Gunn, p. 277.

Chapter 8 – Traveling Again as Unrest Grows at Red River

Hunting Season Winds Down

October 9, 1845 – Thursday. We are now beyond the range of hills[557] running parallel with the Cheyenne River. Several bands of buffalo are seen from the camp, but the weather is such that hunters cannot run, I am sorry to say.

October 13, 1845 – Monday. Snowed all day and drifted some. The follow{278}ing day the same.

October 15, 1845 – Wednesday. Encamped at the "Lakes with Timber on One Side."[558] Such is the name given to these lakes by the French. Here I made a buseayu and got the meat of three cows dried.

Gunn tells us that what Garrioch called a "buseayu," and others called a "boskoya," was a bag made of rawhide and filled with [buffalo] fat ... weighing 200 lbs.[559]

October 16, 1845 – Thursday. Encamped at the Horse Hill.[560] This hill is on the River Cheyenne. The circumstances under which the above hill received its present name are as the following tradition among the Sioux Indians indicates: Many years

---

557 Gunn: "My conclusion with regard to the party's itinerary here is that after leaving Devil's Lake, they proceeded on the north side of the Cheyenne River to Butte Moral, this forming the westward limit of their excursion. Here they struck the old trail leading from St. Cloud on the Mississippi, by way of Breckenridge and the big bend of the Souris River, to the Upper Missouri country. This old trail, marked on U.S. Government maps of the sixties and seventies as that followed by Governor Stevens in 1853, crossed the Cheyenne in the vicinity of Butte Moral, which we have identified above as Peter Garrioch's Hill, substantially where that stream is now crossed by the Great Northern Railway Surry to Fargo cut-off. Here they crossed to the south of the Cheyenne, making their way back eastward along the general line of this old trail. They are now probably somewhere in the northeast corner of Foster County or the southeast corner of Eddy County, a few miles to the west of McHenry station on the Northern Pacific Railway; 'the range of hills running parallel with the Cheyenne River' [would be] the elevated country forming the divide between the James and Cheyenne Rivers, which parallels both streams in a north/south direction for many miles along here."

558 Gunn: "I have been unable positively to identify these lakes. There are many small bodies of water on the route we suppose Garrioch's party to be following. The reference is probably to the group which includes Lakes Jessie, Addie and Sibley, about 10 miles to the northwest of Cooperstown. Most of these are timbered only on their south or west sides, and would thus answer to the French designation above."

559 Gunn, p. 278, also refers again to Appendix E, quoted in the text associated with nn. 548-549 of this chapter, in describing this topic.

560 Gunn: "Marked on maps of the sixties and seventies as Horse Butte. This is a conspicuous hill on the west side of the Cheyenne River towards the eastern edge of Griggs County. Its exact location is on the contiguous corners of Sections. 23, 24, 25, & 26, Township 147, Range 58, about six miles

ago, while a war party of that tribe were scouting about this part of the country, they saw at a distance a horse of uncommon size grazing about the foot of the above hill. They advanced as quickly as they could and made several efforts to catch the animal, but failed in every attempt. The horse, being uncommonly fleet, darted from them suddenly, and, the direction of his home being unoccupied by his oppressors, he disappeared the moment he gained the opposite side of the hill, and could not be traced nor seen by the war party any more.

Some years after, another party passing by that way came to the [same] hill. {279} On approaching it, they saw the horse, and some who had been of the former party recognized him as the same animal. They repeated their attempts to get possession of him, but when they could not succeed by reason of the fleetness and increasing ferocity of the creature, they showered their deadly arrows upon him, and brought him dead to the ground. He killed some and wounded several of the party that waged war against him, [but they] at last brought his existence to an end. His mane, they say, reached to his knees, and his tail streamed along the ground. On examining his tail, they discovered the nest of some little bird in it, and the nest was full of fine fresh eggs. The hill is at present thickly surrounded with little hillocks and mole hills. These, they say, were originally the dung of the horse, which has since turned into earth. The internal abode of this strange animal within the bowels of the hill they never could find. From that day this beautiful hill has borne the title Horse Hill.

October 16, 1845 – Thursday. After leaving the above hill, we traveled about six miles and encamped. Most of the riders had to ride back and put out a large fire that was occasioned by some of the fires of our last encampment not being well secured.

The Burnt Ground with two others paid us a visit. He spent the night with us and then returned to his home.[561]

---

    northeast of Cooperstown. The old trail, now being followed by Garrioch and his party, crossed the Cheyenne somewhere near this point."

561 The memorable visit of Sioux Chief Burnt Earth and some of his men to Red River in August is recorded earlier (above, text associated with n. 531). Such visits between, say, Dakotas and "half-breed" traders represented more than a friendly interaction; they were "checking each other out," against a background of occasional violent disputes or informal agreements and more formal peace treaties negotiated between them to help in averting or minimizing conflict. For example, in July, 1840, Sisseton Dakota warriors surprised a sizable "half-breed" hunting party and killed one of its members as he was butchering his kill. The latter gave chase and killed eight of the Sissetons, whereupon their chief Burnt Earth – here visiting Garrioch's party five years later – came to the "half-breed" camp to protest the excessively harsh retribution of eight of his warriors for only one

Chapter 8 – Traveling Again as Unrest Grows at Red River

Hunters Disperse

October 17, 1845 to November 2, 1845. From this place the hunters separated and scattered in every direction in consequence of there being no buffalo. Subsequent report tells me that not a cow was seen by any party, and therefore everyone was thankful to take all the bulls' meat he could get. {280}

I left my carts near La Côte à Pic [Steep Hill]. After remaining a day at home, I started back with two horses and a cart, and met my other carts at the Grand Point. I brought all home on the 1st and 2nd of November.

The Proceeds

The proceeds of this trip was as follows, viz.: 500 tongues, cured; 130 small bosses, cured; 2 bulls of green meat;[562] 5 bags of pemmican; 2 bags of back fat; 9 bladders of marrow fat; 100 sinews; 5 ridge bones; 17 skins and 15 bundles of dried meat.

Winter Descends

November 17, 1845 – Monday. This day our winter commences this year (1845).

November 18, 1845 – Tuesday. Nearly all the snow that fell yesterday went off today before a strong south wind.

November 19, 1845 – Wednesday. Strong north wind and very cold.

November 20, 1845 – Thursday. All the swamps and little lakes are frozen over.

Another Murder Trial

The Grand Jury convened at Fort Garry today, summoned by the Council for the purpose of considering the case of a prisoner who, some weeks ago, occasioned the death of one his own brothers by thrusting a knife into his side. The Grand Jury

---

"half-breed". Burnt Earth was not assuaged until he was given a collection of articles suitable to "even" the score. There was also in the 1840s and 1850s a custom, as seems to be happening here between Garrioch's party and Chief Burnt Earth, of meetings between Dakota chiefs and leaders of mixed descent people prior to the beginning of the summer hunts in order to exchange gifts and to affirm truces. Michel Hogue, *Métis and the Medicine Line: Creating a Border and Dividing a People* (Chapel Hill: University of North Carolina Press, 2015), pp. 35-39.

562   Green meat was fresh meat. The weather must have been cold enough since the time the two bulls were killed to prevent spoilage on the way home.

passed a verdict of manslaughter upon the prisoner, and the judge condemned him to a year's confinement. {281}

Garrioch's description of this trial before a regular session of the General Quarterly Court of Assiniboia attributed rather more responsibility to the Grand Jury than it bore, and he over-simplified the trial process. Under English law, which the Hudson's Bay Company's Charter made applicable in Rupert's Land, serious crimes were usually brought before two quite different types of jury: Grand and Petit. The task of the Grand Jury, which was consulted first, was to determine whether the Crown's evidence was sufficient, without regard to any possible defence evidence, to justify holding a full-fledged trial. If the Grand Jury decided in the affirmative, an entirely different group of men, 12 in number, were assembled as a Petit Jury to hear all the relevant and admissible evidence on *both sides* and decide whether it established guilt beyond a reasonable doubt. In this case, *The Public Interest vs. Newkesequeskik*[563] the Grand Jury found that a full trial for murder – a capital offence – was called for. Such a trial was then held – the same day – before a Petit Jury composed of 12 different men, who found the accused man guilty of the lesser (non-capital) offence of manslaughter.

November 21, 1845 – Friday. Went out to hunt [musk]rats but found none.

November 22, 1845 – Saturday. This evening the river at this place became a sheet of transparent ice.

November 24, 1845 – Monday. A great fall of snow, which commenced at about 10 o'clock in the morning and continued till...[blank space]

Snowed in at Lake Manitoba

November 25, 1845 – Tuesday. I started in company with Gavin and Frederick to the Manitoba Lake with the view of proceeding thence to the Partridge Crop. From the difficulty of getting on, however, we were detained a week at James Monkman's [on or near the southeast shore of the lake] till such time as we could either put snow on the lakes or shoes on our horses, to make our traveling over the frozen but slippery surface practicable. During our stay here we had two little balls, by way of pastime and innocent recreation, with old François'[564] beautiful girls.

---

563   See Gibson, *LLG, I*, p. 361 & *LLG, II*, pp. 31-36: *The Public Interest vs. Newkesequeskik* (Case 8, A38).

564   Gunn: "The 'old François' referred to was probably François Richards, father of the late William Richards of St. Andrews parish. This family, who were of French origin, formerly lived at Lake Manitoba. The old gentleman had quite a family of sons and daughters."

To Partridge Crop & Back with Burnt Belly

After a week's delay, I hired the Burnt Belly[565] to take me to Partridge Crop for 15 shillings. We arrived there on our fifth day from James Monkman's. Gavin and Frederick I left behind [at Monkman's] to trap and catch all they could during my absence. I remained with brother John and his little family a day and a piece, and returned again to the end of the lake, as it is called. During my short stay there I purchased about £8 worth of fur.

While his brothers' hunting and trapping activities were entirely lawful, so long as they did not sell their catch to anyone other than the HBC, Peter Garrioch's purchase of furs from another trapper contravened the trade monopoly clause of the Company's Charter, as well as the resolutions promulgated by the Governor and Council of Assiniboia on June 19, 1845 (Appendix I – Petitions).

Gavin I found still at the same place, but Frederick had eloped to Red River. I spent another day with James Monkman, and then returned to Red River in company with the above Monkman, George Bird, John Irving and {282} young James Knight.

A Warning

On my return home I was favoured with a communication from Mr. James Sinclair warning me to be on my guard, as Mr. [Cuthbert] Grant[566] had received a warrant

---

565   Gunn: "Probably an Indian."

566   "In July 1828 the HBC Council of the Northern Department appointed Grant warden of the plains of Red River, at an annual salary of £200, to prevent 'the illicit trade in Furs within that District.' He had transferred his loyalties to the new masters, and his value was recognized. He was still sufficiently respected by the Métis to be elected captain of the annual buffalo hunts.... From 1840 the Métis and the Sioux were fighting a kind of guerrilla war over infringement of tribal buffalo-hunting territories, and Grant, as 'Chief of the half-breeds and warden of the Plains,' negotiated a peace settlement in 1844.... By the 1840s Grant's influence among the Métis had waned. A new generation of young and rebellious men had appeared, and a French element led by men such as the elder Louis Riel began to take leadership away from the Scots half-breeds such as Grant. The crucial issue was freedom of trade; in defiance of the HBC monopoly, the Métis were beginning to trade furs with Americans at Pembina (N.Dak.) and St Paul (Minn.), following the example of McDermot, whose HBC licence was not renewed in 1843, and James Sinclair. Here Grant, as warden of the plains, magistrate, and sheriff, was on the side of the company." George Woodcock, "Cuthbert Grant," *DCB* VIII, pp. 341-344. After the Sayer trial in 1849, when Grant presided as one of the magistrates, he lost control of the Métis 'playbook,' and his usefulness to the HBC was over. On the Sayer trial and its significance, see below, Chap..10, text at nn. 711-712, and Gibson, *LLG*, II, pp. 113-118: *The Honble Hudson's Bay Company v. Pierre Guilleaum Sayer*, May 12, 1849 (Case #68, A151), & Gibson, *LLG*, I, pp. 155-119.

from the Governor authorizing him to seize all furs that were traded by private individuals, and that were not intended to be delivered to the Hudson's Bay Company. Those who assisted Mr. Grant in this unlawful and infernal affair were to receive one half of the plunder as a compensation for their services. I reached home, however, without being annoyed by these intrusive measures.

December 16, 1845 – Tuesday. On this day I returned from the above trip.

Governor Christie's Anger

December 18, 1845 – Thursday. Went up to see Mr. Christie about John's letter, at which Mr. Christie felt highly insulted.

While the nature of "John's letter" is not known, it would not be unreasonable to speculate that it was a complaint from John Garrioch at the Partridge Crop mission about mistreatment of the native population of that area by HBC employees. Whatever that issue might have been, the Governor's annoyance was clearly exacerbated by his accurate belief that Peter Garrioch, the messenger, had been trading furs while at Lake Manitoba.

He spoke to me about my having traded fur also. I neither denied nor acknowledged the charge. He threatened to clap me in jail before I left the room, to make me an example to the rest. I told him that, as it was in his power to do so, he might do it. He spoke largely on the validity of their Charter, and of the unlimited privileges and power it conferred upon the HBC. As a parting blessing, Governor Christie advised me not to repeat my former conduct, or he would summon me to the Grand Court and have me tried by jury.

As he left Christie's office, Garrioch was accosted by the Governor's much-respected clerk John Black,[567] who might well have been present at the above interview as well, and who now attempted to add his voice of quiet reason to his employer's bombast.

---

567   Gunn: "John Black [...] was at this time Clerk of [both] the Court and Council of Assiniboia, [as well] as a clerk in the [commercial] service of the Hudson's Bay Company." He had come to Red River in 1839 in company with Recorder Adam Thom to serve as Court Clerk. His commercial responsibilities would eventually displace his duties for the Court and Council entirely; and his competence therein, aided, no doubt, by his 1845 marriage to Governor Christie's daughter, ultimately caused him to be promoted to the rank of a Chief Trader. "In 1854," Gunn explained, "he retired from the service and returned to England; subsequently going to Australia, where he occupied the position of Minister of Lands, at Sidney, under the Government of New South Wales. On his return to England from Australia, he was appointed by the HBC to the office of [Acting] Recorder of Assiniboia, and, in 1862, he returned there to enter upon his duties." Black filled that role with great prowess until the final session of the General Quarterly Court of Assiniboia in

On {283} parting with Mr. Black, he told me to take Mr. Christie's advice and trade no more fur. I told him it required a deal of thinking. He then said, "Let people think or not, just as they please; but we must act." "That's the only thing, Mr. Black," said I! So I took up my cap and bade him goodbye.

HBC Claims Challenged in Print

December 19, 1845 – Friday. Mr. James Sinclair favoured me with the perusal of a volume which contains a full account of the difficulties which took place in this country between the HB and North-West Companies; of the trial the partners of the latter company underwent in Canada; of their final and general acquittal; and of the impeachable conduct and procedure of the HBC and his Lordship, the Earl of Selkirk.[568] After perusing this volume, I am persuaded in my own mind that the Charter, so often adverted to by those who are interested in it, is not worth the paper it is written on; or rather what the ink {284} cost with which it was first written.

HBC Investigates & Acts

December 22, 1845 – Monday. The Burnt Belly told me that Antoine[569] had been twice at him, putting all manner of questions to him concerning his trip with me to the Partridge Crop.

December 23, 1845 – Tuesday. I was informed that Mr. [Cuthbert] Grant, [Warden of the Plains] with two men, had gone to seize goods taken out by William Prichard[570] to the [Lake] Manitoba quarter.

October 1869, whereupon he served as one of Red River's representatives in the negotiations with the Canadian Government that resulted in creation of the Province of Manitoba before retiring to his native Scotland. Also Gibson, *LLG, I,* p. 100, *passim,* & Stubbs, *Four Recorders,* pp. 135-187.

568   Unfortunately, it is now not possible to identify the document to which Peter was referring here, but it might be among the early documents on these topics collected in the Bruce Peel Library, University of Alberta.

569   Gunn: "Probably Antoine Moora, or Morin, one of the Company's constables."

570   Gunn: "A party of this name lived on the Assiniboine River near the Roman Catholic church of St. François Xavier, about six miles west of Headingly. This man was a well-known fur trader of those days, and is probably the one referred to."

Roast Mutton, Plum Pudding & New Year's Visits

December 25, 1845 – Thursday. This is Christmas day, and I had roasted mutton and plum pudding for dinner.

January 1, 1846 – Thursday. I went up this day to the White Horse Plain to see Pascal Berlan [Bréland] about getting buffalo for me at the plains, as I intended to fetch a trip of green meat.

Since fresh ("green") meat did not keep well enough in warm weather to be brought back to the Settlement in large quantities from the plains, it was chiefly sought in winter. Bréland, an experienced and highly skilled bullalo hunter, was being recruited by Garrioch to hunt for him on either a fee-for-service or shared-enterprise basis.

I spent the evening with my friend Pascal, in company with Peter Pruden[571] and two others.

January 2, 1846 – Friday. I returned home, and, according to my usual custom, called on several of my friends as I came down.

January 3, 1846 – Saturday. Charles Cummings[572] and I prepared our trains {285} and harness for our trip to the plains.

January 4, 1846 – Sunday. I went only to the Middle Church.

To the Plains with Charles & Pascal

January 5, 1846 – Monday. Charles [Cummings] and I started for the plains with three horses and sledges. The snow having fallen last evening in great abundance, we were under the necessity of making a new track for ourselves this morning as far as the Upper Church [St. John's].

---

571 Gunn: "A son of the Chief Factor Pruden." See entries for January 1, 1846, and February 20, 1847, and n. 621.

572 Garrioch's brother-in-law, whose wedding to his sister Sally in March 1845, it will be recalled, he did not attend. Gunn: "St. Paul's Parish Episcopal [Anglican] church, on the west bank of the Red River, eight miles north of Winnipeg, at what is now known as Middlechurch [sic]. The first congregation was organized here by Reverend David T. James in 1824. The name Middle Church arose out of the circumstance of its being located midway between St. John's and St. Andrew's, which were designated, in local parlance, as the Upper and Lower churches respectively, There is still an English church at this point." Garrioch's use of the word "only" is interesting. It suggests that he had been attending more than one church each Sunday.

Chapter 8 – Traveling Again as Unrest Grows at Red River

January 6, 1846 – Tuesday. Having spent the night at my friend's – Pascal Berlan [Bréland] – we loaded our trains with hay and wheat and prosecuted our journey. We arrived at the Pembina River on the fifth day from home, and found Jack Spence and some of his friends by the banks of the above river, all seated on the ground.

Gunn's note points out that the route to the buffalo plains taken this time was not the same as that taken by Garrioch on his two 1845 buffalo forays. This route – also a well-used one – headed south and southwest from Bréland's home[573] on the White Horse Plains, past the present towns of Starbuck, Carman, and Thornhill, to a point west of the Pembina mountains near Hannah, in what is now Cavalier County, North Dakota.

Whether by pre-arrangement or spur-of-the-moment agreement, Spence and his friends seem to have joined the Garrioch/Cummings/Bréland party for the ensuing hunt.

Excellent Hunt / Uncomfortable Night

After going about ten miles due west of Lake Debransh,[574] we came to a herd of {286} buffalo cows, out of which my friend Pascal managed to get three for us. After getting them cut up and brought to the hut, which was in the open prairie, we put up a little tent which Urba[575] had taken with him, and stowed ourselves as well as we could into it.

The tent, which had to accommodate seven men of us, was scarcely seven feet in diameter. Everyone had to lie down just as he had walked through the day. The only part we took off of our habiliments was our mittens. We had but one kettle in the whole party for cooking, and that a very small one, it holding only two gallons. We were therefore obliged to cook five times the fill of it before our keen appetites could

---

573 The home of Pascal Bréland is now the location of one of Manitoba's Historic Sites, named Medicine Rock Heritage Park. Bréland (1811-1896) married a daughter of Cuthbert Grant in 1836, and they had 14 children. "In 1851 he was appointed magistrate for the White Horse Plains and, in 1857, he became a member of the Council of Assiniboia. During the 1869-1870 insurrection, he withdrew to the Qu'Appelle Valley, reappearing at St. François Xavier in April 1870 to warn that "men should now refrain from associating themselves with the murderers of a helpless prisoner." Not surprisingly, the new leaders of Manitoba found him useful. He was elected MLA [aka MPP] from St. François Xavier in the first elections of December 1870 and served in various positions thereafter: *Memorable Manitobans: Pascal Bréland*. (Manitoba Historical Society.)

574 Gunn: "Clearly Lac des Branchages, now known as Rush Lake. It lies in the northwestern part of Cavalier County, North Dakota, just south of Hannah. The lake, or rather marsh, is about five miles long by one and a half miles wide. In early days it was a quite considerable body of water, but is now a mere marsh. At its south end are two marshy branches that extend out of it southward like a pair of gigantic deer horns, and from these it derived its name of Lac de Branches."

575 Gunn: "This is probably a Christian name. I am informed that this individual – a French Métis – lived up the Assiniboine at White Horse Plains, [and that his full name was] Urban Delorme."

be pacified and permit us to lie down and slumber. Before these five kettles, we had eaten about two fathoms of the biggest gut of the fattest animal killed this day. On the top of all this we drank six quarts of strong tea, highly seasoned or sweetened. As we had to lie upon one another in snake fashion,[576] we did not pass a very comfortable night.

After a few more days of hard and cold traveling, we reached our home in life and health.

Strange & Overbearing Proceedings

On my way home, I should have stated, I was informed that Mr. Grant had seized the goods and fur of several of the traders (private individual traders). Among the plundered was Quewezayse, Antoine Degerlai's [Desjarlais'] brother; St. Germain and one of Shatra's [Chartrand's] sons. These are {287} certainly strange and overbearing proceedings. The HBC appear determined, at all hazards, to establish their points.

January 18, 1846 – Sunday. We arrived late this evening, not being able to reach home on Saturday.

January 21, 1846 – Wednesday. I fixed a pair of ox shafts, and dined on a piece of gut pudding.

The Magistrates Resist

As previously discussed, the Quarterly Court system established back in 1835 (and criticized by young Peter Garrioch on the title page of his then blank journal book) consisted of two divisions. The senior body, which sat only at Upper Fort Garry with the Governor, Recorder, and other high-ranking officials on the bench, was the General Court, of whose proceedings the journal has taken notice several times. The other division comprised several locally-based Petty Courts, staffed by magistrates chosen from among respected community elders. Although those magistrates knew less about law than the Recorder or the Governor, they knew their communities, and they tended to place greater reliance on common sense and fairness than on what Recorder Thom told them was ordained by the letter of the law.

The Hudson's Bay Company knew that enforcing its asserted fur trade monopoly would be very difficult without the co-operative involvement of these on-the-scene magistrates. Obtaining that assistance was not easy, however. Almost a year previously, in apparent response to the resistance by Garrioch and other free traders to the tariff on imports from

---

576 The reference is to the large, tangled balls of hibernating garter snakes that are still seen in parts of Manitoba.

the United States and their suspected unauthorized fur trading, along with an awareness that the magistrates were generally unsympathetic to Company concerns, the Council of Assiniboia had enacted at Thom's behest that "all questions of revenue or prohibition or licence" would be adjudicated by the General Court rather than by the Petty Courts.[577] That did not remove magistrates from the process altogether, since the principal magistrates were members of the General Court as well; but it did mean that those magistrates who continued to be involved were under the watchful eyes of Christie and Thom.

It was not just as adjudicators, however, that local magistrates could be helpful to law enforcement authorities. They were, to a considerable extent, the eyes and ears, as well as the lay father-confessors, of their communities, and Governor Christie sought their assistance in those capacities.

Mr. James Sinclair gave us a call and informed us that a council extraordinary had been summoned by Governor Christie at Fort Garry yesterday, at which he requested cooperation of the magistrates in his plan to continue and extend his plundering, or seizing system. The magistrates, it appears, had wit enough to refuse having anything to do with the business. In the course of these proceedings, Captain Cary[578] told Mr. Christie, that, had Shatra [Chartrand] shot Mr. Grant on the spot, he (Shatra) would have been acquitted the next moment.

What Is Greatness?

I was told this day that it was the opinion of some of my well- {288} wishers, that, if I lived long, I should someday be a great man. What the greatness is to consist in is not indicated by those good opinionists. Whether it is to be in riches, wisdom, goodness, knowledge or influence, I know not; but one thing I know: that my present prospects

---

577 Oliver, *Canadian North-West*, I, p. 314. On the petty courts generally, see Gibson, *LLG, I, passim*.

578 Gunn: "Captain George Marcus Cary, a half-pay British army officer, sent out about 1836 as manager of the third experimental farm at Red River. He brought with him some twenty assistants. The farm, which occupied the point of land between the Red and Assiniboine Rivers, to the north of the latter stream, was not a success; and, after running at a loss for 10 years, Cary threw up his position in disgust and removed with his family to eastern Canada. In Ross' *Red River Settlement*, pp. 212-221, is given [an] account of his activities in this connection. Ross is not correct, however, in fixing 1838 as the time of Cary's arrival in Red River; as, in a copy of the 1837 minutes of the Council of Assiniboia, held at Fort Garry, now before me, George Cary is mentioned as among those present, and his appointment to the position of councillor ratified. [N]ominations as councillor, it may be remarked, had first to be made by the Governor and Committee in London. By these minutes I find also that Cary, at this same meeting, was appointed joint magistrate with Cuthbert Grant for the 'Upper District,' defined as 'upwards from Sturgeon Creek on the Assiniboine River.'" His departure from Red River occurred the year following the incident recorded above by Garrioch.

do not afford me the slightest reason to expect what others are so kind and sanguine as to entertain and hope for me. Were I, however, to be allowed the privilege of choosing that in which my greatness should consist, I would most certainly give the preference to wisdom and goodness. I do not here ape Solomon the Wise. The historic fact of his having preferred wisdom to riches and honour never struck me until I had finished the last sentence.

April in January

January 22, 1846 – Thursday. This day has been quite an April one. The wind has been from the south and continues as strong and warm [at] the present moment, which is about ten o'clock of the night.[579]

Dominique Pambrun[580] has made a start today with his little family towards Red Lake, his wintering quarters. I sold him a bag of soft fat pemmican weighing 100 lbs., today, on credit; and made him a present of a thigh of meat for his dogs, and six tongues, six little bosses, and twenty or thirty pounds of buffalo backfat meat for his own consumption.

I fixed another pair of ox shafts today, and winnowed eight or ten bushels of wheat.

January 23, 1846 – Friday. Wind from the south all day, which causeth the atmosphere to be very warm and pleasant.

January 24, 1846 - Saturday. The wind still to the south. This day has been altogether an April one. The wind has dissolved so much of the snow that water begins to stand in pools at the doors, and the {289} eaves of even barns hung down with lengthy icicles. William, having gone to the foot of [Bird's] Hill today for wood, found many parts of the road quite bare. I put an old wood sled together today and did various other little jobs. It was so wet that I was obliged to put on boots[581] in the afternoon and walked over to William Gaddy's in them.

---

579 This phenomenon, which still occurs with great regularity across the Canadian Midwest, has been called the "bonspiel thaw" in Winnipeg in more recent years, a reference to a curling tournament.

580 This may be Andrew Dominique Pambrun (1821-1895), son of a long-time HBC employee and his wife, the daughter of a fur trader and an Indigenous woman. Dominique married a Mary Cook which may have brought him into kinship with Peter and explain why Peter was making him gifts on this occasion. There is no note from Gunn on the subject. See Peter's entries for September 20, 1846, and January 21 and February 28, 1847.

581 As opposed, probably, to moccasins.

Chapter 8 – Traveling Again as Unrest Grows at Red River

January 25, 1846 – Sunday. The weather still continues to be very mild. Mr. Smithurst[582] preached at the Upper and Middle churches.

January 26, 1846 – Monday. I went up to William McMillan's but did not find him at home. The roads on land are almost entirely bare. James Sinclair was not at home, having gone to Mr. Kittson's at the Pembina.

January 27, 1846 – Tuesday. Weather as yesterday.

A Most Distressing Accident

I am here under the painful necessity of journalizing one of the most distressing accidents that has ever occurred in this Colony. Within the last hour I was informed by Kenneth McDonald, who has been at the Upper Fort, that Peter Hayden accidently shot a boy at about twelve o'clock today. This boy, who is now no more, was {290} the son of Goubah [Gobin], late of this colony but now residing at St. Peter's, whom he had left in the care of Peter Hayden.

The accident was brought about under the following circumstances, if I am rightly informed. Peter Hayden was on the point of riding out, when some person came in and told him that Mr. Grant was on his way down to rob him [seize illegally acquired furs], and that it would therefore be advisable for him to remain at home. Fired at the intelligence he, Peter Hayden, took the advice suggested, and went in to prepare himself for the reception of Mr. Grant; or, in other words, for the defence of his property.

With this in view, he took out his revolving pistol[583] and commenced setting it in order, when, awful to relate, he inadvertently discharged one of the barrels at the juncture when the poor boy was passing between him and the wall, in the direction of the pistol so discharged. The ball, it is stated, passed through the temples of the lad, and he survived but a few moments after it. Poor Hayden! His case is indeed a desperate

---

582   Gunn: "Reverend John Smithurst, a Church of England missionary, came [from] England to the Red River Settlement in 1839. He was, on his arrival, placed in charge of the Indian Settlement on the Red River below the present Selkirk; in which charge, known as St. Peter's, he remained for [over] ten years." See Bumsted, *DMB*, p. 234.

583   His "revolving pistol" was most likely an Allen & Thurber "pepper-box," a revolving, percussion pistol with several separate barrels arrayed around a central axis, rotated manually. This pistol was widely distributed and very popular from the 1830s to the American Civil War. Its inaccuracy and often dangerous unpredictability, however, are hilariously described by Mark Twain in his autobiographical *Roughing It* (1872). The gun's sometimes erratic character nonetheless appeared to play little or no part in Hayden's defense.

one! No wonder, as I am told, that he attempted to lay violent hands on himself. More hereafter, if the Lord will.

Today I hired Jack Ward for a month at 20/-. We took up 17 pieces of frame wood [for my house].

Arrivals from Partridge Crop

January 28, 1846 – Wednesday. Joseph Monkman arrived today from the Partridge Crop. Mr. Cummings, who was to confirm my having traded on my trip to the P. C., came with Joseph.

The reference to "Cummings" is puzzling. This cannot have been Garrioch's brother-in-law Charles Cummings, who did not go to Partridge Crop with him, with whom he had shared an apparently amicable hunting trip less than a month previously, and who would continue to be the subject of future companionable activities. It is likely that this was Robert Cummings, who was Master of the HBC's post at Berens River at the time,[584] and Peter's use of the expression "was to confirm" may well have meant that Cummings had been inveigled by the Company to report on what Garrioch had been up to on such trips.

[Brother] John tells me in his letter {291} that Gavin and Frederick are doing nothing but making hoop journeys every day.

Gavin and Frederick Garrioch journeyed to Partridge Crop when Peter returned to Red River in December. The expression "hoop journeys" puzzled Reverend Gunn, as it does the present editors. Could it refer to barrel hoops and, inferentially, to drinking bouts? More likely it means daily circuits ("hoops") of their traplines.

---

584   Robert Cummings was Master of the Post at Berens River from 1831 to 1856. In Reverend A. Cowley's journal for January 24, 1846, it was recorded that the "past week has been one of great trial and distress" because Mr. Cummings, "Master of the Company's Post Berent's River, Lake Winnipeg" arrived there "to oversee the men stationed here to collect furs for the Company." However, he brought a quantity of rum with him. "He commenced as he told me by giving them a dram or two each as an inducement and stimulus to trade." However, the occasion turned into "a disgusting Bacchanal…in a short time both men and women with one exception were plunged in a state of dreadful intoxication," leading the writer to a dire conclusion: "Should rum be continued as article of trade humanly speaking all our efforts to civilize and Christianize this people are and will be probably in vain.' CMSA/AM: CC1M4 Mission Bk 1845-1850, North-West Canada, 1821-1880. There were a number of Cummings living in Berent's River, so that it is not possible to identify the person in Garrioch's diaries with absolute certainty.

Chapter 8 – Traveling Again as Unrest Grows at Red River

January 29, 1846 – Thursday. The wind has at length shifted to the north, and it begins to feel like winter once more. A raffle today at Mr. Moat's[585] about a horse.

Is Peter Hayden Crazy?

I was informed yesterday that poor Peter Hayden is crazy. I hope the report is not true.

January 30, 1846 – Friday. Heard that P. Hayden is out of prison. I hope so.

Hayden had been released on bail, fears for his sanity having apparently been allayed. His case would be tried at the General Quarterly Court session of February 19, less than three weeks hence. His friend and fellow free trader Peter Garrioch was apprehensive that he too might be brought before the court that day, charged with unauthorized traffic in furs at Partridge Crop and elsewhere.

Meanwhile, Peter was busying himself with arrangements for construction of his new house when weather permitted. His financial ability to proceed with that project may well have been dependent on his fur trade earnings.

Home, Church, & Drunken Party

January 31, 1846 – Saturday. A cold day and it snows some. I went down to see James Valer[586] about lime, Harry Bird[587] about building my house, and Peter Whitford about chopping [clearing the land] before H. B. could put it up.

February 1, 1846 – Sunday. Remained at home in the forenoon and went to the Middle Church in the afternoon. The church was full, and yet there was but old Bunn[588] and

---

585 Gunn: "Andrew Mowat, a native of Orkney, formerly in HBC's service. He lived on the west bank of the Red River in St. Andrews parish, about one-half mile. above the Stone Church, where he kept a store and engaged in the freighting business between Fort Garry and York Factory on Hudson Bay."

586 Gunn: "An English settler of Red River, later for many years gardener to the HBC at Lower Fort Garry. He lived on the west bank of the above stream, in St. Andrews parish, about one-half mile south of the present Lockport. He engaged, from time to time, in the lime-burning business, he, in conjunction with James Swain, another old-time resident of that part, having furnished all of this material required for the building of Lower Fort Garry."

587 Gunn: "A son of the Chief Factor Bird …and father of J.J. Bird, ex-MPP of Pidgeon Bluff; a millwright by trade. He lived on the west bank of the Red River, about one-half mile north of the St. Andrews church."

588 The venerable and omnicompetent Dr. John Bunn, physician, councilor, magistrate, and later the Settlement's Coroner, Sheriff, and Acting Recorder. See Bumsted, *DMB*, p. 39; Stubbs, *Four Recorders*, pp. 91-134; & Gibson, *LLG, I, passim*.

myself to read the responses. I had to read one verse alone while the old gentleman – I suppose – was busy ruminating over the follies of his youthful days.

February 3, 1846 – Tuesday. Made arrangements with Harry Bird to put {292} up the body of my house with the roof, the two floors, and all the partitions in the lower division, for £22.

February 4, 1846 – Wednesday. Half-cleaned about thirty bushels of wheat with old Jack Ward.

February 5, 1846 – Thursday. Rode up to James McKay's. Yesterday Joseph Monkman started back for the Partridge Crop, and last night there was a drunken party at Charles Cook's.[589]

February 6, 1846 – Friday. Today we put thirty bushels of cleaned wheat up in the loft.

Industrial Initiatives or Dust in People's Eyes?

February 8, 1846 – Sunday. Notices at the church doors about cloth prizes and some other stuff as usual. Always a little more dust to throw into people's eyes. The HBC are ever studious to draw the attention of this community from their own rights, by tantalizing them with some specious luminary, at which the poor deluded dupes are so {293} unwittingly attracted, that, ere they are aware, they are soused into some slough of despond which lay hid immediately beneath the luminary.

This competition was an initiative of the Council of Assiniboia's Committee of Economy. It involved awarding prizes from public funds for the best yarn, cloth, cheese, &c, produced by Red River residents. A prize of £20 sterling was offered, for example, for anyone who could produce 100 yards of high-quality cloth of certain types. While Garrioch's cynical view of the motivation behind the competition may not have been justified, even Gunn was sceptical about the scheme: "The net result of this laudable program, outside of the few prizes obtained, was that the settlers were induced to sink their savings, to the extent of £300, in an English fulling mill, which stood and rotted down without ever having fulled a single yard of cloth."[590]

---

589   Gunn: "A son of Chief Factor W. H. Cook [below, n. 603 and associated text]. He lived on the east side of the Red River, just below Middlechurch, where he kept a small store."

590   Gunn cited Seymour, *Sketches of Minnesota*, p. 228, & Ross, *Red River Settlement*, pp. 337-338.

Chapter 8 – Traveling Again as Unrest Grows at Red River

Church Building & House Building

February 9, 1846 – Monday. Went down to see Harry Bird and Sandy Sebiston. The stones for the church at the rapids[591] are all at the building today.

February 10, 1846 – Tuesday. Went down in evening to see James Sandison[592] about the frame of my house.

February 11, 1846 – Wednesday. James Sandison has undertaken to chop the [trees for the] frame of my house for £2.

Another Free Trader Protest

I went up this morning to attend the meeting at Mr. McDermot's, to which I had been invited last evening by Mr. James Sinclair. The purport of the meeting is specified in the following letter, which we (the signers) sent over to the gentlemen addressed.

Regrettably, although Garrioch left space in the journal for a copy of this letter, he seems never to have got around to including it. His entry for February 19, however, mentions, in the context of Peter Hayden's trial, some of the protesters' demands.

Wonderful Trappers

February 12, 1846 – Thursday. Yesterday Gavin and Frederick returned from the Partridge Crop. They brought as little as could be possibly expected. After an absence of nearly three months, Gavin brought one martin, two foxes, two minks and ten rats [muskrats]. Frederick brought one martin and three rats. Wonderful trappers for sure!!!

February 13, 1846 – Friday. The boys brought up from Valer's kiln 80 bushels of lime.

---

591 Old St. Andrews Church on the west side of the Red River north of Winnipeg, the oldest stone church in Western Canada, is still in operation, holding services monthly. Its designer was Archdeacon William Cockran (1798-1865), who organized other churches and schools in the colony, including the school established in 1851 at Portage la Prairie, with Peter Garrioch as its schoolmaster. Old St. Andrews Church is designated as a National Historic Site.

592 Gunn: "A Scotch Métis, born at York Factory on Hudson Bay; a carpenter by trade. He lived on the Red River at Lambert's Point, one and one-half miles south of St. Andrews church." See entry & note for February 17.

February 14, 1846 – Saturday. Frederick started today to Mouse [Souris] River to trade, and to collect debts due to me. I sent goods with him to {294} the amount of £8.2.3.

February 15, 1846 – Sunday. Went to the Middle Church.

Awaiting a Summons

February 16, 1846 – Monday. I have been anxiously waiting for a summons to the next General Court today, but it has not come yet. It may come tomorrow. If it does I am ready to obey it, though were it left to my option, I should prefer it being deferred to the General Court in the spring, when all the hunters and trappers would be present.

Since his testy interview with Governor Christie, Garrioch seems to have been in little doubt that he would be prosecuted for trading in furs on his trip to Partridge Crop. Although he gave no indication to Christie, or to his journal, of the nature of the defence he expected to present, his response on December 19, 1845, to the critical analysis of HBC rights he borrowed from James Sinclair suggest that he was preparing to launch a frontal assault on the legality of those rights.

To the Far Pines for Logs

February 17, 1846 – Tuesday. Went off to the Far Pines[593] with Gavin, Bill and Charles Cummings. I started here a little after sunrise and got to the Pines about an hour before sundown. Sandy Sebiston, as I had apprehended, was not at the place as he had promised.[594] The consequence is that my men will have to cut their loads.

February 18, 1846– Wednesday. Left the Far Pines this morning at 8 o'clock and reached home at 3 o'clock.

---

593   Gunn: "When the 'Pines' were spoken of, usually the spruce and tamarack woods north of Bird's Hill were meant. The 'Far Pines' were woods of a similar kind, but much more extensive, situated to the north of Devil's Creek, some 12 or 14 miles northeast of the present village of East Selkirk. A great deal of the building material used in the Red River Settlement in those days was brought from this quarter. Trips to the Far Pines were almost as much of an institution as the trips to St. Paul or the buffalo hunts."

594   Did he mean James Sandison rather than Sandy Sebiston? See entries for February 10 & 11. Probably not. See entry for March 3. It seems that he contracted with both men to supply him with logs and that both let him down.

Chapter 8 – Traveling Again as Unrest Grows at Red River 293

No Word or Warrant

So there is no summons for the next Court anyhow; for tomorrow is the Court day, and I have received no word or warrant.

Why had no charge been laid against Garrioch? Perhaps it was because the Company had been unable to obtain legally cogent evidence that he had traded in furs, or because they were concerned that the rather persuasive argument he could be counted on raising against the continuing legal validity of the monopoly granted by the HBC Charter might persuade a sympathetic jury. Possibly, also, the Company simply did not want to risk incurring any more embarrassment than that to which the Hayden case had already subjected it.

I shall, however, be up, if the Lord will, and see and hear what has to be said and done to the beer and whiskey sellers, and to poor Peter Hayden. {295}

The Hayden Case

February 19, 1846 – Thursday. I was up to the Grand Court, and glad I am to note down in my day book that Peter Hayden had a regular trial and is discharged. The Grand Jury gave in their verdict unanimously of manslaughter on his case. He was laid under a bond of £50 to keep the peace of the public for two years; and two of his friends, viz.: Thomas Logan[595] and Charles Laraner [Larance] of £5 each, who have become his securities.

The Peter Hayden homicide case[596] was one of the strangest in the annals of the Red River Courts. As Garrioch reported on January 27, Hayden, after a warning that Warden of the Plains Cuthbert Grant was coming to his home to seize furs suspected of having been obtained by trading, was preparing his pistol for possible use defending his property, when the gun discharged accidentally, killing John Gobin, a young boy under his care. Hayden was charged with manslaughter. Causing death by very great negligence, which seems to have been the case here, was and is a form of manslaughter; and although the court record did not employ that term, the absence from the indictment of the words "with

---

595 Gunn: "Eldest son of Chief Factor Robert Logan, one of the pioneer settlers on the site of the present Winnipeg. Robert Logan purchased from Lord Selkirk's heirs the land on which Fort Douglas stood, together with the Colony windmill, where the family continued to reside [for many] years. The family residence was at the foot of Logan Avenue, which was so called from that circumstance. Alexander, a brother of Thomas was afterwards mayor of the city. Thomas lived, at this time, just south of where the Canadian Pacific Railway depot [later stood]. Later, he lived for a time on Lake Manitoba, at what is known as Logan's Point. About 1860 he settled at what was then known as Pointe Coupé, about 15 miles of Winnipeg on the Red River, where he [began to build] a watermill which, however, was accidentally burned before completion."

596 Gibson, *LLG, II*, pp. 37-40: *The Public Interest v. Peter Hayden* (Case 10, A46). See also Gibson, *LLG, I,* p, 91.

malice aforethought" – the hallmark of murder – leaves no doubt that it was this less grave form of homicide that Hayden was accused of – and to which he pleaded guilty.

What Garrioch's account of the trial omits is the penalty awarded: a fine of one shilling! At the previous session of the same court, a young aboriginal man called Newkesqueskik, found guilty of stabbing his older brother to death under pressure of extreme provocation – another common form of manslaughter – was imprisoned in solitary confinement for an entire year.[597] How can that discrepancy be explained? The fact that the earlier killing was intentional, though provoked, rather than accidental, no doubt justified a degree of greater severity, and Newkesqueskik's race was, regrettably, a likely factor as well. But a sentence of one shilling for manslaughter?! More than the foregoing differences must have been involved.

In the editors' view, that sentence had probably been the result of what a later age would call a plea bargain: an agreement between the prosecution and defence that the accused would plead guilty if the prosecutor would recommend a token penalty. What could have persuaded the Governor (who both directed the prosecution and chaired the Court) to treat Peter Hayden – one of the most painful thorns in his side – so leniently? It was, most likely, fear of public outrage.

While few – including Hayden himself – would have denied that the immediate cause of John Gobin's tragic killing had been the accused's carelessness, most – including the Governor – knew that the Company's intensifying campaign of harassment against Hayden and other free traders had provoked that carelessness. On February 11 – just eight days prior to the trial – a protest meeting was held at Andrew McDermot's home, and Peter Garrioch, who attended at least part of that meeting, reported later in his February 19th diary entry that two of the resolutions then agreed upon had been that: (a) Hayden be broken out of jail, and (b) Recorder Adam Thom, known to have devised the draconian policies that led indirectly to the boy's death, be "driven out of the Colony next spring."

Settlement authorities knew that most Red River residents were generally sympathetic to free traders and that, in particular, they empathized with Peter Hayden, driven by distraction over what he considered Company bullying to commit an act of fatal carelessness. The Court's agreement to a lenient punishment could, and apparently did, assuage public anger.

And as for the Governor's belief that Peter Garrioch had trafficked in furs at Partridge Crop and would very much like to have charged him with it: even if he possessed conclusive evidence of a HBC Charter violation, this was no time to be pressing such a charge publicly.

Charles Demarais [Demanais][598] was tried for selling beer but, there being no sufficient evidence against him, he was acquitted. A horse case between Bruno and Francis

---

597   Gibson, *LLG, II*, pp. 31-34: *The Public Interest v. Newkesequeskik* (Case 8, A38). See also Gibson, *LLG, I*, pp. 361 & 373.

598   Gibson, *LLG, II*, p: 40: *The Public Interest v. Charles Desmanais* (Case 11, A48).

Resar[599] [Richard] was also brought before the Court, in a civil trial which the latter lost.

I was informed today that [Reverend] Mr. Cockran had been informed, that, at our meeting at Mr. McDermot's last week, three resolutions had been passed, viz.:

1. That Peter Hayden, then a prisoner, should be taken out of the jail by force.

2. That Mr. Thom should be driven out of the Colony next spring.

3. [Left blank in manuscript][600] {296}

I was also informed that Mr. Fisher[601] had not succeeded in his intention of building alongside of Mr. Kittson at the Pembina. For Kittson, report says, told him he would have the first man bound that dared to cut a willow near his premises for the purpose

---

599 The Court record gives the parties' names as Antoine Morin and François Richard. Gibson, *LLG*, II, pp. 40-41: *Antoine Morin v. François Richard* (Case 12, A48). Might "Bruno" have been the plaintiff's nickname?

600 One wonders why Garrioch did not include this in his journal. Had he perhaps left the meeting early?

601 Gunn: "The Alex. Fisher of [p. 166]. He was born in the US, probably at Prairie du Chien. His father, Henry Fisher was one of the pioneer residents of that place, being there when Pike visited it in 1805; the probability being that he had been there already for a considerable time. The older Fisher was a Captain of the Militia and a Justice of the Peace, and was married to a daughter of Goutier de Verville. He was said to have been a nephew of President Monroe. One of his daughters was married to Joe Rolette, Sr., of Pembina so that the Alex. Fisher of our reference was a maternal uncle of Joe Rolette, Jr. [See Chap. 6, note 340]. Henry Fisher, we are informed (J. Fletcher Williams, *History of St. Paul*, p. 160), subsequently "went to the Red River of the North in the service of the Hudson's Bay Company." In accordance with his statement, we find in the old registers of grants of land in Assiniboia entries 763, 764, [and 779 in Henry Fisher's name]. Just when the Fishers struck Red River, however, or what end they finally made, I have not been able definitely to ascertain. From 1840-1843 the A. Fisher of our reference was with his nephew Joe Rolette, who was then in charge for the American Fur Company [post] at Pembina; the two being engaged in a partnership business transporting goods by Red River cart to St. Paul. On the taking charge there of Kittson, in 1843, Fisher appears to have been eliminated from the business; the above being the result of his attempt to re-establish himself there." Ironically, Kittson's lengthy success in eliminating competition by adroit manoeuvring on both sides of the border from his perch on the Pembina came to an end in 1854 when he was "driven into retirement" by the HBC's tacit withdrawal of its strict trading monopoly *circa* 1849 following the *Sayer* trial, as well as actions taken by the American government, resulting in freer trade and better access to trading goods, which has been described as "a triumph for a superior trading technique, not for any system of exclusive trade based upon chartered rights" by Rich, *Hudson's Bay Company*, III, p. 561.

of building an opposition establishment. The consequence was that Mr. Fisher had to return to the Settlement. He was at the Fort today.

February 20, 1846 – Friday. I went out with my horse and cariole[602] to meet the boys. I came up to them while at their breakfast, not more than twelve miles from the place I expected they would have left yesterday.

February 21, 1846 – Saturday. After spending the night with the boys, we made an early start this morning and reached home by mid-day. We brought home 98 cedar logs on [sleds drawn by] seven oxen. Uncle Joe[603] gave us a call {297} today. It is about 23 months since I last saw him, though the distance of our residing places is not more than eighteen miles apart. That is just the way that relatives ought to treat each other, where they entertain a mutual respect.

I hung four fine large hams this evening to dry for summer use.

February 22, 1846 – Sunday. Weather very cold and a great deal of coughing in church.

A Patriarch's Death

February 23, 1846 – Monday. This day the *father of us all*, Mr. W. H. Cook[604] departed this life. He died from extreme debility. During a {298} course of 76 years he had

---

602 A more or less elegant horse-drawn sleigh; a very popular winter passenger conveyance at the time.

603 Gunn: "Joseph Cook, a son of Chief Factor William Hemmings Cook. Joseph Cook was the first school teacher at the Indian mission of St. Peters. He began to teach there in 1825, and continued in the position up to his death, when one of his sons was made schoolmaster in his place. He lived on the east side of the Red River, near the mouth of Cook's Creek, below East Selkirk. Cook's Creek derives its name from this circumstance."

604 Gunn: "Chief Factor William Hemmings Cook, Garrioch's maternal grandfather. This gentleman was a man of considerable note in his day, attaining a high and responsible position in the service of the Hudson's Bay Company. Of his early history little is known, except that he was of English birth, and that he came to Rupert's Land in the latter part of the eighteenth century. He was the Governor of York Factory, on Hudson Bay, at the time of the founding of the Selkirk Settlement at Red River and is frequently mentioned in connection with the experiences of the colonists at the former place by all historians who have written of those events. Upon the union of the HB and NW Companies in 1821 Cook, like many others, availed himself of the opportunity of retiring from the service. [He moved] with his family, shortly afterwards, to the Red River, and settled on its western bank, on lot 41, St. Paul's parish, about midway between the present Middlechurch and Parkdale. Mr. Cook was an able, though very eccentric, individual. He was well known to and on friendly terms with all the nabobs of the fur trade in the country at that time. Sir George Simpson frequently refers to him in his correspondence. Among his special hobbies were those of painting and floriculture. His flower

never been once confined to a bed of sickness, and never was under the necessity of having recourse to medicine of any kind till within a few months of his demise, when the partial derangement of his constitutional faculties from an unfortunate dose of laudanum required the occasional advice and treatment of medical skill.

February 25, 1846 – Wednesday. The remains of the deceased were conveyed to the Upper Church burying ground. The procession was composed of about twenty men. So much for a great man of this colony. His spirit has gone to its First Author; may his body rest in peace with the clods of the valley, till the grave shall yield up her charge.

The reverential tone of this and the previous entry about Cook's death, when contrasted with the terse, possibly sarcastic, language of references to his father's death in the entries for February 21 and March 6, 1844, together with his father's complete absence from the emotional farewell scene described in the journal's very first entry in 1837, may suggest that Peter had been much closer to his eccentric, earthy, maternal grandfather than to his sanctimonious father[605].

The Half Breed Protest

February 26, 1846 – Thursday. I attended the meeting proposed at Mr. McDermot's. The Reverend Mr. Belcourt[606] presided and addressed the meeting {299} in English

---

garden, it is said, was a wonder for those days; and the inside of his cottage home was covered with paintings in oils of his own composition. He is said to have presented, from time to time, specimens of his artistic work, as mementoes, to all the chief men in the service; but, so far as is known, there is not a single one now in existence. He was one of the members of the Council of Assiniboia; a position which he held from the inception of that body in 1835 until his death on Feb. 23, 1846. Mr. Cook was 80 years of age, at the time of his death, instead of 76 as here stated. His tombstone is still to be seen in St. John's Cemetery, and 80 years is the record thereon inscribed." Cook's age at death was indeed 80, as recorded in the HBCA/AM: Extracts from Registers of Baptisms, Marriages and Burials in Rupert's Land, E.4/2 folio 146. Of the 27 deaths and burials recorded on that page of the Register, it was only William Hemmings Cook's burial that was celebrated by Rev. William Cockran; the rest – several from families prominent in the Settlement – were presided over by John Macallum.

605   Although it was not exactly a unique phenomenon in families where one member pursued illicit trade in furs, it appears the two were estranged over the issue: "When Peter Garrioch became a free trader, his father, William, refused to see him, and in the end Garrioch stayed away from his father's funeral." Frits Pannekoek, *A Snug Little Flock; The Social Origins of the Riel Resistance of 1869-70* (Winnipeg, Watson & Dwyer, 1991), p. 30.

606   Gunn: "Reverend Georges Antoine Belcourt, a Roman Catholic clergyman, well-known on both sides of the international boundary in the Northwest at that time. Mr. Belcourt was born at [Trois Rivières], Quebec, in 1803, and educated at Nicolet College, where he was afterwards, for a time, professor of mathematics and astronomy. Ordained priest in 1827, after serving a number

and French. The meeting was attended by about 100 persons, and only four of that number, viz.: James Sinclair, Thomas McDermot, John Anderson and myself, were English-speaking. The sum and substance of the presiding gentleman's address was contained in the following subjects: [passage not completed]

The tone of this meeting was very angry; lenient treatment of Peter Hayden seems not to have done much to improve the public's mood, at least not among the French Half Breeds. Considered the most influential white man among the Indigenous population of Red River,[607] **Father Belcourt's calming presence at the meeting, and his channelling of participants' anger into a written petition against HBC and Assiniboia policies, probably headed off major violence. Garrioch would later have more to do with the Belcourt petition, which eventually reached the hands of British Government authorities.**[608]

---

of churches in his home district, he was brought, by Bishop Provencher, to Red River, in 1831, as a missionary to the Indians. His first mission was established among the Saulteaux, 30 miles up the Assiniboine River, at a place afterwards known as Baie St. Paul. This was in 1832; and from that time to 1838 he made his headquarters there; although, during that period, he established also a mission on the Winnipeg River. In the midst of his missionary activities, Mr. Belcourt devoted much time to the study of the Ojibwa Indian tongue, preparing a grammar of that language, which he published in 1839. He also prepared a lexicon of the same, in French and Ojibwa. The grammar and lexicon were [edited] and published after his death by Father Lacombe. Although missionary to the Indians, Father Belcourt was not unknown to his own people, the French-speaking element, among whom he soon became a leader, assisting them in their struggle against the oppressive monopoly of the Hudson's Bay Company. By so doing, he drew upon himself the resentment of that body, and Sir George Simpson wrote the Bishop of Quebec demanding [Belcourt's] removal. Before receiving the Bishop's recall, however, in 1848 he left the country for Lower Canada, by way of the US. The evening before his departure, he was arrested by the HBC authorities, on the pretence of having trafficked in furs, and a posse was sent after his carts to overhaul and examine his baggage. The following year, he was appointed to the charge of Pembina, under the Bishop of Dubuque, where he erected a chapel. Shortly after, however, [he removed] to what is now Walhalla and [built] there, the latter point being selected as more favourable, on account of the floods at Pembina. He died [in Eastern Canada in] 1874. Besides the above-mentioned Ojibwa books, Father Belcourt was the author of an interesting article entitled "The Department of the Hudson's Bay," in which [in addition to] other valuable information, he relates in detail his difficulties with the HBC, above referred to. For this article see *Collections of the Minnesota Historical Society* I, pp. 207-244." Belcourt included his autobiography on pp. 240-244 of the article to which Gunn referred, his "The Department of the Hudson's Bay." See Appendix I – Petitions.

607 "Georges-Antoine Belcourt," Historic Resources Branch, Manitoba Culture, Heritage and Recreation, 1984, p. 4. Gluek, *Minnesota and the Manifest Destiny*, pp. 57-58, 72-73, 104-114, describes the activities and possible motives of this complicated clergyman who was "intense, idealistic, though emotionally unstable….a strange, vindictive man….*persona non grata* to the Company," but who was for a time permitted to establish a mission at Pembina, joining Norman Kittson there and operating with him in opposition to the HBC, eventually seeking support for their activities from the federal government in Washington.

608 See entry for May 28, 1846. A note thereto sets out some of the petition's contents, and the petition is set out in full in Appendix I – Petitions.,

February 27, 1846 – Friday. The executors of the late [William Hemmings] Cook's will employed Mr. [William Robert] Smith,[609] the Gentleman,[610] and Roderick Sutherland[611] to take an inventory of the property left by the deceased.

March 1, 1846 – Sunday. Quite a mild and warm day. This month comes in like a lamb, therefore, say the old heads, she will go out like a lion. We shall see. {300}

More Logging

March 2, 1846 – Monday. I started to the Cedars[612] with Gavin and Charles Cummings for [more wood for] the frame of my intended house.

March 3, 1846 – Tuesday. We got to the wood, and found that James Sandison had cut all the short posts at 9 feet instead of 11 feet. A perfect old humbug!

March 4, 1846 – Wednesday. After traveling about three hours from sundown, we were driven to the fatal necessity of tumbling into bed without fire; our touchwood[613] and flint being so bad that we could not kindle one. Fortunately it was a mild night.

March 5, 1846 – Thursday. Got home a little after sundown under a heavy fall of snow.

---

609   See above, text associated with nn. 88-89, n. 476, and below, nn. 702-704, 706.

610   Gunn thought this probably meant Governor Christie, but it is unlikely that the career fur trader was known for his politesse (the "Gentleman") or that he would agree to undertake so relatively menial a task. Nor was it probable that, if it were Christie, he would be listed second. More likely candidates include Recorder Adam Thom, and possibly Chief Trader John Black, both of whom had legal training and were given to gentlemanly airs.

611   Gunn: "A son of Chief Factor [James] Sutherland of the HBC, one of the early settlers of Red River. There were four brothers, William, James, John and Roderick. Of these, James emigrated to Prince Albert on the Saskatchewan, where he died a few years ago at the age of 98. Roderick, of the above reference, settled down and lived for some time in West St. Paul, just north of the present Middlechurch. He taught school there for a period, and had also the custody of half of the first public library established in the Settlement; the other half being kept at the home of Donald Gunn, the historian, at Little Britain. Roderick Sutherland was one of those who left the country and went to Oregon with James Sinclair, in 1841."

612   Gunn: "Also known locally in those days as "Davie's Pines." The reference is to a large tract of coniferous timber, where cedar was plentiful, lying to the south of what is known as Beausejour, about 35 miles east of Winnipeg."

613   Punk, or tinder, used to start fires after being itself ignited by sparks from a flint struck by steel.

Portents of Spring

March 6, 1846 – Friday. Quite a smart shower of rain today, and a beautiful rainbow after it.

March 7, 1846 – Saturday. The snow begins to flow down into running liquid.

March 9, 1846 – Monday. Started again to the Cedars with Charles and Gavin, and encamped near the Second Pines.[614]

March 10, 1846 – Tuesday. Reached the Cedars by sunrise, and, after breakfast, carried 70 cedar logs to our sledges. We returned to our last night's encampment by 8 or 9 o'clock. Mango, the Indian, told us that he heard thunder on the 5th. {301}

March 11, 1846 – Wednesday. We reached home by 8 o'clock. A very large part of the road from the Devil's Creek[615] to the Red River was entirely bare. One of our oxen was entirely fagged, and we were under the necessity of leaving twenty of our logs on the way.

Hawks and other summer birds were seen in abundance the last two or three days.

March 12, 1846 – Thursday. Some of the late Old Gentleman [Cook]'s property was divided among the surviving children this day by Mr. Christie. I am told they received £6 each.[616]

March 13, 1846 – Friday. Samuel Cook's[617] wife was delivered of a child this morning. I went off for five loads of hay this morning with Gavin and William, and they both went with three frames in the afternoon for a second trip.

---

614 Gunn: "Called also, locally Anderson's Pines: a tract of spruce woods lying at the foot, and on the west side of the range of gravel hills, to the northeast of Winnipeg, of which Bird's Hill is a part. Those particular "pines" (so called) or spruce woods, were in St. Andrews parish, east of the Red River, back of what was known as Lambert's Point."

615 Gunn: "A small stream heading near Cloverleaf Station, on the Molson Cutoff of the C. P. Railway, and flowing north by west into the Red River about six miles from Lake Winnipeg. It traverses a marshy country for most of its length, passing about six miles to the east of East Selkirk."

616 Garrioch's mother was one of the beneficiaries: see entry for March 17. The £6 figure mentioned was either a small interim payment or an erroneous reference to £600, since the March 17 entry indicates that Mrs. Garrioch's share was a "few hundred pounds."

617 Gunn: "Another son of W. H. Cook; see entry for February 23 [and endnote 392]. Samuel Cook inherited the old homestead, and lived there, [keeping a general store], during his life."

Chapter 8 – Traveling Again as Unrest Grows at Red River 301

March 16, 1846 – Monday. I cut sixty rails and gathered them, and about twenty fencing posts.

March 17, 1846 – Tuesday. I went up on horseback by land[618] to James Sinclair's. The roads were much better than I expected to find them.

Mother's Extravagance

I have been greatly annoyed this evening on account of my mother's conduct in laying out the money she received on the 12th[619] without even consulting my opinion. Poor old woman, however, I suppose she knows no better. She thinks, no doubt, that her few hund{302}red pounds will enable her to indulge in extravagance during the probable period of her life, and [is] perhaps not so much concerned about those that might live after her. God forgive me, if I judge uncharitably of my mother. For she does not appear even to dream of the possibility of her riches making to themselves wings and flying away.

March 18, 1846 – Wednesday. It blew from the north all day – a very strong and cold wind. After twelve it commenced to snow, blow and drift in a most furious manner, and it continued so to the moment of writing. We cleaned nearly forty bushels of wheat this day ready for the mill.

March 20, 1846 – Friday. The severity of the weather has somewhat abated, and the comparatively serene sky prognosticates more bright and clement days.

March 21, 1846 – Saturday. The English Packet[620] was taken up today to Fort Garry by Francis Muzena.

March 22, 1846 – Sunday. Old Mr. Pruden[621] came into the Middle Church with his usual gait and manner of lordly consequence.

---

618   Gunn: "Ordinarily, the main winter road of the Settlement was on the ice on the rivers."

619   See entry for March 12. "Laying out the money" seems to mean either dividing her legacy among others or spending it on things she could not otherwise afford.

620   Gunn: "The same, probably, as the Norway House Packet, which brought the mail from Hudson Bay, arriving in the Settlement usually about the end of February." See the entries for February 27 & March 2, 1845, for more about the Norway House Packet.

621   Gunn: "Chief Factor John Peter Pruden of the Hudson's Bay Company; progenitor of the numerous families of that name now resident in various parts of Manitoba. He came to the Hudson Bay regions, from England, at an early date; afterwards settling in Red River Settlement. He lived

Imminent War

March 23, 1846 – Monday. I was informed today that the, or a, packet from Canada[622] arrived yesterday or the day before. The news the pack{303}et brings is important. War is likely to be declared between England and the United States of America. The cause is, I believe, still the Columbia [Oregon] boundary line. God only knows where these childish squabbles about lines in a country of almost infinite space will end.

Trifles

March 25, 1846 – Wednesday. My mind was so much occupied about trifles that I do not remember anything of importance transpiring today.

March 26, 1846 – Thursday. The late Old Gentleman's [Cook's] household furniture, farming implements, &c., &c., were distributed this day among his most avaricious and ungrateful children.

March 28, 1846 – Saturday. We cleaned about fifteen bushels of wheat.

March 29, 1846 – Sunday. A great deal of talk today about war between England and the United States of America. Report says that the Americans have challenged the English.[623]

March 30, 1846 – Monday. Heard today that some Indians or Half Breeds were killed by the Sioux out at the Turtle Mountain.

Heard also that the Reverend Mr. Smithurst, in consequence of the impending war, was tremb{304}ling in his breeches for fear, and talked of fleeing down to Lake Winnipeg.

---

on the west bank of the Red River in Kildonan parish, near Matheson Avenue. He subsequently returned to England, and died there."

622   Gunn: "In those days, to the people of the Red River Settlement, 'Canada' meant [Upper and/or Lower Canada, now known as] Ontario [and/]or Quebec; and with this distant country communication was infrequent and precarious. Apart from transportation by sea via Hudson Bay, which was not available at all in winter, there was an overland route from Montreal by canoe or snowshoe; but only one such trek was normally made to Red River and back in winter." Gunn's note goes on, however, to suggest that this might have been a special "express" packet due to "some special purpose" – such as urgent news of impending war would have been accorded.

623   Gunn: "This was what the American jingo cry of that time, 'Fifty-four forty or fight!' sounded like, when it reached the Red River."

Chapter 8 – Traveling Again as Unrest Grows at Red River

March 31, 1846 – Tuesday. Mr. James Sinclair called today and told me that his letters, and likewise Mr. McDermot's, from England, were detained, they know not where.

Interference by the HBC, which operated the mail service, may well have been suspected.

First geese seen to-day.

April 1, 1846 – Wednesday. Gavin went up for ammunition at the Fort but could get no powder. He brings word that Frederick had some forty to sixty robes and some wolf skins when Thomas McDermot last saw him at the Mouse [Souris] River.

April 2, 1846 – Thursday. It rained all day and all last night.

April 3, 1846 – Friday. It continued to rain all last night, and until twelve today. It blew a strong south wind in the afternoon, and the sky became clear. I winnowed about fifteen bushels of barley.

April 4, 1846 – Saturday. As I am writing this on Monday I do not remember what transpired on Saturday. Alas! it must follow the rest. Surely time ought always to be employed to advantage.

April 6, 1846 – Monday. The wind has again got round to its favourite quarter, the old north. It commenced to snow and drift immediately after breakfast, and it continues so to this moment, which is bedtime.

Earthquake at Turtle Mountain?

April 7, 1846 – Tuesday. I was informed this day that the Turtle Mountain has been rent in twain. From what cause it is not stated. The report is from an Indian of that quarter, and therefore I cannot put overmuch confidence in it. He further stated, I am informed, that the rent in the Mountain had entirely choked up the Mouse [Souris] River. If that is the case, the great body of water which that little river disgorges into the Assiniboine every spring must overrun a large space of country and form itself into a lake of no diminutive size, before {305} it can again get round so as to communicate with its former channel.[624]

---

624 Gunn, in a handwritten insertion in the text on p. 305: "Simply a wild rumour."

Home Life

April 8, 1846 – Wednesday. Weather rather milder than the two preceding days, and the wind begins to wear round to the south. The boys took forty bushels of wheat to the mill and brought home from it from twelve to sixteen bushels of flour.[625]

April 9, 1846 – Thursday. I rode up to Sinclair's in a cariole by land. A great deal of the road is covered over with ice in consequence of the late rains and subsequent frosts. I purchased five pounds of [gun]powder from McDermot, and paid him two shillings a pound for it.

April 10, 1846 – Friday. This being Good Friday, of course, I was at church – at the Lower Church moreover.[626]

April 11, 1846 – Saturday. Some more snow today and cold north wind.

April 12, 1846 – Sunday. The Lord's Supper was administered at the Upper Church. I did not join in the communion, from a conviction of my utter unworthiness. God grant that I may be able to join on the next occasion. Carioles went up by land in abundance.

While Garrioch's claim to have been motivated by a sense of spiritual unworthiness – not his first such admission – may have been genuine, one wonders whether he might also have been influenced by a wish to remain in the background at the church he had abandoned almost a year previously.

April 13, 1846 – Monday. Wind southerly in the morning and back to the north before sundown.

April 14, 1846 – Tuesday. Sir Isaac Newton departed this life before I had finished penning this.[627]

---

625 Gunn: "Garrioch's expression, 'from it' here, probably has reference to the mill, and not to the wheat. The amount of flour here stated was undoubtedly not all that was obtained from that quantity of grain. It was quite a common practice at that time, in taking a grist as large as this to mills of the kind then in use, whose grinding capacity was small, to have a portion ground for immediate use, the remainder to be delivered later."

626 Since ceasing to attend the Upper Church the previous May (see notes to entries for May 4 & May 18), Garrioch had usually attended the Middle Church. The word "moreover" probably refers to the extra effort involved in traveling to the Lower Church on this occasion.

627 Gunn's note to this is a handwritten insert: "Don't know what to make of this. Sir Isaac Newton died March 20, 1727." Perhaps it was Peter's way of saying that it had taken him an interminable

Chapter 8 – Traveling Again as Unrest Grows at Red River

April 15, 1846 – Wednesday. The geese have again made their appearance, being driven northward by a strong south wind. {306}

April 16, 1846 – Thursday. A day of wonderful absurdities, hogs eating young lambs, hens eating their own eggs, and stormy fevers raging!

April 18, 1846 – Saturday. This morning Joe Bird's wife died.

A Poor Shoot

April 20, 1846 – Monday. William Gaddy, Charles Heyet, Gavin and I went out to the Shoal Lake to have some [shooting] sport.

April 21, 1846 – Tuesday. We found James Sinclair at the lake. I fired about twenty shots, and not a feather for my trouble.

About this time the river broke up opposite Orkney Cottage.

April 22-23, 1846 – Wednesday and Thursday. I fired about thirty more shots and only one disputed goose and another dead one for all my waste and trouble.

April 24, 1846 – Friday. I and Gavin returned home. My whole hunt was two geese and a common pheasant; and Gavin's, two geese, thirteen ducks and a gull. James Sinclair and his son killed forty-five ducks, nine geese, one swan, one crane and two rabbits.

Family Responsibilities Renounced

This day I discontinued family worship, from various reasons. How far I may be justified or condemned in the sight of Him from whom no secret is hid I know not. To err is mortal; and, if I have done wrong, I earnestly beg for forgiveness, and to be conducted safely in the path of virtue and piety through the remaining part of my earthly pilgrimage.

This must have been a momentous decision for the devout former student of theology. While one of the "various reasons" to which he attributes the decision may have been the feeling of personal "unworthiness" to which he alluded in his April 12 entry, it is probable that he was encountering resistance to the daily devotions – or to his method of conducting them – by at least some family members.

---

time to catch up on his diary writing. If so, it suggests that he wrote this and neighboring entries at a quite later date.

The next day's entry reveals that merely abandoning family worship would not be sufficient to deal with Peter's leadership problems. It also discloses that more than family members were aware of the situation.

April 25, 1846 – Saturday. I have been sadly annoyed, the last two or {307} three days, by rumours which have been maliciously circulated through the Settlement respecting our family affairs. It was said that I was squandering my mother's property, and that I was attempting to rob her of her money bequeathed to her by her late father. Also that the place was going to rack ever since I took charge. It is my intention therefore, if matters cannot be arranged differently, to resume my former method of acquiring a livelihood, and apply to the Missouri Company, or elsewhere, as a trader.

There had been a forewarning of this difficulty back on March 17, when Peter complained to his journal that his mother was spending her inheritance extravagantly, and "without even consulting my opinion." One suspects that this opinionated, uncompromising, man was simply not cut out to be a *pater familias* – at least not at this point in his life. Convivial though he seems to have been, he had no talent for finding the middle ground essential to resolving disputes – domestic or otherwise. His strange behaviour in regard to his sister Sally's marriage in March, 1845 attested to that. And his many absences from home to hunt or trade probably contributed to the farm's "going to rack."

Peter did return to trading and traveling – his next such adventure being one of his most dramatic – but when at home he appears to have continued exercising authority over at least his two younger brothers for a while to come.

April 26, 1846 – Sunday. A great part of the upper neighbourhood were employed in dragging driftwood to the shore this morning before going to church. Even old James Tait,[628] that ought to know better, was among them.

April 27, 1846 – Monday. I commenced [making] a goldeye net[629] – a thing I never did before, and did it at this time without any aid.

April 29, 1846 – Wednesday. I received this day two pounds four shillings of outstanding debts. Yesterday I clipped my whiskers, and Henry and Sam [Cook] commenced their ploughing.

---

628   Gunn: "A pioneer resident of Red River Settlement, a native of Orkney. There were three brothers, William, John and James. The latter, who was a tailor by trade, lived on the west side of the Red River near Middlechurch: Lot 18, St. Paul. He established a private boarding school for boys and girls at that place, which he conducted for some time."

629   A net for catching goldeye fish.

Chapter 8 – Traveling Again as Unrest Grows at Red River

May 2, 1846 – Saturday. We commenced ploughing this morning, and Gavin sowed two bushels wheat.

James Sinclair came up and proposed taking up his fur to Kittson's. Henry and I made up our minds to do the same.

Garrioch made only a few discreet references in this part of his diary to the fur-smuggling adventure on which he was embarking and which is set out in detail in Chapter 9. Some time later, however, he wrote a much fuller, franker, free-standing account of the episode, which he called "The Pleasures of Smuggling," possibly with separate publication in mind. That account will be found, interwoven at chronologically appropriate points with the regular journal entries, in Chapter 9. That chapter opens with the conclusion of the May 2, 1846, diary entry.

Chapter 9

The Pleasures of Smuggling & Family Pressures

1846 - 1847

Secret Preparations

{307} **May 2, 1846 – Saturday** [entry repeated from Chapter 8] James Sinclair came up and proposed taking up his fur to Kittson's. Henry and I made up our minds to do the same.

This was the inception of a clandestine fur-smuggling adventure,[630] about which Peter Garrioch made only a few cautious references in the regular part of his diary. Norman W. Kittson[631] was an American fur trader.

May 3, 1846 – Sunday. This and the last two days have been excessively {308} warm. Mr. Cochran's text [at church] was, "In your patience possess ye your souls."

---

630 Peter's nephew, the Reverend A. C. Garrioch, described this journey succinctly, but with far less colour than Peter himself did: "…as a young man he [Peter] took the stand that the Hudson's Bay Company were not morally entitled to a monopoly of the fur trade, and that they had shown themselves inefficient in their management of the civil affairs of the country. He lived up to his opinions, and on one occasion, he and some others who had some furs to dispose of, resolved that they were to be sold in the neighboring republic where they would command a better price. Organizing a party at Middle Church they loaded their furs on packsaddles and making a wide detour west of Fort Garry, they struck the Assiniboine west of Sturgeon Creek. There they constructed a raw-hide boat with which they made a hazardous crossing of the river. Thence they made all haste to the domains of Uncle Sam, where they disposed of their furs to some American traders at a paying figure." *First Furrows*, pp. 118-119.

631 See Chap. 7, entries for April 24 & 28, 1845, & Chap. 8, entries for January 26 & February 19, 1846, & n. 498. Despite his friendly relations with Peter Garrioch, Kittson did not tolerate competition on his home turf very well, as the entry for February 19, 1846, confirms.

Chapter 9 – The Pleasures of Smuggling & Family Pressures

May 4, 1846 – Monday. Another very warm day. Gavin sowed three more bushels of wheat. I have to start this night at 9 o'clock.

What Peter had to start that evening – and did – was the smuggling project referred to in the May 2nd entry. And while the day-to-day diary entries continued to say little about the caper, he wrote – some time later – a much fuller free-standing retrospective account of it, which he called "The Pleasures of Smuggling," or, with full title: "Seven Days' Experience or the Pleasures of Smuggling, Being the Account of a Fur-Smuggling Expedition of the Free Traders to Pembina, in which the Author took Part, in 1846,"[632] quite possibly with separate publication in mind. That account has been inserted at appropriate points into this concluding portion of Peter's diary, generally tracking concurrent dates. The "Pleasures of Smuggling" interpolations are enclosed by double brackets: ([[ ]]).

Responding to the Rapacious Designs of the HBC

[[{325}[633] About the beginning of April, reports began to be circulated from one end of the Settlement to the other respecting the measures, it was said, the Hudson's Bay Company were about to take in order to prevent the smugglers of fur [free traders] from carrying away to the States such peltries as were in their possession.

[[Apprehending serious consequences [from what] the Company were contemplating, we who had freely indulged in the common right of all men, receiving nothing but what we returned value for, began now to set our wits to work, to frustrate the designs of that company against us, and to secure our trade, without exposing ourselves or any other party to the results of oppression. Various measures were proposed by our party as to what might be the most expeditious method that could be adopted for the transportation of our trade, and for its final security against the rapacious designs of the H.B.C.

[[Mr. James Sinclair, whose superior abilities and circumstances necessarily commanded our confidence, stiffly contended for the opposite [east] side of the main river as being the best adapted [route] for our purpose. But, after learning the usual state of that part of the country in general at {326} that season of the year, he yielded

---

632   Gunn, pp. 325-364, transcribed it as a stand-alone document following the dated diary entries, in contrast to the approach of the current editors who have interwoven the "Smuggling" document entries chronologically into their diary counterparts. Peter refers later in his diaries to writing it: entry for February 22, 1847.

633   Since the extracts from "Pleasures of Smuggling" are taken from a different part of the Gunn typescript (pp. 325-364) than the diary entries in the rest of this chapter, the pagination is different from that of Gunn's diary typescript.

to our suggestion of preferring the west side as being the most practicable for horses to travel through, and as being equally fitted for clandestine traveling.

[[Having arrived at last at a mutual understanding respecting our route, the day – or rather night – of our departure was settled, and every moment, forthwith, groaned under the silence of our adventurous preparations. As the utmost caution was necessary to prevent every suspicion respecting our future intentions, nearly all our movements to accomplish our purposes had to be carried on during the dead of night.

A Shaky Start

[[On the night appointed, we were to leave Mr. Sinclair's[634] precisely at twelve. We were to proceed directly up the Assiniboine towards the Old Crossing Place,[635] where we were to cross the river, and be beyond the public road which leads towards the hunting grounds[636] by break of day. Unfortunately, however, matters had not been so well managed by Mr. Sinclair's confidants as they might have been, the consequence being that we were within a hair's breadth of being detected.

[[Sinclair had a man to bring up to Henry Cook's place[637] by 9 o'clock what furs and peltries were below[638] but, by some mismanagement on the part of the messenger the carrier did not make {327} appearance at Cook's till near twelve. This was the hour appointed for our onset from Sinclair's, which was still nine miles from there. The

---

634 Sinclair's property was on the west bank of the Red River close to the heart of what would later become the town of Winnipeg. A modern historical plaque at the bottom of McDermot Avenue has marked its location.

635 Gunn: "On the Cameron homestead, about a mile below the present Headingly." See Murray Peterson & Georgia Anderson Taillieu, *Headingley: Pioneers, Past and Present* (Headingley Historical Society, n.d.), pp. 114-115. This is one of a network of trails across the rivers heading west; this one was probably near where the Anglican Church of Headingly once stood. For a near-contemporary map of the area showing the crossing near Camerons' and the church and school, see John Arrowsmith, Map of part of the Valley of Red River North of the 49th Parallel to accompany a report on the Canadian Red River Exploring Expedition by H.Y. Hind. Hind, *Papers Relative to the Exploration of the Country Between Lake Superior and the Red Rivers Settlement* (London: Eyre and Spottiswoode, 1859), I, pp. 253 & 440.

636 Gunn: "The old trail leading from Fort Garry, by way of Headingly, Starbuck, Carman, etc., to the plains of [the present] North Dakota."

637 Gunn: "The Cook homestead in St. Paul's parish is meant. Henry Cook did not settle on the Assiniboine until later."

638 North of the Cook property. James Sinclair must have had a hidden stash of furs downriver from his own property.

Chapter 9 – The Pleasures of Smuggling & Family Pressures

old man that brought up the furs thought it better to wait till his neighborhood at last was quiet, as the least movement of his in a canoe after sundown would be very apt to produce questions. He brought all safe, however, after paddling a distance of six miles.

[[The old man gasped for breath as he entered, with streams of sweat & dirt running along his furrowed cheeks (for he was a blacksmith by trade, and only happened to put the wrong iron in the fire when he came among us), his beautiful locks of gray, [being in disarray,] presenting certain indications of guilt and dread. The expression of the old man's first appearance plainly indicated a strong conviction that nature had strangely erred in having placed but two eyes in his head.

[[When everything had been satisfactorily explained by the old man, we settled our horses and slung our hard coverings [earnings] over them. And, having lashed them on as well as we could and with all possible expedition, I and Cook sprang each on his horse, and away we went.

[[We had proceeded but a few hundred yards, however, when Cook's load tumbled from the back of his horse, and this right by a bridge upon the public road. It would not do in such a place, of course, to make any delay. Seeing, therefore, that it was impossible for us to proceed with any expedition with such an unmanageable mountain on the back of his horse, we concluded to retrace our steps, and put one of {328} the horses in a cart.[639]

What a Fix for a Poor Fellow!

[[We then made a second start, and fortune appeared to smile on our designs till we came to the next creek. Here the great part of the bridge had been lately washed away by a flush of the Spring's dissolving snow and, there being no alternative, we were under the necessity of plunging into the stream, which we did in a part we considered most practical to gain the opposite bank without damage. But just as the horse in the cart had gained footing on the opposite shore, one of the wheels unfortunately came in contact with a slight projection of the bank, which very quickly placed it in a zenith position in relation to its neighbour. Away went the beavers, the martens and the coons!

---

639   That is, harness a horse to a cart, and load the furs into the cart.

[['Necessity is the mother of invention.' Cook sprang into the stream the moment his cart inclined to an inverted position, and while detaining what was still in it with one hand, holding it up in the meantime with the other, he stood on one leg in the water, and threw out the other behind him to interrupt a most valuable pack which the force of the current had already drawn away from the cart. Just imagine the position of the poor smuggler. What a fix for a poor fellow to be in!!

[[We got everything again into the cart, however, without sustaining any other damage than getting a little wet [that] which had tumbled into the creek. We arrived at Mr. Sinclair's by three o'clock in the morning, suffering no other inconvenience than that we were at least three hours behind the time we had settled upon.

The Dark & Stillness of the Night

[[It is remarkable that whatever a man does which he studiously endeavours to prosecute in the dark and stillness of the night, in order to prevent detection, notwithstanding his designs and principles {329} of action may be ever so honest, there is always a kind of inward dread which fills him with an increasing apprehension of guilt, though he entertains not the least doubt of the lawfulness and equity of his conduct.

[[Then within a few hundred yards of Mr. Sinclair's premises, I observed two persons a rod or two before me, within a step or two of the public road. Not being able, however, to form any judgment concerning the parties, and deeming it rather curious that men of apparently not the lower order (which I judged from the whiteness of their dress) should be loitering at that unreasonable hour of the night about the public road, I proceeded as coolly and as regardless of their presence as the nature of the occasion and place would allow me. For I certainly did not suspect the men to be other than some of the Fort Garry clerks or constables who had been appointed by the H.B.C. to keep a nightly and constant watch near about Mr. Sinclair's till every prospect of their being able to seize our furs was annihilated.

[[To my unspeakable pleasure, however, it was none other than Mr. Sinclair and his man[640] who was to accompany Cook and me to the Pembina.

[[Finding that Sinclair was not altogether ready, we stowed our horses and pack the best way we could, and as stealthily as possible, in and about the stables. Upon entering his house, Mr. Sinclair told us that the folks at Fort Garry were keeping a

---

640   John Monkman. See the first paragraph of the entry for May 8, 1846, and Gunn, p. 309.

Chapter 9 – The Pleasures of Smuggling & Family Pressures   313

close and strict watch over all our movements. At that very moment, he said, which was then about 3 o'clock of the morning, they had a watch or two constantly passing and repassing between the Fort and Mr. McDermot's premises, a few {330} hundred yards from his.[641] Our conjectures were as various as we afterward discovered they were absurd respecting the unflinching determination of the H.B.C.]]

Overtaken by Daylight

{308} May 6, 1846 – Wednesday. Daylight overtook us before we could leave James Sinclair's, so that we were obliged to fly to the Little Hill.[642]

[[While thus musing, planning and conjecturing, with the greatest attention to any sound above a whisper, and to any motion from the movement of a flash of lightening to that of a snail, Sinclair's man came in and told us, almost breathless, that the day was already making its appearance above the eastern horizon. This intelligence came like a clap of thunder among us, and came well-nigh petrifying our wits for the time.

[[Instant decision and promptitude of action was all that could now save us from detection. Not a moment could be lost. A council was called, but one suggested one thing, and another, another. Consternation, however, [was] speedily assuage[d], and, in a moment, the whole instantaneously and unanimously moved and adopted a precipitate start.

[[By the time we had proceeded about a mile, the light of day had so far advanced that we could easily see the north gate of Fort Garry. But the good folks within were doubtless at that time too well satisfied with the exquisite sweets of a little before-sunrise slumber to trouble themselves about other men's matters. For who has not experienced the pleasure of a morning's nap about the first of May! As for the poor fellows at the gates, I suppose, if someone had gone to tell them of our proceedings, they would have thanked him for inviting them to breakfast. As the watch were Canadians, their appetites, at that hour of the morning, must have been so keen, and their half dozing nerves in such a condition, that, had we been pointed out to them, they would have taken us to be bales of meat and {331} bags of pemmican.

---

641   Sinclair's biographer tells us that his house was "situated between the dwellings of Alexander Ross and Andrew McDermot, near the gates of Upper Fort Garry." Lent, *West of the Mountains*, pp. 199-200.

642   Gunn: "A small rising on the prairie a few miles northwest of the then Ft. Garry, now Winnipeg, now known as Little Mountain [Park]."

[[As the rapid approach of day required us to be as expeditious as possible in gaining some point at which we could suspend our traveling till the convenience of night should again afford us opportunity to proceed, we diverted our course for the Little Mountain in all haste, so as to get beyond the reach of either natural or artificial detectors as speedily as possible. Our horses, when we arrived there, were as if they had been taken out of an Indian sweating house.

Sanctuary at Little Mountain

[[Here we felt pretty safe, being now at least four or five miles from the Settlement. Having very carefully selected a summit on the hill which, from the shrubbery with which it was thickly surrounded, was well adapted for the purpose of concealment and which gave us the advantage also of commanding every prospect in the direction from which only we could apprehend any danger, we unsaddled our horses, and each one made such disposition of his pack as best suited his ideas.

[[We were, as we afterwards learned from experience, in a very critical situation, [and] it [was only from] very strong and urgent appeals from our stomachs that we were finally induced to kindle a fire and put on our kettle. That is what almost ruined us: yielding to the cravings of our bellies rather than to the premonitions of our judgment.

Discovered!

[[We had not been long in our pleasant situation, as we deemed it, when, upon our constant lookout, we espied an object in the form of a rider advancing towards the hill.

[[We are of course lost no time in {332} removing everything from our hut[643] that would lead to a suspicion of our intentions. One took hold of his pack, another of his saddle, and a third of his kettle. But this confusion was but momentary, and everyone, collecting his scattered senses, took up his packs of furs, carried them a few hundred yards from the hut, and concealed them around the brush and falling timber by which we were nearly surrounded.

---

643 At earlier points in the diaries, the term "hut" appears to refer to a transient shelter, little better than a tent in today's parlance. See Chap. 2, entry for June 21, 1837; Chap. 6, entries for October 5, 19 & 22, November 7, 1844; & Chap. 8, entry for January 6, 1846.

Chapter 9 – The Pleasures of Smuggling & Family Pressures

[[I cannot say we were pleasantly disappointed [by learning that] though no rider, it was a man on foot [Meshell Cline, who was out hunting horses [644]]. That made the matter no better. For this same fellow, as we had previously learned, had already made himself very busy in favour of the Hudson's Bay Company's interests.

[[We of course received him as civilly as we could, and with as much composure and equanimity of mind as the nature of our business afforded. But certainly, had the fellow been blessed with but the single sense of smell, he could not have possibly mistaken our trade. For as some of those packs had been opened and strewn over the ground drying, and as the wind was blowing to the spot we had selected, coming first from one point and the next moment from another, it is unaccountable [remarkable] that the man never detected the strong effluvia of the musk in the beaver and rats. In fact, we ourselves, our carts and everything else about us, must have smelt more like rats, minks and coons than anything else.

[[Indeed, had the poor fellow been blessed with the smallest possible share of the most elementary [powers of perception],[645] he could not but have instantly detected something suspicious, and would immediately have concluded himself an intruder in spite of {333} all our manoeuvres to convince him to the contrary. On the first

---

644 Gunn's note, at the diary entry for May 6, p. 308: "Properly, Michael Klyne. The family lived at that time in the neighbourhood of Point Douglas, about a mile north of Fort Garry. We find the name variously spelled. In the U. S. census of the Pembina district (1850) one Mitchel Klayne, age 31, is enumerated, together with 15 other Klaynes, all of which, with the exception of an infant of 6 months and one of one year, are put down as British and hailing from Red River. This may be the Meshell Cline of the above reference. Later, there were two Klyne brothers, George and Ada, living on the west side of the Red River near where Morris now is. George was a member of the first Manitoba Legislature for Ste. Agathe in 1870. Ada, it was said, performed the part of Executioner, in 1845, in the first case of capital punishment inflicted in Assiniboia. The Klynes were of German origin." Michel Kleyne (1781-1868) was a fur trader and interpreter, first with the NWC and then with the HBC. He opened Jasper House and was in charge of the 200-300 horses kept there. At times he was sent to other posts as required when problems arose. By 1826 he was back at Jasper House and retired from there in 1835. There is a trail along the Maligne River named for him as well as a small river called Klyne River. At Port Douglas he owned lots 22g & 227 and ran a prosperous mill and mixed farm. See "Research bares more rich history," *Winnipeg Free Press* (April 23, 1983), and "Michel Klyne," Wikipedia. The likelihood that he didn't know what Garrioch and his companions were up to is rather slim, and one suspects he chose to ignore it. On Ada Klyne serving as executioner, see above, n. 534.

645 Garrioch's phrase was "principles of physiognomy."

appearance of the man, I could read guilt on the faces of my two companions[646] as clearly as if it had been engraved on marble. They no doubt detected the same on me.

[[The question, however, was soon settled, for we knew our man. He gazed about a little while, apparently wishing, from the nature of our equipments, to ascertain the why and wherefore of our being there. To answer this question, which, although not very polite, was quite natural and customary, we were brought to the disagreeable but unavoidable necessity of learning a new trade, viz.: that of lying. We told the man that we were on our way to the Grosse Isle, which, in relation to our present position, happened to be in a direct course from our homes. This Grosse Isle[647] is the name of a lake or marshy place, which is resorted to every spring by wavies [snow geese][648] and other fowl on their way to the northern coasts.

[[This, of course, was quite apropos to our purpose. He received it like pure Gospel, and in an ecstasy of joy, congratulating himself on our mutually-contemplated sport. He exclaimed, "That's right! I and . . . . .[649] are going out tomorrow, too, and we intend to take our families with us, and . . . . . (one of his sisters – a young woman) is to bear us company. That will be a chance for you." addressing himself to me in particular.[650]

[[We, of course, in our turn, questioned him respecting his present {334} object. He told us he was on his way for his horses, which he expected to find some two or three miles west of us.

[[At the mention of this, I confess, I felt somewhat disturbed – as it was in that direction I had concealed my packs, yet not so securely but that they could be detected. However, as our kettle was on boiling, and we had already requested the stranger to stay and take pot luck with us, I made myself easy, calculating on the cravings of his belly, as we had improperly done on ours. In the meantime, in order to prevent any chance of detection on the part of the stranger's ocular and olfactory senses, we kept him almost

---

646   Henry Cook and John Monkman, according to Gunn's note (p. 333).

647   Gunn: "Groo Zele," in the manuscript – another of Garrioch's phonetic spellings of local French pronunciation. This lake or marsh was about 15 miles northwest of Winnipeg."

648   This is a handwritten, apparently Gunn's, insertion into the typescript (Gunn, p. 333).

649   Name omitted from manuscript.

650   This seems to be a reference to the fact that Peter enjoyed female company, and/or to his probably well-known search for a wife.

breathless answering our questions; at least till such time as the more grateful and inviting odours of tea and ham smothered every other.

[[When all the cravings and vacuums of nature had subsided and been fully replenished, according to the custom of the country, tobacco and pipes were produced; and, under the columns of the spreading smoke of that fragrant weed, conversation became doubly animated.

A Terrible Predicament

[[Observing some of the billets of wood on our fire presenting the appearance of wood that had been cut some time before, our intruder jocularly exclaimed: "Why, I think you have been stealing my wood!" It immediately struck me that I had seen some corded wood in the direction I had concealed my packs.

"Where is your wood?" responded two or three voices almost in the same breath.

"A little way over here," said the man, pointing towards the west and adding, "I must see it as I pass."

[[This was a terrible predicament! To think that the man we had treated with so much kindness, at least in effect if not from choice, {335} should finally be the means of exposing and betraying us was almost unbearable.

[[Not a moment could be lost. I rose from my seat, with all the composure and coolness that a crammed full belly and the threatening danger of the moment would allow. Politely excusing myself to the stranger, that I was only going away to obey a call of nature, and saying that I would be back in a few moments, I walked off with a pace quite unreserved, pretending hurried preparations for fear of being overtaken with some foul mistake, when in fact I was busy doing up again what I had undone.

[[[When I] reached a thick cluster of bushes which, soon screened me from the vision of my companions and the stranger, I increased my speed a hundred-fold. When I came to my packs, I found that they were exposed to plain view from the man's wood above alluded to. I threw them over my head and shoulders in an instant, and proceeded in all haste through bushes, brambles, and lying timber, till I reached a spot I conceived to be more secure, and entirely out of the intruder's way. I then walked back quietly to our hut, with all the composure of innocence and all the gravity of an abstruse thinker, busily employed at the same time, of course, in doing up what the [bogus] call of nature had urged me to undo.

The Inestimable Benefits of Feeding Our Enemy

[[I resumed my seat at the hut by the side of the man I so much dreaded and, having joined the "sons of smoke" with a pipe in my cheek, we made ourselves merry at his expense. The poor fellow joined heartily in our merriment and various quaint phrases, supposing that our merriment was excited by his smart {336} sayings and pithy anecdotes. Our subjects were as various as they were foreign to our present pursuit. One congratulated himself on the pleasant prospect of enjoying the company of a worthy and respected young lady from some days together. Another was very curious and eager to learn the exact situation and appearance of the lake, the quantity of fowl that generally resort to it, and the best way of decoying them. The third, with gestures that gave expression to his words, confidently assured the stranger that he, the third person, was a first rate sportsman, and that we should all eat our fill of fowl ere the sun of the morrow set. We parted, for the present with the last question and answer: "When shall we expect to see you at the lake?" and "To-morrow, about noon!"

[[Poor fellow! That tomorrow never came. We never saw him at the lake. And, I am very certain, they have not yet seen us there.

[[As the man had said, so he did. He went straight out by his wood. Not that he really suspected us of having taken any, for there was abundance about us without going so far out of our way, but to see if none of it had been taken away by those who might have been hauling wood from the same place the preceding winter. If I ever had reason to bless my stars for having treated an intruder with apparent pleasure and becoming civility, it was on this occasion. For, had we yielded to the impulse of the first moment, and paid no attention to the man that we could have wished a thousand miles from us, he probably would have taken a hint from our coldness and have walked on direct to his wood, as he afterwards did, and have come right upon my packs. This, of course, would have disclosed us all, and have de{337}feated our whole plan. This itself ought to teach men what inestimable benefits may be reaped from the feeding of one who is hungry, even though he be our enemy.]]

Chapter 9 – The Pleasures of Smuggling & Family Pressures

Moving On

{308} **May 6, 1846 – Wednesday** We proceeded towards the head of the Sturgeon Creek,[651] when Sinclair came to us a little before sundown.

[[{337} As soon as we had managed to get rid of our companion, as he conceived himself, we lost no time in collecting all our effects, lest we should be again annoyed by some other intruder, and proceeded in a direction which would convince our late visitor, should he chance to see us on the march, that we were really going, as we had said, to the Grosse Isle.

[[As we had to cross the Sturgeon Creek on our expedition, which at this season of the year, is very deep, and only certain parts of it fordable, we had taken the necessary precaution of making ourselves acquainted with the source and various branches of the stream, by the instructions of our friend [the intruder]. He himself had been very particular in reminding us that, if we intended to go only to Grosse Isle, it would be better for us to cross the Sturgeon Creek. This he gave for two reasons: first, the country lying on the other side was much drier at that season of the year; and second [that] the south side of Lake Grosse Isle was generally more resorted to by wavies [snow geese] than the north, on account of its being better adapted for their safety, and affording them a greater range of marshy country for feeding upon. After these particular instructions, our traveling towards a point which was in perfect unison with our feelings and wishes would not in the least arouse the suspicions of the man with regard to the correctness of our previous statements to him. This was certainly, as the Frenchman would say, apropos, and extremely favour{338}able to our designs. Aided with such particular instructions, [we] found but little difficulty in fording the above creek.

Another Intruder?

[[We had not gone, however, more than a mile or so after crossing the creek when, on looking back, we detected an object which appeared to be one on horseback, and apparently right on the trail we had left behind us. This, of course, urged us to double our speed; so that, if what we perceived with eagle eye should prove to be what we constantly expected – a hireling of Fort Garry – we might be enabled to reach a point

---

651 Gunn: "A small stream joining the Assiniboine River from the northwest in the parish of St. James, about six miles above its junction with the Red."

which would at least afford us an ambush for detecting the reality or mere fancy of our apprehensions.

[[Mr. Sinclair, previous to our leaving, had told us that should the aspect of things be tranquil as usual when the hour of business had been ushered upon the Fort Garry folks, he would ride out to The Hill to see us, and to hold 'a bit of a council with us.' This, of course, would naturally buoy up our expectations at times, and would for a moment relieve us of our apprehensions. But the apparent furious driving and superior speed of our pursuer – for the object became so rapidly more and more distinct that we were satisfied he was a rider – could not but lead us to suspect the nature of the embassy.

"It is Mr. Sinclair"

[[No sooner had we reached our much-desired retreat than we eagerly and cautiously brought all – man, beasts, carts and packs – to a point in the heart of the little forest that would, in case of necessity, enable us to dispose of and secrete what was most valuable. While thus hastily engaged in endeavouring to secure what we had acquired in midst of so many sacrifices, one of my companions who was on the look-out suddenly cried out, "It is Mr. Sinclair." On the sound of {339} this pleasing intelligence, our operations were immediately suspended. And, after Mr. Sinclair had assured us that we had not the least reason to be under any apprehension as to the Company's being privy to our proceedings, we made instant preparations for a repast.]]

{306} **May 6, 1846 – Wednesday [continued]** We left there at dusk and proceeded to the Assiniboine River, where we crossed our baggage at midnight.

An Oilcloth Boat

[[{339} While some were making ready something for the belly, the rest were busily engaged in contriving a craft of some sort, which might enable us to cross such rivers, on our way to Pembina, as were not fordable. We speedily constructed one after the fashion of the buffalo-hide canoes made and used by the Rees and Grosventres on the Missouri, or, which will be better understood, a canoe without any end (not everlasting but having the shape of a common washing tub). This we effected by binding a number of willows, brought to lie crosswise on each other about a foot apart, by drawing up the projecting ends in the form of the stern of a craft and enveloping it in an oilcloth or boat covering.

Chapter 9 – The Pleasures of Smuggling & Family Pressures 321

[[When our craft had been constructed and our repast completed, we replaced our effects in the cart and impatiently waited for the approach of the gracious twilight; for the majestic sun, as if favourable to our designs, had withdrawn its last dimpling effulgence behind the horizon just as our masticating operations were coming to a close.

[[As we had been driven to the necessity of resorting to this spot for the purpose of evading contact with travelers on the public road between the upper and lower settlements[652] on the Assiniboine, we now had to retrace our steps, in order to cross the Sturgeon Creek again where we had previously forded it. Two of our party, we concluded, {340} should go ahead and make a halt at the bridge over the Sturgeon Creek,[653] with the view of awaiting the approach of travelers and then reporting the intelligence to those who were behind with the cart, through signs already agreed upon by the party. Fortunately, however, the hour of traveling between the two settlements was already out of date; and such was the darkness of the night that detection would be very difficult, even to the most prying and acute observer. We reached and crossed the bridge without meeting with anything to molest us; and, after following the public road a few hundred yards, we veered to the left in order to reach the bank of the Assiniboine as speedily as possible and thus to conceal ourselves more effectually, by the shrubbery along the bank of the river, from the detection of any person who might be traveling on the public road, in that still hour of the night.

---

652 Gunn: "The "upper" settlement was that known as White Horse Plain, the "lower" extending along the Assiniboine just west of Fort Garry, now St. James and St. Charles." Gunn, p. 339. Father Belcourt, who had a Catholic mission in the area in the 1830s, described its history: "The parish of St. Francis Xavier, of Prairie du Cheval Blanc, [White Horse Plains,] about 18 miles from the mouth of the river Assiniboine, existed as early as 1830. This spot is the least exposed to inundation of all the surrounding country. This parish is composed of emigrants from Pembina, where there were several commercial houses, and quite a number of farmers. But when Maj. LONG, of the United States, had verified the point of the 49° degree of latitude, Pembina proving to be on the American territory, the Hudson's Bay Company caused the whole population to remove to their side, by menacing them with a refusal to let them have any supplies from their stores if they remained. Their missionary, Mr. DUMOULIN, being returned to Canada, the whole colony finished by emigrating, though very reluctantly, to Prairie du Cheval Blanc." Belcourt, "The Department of the Hudson's Bay," p. 224.

653 Gunn: "Probably where Portage Avenue, Winnipeg, now crosses that stream."

Thundering Hoofs

[[We had not proceeded far here, after we had left the public road, when suddenly a loud and sharp whistle from one of our party, from behind, grated my ever-listening ears; and that [was] accompanied with the thundering noise of horses' footsteps in the direction of the highway we had left. I immediately called upon Sinclair, who was a few yards before us, to halt. I had no sooner communicated [that] than he prepared to put spurs to his horse towards a poplar hammock before us. It was not without some expostulation on my part, both as to the impropriety of his conduct in leaving us, should danger be really at hand, to shift for ourselves, and to the impractica{341}bility of attempting an escape were we indeed discovered that he was at last induced to rein in his horse to await the issue of matters.

[[A few moments explained the whole; and, to our great satisfaction, we were most pleasantly disappointed. The thundering noise from behind which filled us with such alarming apprehensions was really the sudden rush of a band of horses after us. But they were neither saddled nor bridled and, of course, [were] without riders. Nothing but mere curiosity, it appears, was what urged them to follow us - to see who we were and what we were about.

[[Without waiting to put any questions to these fresh quadruped intruders, we marched on our course as before, examining the breadth of the river and its banks as we went along; and, having traveled some eight or ten miles further, we finally came to a point on it which we considered a favourable place for crossing.

On the Bosom of the Swift & Swollen Assiniboine

[[We therefore set to work with all possible expedition, unsaddling our horses, arranging our packs, and casting our newly-constructed barge onto the bosom of the Assiniboine. It acted in its present situation on the surface of the water admirably well; but, by the time we had laden it with but a part of our most valuable fur, we discovered, when too late, that some of the willows had lost their bend from want of sufficient cords to keep them in the bowed position. This, of course, made us somewhat apprehensive lest that side of our craft, which had assumed the shape of a tablespoon, should give admittance to the little swells of water that might be occasioned either by our paddles or the swimming of our horses by its side. Seeing, however, that there was now no remedy for the case, and that {342} the least delay on our part might occasion more serious consequences than we had yet been brought to experience, two of us concluded, at all hazards, to venture into the cranky bark, and to stem the current of the swift and deeply swollen Assiniboine.

[[We had left the shore but a very few yards when we found that steering with such a craft was quite impracticable. We therefore yielded to the impulse suggested by superior force and towed with all our might along the side of the swift-gliding stream, in order to gain the bank of the opposite side with as little loss of distance as possible.[654] Nevertheless we could not effect a landing till the stream had carried us about a quarter of a mile from the line of our march.

[[Here then we unloaded and thrust our packs into the heart of the thickets; and, starting back with our craft from this point to the shore we had left our companions, horses and the rest of our fur and baggage on, we landed a few hundred yards still lower down. From this point we had now to carry our canoe to where we first committed our frail bark to the fearful (at this season of the year) Assiniboine, a distance of not less than a third of a mile.

Daring Temerity

[[Having become somewhat bolder by [reason of] the success of our first attempt, nothing would do with him who had accompanied me, and those that remained behind, to see the fun of our upsetting, than to put everything in the canoe, for all hands to go, and to take all the horses over at the same time, in order to avoid the labour of having to make a second trip. This daring temerity, to avoid what is generally termed 'double trouble,' was well nigh the cause of all our troubles being at an end here forever; and [was] certainly as near [to] putting an everlasting full stop to our clandestine practices as anything could possibly be. {343}

Rebellion of the Horses

[[Just as we had reached the middle of the stream, the horses (we had five of them), who had become impatient by reason of the tardiness of our craft, became entangled in such a manner as to hinder each other in their swimming. Two of us, who were towing with all the sinew and marrow we could command, perceiving our dangerous

---

654 In this context the word "towed," which is repeated in the next paragraph, must mean "paddled," since that is what Garrioch and his companion, probably Henry Cook, were clearly doing. The reference to paddling furiously "along the side" of the river may mean that, having got to the other side they needed to paddle in an upstream direction in order to slow the craft sufficiently to land it.

situation, and doubtless shuddering at the very thought of a watery grave, called to the man that held the horses to let them go, as they would most assuredly upset us. But (and who would have thought of it?) "No!" cried the man in a voice of thunder, "I can't lose the horse I paid fifteen pounds for!" He had purchased the horse he alluded to but a few weeks before, for the sum of fifteen pounds sterling, and such was either his affection for the creature or his regard for the money he had given for it, that he would choose to run the risk of his life rather than forsake the object of his affections.

[[Things [then] happened much quicker than I can write them, for by this time our craft had taken in several gallons of water at a single scoop, right by my side, at that part of the canoe which had preferred the shape of a spoon. This was occasioned by the horses growing rather furious and causing one of the cords which our hostler held to come in contact with one of the projecting points of the willows with which our craft was constructed. At this moment I cried to the man, in despair, to let go the horses. But he held on harder than ever and, as if he heard me not, as mute as a stock and as dumb as a lamb to the slaughter.

[[And now when we thought all was over – just at that moment – the confusion among the {344} horses became so general and so alarming owing to one or two of them having managed to get their heads round to the tails of the rest in spite of our poor hostler, he was at length compelled to let all go, and leave them to shift for themselves. It is but justice to say of our present hostler, that he certainly was either more fearless in the midst of danger, or more regardless of his life and future consequences, than the rest of the crew.

[Despite] our apprehensions and [our] truly critical situation, we providentially reached the shore in safety.

[[The horses, however, having gained their liberty, preferred returning to the shore they had left, after being within a very few yards of that for which we had laboured so hard. We were again under the provoking necessity of going back on account of our horses. We therefore made again for the side of the river they were on, after having deposited all our packs and baggage among the brush; and, having maligned our highly serviceable craft and shackled all our horses, we concluded to spend the night there.

[[Here Mr. Sinclair left us and returned home.]]

Chapter 9 – The Pleasures of Smuggling & Family Pressures

Breakfast with Mrs. Wells

{308} **May 6, 1846** – Wednesday [continued] [We] went up this morning to John Wells' place[655] and crossed ourselves and horses.

[[{344} We were now again in a most dangerous situation, should we happen to slumber too long the following morning. For we were within two or three miles of the commencement of the Upper Settlement[656] and not more than a hundred yards or so from a public road, which was very often preferred by these settlers on their way to and from the Settlement below. It would have been somewhat difficult for us to have answered any questions that might be asked, had we been surprised {345} in our beds, respecting our object and motives in spending the night in such an out-of-the-way place.

[[The morning came, however, without any of these unwelcome circumstances which we constantly dreaded, and which we were ever so studious to avoid. We therefore made as little delay as possible, in order to get into the public road as early as practicable, so as to prevent any suspicions on the part of travelers, should we happen to fall in with any before we reached any point on the lower part of the Upper Settlement. Here again fortune seemed to smile on our harmless designs; for we proceeded on this road without the disagreeable occurrence of hearing, seeing or falling in with any mortal man till we had succeeded in reaching one of the principal public roads.

[[Here we saw a man, apparently on his way home from a visit to the Settlement below. Observing [that] four of our horses had saddles without riders on them, he increased his speed, probably to ascertain who we were and to learn something of our business, and, as a compliment, to offer his services in occupying one of our horses, which gave us so much trouble in leading. Preferring any trouble, however, {346} to the unpleasant necessity of again having recourse to wilful lying, we gave him to understand that his politeness was neither required nor appreciated, by applying the lash to our horses and leaving him to muse and comment on our bad manners.

[[The first house we ventured to set foot in was [that of] John Wells. The man was not home, but his wife was. She could not account for our being so early there, as the

---

655 Gunn: "An English Métis who lived on the north bank of the Assiniboine in the White Horse Plains settlement, six miles west of the present Headingly. The family subsequently moved to the Saskatchewan country."

656 Gunn: "Now St. Francois Xavier."

distance from our homes was, at the very least calculation, twenty-four miles; and, she being well informed as to the number and situations of our friends and acquaintances below, could form a pretty good idea of the distance we would have had to travel, had we spent the night even at the nearest point among these.

[[But here again was something in our favour. The season had arrived when the fowl of the more southerly climates usually flock to these northerly regions, and when the half-starved and half-frozen part of our settlers, invigorated and cheered by the prospect, annually rally to the rendezvous of these fowl, by groups and by parties, urged by the stimulus of hunger or from an inclination towards sportive relaxation. As therefore everything about us strongly indicated our intentions to be in reality what we represented them to be on the first questions ("What is your object, and what point are you bound for?"), we found our present situation comparatively easy and perfectly secure for the time being. We told the woman of the house that we were on our way to Rivière Isle de Bois,[657] for the express purpose and in the character of sportsmen. We then made some enquiries as to our probable success, both {347} as to our being able to cross the river at her place and the prospect of game before us.

"Oh yes," she said, "I think you can; for there is a man on the opposite side that has a canoe; and, if you only call to him, he will assist you. He is a very obliging man. Ducks and geese," she continued, "I believe are very numerous, and the wavies are already beginning to come."

[[One of my companions now got up and handed a parcel with some tea and sugar, bread and butter, to the woman to prepare breakfast for us. She immediately commenced operations; and, while the parcel was still in her hand, (for the women of this country are excessively fond of tea), made a most eloquent speech on the virtues of that gracious plant; and expressed her sincere regret that her husband was not at home, who would have rendered us every assistance in his power; and all this nearly in the same breath. The peculiarly inviting fumes exuded by this most virtuous of all plants, at least in the estimation of my country-women, speedily produced in our kind hostess a variety of subjects, but almost always ending with tea!!, making them as amusing to us as they were uninteresting.

[[When we had appeased the cravings of fasting stomachs, we made ready for a start. As a necessary consequence, we had promised to give our hostess a call on our return;

---

657   Gunn: "Eyil de Buaw in the original."

Chapter 9 – The Pleasures of Smuggling & Family Pressures

for, had we really gone to the river we mentioned we should, in all probability, have been obliged to come back to the same place to cross the Assiniboine. She therefore, very naturally, wished to know when we intended to return; so, as we supposed, she might reserve some of the tea and sugar we left with her, and treat {348} us with a cup of it over the greasy thigh of a wavie when we returned with the fruits of our hunts. For we had promised to treat the poor, harmless and truly kind woman with the fattest one we should kill. Poor girl, that fat wavie never greased her lips – or ours.

[[I saw the above woman a twelvemonth after; and the fat wavie became the subject of an hour's most interesting and amusing conversation. It appears she had made every preparation to receive us with such becoming hospitality as her limited means afforded. Probably all was swept and garnished within (this woman is noted for her superior ingenuity in the art of garnishing with porcupine quills), the day we appointed to return. Be that as it may, the hinges of her door suffered more from friction that day than, perhaps, in any whole month previously or subsequently. She looked and listened and waited, till she concluded the tea would suffer damage by lying too long out of the tea kettle. After waiting, therefore, about a week for our return, and not being able to learn a single syllable about us, notwithstanding her unceasing enquiries, she came to the conclusion to enjoy what she had prepared for us. The first she heard of us [again] was about the time she had arrived at the above conclusion; when she was informed that we had been to Mr. Kittson's on the Pembina, about 70 miles from her place, and that we had again returned home and were prosecuting our farming operations as usual.

On to Stinking River

[[But to return: as soon as breakfast was over, we prepared for crossing; and, bidding our hostess, with counterfeit laughter, adieu for the present, we speedily gained the opposite shore. Two of our horses came well nigh being drowned.

[[We had now no time to lose. And our situation became more critic{349}al than ever, for by this time we had been seen by and [had] conversed with several persons; and, owing to our anxiety about the valuable property we had left the night before in the care of minks and mice, we were compelled to invert our course to the fowling grounds before we had lost sight of all the farmers.

[[It so happened, however, that we arrived safely at the place where we had landed our packs and other effects, the night before. Everything was in a much better condition than we had anticipated; and therefore, as hurry was as much an object with us as secrecy and silence, we arranged our various bundles on the backs of our horses[658] as expeditiously as we could, and with such care as would [preclude] the necessity of having to undo them again, before we halted for encamping.]]

[308] May 6, 1846 – Wednesday [concluded] We then came down to our baggage and passed on through prairies, forests and swamps to the Stinking River, where we encamped.

[[{349} Our intention was now to take a southerly course and make a straight cut for the Stinking River,[659] through a country that none of us knew anything about. But, by the time we had proceeded about a mile, we had again to be very cautious, as we had to cross a public road which runs from the Upper Settlement on the main river[660] to the White Horse Plains. This necessary caution, therefore, again caused our course to be somewhat meandering, and tended not a little to check our onward progress.

[[After a good deal of anxiety arising from our constant dread of coming in any way in contact with our kind, we at last managed to get {350} entirely beyond the reach of all such dangers – at least for the present. For we could not but anticipate similar apprehensions when once we had crossed the Stinking River.

[[Our object in studiously shunning and avoiding every intercourse with our own species, while in and near about the Settlement was to prevent the Hudson's Bay Company from getting any information respecting our proceedings till we had succeeded in getting beyond their reach. Therefore, being now really beyond their knowledge and power, as we were now in the very heart of a country seldom or never visited, except by horse hunters, and then but in the fall of the year, we traveled on smoothly and slowly, just as our poor horses could stand it. But, finding that they could not proceed much further without detriment to us and to themselves, unless we gave them a little time for relaxation, we concluded to let them have an hour or two to graze on what they could, and ourselves on a piece of pemmican and a cup of tea.

---

658 Gunn: "They had evidently left the cart behind. Sinclair may have taken it back with him."

659 Now called the La Salle River.

660 Gunn: "By the Upper Settlement on the main river is meant the French communities now comprising St. Vital and St. Norbert, on the Red River just south of Winnipeg. The "public road" referred to probably cut across the base of the angle formed by the two rivers, between the two points mentioned, and thus would have to be crossed by Garrioch's party on their way south." Gunn, p. 349, n. 2.

[[By the time that we had supped, and our animals had eaten to their satisfaction, the sun had already begun to lower peacefully his orb under the western horizon.

Into the Bosom of a Swamp

[[Now, we congratulated ourselves on the security of our traveling; and we only required the aid of the forthcoming night to render our onward movements more romantic. But such is life. We had not gone more than a mile or so when faithful though painful experience taught us that, while darkness may be generally propitious to the prosecution of unlawful and dishonourable actions, it, like everything else in the world, has its exceptions; for this same darkness, which had hitherto enabled us to conduct our miserable business {351} with such success, now led us right into the bosom of a swamp, whose centre and circumference we knew absolutely nothing about.

[[The case was indeed desperate, but there was no cure. One suggested this course and another that; but how preposterous! As well might one take the word of one blind from his birth for the north or the south. There was no alternative. We went south into the swamp, through water, mire and grass, and trusted entirely to the strength and sagacity of our horses to bring us out of the terrible predicament. The poor animals did their duty and brought us safe to land, after they had toiled and waded through this dismal marsh, sometimes to the knees and sometimes to the belly, for more than a mile.

Puddling Like Turtles

[[We were subsequently informed that we had taken a course too much to the east; and that must certainly have been the case. We continued to travel about three hours after we had effected a passage through the above swamp; and by far the greatest part of that time was occupied in puddling through water and mire, like so many turtles. I could not help thinking, "so much for our wit." As there is nothing, however, which does not in the long run come to some end, so it was with these swamps; for, while thus puddling along, we suddenly perceived something before us of the appearance of clouds and, almost in another instant, we were high and dry – right by the side of a thick forest. We had now to change our manner of marching from puddling to scrambling; and, to all intents and purposes, it certainly was jumping out of the frying pan into the fire; or out of a puddle into a canoe, as our fish here often do. In spite of all these obstacles, however, we finally succeeded in accomplishing what we had {352} so anxiously anticipated: a sight of the Stinking River.

Drowning Vexations in Tea

[[With regard to our situation here, in relation to the crossing place of this river, we were utterly ignorant; and therefore, being rather apprehensive lest the snorting of our horses and the kindling of a fire might be within hearing and smelling distance of any travelers who should chance to be spending the night there, we concluded to encamp as speedily as practicable. With this view, we selected a place which we considered suitable to answer the double advantage of affording pasturage for our animals and preserving us from the olfactory or other senses of our neighbours.

[[There can be but little merit to tell the world that we removed our packs and saddles from the backs of our horses, gave the poor animals full liberty to find food suitable to their respective tastes, kindled a fire, and sat down to eat and drink – drowning the toils and vexations of the past day in a kettle running over with a gallon of the delicious tea plant's juice – or that we went to bed and slept, and rose again the following morning. And yet we did all that. But my nimble pen has here taken undue advantage of my momentary absence. Suffice it to say, as a supplement to the doings of this day, that the succeeding night was as welcome to our fagged bodies and weary minds as ever night was to mortal man.

A Dawn Disturbance

[[But our troubles were yet far from coming to an end; for, as the morning sun was only just beginning to disperse his benign rays, at which time slumber is truly delicious, one of our companions suddenly roused us, apparently quite alarmed. In an instant, we sprang from the Land of Nod to the foot of our beds . . . . . [illegible line][661] {353} ...this cannot but be classed among children's frolics and must be forever forgotten.

[[The effect of this terrible leap seemed for a few moments to have deprived us of our usual physical and mental energies; but when our companion had sufficiently explained the ground of his alarm, which he did in one breath, our scattered and still nodding senses instantly rallied together, and once more we were ourselves. I was almost saying that I suppose some of our senses were rambling about the country of Nod looking for their sweethearts and had not yet returned, when we took that terrible leap, and that that was the cause of our apparently momentary absence. But

---

661 Gunn: "This line of the manuscript was so weatherworn as to be quite undecipherable." Gunn, p. 352.

Chapter 9 – The Pleasures of Smuggling & Family Pressures

I think it will be as well to say these things some other time and adhere for the future more closely to what I set out with.

[[Our companion told us that he distinctly heard people singing and conversing, a few moments previously, somewhere to the west of us.

[[What, I say, is paradox, if this is not? Only but imagine: we considered ourselves in the way of duty; and yet, strange to say, we dreaded the approach of those we knew to be prosecuting their daily and of course lawful occupations. Surely one would be ready to say, there must have been a most terrible persecution in this land.

[[But to return once more: each one took hold of his own packs and, conveying them some two or three hundred yards from our hut, carelessly threw them by the side of the bush he considered most favourable.

[[Not having sufficient time for the exercise of thought, we ran down again [to where] we had encamped near the edge of the river, and now taking hold of our saddles and bridles, we carried them away also {354} and placed them beside our packs. On secondary consideration, however, we detected the impropriety of concealing the latter articles. We therefore ran up the hill again, and, bringing them back to the hut, each one carefully placed his own by his seat, in full view. This, of course, was necessary, in the event of our again being driven to the painful expedient of counterfeiting truth, in sending any intruder away with the conviction that we were really hunting for stray horses.

[[After coming to a mutual understanding respecting the propriety and efficiency of this new concoction, one of our party started in search of our horses, of which we had yet learned nothing since they secured their liberty the preceding night. We who remained in the hut in the meantime kept our seats, in the most apprehensive mood imaginable; and such was the suspense that even silence became a sound, and nothing seemed to be something. We would venture at times, with the stealthy footsteps of a house cat, nearer to the verge of the river with the view of improving our hearing and vision; but nothing more than the friction of our hair about our ears could be heard; and nothing else could be seen than the continuous ridge of each one's nose. This latter, I presume, was effected by the occasional extreme obliquity of our eyes in their sockets, caused by our eagerness to see something.

Men of Our Own Profession

[[After remaining in this state, almost motionless and breathless, for about an hour, our companion returned with our horses. Precisely at that juncture, we really did hear the voices of people in the direction of the crossing place. They were such, however, as we {355} subsequently learned, as we had not the least cause to be afraid of. For they were men of our own profession: men that Sinclair and I had sent out to the Turtle Mountain about three months since for the purpose of trading, and who were now on their way home to the Settlement.]]

Another Oilcloth Canoe

{309} **May 7, 1846 – Thursday.** We crossed the river as before in an oilcloth canoe, and proceeded through the prairies to the Scratching River.

[[{355} However, as we were necessarily excluded from the knowledge of [our neighbours' identities] our operations had still to be conducted upon the fancies of the present, and not by the realities of the future. We therefore concluded to cross the river where we were; and, in order to effect this, we had again to adopt our former method of constructing a canoe in which to convey our packs and baggage to the other side.

[[As this river is in reality but a creek of a large size, we drove in our horses, and found but little difficulty in getting them over. In a few moments more we and all our effects were by the sides of our horses. We again stripped our canoe of its skin and left the skeleton there to bleach in the sun. After taking the necessary precaution of examining every prospect in our view, for we were now on the edge of an extensive prairie through which we were to travel, we packed up everything on the backs of our horses with as much expedition as we could command, and made a precipitate start.

[[Here, of course, we were more liable to be detected than ever, that is, with regard to our being seen as travelers. In some respects, [however], we could boast of a new advantage. If a man on foot, or with a cart, happened to be in our way, as we now had the full light of day and expansive ground with a good, hard surface to go upon, we could very easily avoid his friendly salutations and {356} unlawful enquiries. The only disadvantage we entertained any apprehension about was the possibility of being seen by such as might be traveling through the same prairies on horses fleeter than our own. Under such circumstances, adverting to counterfeits and seeking to evade questions would be as unavailing to us as a straw to a drowning man, for some of our packs had been so hastily bundled up that some two or three dozen tails of our most valuable peltries were flowing by the sides of those of our horses whose privilege it was to carry such valuable property.

[[It happened, however, that we fared better than we expected – "And better than you deserved," some would say. Be that as it may, our own impression was that circumstances alter cases – so much so indeed that what is a virtue under one set of circumstances may be a vice under another, and vice versa. When we had proceeded some three or four miles on this extensive and beautiful prairie, we continued on our way rejoicing, for we were now satisfied that we were entirely beyond the seeing and hearing of any traveler whatsoever, as we were at least three miles from the nearest public road; and anything on that being, for the greater part, intercepted from our view by clusters of poplar hummocks and long ranges of various bushes. Indeed, we considered ourselves now masters of our distance, for we had scarcely thirty miles more to go;[662] and by the time the good folks of Fort Garry could learn anything of our proceedings, even were we here discovered, we well knew we could gain a harbour of safety.

[[We therefore suspended our traveling for the day [with] the sun being {357} still about an hour high. And, after shackling our horses and merrily enjoying ourselves at the expense of our persecutors the H.B.C. over a cup of tea and piece of ham and pemmican, my companions lay down to spend a few moments in jocular reflections, and I prepared to enjoy the grateful [gratifying] sensations produced by the northern traveler's inseparable companion, the pipe – to enjoy, as they say over here, a smoke with myself. Imagine, then, my disappointment, my impatience, my rage, in fact my everything but what ought to be, when I discovered that I had either dropped my pipe on the way or left it, in our confusion, at our last encampment.

Making a Meerschaum Out of a Molehill

[[But, as I [have] said before, necessity is the mother of invention. I turned aside to a mole hill, which had become quite solid and compact from age. I made a hole on its top, sufficiently large to contain about an ounce of cut tobacco; and, cutting down one side so as to produce a face, I inserted the stem of a species of grass, equal in size to a wheat straw, till it reached the tobacco at the bottom of the hole. I then carried a piece of fire in my hand and placed it on the surface of the tobacco; and, placing

---

662   Gunn: "According to p. 358 they were [near] the Scratching River." Gunn, p. 356.

myself on my stomach, in a horizontal position, I applied my mouth to the outer end of the straw forming the pipe stem. One or two pulls were sufficient to remove every doubt respecting the merits of this unprecedented discovery. Indeed, such was the nature of the peculiar flavour deduced from [produced by] this long-unfrequented mole hill that I began to be somewhat apprehensive as to what might occasion so delicious a flavour. Could it really have been the musk, the very essence, of the [long-dead] moles? It mattered not, however: it served all the purposes that a com{358} mon clay pipe would have done; and it certainly was as productive of those delicious sensations which the smoking of tobacco generally creates. Such indeed was the effect of that most luscious of all weeds on my sentimental and cogitative parts, when thus drawn from a mole hill, that I utterly lost all recollection of the past and fell into a most pleasing reverie. Suffice it to say, that such was the overwhelming effect of this instance of my ingenious sagacity, that truth itself would scarcely have convicted [convinced] me of folly.[663]

[[After the above sublime doings we retired to rest, and, as usual, arose when the morning came.]]

Last Crossings

{309} **May 8, 1846 – Friday.** Crossed the last river[s] as usual and proceeded as before to the Pembina.

{358} [[Before we could fairly proceed on our journey, we had again to construct a canoe similar to those I mentioned above. Everything being put into it, one of our party leapt on a horse, and, taking one end of the line that was attached to the canoe, he spurred him into the stream and dragged it to the other side. The rest of us followed his example, and once more we succeeded in a fair start, without having sustained any damage.

[[This last creek goes by the name of Scratching River,[664] and the next we came to Marshy River.[665] We experienced but little difficulty in crossing the latter, and but a

---

663 This humorous episode was excerpted in the *Winnipeg Free Press* (February 11, 1939), by H. C. Knox in an article entitled "When You Gotta Smoke, You Gotta Smoke."

664 Gunn: "The Swamp River. See note." (Gunn, p. 309, n. 1). Gunn, p. 358.

665 Gunn referred to the note about the "several streams of this main tributary" which appears on p. 309, n. 1. Gunn, p. 358.

little inconvenience occasioned by the boggy nature of its bottom. On this account, we were obliged to wade through it, leading and driving our horses.

A Silent & Stealthy Entrance

[[Here again it became necessary to make new arrangements before we could proceed any further; for we had but ten or twelve miles more to {359} travel to come to the point of our destination. Not knowing exactly how we might be able to effect a silent and stealthy entrance into Mr. Kittson's premises so as to avoid any curiosity that an open entrance would likely and naturally enough tend to arouse, we concluded [that] our better plan would be to separate and travel in two parties by different directions.]]

{309} **May 8, 1846 – Friday [concluded]** I took the public road from the Swamp River[666] and went directly to Kittson's, while Henry [Cook] and John Monkman struck for a point on the Pembina some three or four miles above Kittson's.

{359} [[It was agreed that my companions were to take a course . . . . . [illegible passage] then to a point on the Pembina River not more than three miles from Kittson's Post; and I was to strike immediately for the public road which runs from Selkirk's Settlement to Pembina, and proceed openly and directly to Mr. Kittson's at the last point mentioned. My companions took all the packs and, of course, all the traveling materials; and they were to encamp where they should first strike the river, and wait there until they should hear from me.

[[I carried nothing with me but my gun, so that, at my first appearance at Kittson's, the impression would be that I had left the above Settlement that morning. For the distance between the two places has often been made in one day. I arrived at Kittson's a few minutes after the sun had gone to his usual rest, and found the above gentleman "enjoying a smoke with himself," sucking out the brains of his beautiful calumet pipe.[667]

---

666   Gunn: "There are several streams of this name tributary to the Red River. The one here referred to flows into it from the southwest, a little north and east of Letellier, about a mile above the mouth of the Roseau River, which joins the former stream from the east. It was known to the Indians as Petopek River, and to the French as Rivière aux Marais, by which name it is still designated on some maps. The "public road" referred to is that which followed the west bank of the Red River from Fort Garry to Pembina." Gunn, p. 309.

667   A highly ornamented Indian pipe.

Bluffing Inquisitive Rupertians

[[As several Rupertian and Indian families from our Settlement had taken up their residence here, enquiries soon came on faster than I could answer them. One enquired after his father, another after his aunts and grandmothers, and a third, of course, after my business. Here I felt not a little grieved; for I soon found that recourse to {360} the old system was again indispensable. I told them anything but the truth respecting the object of my visit. The task was rather a hard one, and certainly one that required more wit and sagacity than I really could pretend to. My only plan was therefore to make everything as plausible as possible, and not to make one circumstance clash with another. In a word, I pretended and pleaded ignorance in toto, and answered their enquiries by diverting their attention from one subject to another as rapidly as my wits could command and produce them.

Supping & Smoking with Mr. Kittson

[[I was glad when word came that supper was ready. This was a kind of reprieve; for Mr. Kittson was already in possession of all the facts connected with the object of my visit; and therefore I felt easy and at home when alone in his company. By the time that supper was over, and Kittson and I had ravished the calumet, the inquisitive neighbours had nearly all disappeared in their respective abodes, enjoying their pipes with themselves. For the Rupertians and Indians, nearly to a man, smoke tobacco.

The Anguish of Lost Companions

[[Agreeably to arrangements, I took advantage of the absence of these enquirers and went out, Mr. Kittson's clerk having the politeness to accompany me, to hunt for my wandering companions. But it appears they had a more correct notion of miles than I had, for they were not there. Here Rolette[668] and I came to a perfect standstill. For what could we do? We called and bawled and whistled till our lungs fairly fainted within us, but all to {361} no purpose. I therefore concluded to return to Kittson's, with a determination of committing to chance what, as I supposed, had been so badly managed by those on whom I had so confidently relied.

[[My companions, as they subsequently stated, had intended to come to [the rendezvous] swamp, which is scarce two miles from Kittson's, to encamp or to await

---

668 Kittson's clerk, Joseph Rolette.

my appearance. But, hearing the report of [hunters'] guns in and about this swamp and not knowing how near they might approach it with safety, as it was a little after dusk, they suspended their traveling till the opportunity afforded by these sportsmen retiring should enable them again to proceed. This, of course, naturally enough accounts for our not finding them where we expected; for they were only about starting for the swamp when Rolette and I retired from it to return to the post. Some two hours after we had retired, Rolette suggested going out again; but knowing well that old folks in tents are no more chained to their beds during the night than they are during the day, I was afraid that our walking out a second time would be very apt to cause suspicion, and therefore I advised to the contrary.

[[While Rolette and I were thus proposing and [debating] matters within, the dogs on the outside appeared to be equally and indeed more than usually busy barking out their own perceptions in their own peculiar way. But, as people seldom take notice of any common occurrence, which is apt to be the case with regard to the confused barking of dogs, the circumstance was no more heeded by us than the squeaking of some dozen children shut up in a toyshop would be.

[[In this instance, however, we were certainly to blame. For though {362} a confused barking of dogs be quite a common thing, and oftener than otherwise from no other cause than the strange animal propensity for imitating, or the feelings of one agitated by being operated upon by those of another, yet there are times when the barking of dogs, however confusedly and apparently to no purpose, most assuredly has some meaning. That is when neither we nor they can discern anything, either by sight or hearing. At such times, they know there is something in the wind, aided alone by that peculiar faculty which nature has seated in their organs of smelling.

[[Now it appears that my companions came to the place, agreeably to our former arrangements, soon after Rolette and I left it. But after having anxiously waited for some time, and at last despairing of either seeing or hearing anything of us that night, and apprehending certain detection should they remain there till the morning, they concluded, at all hazards, to venture to the Post as stealthily as possible, so as to ascertain the cause of my non-appearance. With this object in view, they quickened their pace, so as to find me, should I have reached Kittson's, still out of bed; but various concurring circumstances prevented them from effecting this purpose of coming within the premises. They scrambled through the brush; and, having reached so near as to hear the voices of those in the neighbourhood who had not yet retired to rest, they suspended their march and, expecting me every moment to pass by, sat still in breathless agitation.

[[It was precisely at this juncture that Rolette suggested the propriety of our going out again, and that the dogs grew uncommonly noisy. The inference is plain. The dogs could not see the men, {363} for the latter were in the midst of thick brush; neither could they hear them, for everything was spoken with smothered breath. Yet they were betrayed. How, and by whom? As I said before, we all savoured more of the scent of rats, minks and coons than of anything else. And the dogs, well knowing that no person from the premises had gone out in the direction I allude to, and that they were not conscious of any fur having been previously deposited there, unerringly detected the approach of strangers through the highly perfumed state of their garments.

[[The poor fellows sat there, as they afterwards told me, shaking in their breeches, till light and sounds all died away; and then they returned to their hut, wondering as they went what had become of me. Their apprehensions for my safety were of the most serious and least pleasing nature. One was afraid that I had accidentally shot myself, though he could not even conjecture how; the other was afraid I had fallen from the back of my horse and broken my neck. Then they both concluded that I must have been overtaken by constables from the Settlement, and that I was detained for the present at Mr. Burke's. Mr. Burke was a trader for the Hudson's Bay Company, and had been stationed by that concern about three miles from Mr. Kittson's. {364} These conjectures were stimulated, no doubt, by the intensity of their apprehension for their own safety, which was linked up with mine.

[[While the poor fellows were thus alternately swimming and sinking, according to the turn of their abstruse conceptions, operated upon by their fears, the writer of these remarks was carelessly and variously extending and distending his limbs on a bed suited to the rank and condition of an Indian trader. The End]][669]

Delivery & Return

{309} **May 9, 1846 – Saturday.** We delivered our parcels to Mr. Kittson. Henry and John left the Pembina immediately after sundown, and I left Kittson's about 9 o'clock of the night. I traveled till near daylight and lay down on the prairie to take a short nap.

---

669   This is the conclusion of Garrioch's "Pleasure of Smuggling" reminiscence (Gunn, pp. 325-364).

Chapter 9 – The Pleasures of Smuggling & Family Pressures

May 10, 1846 – Sunday. I arrived at [James] Sinclair's before sundown, after dining with some friends on the way.

Debt Repayment & Restocking

May 11, 1846 – Monday. I went down to pay Mr. Moat[670] and to see after other small affairs.

May 12, 1846 – Tuesday. I went up to the White Horse Plains to see after debts, and to purchase whatever I might consider saleable in the States.

May 13, 1846 – Wednesday. I went up to Mr. Belcourt's.

This visit was likely in connection with the anti-HBC petition that had originated at a public protest meeting on February 26, 1846.

A severe frost last night.

A Fine Bed at Pascal's Place

May 14, 1846 – Thursday. I returned again to Pascal [Bréland]'s, and a fine bed I had. A blanket as dirty as dirt could make it was carelessly thrown upon the bed on the floor, on which I was to spend the night; and {310} when I awoke in the morning, my shirt was but little better than the blanket.

May 15, 1846 – Friday. I returned home after making two bags of pemmican, one bale of dried meat and one pair of shoes by my trip. These were old outstanding debts.

Preparations for Traveling South Again

May 16, 1846 – Saturday. I commenced fixing up my carts for my journey to St. Peter's.

May 17, 1846 – Sunday. I went to the Middle Church as usual. "A wounded spirit who can bear," was part of the text. Gavin sowed the last of the wheat yesterday: nineteen or twenty bushels.

---

670 Gunn's handwritten note, p. 309: "Probably the Andrew Mowat of p. 291."

May 18, 1846 – Monday. I rode up the main river to Wilkie's[671] to hire a man and exchange my horse. I hired Gabriel Azure,[672] Laball's brother, for £7 to go to St. Peter's and back here again. I am also to furnish him shoes when we leave St. Peter's. During his stay there, one half of what he earns by labour is to be mine and the other half {311} his. I hired George Garrioch[673] yesterday also for the same trip at one pound ten shillings per month till we return. At St. Peter's he is to have his liberty till I am ready to return.

Planted six bushels of potatoes.

May 19, 1846 – Tuesday. Fixed another cart and bought fifteen rats from Bread.[674]

May 20, 1846 – Wednesday. Bought 45 more rats and a cart box for three shillings.

Great Court Days

The Settlement's senior court, chaired by Governor Christie, was officially called the General Quarterly Court of Assiniboia. Garrioch often referred to it the "Grand Court," but in the first of his two following descriptions of that tribunal's current proceedings he called it the "Great Court."

May 21, 1846 – Thursday. This has been a Great Court day. Wonderful things have been done by Mr. Thom and the rest of the Court Bench. . . . . . [blank space] was fined

---

671   Gunn: "Jean Baptiste Wilkie, a noted English Métis who lived at that time on the Red River south of Fort Garry, in what is now St. Vital. He was born in 1801 and, although of English extraction, was brought up among the French and, for the most part, threw in his lot with them. He was a noted buffalo runner and Indian fighter, and a recognized leader among the Métis in all such operations. In the great buffalo hunt of 1840, recorded by Alex. Ross, *Red River Settlement,* pp. 245-272. Wilkie was made Chief Captain, with nine adjutants under him. He is described by Ross as "a man of good sound sense and long experience, and withal a fine, bold looking and discreet fellow – a second Nimrod in his way." In 1847 he moved across the international boundary and settled at St. Joseph, now Walhalla, North Dakota, of which he claimed to be the first town officer. He died in 1886." Gunn, p. 310.

672   Gunn: "The Azures, a French Métis family belonging to Red River Settlement, also moved over to the Turtle Mountain quarter in North Dakota, where the present-day representatives of the clan still reside."

673   The identity of this person is unclear. Gunn, p. 311, n. 1, thought he was Peter's next younger brother John's first son, but that particular George was not born until 1846.

674   Gunn: "Probably an Indian. The original would be Puh-quashi-kun." Gunn, p. 311. Gunn's typescript followed the name 'Bread' with a question mark, suggesting that Garrioch did not know him well and was perhaps using a generic name for the man.

Chapter 9 – The Pleasures of Smuggling & Family Pressures   341

£10 for having sold whiskey to the Indians, while Thomas Logan, for the same offence, was fined the petty sum of £2.[675]

Alexander Dahl was sentenced to a calendar month's imprisonment under a charge of adultery with John Falster Senior's wife through the evidence, and no other than that, afforded by the said Falster's wife herself, who is nothing more or less than a common whore. This woman had previously, at different periods, given birth to three or four bastards. She was and is a perfect idiot, incapable of discerning good from evil; and yet, strange to say, the oath of the Court was administered to her.[676]

---

675   The full report of this General Quarterly Court session will be found in Gibson, *LLG, II, passim,* and there is a series of cases about selling liquor to Indians reported at that session: *The Public Interest vs. Thomas Logan* (Case 14, A54), p. 45; *The Public Interest vs. Henry Cook* (Case 15, A540), p. 45; *The Public Interest vs. Mrs. Cathne. Norne* (Case 16, A54); *The Public Interest vs. Henry Brown* (Case 17, A55); *The Public Interest vs. James McDermot* (Case 18, A56), p. 45; etc.; & see commentary, pp. 47-49. The reason for the discrepancy in fines was that in the first case the sale was to a Métis, and in the second it was to an Indian. Whereas the sale of any intoxicant to Indians was prohibited, there was no racially-based liquor prohibition in the case of white or Métis purchasers. There was a general prohibition, however, on the unlicensed sale of whisky or other "ardent spirits" to anyone. Perhaps Peter Garrioch was unaware of this difference, though his comment might also have been influenced by the fact that the accused in the second case, whose name he left blank in the journal entry, was his cousin and close friend Henry Cook. He also failed to mention that the purchaser in the first case was George Garrioch.

676   In the Court record the complainant's surname is shown as Folster. The evidence against Dahl was indeed flimsy. The only evidence purporting to corroborate Janet Folster's was that of someone who had seen her engaging in an unusually long and friendly conversation with Dahl, and of others who testified to the consistency of her claim that it was he who had impregnated her. Garrioch was probably right in questioning the decision to accept her charges as sworn testimony in spite of her undoubtedly retarded intellectual state. Yet accepting her evidence in unsworn form would have been legally permissible in the circumstances; and that evidence was found to be persuasive by male adjudicators. There had been a preliminary investigation of the charges by Magistrate James Bird, who seems to have decided that the evidence was persuasive enough to justify the prosecution, and who provided the General Court with a rather sensitive report about both the allegations and Mrs. Folster's mental capacity. The guilty verdict was reached by a twelve person, all-male jury, and was accepted by a seven person, all-male Court consisting of the Settlement's most senior elders. The charge laid against Dahl – criminal conversation – was invalid, however; there was no such crime. That designated a civil wrong – the tort of adultery, for which a husband could sue another man who had sexual intercourse with his wife. The term "criminal" simply meant "wrongful" in that context. See Gibson, *LLG, II,* pp. 42-45: *The Public Interest v. Peter Alexander Dahl* (Case 13, A50), (1846).

The Court had made an award of monetary damages in just such a case a few years previously, in 1844. See Gibson, *LLG, II,* pp. 1-6: *Wm. Smith vs. Joseph Kirton* (Case 1, A1). The reason that Recorder Thom and the Court chose to uphold such a charge here was probably that the legally correct charge on this evidence would have been rape, which carried a mandatory death sentence at the time.

Signatures

May 28, 1846 – Thursday. I have been traveling so much the last week that I do not remember what occurred each day. I went up yesterday to Mr. Belcourt's and returned home the same day.

Some of this travel was likely due to Garrioch's preparations for his looming trip to the United States. The visit to Belcourt, however, and no doubt much other travel as well, was almost certainly related to the Métis petition to the Queen protesting against their treatment at the hands of the HBC, which was described as having been circulated for signature later in this same entry. An earlier visit to the Reverend Belcourt was mentioned in the May 13 entry.

This day has been {312} another Grand Court day. Mr. McDermot, I am told, was fined £10 for having sold whiskey at the Stinking River, a distance of about seven miles from the Assiniboine River, and £2 for having detained his son Jemmy from the last Grand Court. [677]

I went about today for signatures to a petition to be presented to her Majesty, Queen Victoria. I added 80 signatures to the said petition.

Gunn had the following to say about this important French language petition: "This petition, which was in French, was drawn up by the Reverend G. A. Belcourt of the Baie St. Paul mission. According to his own statement in his article 'The Department of Hudson's Bay,' it was signed by 977 subscribers, and presented to the British authorities in 1847. The prayer of the petition was:

1. **that as good subjects they might be governed by the principles of the British Constitution;**

---

677   Gibson, *LLG, II*: *The Public Interest vs. James McDermot* (Case 18, A56), & Commentary, pp. 47-49. The accused person in this case was not Andrew McDermot, but his son James (Jemmy), who worked for his father, and appears to have sold whisky for immediate consumption to a group of Métis he met on the plains. James was not in court, but his father appeared, claimed James had acted against instructions, but admitted and took responsibility for the offence. He was fined £8 (not £10) and James was fined £12 in absentia. This was a special session of the Court, convened only a week after its regular sitting, to deal solely with this picayune case. As the title of the General Quarterly Court implies, it normally sat only once every three months. Its records reveal only one prior special session, and that was to try a sensational murder case with public safety overtones. Perhaps the reason for holding a Special Court on this occasion was to exert pressure on Andrew McDermot, the Settlement's most successful free trader, and wealthiest resident. Possibly, though, the explanation may lie in Garrioch's claim, of which there is no suggestion in the Court record, that Andrew ordered his son not to attend the regular sitting of the Court, or – more likely – that the father wanted to make amends for his son's failure to attend and to repair his own relations with Settlement authorities.

2. that as British subjects they demanded their right to enjoy the liberty of Commerce;
3. they requested the sale of lands to strangers and that a portion of the proceeds should be applied to improve the means of transport.

The document was later conveyed to England by James Sinclair."[678]

St. Louis & Bloodthirsty Bulldogs

Almost four months had elapsed, and much travel had occurred, before Garrioch's next diary entry – a retrospective one.

September 20, 1846 – [Sunday] After I had written what is on the bottom of the last page, I was quite busily employed in making the preparation necessary for my journey to the States. When everything was ready, which was accomplished by June 4th, I started for my intended tour. I took with me in animal kind four horses, five oxen, one cow, and ten men whom I hired for the trip at £7 each. I left home with six carts and returned with five, the other having broken down on the way. After a very pleasant journey of 33 days, suffering no damage of any kind, except by the exchange of my Dick (a horse) for Cooters (a horse), and but little inconvenience except by bull dogs [horse flies]. I arrived at St. Peter's on the 7th day of July.

The {313} bull dogs were so numerous and so bloodthirsty that we were sometimes under the necessity of taking our animals out of their carts, in order to shelter them from these infuriated and blood thirsty cannibals by covering them with our robes and blankets. On more than one occasion our animals were annoyed and tormented by these rebels during the whole of the night.

After a delay of some three or four days at St. Paul, I walked onto the steamer Cecilia (Captain … Throckmorton)[679] and landed before the front street of the to-be-great City of St. Louis on the 19th day of July.

---

678 Gunn, p. 312, who added a handwritten addition to the wording of the petition: "For full text of this petition, see Appendix F." Appendix F (Gunn, pp. [388-391]) is a much fuller version of this petition and records that it was signed by 977 persons. Gluek, *Minnesota and the Manifest Destiny*, p. 59, describes Peter's active role in gathering the 977 signatures ultimately affixed to the petition. The full text appears here in Appendix I - Petitions.

679 Gunn: "Captain John Throckmorton and one Shellcross were the first persons who engaged in steamboating on the Upper Mississippi. Throckmorton first brought a small steamer called the "Red River" from Ohio, about 1820. He afterwards built the steamboat "Warrior," at Pittsburgh, and engaged with it in the Upper Mississippi trade, and had much of the Government patronage in transporting troops, supplies and Indian goods for the factory trade. He was in the battle of Bad

Worse than Little Boys

Here I learned to a certainty that the great question between the British and American governments, viz.: the barren Columbia question [Oregon boundary dispute], had been amicably settled. Here also I learned that the Americans and Mexicans were killing each other about a piece of land, just as little boys will knock each other down, bite, scratch and kick each other for the sake of a butterfly.[680] Oh ye would be great ones of the earth, ye are a thousand-fold worse and more to be pitied than little boys for, in that ye know more, ye ought to take more and give less.

Little Nest of Satan

My time in St. Louis was limited to the very short period of four days; and, after becoming security for Dominique Pambrun to the amount {314} of $29.00, in Mr. Martin McLeod's favour, I left this little nest of Satan on the 11th of August.[681]

Distinguished Success

On my 40th day from St. Peter's I arrived home, and my animals and carts on their 43rd.

On the whole, I have abundant reason to acknowledge the kindness of my Creator, who has attended me throughout my journey with so much care and mercy, and who has crowned my undertakings with such distinguished success. Nor is it the least part, though the last, for which I ought to manifest unbounded gratitude to God, in that he has preserved my life in the midst of innumerable dangers, that he has enabled me once more to enjoy the society of my friends and relatives in the midst of plenty, peace and health.

Garrioch did indeed have much to be grateful for. Not only had his trade mission met with "distinguished success," but, as he recorded below, he was also participating in salt-trad-

---

    Axe with this steamer and played quite a part in that affair. He was (about 1850) still navigating the Upper Mississippi, making St. Louis his home. See "Sketches of Indian Chiefs and Pioneers of the Northwest," by Colonel John Shaw, *Wisconsin Historical Collections* X, (1888), p. 222."

680 Gunn: "This refers to conquest of New Mexico and California by the United States, which took place that summer."

681 Having said earlier in the entry that he arrived in St. Louis on July 19 and here that he left "this little nest of Satan" on August 11, it is difficult to see how his stay in St. Louis was limited to "the very short period of four days."

ing on Lake Manitoba, [682] since the 1820s one of its chief locations. This was a lucrative part of the sophisticated web of salt-extraction, sugar-making, fur-trading, and other mercantile activities which, along with farming, were contributing to the accelerating vibrancy of Métis economic and cultural life, despite the fact that the Red River summer Peter had fortuitously missed by travelling south had been marked by excessive heat, drought, a severe influenza epidemic,[683] and a poor buffalo hunt.

Selling, Buying, Traveling, Hunting

From the day I arrived to the period stated below I was variously employed; sometimes selling and buying; sometimes traveling; and at other times doing something because there was nothing else to do.

October 1, 1846 – Thursday. I went out to the Manitoba [Lake] with brothers John and Gavin. I went out with a view to sporting, and they to lay in a stock of white fish. My hunt consisted of 28 ducks, 3 pheasants and 2 bitterns.

I saw Charlotte[684] and received a friendly shake of her delicate hand. Poor Charlotte, I fear the barriers between us are so many and so insurmountable that it will be quite impossible for us to establish any stronger relationship than that which already exists through our great ancestor, Adam the First.

---

682 Gunn: "At that time, a great deal of the salt used in the Red River Settlement was made on Lake Manitoba from natural salt springs." For a case of assault and manslaughter between two salt producers see Gibson, *LLG, II*, pp. 336-338: *The Queen versus Paulette Chartrain* (Case 211, B200), & Commentary. In the *Sayer* case, a high-ranking witness, Chief Factor John Ballenden, testifying on behalf of the HBC, stated that the defendant could have paid his debts in salt if he could not pay in money: Gibson., *LLG, II*, p. 115, p. 738, & n. 57: *The Honble Hudson's Bay Company v, Pierre Guilleaum Sayer* (Case 68, A151). Dr. Anne Lindsay has kindly allowed me to read her comprehensive study of salt-making and the salt economy in 19th-century Canadian territory, "With Salt Springs Almost at Our Doors: The History of Salt Making in the Swan River, Winnipegosis and Lake Manitoba Regions," enriched by its citations to numerous other studies of this topic (draft, copyright 2006). She points out that Sayer was a member of one of four families who made salt from the 1820s at Lake Manitoba and Winnipegosis, and that salt-making and salt-distribution were closely linked with Métis economic free trading and bound up with the fur trade (pp. 17-18).

683 See Ross, *Red River Settlement*, pp. 362-364; Stephen R. Bown, *The Company: The Rise and Fall of the Hudson's Bay Empire* (Toronto: Doubleday Canada, 2020), pp. 145-154; & Lent, *West of the Mountains*, p. 184.

684 Gunn noted that he intended to write a note shedding light on the identity of Charlotte, but failed to do so (Gunn, p.314).

October 10, 1846 – Saturday. I returned today from the Manitoba, bringing with me 121 ducks, 1 grey goose, 3 bitterns and 2 pheasants; also 1 bushel salt which I paid seven shillings [for], and 50 pounds of tallow.

Another Winter Approaches

{315} **October 18, 1846 – Sunday.** We received this day the first intimation of approaching winter by a copious shower of snow. . . . . . **[two pages deleted]**[685]

November 12, 1846 - Thursday. There has been some rain today. Our weather hitherto, since the 18th of October, has been fair and perfectly clear, but rather windy.

Peter Hayden arrived from St. Peter's on the 9th instant.

November 16, 1846 – Monday. The wind blows strongly from the North and brings quite a fall of snow.

November 18, 1846 – Wednesday. The snow is off again, and this day is more like a day in May than one in November.

November 19, 1846 – Thursday. A strong west wind all day. A new moon has made its appearance this evening, and therefore, as old folk who are moon observers say, we may expect a change in the weather. And, of course, there will be snow and cold in the place of summer weather.

November 20, 1846 – Friday. Just as old people always say: snow in abundance and a deal of north wind with it.

Good Fishing

November 21, 1846 – Saturday. Gavin returned from the fishing, and left John with his family a little beyond Monkman's Swamp, or Lake, old Blacky having left them in the lurch. He says that they have caught in all 1,400 white and 100 jack fish. {316}

November 22, 1846 – Sunday. The river opposite to Rowlands[686] set fast this morning.

---

685   Gunn, p. 315, noted this deletion of two pages in the MS.

686   Gunn: "George Rowland lived at Lot 39, St. Paul, on the west bank of the Red River, below Middlechurch, a few lots south of Orkney Cottage, the home of the Garriochs. There is today a ragged creek there, cut[ting] through the prairie into the Red, formerly known as Rowland's Creek. The entire property therealong, lying between the main road and the river, including the

Chapter 9 – The Pleasures of Smuggling & Family Pressures

November 23, 1846 – Monday. The river opposite our own place set fast this morning. We stabled our animals this evening, being the first time this fall.

A Disgraceful Scene

November 26, 1846 – Thursday. This is a day which I cannot soon forget; and the impression which the shameful occurances of it have made on my mind will doubtless, and I hope, continue fresh in my memory until I cease to breathe. Charles Cook Jr. was married today to the late George Spence's daughter Margaret. About supper time …! The scene is too disgraceful to relate. Brothers and brothers-in-law …! Great God, forgive us all our folly, and our deviation from that path of sobriety, chastity and charity, in which Thou has commanded us always to walk. Amen.[687]

Oxicide

November 28, 1846 – Saturday. I was informed today that Mr. James Green arrived from St. Peter's last Thursday. It is stated that one of his oxen, while in the cart, was shot by some of the Chippewas from Red Lake.

November 30, 1846 – Monday. Went up to see Mr. Green. The report of his ox being killed is correct. The reason assigned for this outrage on the part of these usually friendly Indians is that Green would not give them anything to eat, though they very politely requested him for a little. This goes very far to confirm the truth of the {317} old saying: 'Lost a shilling through the avaricious desire to save a penny.'

December 1, 1846 – Tuesday. John and Gavin started this morning for their fish at Manitoba [Lake] with four oxen and carts.

Cook and Garrioch homesteads, is now being laid out as a cemetery proposition. George Rowland, the original settler, came from England, and lived here until his death. He had several sons, one of whom lived on the Red River near Selkirk. Another, William, moved to Oregon, in 1841, with the party of Red River settlers who went there with James Sinclair."

687   There is a reference to a drunken party at Charles Cook's in Peter's entry for February 5, 1846. It may be that the entry for February 20, 1847 (Gunn, p. 322) is a possible further reference to this incident. However, in the subsequent entry for February 23, Garrioch wrote dispassionately about traveling with Charles Cook for four days, and he took a similar calm tone in his March 2 and 6 entries towards Cook. Ens, *Homeland to Hinterland*, p. 64, quotes this paragraph and places it in the context of the large, exuberant wedding celebrations prevalent in Métis communities at the time.

Sally's Firstborn

December 2, 1846 – Wednesday. It commenced to snow and blow about 12 o'clock last night and continued all this day. I went down on foot to see [sister] Sally and her firstborn: a fine little boy with a turned-up nose.

December 3, 1846 – Thursday. The weather continued wild and stormy till about sundown today, when it again assumed its wonted serenity.

December 4, 1846 – Friday. Took home four loads of hay. After sundown it began to snow again, and wind with it as usual made it drift.

December 6, 1846 – Sunday. John and Gavin returned from the Lake Manitoba with their fish. The oxen, as I expected, are very much reduced.

Fetching Stones

December 10, 1846 – Thursday. Gavin, William and myself fetched four loads of stones from the Little Rocky Mountain.....

Little Rocky Mountain, or Little Mountain, which had figured prominently in Garrioch's fur-smuggling adventure earlier in the year, is a rugged hilly region a few miles northwest of the Settlement's location that was used, along with the larger rocky area now known as Stony Mountain to the east, as a source of building stone.

This stone might well have been destined, like that mentioned in Garrioch's February 9 entry, for the new church at St. Andrew's Rapids. If, on the other hand, it was intended for building purposes at Orkney Cottage, this was the first sign of a resumption of the construction preparations that had begun in early 1845 and had ended shortly before Garrioch's apparent abdication of family responsibilities in April 1846. Was he attempting to resume those responsibilities?

Families Without Food

... [two pages deleted from the December 10th entry] ... a little was barely enough to support their families till the opening of the spring. I was informed that one of these improvident families was without a single mouthful in the house; and that another family of the same class was under the disagreeable necessity of going two days without eating a mouthful of food of any kind. Three families, before {318} the setting in of the winter, had supplied themselves with a stock of food, which, with a little care, might have kept them comfortably till the opening of spring; but, unfortunately for them, they were so destitute of economy and forethought, that, as usual,

Chapter 9 – The Pleasures of Smuggling & Family Pressures

they ate, drank and sold till they actually ran themselves aground, and therefore they must now starve.

The drought and consequent crop failure in the summer and fall of 1846 had left the Settlement seriously short of food. In this smug and uncharitable portion of the December 10th entry, Garrioch criticizes certain unidentified poor families for failing to take appropriate advance measures to avoid starving over the winter. As the next entry shows, however, even highly competent, self-sufficient settlers had been affected.

Winter Pastimes & Routines

January 14, 1847 – Thursday. I spent the day with my friend Pascal Berlan [Bréland – at the White Horse Plains]. I never saw him so badly off for provisions. Pascal beat us at playing cards by 50, at the game called by them Grand Major. Weather a little mild today.

January 15, 1847 – Friday. I returned home. I had the loan of a spirited young horse from Cameron[688] and a cariole from Robert Sandison.[689] The horse took fright just as I got home, and broke one of the hinges which connect the shafts with the cariole.

January 16, 1847 – Saturday. I sold thirty pounds of sugar to William and Henry Cook in company, and thirty pounds to brother John.

January 20, 1847 – Wednesday. Mr. McLaughlin called here today, and informed me that Dominique Pambrun returned this morning from his trip to the Red Lake, after having waited there fifteen days for Mr. James {319} Sinclair. Not being able to learn anything about him, he concluded to return.

January 21, 1847 – Thursday. Dominique Pambrun came to see us, and told us, that among all that traveled this winter to and from Pembina he was the only person that

---

688   Gunn: "Hugh Cameron lived formerly on the west bank of the Red River near St. Johns, in North Winnipeg, but subsequently moved up onto the Assiniboine, where he resided until his death. The Cameron farm, a fine piece of property 18 chains wide, was on the north bank of the latter stream, about half a mile below the present Headingly. It was the first homestead to be taken in that part. Garrioch's dealings with C. took place here." Gunn, p. 318.

689   Gunn: "A brother to the James Sandison of p. 320, [entry for February 15, 1847]. He was a carpenter and millwright by trade, and built most of the windmills in the Settlement. He seems, at this time, to have been living near Headingly, but, I believe, subsequently lived in West Kildonan, a few lots south of the present Kildonan Park." See Chap. 8, entries for February 10 & 11, & March 3, 1846. Gunn, p. 318.

did not get frostbitten, and that did not complain of fatigue. He is still what he always was: a piece of made-up bombast.

January 25, 1847 – Monday. I walked up today to Hugh Cameron's and bought one of his horses. I did not pay him for the horse. The bargain is as follows: I have to bring him a No. 1 cook stove, next fall, with all parts and appendages complete and entire, and an eight-day clock. Now the horse is in my possession. The articles with which I am to redeem his price are from a thousand to fifteen hundred miles from here; and the time in which I am to make good that value to the late owner is eight months distant from this date. How then can I accomplish that which is, as it were, enveloped in obscure futurity? In the Lord is my time; in the Lord is my ability; in the Lord is my trust; in the Lord is my hope.

January 27, 1847 – Wednesday. The wind has been south today, and the weather has been milder than usual. The whole of the present month, with the exception of the last three or four days, has been cold to the extreme. No year within the remembrance of the oldest settler has been so cold as this has been.

January 29, 1847 – Friday. Yesterday William Bird's son James was married to Isabella, Red Hugh Gibson's[690] daughter. {320}

February 1, 1847 – Monday. The weather was so mild yesterday that the public road on the river was entirely cut up by horses running on it as usual, on account of the snow becoming quite soft and nearly thawing. This morning the wind turned again to the north and brought along with it: 'Mind your noses and your big toeses!!!'

February 3, 1847– Wednesday. Halcro[691] begins to work tomorrow. I went up to McDermot's with Sam [Cook].

---

690 Gunn's intended note on "Red Hugh Gibson" seems never to have been written. Born around 1780 in Scotland's Orkney Islands, Hugh Gibson arrived at Red River with Lord Selkirk's settlers, and HBC records describe him in 1814-1815 as "sober, honest and active" and: "good, 5'3$^{1/2}$ inches and slender. "A saucy, mischief making fellow." Hugh had children with Christiana, a Cree woman with whom he had six children by 1827, but also married Angelique (Ann) Chalifoux in 1823. Isabella Gibson was born in July, 1829, and married James Bird, son of Venus Rubina "Bennie" Hay (1801-1864) and William Bird (1803-1885) in 1847. Red River Ancestry.ca/GIBSON-Hugh-178.php.

691 Gunn: "Joseph Halcro lived on the west bank of the Red River, in St. Paul's parish, just below Middlechurch. He moved with his family, shortly prior to 1885, to the Northwest, and settled on the south branch of the Saskatchewan, in the neighbourhood of Prince Albert. A son, Joseph H. is

Chapter 9 – The Pleasures of Smuggling & Family Pressures 351

February 4, 1847 – Thursday. Philip[692] married to-day, and Gavin and William are at the wedding.

February 5. 1847 – Friday. Those who were at the above wedding report that they had nothing but a cup of tea at supper time. Some went home discontented; the rest passed away the time as merrily as they could. . . . [two pages deleted][693]

February 15, 1847 – Monday. I started to The Pines with three men, one horse, and eight oxen, for some juniper[694] posts that James Sandison had chopped last winter. I returned on Wednesday evening and my men the following day. The snow was so deep, and the road consequently so bad, that the oxen scarcely dragged home one post each. This is {321} the first trip made to the Far Pines, in the direction of The Cedars, this winter.

A Claim to Aboriginal Title

February 18, 1847 – Thursday. I went up to the Grand Court to hear what had to be said on the several lawsuits that were to be taken into consideration today.[695] Some of the most important cases were Mr. Bird's with his servant maid, Jane Moat;[696] Joseph Robierre's about his presenting false invoices to Mr. [Alexander] Ross;[697] [and] Mr.

---

a well-known resident of The Pas, Manitoba." Halcro was also mentioned in the February 23 entry, Gunn, p. 322.

692 Gunn: "Probably Philip Bird."

693 Gunn, p. 320, notes that two pages of the MS were deleted.

694 Gunn: "By 'juniper' was meant the tamarack (Larix Americana), and not the cedar (Juniperus) as might be supposed. This was a common local misnomer."

695 See Gibson, *LLG, II*, pp.52-58: (A63-A69, A70-A72).

696 Gibson, *LLG, II*, pp. 54-56: *James Brown vs. Thomas Brown* (Case 27, A65), & *James Bird vs. Jane Mowat* (Case 28, A66). A young man called Thomas Brown had been found in bed one evening with James Bird's servant girl Jane Mowat. On the following day, the girl left the premises. In consequence, Bird brought two lawsuits before this session of the Court: against Brown for trespass to his home, and against Jane Mowat for desertion from her contract of service. Both actions succeeded. The girl's plausible, and independently-corroborated defence that she had left her employment because Bird had fired her, was rejected by a jury.

697 Gibson, *LLG, II*, p. 54: *Alexander Ross Esq., Collector of Duties vs. Joseph Robert* (Case 26, A65). This action was brought in his capacity as Assiniboia's Collector of Customs against Joseph Robert, not Robière, for falsifying the documentation for imported goods.

McDermot's respecting a piece of land on which Pascal Berland [Bréland] and some others had committed some depredations.[698]

The latter lawsuit was by far the most important case of the day and, given its nature, it is remarkable that Peter Garrioch did not seem to understand its significance. It was no less than a Métis land claim, and the first time such a case, or any aboriginal rights issue, had come before an Assiniboia court. The Defendants admitted cutting wood on McDermot's land but contended that the HBC had not extinguished aboriginal title before selling the land to McDermot.

The defence, which the Court accepted, was that aboriginal title had indeed been extinguished by Lord Selkirk's 1817 treaty with local Indian bands. The validity of the Selkirk Treaty was not challenged on this occasion, as it would be in later years.

The idea that the Company's title was clouded by unextinguished aboriginal rights, which both the French and English Halfbreeds claimed to share, was not new. It had doubtless been mentioned at the mass protest meeting in February, 1846 (held, ironically, on Andrew McDermot's own premises) which Garrioch had attended. The scant attention he gave to the case in this journal entry is therefore surprising.

Also two or three other cases about beer-selling to Indians, &c., &c.

February 19, 1847 – Friday. This day I was informed that Mr. James Bird drove out his old servant, George, from his premises like a dog. It is stated by several eyewitnesses that Bird struck the old man several times with a stick. The poor old man, trembling on his staff from age, cold, and hunger, with difficulty reached Mr. Clouston's where he was directed by a savage to seek revenge and shelter. Even this {322} savage was moved at the brutal treatment, and most abject condition of the poor, helpless old man.[699]

Memorializing Smuggling

Today I commenced my "Seven Days' Experience, or the Pleasures of Smuggling."

This was the retrospective account that Garrioch wrote concerning the fur-smuggling expedition he recorded so sparsely in his regular entries for May 6 to May 10, 1846, inclusive, and which has been interwoven with those entries in this edition.

---

698   Gibson, *LLG, II*, p. 52: *Andrew McDermot vs. Bapt. Fanyant, Pierre Poitras, Louison Morin, & Pascal Berland* (Case 25, A63).

699   One wonders, admittedly on no better basis than coincidence, whether George might have taken Jane Mowat's part in events related to Bird's foregoing lawsuit against her.

Chapter 9 – The Pleasures of Smuggling & Family Pressures

February 20, 1847 – Saturday. I went down as far as Peter Pruden's enquiring after the man that had seen Mr. Bird strike Old George and, on my return home, I was told that the man had been working for [brother] John all day, not more than three hundred yards from my own door.

I called at Mrs. Isbister's[700] with no other object than to deliver a letter to a young woman of the Indian Settlement, to be presented to my uncle Joe [Cook].

A Great Mistake Regretted

I saw Miss Caroline[701] in her sitting room, or parlor; but, there being no indication on my part that manifested a desire to make any stay, she did not invite me into her parlor. I certainly made a great mistake, and I do sincerely regret it. But what is done cannot be undone. Therefore I have only to wait till an opportunity is afforded me, and then endeavour to make amends for that which I have so badly managed.

Could the "great mistake" that gave rise to Garrioch's regret and wish to "make amends" to the lady have been related to the "shameful occurrences" at Charles Cook's wedding which he recorded with such contrition on November 26?

February 22, 1847 – Monday. I spent a good part of the day in writing my "Seven Days' Experience." I sent up [brother] William to purchase 100 lbs. of dried meat from Fort Garry.

More Building Preparations

February 23, 1847 – Tuesday. I started with William, Charles Cummings and old Halcro to The Cedars, and returned on the 27th with 60 cedar building logs. Weather quite mild during our absence, but a great {323} deal of snow and a good deal of thaw.

February 28, 1847 – Saturday. Dominique Pambrun moved up to James McKay's with his family.

---

700 Gunn: "Mother of A. K. Isbister, the well-known Red River patriot and scholar, founder of the Isbister scholarships of Manitoba. Mrs. Isbister was a sister of the Arctic explorer Captain William Kennedy of St. Andrews parish; and resided at this time on his property: on the west side of the Red River just north of St. Andrews Church. The old stone residence upon it is one of the historic and picturesque landmarks of the Lower Red River." Gunn, p. 322.

701 Not identified.

An Inheritance Dispute

I was under the necessity of going up [to Fort Garry] today to see Mr. W. R. [William Robert] Smith for an explanation of my late father's will and intention respecting the distribution of his property among my mother and his surviving children. I was induced to do so on account of brother John's assuming an entitled claim to a share of the said property.

Although he lacked formal legal training, William R. Smith, who had recently replaced John Black as Clerk of both the General Quarterly Court and the Council of Assiniboia, occasionally provided legal advice to Red River residents. It is possible that he had drafted a will for the brothers' deceased father and was now being asked to explain its contents. William Garrioch had died more than three years previously, but it was only now, after a subsequent series of events, that the matter of the will came up again.

The reason that questions arose now was that a serious dispute, which had been brewing since at least March/April 1846, about Peter's assumption of control over the family and its assets had never been resolved. Although William's widow Nancy Garrioch appears to have inherited his property upon his death,[702] his eldest son Peter immediately assumed the responsibilities and rights of head of the household.

While other members of the family might well have accepted that assumption at first, we know that Peter found himself a minority of one over his sister Sally's wedding in March, 1845,[703] and that a family rebellion of some sort occurred in the spring of 1846, leading Peter to renounce his role as leader of family worship and other family matters, and his

---

702 The entry for February 21, 1845, recorded that a licence to import goods from England was issued to Nancy rather than Peter, likely because the Company, which administered land records, considered her the owner of the family homestead. It may seem odd that a woman could maintain such a licence in her own right, since under British law of the time, women were not persons under the law. As conservative Victorian standards took greater hold in Red River as the 19th century wore on, women lost ground economically and legally. See Brown, *Strangers in Blood*, pp. 151-152, & *passim*.

However, at the same time, the Red River Settlement included Scottish, French, and Indigenous traditions that did not always align with these ideas, in the same way that "marriage" was perceived by settlers and Indigenous peoples differently. Indigenous women could run fur trade posts while their partners did other business and could trade on their own behalf. Local custom was that, when a husband died, as in Nancy's case, the wife inherited the home, household goods, and care of or handled disbursements on behalf of the children. While Adam Thom or the HBC might have preferred that women be confined to the roles they played in Victorian England, the reality was that in Red River neither Thom nor the Company had the strength, control, or probably a good enough reason to try to disrupt everything everywhere all at once by putting the area's resourceful, strong women back into Victorian apron strings and managing teacups. If the HBC had not issued licenses to women such as Nancy, taking the path of least resistance, they might have cut their own throats both in terms of losing trade and fomenting more, needless anger and encouraging disregard for the licensing system.

703 Chap. 7, entries for March 8, 13, & 14, 1845. Gunn, pp. 243-5.

Chapter 9 – The Pleasures of Smuggling & Family Pressures

resolve to return to the fur trade.[704] He did indeed leave the family to its own devices for the next several months, as he traveled, traded, and pursued other personal interests. Now, however, he was back on the scene, once more asserting a leadership role in the housebuilding project and probably in other family matters. Some question relating to his authority must have led John to assert an entitlement to succession rights and caused Peter to consult William Smith.

It seems likely that the reason Peter did not report William Smith's advice to his journal was that he was unhappy about it. John was not the sort of person who advanced empty claims. An honest, cautious man, who would eventually prosper to a much greater extent than Peter, John probably had a legitimate legal claim, either under his mother's will, or – more probably – as the residual beneficiary of his father's estate after the termination of a life tenancy devised to his mother. It would be quite consistent with what (admittedly little) we know of William Garrioch's character that he might have placed greater confidence in steadfast John than in impetuous Peter. It is not entirely out of the question, either, that Nancy Garrioch, miffed by Peter's criticisms of the use she was making of *her* father's bequest, might also have preferred to favour her second son.

It appears to have been from this point onward that the relationship of brothers Peter and John soured.

Seeking the Tendency of a Lady's Affections

March 1, 1847 – Monday. I went down to Harry Bird's, with the view of seeking to obtain an interview with Miss[705] . . . . . or to learn the tendency of her inclinations with regard to the disposition of herself in marriage. I came back as I went, without either seeing the object I desired or learning a single syllable respecting the nature and tendency of her affections.

Wood for Shingles

March 2, 1847 – Tuesday. [Brother] William, Charles Cummings and an Indian boy started to The Cedars to bring home wood for shingles. Snow fell in abundance today; and, the wind being high, we had quite a drifty day. This month has therefore come in like a lion, and, if the grey heads be correct, it will go out like a lamb. I shall see, if the Lord will.

---

704   Chap. 8, entries for April 24 & 25, 1846. Gunn, pp. 306-7.

705   Whether the lady was a daughter of Harry Bird, as one might suppose, or someone else will probably never be known. An intended note on the subject was never provided by Gunn. If it were Harry's daughter, the most likely would have been his eldest daughter, Amelia, who married James Taylor in 1847. Harry's other daughters were married in the 1860s. Red River Ancestry.ca/BIRD-HENRY-1805.php.

March 6. 1847 – Saturday. William, Charles, and the boy returned with six loads of cedar for shingles and two loads of frame cedar wood. It has been drifting furiously all this day; and, now that it is about 9 o'clock of the night, it does not appear to abate in the least. March, I see, is determined to take advantage of old men's sayings. I hope he will yield to mine in the end, and convince them that they are true prophets. {324}

Finis

Reverend George Gunn's final editorial note reads as follows: "This concludes the diary proper. The manuscript originally continued up to about the middle of June, 1847, but the concluding ten pages were unfortunately removed before it came into [my] hands."

So this is the way the journal as we have it ends: with neither a bang nor a whimper; but with workaday preparations for shingle-making – plus the destruction of 10 pages of entries covering a little more than three months of the diarist's life!

Among the doubtless inter-related threads left dangling were: What did those final, obviously sensitive, ten pages disclose? Why were they removed? Were the family tensions that had been prefigured by the disagreement over Sally's wedding and intensified by the inheritance dispute, ever resolved? Were the "shameful occurrences" of November 26, 1846, somehow involved? Was there some other cause altogether? And why did a man who was so dedicated a journal-keeper for a decade, sometimes in severe wilderness conditions, apparently cease writing altogether in mid-1847? A final chapter, describing the second half of Peter Garrioch's life, and written by the editors with almost no input from Peter himself, will attempt to address those questions, together with others posed by the few remaining shards of this remarkable man's storm-tossed career.

Chapter 10

After the Diaries

1847 - 1888

Starting Over

When we lost direct contact with Peter Garrioch on the snow-filled evening of Saturday, March 6, 1847, he had just recorded receiving six loads of cedar logs he intended to use for the manufacture of shingles for a construction project planned or underway at Orkney Cottage, the Garrioch family home on the west side of the Red River north of the Settlement.

We know that, at the time and for several reasons, he was smarting emotionally. Although he had felt entitled, as the eldest of his deceased father's surviving children, to recognition and respect as the new head of the family, at least some his kin seemed to resent, and to resist, that assumption of authority. Peter's criticism of his mother's generosity to others in the use she made of her recent inheritance from her father, William Hemmings Cook, had upset her and had brought Peter censure from the wider community. And when he had attempted to prevent a large celebration of his sister Sally's marriage the previous year, he had ended up as the only family member who did not attend the event. Then, a little later, apparent resistance to the daily family prayers Peter had instituted, or carried on, after his father's death, along with critical community gossip, caused him to renounce his leadership role in the family and return to a full-time trading career.

He seems to have slipped back into the *pater familias* role somewhat more recently, however, and was perhaps hoping to strengthen that position by his proposal of marriage to one "Miss Caroline." But we know that offer had been rejected, possibly because he got drunk at a cousin's wedding and caused what he himself called "a disgraceful scene," and "shameful occurrences."[706]

---

706   Entry for November 26, 1846, and n. 687.

He may well also have been continuing to mourn the earlier demise of his love affair with Isabella McKenzie.

And then, just a week before the final surviving journal entry, Peter recorded a visit to William R. Smith, court clerk and amateur legal adviser, for an "explanation of my late father's will and . . . distribution of his property . . ." in light of "brother John's assuming an entitled claim to a share of the said property." Remarkably, he failed to record Smith's response in the surviving pages of his diary – which surely indicates that he had learned that John, not he, was indeed the favoured beneficiary. He may well have lost control of himself at about that point. It would hardly be surprising if his or some other family member's later excision of the next several weeks' journal entries had been intended to remove evidence of that dark time.

None of these factors quite accounts for Peter's complete abandonment of his journal, however. Could there have been some altogether different cause for that? The editors believe there was. A clue is found in, of all places, the report of the first census of the new Province of Manitoba, taken in 1870, the year of the province's birth. By that time, Peter Garrioch had been married for over twenty years to Margaret McKenzie, the younger sister of his former sweetheart Isabella. Yet although Peter and Margaret were not married until February 28, 1849,[707] they reported to the 1870 census-taker that their first child, Kenneth,[708] was 22, thus showing him to have been born in 1848 or, at the latest, early 1849.

Courtship, entry into a marriage with Margaret (perhaps, initially, a country marriage, followed by the known formal one in early 1849), and a growing cadre of children provide a sufficient and an entirely plausible explanation for Peter's abandonment, perhaps after a few riotous, best-forgotten, weeks in mid-1847, of both his occasionally dissolute life-style and his wilderness adventures – along with the journal in which he had been memorializing the latter for the past decade. Might he not have resolved, as age 40 approached, to settle down with the mother of his

---

[707] Marriage, Peter Garrioch and Margaret McKenzie, 28 February 1849, in HBCA/AM: Extracts from registers of baptisms, marriages and burials in Rupert's Land, E.4/2, f.113, & in the CMS records. See Chap. 7 n.482.

[708] Red River Censuses/ Provisional Government of Assiniboia, p. 03/ 32-12. Kenneth was named for Margaret's father Kenneth McKenzie, a renowned fur-trade leader. According to Pannekoek, *Snug Little Flock*, p. 88, Kenneth McKenzie, for all his powerful status, abandoned his two mixed-ancestry daughters, Margaret and Isabella, to a harsh school master who forcibly kept them from their Indian mother and whipped them when they attempted to give the poor woman desperately-needed clothing. (Drawn from a letter of Letitia Hargrave to Mrs. D. Mactavish (September 14-17, 1843), *Letters of Letitia Hargrave*, pp. 13-14.

child, along with such future additions to their brood as might and did quickly arrive, and to support them from more stable endeavours?

Another Crusade

Be that as it may, Peter saw no reason to steer clear of *political* controversy. A new Governor of Rupert's Land – a career soldier and dunderhead of the first order, by the name of Major W. B. Caldwell[709] – arrived at Red River in September 1848 with instructions from the British Government to replace the previous governor, command the British troops who had accompanied him to the colony, and investigate complaints about Hudson's Bay Company conduct that were arriving in London in growing numbers.

In partial fulfillment of his third mandate, Caldwell devised a questionnaire containing blandly-phrased queries about the company's conduct toward the colony's residents, and sent it in early 1849 to a selected group of men he called "upper class householders." Most of those to whom questionaires were sent, knowing which side their bread was buttered on, found little they thought it advisable to criticize in the company's policies or actions, and the few who did so were not taken very seriously by Caldwell. Regrettably, James Sinclair (presumably treated as an "upper class householder" on the basis of his wealth and perhaps his influence among the mixed-ancestry community), who was greatly opposed to HBC policies, chose not to respond to the survey. As for resident Indians, not even their leaders were sent questionnaires. Instead, the leaders were summoned to a group meeting chaired by a clergyman Caldwell trusted not to unduly arouse them. This worthy explained that the new governor wanted their views, questioned them verbally, and recorded their answers.

Since Peter Garrioch was not considered to fall within the "upper class" category, he was not sent a questionnaire. Unwilling to have his concerns ignored, however, he found a copy of a pamphlet that Adam Thom, the community's judge and only lawyer, had written in defence of HBC policies, penned rebuttals to Thom's claims, and sent them off to Caldwell. The Governor peremptorily returned the letter to the sender the following day, calling it an "unsolicited effusion" that would not assist his enquiry. He added, however, that Peter could submit his

---

709 One example of Caldwell's unsuitability for his role was his acquisition and removal to England of an object of special significance in Indigenous culture – a decorated and dried human hand which still resides in the Cambridge University Museum of Archeology and Anthropology. See Laura Peers and Anne Lindsay, "Governor William B. Caldwell's Souvenir: Exoticism and a Gentleman's Reputation," *Manitoba History* 73 (Fall, 2013). Throughout his long and checkered career in Red River, Major Caldwell lived up, or, rather, down to his reputation for being "destitute of business habits and of the art to govern" and as "an elderly, dull-witted giant, punctilious with respect to his own dignity and comfort, but incapable of maintaining the one or ensuring the other." Rich, *Hudson's Bay Company*, III, p. 544, and Gluek, *Minnesota and the Manifest Destiny*, pp. 71-75.

personal grievances for consideration if he wished to do so. Realizing that it would be useless for him to address issues other than those set out in the questionnaire sent to "upper class" respondents, Peter requested a copy of the questions; but the Governor refused his request. Some time later, however, although Garrioch is not known to have pursued the matter further with Caldwell, newspaper readers would find that the October 3, 1849, issue of an English paper, the *London Morning Chronicle,* contained an anonymous letter, written in a style that readers of Peter Garrioch's diary would find entirely familiar, excoriating the Governor's incompetence in the matter.[710]

Delegate of the People, Counsel for the Defence, Juryman

And, long before that issue of the *Chronicle* was even published in England, Garrioch took a very public stand in support of those who challenged company policies by assisting James Sinclair in Assiniboia's General Quarterly Court in defending four Halfbreed free traders who had defied the company's asserted trade monopoly. That case, *Hudson's Bay Company v. Pierre Guilleaum Sayer et al*,[711] was the most celebrated lawsuit ever tried by the settlement's courts.

Concerned that competition from free-traders in furs, most of whom were persons of mixed ancestry, had become unacceptably prevalent, the company decided to prosecute four of them, the most prominent being one Pierre Guilleaum Sayer, for violation of the trade monopoly set out in the company's 1670 Royal Charter. Although that monopoly was considered by many knowledgeable lawyers to have expired, the company had continued to assert its legality, and Adam Thom, the General Quarterly Court's judge, and the only legally-trained person in the settlement, was known to support that assertion by the company that paid his very generous salary. It was time, HBC officials decided, to establish once and for all, by means of a test case in the court it controlled, that traders who competed with the HBC were in violation of the law.

They had reckoned without the outrage this move would provoke in a large proportion of the colony's population. Early on the morning of the day of the trial, May 17, 1849, unprecedented numbers of men – most of them of half-breed heritage and a high percentage of them armed – began to gather at and near the little courthouse outside the west wall of Upper Fort Garry. By trial time, the crowd had reached close to 300 in number. They had surrounded the small building and were shielding Sayer and his three co-defendants. Recognizing that his troops

---

710   Gibson, *LLG, I*, pp. 112-113.

711   Gibson, *LLG, I*, pp. 115-119 & *LLG, II*, pp. 113-118: *The Hon'ble. Hudson's Bay Company v. Pierre Guilleaum Sayer* (Case 68, A 151). See also Lent, *West of the Mountains*, pp. 207-215, and Morton, *History of the Canadian West to 1871* (London: Thomas Nelson, 1939, 2nd ed., University of Toronto Press, 1973) for more on the Sayer trial. See above, Chapter 7, text atm 464, Chapter 8, text atm 566, 595-600, & Appendix I, text atm 820.

Chapter 10 – After the Diaries

would be no match for this mob of armed buffalo-hunters, Governor Caldwell decided to leave them in their barracks and personally led the small court party on foot to the courthouse from his quarters in the fort. Although bombarded by verbal invective, the court party group was allowed to push through the crowd unharmed, enter the courtroom, and proceed to deal with other scheduled cases.

Meanwhile, the milling protesters had found their leaders in James Sinclair and his younger relative and sidekick Peter Garrioch. The two were in earnest conversation with Sheriff Alexander Ross. What did the crowd want? Ross wanted to know. What could be done to avoid a tragic riot? Describing themselves as "delegates of the people," chosen to present a petition to the court outlining the protesters' grievances, Sinclair and Garrioch were eventually invited to explain the situation to the court.

When asked by Recorder (Judge) Adam Thom in what capacity he and Garrioch appeared before the court, Sinclair again described himself and his colleague as "delegates of the people," and attempted to hand a petition – which contained a number of wide-reaching demands – up to the bench. Thom informed the pair, however, that they could not appear before a court of law in such a capacity, that not being what courts were for. But, correct and courageous though he was, Thom was no fool, and knew that he had to find some way to break the impasse before blood flowed. He therefore explained to Sinclair and Garrioch that although the court could not accept the petition, it would be entirely appropriate for them to present it to the next meeting of the Council of Assiniboia, the settlement's governing body. And in the meantime, he went on, although the trial of Sayer and his fellow-accused persons must proceed that day, the defendants were entitled to have anyone of their choosing act as their counsel in the proceedings.

After consulting with other leaders of the protesting crowd, Sinclair and Garrioch returned to the courtroom, announced that Thom's suggestions were acceptable, and told the court that Sinclair would act as defence counsel during the legal proceedings. Garrioch, who had been offered a position on the jury, probably accepted that role.

Thereafter, Sayer's trial proceeded smoothly. Sinclair successfully challenged five of the previously-selected jurors, who were replaced by more acceptable men. Prosecution evidence was presented by Chief Factor John Ballenden, and Sayer, being an honest man, admitted that he had engaged in the trading with which he was charged. His defence was that he believed he had been given permission by a company officer to engage in trading.

In face of the accused's admission and Thom's statement of the law, the jury had no alternative but to convict. It recommended mercy, however, in view of the accused's mistaken belief that he was not violating the law. The tension in the surrounded courtroom at the moment the guilty verdict was announced must have been immense. Would the outraged mob wreak physical vengeance upon the court and jury?

Happily, quick-thinking prosecutor Ballenden, fully aware of the risk of violence, leapt instantly to his feet and seized upon the jury's recommendation of mercy. The official court transcript describes his intervention:

> Mr. Ballenden immediately stated that the company did not value the furs which had been traded, but it was the principle of the transaction which he looked at. But since the jury has now given a verdict against the illegal trading he willingly acceded to the recommendation of the jury, and should drop the other three cases [as well].[712]

Ballenden also agreed to return to the accused men the furs which the company had seized from them.

While he and the members of the court might have thought initially that the Hudson's Bay Company had emerged victorious with this judicial affirmation of its trading monopoly in hand, what happened in the next few moments rendered that victory illusory. Upon learning that the free traders were not to be penalized, and would be given back their furs, the demonstrators mistakenly assumed that they had been acquitted, and that free trade had therefore been upheld by the court! Someone in the crowd shouted "Le commerce est libre!" which even Anglophones quickly understood meant "Commerce is free!" and those words quickly became a chant reverberating throughout the settlement.

And, despite its origin in error, the chant became the fact. Company officials knew that a trade monopoly could never be enforced so long as the great majority of Rupert's Land's population was fiercely opposed to it, and it never again attempted to do so. Peter Garrioch's role in helping to bring that victory about must have gone a considerable distance toward repairing the damage to his ego and reputation recent events seem to have inflicted on him.

The petition Thom had refused to accept in court also received a sympathetic reception when presented, less than two weeks later, to the Council of Assiniboia. That did not mean that the petition's demands – removal of Recorder Thom from the settlement, use of French as well as English in court when appropriate, abolition of a law restricting the importation of goods from the United States, inclusion of half-breeds and French-speaking members on the Council of Assiniboia, and complete abolition of restrictions on free trade – would all be granted quickly.

---

712 Gibson, *LLG, II*, pp. 113-118: *The Hon'ble. Hudson's Bay Company v. Pierre Guilleaum Sayer* (Case 68, A 151), quoted in the Transcript to the case at *LLG, II*, p. 116 from an anonymous letter, probably from Peter Garrioch, quoted in Gibson *LLG II*, p. 737, n. 50. "The Governor read the document, and handed it to Mr. Thom. Mr. Thom refused to acknowledge the deputation, and made a long, fierce, elaborate, and bombastic sort of an address, of about one hour's duration, speaking in the more fearless sort of manner, and winding up in a climax of tears."

Chapter 10 – After the Diaries

An anonymous newspaper account of the meeting – one that reeked of Garrioch's sarcastic and skeptical style – commented with some justification that although, "the poor councillors were so terrified" that "if anyone had asked for a sinecure on the moon, it would have been granted," it added that the promises made were no more reliable than if, "John Bull were to grant you the Isle of Cuba in perpetuity."[713] All five demands were nevertheless eventually achieved.[714]

Settling Down

We do not know precisely when Peter and Margaret began to share their lives, but it was solemnized by the Reverend William Cockran on February 25, 1849.[715] Nor is it clear why their marriage was said by one of their children to have taken place in December 1850[716], nor whether it was delayed or accelerated by the fact that Margaret gave birth to their second out-of-wedlock child, Kemper Mackenzie Garrioch,[717] earlier that year. Perhaps either he or she – or both – had

---

713   Quoted from the same anonymous letter. The letter, dated June 5, 1849, was written to someone, probably Isbister, who gave it to the *London Morning Chronicle*, where it was published on October 3, 1849. The internal evidence points to Garrioch as the author of this diatribe against the lack of real justice and fair representation in Red River ("For it has long been known that Mr. Thom brings all his resolutions cut and dried in his pocket, and they are all passed without a dissentient voice. The people have no representation. They have no faith in these Councillors of the colony – colony in name, but Company in reality.")   In the letter, Garrioch – if indeed it was he – airs his complaints against Governor Caldwell and gives his account of the *Sayer* trial. The newspaper's editorial commentary which accompanies the letter is remarkably pro-colonist. HBCA /AM: A.71/8, folio 24-29, Newspaper Cuttings 1849-1859 – Reel 10. See Appendix I – Petitions.

714   Gibson, *LLG, II*, pp. 117-118. Gluek, *Minnesota and the Manifest Destiny*, pp. 119-120, asserts that the Métis were unaware of their own strength vis-à-vis the HBC's more frightened assessment of it.

715   Marriage, Peter Garrioch and Margaret McKenzie, 28 February 1849. HBCA/AM: E.4/2, Extracts from registers of baptisms, marriages and burials in Rupert's Land, E.4/2, f.113.

716   Their son, Kemper, represented to Gunn the date of Peter's marriage to Margaret McKenzie as December 24, 1850. Kemper Garrioch to Gunn (September 12, 1914). AM: Gunn Papers.

717   Kemper appears to have been born on October 14, 1852, although his birth year is sometimes listed as 1850 or 1851, possibly from his being confused with older brother Kenneth, who himself may have been born as early as 1848. In the 1881 Census of Canada, Record Group 31-C-1, LAC microfilm C-13162 to C-13286, Kemper's birth year is given as 1850 and his age as 31. In the 1891 Census of Canada, LAC: Ser. RG31-C-1, microfilm T-6290 to T-6427, Kemper's birth year is given as "abt 1849" and his age as 42. In the 1901 Census of Canada, LAC: Ser. RG31-C-1, microfilm T-6428 to T-6556, Kemper's birthdate is given as October 14, 1851, and his age as 49. Conversely, in Manitoba's Vital Statistics records (*Canada Manitoba Death Index 1880-1949*), Kemper's birthdate is recorded as October 25, 1847.   Kemper was named after Bishop Jackson Kemper (Chap. 4, text associated with n. 247), who, upon meeting Peter at Prairie du Chien in 1838, had advised him that Kenyon College would be the best place to study theology, as well as after his maternal grandfather, Kenneth McKenzie. The website https://central.bac-lac.gc.ca/.item/?id=e011273080&app=fonandcol&op=pdf has the records associated with his and his wife's (Mary Jane Caldwell) application

to be persuaded, for a while, at least, that the marriage would work. The delay in formalizing the union may well have been caused by clergy reluctance to condone the couple's perceived promiscuousness. Possibly Kenneth was not Peter's child – or not Margaret's. Many scenarios can be visualized, but none can be proven by known evidence.

Perhaps all this uncertainty concerning the dates or concerning Rev. Cockran's willingness or not to marry them[718] can be most easily explained by the real possibility that they had already entered into a relationship *à la façon du pays*,[719] which, by the time information about the events

---

for money in lieu of scrip, approved in 1885, in which Kemper gave his birthdate as October 14, 1850. Perhaps he and his family simply lost track of precisely when he was born.

His wife, Mary Jane Caldwell, predeceased him on April 22, 1927, as announced in the *Free Press Evening Bulletin*, p. 5. She was the daughter of John Gunn, MLA for St. Andrews and a granddaughter of historian Donald Gunn. Her brother was Henry George Gunn. Kemper was instrumental in procuring the first mail service in Fairford, where he lived, and taught there in the Lower Fairford school. He was said to have done "a great deal of research into the history of Fairford, and has left us the notes from which this article is compiled. He was a trapper and a very well educated man." "*Interlake Pioneers*," Steeprock Manitoba (Altona: D.W. Friesen, 1974), p. 19. Kemper died on May 16, 1934, as announced in the *Winnipeg Tribune* on that date, p. 20.

718 In a report dated April 5, 1833, to the CMS, for example, Cockran railed against Indigenous wedding celebrations "for the abuses which had been creeping in among them," such as the dances and the "revellings" which took the party and their friends away from their work for several days at a time and left livestock and other domestic duties in the hands of children ill-equipped to discharge them and "not steady enough to take care of themselves." The occasions caused further mischief because some of the children were "kept from school" and "lost their relish for learning…. The parents in consequence of these wedding feasts, not only neglect their own duties, but become instruments in leading their children into the same error." Cockran, *Journal*, Aug./32 to Aug./33, CMSA/AM: Missions to the Americas Mission Bk 1, North-West America, p. 565.

719 A pre-existing marriage *à la façon du pays* between Peter and Margaret might possibly have been acknowledged or acceded to by Margaret's father, Kenneth McKenzie, whom Peter may have encountered St. Louis in September, 1846, when he travelled there, although Peter's description of St. Louis was decidedly negative and it was therefore unlikely to have been the scene of a successful interaction with a prospective father-in-law. On the other hand, if Peter had met with a cool reception, once again, from McKenzie (who was known to be imperious and hard-hearted) with respect to what was already an established relationship with McKenzie's daughter, it could explain Peter's rather abrupt desire to leave "this little nest of Satan" as quickly as he could. When Peter was in St. Louis in 1846, McKenzie, the "King of the Upper Missouri," was there, amassing a fortune in the wholesale liquor trade in St. Louis since he had moved there in 1834. McKenzie died in 1861 and is buried in Bellefontaine Cemetery in St. Louis: Chittenden, *American Fur Trade,* I, pp. 384-385; HBCA/AM; Find A Grave Memorial website; & Legends of America website.

Marriages *à la façon du pays* were ubiquitous at Red River, and many prominent officials of the HBC entered into them, including Governor Simpson. Just how common they were in Red River was described in 1861 by A. K. Isbister, himself a person of mixed ancestry and a brilliant, well-educated leader of the community, respected in London for his views: "…it is an interesting fact that the half castes or mixed race, not only far outnumber all the other races in the colony put

in Peter's family's life was being gathered (from Kemper) by Gunn (*circa* 1914), had fallen distinctly out of favour as an acceptable form of "marriage."[720]

---

together, but engross nearly all the more important and intellectual offices – furnishing from their number the sheriff, medical officer, the post-master, all the teachers but one, a fair proportion of the magistrates and one of the electors and proprietors of the only newspaper in the Hudson's Bay territories. The mixed race, from the inter-marriage during many generations of the Company's officers and servants with the native Indians, have, in fact, increased to such a degree that they are at the moment the dominant class in the country. The single fact that every married woman and mother of a family throughout the whole extent of the Hudson's Bay Red River Settlement downwards, is (with the exception of the small Scotch community at Red River, and a few missionaries' wives) of this class, and, with her children, the heir to all the wealth of the country – the fortunes made in the fur trade, and the valuable property accumulated in the Red River Settlement – is alone sufficient to invest the race with a high degree of interest and importance." "The Hudson's Bay Territories," *Nor'-Wester* (August 15, 1861), quoted in Morton, *Manitoba: A History*, p. 91, & in Sarah Carter, *The Importance of Being Monogamous: Marriage & Nation Building in Western Canada* (University of Alberta Press, 2008), p. 37.

Isbister's figures are supported by a census taken in 1849, which reported Assiniboia's population as 5,391 (248 above the 1843 total), excluding "Indians," who were apparently not counted as they were very mobile. Of the 5,391 people counted, 91 percent were of other than Selkirk Settler origin. Nearly half the population was under 15 years of age. Of 1,012 women over 15, only 135 were unmarried. Other statistics reported were that "settlers cultivated 6,392 acres; and had 12,760 head of livestock. Barns and stables numbered 1,201. Outside the 745 houses stood 1,918 vehicles; nearly 3 Red River carts to every home! There were, in addition, 428 canoes. The 2,600 boys and girls were taught in 12 schools. Grain was ground in 2 water-mills and 18 wind-mills. Private subscriptions, exceeding $32,000.00, had built 3 churches of stone, 3 of wood, and 3 meetings houses." Russenholt, *Heart of the Continent*, p. 93.

720 Brown, *Strangers in Blood*, pp. 211-220, & Van Kirk, *Many Tender Ties*, pp. 231-242. On p. 126-127 of *The Importance of Being Monogamous*, Sarah Carter summed up on marriage by writing that there were diverse definitions and practices of marriages in Plains societies. Second wives were also common, with the first wife, the "sit-beside-him wife", normally giving permission. Many believed their marriages *à la façon du pays* were as valid as a marriage through clergy, and it was common to have children together before clergy marriage, sometimes (as possibly in Kemper's case) backdating the marriage. After all, clergy were not always available, and the HBC accepted undertakings that the couple would marry when a clergyman was eventually at hand. After 1821, the HBC introduced a form of marriage contract that emphasized a husband's responsibility for his family, and it could be signed before the Chief Factor. Gradually – the transitions took place while Peter and Margaret were forming their family – the CMS had a policy not to baptize children of any man who had more than one wife, and after 1885, "illegitimate" children of the earlier forms of marriage, i.e., those not sanctified by clergy, were not entitled to participate in scrip entitlement to land, but the courts of the new province did not always agree with these draconian measures, nor did the nescient Department of Indian Affairs. Nevertheless, as the "Victorian" form of marriage took on more and more exclusive legitimacy, children like Kemper undoubtedly found themselves becoming more apologetic or evasive about their origins. See Carter, *Importance of Being Monogamous, passim.*

The editors choose to believe, until contrary evidence surfaces, that the most probable sequence of events was that Kenneth, the natural offspring of Peter and Margaret, remained with his mother while Peter worked earnestly on the Garrioch property for a while to prepare a home there for the three of them. Under this scenario, the little family likely came together sometime before the looming birth of their second son, Kemper, became evident. And so, to demonstrate the likelihood of his becoming a reliable permanent provider, Peter seems to have abandoned his journalizing as a symbol of the old life-style he had foresworn or simply because he no longer had the time for it,[721] given that nine children were born to Peter and Margaret between *circa* 1847 and 1870.

Moving to Portage la Prairie

What is certain is that in early 1853, four years after Peter and Margaret were married in the European fashion, they and their children moved, along with most, if not all, of the Garrioch clan, to the Portage la Prairie area, a little more than fifty miles west of the Red River Settlement. The move, encouraged by the Reverend William Cockran, would have disrupted their previous life and taken even more of now forty-two-year-old Peter's time and energy. The region was named for the ancient overland transportation route it provided, one that linked Lake Manitoba and the vast network of waterways above and beyond it from the Rocky Mountains to the Arctic Ocean, with the huge Assiniboine / Red / Mississippi / Missouri river network below it. As a gathering place of Indigenous peoples since time immemorial, it was also the site of an existing HBC trading post and various predecessor establishments, although the Company had discouraged use of the Portage area for permanent settlement.

Cockran, the large, rough-and-ready Anglican missionary highly respected by the Garriochs and their neighbours since he had attracted them to the St. Andrews area, was not, however, a man who discouraged easily. Born in England of what a biographer[722] called "humble" Scottish stock, Cockran grew up on a farm, and was employed, before taking up missionary work, as a junior agricultural manager, as well as a "teacher of a small school for children." A "very big and vigorous man," whom an official of the Church Missionary Society thought "would not

---

721   See the Introduction for a discussion of the possibility that there were "lost" diaries dating from after 1847, as Kemper Garrioch informed Gunn in 1914 (AM: Gunn Papers).

722   J.E. Foster, "William Cockran," *DCB* IX, pp. 134-137. See also Robert J. Coutts, *The Road to the Rapids: Nineteenth-Century Church and Society at St. Andrews Parish, Red Rive*r (University of Calgary Press, 2000), p. 34, & *passim*, & Raymond Beaumont, "The Rev. William Cockran: the Man and the Image," *Manitoba History* 33 (Spring 1997). Beaumont offers a nuanced view of Cockran as well as a highly critical view of the methods and conclusions of both Frits Pannekoek and George van der Goes Ladd and the latter's twisting of A. C. Garrioch's relationship with Cockran to serve their derogatory opinions of Cockran. See Chap. 3, n. 206.

Chapter 10 – After the Diaries

suit a congregation in England," because "his origin is low, …his manners unpolished and … his accent vulgar even as a Scotchman," Cockran was nevertheless considered an appropriate spiritual leader for members of Rupert's Land's Indigenous population.

And so he was. Believing that both his mixed-blood, English-speaking congregation and the Indian groups to which he increasingly also ministered needed instruction in practical matters – reading, writing, and agriculture – as well as theology, he had since 1825 preached and ministered to, taught, cajoled, threatened, advised, and assisted in every other way he could, both congregations, first at Upper Church (St. John's), then at Grand Rapids (St. Andrews), as well as at a native settlement called St. Peters further north on the river. In doing all of this, he earned the respectful satisfaction and often love of his flocks. He had been close to the Garrioch family from the time of his arrival at Red River, serving the Church Missionary Society alongside William Garrioch Sr. in the early years, and the bond had become firmer after the family followed Cockran northward to the St. Andrews area following the 1826 flood. It will be remembered that when the missionary was building St. Andrews church, Peter's journal recorded efforts to acquire and transport stone for that purpose.[723]

Cockran's attitude toward the Hudson's Bay Company's authorities was somewhat ambivalent. Generally speaking, he was respectful of them, and even agreed to serve as the Company's chaplain for several years; but he was also sensitive to his congregants' complaints about and resentments toward some of them individually, and to the Company generally. On August 4, 1850, Red River Chief Factor John Ballenden wrote to Governor George Simpson, informing him that Cockran had that day submitted his resignation as chaplain, effective June 1, 1851, and remarking: "I am not sorry, as his conduct during the last two years has been such as could never merit the approbation of any officers of the Hudson's Bay Company."[724]

Feeling a need to establish another mission station like St. Peters among Indigenous populations west of the main settlement, Cockran had set out in 1851, with the concurrence of the Church Missionary Society, for the Portage la Prairie area – perhaps in open defiance of Governor Simpson's express wishes, as Peter Garrioch's nephew the Reverend A. C. Garrioch later recounted in print[725] – to locate a suitable site for such a mission and a supportive white / Métis settlement. Wisely, having found what he was looking for along the Assiniboine River and

---

723 February 9, 1846, and probably December 10, 1846. See also A. C. Garrioch, *First Furrows*, pp. 78-79.

724 Ballenden to Simpson (August 24, 1850). HBCA: D5/28. The tension between Simpson and Archdeacon Cockran is described in some detail in A. C. Garrioch, *The Correction Line*, pp. 180-183.

725 "*Governor Simpson*: 'Archdeacon, I wish you to understand that I am quite opposed to your establishing a settlement up there.' *Archdeacon Cochrane* [sic]: 'Sir George, I am going up there to establish a mission, and I am going up this very day.'" A. C. Garrioch, *First Furrows*, pp. 81-2. The reverend gentleman assured his readers at p. 81 that the quotation "can be taken as authentic on the statement of the most reliable of the [unnamed] pioneer patriarchs." Whether or not such a

"the slough" (a severed river loop "oxbow" later called "Crescent Lake") Cockran sought the consent of the native Saulteaux of the area through negotiations with their chief, Pe-qua-ke-kan, and agreement was reached on an annual rental of one bushel of grain per settler per year during the chief's lifetime.[726] Cockran appears then to have encouraged members of his St. Andrews flock to move there.

There were good reasons for them to do so. The soil offered farmland richer than in many parts of the main settlement. Also, the area, being a few miles beyond the fifty-mile radius within which the regulatory jurisdiction of Red River's ruling Council of Assiniboia prevailed, offered some relief from Hudson's Bay Company control. On the other hand, it placed them beyond access to the main settlement's postal, policing, and judicial services. As Gerhard Ens has pointed out,[727] the location offered more convenient, and less conspicuous, access to the prairies, where the lucrative buffalo robe trade in which both French and English-speaking mixed-ancestry hunters were involved was still active. The occurrence of another major flood at Red River in 1852 – the year the St. Andrews migration to the Portage began in earnest – might possibly also have had some influence, although St. Andrews, which stood on much higher ground than most of the settlement, was not seriously affected by the high water.[728]

In any event, a vanguard of some twenty-five, chiefly St. Andrews-area families, made their way to Portage la Prairie in the first year or two after the Reverend William Cockran established the new settlement, taking up homesteads along the shores of the slough and the Assiniboine River. Among them were the households of Peter, John, William, and Gavin Garrioch.[729] Their mother, Nancy Cook, came with them – the hardy woman would live until 1876 – but it seems likely that she did not remain in Peter's household; John's would have been the more probable.

---

conversation ever took place, there can be no doubt that Simpson and the company he served were strongly opposed, and widely known to be opposed, to settlement in the area in question.

726   Eldon Franklin Simms, *The Story of St. Mary's la Prairie Anglican Church, 1853-1953: Commemorating the Founding of St. Mary's la Prairie parish by Archdeacon Cochrane, 1853-1953* (Portage la Prairie: St. Mary's la Prairie Anglican Church, 1953); & Manitoba Legislative Library, Winnipeg, F5649. P77 Sim (Internet Archive).

727   Ens, *Homeland to Hinterland*, pp. 84-6.

728   Bumsted, "Early Flooding," p. 86.

729   All of them were included on the list of those who were members of the first St. Mary's congregation, Only Gavin was not included among the first fifteen on the list who "arrived about the same time as the Archdeacon [Cockran]." A. C. Garrioch, *First Furrows*, p. 80. The book's author, Alfred C. Garrioch, was a son of Peter Garrioch's brother and sometime rival, John. Alfred became a scholarly clergyman of some prominence. Born in 1849, Alfred – at the age of 3 or 4 years – was also one of Portage la Prairie's charter residents (p. 89). As for Peter, his son Kemper told Gunn that "father came to Portage la Prairie on 15 March, 1853, alone, and we followed two months later." Kemper Garrioch to Gunn (September 12, 1914). AM: Gunn Papers. See also Simms, *The Story of St. Mary's la Prairie Anglican Church*, p. 5.

Chapter 10 – After the Diaries

Cockran, who was promoted to archdeacon in 1853, partly in recognition of his Portage la Prairie initiative, did not immediately make the migration to Portage himself. Being too heavily consumed by responsibilities elsewhere to move immediately, he nevertheless remained in close touch with developments at Portage,[730] including construction of St. Mary la Prairie church, completed in 1855, likely with significant involvement by the Garrioch brothers. And in 1857 Cockran and his wife finally moved permanently to the settlement he had conceived six years previously.

Teaching Again

Peter Garrioch appears to have regained at Portage la Prairie at least some of the lost status his unwise behaviour at Red River may have cost him. He and Margaret acquired and began to develop a lot along the Slough Road, as did his three brothers and their families at nearby locations. And when the new church came into being all four brothers were listed as congregation members.[731] When a day school for settlers' children was established in 1854 Peter was appointed its first teacher.[732] In fact, there being no school building in existence for the first year of its operation, classes were held at his and Margaret's home – in Peter's workshop in warm weather, in the kitchen when it was colder.[733]

By the school's second year of operation a purpose-built schoolhouse had been constructed, doubtless with the Garrioch brothers' participation, and certainly with Peter as teacher, a mile distant from his and Margaret's farm.[734] It was a log building with thatched roof that Peter's nephew Alfred tells us was forty feet by twenty, with nine-foot-high walls, a ceiling, and three large hinged windows, under which, attached to the wall, extended a twenty-five-foot continuous desk at which all the children sat. And he also recalled, with some apparent bitterness, that the

---

730   A. C. Garrioch, *First Furrows*, pp. 77-79.

731   *Ibid.*

732   *Ibid.*, pp. 118-12, & A. C. Garrioch, *The Correction Line*, pp. 374-375. The descriptions therein of Peter's classes by his nephew Alfred, who was a member of the first one and seems from the richness of his accounts to have been in attendance throughout his uncle's tenure and beyond from the age of seven years onward, have the ring of authenticity, albeit somewhat too precisely embroidered in places. Peter's son, Kemper, in response to Gunn's query, said Peter began teaching there in winter, 1855, not in summer, since all of the people thereabouts were on the buffalo hunt. Kemper Garrioch to Gunn (September 12, 1914, AM: Gunn Papers). Oddly, it was said that after the school was constructed, Peter "for the space of three years, taught the young how to shoot." Robert B. Hill, *Manitoba: History of its Early Settlement, Development, and Resources* (Toronto: William Briggs, 1890), p. 136.

733   *Ibid.*, p. 120.

734   Not to be confused with the residential Indian school, which was not established until later, and was taught by others. *Ibid.*, p. 120.

large classroom stove stood closer to the end where the girls sat than to the boys' section! "What was worse, it had no floors. There were no desks, and when we wanted to write we knelt down, on the mud, put our slates on the bench and did our lessons.[735]

His assessment of his uncle Peter's teaching was mixed, at least initially:

> These inconveniences would not have prevented us from learning something if we had only had a desire to learn, but what with our thoughtless indolence and the carelessness of our master (this seems to be some childish impression which soon changed), we left school in six months about as wise as when we first went.... For the next two years school was kept only during the winter months and during the last six months, the young pupil decided that his uncle was improving as a school teacher. In fact, he gets a flogging merely because he had looked away from his slate for a moment....

> The next teacher was Henry Laronde, then Joseph Tait, next Benjamin McKenzie, and then Peter Garrioch again. 'At which time,' the diarist writes, 'he was everything I could wish. He and I were always good friends, excepting once.'

> It was the teacher's custom every evening before prayers were said, to tell the pupils to put away their books and turn away from their desks, then he lectured them on some subject which he thought would be useful to the children then and in after life.

> Although the pupil later realized what a fine man his uncle was, he says, 'I did not always think so then, and was often very indignant with him for wasting so much time, as I thought, at his babbling.'

> On this particular day he was lecturing the bigger boys about the cruel practice of ducking the smaller ones under the snow. The nephew was sitting next to the teacher's son and turned round and said to him, 'I haven't dived any of the smaller boys under snow, but if I wanted to, I could dive Mr. Peter Garrioch himself under the snow.' The teacher saw his lips moving and, of course, questions followed, which ended up in his son saying that the culprit had said he could duck all the boys in the school if he chose to.'

> As it was against the rules to talk, the teacher bumped the heads of the two boys soundly together, saying that although he had not yet done much flogging, he would, if they put him up to it, flog them all round.

> The next school teacher was Rev. Thomas Cochran, and Mr. Garrioch [A. C.] records that he set his heart and soul towards learning during that six months, and was sorry he had wasted so much time previously, 'for he already began to feel what an awkward thing it was to have only half an education.' He planned to devote as much time as he possibly could to reading, but over grammar and arithmetic he did not write so enthusiastically.

---

735   From the Journal of Rev. A. C. Garrioch, quoted in an article drawing on what he had to say about his school experiences, written by his daughter, Verena L. Garrioch (a reporter with the *Winnipeg Tribune*). The editors have not been able to locate the journal itself – it may still be in the hands of Verena's descendants - and suspect that its contents may have been confused by researchers with A. C. Garrioch's other accounts of his upbringing, such as *The Correction Line* and *First Furrows*.

Chapter 10 – After the Diaries

> And that is the way youths received their schooling in the early settlements seventy years ago. If they were not of a studious nature, as Mr. Garrioch was, they might not learn a great deal in the six-month period. Besides, when they were not studying there was much work to be done – setting stones in a kiln and firing it, picking over vegetables in cellars, hauling fuel, a canoe to be made, and field work.[736]

Quite in contrast to his uncle Peter, whose affinity for his and others' oxen and other animals, both wild and domestic, is manifest throughout his diaries,[737] A. C. Garrioch professed a dislike of farming rooted in his distrust in the animals: "…as I have often resolved before, that I will never be a farmer unless I can afford to be one without the trouble of holding the plough or having anything to do with those wayward creatures, oxen…."[738]

Alfred Garrioch also tells us that Peter taught at the Portage parish school for three years,[739] following which he says, coyly, that his uncle "took a rest."[740] Peter's son Kemper, on the other hand, told the Reverend George Gunn in his 1914 letter[741] that he was age 11 "when I attended his last school" at Portage, and Kemper would not have turned 11 until 1861, having been in attendance at the school for at least seven years.

The Portage la Prairie population had expanded considerably by that time. One historian tells us that, "The settlement in the parish of Portage in 1862 consisted of some sixty houses with an average of five persons in each house. After 1862 settlement came on apace."[742] Three more

---

736 Verena Garrioch, "First Schools," p.8.

737 E.g., Chap. 2, entries for June 14, 17, 19-21, 1837, and nn. 106, 109, to June 15; Chap. 5, entry for April 13, 1844; Chap. 6, entries for November 16, 17, 20-25, December 1-4, 7, 1844; Chap. 8, entries for October 16, 1845, and March 1, 1846; Chap. 9, entries for November 28, 30, 1846, February 15, 1847.

738 Verena Garrioch, "First Schools," p. 8.

739 The periods in which Peter taught school are not easy to determine. For example, A. C. Garrioch states in *First Furrows*, p. 126, that Peter taught in the Portage school until the spring of 1864, when he was succeeded by Joseph Tait of St. Peter's. In *The Correction Line*, which he described as "practically a new history …not a mere revision of 'First Furrows,'" he included a section on "Portage School Teachers from 1851 to 1870" (pp. 374-379), where he stated that Peter taught in the winter of 1851-1852 in the earliest days of the settlement, as well as following the retirement as teacher of Thomas Cochrane after which he taught until 1864.

740 *First Furrows*, p. 122. Whenever Peter stopped teaching at Portage he was much more likely to have turned back to trading or hunting than to have "rested." In his Journals, described as such in Verena Garrioch, "First Schools," p.8. A. C. Garrioch recalled his time under Peter's tutelage, which could have been either during this earlier period, c.1855-1861, or later, c.1866-1871, or 1872.

741 Kemper Garrioch to Gunn (September 12, 1914). AM: Gunn Papers.

742 J. H. Metcalfe, *The Tread of the Pioneers, under the Distinguished Patronage of the Government of the Province of Manitoba, the Corporation of the City of Portage La Prairie, [&] the Council of the Rural Municipality of Portage La Prairie* (Toronto: Ryerson Press, 1932), p. 19.

children had been born to Margaret and Peter Garrioch by then: Laura Louise in 1854 and twins Emeline and John West in 1858. Naming the latter after the brother who by now seems to have supplanted Peter as the family's leader might indicate that if relations between the two elder Garrioch men had been ruptured previously they were now healed, at least for the time being.

By then John Garrioch was no longer just the leader of his own clan. His energy and resourcefulness had already brought one of the area's most productive farms into existence, and he was building a reputation as a community leader. His son Alfred C. Garrioch would later write that the Red River newspaper *The Nor'-Wester*, whose Portage correspondent John had become,[743] had described him in 1864 as: "one of the largest and …one of the wealthiest farmers at la Prairie," adding, "and Mr. Peter Garrioch, sorry to say, one of the contrary…."[744] Some corroboration of the latter assertion might be found in the fact that in 1862 Peter sold a strip of his property 10 chains (660 feet) wide to a neighbour.[745] It probably also confirms that agriculture was not a high priority for him.

If Peter was not farming, what was he doing? The most likely probability, at least after he ceased teaching in 1861, and perhaps also in the summer months between teaching sessions before that, is that he was once more trading and/or buffalo-hunting. Perhaps the sale of part of his property in 1862 was motivated by a wish to purchase equipment for another foray to the prairies. Another possibility will be considered below.

---

743 *Nor'-Wester* (April 16, 1862), as recorded by A. C. Garrioch, *The Correction Line*, p. 228. However, a perusal of the newspaper of that date shows merely that it published a letter of his on unrelated topics, not that he had been hired as a correspondent in the sense in which the term is used today.

744 *The Correction Line*, pp. 243-244. The statement comes from "*Whitford v. McBain*. A Complete Statement", signed by John, Kenneth, and Robert J McBain, was dated September 11, 1864, and was published as an "extra" to the September 16, 1864 edition of the *Nor'Wester* The authors state that they were writing the full account of the trial in order to correct, "a letter signed by three of our disappointed, but most worthy jurors of Portage Laprairie, Mr. P. Garrioch, Mr. M. Cumming, and Mr. B. McKenzie, who not only write humorously, but actually stigmatize Mr. J. Garrioch with perfect falsehood…." The McBains' account concludes with a caustic statement supposedly quoted from John Garrioch: "Thanks be to my kind brother, who has laid before me such a useful and important moral, and I earnestly pray that the eyes of my poor brother may be opened, that he may so conduct himself for the future that the wise may no more be heard to say, as they too often have, with too much truth: 'He stands in his own light.' In conclusion, we would beg to say that Mr. John Garrioch is one of the largest farmers at Lapriarie, and so in every respect one of the wealthiest, and Mr. Peter Garrioch, sorry to say, one of the contrary."

745 Metcalfe, *Tread of the Pioneers*, p. 19.

Chapter 10 – After the Diaries

Westbourne Mission Created

In the meantime, something was happening a short distance northwest of Portage that would, before very long, have a major impact on the future of Peter and his family. Reverend William Cockran's son-in-law, Henry George, also a Church Missionary Society missionary, apparently began his career at an Ojibway community called Fort Alexander on the Winnipeg River, a short distance east of the southern end of Lake Winnipeg.[746] He had served elsewhere thereafter, but in 1859, he was authorized to find a suitable location for a new mission station. After traveling "upwards of 360 miles – the length of England itself," as he put it, he recommended a location he described as "rich in natural resources, …distant enough from a trading post, but not too far from the abodes of civilized men to render it isolated or dangerous."

He might have added that the place he chose – a long-established gathering area for both Saulteux and Cree Indians located on the Whitemud River southwest of Lake Manitoba and only a relatively short distance northwest of Portage la Prairie – had been previously visited by itinerant Roman Catholic missionaries, but that there was no permanent Christian mission, Catholic or Protestant, nearby as yet. He and Cockran were eager to establish one before the Catholics got around to doing so. George's choice was subsequently approved by a local Church Missionary Society committee, and he was soon on his way to begin building, "my cheerful undertaking at White Mud River."[747] By early 1860 the Reverend George had much to report:

> I am thankful to report that what has been done up to this date is beyond my most sanguine expectations. My buildings have rapidly progressed, & the most satisfactory trait in my operations is the gathering of many souls around me, and my success in gaining the respect & goodwill of heathen & Roman Catholic Indians. For the most part there has, without intermission, been 60 souls residing. These now claim an inheritance in the soil. Our number will be greatly augmented in the course of time. My school, which I personally superintend, averages 14, a number not to be despised in the very first beginning of a new station. Five Indians with families have already applied for assistance in raising their houses, and in opening farms.

---

746 On a map that purports to show Garrioch's peregrinations in north-central North America (see Appendix II - Map), only one trip is not described in his diary entries. That journey was to Fort Alexander. Might the young missionary have retained the seasoned wilderness traveler to guide him to his first posting, and Peter have accepted the assignment in preference to staying home and ploughing his rock-hard prairie fields or building fences? While no evidence to that effect has been found, it's an intriguing, if slim, possibility. George was not married to Cockran's daughter when he first went to Fort Alexander, but George might nevertheless have known, or known about, Garrioch by then.

747 George to CMS, January 23, 1860, CMSA/AM: Microfilm Reel 87. On Reverend Henry George in Westbourne, see A. C. Garrioch, *The Correction Line*, pp.288-289. See also Westbourne-Longbourne History Society, *When the West was Bourne*, pp. 21-28.

> A Cree Indian service is every Sunday well attended. Likewise, divine service in English is performed for the benefit of the domestics & half breeds resident. The attendance on the services is satisfactory. At the former, however, we cannot look for a very large number, nor great regularity, as they are necessarily prejudiced in their own particular belief. But, being teachable, they are within my reach. The young especially are my hope & encouragement [...]
>
> You will doubtless look for a few words about the location I have chosen.... I chose one where the means of life are certain, and w[h]ere an Indian population can take root and flourish.... I did not act precipitately, & was not satisfied with my own judgment [only]. I laid the case before Arch'd Cochrane in the absence of the Bishop. I felt sure that his wisdom & sound practical view of the question would secure approval. I believe he wrote to your Committee that White Mud River was the only safe position I could fix upon, safe as to permanency and useful success.[748]

Two weeks later[749] he reported that: "I am increasingly persuaded that the advantages of my position cannot be overrated," and offered considerably more detail about the station:

> The small river, characteristic for its winding, reminds one of a rural spot in England, both sides lined with the sturdy oak, occasional bluffs of poplar, the maple & ash [which] afford us an abundance of what is necessary in raising buildings & supplying fuel. Limestone in the bed of the river will meet the wants of the farmer. And the prairie lying before us will enable a people wishing to support themselves to raise the produce of the farm to any extent. Two American citizens who happen to be with me ...have declared that they have not beheld any grazing country to equal it in richness & fertility. [...]
>
> The river throughout the year abounds with fish, and we are no great distance from a fall fishery which will supply us annually with an ample store of food for the winter. In choosing a location, I have thought of food as ...the grand secret of mission success. I am aware that some would regard this as secular, beneath the consideration of an Evangelist, but I maintain most firmly that there is no evangelizing a starving, pinched, & discontented people.... A further recommendation to the place is that I am on the Indian pass to the great buffalo prairies, and... on the highway to the Rocky Mountains [where] I have the opportunity of seeing the Cree, Stoney, & Saulteaux tribes.

This letter concluded with reference to two problems. His "greatest difficulty," George reported, was to "find an able teacher for my school." Until he did so, he had to do the teaching himself, although he admitted it was a task he enjoyed. His other problem was picayune by contrast: that "the name 'White Mud River' offends the ear," and he accordingly requested the Society to substitute "the Indian name 'Wahputumesleeseepee'" until a better identifier could be found!

---

748 CMSA/AM: Microfilm Reel 87 (February 2, 1860).

749 *Ibid.* (February 15, 1860).

Chapter 10 – After the Diaries 375

Church Missionary Society officials must have been relieved when the Reverend George's July 28, 1860 letter[750] reported that a better identifier had indeed been found: the non-euphonious name "Whitemud" had been replaced by Bishop's decree with "Westbourne" in honour of John West, the first Protestant missionary in the area.

The same report stated that the school by now contained "35 souls," comprising "25 Christians & 10 Romanists" [sic], and that construction of "a strong & capacious resident house," as well as the mission school, chapel, and store, were now complete. These achievements had consumed more than George's £50 budget, however, and he had therefore found it necessary to request that the budget be doubled for the following year. The next year's report revealed that a boarding school serving nine children had been added to the mission.[751] Nonetheless a suitable teacher did not appear to have been found yet.

Peter and John at Odds Once More

In 1863 or thereabouts, under the leadership of the Reverend Cockran and his son-in-law, the burgeoning Portage la Prairie community organized a local government and court structure resembling that of the Red River Settlement, except that the Portage version was democratically designed and chosen. This was due to the fact that Portage had been refused government service of any kind from Red River.[752] Garrioch and his neighbours therefore decided to create *their own* governing Council and Court. The Court met first on January 6, 1864, and the initial case occupied both that sitting and the next one in April. Both John and Peter Garrioch were involved, John as Vice-Chairman of the three-member Court, and Peter as foreman of the jury.

---

750   Ibid. (July 28, 1860).

751   Ibid. (October, 1861).

752   In 1864, the Portage la Prairie settlers petitioned the Governor & Council of Assiniboia to become "annexed" to the Red River Settlement and to come within its jurisdiction, but, acknowledging that there was a need for, "some comprehensive measure for the government of the country generally" in the face of the fact that there were numerous unregulated settlements springing up across the country, it was unanimously rejected on the basis that there was insufficient money and military presence to govern any such extension until provision for it could be effected in London. Oliver, *Canadian North-West*, I, pp. 538-539. By the time this petition arrived in Red River, it is likely that at least some of the notorious events of the *Whitford v. McBain* imbroglio had come to the attention of the Governor & Council and, if so, may have coloured the rejection of the Portage la Prairie petition as 'inviting trouble.' Another description of the creation, operation, and fate of the Council of Portage la Prairie, touching on the *Whitford* case, is found in A. C. Garrioch, *The Correction Line*, pp. 238-244.

The case brought before that inaugural sitting of the court was *Whitford v. McBain*,[753] in which one Mrs. Whitford, a widow, sued McBain, a man she alleged was unlawfully occupying property she claimed to have inherited from her husband. As soon as the jury was empaneled, the plaintiff's son-in-law, David Cusiter, announced that he was her attorney. He went on to state that the wrong person had been sued and that although McBain was occupying the land in question, he was doing so because it had been sold to him by the plaintiff's son without his mother's authority, so the son should have been the defendant and had declared himself willing to be sued. If this weren't confusing enough, the Court had just been launched and no one knew a thing about legal procedure.

It quickly became apparent that the proceedings were stirring up the bad blood between the Garrioch brothers since each was backing a different side in the case. Jury foreman Peter Garrioch urged loudly from the jury seats that the plaintiff's change in defendants be allowed – it was his insistence suggesting strongly that he had been involved in initiating the plaintiff's ploy. And ploy it almost certainly was, designed with the apparent intention that the son would admit his wrongdoing, acknowledge that his mother was the owner of the land, the mother would not ask for damages, and McBain would be ordered off the land, probably without getting his money back.

After 'counsel' Cusiter had closed his case for the plaintiff, Mrs. Whitford, he suddenly remembered a certain document he had forgotten to introduce into evidence. The Chairman, likely John Garrioch, who took over at one point to allow the regular Chairman to be a witness for the defense, refused to allow the document to be considered. Whereupon jury foreman Peter threatened that the jury would resign if it was not. So it was entered, though it turned out to be irrelevant.

That day's confused proceedings continued with acting-Chairman John Garrioch's pro-defence charge to the jury which then retired to consider their verdict. After a while they returned, and Peter announced that eleven of them were in agreement, but the twelfth was stubbornly refusing to co-operate. Therefore, he said, unless a replacement juror was appointed, the other eleven would resign. Outraged, but intimidated, the Court complied, and minutes later the jury announced a unanimous verdict for the plaintiff Mrs. Whitford. Peter and the other jurors and Whitford supporters then rushed from the courtroom, bringing the proceedings to a sudden conclusion. In the hubbub that followed, the Court adjourned without remembering to impose a sentence or damage award on the (new) defendant. John fumed as Peter exulted.

During the interval before the next court session, however, John did more than fume. Visiting Red River before the next sitting of the Portage court, he consulted an English law book and

---

[753] Gibson, *LLG*, I, pp. 190-194. Note that this case is not covered in *LLG, II* since it was not tried under the jurisdiction of the Quarterly Court of Assiniboia in Red River and so did not form part of that court's records.

Chapter 10 – After the Diaries

learned that jury verdicts cannot come into legal effect until they have been made formal orders of the court. Since that had not happened in the *Whitford* case, everyone having assumed that the proceedings were over when the jury rushed out to celebrate its victory, the parties would have to return to the courtroom, if only briefly, before the decision could be brought into force. This turned out to be a far from perfunctory step, as the next phase of the case was to demonstrate.

At the Court's second sitting, in April, proceedings were just starting when Cusiter strode in with many supporters of Mrs. Whitford and demanded that the case then before the Court be postponed until the sentence was imposed in the January case. The Chairman asked the interloper to sit down and promised to put the matter on the day's list – at the bottom. But that wasn't good enough for the intruders, whose numbers and vociferousness (plus support from, again, jury foreman Peter) were enough to bend the court to their wishes. "Very well," said acting-Chairman John Garrioch, "Here's how I'll deal with the jury verdict: it's based on perjury and fraud, so I will not accept it!" (or words to that effect).

John had come armed with more lawbook revelations. One was to the effect that a court can refuse to formalize a jury verdict it considers to be contrary to law. John accordingly challenged Cusitor to prove that the jury's verdict had *not* been illegal. Although that was a highly dubious demand, Cusitor attempted to comply with it by producing a letter from a witness to the deceased Mr. Whitford's will. The letter stated in part: "When the old man died I was at his bedside, and heard him say: 'I leave all to my wife.'"

That was when John Garrioch pounced – with yet another lawbook quotation to the effect that wills, to be legally valid, must be in written form! Scandalized, jury foreman Peter Garrioch leaped to his feet, denounced his brother John's decision, chased him from the courtroom, resigned his juridical duties, and led the other former jurors and supportive spectators, shouting, from the room. The hearing ended in chaos, and the Court ceased to function altogether after such a tumultuous start.[754]

The land in question appears to have remained in Mrs. Whitford's hands, which would have been the correct legal result under applicable succession legislation regardless of the illegality of verbal wills, but whether McBain ever got his money back, as he certainly should have, is not known.

A more important question for the purposes of this account is whether the re-opened rift between Peter and John was ever mended. Although very little evidence on that subject exists, we will return to the question at a later point.

---

754   In a February 27, 2013, email to Lorna Turnbull, then Dean of Law at the University of Manitoba, Dale described Peter's behaviour on that occasion as that of an "outrageously disruptive jury foreman in a notorious vigilante trial by citizens of Portage La Prairie."

The *Whitford* case continued to reverberate between the brothers, in the form of a series of letters published in the *Nor'-Wester* on May 31, August 18, September 16, 1864, and February 6, 1865, in which the two sides, one John's and the other Peter's, continued to snipe at each other in full public view. In doing so, each side provided fulsome tirades against the other concerning the *Whitford* imbroglio, thus affording us enough details to furnish a complete picture of the chaotic proceedings and their effect on the Garrioch family. The fraternal (near-fratricidal?) exchange was initiated by the *Nor'-Wester's* May 10, 1864 report of the trial, under the rubric: "Rich Scene in a Court of Justice:"

> We have received an account of a rich scene which took place at a recent meeting of the Court at Portage Laprairie. The Associate on the bench, Mr. J. Garrick, roundly charged one of the juries with having perjured themselves because they brought in a certain verdict. This gave rise to much violent talking; and when the next case came on, a general row commenced. The President of the Court, Mr. F. Bird, being summoned as a witness, left the Bench and his place was taken by Mr. J. Garrick who, when he began to state the case to the jury, was stopped by attorney for defence – on what ground we know not. Others in the room cried out that he should go on, and then ensured a scene of confusion and disorder, in the midst of which, and in some way of which we are not informed, the presiding magistrate was driven from the Bench; - and from his seat in the local Council, at the same time. The people up there have a very prompt and determined way of dealing with their magistrates, surely! And, we must say, on the other hand, that the utterances from the Bench appear to have been decidedly novel and startling for a Court of Justice. Of course, this row brought the proceedings to a standstill. Next day the voting for a new Magistrate and Councillor commenced. Some of the Portage people are now strongly in favor of annexation to this Settlement.[755]

This anonymous account cast John in a negative light while relegating Peter's role to the background. It provoked a response from John in the form of a letter published in the *Nor'-Wester* on May 31, 1864. In particular, John was offended by the statement that 'J. Garrick roundly charged the jury with having perjured themselves because they brought in a certain verdict."[756]

The next letter, dated June 15, 1864, but not published in the *Nor'-Wester* until August 18, was described as a "lengthy but humorous reply to Mr. John Garroch's [sic] last letter" and signed by "P. Garroch, M. Cummings and Benj. McKenzie." In their response, likely penned by Peter, it was conceded (with much invective) that John may not have made the charge of perjury against the jury in those very words, but, more fundamentally, John:

---

755 *Nor'Wester* (May 10, 1864).

756 *Nor'-Wester* (May 31, 1864).

Chapter 10 – After the Diaries

> ...failed to recognize the verdict of the jury by withholding the decision of the Bench.... [and by] gravely put[ting] the following question to Mr. D. Cusiter, the attorney for the plaintiff: 'Can you produce evidence to prove that the verdict is not illegal?' And was not that paramount to roundly charging the jury with perjury?

Objecting to John's assumption of the two roles of judge and pleader, Peter asked, rhetorically: "What did he mean when he made use of the words fraud and perjury?" Peter called John's language "insulting" and "abusive" and as foreman sprang up to be heard, supported by members of the audience. Avowing a strong desire that the truth should come out, in a public newspaper as seemed necessary, Peter fulminated over the sacred duty of the jury – in this case a unanimous one – and charged John and his faction with, "a course of political intrigue and chicanery," ending with the astonishing award of 300£ to the loser, "which makes one's very blood to ache, and his bones to palpitate."[757]

The penultimate exchange in the series was from three allies of John and published in the *Nor'-Wester* on September 16, 1864. The signatories, John, Kenneth, and Robert J. McBain (probably all ghosting for John), billed their long missive as "A Complete Statement" about the *Whitford* case, perhaps to avoid the appearance that it was just another response to Peter's faction and opening the possibility that the newspaper would grant Peter another right of reply. It does place the *Whitford* proceedings in an authoritative context, the councillors having been "nominated by Reverend Thomas Cochrane and elected by the public without one contrary vote, and all in the presence of the good old Ven. Archdeacon Cochrane," a swipe at Peter who had long been close to the latter. There followed a detailed description of the events in the hearing(s) and of the Chairman's having "manifested the greatest forbearance" in the face of various assertions that the parties were not the correct ones, and other irregularities, etc., casting John as the soul of reasonableness who was just allowing the proceedings to play out as best he could. The "Complete Statement" summed up: "...we would beg to say that Mr. John Garrioch is one of the largest farmers at Laprairie, and so in every respect one of the wealthiest, and Mr. Peter Garrioch, one of the contrary," a statement all the more hurtful the more true it may have been.[758]

Finally, Peter's allies, fellow *Whitford* jurers B. McKenzie, Allan McIver, Jno. D. McKay, Malcolm Cumming, Thos. Anderson, Chas. Cumming, P. Henderson, plus David Cusiter, Counsellor, penned a lengthy riposte, dated December 1, 1864, but not printed (in the format of a *"Nor'-Wester Extra"*) until February 6, 1865. After opening salvos attacking the writers of the previous September 16, 1864, "Extra," the writer(s), again likely Peter himself, says:

---

757 *Nor'-Wester* (June 15, 1864).

758 *Nor'-Wester* (September 16, 1864). The suggestion that Peter was impoverished seems strange when one considers that his wife Margaret was the daughter of Kenneth McKenzie, who was a prominent American trader described as the King of the Missouri (above n. 503.) McKenzie died in April, 1861; did he leave no legacy to his daughters and their families?

> The sum total of the contents of the Extra in question may be briefly stated in a few words – misconstruction, misrepresentation, detraction, disgusting personality, low wit, extreme arrogance: and we hope not deliberate, but we fear direct falsehood, with a sparse sprinkling of truth here and there....They are woefully mistaken if they suppose P. Garrioch stands alone. They ask: why then the controversy between such two parties? We answer, – From no other cause whatever but from the inability of the leading men of the Bench to prosecute and conduct matters of a legal character." Then follows a series of alleged corrections to the other (John's) side's presentation of the goings-on during the *Whitford* trial, ending with a summing up the impugned conduct of the presiding magistrate *pro tem* (John): "The sentence had been passed and pray what earthy right had J Garrioch to read or say anything more on the subject? What business had he to ask questions so insolent and irrelevant of the plaintiff's attorney when the verdict of twelve sworn men and the sentence of seven sworn judges had forever settled the case? Here it is whence those 'fiendish flames' emanated with which they charge their more innocent neighbors....

Then the writer uses language which convinces the modern reader (at least) that it is Peter writing in bitter personal terms about his brother:

> As to the simple tale they allude to, we are sorry to say it was quite misunderstood and therefore misapplied. The Editors perhaps are somewhat to blame for this as the leaving out so much of our former communication necessarily destroyed the connection of various parts. The person intended by the wrong ass bridled, is David Cusiter, whom John Garrioch vituperated in full court. We are happy to learn however, that J. Garrioch is apparently grateful for any useful hint which drops from his older brother's pen. It is to be hoped that he will 'so conduct himself in the future' as to afford no reason to his friends or enemies to say of him he is blinded by his extreme arrogance and excessive vanity. Mr. P. Garrioch thinks that though praying for each other is a divinely-inculcated precept, his brother John had better offer up that prayer for himself in the first place, and then think of his poor brother in the second place, for though charity should not be confined *to** certainly it ought to begin at home. ...the Extra worthies ...seemed to have arrogated to themselves a complete triumph in not only putting on the harness but in taking if off, by the mere force of hair splitting, grasping at straws and mountain-top declamations....[759]

It would be hard to conclude otherwise than that this very public and heated dispute between the brothers and their respective allies hardened their differences into a concrete block for a very considerable time, if not for the rest of their lives.

---

759   The asterisk is in the original. *Nor'-Wester* (February 6, 1865).

Chapter 10 – After the Diaries

Catechist & Teacher

In the spring of 1865, the Garriochs' spiritual leader and friend Reverend William Cockran took ill and decided to retire to Toronto. He recovered very quickly after his arrival there, however, and returned to the West in late summer of the same year, determined to settle at the Westbourne mission, from where his son-in-law Henry George had apparently decided it was time to move on.

Perhaps by coincidence, but very likely at Cockran's suggestion, Peter Garrioch also moved to Westbourne at about the same time – in the role of the mission's catechist[760] and teacher. Peter and Margaret's family had expanded again in the previous year with the birth of Isabel Margaret, and of course the other children were all getting older and more expensive to feed and clothe. If whatever Peter had been doing since leaving the Portage school was bringing in much income there is little evidence of it. The pressure from Margaret, and probably from his own conscience, to increase his income must have been growing insistent. It should not be surprising, therefore, that an opportunity to return to teaching on a salaried basis would have been attractive, especially as part of a missionary enterprise led by his old friend and advisor William Cockran in a location at some distance from where his younger brother's accomplishments were now so obviously outshining his.

Garrioch and Cockran had not been in Westbourne long, however, before fate took a cruel turn. The Reverend William Cockran, then in his late sixties, went swimming in the Whitemud River, but caught a chill in the cool September weather and became seriously ill. Peter, realizing that his friend needed medical attention, drove him (in his 'democrat carriage' according to one account, adding that it was "the only one in Westbourne")[761] to Cockran's daughter's home at Portage la Prairie, where he died October 1, 1865.

Peter remained at Westbourne, however, soon to be joined by Margaret and the children, and become head of one of the earliest of the area's settler families. Although Kemper Garrioch recalled, much later, that the move from Portage was not made until April 6, 1866,[762] there can be no doubt that Peter spent considerable time at the mission during the preceding winter, preparing his charges for confirmation by the new bishop, Robert Machray, upon his anticipated

---

760 Religious instructor.

761 Westbourne-Longbourne History Society, *When the West was Bourne*, p. 136. A democrat was a type of light, four-wheeled, four-seat, horse-drawn carriage that was fashionable at the time. Might Peter have purchased the carriage with proceeds from his 1862 sale of land?

762 Kemper Garrioch to Gunn (September 12, 1914). AM: Gunn Papers. This was the time it was decided to build a new school, which was dedicated in July of that year by a great community celebration, according to A. C. Garrioch (Kemper's first cousin), as described in Verena Garrioch, "First Schools."

inaugural tour of inspection at Westbourne in early 1866.[763] What probably happened was that Peter and Cockran had come to the mission station without Peter's family in the fall, with Peter remaining chiefly in Portage for the winter but visiting the mission alone from time to time to conduct catechism training. The permanent move with his family occurred in April.

Interestingly, when the first election of vestrymen for St. Mary's church in Portage occurred on April 9, 1866, Peter was one of those chosen, along with brothers John and William, even though he and his family were now at Westbourne.[764] Whether he retained that position at St. Mary's for a significant length of time is not clear. What is well established is that Peter and his family resided at the Westbourne mission from April, 1866, onwards. While his official responsibilities as catechist and teacher were chiefly pedagogical, Peter was frequently – most of the time, in all likelihood – the sole Church Missionary Society representative present at the mission. It would be difficult for anyone familiar with his leadership impulses and theological ardour to believe that he did not engage in at least occasional preaching as well. Even without the full theological training he had sought at Kenyon College, he had finally attained a position somewhat akin to the missionary career he had set out from Orkney Cottage almost thirty years earlier to establish.

Margaret bore their youngest children, William Cockran Ridley in 1869, and Alice Jane in 1870. They were born at Winnipeg, now the name of the former Red River Settlement, as had those of all or most of the couple's children – presumably to be closer to medical and/or midwife assistance – but she brought them home to the Westbourne parsonage. And although the older children would be soon venturing out on independent lives, they do not seem to have been overly eager to do so. For example, Kenneth, their eldest at age 22, was still living with his parents at the time of the 1870 census.

Insurrection & Provincehood

The years 1869 and 1870 were ones of turbulence and political rebirth in what is now Manitoba. Anyone aware of Peter Garrioch's previous outspoken dissatisfaction with the Hudson's Bay Company's governance of Rupert's Land might have expected him to become an active participant in the 1869 Métis insurrection led by Louis Riel. The reason is that, like Riel, Peter had long railed against the Company's plan to sell the vast area back to Great Britain, with a view to its being ceded to the newborn nation of Canada with no prior stipulations as to its status. Worse, the Company's plan was negotiated without the participation or even knowledge of Rupert's Land's inhabitants.

---

763   See Robert Machray, *The Life of Archbishop Machray* (Toronto: Macmillan, 1909), p. 129.

764   Simms, *The Story of St. Mary's la Prairie Anglican Church, 1853-1953*. (Internet Archive).

Chapter 10 – After the Diaries

No evidence of any such activity on Peter's part has been found, however. Brothers John and William, on the other hand, were significantly involved – not as Riel opponents, as one might have thought, but as representatives of Portage la Prairie at the two meetings of community spokesmen convened by Riel to discuss the Settlement's demands to Canada: the "Convention of 24," held in November, 1869, and the "Convention of 40," which took place in January/February, 1870.[765]

John Garrioch was present at the first of those meetings. The delegates insisted upon and unanimously approved a carefully-phrased "List of Rights." At the second, with brother William replacing John, the List of Rights was revised somewhat, and three representatives of the Settlement were unanimously chosen to travel to Ottawa to negotiate Rupert's Land's future.[766]

---

[765] John, but not Peter, was listed as a member in the March 9, 1870, proclamation of the First Legislature of Rupert's Land, of which Riel was President. The proclamation is reproduced in Bruce Peel, *Early Printing in the Red River Settlement 1859-1870* (Peguis Pubishers, 1970), p. 53. John's son, John, the brother of A. C. Garrioch, was one of the "Portage la Prairie Gang" that attempted to free Riel's prisoners in February, 1870, and ended up being captured themselves. Lawrence Barkwell, "*Alfred Campbell Garrioch*," Virtual Museum of Metis History and Culture, 2011. metismuseum@gdi.gdins.org.

[766] Alexander Begg, *Begg's Red River Journal and Other Papers Relative to the Red River Resistance of 1869-1870*, edited with an Introduction by W. L. Morton, Champlain Society Publications XXXIV (1956), pp. 166, 285, 323, & 333. On the Conventions themselves, see W. L. Morton's Introduction, pp. 59-100, which explains how, between the two Conventions, events led to misunderstandings between the English Métis, led by James Ross, and the French Métis, led by Riel, over Riel's plan to declare a Provisional Government to fill the governmental "gap" (or "abandonment") to be created by the hand-over by the HBC on December 1 and Canada's future acquisition of Rupert's Land as a Province. Eventually it became clear that it would be in the best interest of all Métis to possess the power to negotiate terms, especially to preserve their interest in the lands they occupied/owned. The English Métis delegates said they needed to consult the communities they represented, and this is the point where John Garrioch may have discovered that his Portage la Prairie constituents and his employer, the CMS, considered that he was not welcome to participate on their behalf in the Convention of 40, the next iteration of the Métis struggles for meaningful negotiation of the terms by which their lands were to be taken into Confederation, especially once Riel had captured the Schultz party and proclaimed the Provisional Government on December 8, 1870.

John Garrioch, however, still played a role, however informally, in the transition from Provisional Government to Province. As the fourth "List of Rights" as drafted by the Provisional Government morphed into the *Manitoba Act*, the lands of the new province were kept under federal control, with Indian title granted and Dominion titles issued to land holders, without reconciling Métis claims to both Indian title and to a block of land exclusively in the possession of each of them. The *Manitoba Act* provided that 1.4 million acres should be reserved to children of half-breed families in the same way as to the Crown's Indian wards: W.L. Morton's Introduction, pp. 136-137. Unhappily, the claims of Indians and the Métis were vexingly irreconcilable, and there were petitions from all sides on the issue, one of which was from Pie Wasch, Cha-Wa-We-Ash to Governor McDougall, dated September 26, 1869, and reproduced in Begg's diary, pp. 180-181.

While no evidence of Peter's involvement in those historic events has been found, it seems highly likely that he would have approved of his brothers' roles.

Prominence Regained

And it was not long before Peter Garrioch was also to make a personal and vital contribution to his community. Shortly after the birth of Manitoba – the new Canadian province that these events caused to be brought into being in May, 1870 – Peter performed a very valuable service for both his community and his province that Westbourne's official history describes as follows:

> In 1870 the smallpox epidemic reached such proportions in the Northwest Territories that a quarantine station was built on the Fort Carlton Trail on the outskirts of the Whitemud River Settlement, on the north side of the river. This building was erected to house any furs, etc. that HBC men and free traders would try to bring down to Fort Garry. Peter Garrioch was in charge of the Whitemud River post, with several 'policemen' under him.[767]

Peter's performance in that essential role at a time of great peril to Manitoba's public health was considered so satisfactory that the chief quarantine officer for the district recommended to the Lieutenant-Governor of the province, in November, 1870, that he be appointed as a justice of

---

Apparently because he was considered influential, another petition was addressed to John and posted on a church door. John in turn sent it to the *Manitoban and Northwest Herald*, where it was published on July 1, 1871: "To the Editors of the Manitoban. Portage La Prairie, 16th June, 1871. Gentleman: As I consider the public have an interest in this day[']s publication, or in the notice which was posted on our church-door to day, I shall give you an exact copy of what we may consider as an Indian protest, and since they have had the politeness to address me before the public, I give you leave to use the following as you please. 'Portage La Prairie, June 14, 1871. To Mr. John Garrioch and the public, NOTICE. As you have encroached somewhat on our rights, both from one side and the other, we have thought it proper to say a few words. We are expecting to see something done every day, and therefore we wish nothing to disturb us for the present. This land that you are wanting to take without our permission, don't you think the government would ask how did you get it? Why we speak to day, is because we are poor but we still hold the land for our children that will be born afterwards. When we speak first we speak softly; but when we speak again we will speak louder. We hardly need say that this alludes to an attempt that has been made to claim and occupy lands that does not yet belong to them, for they know that we have not yet received anything for our lands, therefore they still belong to us. We now beg of you, one and all, to give us no more trouble until we are spoken to by the person with whom we expect to treat with. We think well to advise the settlers who are now on claims to keep them and not sell them yet. We don't say we have already given you these lands, but allow you to remain on them. (Signed) Yellow + Quill (his mark) I-ee-be x Pee-Tang (his mark) Zhoo x Shou (his mark) Moose x Oris (his mark).' JOHN GARRIOCH."

767 Westbourne-Longbourne History Society, *When the West was Bourne*, p. 98.

Chapter 10 – After the Diaries

the peace, in charge of "two or three constables," who "would answer the purpose of police...."[768] That recommendation resulted in an even more prestigious appointment: as President of the Court of Petty Sessions for the County of Marquette West. Those duties apparently proved too onerous for Peter; he resigned as President in October, 1871, but remained a judge of the Court.[769] And although it is not certain how long he held a position on that court, he continued to be re-appointed as a justice of the peace until at least April, 1876, even though he had tried to resign earlier.[770]

Justices of the Peace were not just judicial officers and directors of police. Their public prominence placed them in a position of general community leadership. An item in the May 3, 1873, issue of the *Manitoban and Northwest Herald* tells us, for example, that: "Pursuant to a notice issued by the magistrate at ...White Mud River, a public meeting was held at the said place ...for the purpose of taking local and other matters into consideration. [With] Mr. Peter Garrioch, as chairman, the following resolution was moved ...and carried unanimously...."

Peter had sought even greater prestige than that judicial rank bestowed by contesting Manitoba's first election for members of the Parliament of Canada – a special by-election for the new province only – on March 2, 1871. Living, as he did, in an area of Manitoba where many voters of mixed ancestry resided, facing two opponents in whom no Ingenious blood is known to have flowed, and running as a candidate for Sir John A. Macdonald's governing Conservative Party, his chances of election might have appeared favourable. Peter's nephew, the Reverend A. C. Garrioch, admittedly not unbiased in the matter, observed of his uncle Peter as he stood for election:

> ...it could only have been due to inimical representations that Peter Garrioch was not preferred. Native born, an older man, and much older in services to the country, a splendid conversationalist, a good public speaker, well acquainted with the Metis and as much as home as themselves in their mother tongue, he was probably an equally good man among the English, and by far the more likely man to have captured a good share of the French vote.[771]

---

768 AM: Finding Aid M781, #72 – Archibald Papers [Incoming] Calendar, (November 1, 1870).

769 *Le Métis* (November 9, 1871).

770 *Winnipeg Daily Free Press* (April 3, 1876); *Le Métis* (April 13, 1876), AM: MET 711109, 1 nr 23. Reproduced on p. 311 of Westbourne-Longbourne History Society, *When the West was Bourne* is a letter, dated July 26, 1872, from the Royal Provincial Society to Peter Garrioch, acknowledging his request to be relieved of his duties as Justice of the Peace, but denying the request, since "the Government cannot dispense with the services of good men and leading citizens." Appointed: *Le Métis* (June 29, 1871); Reappointed *Manitoban & Northwest Herald* (February 28, 1874); & Reappointed for the County of Marquette. *The Daily Free Press* (April 3, 1876).

771 A. C. Garrioch, *Correction Line*, p. 341.

But when the ballots were counted, candidate Garrioch stood last. Some consolation must have come from learning later that neither of his opponents ended up being elected either. They had finished in a tie, and had both traveled to Ottawa hoping to have the problem sorted out, but before that could happen, the matter was made moot by Prime Minister Macdonald's calling a general election.[772] And whatever residual disappointment Peter might have experienced by reason of his electoral loss would have been assuaged to some considerable extent by his appointment as Westbourne's Postmaster in July 1871, a position he held for the next two years.[773]

Having become a relatively big fish in a small pond, Peter was apparently content with his lot for the time being and does not seem to have attempted to run for Parliament again in 1872. He did, however, contest the 1873 election[774] – called after the Macdonald government was forced from office by the Pacific Scandal – but he was again defeated, this time along with a majority of Conservative candidates country-wide. Nevertheless, he was active in local affairs, elected, for example, to chair the meeting of area citizens on April 11, 1873, at which a resolution was passed which led to the incorporation of the Township of Westbourne that year.[775]

Unemployed & Homeless

Peter's second electoral loss would have been more painful than the first, because he now found himself without any paid employment other than his stipend as Justice of the Peace. The federal Conservatives' decimation at the polls had ended any hope that his commission as Postmaster would be renewed, of course, such positions being patronage appointments, and his post as teacher, catechist, and probable occasional lay preacher at the Westbourne mission had ended in 1871 or 1872,[776] when his cousin the Reverend Thomas Cook, another grandson of William

---

772 *Ibid.*, pp. 340-2.

773 LAC: PSFDS03-(8630), item 17302. Or longer. In another source for post offices and postmasters, Garrioch's date of appointment is given as July 1, 1871, and his date of resignation as April 1, 1876, a period of nearly five years. It has been noted that the office of postmaster had been in part created as a kind of compensation for those of the labouring classes who failed to achieve the respectability of middle-level fur trade tasks, such as clerkships, and it was a convenient cost-cutting measure as well, since postmasters received wages of half to two-thirds of a clerk's salary. Brown, *Strangers in Blood*, pp.205-206.

774 The *Manitoban and Northwest Herald* (January 31, 1874) noted his nomination as having occurred on December 31, 1873.

775 *Manitoban and Northwest Herald* (May 3, 1873), p. 2, and AM: website for "Westbourne (MB: Rural Municipality)."

776 Kemper Garrioch (AM: Gunn Papers) stated to Gunn in 1914 that his father's employment as teacher and catechist under the CMS ended in 1871, but a report of a late-1871 survey of the CMS lands states that: "Peter Garrioch lived there since 1865 as a catechist in the parsonage and have [*sic*] the lands [. . . of] the CMS for his use while under pay of the Society. [. . .] [H]as to leave the

Hemmings Cook, took charge of the mission,[777] and became its sole senior employee. Moreover, Peter's loss of his mission job also meant the loss of his large family's home at the parsonage – and perhaps their use of parsonage land for crops and kitchen garden as well.

What to do? Finding land on which to build a new home and grow new crops, which had to be given first consideration, might not be easy. Prior to provincehood, most incoming settlers to the area had simply squatted on unoccupied land, set about clearing as much of it as was immediately required, built simple houses, and planted crops. After a time some such owners sold or leased their land to others, and the legality of such transactions, as well as of the initial unauthorized occupation, was eventually confirmed by legislation.[778] When Kemper Garrioch began to feel urges of independence, for example, he either squatted on or purchased land adjacent to the Canadian Missionary Society lot his father was using as a privilege of his employment by the mission – and then sold it to someone else after his plans apparently changed.[779] Peter Garrioch had not been as prudent as his son, however, and by this time much of the best land near Westbourne was occupied.

The family could have been in serious trouble. While the children could at least look forward to eventually receiving land grants from the government of the new province when they reached adulthood under the "Grant for Halfbreeds" provision of the provincial constitution negotiated by Louis Riel's provisional government's representatives in 1870, that benefit applied only to "*children* of . . . Halfbreed heads of families," not to the heads of families or their spouses themselves.[780] And, of course, most of the children were still minors at this point, too young to exercise their constitutional rights for some time to come.

As it happened, however, Peter dealt with the problem in a very simple manner. Kemper's 1914 letter to George Gunn states that: "In 1872 he took up his residence on his farm in Westbourne, where he resided until his death."[781] Since "his farm" could only have meant the Canadian Missionary Society mission property he had been cultivating as a perquisite of his employment

---

parsonage next year": Westbourne-Longbourne History Society, *When the West was Bourne*, pp. 37-8. Perhaps Peter and his family were allowed to remain in the parsonage for a period after his employment had ceased. Perhaps, too, Peter's employment was voluntary; Kemper's letter refers to his having "retired."

777 Westbourne-Longbourne History Society, *When the West was Bourne*, p. 136. Peter's nephew, A. C. Garrioch, reported in his book *The Correction Line*, p. 101, that he himself taught in the parish day school in St. John's parish, Red River settlement, from 1869 to 1871, the school where Peter had taught in 1836-1837.

778 *Manitoba Act*, 1870, s. 32(3) & 32(4).

779 Westbourne-Longbourne History Society, *When the West was Bourne*, p. 37-42.

780 *Manitoba Act*, 1870, s. 31, emphasis added. However, Nancy Cook was successful in applying for her scrip entitlement; her claim was marked issued October 2, 1876.

781 Kemper Garrioch to Gunn (September 12, 1914). AM: Gunn Papers.

since 1865 or 1866, we must conclude that he just built a house there, moved his family into it, and continued living on and farming Society land. Apparently neither the Reverend Cook (who was Peter's cousin, after all), nor anyone else objected to their continued presence; and the situation must have prevailed unchallenged for the next six years.

Peter's Last Battle

Then, in 1878, Peter Garrioch made an interesting discovery. Searching the provincial land records respecting the Church Missionary Society's title to the Westbourne mission, he discovered that although the Hudson's Bay Company had agreed in 1859 to give the land in question to the Society, no steps had ever been taken to issue a formal patent for the property. So, in February, 1879, Peter applied for a patent in his own name for the land he and his family had been occupying since he left the employ of the Church Missionary Society – and perhaps for the rest of the mission's land as well! The Society, unwilling to cede ownership to its former employee, objected to his application,[782] sought evidence that the Society had been at least in "peaceable possession" (squatter's occupation) of the land since long before the Garriochs came along, and filed a competing patent application.

The dispute dragged on for six years, but it does not appear to have been very rancorous. When the Society decided to build a new church in place of the dilapidated old one, for example, Peter and his son John West were both donors to the building fund.[783] And although the Society was eventually granted a patent for all the land the Hudson's Bay Company had originally agreed to give it, Garrioch sympathizers within the organization persuaded the Bishop of Rupert's Land to grant Peter a deed for 60 acres: presumably the land he was then occupying. That deed was dated October 7, 1884; Peter had just four more years to live.

The Final Years

All that Kemper Garrioch told George Gunn about his father's concluding years, other than the date of his death, was that: "For the last decade of his life he was a victim of asthma, and unable to follow his avocation."[784]

---

782 On March 24, 1879, "the full impact of land ownership created chaos at the CMS meeting … when it was finally realized that Westbourne, along with their other church properties, had to be patented." Westbourne-Longbourne History Society, *When the West was Bourne*, p. 228.

783 "The 'Subscription List' found in their new Treasurer's Book reads like a Manitoba *Who's Who*: … the list of 22 persons included the Bishop of Rupert's Land, A.G.B. Bannatyne, the Rev. Thomas Cook, Peter Garrioch, John West Garrioch (Peter's son), & Hon. John Norquay (Premier of Manitoba)." Westbourne-Longbourne History Society, *When the West was Bourne*, pp. 228-229.

784 Kemper Garrioch to Gunn (September, 12, 1914). AM: Gunn Papers.

Chapter 10 – After the Diaries

By "avocation" Kemper might only have meant Peter's day-to-day work on the farm; but the primary meaning of the word is a "secondary activity undertaken in addition to one's main work,"[785] and we know that Kemper used words carefully (even if not always accurately). We also know that at some point after he stopped making entries in his diary, a careful fair copy of its centrefold map of his travels was made, on which he was referred to as "author" (see Appendix II). Might it not have been possible – perhaps even likely – that what Peter's son was telling his nephew in this letter was that asthma had prevented Peter's intended *polishing and publication of the diaries – his "avocation"* – in whole or in part? The second editor, Dale, believed so. After all, it was Reverend Gunn's own decision to do just that himself on behalf of the deceased author that caused him to request Kemper's assistance with *his* avocation.

Peter Garrioch died, well into his 77th year, on November 20, 1888, at his Westbourne home. Although it is not known where he was buried, the likelihood is that it was near the family farm, possibly without a monument. Margaret survived him by many years, dying at age 89 on July 20, 1914, in Portage la Prairie, where her remains lie, marked by a handsome stone, amid the well-marked graves of numerous other Garriochs in the cemetery established by the Reverend William Cockran, the Garrioch brothers, and the other charter members of St. Mary's la Prairie Anglican church.[786]

Had the stormy feelings that embittered relations between Peter and some of his family members from time to time healed before his death? No certain answer can be offered. The fact that no monument to Peter's memory appears to exist,[787] as it does for so many others of the family, including Peter's wife, suggests that hostility might have prevailed until the end. On the other hand, Reverend Alfred Campbell Garrioch – John's son and Peter's nephew – described Peter

---

785 *Canadian Oxford Dictionary*, 2nd ed.

786 The charter members of St. Mary's congregation are listed in Garrioch, *The Correction Line*, pp. 179-180.

787 When Dale visited Westbourne in August, 2014, he initially went to the most logical place for the cemetery, St. George's Anglican church, a replacement for a church totally destroyed by fire in 1928, but it had a very large padlock on its door and looked, with its flaking paint and cracked windows, as if it were now used only on rare special occasions, if ever. The small churchyard contained no gravestones whatsoever. After being directed to the original Westbourne Cemetery, some distance west of the village, he, like Durlene before him, found only one gravestone for a Garrioch (Jemima Garrioch) among the relatively few gravestones there. Nevertheless, the secondary sources, including the substantial 1985 Westbourne local history project, state that Peter was buried, as was his wife, who died on July 20, 1914, in Westbourne Cemetery: Westbourne-Longbourne History Society, *When the West was Bourne*, p. 311; G. A. McMorron, ed., *Souris River Posts*; & Métis Museum, entry for "Peter Garrioch", https://www.metismuseum.ca/media/document.php/12571.Peter%20Garrioch%20ASC.doc.; & Métis Dictionary of Biography, Vol. E to G, ed. Lawrence J. Barkwell, entry for "Peter Garrioch," Scribd, entry for "Garrioch, Peter (b. 1811): *Métis Free-Trader*," scribd.com/document/30044709/Garrioch-Peter.Law.

in his first book, *First Furrows,* as a man "of a philosophic turn of mind" and "an even temper,"[788] and in his second book, *Correction Line,* as "a splendid conversationalist," at home with both English and French speakers, and praised his many "services to the country."[789] Such admiration by the son of Peter's chief fraternal competitor does not suggest that the intra-family hostility was long-lasting or shared by all of Peter's family members.

In any event, A. C. Garrioch's words of praise for Peter Garrioch provide a fitting epitaph in place of what may never, but ought to have been, engraved about him in stone.

---

788   *First Furrows,* pp. 118-119.

789   *The Correction Line,* p. 341.

Appendix I

Petitions

At the time Peter Garrioch was recording his thoughts and experiences in his diaries, Red River society was particularly unsettled. There was growing dissatisfaction with the paternalism and patronizing attitudes shown towards the local population by Hudson's Bay Company officialdom, as it operated both on the ground in Rupert's Land and in London, growing as that population was in economic strength, education, and cultural sophistication. Free traders and free-trade proponents, such as Alexander Kennedy Isbister, Guillaume Sayer, James Sinclair, John McLaughlin, and Peter Garrioch, aided and abetted by their trading partners over the border, such as Norman Kittson and Kenneth McKenzie, were increasingly influential and hostile to the strictures on commerce imposed by the Company on their activities. They were doing the work, while the Company sat back and insisted it should get its cut through duties, unfair bartering practices, and customs and supply restraints. Where could they turn?

In the Company's huge territory, there were no elected governments as yet through which political expression and influence could be exerted. There was only the sclerotic Company monopoly, exerting dominance over every aspect of life in Rupert's Land to the extent that it was able to do so and stifling meaningful communication with its inhabitants.[790]

---

790 When John McLoughlan, Andrew McDermot's nephew and Peter Garrioch's erstwhile trading companion, was testifying in London in 1857 to the Select Committee on the Hudson's Bay Company, he was asked about the justice system at Red River, including the one capital execution ordered by Adam Thom (Capenessesweet; see Chap. 8, entries for September 1 through 5, 1845). One of the Select Committee members expressed puzzlement about why, if it was, as McLoughlin said, "perfectly well" known that the Company was bound by law to send all capital cases to be tried in Canada, the colonists of Red River did not "remonstrate against this execution?" McLoughlin answered: "It is impossible for them to remonstrate there; they are too much under the control of the Company; the Company would stop the supplies." *Report from the Select Committee,* Question 5027, p. 280. One of the few means of public communication, notices posted on church doors, served as a poor substitute for interaction between citizens and the authorities. See Chap. 8, entry for February 8, 1846, and Chapter 10, n. 766

Moreover, these restive Rupertslanders believed with justification that the Company-established courts, even where they existed, were not offering impartial justice, certainly not in cases where the Company's interests were at stake, and this view was growing stronger in the 1840s and 1850s when the *Sayer* trial brought the matter to a head.[791]

As a result, it is no wonder that, by mid-century, petitions and formal letters directed at the Company both locally and in London became an important way – indeed, the only peaceful way[792] – to let off steam for those experiencing destabilizing political, social, and economic pressures, in the hope that this would amount to a workable and genuine vehicle for communicating with the Company. Such manifestos giving voice to the accumulating dissatisfaction were relatively common in those years, and it was not surprising that the commercial and cultural leaders of the people were involved in drafting, circulating, posting, and presenting them. Peter Garrioch was no exception. His diaries make frequent mention of such activity on his and others' part, and it seems useful to present his role in extracted format, as an appendix to his diaries, both to serve as one example, by no means comprehensive or definitive (as would be desirable), of that form of expression as well as to reflect the significant role Peter played as a leader in promoting such limited political expression as was available to Red River society at the time.

Once Peter Garrioch had left his early teaching and had given up on obtaining theological training at Kenyon College, he launched himself with gusto into trading activities throughout a large swath of porous-border territory in what are now parts of Manitoba and U.S. states such as Minnesota and the Dakotas (See Appendix II – Map). Initially, he contracted in the fall of 1842 to trade for the Missouri Fur Company (MFC), and then the American Fur Company (AFC) a post assigned to him at the Mouse (Souris) River,[793] where he could trade freely on American soil, until he learned in early 1844 that the U.S. government was discouraging the sale of liquor to the Indigenous population by retrenching the MFC's and AFC's operations and confiscating goods sold in posts such as the Souris one.

Nevertheless, traders such as Peter continued to do brisk business across the territory along the Missouri and back to Red River without governmental molestation, so long as they were

---

791   Chap. 10, text accompanying nn. 711-713. See Gibson, *LLG*, I, p. 112, & *passim*.

792   When John McLoughlan was testifying in London in 1857 to the Select Committee on the Hudson's Bay Company, he was asked: "Q. 4966: While you were at the Red River Settlement what means had the settlers of knowing the regulations of the Company? – By proclamations, those that have been read. Q. 4967: Proclamation, such as we have had before us to-day, was the means of communication with the settlers by the council? –Yes. Q. 4968: And the only means? – The only means." *Report from the Select Committee*, p. 277. Posting by the authorities of other communications was common as well; see Chap. 8, entry for February 8, 1846.

793   Chap. 5, text associated with nn. 267-268, 293-303.

Appendix I – Petitions

careful about fur cargoes.[794] Indeed, in June, 1844, Peter and other prominent free traders James Sinclair, Peter Hayden, James Green, and Henry Cook opened up a major new trade route along the Crow Wing Trail, returning to Red River with U. S. goods, effectively showing that the Settlement was no longer so exclusively dependent on the Hudson's Bay Company for its supplies, despite the fact that these and other vigorous undertakings by the free traders to escape the Company's restrictions were strengthening the Company's determination to defeat their efforts.[795]

In early 1845, the Company, through Custom Collector James Bird, was starting to seize what it thought to be illicit trade goods.[796] As he described it pungently in his diaries, Peter came within the Custom Collector's cross-hairs, exchanged several letters with him and found in the course of doing so that Bird was attempting to set Peter and his fellow free-traders against each other by misrepresenting them to each other as to who was actually going to pay the demanded duties This tactic was defeated because the free-traders were comparing notes with each other, as well as holding strategy meetings.[797]

It was the Reverend William Cockran who suggested a way forward:

> His Reverence, Mr. Cockran called this morning and paid me 9/2 for Mr. Cowley. I handed him Mr. Bird's note, and he gave his opinion, by way of advice, that we who were importers of American goods should either pay the tax demanded now and petition Governor-in-Chief George Simpson for a repeal of 'the tax law on American goods; or present a written petition to Mr. Christie, the [Assiniboia] Governor, to be laid before the Council [of Assiniboia] on the arrival of Governor Simpson.'[798]

Peter's diary entries for May 3 and May 6, 1845, show that he composed the suggested petition, probably by agreement among his fellow free-traders that he do so, then left it with Sinclair on May 7, 1845, to have it "copied and corrected."[799] His entry for May 9, 1845 recorded that "it was signed by seven of us who had imported goods from St. Peter's, viz.: Peter Hayden, Henry Cook, Alexis Goulet, Dominque Ducharme, Alexander Ducharme, Charles Laurence and myself."

---

794   Chap. 5, entry for January 2, 1844.

795   Chap. 7, entries for March 28 through April 9, FN 491, and May 8 & 9, 1845.

796   Gibson, *LLG, I*, p. 90.

797   Chap. 7, entries for March 28 – April 8 & 24, 1845.

798   Chap. 7, entry for April 9, 1845.

799   Chap. 7, entry for May 7, 1845.

The editors of the present work have noted that neither Andrew McDermot nor James Sinclair signed it, having been co-opted or even bribed (in McDermot's case) by Governors Simpson and Christie to remain distant from the more rabid free- traders.[800]

Gunn noted his regret that he was unable to find a copy of Peter's petition after thorough searching.[801] That likely means that it was not printed and circulated in the community, at least not widely, but was, rather, presented directly to those it was petitioning, the Governor and Council of Assiniboia. Peter relied on its existence to rebuff another of Collector Bird's approaches to him by stating that their "petition, stating our reasons for refusing to comply with the requisition of import duty; and requesting that requisition to be repealed on certain weighty considerations" was still under consideration.[802] The Company's reception of it appears in the June 16, 1845, minutes of a meeting of the Council of the Governor and Council of Assiniboia:

> At the President's request, there was read a petition from Charles Laurence, Dominique Ducharme, Peter Garriock, Henry Cook, Peter Hayden and Alexis Goulait, to the Governor and Council, praying for relief from the payment of the usual duty on their imports from the United States….[803]

The matter was referred to the next meeting, on June 19, where extensive resolutions by Mr. Thom, including on "Import Duties," were adopted, and the petition dealt with:

> With reference to the petition of Charles Larance [sic] and others, which was read at the preceding meeting, and again fully considered, it was resolved …that the petitioners be referred, for an answer, to the first three resolutions of this date; and it was further resolved …that the said petition abounds in imputations and opinions which are equally irrelevant and erroneous.[804]

The "first three resolutions" adopted at that time, presumably for the purpose of underscoring the Company's answer to such a cheeky petition, made minor concessions, but *not* to the petitioners:

> Resolved,
>
> 1. That, once in every year, any British subject, if an actual resident *and not a fur trafficker*, may import, whether from London or from St. Peters (in the United States), stores free

---

800 Chap. 7, entry for May 9, 1845, & n. 506-507.

801 Gunn, p. 258.

802 Chap. 7, entry for May 12, 1845.

803 Oliver, *Canadian North-West*, I, pp. 315, & 326-327.

804 *Ibid*.

of any duty now about to be imposed, on declaring truly that he has imported them at his own risk.

2. That, once in every year any British subject, *if qualified as before*, may exempt from duty as before, imports of the local value of ten pounds, on declaring truly that they are intended to be used exclusively by himself within the Red River Settlement, and have been purchased with certain specified productions or manufactures of the aforesaid Settlement, exported in the same season, or by the latest vessel at his own risk.

3. That, once in every year, any British subject, *if qualified as before*, who may have personally accompanied both his exports and imports, as defined in the proceeding resolutions, may exempt from duty, as before, imports of the local value of £50, on declaring truly that they are either to be consumed by himself, or to be sold by himself to actual consumers within the aforesaid settlement, and have been purchased with certain specified productions or manufactures of the settlement, carried away by himself in the same season, or by the latest vessel at his own risk." [emphasis added]

Additional resolutions continued in similar byzantine language. Gunn appended a version of these resolutions, as Appendix A to his typescript of Peter's diaries.[805] He also included the resolutions that followed the first three, ending with the ninth: "That, henceforth, furs shall be purchased from none but the actual hunters of the same."

In the apparently most formal version of the Council's resolutions from the June 19 minutes, the term "public defaulter" is used instead of "fur trafficker." Whichever words were used, it was clear that "fur traffickers" such as the petitioners, were considered "public defaulters" and placed outside the conferring of whatever benefits these resolutions purported to confer. In short, the resolutions, for all their elevated phraseology, were a slap in the face of those malcontents whose petition was adjudged to be both "irrelevant" and "erroneous."

Not recorded in Peter's diaries is the reaction of the petitioners to this rebuff. It must have stung even more because they had received an early assurance that their petition would be taken seriously; as a result they were prepared to meet the Company's demands:

May 13, 1845 – Tuesday. Peter Hayden came down with instructions from Governor Christie, advising us to pay the tax on American goods, and that our petition would be duly attended to. Relying on the promise of the Governor, we yielded, and addressed the following note to his Excellency, signed by our party:

Alexander Christie Esq., Governor of Assiniboia   May 13, '45.

Sir:-

We the undersigned, your late petitioners, take this opportunity of returning you our sincere thanks for the friendly advice you have transmitted to us by Mr. Peter Haydon,

---

805   Gunn, pp. 365-366. Two other, more formal versions appear in Oliver, *Canadian North-West*, I, pp. 318-323 & II, pp. 1303-5. Gunn may have been working from a broadsheet version in his own possession or in Peter's.

and likewise for the impartial and favourable consideration which you assure us shall be bestowed on our said petition by your Honourable Council. And therefore, fully relying on the favourable prospect before us, we do hereby assure your Excellency that it is our intention, forthwith, to settle our accounts on our imported American commodities.

Two or three hours after we had signed the above note, Mr. Bird popped in, and I settled with him without a murmur or a groan.[806]

Perhaps fortunately for his peace of mind, considering how his petition was concurrently faring, Peter left on June 10, 1845, for the buffalo hunt and didn't return until August 12, 1845.[807] He made no subsequent mention of the petition he had written, instead moving on to note, on August 15, 1845, that "a petition was prepared for the Half Breeds in general, to be presented to the American Government,"[808] but offered no further comment about it. It was drafted by McDermot's nephew, John McLaughlin, seeking that government's assistance against the Company's allegedly illegal suppression of democracy and free trading in furs. McLaughlin was supposed to deliver it to Washington, but instead mailed it to the American Secretary of State, James Buchanan, who passed it on; it eventually disappeared,[809] despite the fact that, as J. M. Bumsted writes, it was "purportedly signed by 1,250 'half breeds and Canadian settlers."[810]

The next move on the petition front came in the form of an open letter to Governor Christie asking him to clarify Indigenous rights. Since he signed it and its author was a close friend of his, Peter may have had a hand in drafting it, too. He described it in his diary entry of September 5, 1845:

> …on Monday last, a document was presented to the Governor [Christie] containing a number of questions from a number of the Half Breeds. The questions had particular reference to fur trading and the peculiar rights and privileges of the Hudson's Bay

---

806   Chap. 7, entry for May 13, 1845.

807   Chap. 8, entry for August 12, 1845.

808   *Ibid*. According to Rich, *Hudson's Bay Company*, III, pp. 723-724, this petition fed Governor Simpson's fear at the time that the Métis were succumbing to the lure of admission of their territory into the United States, with the advantages of American citizenship and access to American goods acting as tempting baubles. Rich wrote, at pp. 794-795: "The issue to be fought out in the last ten years of the Company's chartered history was precisely this, whether the old geographical allegiance to the Bay [HBC] should be replaced by ties to the south or by ties to the east; whether the prairies should go to the United States or to Canada."

809   Chap. 8, commentary to entry for August 15, 1845, & n. 529; see Gibson, *LLG, I*, p. 91, & nn. 48 & 50.

810   Bumsted, *Trials & Tribulations*, pp. 99-100.

Appendix I – Petitions

Company, and of the Half Breeds. The answer to the above document, of which I have preserved a true copy, was returned in a few days.[811]

Although framed as a letter, dated August 29, 1845, to Alexander Christie, Esq., Governor of Red River Settlement, its author, James Sinclair, was promulgating the view of the Métis community that free trade in furs was fundamental to their identity and innate rights and that the Company should endorse their position. Gunn appended it and the Governor's response to it, in the form of Appendix D to his typescript of Peter's diaries:

> Sir: Having at this moment a very strong belief that we as natives of this country and as Halfbreeds have the right to hunt furs in the Hudson's Bay Company's territories whenever we think proper, and again sell those furs to the highest bidder; likewise having a doubt that natives of this country can be prevented from trading and trafficking with one another, we would wish to have your opinion on the subject, lest we should commit ourselves by doing anything in opposition, either to the laws of England, or the honourable company's privileges, and, therefore, lay before you as Governor of the Red River Settlement a few queries which we beg you will answer in [due] course:
>
> Has a Halfbreed, a settler, the right to hunt furs in this country?
>
> Has a native of this country (not an Indian) a right to hunt furs?
>
> If a Halfbreed has the right to hunt fur, can he hire other Halfbreeds for the purpose of hunting furs?
>
> Can a Halfbreed sell his furs to any person he pleases?
>
> Is a Halfbreed obliged to sell his furs to the Hudson's Bay Company at whatever price the Company may think proper to give him?
>
> Can a Halfbreed receive any furs as a present from an Indian, a relative of his?
>
> Can a Halfbreed hire any of his Indian relatives to hunt furs for him?
>
> Can a Halfbreed trade furs from another Halfbreed in or out of the Settlement?
>
> Can a Halfbreed trade furs from an Indian in or out of the Settlement?
>
> With regard to trading or hunting furs, have the Halfbreed, or natives of European origin, any rights or privileges of Europeans?
>
> A settler having purchased lands from Lord Selkirk, or even from the Hudson's Bay Company, without any conditions attached to them, or without having signed any bond, deed, or instrument whatever whereby he might have willed away his right to trade in furs, can he be prevented from trading furs in the Settlement with settlers or even out of the Settlement?
>
> Are the limits of the settlement defined by the municipal law, Selkirk grant, or Indian sale?

---

811   Chap. 8, entry for September 5, 1845.

If a person cannot trade furs either in or out of the Settlement, can he purchase them for his own and family use, and in what quantity?

Having never seen any official statements, nor known, but by report, that the Hudson's Bay Company has peculiar privileges over British subjects, natives, and half-breeds, resident in the settlement, we would wish to know what those privileges are, and the penalties attached to the infringement of the same?

We remain your humble servants,

James Sinclair,	William Bird,
Baptiste La Roque,	Peter Garech,
Thomas Logan,	Henry Cook,
John Dease	John Spence,
Alexis Gaulat,	John Anderson,
Louis Letendre de Bateche,	Thomas McDermot,
William McMillan,	Adall Trettier,
Antoine Morran,	Charles Hole,
Bat. Wilkie,	Joseph Monkman,
John Vincent,	Baptiste Farman.

This letter with its multiple questions and air of innocent inquiry was no more popular with the Company than its predecessors had been. Governor Christie responded in a letter dated September 5, 1845, redolent with condescending language and dismissing the notion that the letter-writers could possibly be so ignorant as they were claiming to be.[812] Gunn appended the Governor's answer in full:[813]

---

812 No less an authority than Alexander Ross wrote in 1852, about the time when "all points hitherto in dispute were settled by the Governor himself, or not settled at all – as often the one as the other – and yet peace was maintained. But the time having come, when the smoothing system would no longer work satisfactorily, other means were necessary, by the adoption of which law and order were for the first time established in the settlement [i.e., *circa* February, 1835, when the Governor and Council of Assiniboia was constituted].... During all these political changes the colonists were kept in the dark, never having been put in possession of their intellectual rights, by knowing what was going on, or to whom the colony belonged. Nor was it till many years after the settlement became virtually the Company's own property, that the fact was made known to the people, and then by mere chance. Till this eventuality, the people were under the persuasion that the colony still belonged to the executers of Lord Selkirk and were often given to understand so. By this political finesse, or shall we rather call it, political absurdity, the Company preserved themselves clear of all responsibility, whatever transpired. Did they remove any grievance or assist the colonists? It was looked upon as purely gratuitous on their part. Whereas had the people known the relative position in which they stood to the Company, they would no doubt, as a matter of course, have insisted at an earlier period on what was their undoubted right, as subjects." Ross, *Red River Settlement*, pp. 173-174.

813 Gunn, pp. 383-385, Appendix D.

Appendix I – Petitions

Gentlemen – I received your letter of the 29th ultime, on the evening of the 3rd instant, and I am sure that the solemn and important proceedings in which I was yesterday engaged [Gunn: the hanging of an Indian murderer at Fort Garry[814]] will form a sufficient apology for my having allowed a day to pass without noticing your communication.

However unusual it may be for the rulers of any country to answer legal enquiries in any other way than through the judicial tribunals which can alone authoritatively decide any point of law, I shall, on this particular occasion, overlook all these considerations which might otherwise prompt me to decline, with all due courtesy, the discussion of your letter; and I am the rather induced to adopt this course, by your avowal, for which I am bound to give you full credit, that you are actuated by an unwillingness to do anything in opposition, either to the laws of England, or to the Hudson's Bay Company's privileges.

Your first nine queries, as well as the body of your letter, are grounded on the supposition that the half breeds possess certain privileges over their fellow citizens, who have not been born in this country. Now, as British subjects, the half-breeds have clearly the same rights in Scotland or in England as any person born in Great Britain, and your own sense of justice will at once see how unreasonable it would be to place Englishmen and Scotsmen on a less favourable footing in Rupert's Land than yourselves.[815] Your supposition, further, seems to draw a distinction between half-breeds and persons born in the country, of European parentage, and, to men of your intelligence, I need not say that this distinction is still more unreasonable than the other.

Your tenth query is fully answered in these observations on your first nine queries.

Your eleventh query assumes that any purchaser of lands would have the right to trade furs if he had not 'willed' it away by assenting to any restrictive conditions. Such an assumption, of course, although admissible of itself, is inconsistent with your general views; the conditions of tenure which, by the by, have always been well understood to prohibit any infraction of the company's privileges, are intended not to bind the individual who is already bound by the fundamental law of the country, but merely to secure his lands as a special guarantee for the due discharge of such, his essential obligations.

---

814   Chap. 8, entry for September 5, 1845.

815   This appeal to the petitioners' sense of fairness that all British subjects should be treated alike was the epitome of hypocrisy on the Governor's part, since he and Thom were actively scheming against Peter, Sinclair, and their fellow free traders to thwart their trade in furs by any means possible. See Chap. 6, text associated with n. 356. As their companion John McLaughlin testified in 1857 before the Parliamentary Select Committee, the Company interfered in the fur trade by stopping their supplies, seizing and impounding the furs, requiring forfeit of their furs, preventing parties from making gifts of furs among themselves, imprisoning fur traders, and even enlisting the missionaries (e.g., the Reverend John Smithurst) to persuade their flocks not to wear furs. McLaughlin even asserted that, as one of the petitions showed, the Company was not only seizing goods from traders who did not adhere to the Company's prohibition on trading in furs, but imposing a 20 percent duty on imported American goods, in the case of those trafficking in furs, or even suspected of doing so, rather than the 4 percent duty imposed on others. *Report from the Select Committee*, Q. 4738-4761, pp. 263-264; & Q. 5030-5046, 5054, pp. 280-281.

After what has been said, your twelfth query becomes wholly unimportant.

Your fourteenth query, which comprises your thirteenth, and, in fact, also all the other queries that you either have, or could have, proposed, requests me to enumerate the peculiar privileges of the Hudson's Bay Company, on the alleged ground that you know them only through report. Considering that you have the means of seeing the Charter and the Land Deed, and such enactments of the Council of Rupert's Land as concerns yourselves and your fellow citizens; and consideration further that, in point of fact, some of you have seen them, I cannot admit that you require information to the extent which you profess; and even if you did require it, I do not think that I could offer you anything more clear than the documents themselves are, on which my enumeration of the company's rights must be based. If, however, any individual among you, or among your fellow citizens, should at any time feel himself embarrassed in any honest pursuit, by legal doubts, I shall have much pleasure in affording him a personal interview.

> I am, gentlemen,
>
> Your most obedient servant,
>
> Alexander Christie,
>
> Governor of Assiniboia

Again, Peter coped by going about his business, leaving for the fall buffalo hunt on September 9, 1845,[816] without recording, in his diaries anyway, his reaction to this piece of evasive sophistry. By that point, he and his confrères must have expected nothing more.

What they did get was action by the Company to seize contraband furs. Peter received timely warning from Sinclair, as he noted in his diary entry for November 25, 1845:

> On my return home I was favoured with a communication from Mr. James Sinclair warning me to be on my guard, as Mr. [Cuthbert] Grant had received a warrant from the Governor authorizing him to seize all furs that were traded by private individuals, and that were not intended to be delivered to the Hudson's Bay Company. Those who assisted Mr. Grant in this unlawful and infernal affair were to receive one half of the plunder as a compensation for their services. I reached home, however, without being annoyed by these intrusive measures.[817]

However, Peter was subsequently confronted personally by the Governor, who threatened to have him jailed if he continued to trade in furs. Peter recorded this dramatic encounter in his diary entry for December 18, 1845:

> He spoke to me about my having traded fur also. I neither denied nor acknowledged the charge. He threatened to clap me in jail before I left the room, to make me an example to the rest. I told him that, as it was in his power to do so, he might do it. He spoke

---

816 Chap. 8, entry for September 9, 1845.

817 Chap. 8, entry and notes for November 25, 1845.

largely on the validity of their Charter, and of the unlimited privileges and power it conferred upon the HBC. As a parting blessing, Governor Christie advised me not to repeat my former conduct, or he would summon me to the Grand Court and have me tried by jury.[818]

This empty threat was immediately followed by a conversation with Christie's less-bombastic clerk, John Black, who,

> ...told me to take Mr. Christie's advice and trade no more fur. I told him it required a deal of thinking. He then said, 'Let people think or not, just as they please; but we must act.' 'That's the only thing, Mr. Black,' said I! So I took up my cap and bade him goodbye."[819]

On February 11, 1846, Peter met with Sinclair and others at McDermot's house to prepare still another protest in letter form, signed by Peter and others. This time, the protest was against the Governor's increasingly harsh measures against the free traders, in particular, Peter Hayden, which had led to the unfortunate incident in which Hayden, hastily preparing himself for a raid on his goods by the Company, accidently discharged his pistol and killed a young man in his charge. Hayden was shortly to be facing trial, and the protesters prepared resolutions demanding, first, that Hayden be broken out of jail and, second, that Recorder Thom be "driven out of the Colony." The letter has, unfortunately, been lost, even though Peter noted in his diary entry that it had been delivered to its intended recipient. He was also informed that the resolutions it contained had been made known to the Reverend Cockran.[820]

Hard on the heels of the protest letter and Peter Hayden's trial, from which Hayden emerged with a negligible penalty, the core protesters, James Sinclair, Thomas McDermot, John Anderson, and Peter Garrioch, were joined by a large contingent ("about 100") of French-speaking Métis at a meeting at McDermot's on February 26, 1846, presided over by Reverend George-Antoine Belcourt, the widely-travelled Roman Catholic priest known for his vocal opposition to the Company's policies. Father Belcourt managed to channel the angry mood into a decision to prepare another petition against the Company and its policies, this time addressed to Queen Victoria.[821]

---

818   Chap. 8, entry and notes for December 18, 1845.

819   *Ibid.*

820   Chap. 8, entry for February 19, 1846.

821   Chap. 8, entry for February 26, 1846; Chap. 9, entry and commentary for May 28, 1846. In his Autobiography, penned in 1853, Belcourt described his role in this meeting (although misdating it having occurred in 1837) and its eventual outcome: "In 1837, the exactions of the Hudson's Bay Company, and their abuse of power, having excited the indignation of the colony, many of them were disposed to go into excesses, which were of a nature to be of no utility to any party. As he

Gunn included an English translation of the Belcourt petition as Appendix F to his typescript of the Garrioch diaries:

> Text of Petition Prepared by Rev. G. A. Belcourt of the Baie St. Paul Mission and Signed by 977 Red River Settlers in May, 1846. Translated from the French.
>
> We, the undersigned humble and loyal subjects of her majesty Victoria, Queen of the United Kingdom of England, Scotland, and Ireland, etc., inhabiting a remote corner of her vast domain on the Red River, Department of the Hudson's Bay, have dared, with complete confidence to apply to your Lordship to lay at the foot of the throne and to support with your influence the representations and demands which we set forth with humble deference in the present petition.
>
> Drawn by pompous promises to this spot in the vast territory of Hudson's Bay, our fathers hoped that the plans of the late Lord Selkirk would be punctually carried out; that according to the contracts in favour of the colonists, their commodities, etc., would be sold at a satisfactory price, fixed in the said contracts, and that the toil of the laborer would not be paralyzed by his inability to sell his productions. All these promises have been evaded, all hopes frustrated.
>
> The monopoly, which has weighted heavily on us for about one hundred and seventy-six years, is getting heavier all the time, to the degree that we are no longer permitted to exchange the peltries of our country for imported goods, or vice versa, under pain of being imprisoned, or of seeing our goods seized on the mere suspicion that they are to be exchanged for furs. This severity had been pushed to the extent of prohibiting us from receiving payment for food procured by Indians perishing of hunger, at long distances from all succour, considering that such payment can only be made in furs, and notwithstanding the assurance that we will deliver up the said furs at the very store of the Company and at whatever price they wish to give. A severity, so revolting, not to say inhuman, has irritated all, and although we are in part disposed to suffer for a still longer time in order to prevent disturbances and to evade the direful consequences of an irritation very nearly general, not being able to address our complaints to the Governor of the Company, in whom the people no longer have confidence, we take the only means which remains to us of avoiding carnage and bloodshed, by depositing at the foot of the throne our humble and respectful supplications.
>
> As British subjects, we desire ardently to be governed according to the principles of that constitution which makes happy all the numerous subjects of our august Sovereign.

---

possessed all the confidence of the inhabitants, Mr. BELCOURT proposed to them to adopt legal measures, and not such as their conscience, and a spirit of honesty must reprove. A petition to the Queen was the means he proposed to try. As no one else felt himself capable of drawing up this document, rather than see things come into an extremity, he undertook it himself. This petition was carried to England by Mr. JAMES SINCLAIR, and presented to the government by a society of advocates, the zeal of whom merits the warmest praises, particularly Mr. ISBISTER. This cause made a considerable noise in England. It was vigorously sustained by Mr. BLACKSTONE and others; but favor and money put an end to the discussions." Belcourt, "Department of the Hudson's Bay," pp. 241-242.

Justice being administered by a judge paid by the Company, the Councillors who make the laws being creatures of the Company, or interested only in not displeasing it in any way, being all of them, moreover, elected by the Governor and Committee of the said Company, it follows that the people feel a lack of confidence, and do not believe at all in the possibility of winning a suit in any case which concerns the Company, or a friend, or a favorite of theirs. This disposition of minds, so dangerous to the peace and public tranquility, will not exist if the people, as is the case elsewhere in the British possessions, had a part in making the laws and if they were independent of the Company.

We dare humbly to express the thought that justices of the peace or magistrates, chosen from among those whom the people respect and consider upright, would be a mode of justice sufficient for a long time yet, or at least until the municipal revenues are great enough to meet the expenses demanded by a regular court of justice.

As British subjects we desire and demand urgently that there be accorded to us that liberty of trade, so necessary to the prosperity of states and so powerfully maintained by the laws in all other possessions of our august Sovereign.

By reason of the monopoly accorded to the Hudson's Bay Company, the natives have the painful imposition of seeing exported all the wealth of their country for the exclusive profit of foreign traders, and all the colonists find themselves under the necessity of using imported goods, without being able to export in exchange any of the productions of their country; if sometimes certain individual traders have wished to attempt to transport some of the goods of the country, the Company has caused them so much embarrassment that they have been compelled to desist, and always to the detriment of the country. Under such a rule people are reduced to a kind of slavery; the efforts of the most energetic of those persons who are industrious and who are endowed with ability along commercial lines are neutralized,; and under this state of affairs, public discontent can only go on increasing all the time until there is an explosion fatal to all the parties.... A word of clemency from the lips our Sovereign will spare us these dangers by establishing happiness and peace in our country; then in giving to trade the energy which it draws from liberty, will deposit on our soil the germ of prosperity.

We beg also that our municipal Council may be permitted to sell lands to those who emigrate from a foreign country to ours; and we make urgent demand that for a time and at a rate fixed according to the pleasure of her Majesty, a sum may be taken from this sale, in order to better means of transportation.

Placed in the center of North America, about six hundred miles from Hudson's Bay, the waterway which communicates with that place is obstructed in various places by impracticable passages, where all the goods are carried....which requires a great many men, a great deal of time and expense and definitely renders impossible the exports of a great part of our produce.

Our lands are fertile and easy to cultivate. The laborer only awaits the hope of being able to sell in order to give himself up to the work which can make this country a granary......

We are near the boundary line; we can go over to the neighboring territory; we are invited there; but we admire the wisdom of the British Constitution, and we desire its privileges.

The sincere desire which our august Queen has of making her subjects happy is known as far as this place and even beyond; we hope everything then from her clemency. In granting our prayers, she will make us happy; and we beg,' etc., etc.

(With 977 names attached).

[Hudson's Bay Company, Return to an Address of the Honorable the House of Commons, April 23, 1849, p. 4][822]

This missive was intended to secure as many signatories as possible, and Peter reported later, on May 28, 1846, that he, "went about….for signatures to a petition to be presented to her Majesty, Queen Victoria. I added 80 signatures to the said petition."[823] His efforts in that regard were apparently not limited to that day, since on May 13, 1846, he recorded in his diary that he, "went up to Mr. Belcourt's," so Peter's work on collecting signatures took place over a period of weeks.[824]

Undoubtedly others worked to the same end. Once the petition had been made known, the combustible character of Father Belcourt's rhetoric, not just in the language of the petition but also in a broadside he unleashed in 1853 against the Company from his refuge in Pembina, to which he moved in 1849,[825] had its most immediate effect on his career. Already detested by Company

---

822   Gunn, four unnumbered pages, titled Appendix F, following the 387 consecutive pages of his typescript of the Garrioch diaries and Appendices A-E. The dotted lines are as they were in Gunn's typescript of Appendix F.

823   Chap. 9, entry and commentary for May 28, 1846.

824   Ibid.

825   Belcourt, "Department of the Hudson's Bay," pp. 207-244. It begins with a passage reflecting a considerable degree of legal and moral fervour:"This last company took advantage, as it still does, of a charter granted by CHARLES II, to his cousin RUPERT. This document, although illegal according to the British constitution, has been strongly sustained. It grants the most absolute powers, and concedes a sovereignty more despotic than CHARLES himself possessed. Though the governmental department has sufficiently expressed themselves upon the subject of the illegality of this contract, yet the friends of this company have always been so powerful as to prevent any official declaration to this effect, by contending that the subject should first undergo a discussion in court. Thus, those who are opposed to the pretentions of this company, not having enough of money to sustain the process; fearing that gold and favor would prove the stronger argument, find themselves obliged to submit to a usurpation which they cannot prevent."Though they complained of these abuses a few years ago by petition, which was ably sustained at London, and which occasioned a great deal of excitement in England, the only effect produced here, was to abate in a small degree the boldness of the pretentions of this company, which tended to a perfect tyranny. In proof of this, I will adduce a few instances of their impositions: On one occasion, they seized the effects of a hunter, upon suspicion that he might exchange some of them with the Indians for furs. On another occasion they caused a hunter to be imprisoned for having given one of his overcoats to a naked Indian, for about its value in rat skins. They also refuse to allow the missionaries to receive furs to sustain the expenses of public worship; whilst the Indians cannot obtain any money from

Appendix I – Petitions

officials for his strong support for Rupert's Land's Indigenous people, Belcourt's promotion of their interests had become such a threat to the Company's economic position that Governor Simpson made representations to the Archbishop of Québec, Msg. Signay, to prevent Belcourt from returning to the Settlement. The result of this was that in 1848 Father Belcourt ended up stationing himself at Pembina, on the American side of the border, where he "continued to be the rallying centre of half-breed discontent"[826] and to be an ally of sorts to Norman Kittson who was contributing to the challenges against the legitimacy of the Company's fur trade monopoly.[827]

The petition itself was conveyed by James Sinclair to the highly-respected leader of the mixed-ancestry community at Red River, Alexander Kennedy Isbister (1822-1883), who was expected to know how to bring it to the attention of London authorities. The accomplished and highly-intelligent Isbister had resided in London since leaving the Company's dead-end employ in 1842, although for the remainder of his life he maintained communications with the Red River settlers "continuously and uninterruptedly."[828] In the United Kingdom he received a first-rate education, became a prominent teacher and text-book writer, and "was the recognized authority on all matters concerning the Hudson's Bay Territories"[829]

---

the company for their furs; and forbid the missionaries to buy leather or skins to protect their feet from the cold. These, and a thousand other grievances call so loudly for redress, that I think a small increase of the burden will cause the evil to correct itself." At p. 224, Father Belcourt referred to his removal to Pembina in 1849, from his mission in the White Horse Plains area. This "lenience" on the part of the Archbishop of Quebec to permit him to come back to the area appears to have been in part stimulated by a letter petitioning for his return addressed to Bishop Signay, dated November, 1847, at White Horse Plain, and signed by large numbers of the French-speaking Métis community: Assumption Abbey, Richardton, N.D., Belleau Collection, Roll 2, 1847: pp. 19-21. [Provided to the Louis Riel Institute by Émilie Pigeon.]

826   Morton, *Manitoba: A History*, pp. 75-77; A.S. Morton, *Sir George Simpson: Overseas Governor of the Hudson's Bay Company – A Pen Picture of a Man of Action* (London: J. M Dent, 1944), pp. 200 & 202; and Rich, *Hudson's Bay Company*, III, p. 548.

827   For a detailed description of Belcourt's activities and his alliance with Kittson and the free traders, see W. L. Morton, "George-Antoine Bellecourt (Bellcours, Belcourt)," *DCB* X, pp. 46-48, & "Georges-Antoine Belcourt," Historic Resources Branch, Manitoba Culture, Heritage and Recreation, 1984, p. 8.

828   Isbister's own statement in 1857 in answer to a question (Q. 2477, p. 126) during the sittings of the Select Committee on the Hudson's Bay Company. See H.C. Knox, "Alexander Kennedy Isbister," *Papers Read Before the Historical & Scientific Society of Manitoba*, Ser. 3, nr. 12 (Winnipeg, 1957), pp. 17-28 and *Alexander Kennedy Isbister: A Respectable Critic of the Honourable Company* (Ottawa, Carleton University Press, 1988), *passion*. Indeed, Peter Garrioch knew the family well enough to go to Isbister's mother's house in Red River to enlist her assistance with a young woman he was hoping to woo, as he recorded in his diary on February 20, 1847 (Chap. 9).

829   Knox, "Alexander Kennedy Isbister." Isbister attended the Reverend Macallum's school in Red River and his sister Caroline was married to Governor Alexander Christie.

Isbister's Memorial of Grievances was entitled: *A Few Words on the Hudson's Bay Company; with a Statement of the Grievances of the Native and Half-Caste Indians, addressed to the British Government through their Delegates Now in London* (C. Gilpin, n.d. but 1846). Its twenty-four pages begin with a three-page unsigned introduction. It is a general statement of grievances against the Company, and it does not mince words. The opening paragraph states that the Company

> is now the only survivor of the numerous exclusive bodies which at one time depressed almost every branch of British commerce. …it reigns supreme over 50 native tribes of Indians, who are the slaves of its laws and policy, and scarcely removed but in name from being its actual bondmen; it is, however, not upon that point we purpose to dwell, but rather upon a far more important and hitherto unpublished fact, namely that although exercising commercial and territorial sovereignty over so wide a range of country, the Charter under which it claims this right of despotic sway is *illegal*.

Then follow cogent arguments: first, that the Company's Charter had long since expired; second, that the 1821 licensing arrangement with the Company was insufficient to confer the authority it claimed; third, that the profits generated by the Company resulted in negligible revenue for the mother country; and fourth, that the avowed objects of the 1821 arrangement (a) to enable the removal of the supply of "spirituous liquors to the Indians as an article of commerce;" and (b) to provide facilities and means of support for chaplains, missionaries, and schoolteachers for "civilizing and evangelising the Indians, and improv[ing the] condition of the native population generally throughout the territory" were abject failures, despite Sir George Simpson's representations to the contrary when he submitted his report to the House of Commons in support of the Company's renewal of its licence in 1842. Moreover, Isbister charged, "…[S]uch [of the reports] as have been made public, are destitute of truth, and were evidently framed with a view to mislead the colonial authorities and avert further inquiry."

On pages four through eight of "A Few Words," the Memorial itself appears, signed by A. K. Isbister (the likely author), Thomas Vincent, John McLeod, D. V. Stewart, James Isbister, and "a sixth Memorialist, Mr. Sinclair, [who] has been under the necessity of returning to America." It sets out the grievances of "the unfortunate people who are compelled to appeal to their Sovereign for protection against the ruinous effects and consequences of the monopoly" the Company was able to enjoy under a Charter that had "long since lost its force," exercising "the harsh administration [under which] discontent and misery prevail amongst the natives of Rupert's Land to an unparalleled extent." Where schools and churches existed, it was due to the exertions of the Church Missionary Society, not the Company, nor did the Company open up the mineral and agricultural resources necessary to improve the country. Due to "the exorbitant prices demanded by the [Company's] traders for the wretched and almost valueless articles given in a mockery of exchange for the richest and most valuable furs," Indigenous fur traders were having

Appendix I – Petitions

to slaughter ever more animals to eke out a meagre subsistence, which in turn had led to the near-extinction of the "animals which supply the food of man" and putting them perpetually in the Company's debt.

Before closing by reference to "the precarious state of the public peace," the Memorialists set out the position of the free-traders (such as Peter Garrioch):

> That feeling the utter inadequacy of the remuneration for their furs from the Company, many of the more enterprising of the natives have formed a resolution to export their own produce and import their own supplies independently of the Company. They urge, that even supposing the Charter were still valid, and that it vests in the Company an exclusive right of trade to Hudson's Bay as against all other traders from Britain, none of its provisions are, or can be binding on the natives to trade with the Company exclusively, or can prevent them from carrying their furs or other property out of the country to the best market. Where this course has been adopted, however, the Company's agents have seized the furs of such parties as refused to sell them at the prices fixed by the Company, and in some instances have imprisoned the recusant natives. Against such gross aggressions on the rights and liberties of the natives your Memorialists most vehemently protest. Being unable to obtain redress from the local courts of the country, your Memorialists feel entitled to claim the protection of the British Government, and humbly intreat [sic] your Lordship to take the case into your kind consideration.

On pages eight to eleven, the actual Belcourt petition appears, in the original French, ending with (in English) "[Here follow about 1000 signatures]" and signed by William Dease, J. Baptiste Payette, J. Louis Rielle, Charles Montiony, and Cuthbert McGillis, "Membres d'un Commité élu par le people."

The remaining pages are devoted to various statements and evidence relating to the propositions set out in the Memorials, including the Company's "exorbitant" chart of tariffs, as described above in Chapter 6, note 346.

The Belcourt petition was not translated nor placed in the hands of the Colonial Office (which never really considered it) until late in 1847, and the Company lost no time in communicating its refutations of its premises.[830] Isbister's Memorial of Grievances was quoted in: *Great Britain. Parliament. House of Commons. Papers* (1849), nr. 227. It took the British government two years to refer the whole matter to – unsurprisingly – the Hudson's Bay Company, which eventually concluded that everything was just fine in the Red River Settlement. Isbister objected to these signs of official inaction in an 1849 letter to Lord John Russell, following which it was

---

830   Bumsted, *Trials & Tribulations*, pp. 101-108. On pp. 108-111, Bumsted discusses the *Sayer* trial as part of the same rebellious spirit which led to the Belcourt petition and the Isbister Memorial.

determined that the subject could only be raised by petition and the petitioners would have to pay all expenses associated with it. The matter was dropped – for the time being.[831]

Ultimately, the discontent in the North American colonies found its way into the British Parliament which, in an ironic twist, was reminded by the Company itself in December, 1856, of the need for renewal of the twenty-one-year licence it was granted in 1838 for exclusive trade, a licence due to expire in 1859. Instead of simply granting another licence based on the Company's claim that it had maintained peace, suppressed the liquor trade, and provided moral and religious instruction to the populace, Parliament passed a motion from Henry Labouchere, Secretary of State for the Colonies, to appoint a Select Committee to inquire into the issues such renewal raised. The Select Committee was comprised of members both favourable to and opposed to the Company's conduct in its territory. Extensive hearings were held beginning February, 1857, and its report was printed on July 31 and August 11 of the same year as the *Report from the Select Committee on the Hudson's Bay Company; together with the Proceedings of the Committee, Minutes of Evidence, Appendix and Index*, amounting to 547 pages.

Early on, the Select Committee called Governor Simpson to give evidence. Over several days, Simpson was put through gruelling questioning by knowledgeable Committee members (Questions 702-2125, pp. 44-108), including questions about Governor Christie's actions in 1845 (p. 103), the failure of the Company to make any provision for schools (p. 91) or the education of the "55,578 Indians" who were hunting furs for the Company ("they are a bold, warlike people, over whom we have no control") (p. 102), the rebuff by the Company to requests by traders such as McDermot and Sinclair to ship their goods to Britain on Company ships ("I have suggested to Mr. McDermot and Mr. Sinclair, and various other people, that they had better charter a ship for themselves.... No, not for the purpose of trade; I said that the inhabitants of Red River are quite at liberty to import their own supplies in their own ships") (p.80), and duties imposed and collected by the Company (pp. 103-104). He asserted that neither "the Indian tribes" nor the "half-breeds" were subject to Company restrictions on trade, but was evasive when asked about details.[832]

Three days later, on March 5, 1857, A. K. Isbister was called to testify before the Select Committee (Questions 2391-2655, pp. 120-137) and was recalled again for more evidence on June 23, 1857, as the last witness (Questions 6072-6098, pp. 353-356). His oral testimony was less impressive than his memorials and petitions. He prevaricated when asked by Secretary Labouchere, in

---

831 *Ibid.*

832 For example, when Lord John Russell asked (Q. 1757, p. 92): "Supposing any person was to come from the United States to trade with them, would you interfere?" Simpson's answer was "We should oppose it by every means in our power, but not by violence." Simpson's answer is inconsistent with descriptions of the actions the Company took against the fur traders as described before the Select Committee by, for example, free trader John McLaughlin; see above, n. 815.

Appendix I – Petitions 409

the chair, if it would be to the advantage of the "red man" that the Company's monopoly in fur trading should be abolished and the country be opened to unlimited competition by anyone who wished to engage in trade in it, but he did state that the peace and good order necessary for that state of affairs to succeed could and should be supplied by the Government of Canada: "I am afraid there will be no other way of settling the difficulty [of governance]" (pp. 123-124). He gave as his view:

> I presume that the Red River Settlement. . . .would send representatives to the Canadian Parliament immediately; that there would be townships erected in cultivated districts in the same way as in Canada, and that the people living in those settlements would spread themselves northward and engage in the fur trade; and that eventually the fur trade, which is now forced through the unnatural channel of Hudson's Bay, would be brought down through the route that connects Lake Superior with Lake Winnipeg. (p. 130, Question 2528).

Questioned about Father Belcourt's petition[833] and accompanying documentation, Isbister acknowledged that he was not the author of the petition, but had agreed and still agreed with its contents, had played the chief role in collecting papers with supporting evidence for it, and had had a long correspondence with the Colonial Office concerning it (pp. 125-127, Questions 2459-2481). It is clear from these questions and answers that most and likely all the material which accompanied the petition, as well as the petition itself, were in the hands of the Select Committee, which was aware of their significance and context, as shown in the following exchange between Select Committee members and Isbister:

> Q. 2552: "Is it within your knowledge that the settlers of the Red River Settlement complain of the existing form of government?" – "They have done so; they did so when the petition was sent over here."
>
> Q. 2553: "Do they still adhere to the complaint which they made at that time?" – "I believe they have practically taken the government into their own hands."
>
> Q. 2554: "Is it within your knowledge that any application or complaint was ever made to the Government of America on the subject?" – "There was a petition addressed by the Red River settlers to the American Government, I believe."
>
> Q. 2555: "Did you ever see a copy of that petition?" – "I have a rough copy of it, but whether it is authentic or not I have no means of saying."
>
> Q. 2556: "You are not able to speak of your own knowledge?" – No, but there is a gentleman who can do so: Mr. [John] McLoughlin."[834]

---

833   Described in detail in nn. 821, 825, 828, and 832, and text associated with them.

834   McLoughlin also clarified for the Select Committee that the Governor and Council of Assiniboia was not a representative public body nor an expression of local government; rather, after reading out the names of the Council members, he said that "they were every one in some way or other

Q. 2557: "What is the date of the petition?" – "It was about 1846, at the time of the excitement connected with the Oregon boundary question."

Q. 2558: "What was the general purport of the petition?" – "I believe that they desired the American Government to annex the Red River territory to the United States, and promised them assistance against the Hudson's Bay Company, in the event of a war; I believe that was the object of it."[835]

In his second appearance before the Select Committee during which he served as a kind of expert on the physical characteristics and resources of the HBC territory, Isbister concluded by asking to lay:

> a petition which I have recently received from the Red River settlers, signed by some hundred names, which will be found appended to it, …addressed to the Legislative Assembly in Canada, and sent here to me by a Member of that Assembly …by Mr. Macbeth, who presented the petition to the Legislative Assembly, and who is himself a native of the Red River Settlement (Q. 6094-6098, p. 356).[836]

---

connected with the Company." (Q. 4800). "Then in your opinion that council did not fairly represent the colonists of the Red River? – Not at all; it represented the Company" (Q. 4801, p. 267).

835 Pp. 131-132. It is easy to imagine the impression a petition from the Red River colonists addressed to the American Government must have had on the members of the Select Committee, once they learned of it, as they contemplated the boost the petition could have provided to American aspirations to acquire large swaths of land north of the border, resulting in enormous loss in territory to the British empire – and all because of unrest generated by the HBC's mismanagement.

836 This appears to be the same petition submitted to the Select Committee by Alfred Robert Roche, a English clerk who had spent 15 years in Montreal, Kingston, and Toronto, but had never travelled into the HBC's territories, although he had been charged with assisting with research into the HBC's situation, as a result of Canada having received the Petition to the Legislative Assembly of the Province of Canada. This one was entitled "*Petition from Inhabitants and Natives of the Settlement situated on the Red River, in the Assiniboia Country, British North America* [n.d., n. p.], *signed by Roderick Kennedy and 574 others,*" and was printed in the Select Committee's report on pp. 437-439.

Roche gave evidence about this wide-ranging petition on June 9, 1857, summarizing the undated petition. He described the petitioners' grievances about the HBC's failure to grant proper deeds to land for which they had paid or to force illegal deeds upon them. "Q. 4556. Do they speak generally with regard to their property, or describe what particular property has been taken from them?" – "'They searched our property, even by breaking open our trunks, and all furs found were confiscated.' Furs they speak of. Then they complain that the valuable commercial productions of the country are exported for 'the exclusive benefit of a company of traders, who are strangers to ourselves and to our country.' They also complain of being obliged to import everything through the Company, and then they speak of the rule of the Company paralysing the whole of their energies, and therefore they wish to be attached to Canada. They say that they have appealed to the Imperial authorities without effect, and therefore they petition the Parliament of Canada."

Appendix I – Petitions

Although the Select Committee's printed report does not appear to include Isbister's materials in its collection of evidence, this is explained by an exchange on May 19, 1857, between the Select Committee and witness Colonel J.F. Crofton who had commanded the troops who went out to Red River in 1846:

> Q. 3412: "On your return to England, you were called upon by the Secretary for the Colonies to report upon certain complaints made by settlers in Hudson's Bay?" – "Yes; I remember that perfectly well; I was quartered at Fermoy, and that question was afterwards discussed in Parliament. As well as I remember, it was Mr. Isbister's memorial."
>
> Q. 3413: "You made nine or ten answers, I think, to certain questions?" – "Yes; I remember perfectly making replies to Sir Benjamin Hawes, then Mr. Hawes."
>
> Q. 3414: "Do you adhere to the opinions which you then gave?" – "I am sure I must, for I took great pains to be accurate then…."
>
> Q. 3423: "I think there were nine questions put to you, and you gave answers to all those in your report to the Secretary of State?" – "I have no copy of them. I lost or was robbed of most of my papers when I was in Ireland, and among the rest a copy of those answers relating to Mr. Isbister's memorial, and therefore I am depending upon my memory entirely for it."
>
> Q. 3424: "You know that they were furnished to the House of Commons?" – "I heard so, but never saw them."
>
> Q. 3425: "And they have been printed?" – "I never heard that. I never saw them." (pp. 182-183).

Another Red River free trade sympathizer, the knowledgeable John McLoughlan, Andrew McDermot's nephew, gave his testimony on June 11, 1857 (Questions 4710-5096, pp.262-285), and it was certainly more combustible and forthright than Isbister's had been, emphasizing, for example, in response to a question about what he had meant by referring to the Company's "persecution" of Red River inhabitants, that:

Roche went on to explain that the Canadian Legislature had just appointed a committee to look into the matter, a "very wide" inquiry, including into the validity of the Company's charter. "Q. 4563. Do you know whether the practice has been to transmit any grievance to the Crown, to the Government of this country, and not to the Imperial Legislature?" – "Do you mean from Canada, or from the Red River?" "Q. 4504. From the Red River; not from Canada?" – "Yes, I think they appealed to the Colonial Office in 1849." Then Roche concluded his testimony by bringing the Select Committee back from such legalistic distractions: "Q. 4565. Do you know under what authority the Colonial Legislature assume the power of inquiring into charters granted by the Imperial Government, in territories not belonging to Canada?" – "I do not know that it is any authority which they assume; they inquire into it with the object of ascertaining whether this charter does conflict with any rights which they may have." (pp. 254-255).

In 1845 and 1844, at the time that this trading was carried on to such an extent, the Indians and the settlers, or those parties who traded in furs, received immense annoyance in that way from the Hudson's Bay Company in their refusing to sell them goods and to give them certain supplies....for two years, there was quite a ferment in the settlement, owing, in a measure to this trading in furs; and not only that, but other disadvantages under which they laboured, created this excitement. There were prohibitory duties placed upon goods coming into the settlement; upon manufactured goods entering the country." (Qs., 4763, 4765, p. 264).

McLoughlin elaborated on these matters at the request of Select Committee members, producing or being shown various documents:

Q. 4766. Mr. Edward Ellice: "Will you state of what these prohibitory duties consisted, and how they were put on?" – "I shall refer to them again if you will allow me. I have the original documents on the subject in my possession. They were prohibited from trafficking, or importing goods from the United States except once a year, and that only to the amount of 50£.Sterling. There was a complete discouragement thrown in the way of an export trade with England in tallow and hides and tongues; there was an issue of land deeds of the most peculiar and ridiculous nature, and of such a character as no British subject could possibly submit to. In fact, there was a licence of a very severe nature, and no person could trade at all except under this licence. With regard to these land deeds, one peculiarity in them was – I might mention, that the parties had received this land, and purchased it some 20 years previous to this from another proprietor entirely, and they were called upon then to sign away their powers – one provision of the deed was, that the Hudson's Bay Company should grant them permission before they could sell their land to any other party. They could not even trade in furs in any other part of North America, and there were some other things like that. Then again there was a total prohibition of the fur trade, the only natural production of the country in its present wild state, with a great many other things that they had to complain of. These proclamations perhaps were contingent upon the fur trade, but at the same time they kept the settlement in a state of ferment." (pp. 264-265).

When asked for proof of these assertions, he produced among other things the original of a proclamation by Governor Christie dated December 20, 1844,[837] that letters by unrepentant fur traders would have to be submitted, open to the scrutiny of Company officials, before being sealed and delivered to their recipients, a proclamation to which exception was taken "from one end of the settlement to the other" (Q. 4779, p. 265). McLoughlin also told the Select Committee that Mr. Sinclair's letters had been refused by Governor Christie.[838] He then read

---

837   Included at p. 373 in the Select Committee's report's papers. It was furnished by the Reverend G. O. Corbett as *Extract from the Minutes of Meeting of the Governor and Council of Rupert's Land, held at Red River Settlement*, 10 June, 1845.

838   Q. 4780, p. 265; see Chap. 8, commentary and notes at entry for September 5, 1845.

Appendix I – Petitions

the text of a 1848 petition from "the undersigned American importers" (Q. 4791, p. 266) against the practice of licencing permits for furs, promulgated by the Governor on December 7, 1844, and then read into the record certain resolutions, passed by the Governor in Council on April 3, 1845, on motion from Mr. Thom and seconded by Dr. Bunn, to deal with the refusal of "certain importers of American goods [who] had refused to pay the duty on their imports," as well the attempts of Collector Bird to collect them.[839]

One of the Select Committee members, examining the document, said to McLoughlin:

> Q. 4804. "There is a note upon the name of Mr. Thom, and as that note contains a very important statement, I wish you to look at it and tell me in whose handwriting it is?" –"That is Peter Garrick's writing in the settlement [statement?], if I am not mistaken in the writing." (p. 267).

Since McLoughlin had indeed spent a fair amount of time in Peter's company,[840] it is likely that he was indeed in a position to recognize Peter's handwriting.

Unfortunately, the subsequent exchange did not clarify whether the resolution (petition) read into evidence (Q. 4806, p. 268) was Peter's work or that he simply wrote something upon it; it had to do with measures to improve the functioning of the Quarterly Court.

On July 31, 1857, the Select Committee on the Hudson's Bay Company issued its two-page report to the House of Commons, in the form of a short preface to the extensive evidence it had assembled. It concluded that not only the imminent expiry of the Company's licence of exclusive trade made its inquiry necessary, but also certain other circumstances, such as the desire of "our Canadian fellow-subjects" to have extended to them regular settlement in this territory, the need to administer the affairs of Vancouver's Island, and "the present condition of the settlement which has been formed on the Red River." The Select Committee recognized the value of "the evidence taken before a Committee of the Legislative Assembly, appointed to investigate this subject containing much valuable information in reference to the interests and feelings of that important Colony, which are entitle[d] to the greatest weight on this occasion."[841]

The Select Committee's first conclusion was that Canada should be enabled to annex parts of the territory over which the Company then held rights for purposes of settlement, bringing in trans-

---

839   As described in Chap. 7, commentary and entries for March 2 & 28, April 6, 7, & 9, 1845

840   See diary entries for September, 1845.

841   This conclusion was arrived at despite the acerbic questions put to Roche about whether the Canadian Legislature even had authority to look into the HBC's governance; above, n. 824. The context was that body's receipt of the June 9, 1857, petition outlining the grievances of Red River's inhabitants, information which the Select Committee also had. However, it is not clear whether the "importance" here was being ascribed to Canada's views or to those of the Red River inhabitants.

portation and local administration to secure peace and good order, particularly in the Red River and Saskatchewan districts. Those districts would be ceded to Canada and, "the authority of the Hudson's Bay Company would of course entirely cease." The Select Committee refrained from providing detailed recommendations for the implementation of these and other goals, calling on the Government, in the next session of Parliament, to bring in a bill, after consultation with Canada and the Company, to achieve these ends.

It might be thought that the complaints and petitions of Garrioch and his fellow Red River inhabitants had born rich fruit, but although at least some of their petitions had reached the powers-that-be in London and sympathetic witnesses had been heard, the central propositions of free trade in furs and responsible government had been rejected or at least postponed – for an unexpected reason: the potential for free trading to lead to wider distribution of alcoholic spirits to Indigenous peoples:

> [T]he opinion at which Your Committee have arrived in mainly founded on the following considerations:
>
> 1. The great importance to the more peopled portions of British North America that law and order should, as far as possible, be maintained in these territories;
>
> 2. The fatal effects which they believe would infallibly result to the Indian population from a system of open competition in the fur trade, and the consequent introduction of spirits in a far greater degree than is the case at present; and
>
> 3. The probability of the indiscriminate destruction of the more valuable fur-bearing animals in the course of a few years.
>
> For these reasons Your Committee are of the opinion that whatever may be the validity or otherwise of the rights claimed by the Hudson's Bay Company, under the Charter, it is desirable that they should continue to enjoy the privilege of exclusive trade, which they now possess, except so far as those privileges are limited by the foregoing recommendations.[842]

The next few years brought twists and turns in the fate of the Red River settlement after Governor Simpson died and the influence of the Company waned in the wake of its intransigence against making proper arrangements in its territory for effective government and administration of justice. A dispute arose over referring the licencing renewal issue for ultimate adjudication by the Judicial Committee of the Privy Council. Sensing change, Canadian and American parties began to form in the Red River territory to support the respective claims of those governments, and the *Nor'-Wester*, founded in 1859, took a prominent role (and won readers) in urging emancipation from the Company and the development of self-government. In 1863, the London HBC Committee sold its interests to the newly-formed International Financial Society, which

---

842   *Report from the Select Committee*, p. iv.

Appendix I – Petitions 415

proved itself not particularly interested in the original character of the HBC as a fur-trading company.[843] The Red River territory was well along on the bumpy road towards provincehood.

These events in London took years to manifest themselves in distant Rupert's Land and to convey to the Red River protesters that they would ultimately be thwarted in their approach to London for succor. At the launch of that lengthy process, in 1846, the Company was clamping down as best it could on the free traders. Peter summarized the situation at the outset of his forthright essay, "Seven Days' Experience or the Pleasures of Smuggling":

> About the beginning of April, reports began to be circulated from one end of the Settlement to the other respecting the measures, it was said, the Hudson's Bay Company were about to take in order to prevent the smugglers of fur [free traders] from carrying away to the States such peltries as were in their possession.
>
> Apprehending serious consequences [from what] the Company were contemplating, we who had freely indulged in the common right of all men, receiving nothing but what we returned value for, began now to set our wits to work, to frustrate the designs of that company against us, and to secure our trade, without exposing ourselves or any other party to the results of oppression.[844] Various measures were proposed by our party as to what might be the most expeditious method that could be adopted for the transportation of our trade, and for its final security against the rapacious designs of the H.B.C.
>
> …Having arrived at last at a mutual understanding respecting our route, the day – or rather night – of our departure was settled, and every moment, forthwith, groaned under the silence of our adventurous preparations.[845]

---

843   There are many more details about this period provided in Rich, *Hudson's Bay Company*, III, pp. 798-816.

844   Peter's conclusion in this paragraph about the Company's rapacious designs on the profits of the free traders because the HBC was the sole purchaser of their goods and could set whatever prices it wished was echoed by Alexander Ross in his expansive descriptions in 1853 of the summer hunts, in which he himself participated, concluding the chapter with: "The reader has already been advised of the fact that the Company's demand affords the only regular market or outlet in the colony, and, as a matter of course, it is the first supplied. The Company being served, there is really no sale except to a few private individuals.… In less than a month, therefore, they have to start on the second trip, as destitute of supplies, as deeply in debt, and as ill provided as at first. Such was the result of the expedition we have described in detail, and such is the result of every expedition. The writer is not acquainted with a single instance, during the last twenty-five years, of one of these plain-hunters being able to clear his way or liquidate his expenses, far less to save a shilling by the chase; the absence of a proper system, and want of a market, render it impossible:" Ross, *Red River Settlement*, pp. 273-274.

These observations go a long way towards providing an explanation for Peter's near-poverty later in life. Unlike his brother John, who made a career in farming, Peter had bet his future on the fur trade.

845   Chap. 9, beginning of Smuggling account.

Once again, Peter took refuge in his entrepreneurial activities. Instead of merely petitioning once more and seemingly to no avail, Garrioch and his fellow free-traders were now taking action by deliberately engaging in the very pursuits the Company was determined to prevent and by labelling those pursuits in a cheeky epithet as "smuggling" in which the free traders were taking "pleasure." Despite the fact that it is infused with Peter's innate good humour and considerable talent for vivid description, "Seven Days' Experience or the Pleasures of Smuggling" was a giant step further along the road to the eventual demise of the HBC's monopolistic rule and the ultimate incorporation of Rupert's Land into the new Dominion of Canada. It is no wonder that Peter Garrioch must have hesitated to publish it after he had finished writing his smuggling manifesto. For a man about to settle down to marriage and a life with a large family in a close-knit community, his account was as yet too incendiary for that moment, its subject matter being a form of lived petition, one which had moved from requests to action, on fire with purpose.

Appendix II

Peter's Peregrinations: The Map

At some point, presumably after Peter completed the trading trip he chronicled in "Seven Days' Experience or the Pleasures of Smuggling, Being the Account of a Fur-Smuggling Expedition of the Free Traders to Pembina, in which the Author took Part, in 1846" (Chapter 9), following which he laid down his pen and brought his bulky diary books back to his home, a map relating to his journeys was drawn. Or more accurately, a map and a free-standing, unbound copy of it. Is either one of these maps Peter's handiwork?

Illustration 1: The Bound Map

Pictured above, Illustration 1, is the bound, less embellished version. It shows a large area, with rivers, lakes, mountains, as well as settlements or forts, most represented by small square boxes next to identifying names.

The Green-Covered Diary with the Bound into it Map

In the Peter Garrioch *fonds* in the Archives of Manitoba, MG2-C38, this map – we'll call it the "Bound Map" - is bound into a green-covered diary book on deposit there. The book – approximately 1.5 inches thick and measuring 12 5/8 by 8 inches – contains the bulk of Peter's extant diary entries. It appears to be several parts of the diaries bound at some later time into one book, but out of sequence.

The entries begin with January 1, 1843, but the green book does not contain what Gunn referred to as Part I ("A Journal of a trip from Red River to St. Peter's Minn and Prarie du Chien 1837-1838", Gunn pp. 43-135) nor Part III ("Fur Trading on the Missouri 1842-1844", Gunn, pp. 148-179). Since Gunn's typescript contained several more parts (listed above, Introduction), it appears that a later possessor of portions of the diary, perhaps someone after Gunn's time, bound together what he or she had into this one book. The green cover shows little sign of heavy wear, such as having been carried on an overland journey, which also supports the conclusion that the green book was not an original repository for Peter's diary pages, as does the fact that, if Gunn had bound it, he would undoubtedly have been careful to have bound the parts he had obtained from various sources in chronological sequence.

The green-covered diary book does contain what Gunn called Part IV: "Account of a Trip Made by Steamboat and Red River Cart from Fort Garry to Galena, Illinois, and Back, in 1844." That part of Gunn's transcript is assigned page numbers 180 – 234. The Bound Map is inserted in such a way as to break Peter's entry of November 6, 1844, into two parts, interrupted mid-stream as though the map had been inserted between diary pages merely for purposes of binding it in the book, not because it logically belonged where it is.

Gunn makes no mention of a map, Garrioch-made or otherwise. In fact, there is no indication in Peter's original diary pages, nor in Gunn's typescript of the November 6 entry on p. 220, that a map exists, let alone that one should be inserted just there. In view of Gunn's proclivity for copious notation on the geographical features of Peter's travels, it is impossible to believe that he would not have mentioned coming across such a relevant, even Peter-made map, whether found there or elsewhere, and would not have included it prominently in his collection of materials about his uncle.

Nor does the pagination confirm that the Bound Map originally belonged where it is now, appearing to show that it was arbitrarily bound into the diary book sometime in the more recent past. The two-page map is assigned page numbers 40 and 41 on the upper outer corners

Appendix II – Peter's Peregrinations: The Map

(Illustration 1). The two pages immediately preceding (Illustration 2) and following (Illustration 3) the inserted Bound Map are numbered on both top and bottom, but in a way that shows the inconsistency of the page numbering on the Bound Map:

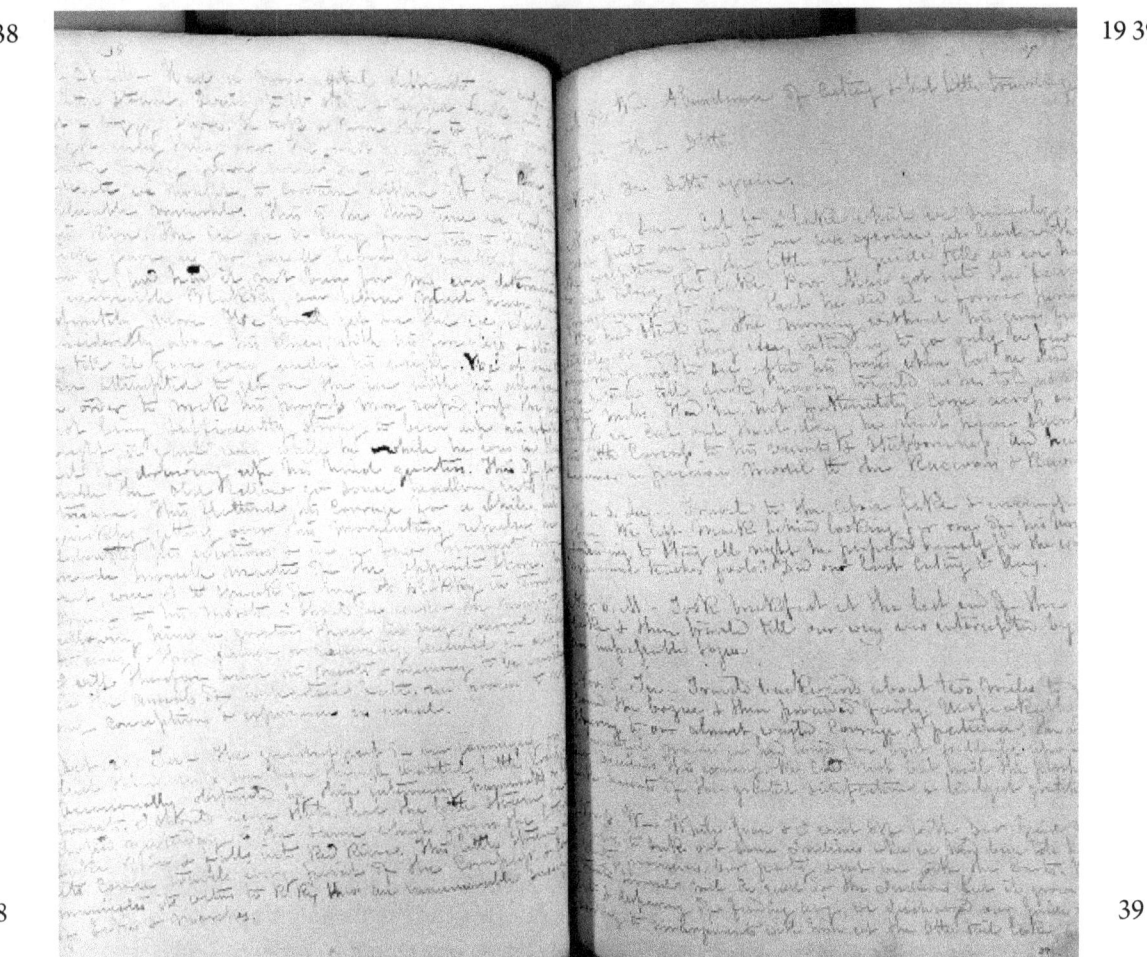

Illustration 2: The Two Pages Preceding the Bound Map

The numbers on the top of these pages (noted outside the edges of both illustrations) differ in appearance from those on the bottom. Both sets seem to be later additions, as are the numbers "40" and "41" on the Bound Map depicted in Illustration 1. Of note are the page numbers "18" and "20" encased in circles on the upper left corners of the pages preceding and following the map page. They are faded and the ink is coloured in such a way that suggests they are original numbers, or certainly older than the later numbers superimposed on the pages, including the

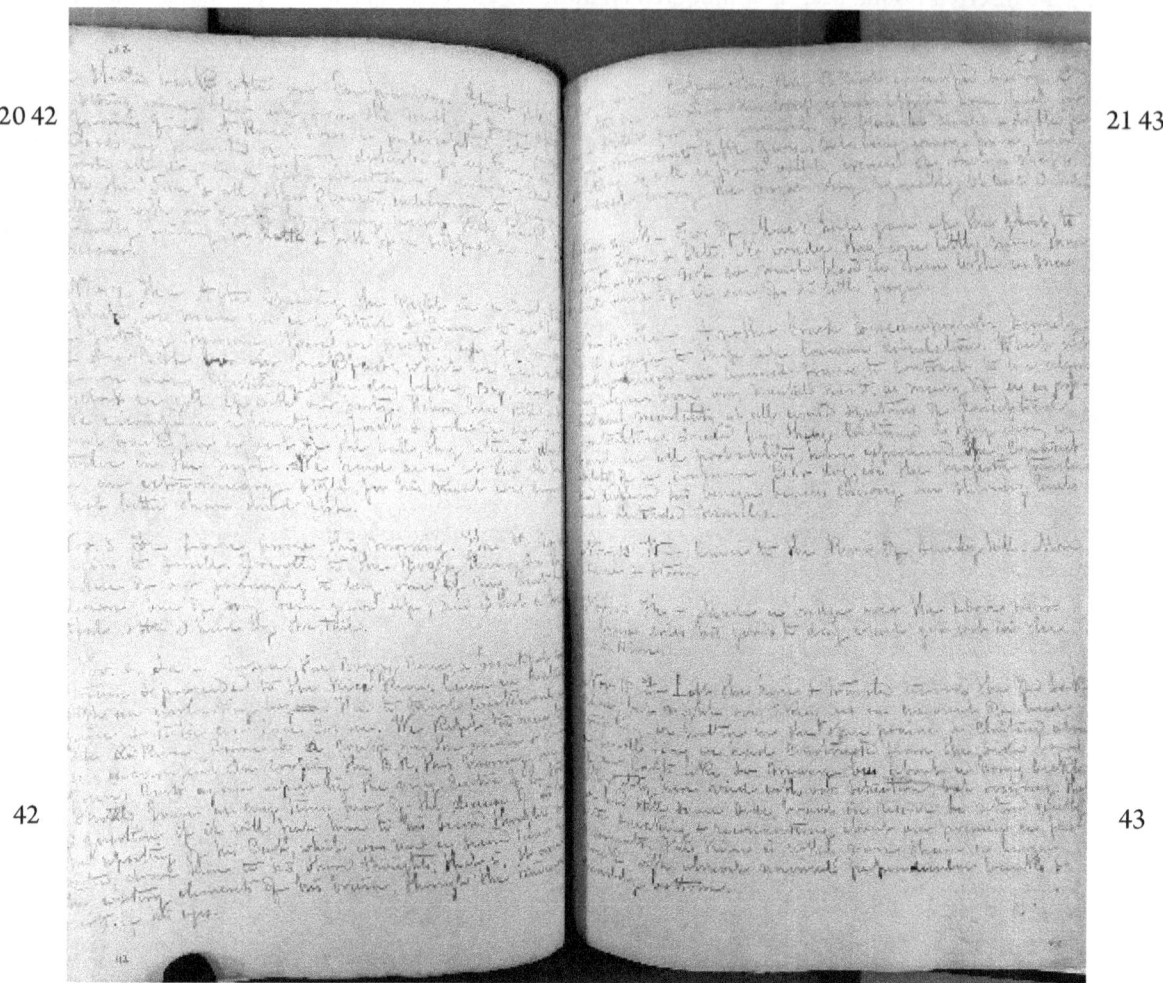

Illustration 3: The Two Pages Following the Bound Map

Bound Map page. The numbers "38" and "39" on the lower corners of Illustration 2 and the numbers "42" and "43" on the lower corners of Illustration 3 appear to be the compiler's attempt to renumber those pages to account for the map's insertion and the pagination sequence assigned to it. The original-appearing consecutive numbers "18" ("19") and "20" ("21") on the pages immediately preceding and following the Bound Map point to the conclusion that there was nothing inserted between them before the insertion of the Bound Map. This instructive page numbering as well as the fact that the November 6, 1844, diary entry was artificially broken into two parts by the map's insertion, both underscore the conclusion that there were no additional pages, such as the inserted Bound Map, in the original diary pages when Gunn had them. In short, the map must have been a later interpolation at a time when portions of Peter's diary were bound into the green-covered diary book.

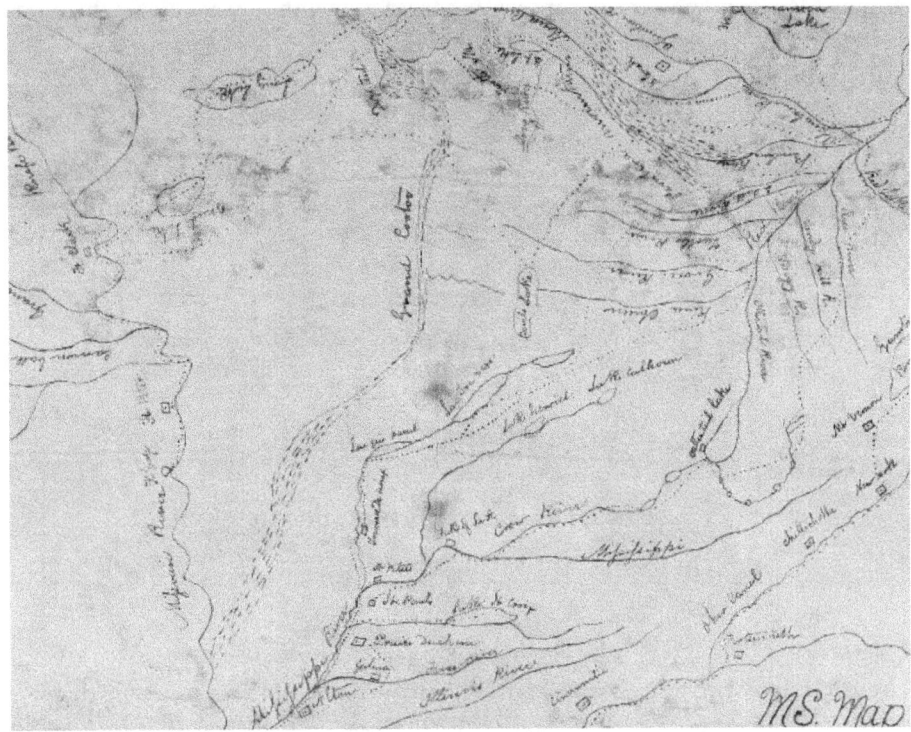

Illustration 4: The Freestanding, Captioned Map

The Free-Standing, Captioned Map

Of course, that doesn't address the question of *who* made the map. For that, it will be necessary to examine internal evidence. First, however, there is a detour to be taken in order to examine another map. This second map, the "Captioned Map,"[846] is virtually identical to the Bound Map, except that it is freestanding and stored in a separate location, D/279/1, at the Archives of Manitoba. It shows evidence of having been folded, despite not having been pasted into one of the diary books:

As one might expect from a freestanding map, this Captioned Map, Illustration 4, is overall larger than the other extant diary books. However, the size of the map itself inside the surrounding borders is roughly the same as that of the Bound Map. Since the numbers "40" and "41" are

---

846   Professionally photographed in 2016 by staff at the Archives of Manitoba, whose unfailing courtesy and assistance on this and on many other occasions the editors have greatly appreciated. The other photographs in this Appendix were taken at the Archives in 2023 by Josephine Sallis, and I (Sandra) am indebted to her for her assistance with that and other archival tasks.

missing from the corners of this freestanding map, it is likely that the borders were cut off a copy of the map to fit the size of the green-covered diary book and that page numbers were then added to the Bound Map in order to create consecutive pagination unnecessary on a stand-alone map, but desirable in a map included in a printed book. In short, this free-standing map is physically a separate item, whereas its counterpart copy was altered slightly to fit into the diary book in which it is bound.

The most striking addition is the prominent caption which embellishes the lower righthand corner of the free-standing map, Illustration 4. It reads:

MS Map
accompanying
Journal of Trip from R. R. Settlement to
Galena Ill. and Back, in 1844,
&
Showing Routes Taken by Author in
His Various Travels

The phraseology of the caption suggests that it was a later addition: "A MS. Map *accompanying* Journal, etc." It states two purposes: not only does it purport to depict a particular journey, that of Peter's trip to Galena and back (Chapter 4), but his routes – presumably all of them – during his various travels. How could that wider purpose even be effected until *after* those travels had been taken? And why would such an accomplished traveler as Garrioch even *need* to draw or place a map in his diary book, especially after the fact, unless it was for the benefit of later readers considerably less acquainted with the territory than he? Why would he have bothered to make a map after the fact which was of no practical value to him personally, other than for promotional purposes or postering?

It is odd, too, that Peter would have described himself as the "author" of a map to show the routes he had already travelled. Why not affix his name to the map if he had in fact drawn it himself? This observation is undercut somewhat by the fact that the description of himself as "author" also occurs in the Smuggling document he wrote during the closing days of his diary-writing: "Seven Days' Experience or the Pleasures of Smuggling, Being the Account of a Fur-Smuggling Expedition of the Free Traders to Pembina, in which the *Author* took Part, in 1846" (emphasis added), which the editors integrated into Peter's concurrent diary entries in Chapter 9. Still, the description of Peter as "author" in both cases has a kind of self-promoting quality to it, as though signalling that the item in question was not for Peter's use, but to exhibit his activities to others.

The diaries contain no internal evidence that Peter had any interest in map-making or that he even used or carried a map during his travels, much less drew one. Instead, as the diaries amply

Appendix II – Peter's Peregrinations: The Map

illustrate, Peter relied on landmarks and on passing travelers, especially Indigenous ones, for information about routes, supplies, and dangers along the way. He often hired guides. Nor does it seem possible for him to have carried or made a map showing the routes taken on his "various travels" *before* he was finished making them.

No, this was an after-the-fact sketch map. The wording of the map caption points to the hand of someone who intended to publish the diaries and thought a sketch map would be a useful addition for readers to see the terrain as a whole. But we have seen that, except for "Smuggling", which he ultimately refrained from publishing, Peter seems not to have contemplated publication.

On the other hand, Peter did live another 41 years after he completed the extant diaries in 1847, so it is possible that, as the remaining years of his life wore on, he began to consider publishing them. Further evidence in favour of that eventuality is that pages about sensitive topics were removed from the diaries, either by Peter or someone else, which makes more sense if publication was being contemplated. Moreover, a cursory comparison of the handwriting in which the place names were written on the map shows a similarity to Peter's handwriting in his diary books.

Common Features of the Bound and Captioned Versions of the Map

The two maps, Illustrations 1 & 4/5, have identical, or nearly-identical, internal features. However, on the Bound Map, but not on the Freestanding, Captioned Map, there is an addition to the lower right centre of the map, to the right of "Ohio River," of a box signifying a post and labeled "Cincinnati"; both the box and the name are scribbled out.

The two versions of the map – like its presumed creator – are certainly unorthodox, with North in the upper right-hand corner and the south in the lower left, for example. Dotted lines appear to show Peter's travel routes, but the locations of places visited are only approximate, and the distances are sometimes disproportionate and out of scale. But it illustrates with easily-understood visual eloquence a remarkable tale of one man's ten-year odyssey by horseback, ox cart, canoe, steamboat, and on foot, over a vast expanse of north-central North America at the point in its history when it was about to be overwhelmed by European and European-influenced immigrants.

The only trip illustrated that is not described, or even referred to, in the extant diaries is a journey (upper right-hand corner) to Fort Alexander, a Saulteux community and Church Missionary Society mission station on an unlabelled river (actually the Winnipeg River) flowing into Lake Winnipeg. The editors speculate in Chapter 10 that it might illustrate a journey on which Peter may have guided the Reverend Henry George to his first posting at Fort Alexander in the mid to late 1850s, where George was establishing a school.[847]

It is curious that, so far as is known to the later editors, the Reverend George H. Gunn made no mention of either of these maps, although one was inserted or bound in and the other perhaps kept with the diary books of his uncle, the very books from which Gunn laboured so meticulously to make a typescript. If either or both of the maps had been there when Gunn was working with those diary books, why did he neither mention, nor include them in his otherwise thorough work on his uncle's *oeuvre*? This omission makes it even more likely that they were created after the diaries were written and after whatever role Gunn may have played in assembling the green-covered book, with the loose map page cut down and inserted in it, as it exists today. Thus there is a strong possibility that neither copy of the map was Garrioch's work, or at least that he did not draw or put them with his diary materials as he wrote or completed his diaries, and in the circumstances, it is highly unlikely that the map was Gunn's work.

Opposite is Illustration 5, which is a copy of Illustration 4, but enlarged, and with the original stains Photoshopped out (by Dale) for better visualization.

Sometime later, notably, this freestanding map, unlike its bound counterpart in the green-covered diary book, was embellished with a prominent caption in the lower right corner, to be discussed below. It is the most striking difference between the bound and freestanding versions of the map.

Internal Evidence against Peter Garrioch Being the Author of the Map Attributed to Him

Dale Gibson and Durlene Germscheid, the second and third editors, proceeded on the basis that it was indeed Peter himself who drew the map, but I (Sandra) have concluded that he was not the author of the map, nor of the later large caption affixed to it. Along with the physical characteristics already discussed which suggest that the map was a later fabrication, there are several reasons for that conclusion arising from the map's contents themselves. The first reason is that the map does not, in fact, accomplish its stated purpose of "Showing the Routes Taken by Author in His Various Travels," or, at the very most, only approximately.

---

847 Whether or not accompanied by Peter Garrioch, Henry George went to Fort Alexander *circa* 1855, first teaching there, then dedicating his life to missionary work, described in his reports to the CMS. Perhaps the fact that Peter had also taught school in such communities was an inducement for both men for Peter to accompany Henry George, along with the fact that George had married the Reverend Cockran's eldest daughter. Like many teachers of "Indian children," George found the children in his Fort Alexander school "indolent" and the parents "not too anxious themselves of becoming followers of the Lord Jesus Christ, as I believe they seek more for the loaves and fishes than for the true bread of life." CMSA/AM: Mission Bk, CC1M6, 1885-1862, 1865.

Appendix II – Peter's Peregrinations: The Map

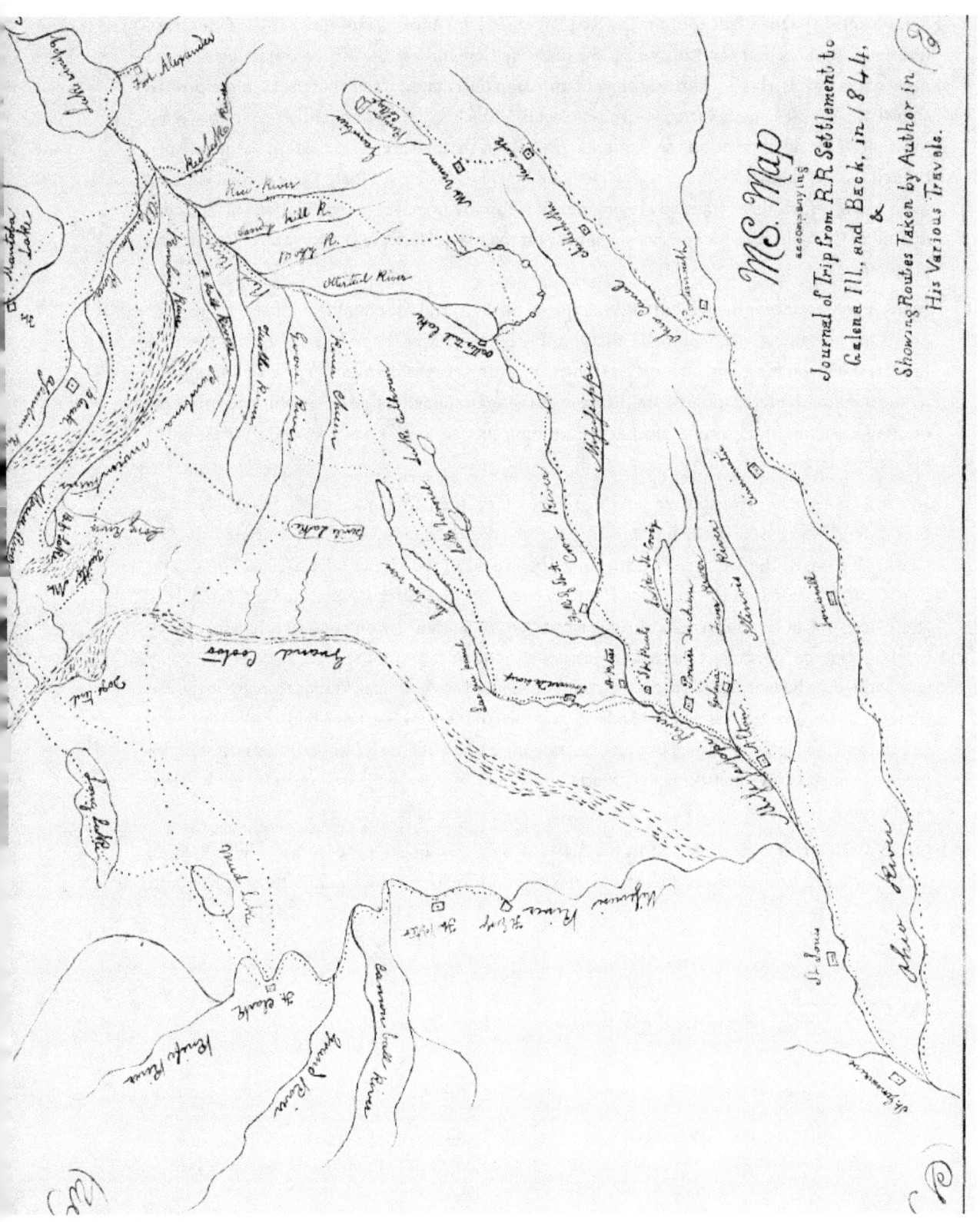

Illustration 5: The Freestanding, Captioned Map

Significantly, the map fails to show the Red River settlement or its environs, where Peter lived during most of his diary-writing years. Since the settlement was the ultimate starting and end point of his travels, this is a fairly significant omission on a map stated as having as its purpose to show Peter's routes on his various travels. As well, while his diaries frequently refer to traveling to Kittson's establishment on the Pembina, no post of that nature is marked on the map, even though the Pembina River itself is depicted and labeled as such. In fact, many of the locations from and to which Peter traveled are not identified on the map, yet many locations he does not mention visiting in his diary entries do appear on the map. Here are further examples of these peculiarities:

In his diary entries for the fall of 1842, the spring of 1843, and March of 1844, Peter elaborated on his having "a post assigned to my charge at the Mouse River."[848] While the Mouse (Souris) River is shown on the maps, no "post" is shown, in contrast to the many other posts which appear on the map, distinctly marked by small boxes. It is hard to imagine that Peter would have simply omitted the name and location of what was, to him, such an important post and a milestone in his trading career.

In April, 1843, Peter transported goods to Fort Clark, then continued down the Missouri to Fort Pierre[849] which he described in some detail, including comparing it favourably to Fort Clark. He stayed there for ten to fifteen days before taking the steamboat back to Fort Clark. Fort Clark is named on the map, as is Fort Pierre – but the latter is identified on the map as "St. Peter," not as "Fort Pierre," a strange alteration for someone who consistently wrote diary entries about the fort as Fort Pierre and was as well acquainted with the place as Peter obviously was and where he learned later that he could have met the American trader to tussle over the removal of his Mouse River post.[850] Indeed, the town of Pierre was established in 1880 opposite Fort Pierre, the former trading post, and became the capital of South Dakota. The author of the maps was mistakenly identifying Fort Pierre by a name, St. Peter, it never bore in Peter's lifetime nor beyond.

On that same trip, Peter referred in his diary to the steamboat's proceeding to Fort Union, an important trading post on the Missouri River and for years the headquarters of Kenneth

---

848 Chap. 5, entry and commentary for January 2, 1844 (retrospective) and *passim*.

849 *Ibid.*

850 Chap. 5, January 2, 1844 (retrospective), under the subtitle "Complex Motivation:" "In consequence of these new regulations, I was deprived of my post at Mouse River; and the only alternative[s] I had [were] to go down to *Fort Pierre* to await Mr. Picotte's arrival from St. Louis, or to return to Red River immediately. Mr. Picotte had told me in the summer to consider myself as engaged for a twelvemonth at the rate of $40." (italics added).

Appendix II – Peter's Peregrinations: The Map   427

McKenzie, the powerful free trader who became his father-in-law.[851] Fort Union does not appear on the map at all, and it is highly unlikely that Peter would simply have omitted such a key place from a map of his travels.

In April, 1844, Peter described his travels to Rivière aux Isle de Bois to trade for sugar, a place of some significance to him. Over the course of several days' entries, April 9-15, he described in detail [852] the considerable difficulties he had getting his animals and equipment to where the sugar-workers were working and celebrating, yet the location is not shown on the map. Nor is Back Fat Lake, where he went hunting on April 19, 1844.[853]

In September, 1844, Peter hired a guide to travel back to Red River via the Sauk Rapids,[854] and, although the route was eventually abandoned in favour of the Crow Wing Trail, the Sauk Rapids do not appear on the map.

In his diary entry for November 25, 1845, Peter described a trading trip to Partridge Crop (since 1851, Fairford),[855] but it is not identified (under either name) on the map.

In "Pleasures of Smuggling", on approximately May 6, 1846, Peter described in detail the process of fording Sturgeon Creek, and on the same date in his diaries, the experience of crossing the Stinking River,[856] but neither tributary appears on the map. The same is true for the following day with the Scratching River and the Marshy River.[857]

There are two thickened areas of flowing broken lines on the map, one identified and the other not. The name of the one at the centre left of the map is "Grand Cootoo," a label of some mystery until one discovers that Aaron Arrowsmith's 1814 map of North America included the Coo-too-nay River, one of the many ways to spell Kootenay, in Blackfoot.[858] This makes no sense on a map purporting to be a record of Peter's travels, since they were confined to an area encompassing roughly Manitoba, Minnesota, Illinois, and the Dakotas, while the Kootenay River's most easternly location is northwestern Montana. On the other hand, it is possible that "Grand Cootoo" is a rendition of Grand Coteau in North Dakota, the site of the great Métis-Sioux battle

---

851   Chap. 5, n. 482. On McKenzie's place in Peter's life, Chap 10, nn. 708 & 719. Built by McKenzie, Fort Union Trading Post is now a U.S. national historical sight (Wikipedia)

852   Chap. 5, entries and commentary for April 9-15, 1844.

853   Chap.5, entry for April 19, 1844.

854   Chap. 6, entries, notes, & commentary for September 4-16, 1844.

855   Chap. 8, entry & notes for November 25, 1845.

856   Chap. 9, extensive entry for May 6, 1846.

857   Chap. 9, extensive entries for May 7 & 8, 1846.

858   Greg Nesteroff, *Castlegar News* (March 7, 2020).

of July, 1851.[859] If so, it again supports the conclusion that the map was made sometime after Peter completed his diary-writing, at least in terms of the diaries we have.

In sum, the failure of the map maker to track and record the actual places, even important ones, identified by Peter throughout his diaries, as well as the fact that rivers, lakes, mountains, and forts not named in the diaries were included on the map cannot but lead to the conclusion that whoever made the map had not read the diaries closely in order to ensure that the readers of the map would be able to follow Peter's travels in what must have been meant to be close detail. It is hard to imagine that Peter himself would have been content with fabricating such an imprecise map about his own travels. Far from "showing the routes taken by the author in his various travels," the map is instead a generic map of the huge area, designed to give some visual emphasis to Peter's wide-ranging trading trips, probably at a time in the future when such individual exploits had become rare and romanticized and were thought to need illustrating.

Finally, it should not be forgotten that Peter had no need for a map for the purpose for which modern travelers use them: to visualize an area or to find their way to a desired destination. The diaries show no indication that Peter set his course by written directions, instead relying on the terrain and the people he encountered along the way or whom he hired as guides, as, for example, the Suza Bruno he had hired at Crow Island (entries for September 24-30, 1844, above). Given the vagaries of weather, the varying difficulties in crossing rivers he encountered, the need at times to detour in order to secure necessary food and other supplies before proceeding, delays due to recalcitrant oxen and horses and unexpected swamps, and detours necessitated by the presence of dangerous persons on a given route, a "European" style map of this type would have been of limited or no use to him, resourceful and experienced as he already was. He would have considered irrelevant to himself the function of maps as described by a modern scientist: "A map is an abstraction. It reduces something in the original dimensionality of the world, but it still preserves the salient and relevant information."[860]

By contrast, early Indigenous and Métis map-makers worked from memory, not abstractions, and tended to include physical features important to way-finding, such as the location and length of portages or numbers of days for a journey, rather than just depicting locations with place names as this map does.[861] Their work was often in the service of surveyors such as

---

859   The latter suggestion is courtesy of Jennifer S. H. Brown.

860   Dr. Aviv Regev, a computational biologist, was referring to the Human Cell Atlas mapping of the human body at the level of individual cells, "With cell atlas, researchers set out to map the human body, shed light on causes and effects of disease." *Globe & Mail* (August 2, 2023), p. 1.

861   Judith Hudson Beattie, "Indian Maps in the Hudson's Bay Company Archives: A Comparison of Five Area Maps Recorded by Peter Fidler, 1801-1802," *Archivaria* 21 (Winter, 1985-1986).

Appendix II – Peter's Peregrinations: The Map

Peter Fidler,[862] who preserved them, or David Thompson, who, in order to survive in unknown territory, badly needed a record of the most basic information initially possessed only by the Indigenous people.

In contrast to the case of the early explorers, who had to rely on the deep knowledge of their Indigenous guides before they could even think about embarking on their travels, the map found with or in Peter's diary book was not likely to have been created after the fact by, or for, a man of mixed ancestry who already knew the terrain he had travelled. Instead, it was more likely to have been created by someone else, perhaps a descendant or a colleague, for an audience of bystanders. Despite some superficial similarities to Indigenous maps, the map found in the green diary book and its free-standing analogue was an artificial construct, an illustration, not something that was designed to serve a practical way-finding purpose.

Who drew the map and for what reason? There is no definitive answer. From the evidence we have, particularly the fact that the map is inconsistent with Peter's accounts of his travels, it is unlikely that Peter himself drew it. The authorship of the rather pompously-named "MS Map accompanying Journal of Trip from R. R. Settlement to Galena Ill. and Back, in 1844, & Showing Routes Taken by Author in His Various Travels," found both as a free-standing artifact and bound into the green-covered diary book, remains a mystery, among many other mysteries in Peter Garrioch's life.

---

862   J. G. MacGregor, *Peter Fiedler: Canada's Forgotten Surveyor, 1769-1822* (Toronto: McClelland & Stewart, 1966), *passim*. "The Old Red River Library, A Precious Historic Remnant," n. d. MG9 A78-1, A78-3, recounts how upon his death in 1821, Fiedler left his library of 500 precious books to the HBC in trust for the people of Red River, a fact traceable to Fiedler's signatures on the twelve old volumes he had in his own book collection. Names recorded on some of the volumes attest to the fact that they were circulated in the community in a kind of lending library fashion.

Appendix III

Garrioch Family Photographs

When I (Sandra) learned during the course of preparing this book for publication that the Archives of Manitoba does not possess a photograph of Peter Garrioch, I found it surprising, since Peter, who died in 1888, lived well into the era of photography and was a respected citizen of the Red River settlement and later the Province of Manitoba. Fortunately, I took another look in Dale's laptop and found, to my great pleasure, a folder labeled "Garrioch photos" containing the first three photographs below. Sadly, however, there are no captions or explanatory notes that would permit firm identification or disclose their provenance. I do know that Dale and Durlene visited Garrioch family members and suspect these photographs were supplied by one or more of them. This, too, is uncertain because, surprisingly, Dale left behind almost no notes about these visits, at least none that I can find.

The fact that there are so few relevant photographs in the "Garrioch photos file" and that there is a family resemblance to the clearly-identified public photographs of Peter's three literary nephews (below) made me initially hopeful that the first three photographs do indeed depict Peter Garrioch.

The first appears to have been taken around 1849, at the time of Peter's and Margaret's marriage. Their hands are featured, and their position suggests that the two of them were or were about to be wed, despite the absence of visible wedding rings. At the time Peter, born on July 5, 1811, would have been 38 years old, and Margaret, born on September 1, 1825, would have been 24. The couple depicted in the photograph do appear to be of those ages. And the man shown here certainly matches the description of Peter by Alexander Ross as "an English half-breed, a comely, well-behaved young man of respectable connections."[863]

On the other hand, as Anne Lindsay points out,[864] the cut of the woman's jacket or bodice seems to date from a later time, as does her hairstyle.

---

863   Chap. 5, nn. 335 & 336 and accompanying text.

864   Email from Lindsay to Anderson (September 17, 2023).

Appendix III – Garrioch Family Photographs 431

The second photograph seemingly shows the man in the first photograph, now several decades older, still vigorous and genial, as one might have expected Peter to have remained during his sixties and early seventies.

The third photograph above shows the same elderly man, this time standing second from right within a family grouping. The rest of the family members are not identifiable, and the men appear too much of Peter's age to be his nephews, with the exception of the man standing second to the right of Peter, who most resembles George Henry Gunn, Peter's amanuensis, except that Gunn was born in 1865 and was a young man when Peter died in 1888.

However, thanks to the efforts of the knowledgeable Anne Lindsay, the same photograph has been determined to be part of the St. John's Cathedral Archives (VI MA 002), where it is identified as "Red River Settlement Descendants 1920, 100th Anniversary of Beginning CCSJ." Therefore, the man second from right cannot be Peter even though it could be one of his nephews or sons.

A better copy of the photograph than Dale's is reproduced below:

The following seven photographs are of Peter's three literary nephews, George Henry Gunn (1865-1945), his brother John J. Gunn (1861-1907), and their first cousin Alfred Campbell Garrioch (1846-1934), described in the Introduction, at note 8. Unlike the first three photographs, their subjects are readily identified.

The initial set depicts George Henry Gunn. The first of the two photographs was published in the Winnipeg *Weekly Free Press & Prairie Farmer* (February 16, 1910), p. 6, in connection with his abundant contributions to Manitoba's history. The second is found in *East Side of the Red: A Centennial Project of the Rural Municipality of St. Clements, 1884-1984* (East Selkirk, Man.: St. Clements Historical Committee, 1984). p. 571.

Appendix III – Garrioch Family Photographs

The second set of photographs depicts the Reverend Alfred Campbell Garrioch. The photograph showing him wearing a hat was published in the *Winnipeg Tribune* (February 10, 1933), p. 4, while the photograph on the right is the frontispiece from his book, *The Correction Line*, published in 1933.

Another photograph of a younger A. C. Garrioch with his wife is held by the Provincial Archives of Alberta:

The third set depicts John J. Gunn. The lefthand photograph is the frontispiece to his collection of essays, *Echoes of the Red*, published posthumously by his widow in 1930. The photograph on the right appeared in the *Manitoba Morning Free Press* (December 26, 1906), p. 15, and in the *[Winnipeg] Weekly Free Press & Prairie Farmer* (January 2, 1907), p. 20, in connection with his work as the President of the Manitoba Beekeeper's Association, and then more widely published after his untimely death, gored by a bull on his East Selkirk farm on September 22, 1907. It appeared, for example, in the *Weekly Free Press & Prairie Farmer* (September 25, 1907), p. 4, along with his obituary.

Appendix III – Garrioch Family Photographs

It is fortunate that these published photographs of three of Peter's nephews exist, since their striking resemblance to each other and to the man who may be (or may not be) Peter Garrioch presents a clue to Peter's physiognomy and provides a tantalizing possibility that the first three photographs are of another of Peter's close relatives, perhaps one of his sons.

It is hoped that the publication of the unidentified "Peter Garrioch" photographs here, along with those of his nephews, will result in more exact identification of the former and the eventual coming to light of actual, verifiable photographs of the man himself.

Bibliography

1: Archival Sources

Archives of the Ecclesiastical Diocese of Rupert's Land (Winnipeg)

    Reminiscences of Reverend Benjamin McKenzie. PRL-84-59 7953

Archives of Manitoba (Winnipeg)

    Alexander Ross Family *Fonds*

    Adams, G. Archibald *Fonds*

    Cockran, Reverend William. *Journal*. Church Missionary Society Archive. Missions to the Americas Mission Book 2, North-West America.

    _____ Original Papers, Letters and Papers of Individual Missionaries. Catechists and Others 1825-1865, North-West Canada 1821-1880 CC1O16 (148-163).

    _____ "Report of the state of Religion, Morality, and Education at the Red River Settlement and Grand Rapids by the Revd Messrs Jones and Cockran," [1835] in Church Missionary Society Archive, Section V, Missions to the Americas Mission Book 2, *North-West America*.

    Garrioch, Peter, *Journals*. MG2 C38

    Gunn, George Henry *Fonds,* HBC Archives MG9 A78-1, A78-3.

    _____ . "Adam Thom," n. d.

    _____ . "Buffalo Hunting in the West," n. d.

    _____ . "Correcting the Correction Line; a Review of A.C. Garrioch's book, The Correction Line," n. d.

    _____ . "Correspondence, 1891-1942."

    _____ . "Lists of Inland Posts established by the Hudson's Bay Co., with dates of establishment," n. d.

    _____ . "Martin McLeod," n. d.

    _____ . "Note re James Green," n. d.

    _____ . "Note re Rev. William Cochrane," n.d.

    _____ . "Our Country, Its People & Industries at The Beginning of the Nineteenth Century," n. d..

    _____ . "Peter Garrioch and the Founding of Saint Paul," n. d

    _____ . "Peter Garrioch, His Life and Times," n. d.

    _____ . "Peter Garrioch: Teacher, Trader, Traveler, Diarist," n. d.

    _____ . "Peter Garrioch's School, An Unwritten Chapter of Minnesota History," n. d.

    _____ . "*The Journal of Peter Garrioch,* edited with notes by George H. Gunn."

    _____ . "The Old Red River Library, A Precious Historic Remnant," n. d.

    _____ . "Verse, Psalms, Hymns."

Appendix III – Bibliography

Hudson's Bay Company Archives

    Jones, David, *The Missionary Register, Missionary Papers, Mission Book, North-West Canada*, CC 1 M 1, empire.amdigital.co.uk, December, 1826.
  Northern Department missionary and mission station accounts, including
    Church Missionary Society Archives, North West America Mission (Canada) (1822)
    Church Missionary Society Archive, Missions to the Americas Mission Book, North-West America
    Original Papers, Letters and Papers of Individual Missionaries, Catechists and Others 1825-1865, North-West Canada 1821-1880
    empire.amdigital.co.uk
  Thomas Douglas, 5th Earl of Selkirk Collection

Historic Resources Branch, Manitoba Culture, Heritage and Recreation (Winnipeg)

Library and Archives Canada (Ottawa), Census of Canada, 1881, 1891, 1901

Louis Riel Institute (Winnipeg)

    Pigeon, Émilie, *Assumption Abbey, Richardton, N.D.*, Belleau Collection, Roll 2, 1847: 19-21

Minnesota Historical Society (Saint Paul)

    Stephen Riggs & Family Papers, *Mary Anne Longley Riggs Correspondence, 1837-51*, 144.G.7.2F.

2: Other Unpublished Sources

Gibson, Dale. Email to Lorna Turnbull. February 27, 2013
Lindsay, Anne. Emails to Sandra Anderson. June 7, June 19, & September 17, 2023
Lindsay, Anne. "With Salt Springs Almost at Our Doors: The History of Salt Making in the Swan River, Winnipegosis, and Lake Manitoba Regions." Manuscript draft. © Anne Lindsay, 2006.

3: Newspapers and Periodicals

Alberta Native News (Edmonton)
Castlegar News (British Columbia)
Daily Free Press and Prairie Farmer (Winnipeg)
Edmonton Daily Bulletin
Forbes Magazine (Jersey City, New York)
Free Press Evening Bulletin (Winnipeg)
Globe & Mail (Toronto)
Le Métis (St. Boniface)
Lethbridge Herald
London Morning Chronicle
Manitoba Free Press
Manitoba Morning Free Press (Winnipeg)

Manitoba Pageant (Winnipeg)
Manitoban & Northwest Herald (Winnipeg)
Missouri Gazette (St. Louis)
The Nor'-Wester (Fort Garry, Red River Territory)
Portage la Prairie Weekly
The Province (Vancouver)
Saint Paul Pioneer Press
Saint Paul Weekly Minnesotan
Spirit of the Times: A Chronicle of the Turf, Agriculture, Field Sports, Literature and the Stage (New York City, N. Y.)
U.S. News and World Report (Washington, D. C.)
Victoria Times Colonist Weekly
Windsor Star (Ontario)
Winnipeg Daily Free Press
Winnipeg Evening Tribune
Winnipeg Free Press
Winnipeg Free Press & Prairie Farmer
Winnipeg Tribune
Winnipeg Tribune Magazine

4: Online Resources

1838-39 Catalogue of Kenyon College's Theological Seminary of the Diocese of Ohio
Ancestry.com
Beaumont, Raymond M. & Lawrence Barkwell, The Virtual Museum of Metis History and Culture and Applied Research.
Barkwell, Lawrence, *"Alfred Campbell Garrioch."* Virtual Museum of Metis History
Canada Manitoba Death Index 1880-1949
Canada Statutes
Canadian Encyclopedia
Canadiana.Org
Catholic Encyclopedia
Church Missionary Society records
Culture, 2011. metismuseum@gdi.gdins.org
Dictionary of Canadian Biography (*DCB*)
Dictionary of Manitoba Biography (*DMB*), ed. J. M. Bumsted. Winnipeg, University of Manitoba Press, 1999.
Gabriel Dumont Institute of Native Studies (Saskatoon)
HathiTrust Digital Library
Internet Archive
JStor
Legislative Assembly of Assiniboia.
Manitoba Culture, Heritage and Recreation, 1985.
Manitoba Historical Society: Memorable Manitobans
Manitoba Names, Winnipeg, Manitoba Conservation, 2001.
Métis Dictionary of Biography, ed. Lawrence J. Barkwell, Métis Museum
Red River Ancestry.ca
Red River Censuses, Provisional Government of Assiniboia

Appendix III – Bibliography

Scribd, scribd.com
University of Alberta, Bruce Peel Special Collections & Archives Library, Edmonton
Wikipedia
WorldCat

5: Published Sources (including selected sources cited* by G. H. Gunn)

*The later editors made no attempt to correct Gunn's sources as they appear in his quoted notes. Since Gunn did not always cite his sources completely or in modern convention, the reader of his notes is referred to the more complete bibliographical information below)

[Anon.] *Interlake Pioneers, Steeprock Manitoba*. Altona, Manitoba: D. W. Friesen & Sons, 1974.

Arrowsmith, John. *Map of part of the Valley of Red River North of the 49th Parallel to accompany a report on the Canadian Red River Exploring Expedition by H.Y. Hind [facsimile]*. 1:253,440. In: Henry Youle Hind. *Papers Relative to the Exploration of the Country Between Lake Superior and the Red Rivers Settlement*. London: G. E. Eyre & W. Spottiswoode. 1859. Also available at https://www.flickr.com/photos/manitobamaps/2089812938.

Baker, D. A. J. "Early Schools of Minnesota." *Collections of the Minnesota Historical Society* I. St. Paul, Minn.: MHS, 1872. Pp. 81-83.

Baker, James H. "Lives of the Governors of Minnesota." *Collections of the Minnesota Historical Society* XIII. St. Paul, Minn.: MHS, 1908. Pp. 77-105.

Barclay, Krista. "From Rupert's Land to Canada West: Hudson's Bay Company Families and Representations of Indigeneity in Small-Town Ontario, 1840–1980." *Journal of the Canadian Historical Association* 26:1 (2015). Pp. 67–97.

Barkwell, Lawrence. "Alfred Campbell Garrioch." Virtual Museum of Metis History and Culture, 2011. metismuseum@gdi.gdins.org.

Beattie, Judith Hudson. "Indian Maps in the Hudson's Bay Company Archives: A Comparison of Five Area Maps Recorded by Peter Fidler, 1801-1802." *Archivaria* 21 (Winter, 1985-1986). Pp. 166-175. https://archivaria.ca/index.php/archivaria/article/view/11246/12185.

Beaumont, Raymond M. "The Rev. William Cockran: the Man and the Image." *Manitoba History* 33 (Spring, 1997). https://www.mhs.mb.ca/docs/mb_history/33/cockran_w.shtml.

Begg, Alexander. *Begg's Red River Journal and Other Papers Relative to the Red River Resistance of 1869-1870*. Edited with an Introduction by W. L. Morton. Champlain Society Publications XXXIV. Toronto: Champlain Society, 1956.

Belcourt, Father G. A. "The Department of the Hudson's Bay." *Collections of the Minnesota Historical Society* I (1872). Pp. 207-244.

———. "Letter dated November 25, 1845" in Executive Documents, United States, 31st Congress, 1st Session 8, nr. 51 (1849-50). P. 44. (Gunn's Appendix E.)

Bell, Charles Napier. *The Old Forts of Winnipeg, 1738-1927*. Manitoba Historical and Scientific Society Transactions, new series, nr. 3. Winnipeg: Dawson Richardson, 1927.

Blanchard, Jim, ed. *A Thousand Miles of Prairie: The Manitoba Historical Society and the History of Western Canada*. Winnipeg: University of Manitoba Press, 2002.

Bond, J. Wesley. *Minnesota and its Resources.* New York: Redford, 1853.

Bown, Stephen R. *The Company: The Rise and Fall of the Hudson's Bay Empire.* Toronto: Doubleday Canada, 2020.

Brown, Jennifer S. H. "Documentary Editing: Whose Voices?" *Occasional Papers of the Champlain Society.* Toronto: Chaplain Society, 1992. Pp. 1-13.

———. *Ethnohistorian in Rupert's Land: Unfinished Conversations.* Edmonton: Athabasca University Press, 2017.

———. "Partial Truths: A Closer Look at Fur Trade Marriage." *From Rupert's Land to Canada* Theodore Binnema, Gerhard J. Ens, & R. C. MacLeod, eds. Edmonton: University of Alberta Press, 2001. Pp. 59-77.

———. *Strangers in Blood: Fur Trade Company Families in Indian Country.* Vancouver: University of British Columbia Press, 1980.

Brunson, Alfred. "A Methodist Circuit Rider's Horseback Tour from Pennsylvania to Wisconsin, 1835" Reuben Gold Thwaites, ed. *Collections of the State Historical Society of Wisconsin* XV (1900). Pp. 264-291.

Bryce, George & Charles N. Bell. "Original Letters and other Documents relating to the Selkirk Settlement." *Manitoba Historical and Scientific Society Transactions,* series 1, nr. 33 (January, 1889).

Bumsted, J.M., ed. *Dictionary of Manitoba Biography (DMB).* Winnipeg, University of Manitoba Press, 1999.

——— "Early Flooding in Red River, 1776-1861." "Another Look at the Buffalo hunt," in: *Thomas Scott's Body and Other Essays on Early Manitoba History.* Winnipeg: University of Manitoba Press, 2000.

———. *Trials & Tribulations: The Red River Settlement and the Emergence of Manitoba, 1811-1870.* Winnipeg: Great Plains Publications, 2003.

Canada. Minister of Supply and Services. *Report of the Royal Commission on Aboriginal Peoples.* 5 vols. Ottawa: Canada Communication Group, 1996.

Carter, Sarah, *The Importance of Being Monogamous: Marriage & Nation Building in Western Canada.* Edmonton: University of Alberta Press, 2008.

Case, John H., ed. "Historical Notes of Grey Cloud Island and the Vicinity." *Collections of the Minnesota Historical Society* XV. St Paul, Minn.: MHS, 1915. Pp. 371-376.

Chittenden, Hiram M. *History of Early Steamboat Navigation on the Missouri; Life and Adventures of Joseph La Barge.* 2 vols. New York: Francis P. Harper, 1903. (Reprinted in a single volume edition in 1962 under an expanded title: …*Joseph La Barge, Pioneer Navigator and Indian Trader, for Fifty Years Identified with the Commerce of the Missouri Valley.*)

———. *The American Fur Trade of the Far West: A History of the Pioneer Trading Posts and Fur Companies of the Missouri Valley and the Rocky Mountains and of the Overland Commerce with Santa Fe.* 3 vols. New York: Francis P. Harper, 1902. (Reprinted twice in 2 volumes in 1935 and 1954, the latter with an Introduction by Minnesota historian Grace Lee Nute.)

Coles, Laura Millar. "Looking Backward; Reaching Forward: The Champlain Society and Documentary Publishing." *Occasional Papers of the Champlain Society.* Toronto: Chaplain Society, 1992. Pp. 15-35.

Appendix III – Bibliography

Collier, Anne M. *A History of Portage la Prairie & Surrounding District*. Altona, Manitoba: W. Friesen & Sons, 1970.

Cooper, Barry. *Alexander Kennedy Isbister: A Respectable Critic of the Honourable Company*. Ottawa: Carlton University Press, 1988.

Coutts, Robert J. *The Road to the Rapids: Nineteenth-Century Church and Society at St. Andrews Parish, Red River*. Calgary: University of Calgary Press, 2000.

Devine, Heather. *The People who Own Themselves: Aboriginal Ethnogenesis in a Canadian Family, 1660-1900*. Calgary: University of Calgary Press, 2004.

Dick, Lyle. "Manitoba History: Red River's Vernacular Historians." *Manitoba Historical Society* 7 (Winter, 2013). Pp. 3-15.

Dye, Eva Emery. *McLaughlin and Old Oregon*. Chicago: A. C. McClung & Co., 1900.

Edmunds, R. David. "'Unacquainted with the laws of the civilized world': American Attitudes toward the Métis Communities in the Old Northwest." *The New Peoples: Being and Becoming Métis in North America*. Jacqueline Peterson & Jennifer S. H. Brown, eds. Winnipeg: University of Manitoba Press, 1985. Pp. 185-194.

Ellet, Elizabeth Fries. *The Pioneer Women of the West*. Philadelphia: Porter & Coates, 1873. Pp. 305-338. (Mrs. Snelling's reminiscences, first published in 1852.)

Ens, Gerhard J. *Homeland to Hinterland: The Changing World of the Red River Métis in the Nineteenth Century*. Toronto: University of Toronto Press, 1996.

Faiers, Jonathan. *Fur: A Sensitive History*. New Haven: Yale University Press, 2020.

Fairbanks, Carol. *Prairie Women: Images in American and Canadian Fiction*. New Haven: Yale University Press, 1986.

Ferguson, Barry, ed. *The Anglican Church and the World of Western Canada, 1820-1970*. Regina: Canadian Plains Research Center, University of Regina, 1991.

Galbraith, John S. *The Little Emperor: Governor Simpson of the Hudson's Bay Company*. Toronto: MacMillan, 1976.

Garrioch, A. C. *A Hatchet Mark in Duplicate*. Toronto: Ryerson Press, 1929.

–––. *The Correction Line*. Winnipeg: Stovel Company, 1933.

–––. *The Far and Furry North: A Story of Life and Love and Travel in the Days of the Hudson's Bay Company*. Winnipeg: Douglass-McIntyre, 1925.

–––. *First Furrows: A History of the Early Settlement of the Red River Country, Including that of Portage la Prairie*. Winnipeg: Stovel Company, 1923.

Garrioch, Verena L. "First Schools on Portage Plains." *Winnipeg Tribune Magazine*, July 27, 1935. P. 8.

Gibson, Dale. *Law, Life, and Government at Red River, Vol. 1: Settlement and Governance, 1812-1872; Vol. 2: Annotated Records of the General Quarterly Court of Assiniboia*. Osgoode Society for Canadian Legal History & Rupert's Land Record Society Series nrs. 13 & 14. Montreal & Kingston: McGill-Queen's University Press, 2015.

–––. "The First Hanged Was Indian: Capital Punishment in the Quarterly Court of Assiniboia." *Papers of the Rupert's Land Colloquium*. Issued as a Compact Disk (CD). Winnipeg: Centre for Rupert's Land Studies, University of Winnipeg, 2008.

Gibson, Dale, & Lee Gibson. *Substantial Justice: Law and Lawyers in Manitoba, 1670-1870*. Winnipeg: Peguis Press, 1972.

Gilman, Rhoda R., Carolyn Gilman, & Deborah L Miller. *The Red River Trails: Oxcart Routes between St. Paul and the Selkirk Settlement, 1820-1870*. St. Paul: Minnesota Historical Society, 1979.

Giraud, Marcel. *The Métis in the Canadian West*. George Woodcock, trans. 2 vols. Edmonton & Lincoln, Neb.: Alberta & Nebraska University Presses, 1986.

Gluek, Alfred J. *Minnesota and the Manifest Destiny of the Canadian Northwest: A Study in Canadian-American Relations*. Toronto: University of Toronto Press, 1965.

Great Britain. Parliament. House of Commons. *Report from the Select Committee on the Hudson's Bay Company; Together with the Proceedings of the Committee, Minutes of Evidence, Appendix, and Index*. London: Ordered, by the House of Commons, to be Printed, 31 July & 11 August 1857.

Gunn, Donald. *History of Manitoba from the Earliest Settlement to 1835; &* [by Charles R. Tuttle] *from 1835 to the Admission of the Province into the Dominion*. Ottawa: Maclean, Roger & Co., 1880. Also available at http://www.ourroots.ca/e/roots/113c0005.jpg

Gunn, George Henry. "Peter Garrioch at St. Peter's, 1837." *Minnesota History* 20 (1939), Pp. 119-128.

Gunn, John J. *Echoes of the Red: A Reprint of Some of the Early Writings of the Author Depicting Pioneer Days in the Red River Settlements*. Toronto: Macmillan, 1930.

Hargrave, Joseph James. *Red River*. Montreal: J. Lovell for the author, 1871.

Hargrave, Letitia Mactavish. *The Letters of Letitia Hargrave*. Edited with an Introduction by Margaret Arnett Macleod. Champlain Society Publications XXVIII. Toronto: Champlain Society, 1947.

Healy, William J. *Women of Red River: Being a Book Written from the Recollections of Women Surviving from the Red River Era*. Winnipeg: Russell, Lang for the Women's Canadian Club, 1923.

Henry, Alexander. *New Light on the Early History of the Greater Northwest: the Manuscript Journals of Alexander Henry, Fur Trader of the Northwest Company and of David Thompson, Official Geographer of the Same Company, 1799-1814: Exploration and Adventure among the Indians on the Red, Saskatchewan, Missouri, and Columbia Rivers*. Elliott Coues, ed. 3 vols. New York: Francis P. Harper, 1897. (Reprinted as a two-volume edition in 1965.)

Hill, Robert B. *Manitoba: History of its Early Settlement, Development, and Resources*, Toronto: William Briggs, 1890.

Hogue, Michel. *Métis and the Medicine Line: Creating a Border and Dividing a People*. Chapel Hill: University of North Carolina Press, 2015.

Holcombe, Return Ira. "Narration of a Friendly Sioux." *Collections of the Minnesota Historical Society* IX (1901). P. 427.

Howe, Henry. *Historical Collections of Ohio: An Encyclopedia of the State; History Both General and Local; Geography With Descriptions of Its Counties, Cities, and Villages; Its Agricultural, Manufacturing, Mining, and Business Development; Sketches of Eminent and Interesting Characters, etc.; With Notes of a Tour over It in 1886*. Ohio Centennial Edition. Cincinnati: State of Ohio, 1904.

Hubbard, Lucius F., William Pitt Murray, James H. Baker, Warren Upham, Return Ira Holcombe, & Frank R. Holmes. *Minnesota in Three Centuries, 1655-1908*. 3 vols. New York: Society of Minnesota, 1908.

[Isbister, Alexander Kennedy.] *A Few Words on the Hudson's Bay Company; with a Statement of the Grievances of the Native and Half-Caste Indians, addressed to the British Government through their Delegates Now in London*. London: C. Gilpin, 1846. Also available at https://www.canadiana.ca/view/oocihm 16731.

Keating, William H. *Narrative of an Expedition to the Source of St. Peter's River, Lake Winnepeek, Lake of the Woods, &c. Performed in the Year 1823, by Order of the Hon. J.C. Calhoun, Secretary of War, under the Command of Stephen H. Long, U.S.T.E. Compiled from the Notes of Major Long, Messrs. Say, Keating, & Colhoun*. 2 vols. London: George Whittaker, 1825.

Kemp, Douglas. "The Red River Parish." *Manitoba Pageant* 8:1 (September, 1962). Pp. 20-23.

Kemper, Jackson. "Journal of an Episcopalian Missionary's Tour to Green Bay, 1834." *Wisconsin Historical Society Collections* XIV (1998). Pp. 394-449.

Knox, Harold C. "Alexander Kennedy Isbister." *Papers Read Before the Historical & Scientific Society of Manitoba*, series 3, nr. 12. Winnipeg, HSSM, 1957. Pp. 17-28.

———. "When You Gotta Smoke, You Gotta Smoke." *Winnipeg Free Press* (February 11, 1939).

Knox, Olive Elsie. *Red River Shadows*. Toronto: Macmillan, 1948.

Ladd, George van der Goes. "Father Cockran and His Children: Poisonous Pedagogy on the Banks of the Red." Barry Ferguson, ed., *The Anglican Church and the World of Western Canada, 1820-1970*. Regina: Canadian Plains Research Center, University of Regina, 1991. Pp. 61-71.

Larpenteur, Charles. *Forty Years a Fur Trader on the Upper Missouri, the Personal Narrative of Charles Larpenteur, 1833-1872*. Elliott Coues, ed. 2 vols. New York: Francis P. Harper, 1898. (A two-volumes-in-one, facsimile reprint was published in 1962.)

Lent, D. Geneva. *West of the Mountains: James Sinclair and the Hudson's Bay Company*. Seattle: University of Washington Press, 1963. Long, John S. *Treaty No. 9: Making the Agreement to Share the Land in Far Northern Ontario in 1905*. Montreal & Kingston: McGill-Queen's University Press, 2010.

MacGregor, J. G. *Peter Fiedler: Canada's Forgotten Surveyor, 1769-1822*. Toronto: McClelland & Stewart, 1966.

Machray, Robert. *The Life of Archbishop Machray*. Toronto: Macmillan, 1909.

MacLeod, Margaret Arnett. "Manitoba Sugar Maple." *The Beaver* 286 (Spring, 1955). Pp. 10-13.

MacLeod, Margaret A. & W. L. Morton, *Cuthbert Grant of Grantown: Warden of the Plains of Red River*. Toronto: McClelland and Stewart, 1963. (Reissued in M&S's Carleton Library in 1974 with a New Introduction by W.L.Morton.)

Manitoba Village History Committee. *Many Trails of Manitou-Wapah*. Alonsa, Manitoba: The Committee, 1993.

McDermott, John Francis, ed. "A Journalist at Old Fort Snelling: Some Letters of 'Solitaire' Robb." *Minnesota History* 31:4 (December, 1950). Pp. 209-221.

McLaren, John, A. R. Buck, & Nancy Wright, eds. *Despotic Dominion: Property Rights in British Settler Societies*. Vancouver: University of British Columbia Press, 2005.

McMorron, G. A., ed. "Souris River Posts & David Thompson's Diary of His Historical Trip Across the Souris Plains to the Mandan Villages in the Winter of 1797-98." *Annual Report of the Manitoba Historical and Scientific Society* (1950). Pp. 17 & 21. (Peter Garrioch's burial in Westbourne.)

———. "Souris River Posts in the Hartney District." *Transactions of the Manitoba Historical and Scientific Society* series 3 (1948-49): p. 21. https://www.mhs.mb.ca/docs/transactions/3/sourisriverposts.shtml;

Metcalfe, Joseph H. *The Tread of the Pioneers, under the Distinguished Patronage of the Government of the Province of Manitoba, the Corporation of the City of Portage La Prairie, [&] the Council of the Rural Municipality of Portage La Prairie.* Toronto: Ryerson Press, 1932.

Mitchell, W. H. & J. H. Steven., *Geographical and Statistical History of Hennepin County: Embracing Leading Incidents in Pioneer Life, the Names of the Early Settlers, and the Progress in Wealth and Population to the Present Time.* Minneapolis: Russell and Belfoy, 1868.

Morton, Arthur S. *History of the Canadian West to 1871.* London: Thomas Nelson, 1939, 2nd ed., University of Toronto Press,1973.

_____, *Sir George Simpson: Overseas Governor of the Hudson's Bay Company – A Pen Picture of a Man of Action.* London: J. M Dent & Sons, 1944.

Morton, W. L. "Introduction." E. E. Rich, ed., *London Correspondence Inward from Eden Colvile, 1849-1852,* Hudson's Bay Records Society Publications XIX. London: Hudson's Bay Record Society, 1956. Pp. lviii – lix. (Also issued as Champlain Society Publications XXX. Toronto: 1956.)

_____ *Manitoba: A History.* Toronto: University of Toronto Press, 1957.

Murphy, Lucy Eldersveld. *A Gathering of Rivers: Indians, Metis, and Mining in the Western Great Lakes, 1737-1832.* Lincoln: University of Nebraska Press, 2000.

Neill, Edward Duffield. *The History of Minnesota from the Earliest French Explorations to the Present Time.* Philadelphia: J. B. Lippincott, 1858.

———. *History of Minnesota: from the Earliest French Explorations to the Present Time.* Revised and enlarged 5th ed. Minneapolis: Minnesota Historical Company, 1883.

Newson, Thomas McLean. *Pen Pictures of St. Paul, Minnesota, and Biographical Sketches of Old Settlers from the Earliest Settlement of the City, Up to and Including the Year 1857.* St. Paul: The author, 1886.

Nute, Grace Lee, ed. "The Diary of Martin McLeod." *Manitoba History Bulletin* 4:7-8 (August.-November, 1922). Pp. 351-439.

Oliver, E. H. *The Canadian North-West: Its Early Development and Legislative Records: Minutes of the Councils of the Red River Colony and the Northern Department of Rupert's Land.* 2 vols. Ottawa: Government Printing Bureau, 1914.

Palliser, John, *Solitary Rambles and Adventures of a Hunter in the Prairies,* London, John Murray, 1853. (Reprinted in facsimile (Edmonton: Hurtig, 1969) with an Introduction by Alberta historian Hugh A. Dempsey.)

Pannekoek, Frits. *A Snug Little Flock: The Social Origins of the Riel Resistance of 1869-70.* Winnipeg: Watson & Dwyer, 1991.

Peel, Bruce, *Early Printing in the Red River Settlement, 1859-1870*. Winnipeg: Peguis Publishers, 1970.

Peers, Laura & Anne Lindsay, "Governor William B. Caldwell's Souvenir: Exoticism and a Gentleman's Reputation." *Manitoba History* 73 (Fall, 2013). Pp. 2-8.

Peterson, Jacqueline & Jennifer S. H. Brown, *The New Peoples: Being and Becoming Métis in North America*. Winnipeg: University of Manitoba Press, 1985.

Peterson, Murray & Georgia Anderson Taillieu. *Headingley: Pioneers, Past and Present: A Historic Look At Life in Headingley, Manitoba*. Headingley: Headingley Historical Society, 2003.

Raffan, James. *Emperor of the North: Sir George Simpson & the Remarkable Story of the Hudson's Bay Company*. Toronto: Harper Collins, 2007.

Rich, E. E. *The History of the Hudson's Bay Company, 1670-1870*. 2 vols. Hudson's Bay Records Society Publications XXI & XXII. London: Hudson's Bay Records Society, 1958.

———. *The History of the Hudson's Bay Company, 1670-1870*. 3 vols. [Trade edition.] New York, Macmillan, 1960.

Richardson, Brian. "Manitoba History: The Quality of Friendship: Andrew McDermot and George Simpson." *Manitoba History* 46 (Autumn/Winter, 2003-2004). p. 27-36.

Riggs, Stephen R. *Mary and I: Forty Years with the Sioux*. Boston: Congregational Sunday-School & Publishing Society, 1888. (First published: Chicago: W.G. Holmes, 1880).

Rodolf, Theodore. "Pioneering in the Wisconsin Lead Region." *Collections of the State Historical Society of Wisconsin* XV (1900). Pp. 338-389.

Ross, Alexander. *The Red River Settlement: Its Rise, Progress, and Present State, With Some Account of the Native Races and Its General History to the Present Day*. London: Smith, Elder, 1856. (Edmonton: Hurtig, 1972 facsimile reprint includes an Introduction by W.L. Morton.)

Russenholt, E. S. *The Heart of the Continent, Being the History of Assiniboia – the Truly Typical Canadian Community*. Winnipeg: MacFarland Communication Services, 1968.

Schultz, John C. *The Old Crow Wing Trail. Manitoba Historical and Scientific Society Transactions* series 1, nr. 45. Winnipeg: MHSS, 1894. Reprinted in Jim Blanchard, ed., *A Thousand Miles of Prairie: the Manitoba Historical Society and the History of Western Canada*. Winnipeg: University of Manitoba Press, 2002. Pp. 107-127.

Seymour, E. Stanford. *Sketches of Minnesota, the New England of the West, with Incidents of Travel in that Territory during the Summer of 1849*. New York: Harper & Brothers, 1850.

Shaw, E. C. "The Kennedys – An Unusual Western Family." *Manitoba Historical Society Transactions*, series 3, nr. 29 (1972-1973).

Shaw, John. "Sketches of Indian Chiefs and Pioneers of the Northwest." *Wisconsin Historical Collections*. X (1888). P. 222. (Captain John Throckmorton.)

Simms, Eldon Franklin. *The Story of St. Mary's la Prairie Anglican Church, 1853-1953: Commemorating the Founding of St. Mary's la Prairie Parish by Archdeacon Cochrane, 1853*. Portage la Prairie: St. Mary's la Prairie Anglican Church, 1953.

Simpson, Alexander. *The Life and Travels of Thomas Simpson, the Arctic Discoverer*. London: Richard Bentley, 1845.

Simpson, George. "Character Book of George Simpson." Glyndwr Williams, ed., *Hudson's Bay Miscellany, 1670-1870*. Winnipeg: Hudson's Bay Records Society Publications XXX, 1975.

Simpson, Thomas. *Narrative of the Discoveries of the North Coast of America: Effected by the Officers of the Hudson's Bay Company, During the Years 1836-1839,* London: Richard Bentley, 1843.

Sprague, D.N. & R. P. Frye. *The Genealogy of the First Métis Nation: The Development and Dispersal of the Red River Settlement, 1820-1900*. Winnipeg: Pemmican Publications, 1988.

Spry, Irene M. "The Métis and Mixed-Bloods of Rupert's Land before 1870." *The New Peoples, Being and Becoming Métis in North America*. Jacqueline Peterson & Jennifer S. H. Brown, eds. Winnipeg: University of Manitoba Press, 1985. Pp. 95-118.

St. Clements Historical Committee. *The East Side of the Red: A Centennial Project of the Rural Municipality of St. Clements, 1884-1984*. East Selkirk, Manitoba: St. Clements Historical Committee, 1984.

Stubbs, Roy St. George. *Four Recorders of Rupert's Land: A Brief Survey of the Hudson's Bay Company Courts of Rupert's Land*. Winnipeg: Peguis Publishers, 1967.

Sunder, John E. *The Fur Trade on the Upper Missouri, 1840-1865*. Norman: University of Oklahoma Press, 1965.

Talbot, Robert J. *Negotiating the Numbered Treaties: An Intellectual & Political Biography of Alexander Morris*. Saskatoon: Purich Publishing, 2009.

Taliafarro, Lawrence. "Auto-biography of Major Taliafarro." *Collections of the Minnesota Historical Society* VI (1894). Pp. 189-255.

Upham, Warren. *Minnesota Geographic Names, Their Origin and Historic Significance. Collections of the Minnesota Historical Society* XVII. St. Paul: Minnesota Historical Society, 1920.

Upham, Warren & Rose Bareteau Dunlap. *Minnesota Biographies, 1655-1912. Collections of the Minnesota Historical Society* XIV. St. Paul: Minnesota Historical Society, 1912,

Van Cleve, Charlotte Ouisconsin. *Three Score Years and Ten: Lifelong Memories of Fort Snelling, Minnesota, and Other Parts of the West*. Minneapolis: Harrison & Smith, 1888.

Van Kirk, Syvia, *"Many Tender Ties": Women in Fur Trade Society, 1670-1870*. Winnipeg: Watson & Dwyer, 1980 & Norman: University of Oklahoma Press, 1983.

Westbourne-Longburn History Committee. *When the West was Bourne: A History of Westbourne and District, 1860-1985*. Westbourne, Manitoba: Westbourne-Longbourne [sic. Longburn] History Society, 1985.

Willand, Jon. *Lac Qui Parle and the Dakota Mission*. Madison, Minnesota: Lac Qui Parle County Historical Society, 1964.

Williams, Glyndwr, ed. *Hudson's Bay Miscellany, 1670-1870*. Winnipeg: Hudson's Bay Records Society Publications, XXX, 1975.

Williams, J. Fletcher. *History of St. Paul to 1857*. Saint Paul: Minnesota Historical Company, 1876.

Winchell, H. N., Edward Duffield Neill, John Fletcher Williams, & Charles S. Bryant. *History of the Upper Mississippi Valley*. Minneapolis: Minnesota Historical Company, 1881.

www.ingramcontent.com/pod-product-compliance
Lightning Source LLC
Chambersburg PA
CBHW082032230426
43670CB00016B/2637